LATIN AMERICA

ITS PROBLEMS AND ITS PROMISE

The Western Hemisphere

Reprinted, with permission, from Margaret Daley Hayes, *Latin America and the U.S. National Interest: A Basis for U.S. Foreign Policy* (Boulder, Colo.: Westview Press, 1984).

LATIN AMERICA

ITS PROBLEMS AND ITS PROMISE

A Multidisciplinary Introduction

FOURTH EDITION

EDITED BY

Jan Knippers Black

Monterey Institute of International Studies

Westview
PRESS

A Member of the Perseus Books Group

Copyright © 2005 by Westview Press, a Member of the Perseus Books Group.

Published in the United States of America by Westview Press, A Member of the Perseus Books Group.

Find us on the world wide web at www.westviewpress.com

Westview Press books are available at special discounts for bulk purchases in the United States by corporations, institutions, and other organizations. For more information, please contact the Special Markets Department at the Perseus Books Group, 11 Cambridge Center, Cambridge, MA 02142; or call (617) 252–5298, (800) 255–1514; or email special.markets@perseusbooks.com.

Library of Congress Cataloging-in-Publication Data
    Latin America, its problems and its promise : a multidisciplinary introduction / edited by Jan Knippers Black.—4th ed.
        p. cm.
    Includes bibliographical references and index.
    ISBN 0-8133-4164-7 (pbk. : alk. paper)
    1. Latin America.   I. Black, Jan Knippers, 1940-
    F1406.7.L38   2005
    980—dc22

                                                                2004027268

The paper used in this publication meets the requirements of the American National Standard for Permanence of Paper for Printed Library Materials Z39.48–1984.

10 9 8 7 6 5 4 3 2 1

*This fourth edition is dedicated to all of the
contributors to earlier editions—our esteemed colleagues
and my cherished friends—who are now deceased:*
E. Bradford Burns
Eldon (Bud) Kenworthy
John D. Martz
Brady Tyson
Rene A. Dreifuss

Contents

List of Maps, Tables, and Figures   *xi*

1   Introduction: Understanding the Persistence of Inequity,
    Jan Knippers Black   1

I   THE LAND AND THE PEOPLE

2   Landscape and Settlement Patterns, *Alfonso Gonzalez*   22

3   The Indigenous Populations of Latin America, *Karl H. Schwerin*   41

4   Harmonizing and Disharmonizing Human and Natural
    Environments, *David Stea* and *G. Shane Lewis*   59

II   HISTORICAL SETTING

5   Colonial Latin America, *Peter Bakewell*   78

6   Latin America Since Independence: An Overview,
    Michael Conniff   88

III   ECONOMIC AND SOCIAL STRUCTURES

7   The Latin American Economies Restructure, Again,
    William P. Glade   102

8   Social Structure and Change in Latin America,
    Henry Veltmeyer and *James Petras*   119

9   Emerging Social Movements and Grassroots Change,
     Wendy Muse Sinek   139

IV   POLITICAL PROCESSES AND TRENDS

10   Participation and Political Process: The Collapsible Pyramid,
     Jan Knippers Black   158

11   Women in Latin American Politics: Progress Toward
     Gender Equity, *Jane S. Jaquette*   189

12   Globalization and Insecurity in the Americas, *Jorge Nef*   207

V   EXTERNAL RELATIONS

13   International Relations in Latin America: Conflict and
     Cooperation, *James Lee Ray*   232

14   The United States and Latin America: Into a New Era,
     Wayne S. Smith   249

VI   MEXICO AND CENTRAL AMERICA

15   Mexico: A Revolution Laid to Rest? *Fred R. Harris* and
     Martin C. Needler   280

16   Central America: From Revolution to Neoliberal "Reform,"
     Thomas W. Walker and *Christine J. Wade*   311

17   Panama and the Canal, *Steve C. Ropp*   333

VII CUBA AND THE CARIBBEAN

18   The Cuban Revolution, *Nelson P. Valdés*   348

19   The Caribbean: The Structure of Modern-Conservative Societies,
     Anthony P. Maingot   375

VIII THE ANDES

| 20 | Colombia's Split-Level Realities, *Jan Knippers Black* | 392 |

| 21 | Venezuela: A "Model" Democracy in Crisis, *Steve Ellner* | 409 |

| 22 | Ecuador: Political Turmoil, Social Mobilization, and Frustrated Reform, *Pablo Andrade A.* and *Liisa L. North* | 423 |

| 23 | Peru: Economic Vulnerability and Precarious Democracy, *Cynthia McClintock* | 441 |

| 24 | Bolivia: A Resuscitated Indigenous Movement, *José Z. García* | 457 |

IX BRAZIL AND THE SOUTHERN CONE

| 25 | Brazil: From Military Regime to a Workers' Party Government, *David Fleischer* | 470 |

| 26 | Chile: The Development, Breakdown, and Recovery of Democracy, *J. Samuel Valenzuela* and *Arturo Valenzuela* | 501 |

| 27 | Argentina: Decline and Revival, *Peter Calvert* | 541 |

| 28 | Uruguay and Paraguay: An Arduous Transition, *Diego Abente Brun* | 556 |

| 29 | Conclusion: A Troubled Neighborhood, *Jan Knippers Black* | 580 |

Acknowledgments	593
About the Book and Editor	595
About the Contributors	597
Index	605

Maps, Tables,
and Figures

*(All photographs that introduce part openers
are courtesy of Jan Knippers Black.)*

Maps

The Western Hemisphere   *frontispiece*
Central and Middle America and the Caribbean   *xiii*
South America   *xiv*

Tables

2.1   Latin America: Population characteristics   25
2.2   Natural Regions of Latin America   29
2.3   Altitudinal Zonation of Climates in Latin America   34

3.1   Amerindian Population of Latin America, ca. 2000   46

7.1   Economic Dimensions of Selected Latin American
        Countries, 1994   103

8.1   The Population of Latin America and the Caribbean:
        Some Basic Distributions, 1994   121

8.2   The Structure of Economic Activity, Selected Countries,
        Ranked (out of 132) in Reverse Order of Per Capita
        Income, 1994   122

8.3   Distribution of National Income, by Top/Bottom Quintiles
       (1–2) and Top Decile (3), for Selected Countries, Listed in
       Rank Reverse Order by Per Capita Income Levels, 1993   122

8.4   Latin American Class Structure in the 1990s
       (% distribution of the EAP)   123

12.1   Indebtedness: Selected Countries 1970–1985 and 1985–2000   215
12.2   Latin America: Foreign Debt 1990, 1992, and 2000 Figures   215
12.3   Growth of the Estimated % of Population in Poverty
       and Indigence in 19 Countries in Latin America, 1980–1990   220
12.4   Region Military Balance   221
12.5   Electoral Participation (as percentage of those registered)   223
12.6   Comparative Indicators for Latin America and the Caribbean   226

18.1   Imports, Growth Rate and Total by Year (in millions USD)   367
18.2   Gross Internal Investments, Growth Rate   368
18.3   Gross National Product, Growth Rate by Year   368
18.4   Population Growth Rate by Year   369

19.1   The Insular Caribbean: Basic Statistics   376

2.1   Latin America: Natural Regions   28
22.1   Ecuadorian Heads of State and Their Political Affiliations   428
22.2   Ecuador in Context   438

Figures

2.1   Latin America: Natural Regions   28

10.1   Political Participation by Social Strata:
       The Collapsible Pyramid   163

South America

Reprinted, with permission, from Howard J. Wiarda and Harvey F. Kline, eds., *Latin American Politics and Development*, Second Edition (Boulder, Colo.: Westview Press, 1985).

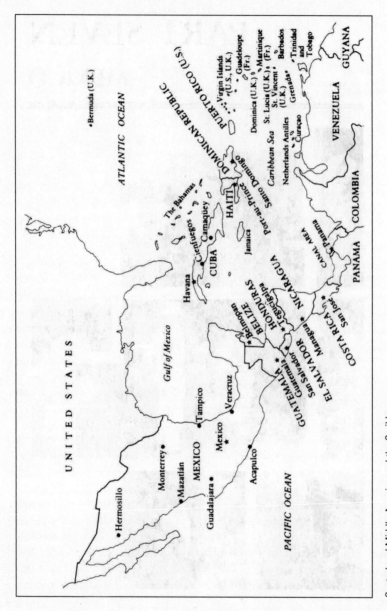

Central and Middle America and the Caribbean

Reprinted, with permission, from Howard J. Wiarda and Harvey F. Kline, eds., *Latin American Politics and Development*, Second Edition (Boulder, Colo.: Westview Press, 1985).

Chapter 1

INTRODUCTION:
UNDERSTANDING THE PERSISTENCE
OF INEQUITY

JAN KNIPPERS BLACK

A MEASURE OF THE PACE and direction of social change in Latin America, as elsewhere, is how long it takes a word or phrase that carries positive connotation to come to mean the opposite of what it once did. When the first edition of this book came off the presses two decades ago, in 1984, the word *reform* still meant change in the direction of greater equity, that is, change favoring the have-nots. Now it refers more often to change favoring the haves, particularly foreign creditors and investors. And the demand from below for structural change—legal and institutional change to lock in that enhanced equity—has given way to demand from above for structural adjustment to push costs downward in the social pyramid and benefits up.

Latin America, as the first region of what is now called the Third World to be thoroughly subjugated by European colonialism and the first to throw off that subjugation, has long been the Third World's pacesetter and harbinger. It was first to adopt the trappings of a republic and first, in varying degrees and by varying means, to bring some reality to the rhetoric of popular participation.

Latin America was first to elaborate legal, institutional, and political bases in support of national economic sovereignty, and first to see those bases obliterated and constitutions shredded by military dictatorship. Thus, it was first, particularly under the dictatorships of the Southern Cone, to be forced open for "free trade"—in fact, very costly debt—and its attendant conditions, and, in the 1980s, first, along with Africa, to experience shock therapy and economic meltdown.

A trend to limited redemocratization and sporadic economic growth that raised hopes in the 1990s has given way in the new millennium to widespread cynicism, anger, and desperation, as prices rise, wages fall, and income gaps widen. New parties and new categories of social movements generated in response may lead to more meaningful political participation in the long run. In the short term, however, new manifestations of social discontent keep governments enfeebled and economies off-balance. Ahead of the curve, at this point in time, is not a very comfortable place to be.

Meanwhile, Latin America is never very far removed from the moods and manias of its more ambitious northern neighbor. Like a long-suffering and not necessarily willing spouse, Latin America has been occasionally courted with false promises, but more often taken for granted when the United States was feeling confident and battered or suffering from insecurity or delusions of invincibility.

For Latin America, as for the United States, the onset of a new millennium represents both the best and the worst of times—a new age of democracy but perhaps also a new kind of democracy: one that allows for election to office but not to power; one in which the vestment of office is all too often a straitjacket. Since the early 1990s, most of the Latin American countries have been under elected, constitutional, and more or less democratic governments. These democracies, however, are for the most part limited and very fragile. Although the middle classes have regained participation and relief from intimidation, the more numerous poor lack effective representation and remain vulnerable to abuse. Moreover, a debt crisis compounded by deep economic recession has left newly elected leaders at the mercy of foreign creditors and thus with precious little latitude for national economic decisionmaking. Their failure to follow through on popular mandates has left them at the mercy also of social movements born of hunger as well as of old grievances and new organizational skills.

The same pressures and perceptions of the times that are brought to bear on U.S. and Latin American policymakers set the agenda and the parameters that govern academic discourse. Thus to the student who must launch his or her exploration of Latin America through the eyes and ears, the assumptions and perspectives, and the theoretical and ideological filters of others, it would be useful to know something of the intellectual paths that have been traveled by the specialists in the field. Those paths have circled, dead-ended, and U-turned, merged and diverged; they are now, as always, subject to turns in new directions. The attempt to understand social relations, especially in an area so diverse and complex as Latin America, can never be a simple matter of learning "the facts." There will always be many facts in dispute; answers depend on the nature of available data, on the interests of the sources consulted, and on how questions are asked. Confronted, as one must be in a text having many authors, with differing points of view and thus differing interpretations of the same historical and social data, the student may find it worthwhile to begin the study of Latin America with a study of Latin Americanists.

It is to be expected that interests and interpretations of social phenomena will vary from one discipline to another. The geographer may find, for example, that soil quality, climate, and topography determine settlement patterns and socioeconomic relations, which in turn configure political systems. The anthropologist may find explanation for social harmony or social conflict in ethnic and cultural patterns. The economist may find that political trends derive from economic ones, while the political scientist may see power relationships as overriding. In the study of Latin America, however, there has always been a unifying theme.

From the perspectives of U.S.- and European-based scholars, as well as from those of Latin America's own creative and scholarly writers, the study of Latin America has been approached as the study of a problem, or set of problems. The problems might be capsulized as underdevelopment and political instability or, more simply, as poverty or inequality and the failure of democratic systems to take hold. The search for the roots, causes, and progenitors of these problems has generally led in one of three directions: to the Iberians—the conquistadores and the institutions, attitudes, and cultural traits they brought with them to the New World; to the Latin Americans themselves—the alleged greed of the elites, absence of entrepreneurship in the middle classes, or passivity of the masses; or to the United States and the international capitalist system it promotes and defends.

Long before U.S. scholars began to direct their attention to Latin America's problems, the area's own intellectuals were absorbed by the question of where to place the blame. Domingo Faustino Sarmiento and other nineteenth-century intellectual and political leaders of cosmopolitan Buenos Aires blamed the cycles of anarchy and tyranny their newly independent country was suffering on Hispanic influences.[1] Sarmiento in later life directed his scorn toward Latin America's own "melting pot." Influenced by social Darwinism, he diagnosed "the decadent state" of Argentine society as deriving from its racial components of Spanish, Mestizo, Indian, and Negro.

Turning the tables at the turn of the twentieth century, José Enrique Rodó, Uruguay's foremost literary figure, urged the youth of his country—in his masterpiece, *Ariel*—to shun the materialism of the United States and to cling to the spiritual and intellectual values of their Spanish heritage. A strong current of Latin American social thought, reflected in art and music as well as literature, that gained momentum a few decades into the twentieth century has touted the strengths of native American cultures and blamed both Hispanic and North American influences for the prevailing instability and social injustice. Likewise, in the Caribbean, the Black Power movements of the 1960s and 1970s called Europe and Anglo-America to task for the region's underdevelopment.

Latin American studies as an interdisciplinary field in the United States and, by extension, the coming of age of analysis of Latin American social and political systems are clearly the illegitimate offspring of Fidel Castro. Prior to the Cuban Revolution, historians, anthropologists, and literary scholars had generally pursued their studies of Latin American subjects in disciplinary isolation. Political analysis had been largely limited to formal legal studies, highlighting the fact that Latin American regimes rarely lived up to the standards, borrowed from France and the United States, embodied in their constitutions. Such studies generally drew their explanatory theses from the distinctive historical and cultural traditions of the United States of North America and the disunited states of Latin America and, in so doing, contributed to the mystification of the political process in both areas.[2] The Iberian heritage of feudalism, authoritarianism, and Catholicism was seen as the major obstacle to democratic and socioeconomic reforms.

The surge of interest in Latin America on the part of U.S. politicians and academics (encouraged by newly available government-funded fellowships and contracts) that accompanied the Cuban Revolution coincided with the acceleration of decolonization elsewhere and the expansion of attention to the Third World generally by the previously parochial disciplines of economics and political science. Thus, development and modernization theory, formulated to address change processes in other parts of the Third World, came to dominate the study of Latin America as well. Studies falling under these rubrics generally posited that either the economic and political systems of Latin America would increasingly approximate those of the United States and Western Europe or the area would be engulfed in violent revolution.

The invalidation of many of the assumptions of development and modernization theorists by the onrush of events—particularly by the fall of democratic regimes and their replacement by military dictatorships—resulted in a theoretical backlash as well as in long overdue attention to the work of Latin American theorists. The backlash was expressed in a reassertion of the tenacity of tradition, of the fundamentally conservative character of Latin American society. This perspective has been endowed with greater theoretical and conceptual sophistication in studies using the corporatist model. Corporatism stresses the hierarchical organization of modern institutions and the persistence of control from the top.

There existed a large body of literature by Latin Americans, dating back to "the black legend" of Spanish rule, to support the historical and cultural explanations for the failure of democracy. But the trends that had dominated the social sciences in the major Latin American countries were variations on the Marxist themes of class conflict and imperialism. One such body of thought, known as dependency theory, came to rival development and modernization theory for predominance among U.S. and European specialists in Latin American studies. Dependency theory held that Latin American underdevelopment should be understood as a by-product of the international capitalist system.

With the end of the Cold War, that system struck back with a force that suppressed all previously contending paradigms. Some Latin American theorists continued to urge attention to national and local markets, to social and economic democracy, and to a new kind of nationalism; but a triumphalist neoliberalism that stressed open markets, privatization, and elections-as-democracy and gave no quarter to social concerns came to dominate elite institutions throughout the hemisphere through the end of the century.

These theoretical trends and approaches have permeated all aspects of Latin American studies, because—to a far greater extent than in Europe or the United States—philosophy, literature, the arts, and other pursuits of the intelligentsia in Latin America tend to reflect national or regional concerns. It could hardly be otherwise; the cataclysmic episodes of insurgency and repression, revolution and counterrevolution, leave no one untouched.

BLAMING THE IBERIANS: CORPORATISM AND CULTURE

The historical-cultural approach to the study of Latin America and its problems draws attention to the persistence in contemporary Latin America of attitudes, institutions, and social relations that are said to have been characteristic of the Iberian peninsula in medieval times.[3] According to this view, the Spanish conquistadores, crown officials, and Roman Catholic missionaries transplanted in the New World a social system firmly based on elitism, authoritarianism, and militarism.

The Portuguese legacy differed from that of Spain in its greater tolerance of racial and cultural diversity, but, like the Spanish, the Portuguese inculcated in their New World offspring a rigid sense of social, political, and cultural hierarchy. The patriarchal view, deriving from Iberian monarchism, held that culture and personality were functions of education and that the uneducated man was incapable of participating in the dominant political culture. (That women, educated or otherwise, were to be seen but not heard was taken for granted.) The uneducated man was expected to accept his status in society as a function of a divinely ordered hierarchy. However, as the uneducated were not expected to be responsible for their own welfare, the dominant class was obligated to contribute to the amelioration of their suffering. Public morality was an integral part of the political culture, and the Catholic Church, also hierarchical in structure, absolutist in doctrine, and authoritarian in practice, shared with the institutions of government the responsibility for the maintenance of the political and moral order.

During the early colonial period—the sixteenth and seventeenth centuries—a great debate raged among intellectuals and governmental and spiritual leaders in Spain and its colonies as to whether native Americans were fully human. It was finally concluded that the Church's Christianizing mission implied recognition of the fundamental human attributes of the Indians. But in much of the empire, the slaughter or enslavement of the Indians proceeded nevertheless, and it is clear that many contemporary Latin Americans continue to see the Indians as belonging to a lesser order of humanity.

Corporatism

The corporatist model, drawn primarily from medieval Catholic thought and observed, to some degree, in Spain under Franco and Portugal under Salazar, was found to "fit" mid-twentieth-century Latin American politics to a greater degree than some of the models derived from development and modernization theory. The model, elaborated in works by Wiarda, Schmitter, Malloy, Erickson, and others, has called attention to the tendency to vertical, as opposed to horizontal, organization among politically active groups in Latin America.[4] Such groups, in corporatist systems, are controlled and manipulated by authoritarian governments so that communications and power flow from the top down rather than from the bottom up.

Few Latin Americanists would dispute the observation that vestiges of medieval Iberia are still to be found in Latin America. Nor is the existence of corporatist tendencies a subject of great controversy. The point at which many Latin Americanists depart from the findings of some scholars pursuing historical-cultural or corporatist approaches is the supposition that contemporary manifestations of elitism and authoritarianism are due primarily to colonization by Spain and Portugal.

Critics note, for example, that some countries that experienced fiercely authoritarian, military rule in the 1970s and 1980s (Chile and Uruguay, for example) had enjoyed constitutional and more or less democratic rule throughout most of the twentieth century. Furthermore, the Southern Cone (Argentina, Uruguay, and Chile) was among the areas least influenced by colonial Spain. In Argentina, descendants of Italian immigrants, who arrived in great waves around the turn of the twentieth century, now outnumber the descendants of Spanish settlers. Surely some common denominators of vintage more recent than the colonial period are needed to explain the resurgence of authoritarianism in Latin America in the late twentieth century. Moreover, the qualitative difference between traditional corporatism and the modern bureaucratic-technocratic variety has often been understated. By the end of the 1980s, the popularity of the corporatist paradigm appeared to be waning, and some of its former proponents, including Howard Wiarda, had turned to an emphasis on cultural causation.

Cultural Causation

The late 1980s saw a revival of interest in the explanatory power of culture as an independent variable. Samuel Huntington began to suggest that development and modernization may be distinctively Western goals. He alleged that aspirations to wealth, equity, democracy, stability, and autonomy emerge from Western, particularly Nordic, experience, and that other cultures may prefer simplicity, austerity, hierarchy, authoritarianism, discipline, and militarism.[5] This view represents a considerable retreat for a theorist who once believed Western-style modernization to be irresistible. Huntington had retreated even farther by the turn of the century. In his own works and in *Culture Matters: How Values Shape Human Progress*, which he co-edited with Lawrence Harrison, one finds echoes of the sentiments of Sarmiento.[6]

BLAMING THE LATIN AMERICANS: DEVELOPMENT AND MODERNIZATION THEORY

Whereas analyses of contemporary Latin America based on the traditional, or historical-cultural, approach tended to have a static quality, development and modernization theory introduced a new dynamism into the field. The new approach highlighted the facts that, for better or worse, social change was indeed under way and that to a great extent, that change was in response or in reaction to the spread of the ideas and technologies of the more industrialized world, primarily the United States and Western Europe, to the Third World.

The body of thought that came to be known as development and/or modernization theory—terms often used interchangeably—was pioneered primarily by U.S. scholars in the late 1950s and the first half of the 1960s. In economics, development theory presumed that with the infusion of capital and the acquisition of business skills, and with the advantage of not having to reinvent the wheel, the nations that had yet to experience their industrial revolutions would pass at an accelerated pace along paths already broken by Western Europe and the United States. Walt W. Rostow further assumed that economic development, at least beyond a stage he called "take-off," was irreversible.[7]

From the perspective of anthropologists and sociologists, "modernization" generally meant the ingestion of the supposedly Western attitudinal traits of rationalism, instrumentalism, achievement orientation, and the like. This approach stressed the felicitous consequences of the spread of modern communications media, of education in science and the liberal arts, and of technology transfer. And it implied that Third World societies could (and should) become developed through the accelerated absorption of individuals into the middle class or the modern industrial sector.

Political scientists borrowed liberally from the other social sciences, often without seeming to notice that in their extreme formulations these theories amounted to a virtual denial of the stuff of their own discipline: power relationships. Political scientists did, however, add their own set of indices of development and/or modernization to those compiled by scholars of other disciplines. Gabriel Almond, for example, stressed structural differentiation (the elaboration of economic and political roles), whereas Samuel Huntington stressed the strengthening of political institutions.[8] Other scholars focused on participation, egalitarianism, and governmental capability. Some assumed that such attributes were mutually reinforcing. Huntington, however, seeing expanding participation in the absence of institutionalization as destabilizing, stressed the importance of stability. Martin C. Needler, perceiving the same contradiction, placed higher priority on participation but noted that in the absence of steady economic growth participation would have a destabilizing effect on systems of limited democracy, threatening the imposition of authoritarianism.[9]

These trends in the social sciences coincided with the Cuban Revolution and thus with the Alliance for Progress and the emergence of interdisciplinary programs in Latin American studies. Development came to be one of the major goals of the Alliance for Progress; the other was security—the prevention of "another Cuba." These goals were deemed to be interdependent; it was rarely imagined that they might be contradictory. The few critical voices, such as that of Albert O. Hirschman, who argued that popular pressure, sometimes assuming violent form, was essential to the achievement of reform, were generally ignored.[10] The prevailing view, that "unrest" was an impediment to progress and had to be contained by strengthened security forces, won out in academic as well as in governmental circles until a wave of military takeovers forced a reevaluation.

Critics of development and modernization theory have pointed out that its adherents often emitted an optimism bordering on euphoria. Huntington had said that "modernization is not only inevitable, it is also desirable."[11] Such positivistic assumptions, that what was good was inevitable and vice versa, had predictable consequences for analysis. Researchers were inclined either to see what they wanted to see or to label whatever they saw as progress. Economists, for example, measured development by using aggregate data on the growth of gross national product or per capita income, data that were blind to the skewed distribution of income. While U.S. economists lavished praise on Brazil's "economic miracle," Brazil's own dictator, General Emilio Garrastazú Médici, commented in 1970 that "the economy is doing fine, but the people aren't."[12]

Critics have also argued that many of the supposed attributes of modernity are not even characteristic of the industrialized countries, much less of what they project to or promote in the Third World. Nor does the undeniable influence of the so-called developed countries necessarily contribute to the kind of development desired by leaders and peoples of the so-called underdeveloped ones. Technology transfer, for example, has generally meant a transition from labor-intensive to capital-intensive industry in areas where labor markets are glutted and capital is scarce.

A tendency common to much of the work based on development and modernization theory was a peculiar sort of ethnocentricity based on an idealized and class-delimited national or North Atlantic self-image. The terminology employed in such work, for example, was often charged with unacknowledged value judgments. All cultures other than our own, from a sophisticated ancient civilization such as China's to a preliterate society of nomads, were lumped together under the single epithet "traditional." Such terms as "secularism" and "rationalism" carried the thinly veiled implication that they referred to the thought processes of clear-headed folks like us. If Latin Americans and other peoples of the Third World had failed to achieve development or modernization, it was assumed to be because they lacked our industriousness and had failed to see their own problems as clearly as we saw them. In effect, the blame for poverty and powerlessness was placed squarely on the poor and powerless.

There were those, of course, who used some of the concepts and models of the developmentalists but rejected such ethnocentric assumptions. Scholars of the period were not necessarily in accord as to which of the indices of development and modernization were most relevant and useful. Nevertheless, distinctions between value-free and value-laden concepts were rarely well drawn. The behaviorist tendency in the social sciences, which was also coming into its own in the 1960s, sharpened the inclination of social scientists, attempting to be "scientific," to hold acknowledged bias in disdain. Thus, those scholars who argued that economic growth and stability were the most important indices of development and those who, in contrast, contended that redistribution of wealth and the expansion of political participation were more important tended to maintain the pretense that they were arguing over facts rather than over values.

As military regimes swept the hemisphere in the 1960s and 1970s, replacing democratic ones, the development approach was discredited and superseded by newer theoretical trends, particularly dependency. Some of the theorists once attracted to the development paradigm became persuaded by the arguments of dependency theory. Others came to stress the interdependence of First and Third Worlds or to look for cultural causation in differing levels of development. Many of the attitudes and assumptions associated with development theory were revived in the 1990s through the currency of neoliberalism, but the latter also embodies striking differences.

BLAMING THE UNITED STATES:
DEPENDENCY AND RELATED THEORIES

In his earlier ideological incarnation as one of the originators of dependency theory, Brazilian social scientist Fernando Henrique Cardoso responded to the question, "What is dependency?" by saying, "It's what you call imperialism if you don't want to lose your Ford Foundation grant." (Elected president of Brazil in 1994, Cardoso now calls dependency theory his Frankenstein.) More precisely, as Susanne Bodenheimer Jonas has noted, dependency refers to the perspective from "below," whereas the Marxist theory of imperialism provides the perspective from "above."[13] As the Marxist theory of imperialism seeks to explain why and how the dominant classes of the dominant capitalist powers expand their spheres of exploitation and political control, dependency theory examines what this relationship of unequal bargaining and multilayered exploitation means to the dominated classes in the dominated countries.

Like most of the other trends and perspectives that have been designated theory, dependency by no means refers to an integrated set of if-then propositions. Rather, it is a focus of inquiry and a body of thought built upon common assumptions. Unlike the behavioral approach that has held sway over most aspects of social science in the United States since the mid-1960s, dependency is unabashedly normative. Its impulse derives largely from the attempts of the United Nations Economic Commission for Latin America (ECLA), under the leadership of Argentine economist Raúl Prebisch, to understand and counteract such problems as the deterioration in the terms of trade for producers of primary (nonindustrial) products. A renewed awareness of economic exploitation and dependency followed upon disillusionment with industrialization through import substitution, Latin American economic integration, and other solutions proposed by ECLA. Thus, a number of Latin American political scientists and sociologists, including Brazilians Cardoso and Teotonio dos Santos and Chilean Osvaldo Sunkel, renewed their efforts to explain patterns of social class structure and predict the structural changes that are inherent in the process of capitalist development in a dependent state. This new focus derived in part from a recognition that the form of this exploitative relationship was constantly subject to change and that the consequences of the industrialization of the periphery—that is, the Third World—through the medium of multinational corporations had not been adequately addressed by previously prevalent theories.

Among the assumptions that underpin dependency theory are the following. First, the distribution of power and status in national and international arenas is ultimately determined by economic relationships. Second, the causes of underdevelopment are not to be found in national systems alone but must be sought in the pattern of economic relations between hegemonic, or dominant, powers and their client states. The perpetuation of the pattern of inequality within client states is managed by a clientele class, which might be seen as the modern functional equivalent of a formal colonial apparatus. Third, both within and among states, the unfettered forces of the marketplace tend to exacerbate rather than to mitigate existing inequalities. That is, the dominant foreign power benefits at the expense of its client states, and the clientele class benefits at the expense of other classes.

Dependency theorists further held that development would not take place through the "trickle-down" of wealth nor through the gradual diffusion of modern attitudes and modern technology; that the upward mobility of individuals expressed by their gradual absorption into the modern sector is no solution to the problem of the impoverishment of the masses; and that stability is no virtue in a system of pronounced inequality. In fact, most dependency theorists, or, in Spanish, *dependentistas,* believed that only by breaking out of the international capitalist system and establishing socialist regimes would Latin American nations gain control over their own decisionmaking and expand the options available to them.[14]

Whereas modernization and development theorists see foreign investment and foreign aid as critical to development in the Third World, *dependentistas* see such investment and aid as means of extracting capital from client states. *Dependentistas* would probably agree with the observation of U.S. congressman Dante Fascell (D-Florida) that aid is a means whereby the poor of the rich countries contribute to the rich of the poor countries. They might also add that aid is yet another means whereby the poor of the rich countries contribute to the rich of the *rich* countries.

Andre Gunder Frank, comparing the experiences of the Latin American states during World War I and the depression of the 1930s with their experiences during periods when the links were stronger between those states and the industrialized West, concluded in 1970 that satellites, or client states, experience their greatest industrial development when their ties to the more developed states are weakest.[15] Other scholars, noting, for example, the industrial expansion of Brazil in the late 1960s and early 1970s, maintain that rapid industrial growth may take place under conditions of dependency. There is general agreement, however, that to the extent that economic growth takes place under conditions of dependency, it is a distorted pattern of growth that exacerbates existing inequalities among both classes and regions within client states.

Like development theory, dependency theory has been limited by an excessive reliance on aggregate data and a "black box" approach—which treats nations like black boxes, shedding no light on internal dynamics or relationships. Such an approach deals with the outcome of unequal relations between nations but fails to elaborate the political mechanisms whereby dependent relationships are perpetuated. Furthermore, in assigning primacy to economic relationships, *dependentistas* tend to give short shrift to other factors, such as the pursuit of institutional, or bureaucratic, interests, which may have an important bearing upon relations between dominant powers and client states and upon relations among political actors within client states.

Penetration Theory and Bureaucratic Authoritarianism

Other approaches that share many of the assumptions of dependency theory and serve to elaborate or refine our understanding of politics in dependent states include penetration theory and the model of bureaucratic authoritarianism. Penetration theory seeks to identify the means whereby a dominant foreign power influences policy in a client state not only directly, through diplomatic pressures, but also indirectly, through the manipulation of political competition within the client state.[16] Bureaucratic authoritarianism, according to Argentine political scientist Guillermo O'Donnell, who coined the phrase, is the likely outcome of social and economic modernization in the context of delayed, or dependent, development. Such impersonal, institutional dictatorship is not a vestige of the feudalistic rule imposed by Spain or Portugal but rather a response to a perceived threat to the capitalist system. According to O'Donnell, the levels of coercion and of economic orthodoxy that are imposed depend upon the level of perceived threat.[17]

The Center-Periphery Model

The relationships hypothesized or described by dependency theorists have been incorporated by Norwegian scholar Johan Galtung into a model of elegant simplicity.[18] According to the center-periphery model, elites of the center, or metropolis, draw bounty from the periphery of their own state system (through taxes, for example), which they devote to the nurture and support of co-opted elites of client or "peripheral" states. In turn, elites of those client states, dependent upon elites of the center for assistance in exploiting and suppressing their own peripheral, or nonelite, populations, have no choice but to allow center elites to participate in, or share in the product of, the exploitation of the peripheral peoples of the peripheral states.

World Systems Theory

World systems theory, pioneered by Immanuel Wallerstein, also views the world economy as segmented into core and periphery areas.[19] Rather than focusing on the interactions of governments, however, this approach calls attention to the transnational interactions of nonstate actors, particularly multinational corporations and banks. The international economy is said to be driven by the initiatives of economic elites, particularly of the developed capitalist states, whose governments normally do their bidding. The control centers of the world economy then are financial rather than political capitals. The farther one lives from such a center, the less the "trickle-down" of its wealth will be experienced.

Wallerstein, who sees the ideas of *dependentistas* as falling within the world system perspective, takes issue with more traditional Marxists and liberals alike for what he calls a rigidly developmentalist approach. That is, both schools assume that each nation-state must pass through the same set of stages, or modes of extracting surplus, in the same order. As Wallerstein sees it, the nation-state system, which came into being in part as a convenience to economic elites of an earlier era, has ceased to be the essential institutional base of the global economy. The contemporary struggle, then, is not between rich and poor states, but rather between rich and poor classes in a global society.

Seeking Common Ground

None of the approaches, models, and theories discussed above wholly excludes the others. The differences among them are largely differences of perspective, emphasis, and value judgment. Adherents of development and modernization theory, like those of the historical-cultural approach, tend to focus on the attitudes of individuals and the behavior of institutions, though the former are more attuned to the indices of change whereas the latter more often stress continuity. Both pay tribute to the achievements of the modern West and deplore the antidemocratic influences of the Iberian tradition, but development and modernization theorists, more readily than historical-cultural analysts, see approximation to the Western model as a plausible solution.

Drawing explicitly on Marxist concepts, dependency theory looks to material interests and class conflict as well as to international patterns of trade, aid, and political control for explanations of political process at the national level. Thus, even when scholars of differing schools can agree as to what happened, they are likely to disagree as to why it happened. Whereas development and modernization theorists, for example, have generally viewed the public and private vehicles of U.S. influence as forces for democratic and social reform, dependency theorists have viewed them as antidemocratic and anti-egalitarian forces.

In the late 1980s, a number of scholars sought to resolve the debate between development and dependency theorists by seeking common ground or sought to supersede the debate by asking a different set of questions. One consequence has been a new emphasis on "interdependence." Another has been a wide-angle focus, reaching across disciplines and deep into the history of industrialization to explore, in particular, relationships between the state and the private sector, domestic and foreign. That approach has been labeled the new international political economy.

Interdependence

Whereas scholars dealing with relations between developed states and the Third World tended to focus in the 1960s on the benefits of such relations for the Third World and, in the 1970s, on the detriment of such relations to the Third World, many scholars in the 1980s began to focus instead on complementary needs and common problems. Some noted, for example, an increasing vulnerability on the part of the industrialized states to economic problems in the Third World. The high interest rates of the early 1980s in the First World, particularly the United States, were devastating to Latin American economies. The consequent debt crisis in Latin America has threatened the solvency of U.S. banks and closed markets for U.S. manufactured goods.

International Political Economy

The international political economy (IPE) agenda recaptures the scope of nineteenth-century social concerns for the purpose of addressing contemporary policy issues. Thus, the assumptions and findings of IPE theorists tend to cut across, and perhaps defuse, the development-dependency debates. In addressing Third World issues, IPE theorists, like dependency theorists, seek explanation for means and levels of development in class conflict rather than in assumptions about attitudes. Like modernization and development theorists, however, they generally find a positive relationship between development and democracy. They accept, to a point, the *dependentista* assertion that Third World countries have been disadvantaged by their participation in the global economy, but hold that positive results have on occasion been achieved where Third World governments had the capacity to negotiate the conditions of their participation.

International political economy shares with the world system school the conviction that development follows no preordained sequence of stages. IPE, however, faults the world system approach for underestimating the role of the state in determining economic outcomes. Rejecting both the liberal preference for an unfettered market and the Marxist choice of state dominance of economic decisionmaking, international political economy theorists contend that both state and market have important roles to play and that on occasion they are mutually reinforcing. Effective operation of the market may in fact be dependent upon the vigilance of a strong state, prepared to intervene where necessary.

Like dependency theorists, adherents of the IPE approach concern themselves with the contradiction between the territorial character of state power and the transnational character of economic power, but IPE theorists argue that the penetration of foreign capital does not necessarily shrink the economic role of the state. Studies of petrochemical and iron industries in Brazil by Peter Evans, of the oil industry in Venezuela by Franklin Tugwell, and of the copper industry in Chile by Theodore Moran have shown that foreign-owned extractive sectors may stimulate state entrepreneurial activity. That in itself, however, does not necessarily advance living standards or other indices of development.[20]

THE POST–COLD WAR PARADIGMATIC SHIFT

Though the Cold War ended with a whimper rather than a bang, the postwar period has had much in common with the aftermath of other wars—shifting boundaries and trade patterns, new categories of the displaced and the deprived. The winner in this case was not a country or set of countries but an economic system. That system is not just capitalism; it is a socially premodern version of capitalism bulwarked by postmodern technology.

Spencerian capitalism, emerging triumphant, has demanded unconditional surrender not just of socialism in its extreme forms but also of many experiments in state planning and regulation, state-run enterprise and protected domestic industry, and welfare provision—in Latin America, and particularly the most developed Latin American states, survivals of several decades of political development and economic nationalism. Such globalization of economic power and planning has meant also a level of hegemony in the realm of ideas unprecedented perhaps since the era of scholasticism. That is not to say that there is no dissidence or heresy. So long as there have been spokesmen of the haves proclaiming that trends and policies in their interest were in the interest also of the have-nots, there have been defenders of the have-nots having the nerve to say "not so." But one thing the have-nots do not have in times like these is a forum.

The kind of economic devastation that followed the final cataclysms of the Cold War in the region of its epicenter got a long head start in Latin America. The debt crisis of the early 1980s left Latin American leaders at the mercy of creditors and currency speculators. The state itself, as a representative of a sovereign people, was so weakened that any line of policy, or even rhetoric, that smacked of economic nationalism threatened to set off a stampede of fleeing capital.

The surrender of economic policymaking seemed not to be a matter of choice, but domestic constituencies nonetheless demanded explanation and justification, which was scripted in neoliberal terms. Dependency theorists might claim that this turn of events had validated their analysis of the problem; but in a globalized economy—that is, without an alternative market or credit source—they were left without politically feasible solutions.

Liberalism and Neoliberalism

Like persons and places and religions, theories that acquire celebrity status—and thus usefulness to the powerful—become caricatures of themselves or their original versions; and liberalism was no exception. As elaborated in 1776 by Adam Smith, it was a progressive proposition, designed to redistribute wealth and opportunity from opulent courts and colonizers monopolizing trade under a system known as mercantilism to a new class of merchants and entrepreneurs whose interests and power would be limited by competition. Smith, however, recognized the danger of the evolution of monopolies and advocated strict governmental regulation to prevent such a development.

As liberalism came to be championed by an expansive Great Britain in the nineteenth century and the United States in the twentieth century, its qualifiers faded and its progressive features were transformed. The surviving core of the theory held that states had a common interest in the free flow of goods, services, and capital across national borders. Smith's laissez-faire principle was reinforced by David Ricardo's theory of comparative advantage. That theory posited that states should take advantage of their raw materials, low labor costs, technologies, or other strengths in order to specialize in those goods they could produce most efficiently, while trading for goods in which other states had the advantage. In colonial and neocolonial systems, the advantage accrued, of course, to mother countries, not colonies.

Development and modernization theory was a legitimate offspring of liberalism, and like its sire it served to explain and legitimate the seemingly limitless opportunities and responsibilities of an imperial power at its peak. Like liberalism also it sought to promote social and political change in adversary or client states, within limits dictated by economic interest.

Though its power center does not reside in a state, neoliberalism shares those circumstances and attributes of its forebears. But whereas development theory sought to strengthen state institutions, neoliberalism as expressed in policy tends to eviscerate them. Governments in general are seen as wasteful and corrupt, their deficits inflationary, their budgets a drain on resources that might otherwise be directed to servicing debt and attracting investment. And privatization of government enterprises or services that might bring in a profit has commonly been a condition for the extension of credit. These and other measures that have come to be known collectively as "structural adjustment" are in the context of neoliberalism both policy prescriptions and factors in explanation and prediction of economic growth and stability or their absence. It is also assumed that an economy restructured along the lines prescribed is a prerequisite for a smoothly functioning electoral democracy. It has been conveniently forgotten that in general the "opening" of Latin American economies coincided with the shutdown of democratic systems in the 1970s rather than with their return.

Critics and Heretics: What's Left of the Left

With the end of the Cold War, the right had lost its cover story, but the left had lost something harder to come by; it had lost its dream.

Criticism of neoliberalism as theory and as policy has exhibited little in the way of romanticism or radicalism. It is not in spite of the enormity of Latin America's problems and the pressures that private interests are able to bring to bear against the public interest but *because* of them that political strategies and policy alternatives from the left in the 1990s have been measured and modest.

The *dependentista* school has not vanished, though some might argue—since Cardoso was elected president of Brazil as a born-again neoliberal—that it has gone under deep cover. Osvaldo Sunkel, in his influential book *Development from Within*,[21] argues that while a strategy of export promotion may be unavoidable, a healthy economy, resistant to the effects of global market volatility, demands priority attention to the development of the domestic market. Andre Gunder Frank, who has joined world systems scholars in the study of long cycles of history, found Latin America in the early 1990s to be increasingly marginalized from world trading systems. More important, he sees commerce centering once again in the twenty-first century in the Orient, and particularly China.

Mexican scholar and political columnist Jorge Castañeda, in *Utopia Unarmed*,[22] observes that the entire political spectrum shifted sharply to the right in the 1990s. In that context, he finds the left alive and well and living in the center—or what used to be the center. He does not interpret such repositioning, however, as surrender or battle fatigue; rather, he sees it as the outcome of learning through painful experience to see politics as the art of the possible. Castañeda calls for a revival of nationalism, but reformulated so as to promote transnational coalition building and to accommodate regional economic integration.

A MESSAGE FROM THE STREET

While the left in the ivory towers of academia, politics, and punditry may have been, at the turn of the twenty-first century, alive and well and living in the center, the disadvantaged people for whom they proposed to speak had taken to the streets; and momentum with respect to the articulation and projection of their message had shifted to the street-level world of social activists and social movements.

Throughout the hemisphere, from Mexico to Argentina, those whose resources and livelihoods and safety nets had been usurped by the faceless corporate and institutional predators who came to be identified with neoliberal globalization found new means of organizing and making themselves heard. The Zapatistas of the Mexican state of Chiapas garnered support from around the world as the virtual version of their revolution was played out in poetry on the Internet. In Colombia, "peace communities" put up unarmed resistance to guerrillas and government-supported paramilitaries alike. In Ecuador and Bolivia, indigenous communities coalesced to bring down elite-based governments. In Argentina, barter clubs, co-op factories, and neighborhood support groups overcame anarchy when government collapsed. And in Brazil, landless workers, more than a million strong, helped to propel the leader of a genuine workers' party into the presidency.

All of this newly effective commotion in the streets and fields and forests provided a new focus for Latin Americanists. Sonia Alvarez was among the first to call attention to the potential of popular, grassroots movements in Latin America.[23] Such movements, in Latin America and elsewhere, have benefited greatly from the work of a multifaceted thicket of nongovernmental organizations, operating at all levels from local to global. Henry Veltmeyer is among the Latin Americanists who have envisioned an important role for such organizations.[24]

Activists' Alternative Perspectives

The last decade of the twentieth century and the first decade of the twenty-first have, in fact, seen the amassing of a great body of scholarly and popular literature inspired by needs and interests that run counter to those advanced by neoliberalism. This intellectual flourishing, particularly on the part of environmentalists, feminists, and advocates of grassroots community development, was, however, slow to generate a great debate, mainly because until recently economists, who enjoyed unchallenged disciplinary primacy in the business of theoretical legitimization, generally ignored it.

Between these concerns and neoliberalism as now advanced there is little common ground. From the perspective of environmentalism, the global village is being stripped of resources by a feeding frenzy set off by deregulation and the new openness of markets and fueled by hard-currency debt-service requirements. Globe-hopping investors deplete, despoil, and depart, leaving communities and ecosystems devastated.

Likewise, scholars engaging in gender analysis, along with chroniclers and supporters of the international women's movement, have noted that the front-line victims of the economic restructuring now sweeping the global village are women. Shrinkage of the public sector has cost women their best professional jobs at the same time that loss of family services, pensions, and benefits has expanded their responsibilities. While women are being squeezed out of the better-paying formal economy, they are being drawn in ever greater numbers into exploitative informal-sector work. Jane Jaquette has done seminal work on the mobilization of women to confront social and political crisis.[25] Mala Htun represents a new generation of women focusing not only on women in politics but on the politics of gender issues.[26]

As governments, bound first to distant creditors, default on their obligations to their own citizens, the newly displaced and deprived are discovering what the long-suffering have always known—that the last bastion of security is the community, a community organized and aware of the need for general commitment and mutual support. Theorists of grassroots development note that such awareness and commitment runs counter to the dog-eat-dog or all-eat-dog options suggested by neoliberal individualism. Moreover, globalization—the alienation or distancing of decisionmaking about priorities and livelihoods—presents a dire threat to the ideal of individual and collective self-sufficiency, or "empowerment," that is the philosophical foundation of community development.

Globalizing Justice?

With increasing success, since the first major street demonstrations against the World Trade Organization (WTO) in Seattle in 1999, opponents of neoliberal globalization have broadened their constituencies, united diverse groups and causes, and made their voices heard. Since the Seattle meeting, massive demonstrations have regularly dogged the deliberations of international financial institutions and other global money movers, and after several years of covering the action, media analysts finally began to ask why. A new threshold was crossed at the WTO Forum in Cancun in 2003, when for the first time NGOs moved up from the street to work directly with delegations of Third World governments. Under Brazilian leadership, a coalition including China and India as well as Argentina and several other Latin American countries blocked the next round of the WTO's proposed reforms and derailed, at least temporarily, the proposed Free Trade Agreement of the Americas (FTAA).[27]

Thus, the surge of events, prompted by bottom-up initiatives, seems finally to have broken the paradigmatic monopoly of neoliberalism. Though advocates and critics rarely engage each other in straightforward debate or in pursuit of theoretical synthesis, perspectives alternative to or critical of neoliberal globalization are gaining increasing attention in the media and in academia and perhaps laying the groundwork for a vibrant new dialogue on the fundamentals of democracy and development.[28]

Many of those concerned about the dark side of globalization point out that the issue is not globalization—global interaction or togetherness—itself, but rather what is being globalized. They say that, in contrast to their intellectual detractors and political adversaries, they would advance the globalization of social justice, biological and cultural diversity, and respect for human rights. In fact, as anti-terrorism replaces anti-communism as the new all-purpose trump card of the powerful, Latin Americanists are once again edging into the forefront of social criticism. It could hardly be otherwise; the New American Century declared by the George W. Bush Administration sounds to Latin Americans and Latin Americanists like a century with which they are already all too familiar.[29]

Notes

1. Sarmiento's best-known work is *Facundo* (in English translation, *Civilization and Barbarism: The Life of Juan Facundo Quiroga* [New York: Collier Books, 1961]).

2. This author submits that one of the reasons that Latin American politics has been so poorly understood by North Americans is that North American politics is also poorly understood by them.

3. Among the Latin Americanists whose works have tended to be in this vein are Fredrick Pike, John Mander, Charles Wagley, Claudio Veliz, Ronald Newton, William S. Stokes, and William Lyle Schurz.

4. Works highlighting corporatism or employing corporatist models include Howard J. Wiarda, *Corporatism and Development: The Portuguese Experience* (Amherst: University of Massachusetts Press, 1977); Howard J. Wiarda, ed., *Politics and Social Change in Latin America: The Distinct Tradition* (Amherst: University of Massachusetts Press, 1974); Philippe C. Schmitter, *Interest Conflict and Political Change in Brazil* (Stanford, Calif.: Stanford University Press, 1971); James M. Malloy, ed., *Authoritarianism and Corporatism in Latin America* (Pittsburgh: University of Pittsburgh Press, 1977); and Kenneth Paul Erick-

son, *The Brazilian Corporative State: Working Class Politics* (Berkeley: University of California Press, 1977).

5. Samuel Huntington and Myron Weiner, eds., *Understanding Political Development* (Boston: Little, Brown, 1987), pp. 21–28.

6. New York: Basic Books, 2000.

7. Walt W. Rostow, *The Stages of Economic Growth* (London: Cambridge University Press, 1960).

8. Gabriel Almond and G. Bingham Powell, *Comparative Politics: A Developmental Approach* (Boston: Little, Brown, 1966); and Samuel Huntington, *Political Order in Changing Societies* (New Haven, Conn.: Yale University Press, 1968).

9. Martin C. Needler, *Political Development in Latin America: Instability, Violence, and Evolutionary Change* (New York: Random House, 1968).

10. Albert O. Hirschman, *Journeys Toward Progress: Studies of Economic Policymaking in Latin America* (New York: Twentieth Century Fund, 1963).

11. Samuel Huntington, "The Change to Change," *Comparative Politics* 3 (April 1971), p. 290.

12. Cited in Dan Griffin, "The Boom in Brazil: An Awful Lot of Everything," *Washington Post,* May 27, 1973.

13. Susanne Bodenheimer Jonas, "Dependency and Imperialism: The Roots of Latin American Development," *Politics and Society* 1:3 (May 1977), pp. 327–357.

14. Richard Fagen, "Studying Latin American Politics: Some Implications of a Dependency Approach," *Latin American Research Review* 12:2 (1977), pp. 3–26.

15. Andre Gunder Frank, *Development and Underdevelopment in Latin America* (New York: Monthly Review Press, 1968).

16. For an elaboration and application of penetration theory, see Jan Knippers Black, *United States Penetration of Brazil* (Philadelphia: University of Pennsylvania Press, 1977), forthcoming in Portuguese edition from Fundação Joaquim Nabuco, Editóra Massangana, Recife.

17. Guillermo O'Donnell, *Modernization and Bureaucratic-Authoritarianism: Studies in South American Politics,* Politics of Modernization Series, no. 9 (Berkeley: Institute of International Studies, University of California, 1973).

18. Johan Galtung, "A Structural Theory of Imperialism," *Journal of Peace Research* 8:2 (1972), pp. 81–117.

19. Immanuel Wallerstein, *The Modern World-System: Capitalist Agriculture and the Origins of the European World-Economy in the Sixteenth Century* (New York: Academic Press, 1974).

20. See Peter Evans, *Dependent Development: The Alliance of Multinational, State, and Local Capital in Brazil* (Princeton: Princeton University Press, 1979); Franklin Tugwell, *The Politics of Oil in Venezuela* (Stanford, Calif.: Stanford University Press, 1975); and Theodore H. Moran, *Multinational Corporations and the Politics of Dependence: Copper in Chile* (Princeton: Princeton University Press, 1975).

21. Osvaldo Sunkel, ed., *Development from Within: Toward a Neostructuralist Approach for Latin America* (Boulder, Colo.: Lynne Rienner, 1993).

22. Jorge B. Castañeda, *Utopia Unarmed: The Latin American Left After the Cold War* (New York: Knopf, 1993).

23. See Alvarez and Arturo Escobar, eds., *The Making of Social Movements in Latin America: Identity, Strategy, and Democracy,* (Boulder, Colo.: Westview Press, 1992).

24. Henry Veltmeyer, *Nongovernmental Organizations and Development* (Halifax, Nova Scotia: Fernwood Books and London: Zed Books, forthcoming 2005).

25. Jane S. Jaquette, *The Women's Movement in Latin America* (Boston: Unwin Hyman, 1989).

26. Mala Htun, *Sex and the State: Abortion, Divorce, and the Family Under Latin American Dictatorships and Democracies* (Cambridge: Cambridge University Press, 2003).

27. The coalition was offended, particularly by the hypocrisy of First World protectionism and by the increasing shift of power and initiative through such agreements from the public to the private sector.

28. See, for example, Réne Armand Dreifuss, *A Epoca Das Perplexidades* (Petropolis, Editora Voces, 1996); William Robinson, *Transnational Conflicts: Central America, Social Change, and Globalization* (London: Verso Books, 2003); and Jan Knippers Black, *Inequity in the Global Village: Recycled Rhetoric and Disposable People* (Westport, Conn.: Kumarian Press, 1999).

29. See Virginia Bouvier, ed., *The Globalization of U.S.–Latin American Relations: Democracy, Intervention, and Human Rights* (Westport, Conn.: Praeger, 2002).

PART I

THE LAND AND
THE PEOPLE

LANDSCAPE AND
SETTLEMENT PATTERNS

ALFONSO GONZALEZ

LATIN AMERICA IS AMONG the largest world culture regions, with an area of 20.5 million square kilometers (7.9 million square miles), more than double the size of the United States. It has the greatest latitudinal range of any world region, extending from 32 degrees north latitude to 56 degrees south latitude. The airline distance from northwestern Mexico to northern South America is nearly 5,000 kilometers (more than 3,000 miles), and from there to Cape Horn, following the general curvature of the continent, is an additional 7,500 kilometers (more than 4,600 miles). As a consequence, the region has a highly diversified ecology. Although it is primarily tropical, it encompasses some mid-latitude environments, and there is great variation in the physiography, climate, vegetation, soil types, and minerals that are encountered in the region.

OUTSTANDING PHYSICAL CHARACTERISTICS

There are some outstanding physical characteristics in Latin America that combine to render a uniqueness to the region. The Andes, for example, constitute the highest continuous mountain barrier on earth with a lineal extent of more than 7,000 kilometers (4,400 miles). The chain includes the highest summits outside of central Asia, with at least three dozen peaks higher than Mount McKinley (6,194 meters, or 20,320 feet), the highest summit in North America. Virtually every maximum or near-maximum elevation for most of the world's features (except summits) occurs in the Andes—the highest settlement, capital city, railroad, highway, mining activities, commercial airport, volcanoes, navigable lake, and snowline, among others. Furthermore, the steepest coastal gradient anywhere occurs in Colombia.

The Amazon is physically the world's greatest river. Although second to the Nile in length, it has by far the greatest discharge volume, drainage basin, and length of navigable waterways of any river on earth. The highest and most voluminous waterfalls are located in South America. Two or three of the world's highest falls occur in the Guiana Highlands, and five of the seven greatest waterfalls in the world in volume of flow are in the Brazilian Highlands. Although the waterpower potential of Latin America is somewhat less than that of Asia, one-fifth of the world's potential hydroelectric power is found in Latin America.

Latin America is a unique faunal region, the Neotropical Zoogeographical Realm, which covers all of Latin America except northern and central highland Mexico and the Bahamas. Although the diversity of mammalian animal life is somewhat greater in the African region, no world region has so many unique mammalian families. Furthermore, Latin America has the most diverse bird life and a highly varied and complex collection of lower animal forms.

Latin America has the highest proportion of any world region of its area in forests (nearly one-half), and the regions of Amazonia and the Guiana Highlands represent the largest continuous tropical rain forest area on earth. Latin America also contains the greatest absolute area in forest, almost one-quarter of the world total, and the highest per capita forested area of any world region. Unfortunately, perhaps only one-third of this forested area is both economically productive and accessible, so that Latin America, in reality, is a net importer of forest-based products. Currently, the reduction of the forests is occurring at an unprecedented rate: more than 400,000 square kilometers (more than 150,000 square miles) of forested area were cleared for other uses during the 1990s. This reduction is essentially in tropical South America and Mexico. This is approximately one-half of the world's net total loss of forests.

There are a number of extremes that distinguish the climate of Latin America. Some of the coastal lowlands and island stations approach the world record of only approximately 13 degrees C (23 degrees F) between the highest and lowest temperatures ever recorded. Probably the driest region on earth is the Peruvian-Atacama Desert, especially in northern Chile. Nevertheless, southern Chile is one of the rainiest places on earth, receiving measurable precipitation for as many as 325 days a year. The wettest place in the Western Hemisphere is located in the western Colombian Andes, which receive more than 8.5 meters (335 inches) of rainfall annually.

Latin America is periodically beset by major natural disasters that are destructive of both lives and property, second only to the Orient. Earthquakes occur with great frequency along the western highland margin of the region. Two of the greatest quakes outside the Orient occurred in 1868 and in 1970 in highland Peru, each causing the loss of 50,000 to 70,000 lives. More recently, devastating quakes occurred in 1972 at Managua, Nicaragua, in 1975 in central Guatemala, and in 1985 in Mexico City. Fifty or more active volcanoes exist in the region, approximately one-quarter of the world total. The eruptions of Mt. Pelee (Martinique) in 1902, which resulted in the deaths of at least 30,000 people, and of Nevado del Ruiz (Colombia) in 1985, with more than 22,000 killed, rank among the greatest volcanic eruptions of modern times. Hurricanes occur regularly within the Caribbean Basin and with less frequency on the Pacific coast of Mexico, often causing thousands of deaths. Perhaps the greatest avalanche ever recorded occurred in the Andean region of Peru.

Outstanding Population and
Settlement Characteristics

The population and settlement pattern of Latin America is also distinctive. The population in mid-2003 was approximately 540 million (see Table 2.1). More than 8 percent of the world's population now resides in Latin America, compared to less than 2 percent during the colonial period. It is the only world region that, since the mid-eighteenth century, has consistently increased in population faster than the world average. For half a century beginning in the early–World War I period, Latin America was the fastest growing region in the world. It was equaled or surpassed by the Middle East and sub-Saharan Africa during the 1970s, or even earlier.

Latin America's rate of population growth has been gradually decreasing since the early 1960s, and the decline has been more significant recently. Nevertheless, the region's population continues to increase by more than 8 million annually. During the early–World War II period, the average rate of growth was 2.7 to 2.9 percent per year. Now the population is expanding at less than 2 percent annually. The greatest rates of growth occur in northern Central America and in Andean South America. Traditionally, the slowest growth has occurred in Argentina and Uruguay, although more recently these countries have been joined by Chile, most of the Antilles, Brazil, and some smaller countries. The potential for further population growth remains in those few countries in which the death rate remains relatively high, notably in Haiti. Family planning programs in the region became generally significant in the late 1960s.

The age structure of the population is characteristic of underdeveloped regions generally—a high proportion of the younger ages (now 32 percent or more younger than fifteen) and a low proportion of older people (now 6 percent sixty-five years or older). Dependency ratios (proportions of the very young and very old in relation to the productive ages, fifteen to sixty-four) are somewhat high (but declining) in the region, placing an additional burden on the economy. Partially related to this situation is the fact that only approximately two-fifths of the population is economically active (compared with about one-half in developed regions). With reduced mortality, increasingly large numbers will be entering the labor force, currently probably more than 3 million annually, which will result in heavy demands on employment opportunities as well as on educational and health facilities and housing.

In Latin America, infant mortality rates are the lowest of any underdeveloped region, and life expectancy is the longest. (A subregion of the Orient, East Asia, however, now has rates that approximate the Latin American average.) Mortality aside, there is still a significant gap between the levels of living in Latin America and in the more developed regions.

The population density of Latin America averages approximately twenty-six inhabitants per square kilometer (more than sixty-seven per square mile), which is only slightly more than half the world average and is comparable to a

TABLE 2.1 Latin America: Population Characteristics

	Area (thousand) km²	Population (million) 2003	Density (per km²) 2003	Percent Annual Population Increase 1995–2000	Projected Population (million) 2025	Birth Rate a	Death Rate b	Infant Mortality Rate c	Composition of Population by Age -15	65+	Percent Population Urban	Agricultural
Mexico	1958	104.9	54	1.4	133.8	29	5	25	33	5	75	21
Guatemala	109	12.4	114	2.6	19.8	33	7	41	42	4	39	60
El Salvador	21	6.6	315	2	9.3	29	6	30	38	5	58	39
Honduras	112	6.9	61	2.6	10.7	34	5	34	42	4	46	46
Nicaragua	130	5.5	42	2.7	8.3	32	5	31	42	3	57	44
Costa Rica	51	4.2	81	2.8	5.6	18	4	10	30	6	59	20
Panama	76	3	39	1.6	4.2	23	5	21	32	6	62	44
Belize	23	0.3	12	2.9	0.4	29	6	21	41	4	45	52
Cuba	111	11.3	102	0.4	11.8	12	7	6	21	10	75	25
Dominican Republic	49	8.7	179	2	11.1	25	6	31	35	5	61	34
Haiti	28	7.5	271	2.1	11.1	32	14	80	40	4	36	64
Puerto Rico	9	3.9	434	0.8	4.2	16	7	10.6	24	11	71	24
Jamaica	11	2.6	241	1	3.3	21	7	24	31	7	52	44
Trinidad/Tobago	5	1.3	255	0.5	1.3	13	7	18.6	25	7	72	26
Guyana	215	0.8	3.5	0.4	0.7	23	9	53	30	4	36	63
Suriname	163	0.4	2.7	1.3	0.4	23	7	27	32	6	69	25
French Guiana	90	0.2	1.9	3.6	0.3	31	4	12	33	5	79	25

(continues)

TABLE 2.1 (continued)

	Area (thousand) km² 1958	Population (million) 2003	Density (per km²) 2003	Percent Annual Population Increase 1995–2000	Projected Population (million) 2025	Birth Rate a	Death Rate b	Infant Mortality Rate c	Composition of Population by Age		Percent Population	
									-15	65+	Urban	Agricultural
Venezuela	912	25.7	28	2	35.2	24	5	19.6	34	4	87	13
Colombia	1139	44.2	39	1.9	58.1	23	6	28	33	5	71	25
Ecuador	284	12.6	44	2	17.5	27	6	35	36	4	61	37
Peru	1285	27.1	21	1.7	35.7	26	7	33	34	5	72	27
Bolivia	1099	8.6	8	2.3	12.2	32	9	61	39	5	63	37
Paraguay	407	6.2	15	2.6	10.1	31	5	37	39	5	54	43
Chile	757	15.8	21	1.4	19.5	18	6	10.1	26	7	87	14
Argentina	2780	36.9	20	1.3	47.2	19	8	16.6	31	9	89	12
Uruguay	175	3.4	19	0.7	3.8	16	9	13.5	24	13	93	8
Brazil	8514	176.5	20	1.5	211.2	20	7	33	30	6	81	18
Latin America	20533	540	26	1.6	690	23	6	29	32	6	75	24
Canada	9971	31.6	3.1	0.9	36	11	7	5.3	18	13	79	21
United States	9629	291.5	30	1	351.1	14	9	6.9	21	13	79	23
Underdeveloped Countries	84933	5105	62		6638	24	8	61	33	5	40	
WORLD TOTAL	135641	6314	47	1.4	7907	22	9	55	30	7	47	52

a Number of births annually per 1000 population
b Number of deaths annually per 1000 population
c Number of deaths of infants (less than 1 year of age) annually per 1000 live births

Sources: United Nations, Demographic Yearbook 2000; Population Reference Bureau, Inc., 2003; World Population Data Sheet; Britannica Book of the Year 2003, Britannica World Data; Food and Agriculture Organization, Production Yearbook 2002.

number of other world regions. Most of the countries of Latin America are, therefore, below the world average in density; exceptions include the Antilles, El Salvador, Guatemala, Costa Rica, and more recently, Honduras and Mexico. Partly as a consequence of relatively low crop yields, population pressure on available cropland is greater in Latin America than in any developed world region, but such pressure is less than in any other underdeveloped area.

The pattern of population distribution in Latin America includes a concentration on the periphery, especially in South America and on the Pacific margins of Central America. Population is also concentrated in the highlands within the tropics, with one-half to three-quarters of the national populations in the upland areas. Major exceptions are the Antilles, Nicaragua, Panama, Belize, and the Guianas. Latin America has a larger population in the highlands than any other world region.

The region has a nucleated pattern of settlement, with semi-isolated population clusters and national population cores. Population clusters have been detached, although this is diminishing with increased population and improved transportation. Generally 10 to 25 percent of the national area of a Latin American country contains one-half or more of the national population. As a result, in most countries there are large areas that are very sparsely settled—half of the area of Latin America contains only about 5 percent of the region's total population. But many outlying areas are growing faster than the overall growth rate.

A rapid process of urbanization has characterized Latin America, especially since World War II. It is, by far, the most highly urbanized underdeveloped region. Its population was one-half urban by 1965 and was by early twenty-first century about three-quarters urban, the result of both natural increase (excess of births over deaths) and internal migration, with probably 3 to 4 million migrants recently moving into the urban centers. The causes of rapid urbanization include rural poverty (the "push" factors—expulsion from the countryside); the fast rate of natural increase in the rural areas; the scarcity of available arable land, especially in the traditional areas of settlement; the land tenure system (*latifundia*, the predominance of large estates, and *minifundia,* the prevalence of many very small landholdings); limited rural employment opportunities and low wages; and restricted social services in rural areas. Also, the attractions of the city (the "pull" factors)—the possibility of employment, higher wages, and improved social services—make the cities, especially the capitals, appealing to impoverished rural residents.

The largest city of each country (the capital, except in Brazil, Ecuador, Belize, and also now possibly Bolivia) tends to dominate the life of the country and is generally several times larger than the second largest city. This degree of primacy is more accentuated in Latin America than in any other world region. Some countries are highly urbanized, notably Venezuela and the Southern Cone countries of South America, while the most rural areas are Central America, Haiti, and the Guianas.

Compiled by Dr. Gonzalez and M. Styk, U of Calgary

FIGURE 2.1   Latin America: Natural Regions

Natural Regions

Although there is a great variety of physical habitat in Latin America, it is possible to subdivide the area into thirteen natural regions (see Map 2.1). These regions, although based fundamentally on physiographic characteristics, also possess some unifying characteristics of climate, natural vegetation, and soils. Therefore, since these natural regions present differing sets of problems for human settlement and economic development, the human patterns are often in

TABLE 2.2   Natural Regions of Latin America

	Area (thousand km²)	Population (thousand) 2002	Percent Annual Growth 1995–2002	Density (per km²)	Percent of Total Area	Percent of Total Population 2002
Gulf-Caribbean Coastal Lowlands	763	35134	2.94	38.6	3.7	6.7
Pacific Littoral	487	24102	1.32	49.5	2.4	4.6
Cordilleran Highlands	3234	167173	1.42	51.7	15.7	31.7
Antilles	234	37393	0.81	159.6	1.1	7.1
Llanos (Orinoco)	641	5985	3.71	9.3	3.1	1.1
Guiana Highlands	1103	2889	1.89	2.6	5.4	0.5
Amazonia	4956	16630	3.19	3.4	24.1	3.2
Brazilian Highlands	4335	160363	1.51	37.0	21.1	30.5
Peruvian–Atacama Desert	402	14546	2.67	36.2	2.0	2.8
Middle Chile	255	13640	0.78	53.5	1.2	2.6
South Chile	241	239	-0.03	1.0	1.2	0.05
La Plata–Parana Basin	2356	40441	1.46	17.2	11.5	7.7
Northwest Argentina–Patagonia	1538	8099	1.51	5.3	7.5	1.5
Total Latin America	20544	526634	2.51	25.6	100.0	100.0

Note: Figures are estimates and totals may not coincide with above data or with other data for Latin America because of changing boundaries, estimates, and rounding.

large measure a response to the prevalent locational and physical factors. Crude approximations of the areas, populations, and densities for the natural regions of Latin America are presented in Table 2.2.

GULF-CARIBBEAN COASTAL LOWLANDS

The Gulf-Caribbean Coastal Lowlands are a continuation of the Atlantic-Gulf Coastal Lowlands of the United States, but south of the Rio Grande (Rio Bravo to the Mexicans) the coastal plain is narrower and interrupted. In the northernmost section, in the Mexican state of Tamaulipas, the climate is mostly subhumid (low-latitude steppe). This section is relatively sparsely settled, although the lower Rio Grande Valley has dense settlement because of agriculture and the newly developed gas fields. South of Tamaulipas, the coastal lowland is tropical in climate, vegetation, and soils.

The coastal plain becomes very restricted in portions of Veracruz and along sections of Central America; it becomes broadest in Yucatán and is fairly broad in Nicaragua and adjoining sections of Honduras and Costa Rica. Many portions of the coastal plain are characterized by poor drainage, resulting in swamps and marshes. Precipitation occurs throughout the year, but it is concentrated in the warmer months and is often twice as great as on the Pacific littoral. Many parts of the coastal lowlands are subject to violent tropical storms, especially from August through November. These hurricanes sometimes cause losses of thousands of lives and (unnecessary) extensive property damage.

The soils generally are not highly productive under continuous tillage. These lowland areas have traditionally had only scattered areas of settlement, frequently associated with commercial plantation agriculture, especially of bananas, and with fishing and logging. However, in recent decades, there has been an influx of migrants into the lowlands.

The Yucatán peninsula, a platform of coral rock with limestone beds, is characterized by shallow, dry rendzina soil, with many sinkholes (*cenotes*) and few surface streams. The eastern and southern sections of the Mexican portion of the peninsula, Belize, and the northern third of Guatemala (the Petén) comprise one of the most sparsely settled areas of the coastal lowlands. Nevertheless, in pre-Columbian times, this area was the cultural hearth of the Mayan civilization, with population densities significantly above current levels.

The older petroleum fields of Mexico were centered in northern Veracruz. Reduced production continues from fields near Tampico, Tuxpan, and Poza Rica, but the great petroleum and natural gas fields were opened in the 1970s in southern Veracruz, Tabasco, and adjacent Campeche and on the offshore banks. Agricultural expansion in this region predates the development of the petroleum and natural gas industries.

The Gulf-Caribbean Coastal Lowlands extend into neighboring Colombia and Venezuela in South America. There they mainly comprise the Atrato and Magdalena valleys of Colombia and the Maracaibo Basin of Venezuela, which contains Latin America's largest lake. These areas have been attracting migration from the more traditional highland centers of settlement because of the production of bananas and other tropical crops in Colombia and the great petroleum production in the Maracaibo district of Venezuela.

Antilles (West Indies)

The Antilles comprise one of the world's most important archipelagoes. The total area of the islands is only about 238,000 square kilometers (92,000 square miles), approximately the size of Oregon. Cuba alone embraces one-half of the area; most of the remainder consists of the other Greater Antilles: Hispaniola, Jamaica, and Puerto Rico. The islands enclose one of the world's largest seas, the Caribbean, on the north and east.

The Greater Antilles are a complex folded and block-faulted mountain system that is mostly submerged. They consist of two ridges, separated by a deep trough. The Lesser Antilles, extending from east of Puerto Rico to the Netherlands Antilles off the coast of South America, consist of a great number of much smaller islands with an arcuate shape, convex toward the Atlantic Ocean and structurally connected with the highlands of Venezuela. In the north, the Leeward Islands extend from the Virgin Islands to north of Guadeloupe, or possibly as far south as Martinique. The southern islands are the Windwards. The total area of the Lesser Antilles is less than 13,000 square kilometers (5,019 square miles), about the size of Connecticut. The Antilles region, like the northern mainland of Central America and most of Mexico, is regularly exposed to hurricanes. The climate throughout the Antilles gives rise to either tropical rain forest or tropical savanna.

The Antilles, except for the Bahamas and the Turks and Caicos, are far more densely settled than any other area of Latin America. Their populations are predominantly of African descent. The geographic location, combined with an equable climate and productive soils, gave rise to the earliest plantation economies of the New World. These were based primarily on sugar, although later bananas, coffee, and other crops were added.

The plantation agricultural economy has declined recently, especially on the smaller islands. Other economic activities, including tourism, subsistence agriculture, and commerce, have generally proved inadequate to support the dense populations. Mineral wealth in this region overall is minor but is of importance in eastern Cuba, Jamaica, and Trinidad. Relatively rapid population growth in the post–World War II period without compensating socioeconomic development caused a large exodus of emigrants to the United States, the United Kingdom, France, the Netherlands, and Canada.

Pacific Littoral: Coastal Plains and Valleys

The Pacific margins of Middle America and the northern section of South America represent a narrow zone of diverse physical landscapes. The peninsula of Baja (Lower) California, in Mexico, represents the southern extension of the Pacific mountain system of North America and consists of a long series of blocks tilted toward the Pacific Ocean with a steep fault scarp to the east on the Gulf of California side. This essentially desert, shrub-covered region has been, with parts of Yucatán, the most sparsely settled and isolated area of Mexico. However, in 1972 a paved highway was opened, and it runs the length of the peninsula, nearly 1,900 kilometers (1,180 miles).

Across the Gulf of California lies the almost equally arid Sonoran Desert, the southward extension of the basin-and-range topography of the United States. Although the population is greater toward the more humid south, many of the river valleys of southern Sonora and northern Sinaloa are densely settled and intensively utilized due to the irrigation projects developed since the Mexican Revolution of 1910.

From approximately Mazatlán southward, the remainder of the coastal margin of Mexico, Central America, Colombia, and Ecuador is generally narrow; in places it disappears completely as the highlands reach the shore. The population along the Mexican section of this coastal zone is relatively sparse but increasing. The Pacific coastal margins of Central America tend to have greater population settlements than the Caribbean coasts, except in Honduras, but the coastal lowlands on both sides of the isthmus are undergoing a rapid increase in settlement. The great majority of the population of Panama is located in the Pacific lowlands, whereas that of Nicaragua is in the lake district lowlands close to the Pacific.

The extremely humid Pacific coastal margins of Colombia are sparsely settled and relatively isolated from the country's national settlement core. However, the growing commercial importance of the port of Buenaventura has stimulated population migration into this heavily forested area. The coastal margins and Guayas lowlands of Ecuador contain approximately half of that country's population and constitute a very rapidly expanding area of development.

The cultivation of a number of tropical products, especially bananas, since World War II has encouraged settlement in this region, where the ports and the largest city (Guayaquil) of the country are located.

CORDILLERAN RANGES:
INTERMONTANE BASINS AND PLATEAUS

The highland spine of the American Cordillera extends the length of Latin America near the Pacific margin of the region. Clearly, this is the most extensive of all the natural regions, with an airline distance of more than 12,000 kilometers (7,458 miles); it is also one of the most populous, with about 170 million inhabitants. From Mexico to Bolivia, this highland zone contains from about half to more than three-quarters of the populations of every country except Belize, Nicaragua, and Panama.

The Cordillera is a young, complex mountain system with a considerable diversity of features, rock types, and geologic structures. Peaks attain elevations of nearly 7,000 meters (22,966 feet). Aconcagua, rising 6,960 meters (22,835 feet) on the Chilean-Argentine border just north of Santiago, is the highest summit in the world outside of central Asia. The passes are extremely high in the Andes, and throughout most of the Cordillera the high elevations, steep slopes, and extremely rugged terrain present very serious obstacles to transportation. Glacier and ice fields occur throughout much of the mountain system, even at the equator, and reach sea level in southern Chile. There are snowcapped peaks in the highland zones of Mexico and of every country of South America within the Cordilleran system.

Within Latin America, the Cordillera attains its greatest width in northern Mexico (1,000 kilometers [more than 600 miles]) and Bolivia (800 kilometers [500 miles]). It becomes very narrow in portions of southern Central America and again in Chile. There are only four major topographic breaks in this formidable barrier: (1) the Isthmus of Tehuantepec in Mexico; (2) the Nicaraguan graben lowlands, which run from the San Juan River in the Caribbean coastal zone through the lake district northwest to the Gulf of Fonseca (part of this route was considered an alternate for a canal during the last century); (3) the Panamanian isthmus, where the canal is located; and (4) the Atrato–San Juan river valleys across northwestern Colombia.

The mountain system also contains numerous intermontane basins and plateaus, the largest being those of northern and central Mexico and the Altiplano of Peru and Bolivia. These plateaus are the major population zones of Mexico and Bolivia. The system contains some fifty active volcanoes—the greatest concentration in the world outside the Orient—concentrated in five zones: (1) the volcanic axis of Mexico, along the southern margin of the Mexican Plateau; (2) the Central American Pacific volcanic belt, extending from just inside the Mexican border to Costa Rica; (3) southern Colombia and Ecuador, including the Galápagos Islands; (4) central and southern Peru; and (5) Chile, where the two highest active volcanoes in the world are found. The only volcanic activity in Latin America outside the Cordilleran system occurs on three of the lesser Antilles. Throughout its length, the Cordilleran region is one of the most earthquake-prone regions on Earth, except in northern Mexico. Very strong quakes occur regularly and cause considerable loss of life.

Most of the population in the western Cordilleran highlands of Latin America is found in the tropical zone or just on its margins, where there is a considerable range of climate. Climates and vegetation vary with altitude and temperature. The altitudinal boundaries of the climatic zones vary among localities because of latitude, windward/leeward location, exposure, precipitation, and humidity. In the highlands, although the seasonal range of temperature is comparable to that in the adjacent lowlands, the diurnal range is usually considerably greater, especially during the dry season. Table 2.3 gives a general overview of the major altitudinal zones in Latin America.

Throughout the Cordilleran highlands, the more productive basins have numerous urban communities and high rural densities. Increasing population pressure and the land-tenure system have stimulated a massive rural-to-urban migration, and, to a lesser degree, agricultural colonization of the more sparsely settled lowlands. The region has a great diversity of mineral wealth, but that wealth is concentrated in northern and central Mexico and in Peru and Bolivia.

The higher zones have a very high proportion of Amerindians, especially in Guatemala and the central Andean counties. The *tierra caliente* zone, especially the Caribbean lowlands of Central America, the lowlands of Colombia, and to a lesser degree, the coastal zones of Venezuela and Ecuador, has the greatest concentration of blacks.

Orinoco Llanos

The Llanos ("plains") lie between the Venezuelan-Colombian Andes and the Guiana Highlands and are drained by the Orinoco River system. This basin, nearly evenly divided between Venezuela and Colombia, is the third largest in Latin America, accommodating the third greatest river discharge of the region. In size, the Llanos region approximates the state of Texas; it is one of the five very sparsely settled natural regions of Latin America.

Petroleum and iron ore have been exploited for some time in the eastern Llanos of Venezuela, but the most widespread activity, by far, is cattle ranching. In recent decades, there has been migration in both countries from the densely settled highlands to the forested margins and the open grassland districts of these lowlands. The settlers have reportedly encountered resistance from a few nomadic Amerindian tribes in the area.

Guiana Highlands

The Guiana Highlands, and the associated coastal lowlands, are perhaps two-thirds larger than the Llanos but contain even less population, making the Guiana region, Amazonia, and South Chile the most sparsely settled regions in

TABLE 2.3 Altitudinal Zonation of Climates in Latin America

Lower Altitudinal Limit	Zone	Average Monthly Temperature	Major Agricultural Commodities
4,500 m (14,000 ft)	permanent snowfields (*nevados*)	<0°C (<32°F)	
3,000/3,500 m (10,000/ 11,500 ft)	alpine meadows (*tierra helada, páramos*)	6°–10°C (43°–54°F)	livestock grazing (especially sheep and goats, with llamas and alpacas in the central Andes) (above treeline and general crop cultivation)
2,000 m (6,000/ 6,500 ft)	temperate (*tierra fría*)	10°–17°C (54°–65°F)	midlatitude crops: wheat, barley, white potatoes, apples, and other deciduous fruits
600/1,000 m (2,000/ 3,000 ft)	subtropical (*tierra templada*)	17°–24°C (65°–75°F)	coffee, maize, cotton, rice, citrus, sugarcane
Sea level	tropical (*tierra caliente*)	24°–28°C (75°–83°F)	bananas, cacao, rubber, palms (coconut, oil), pineapples, mangoes (crops of subtropical zone also, except for coffee)

Note: Metric and English measure figures are rounded so conversion is not exact.

Latin America. There is a narrow coastal lowland along the Guianas, which contains approximately nine-tenths of the population of those countries. There is also a narrow riverine lowland between the Guiana Highlands and the Orinoco River, which contains the greater part of the population and economic activity of the Guiana Highlands of Venezuela, nearly one-half the area of that country.

Much of the upland surface has been dissected by streams, and the world's highest waterfalls are located near the Venezuelan-Guyanan border. This highland massif and the Brazilian Highlands are composed of remnants of the oldest rocks on the continent—primarily a granite base partially capped by a resistant sedimentary layer. Bauxite, iron ore, and manganese are the most important mineral deposits of the area, but gold and diamonds are also found there.

AMAZONIA

The Amazon Basin is the largest natural region of Latin America and one of the most homogeneous. Although nearly three-quarters of the basin lies within Brazil, portions of the region extend into Peru, Bolivia, Colombia, and Ecuador. Despite the basin's immense area, its population is extremely sparse: Only about 3 percent of the population of Latin America resides in this largest river basin on earth.

The Amazon River is, in volume, the greatest river on earth, although it is slightly shorter than the longest river, the Nile. The Amazon accounts for nearly one-fifth of the total world river discharge into the oceans. The outlet of the river is more than 300 kilometers (186 miles) wide and contains an island the size of southern New England. It is the most navigable river system on earth. There is no bridge across the Amazon in its entire lowland traverse of the continent. Despite the river's immense silt discharge, the delta has undergone little development because of coastal subsidence and coastal currents. Few places on earth can match Amazonia with regard to diversity of life-forms.

The Amazon Basin can be generally divided into two major parts: the low-lying, level alluvial lowlands, or floodplain, and the upland plains. The floodplain is of varying width and constitutes approximately one-tenth of the basin's area. This zone consists of a series of broad, disconnected swamps with natural levees. Much of the area is inundated at various times of the year. The most fertile soils, replenished by river silt, are the best agricultural land, and by far the greater part of the settlements lie within this zone. The upland plains are generally above the periodic river floodings and contain the highly leached and laterized soils typical of many tropical environments. The population in this zone is extremely sparse.

Recently deforestation of the Amazon Basin has accelerated to alarming proportions. Increasing areas are being devoted to crop cultivation and cattle ranching. Beginning in the 1970s, extensive highway network have been constructed, along with hydroelectric dam projects. Considerable mineral wealth has been discovered and is being exploited, especially iron, ferro-alloys, bauxite, gold, and petroleum. The destruction of the habitat is of serious concern for the aboriginal Amerinds; soil erosion, the loss of wildlife and plant species, and the alteration of regional and global climates are also sources of global concern.

BRAZILIAN HIGHLANDS

The dissected Brazilian Plateau and its associated coastal lowlands make up the second largest natural region of Latin America and, with the Cordilleran Highlands, have the largest population of the entire region. Nearly one-third of Latin America's population is in this natural region, which accounts for half of Brazil's area and almost all of that country's population.

The diverse Brazilian Highlands consist of (a) a prominent seaward escarpment, the Serra do Mar of the southern section, which acted as a transportation handicap and barrier to early penetration of the interior; (b) the rolling, dissected plateau of the interior of this highland zone, which is inclined away from the ocean so that drainage is generally toward the interior before it eventually reaches the ocean; and (c) the old, eroded, and rounded mountain ranges that are found in different sections of the uplands. The east-central section of this Brazilian shield, notably in the state of Minas Gerais (General Mines), is highly mineralized with significant deposits of iron, ferro-alloys, diamonds, and gold.

The narrow and discontinuous coastal plain accounts for only 5 to 10 percent of the area of Brazil but about a third of the population, including five of the largest cities—Rio de Janeiro, Recife, Salvador, Fortaleza, and Porto Alegre. The coastal lowlands have a tropical rain forest, or monsoon, climate and broadleaf evergreen forests. Tropical savanna occurs along much of the northeastern coast and the northern and central portions of the interior highlands. However, the interior northeastern section is a comparatively subhumid region. Its periodic droughts have had devastating effects on the nearly 30 percent of the national population residing in the poverty-stricken nine states of this section. This has been a zone of out-migration, primarily to the coastal plantation zone and the industrial and commercial centers in the south and southeast.

The southern highland section has a humid subtropical climate and, on the Paraná Plateau, soil hospitable to coffee. Population growth is somewhat faster in São Paulo—which, combined with the three southern states, contains nearly two-fifths of the national population—than in the other eastern sections of the country. The interior plateau is also undergoing in-migration and rapid growth and development, although the region is still sparsely settled.

PERUVIAN-ATACAMA DESERT

The Peruvian-Atacama Desert region consists of a narrow coastal zone that extends 3,000 to 3,500 kilometers (more than 1,800 to more than 2,000 miles) from near the Ecuadoran-Peruvian border to Coquimbo, Chile. The coastal plain is extremely narrow or absent, and the coastline generally lacks enclosed, protected harbors. Isolated blocks and low coastal hills also characterize parts of the zone, and in places, there are low, but steep, escarpments behind the shore. There are few perennial streams, especially toward the south.

The combination of the Pacific anticyclone, the cool Humboldt current, and winds that parallel the coast makes this coastal zone perhaps the driest on Earth. Arica, Chile, at the border with Peru, has the lowest average annual precipitation (0.5 millimeters [0.02 inch]) of any weather station on Earth. Another station, Iquique, less than 200 kilometers (about 100 miles) to the south, has experienced a period of fourteen years without measurable precipitation. However, the El Niño phenomenon occurs occasionally and brings heavy rains and floodings. Atmospheric and oceanic disturbances displace the cool Humboldt (or Peru) current farther offshore, permitting warmer water from the equatorial region to move southward off the coast of Ecuador and Peru. When this happens, the loss of fisheries and marine birds can also be catastrophic.

The great mineral wealth in what is now Chile, first of nitrates and later of copper, opened sections of the arid north to development. However, this one-third of the country contains less than one-tenth of the national population. Significant iron ore is exploited in southern Peru and the extreme south of the Atacama in Chile. In Peru, as in Chile, many stretches are barren both of vegetation and habitation, but fairly dense settlement occurs in the irrigated narrow coastal valleys, especially from Lima north.

Middle Chile

The relatively small Middle Chile region, lying between Coquimbo and Puerto Montt, comprises only one-third of the national area but contains slightly more than nine-tenths of the country's population, most of the agricultural land and industrial production, and much of the mineral wealth.

The northernmost section of this region is desert/steppe, a transition to the very arid region of the Atacama. Most of northern Middle Chile, however, has essentially a Mediterranean climate. In this sector, the summers remain dry; the mild winter is the season of precipitation. In some places, irrigation is necessary during the summer. This sector, which includes the capital, Santiago, contains more than 70 percent of Chile's population. The remainder of Middle Chile, south of Concepción, is less densely settled. Precipitation is greater in this area and occurs throughout the year. Southern Middle Chile is the most important forest-producing region of the country. The major mineral wealth is copper.

South Chile

South Chile, another small natural region, has a very sparse population. The coastal range is now partially submerged to form an archipelago, and much of the longitudinal valley is drowned. Andean glaciers reach sea level in this region, which is one of the four major fjorded coasts on earth. The region is rugged and isolated, cold, rainy, and dreary. There are no road or rail extensions south of Puerto Montt.

Only 2 percent of Chile's population resides in this third of the country. Most of those people are concentrated in the northern sector, on Chiloé Island—where forest quality and soils are relatively good—and in the Atlantic portion of Chile. There, in the rain shadow of the low Andean chain along the Strait of Magellan, the main economic activities are sheep raising, forestry, and the production of coal and petroleum.

NORTHWEST ARGENTINA AND PATAGONIA

Patagonia and Northwest Argentina compose one of the larger of the natural regions of Latin America and lie entirely within Argentina. The Northwest is larger and more populous than Patagonia, yet the two subregions contain less than a quarter of the country's population in more than half the national territory. In addition to sparse settlement, aridity and uplands characterize this natural region.

Northwest Argentina contains a series of pre-Cordilleran and Pampan ranges that attain their greatest breadth at 30–35 degrees south latitude and extend into the provinces of San Luis and western Córdoba. Most of the settlement and irrigated agriculture occur in the basin oases of the foothills.

The desert and steppe area of Patagonia is unique in that it is the only mid-latitude arid climate in the Southern Hemisphere and the only major arid region on the east coast of a continent. The soils of Patagonia and part of Tierra del Fuego, like those of arid northern Mexico, are typical desert soils—productive when irrigated—and important agricultural output, especially of fruits, is obtained from the densely settled and intensively cultivated oases. There are some mining communities in Northwest Argentina. Petroleum is produced in both coastal Patagonia and in the Andean foothills of the Northwest. Much of the region, however, is sparsely settled and devoted to livestock ranching.

LA PLATA–PARANÁ BASIN

The La Plata–Paraná Basin, the third largest in the Western Hemisphere, after the Amazon and the Mississippi, encompasses the La Plata estuary, the master stream—the Paraná—and its tributaries, notably the Paraguay and Uruguay Rivers. The basin lies mostly within northeastern Argentina but also includes all of Uruguay and Paraguay and a portion of southeastern Bolivia. (A significant portion of Brazil is also drained by this river system, but most of that region of Brazil is included in the Brazilian Highlands natural region.) The La Plata–Paraná Basin is also one of the most populous of the natural regions and contains the Argentine nucleus of settlement.

This natural region has several subregions: the Gran Chaco (west of the Paraná and Paraguay Rivers from 29 degrees to 30 degrees south latitude northward to Bolivia); eastern Paraguay (east of the Paraguay River); Mesopotamia (Argentina between the Paraná–Alto Paraná and Uruguay Rivers); the Pampas (grasslands radiating outward from Buenos Aires for more than 600 kilometers [400 miles]); and Uruguay. The soils over much of the area are mollisols, deep and dark with organic matter and minerals, that develop near the humid-dry climatic boundary in the midlatitudes. These are the richest soils in Latin America and among the best in the world. The Pampa is the major food-surplus-producing region of Latin America. However, soil quality deteriorates toward the drier Northwest and Patagonia and, especially, northward into the humid tropics. The prevailing climate over most of the region is humid subtropical, comparable to the southeastern United States, with hot, rainy summers and mild winters.

SUMMARY AND CONCLUSION

The natural environments of Latin America are diverse and display varying degrees of settlement and development. The three largest regions—Amazonia, the Brazilian Highlands, and the Cordilleran system—comprise nearly two-thirds of the total area of Latin America. The Cordilleran highlands are very rugged, presenting enormous problems for cultivation and transport, but this has been the traditional area of settlement since pre-Columbian times for most of the countries that lie within the region. The Cordilleran and Brazilian highlands contain nearly two-thirds of Latin America's population. At the other extreme, five regions—Amazonia, Guiana Highlands, Northwest Argentina and Patagonia, Llanos, and South Chile—comprise more than two-fifths of Latin America but contain about 6 percent of the population. Rates of population growth in these sparsely settled areas, however, are rapid (except in the midlatitudes), as pressures on land and resources in the traditional settlement areas stimulate internal migration. Despite this significant movement, the great migration within Latin America is into the major urban centers. This rural-urban migration is many times greater than the migration into sparsely settled regions.

SUGGESTED READINGS

Physical Geography

Clawson, David L. *Latin America and the Caribbean: Lands and Peoples.* McGraw-Hill, 2004 (3rd ed.). Chapters 2–4.

Blouet, Brian W. "The Environment" in Blouet, Brian W., and Blouet, Olwyn M., eds., *Latin America and the Caribbean: A Systematic and Regional Survey.* Chichester, NH: John Wiley & Sons, 2002 (4th ed.). Chapter 2.

Handbook of Middle American Indians. Vol. 1, *Natural Environment and Early Cultures,* ed. Robert C. West. Austin: University of Texas Press, 1964. 570 pp. Eight of the chapters provide a good detailed study of the different aspects of the physical environment of Middle America. Probably the best overview of the physical geography of this part of Latin America.

Handbook of South American Indians. Vol. 6, *Physical Anthropology, Linguistics, and Cultural Geography of South American Indians.* U.S. Bureau of American Ethnology, ca. 1948/1949; reprinted New York: Cooper Square, 1963. 715 pp. The section by Carl O. Sauer, "Geography of South America" (pp. 319–344), pertains to the physical landscape of the continent and can serve as a companion piece (although not as detailed) to the *Handbook of Middle American Indians* to complete the coverage of all of Latin America.

Kendrew, Wilfrid George. *The Climates of the Continents.* 5th ed. Oxford: Clarendon Press, 1961. 608 pp. Part 6, "South America, Central America, Mexico, the West Indies" (pp. 464–527). Probably one of the best accounts, although perhaps too detailed, of meteorological and climatic conditions in Latin America.

Robinson, H. *Latin America.* 4th ed. London: MacDonald and Evans, 1977. Chapter 1.

Verdoorn, Frans, ed. *Plants and Plant Science in Latin America.* Waltham, Mass.: Ronald Press, 1945. 381 pp. Despite this work's age, it is still an informative source, not only for the phytogeography and agriculture of the region, but also for other aspects of the physical environment.

Population

Blouet, Brian W. "Population: Growth, Distribution, and Migration," in Blouet, Brian W., and Blouet, Olwyn M., eds., *Latin America and the Caribbean: A Systematic and Regional Survey.* Chichester, NH: John Wiley & Sons, 2002 (4th ed.). Chapter 5.

Gonzalez, Alfonso. "Latin America—Population and Settlement," in Boehm, Richard G., and Visser, Sent, eds., *Latin America: Case Studies.* Dubuque, Iowa: Kendall Hunt Publishing Co., 1984. Chapter 6.

Merrick, Thos. W., et al. "Population Pressures in Latin America." *Population Bulletin* 41:3 (1986).

Sánchez-Albornoz, Nicolás. *Population of Latin America: A History.* Berkeley: University of California Press, 1974. 299 pp. A very good and thorough study of the growth and development of Latin America's population (chapters 1–4) but also contains chapters (6–8) that deal with recent trends and prospects.

Sargent, Charles S. "The Latin American City," in Blouet, Brian W., and Blouet, Olwyn M., eds., *Latin America and the Caribbean: A Systematic and Regional Survey.* Chichester, NH: John Wiley & Sons, 2002 (4th ed.). Chapter 6.

Chapter 3

THE INDIGENOUS POPULATIONS
OF LATIN AMERICA

KARL H. SCHWERIN

In order to understand the contemporary character and distribution of Indian populations in Latin America, it is necessary to know something about the nature of indigenous societies at the time of European discovery. The native inhabitants of the New World represented a great range of cultural development, from simple hunting and gathering bands to complex and literate civilizations. Within the area of present-day Latin America, the great majority of the peoples had reached levels of significant cultural achievement. Most societies were food producers, and in many respects, the region from central Mexico southward was far more advanced than the area lying to the north in what is today northern Mexico, the United States, and Canada. In fact, North America is the only major world region where the majority of the aboriginal peoples relied on gathering, hunting, and fishing for their subsistence. By contrast, South America was inhabited by predominantly agricultural societies.[1]

Nonetheless, a full range of cultural variability also existed in the Latin American region. Although specialists might want to differentiate a great number of categories, it is more instructive for our purposes to treat the early Indian societies as belonging to one of three major types. Marginal hunters and gatherers were restricted for the most part to Argentina, Uruguay, and parts of coastal Brazil. They were also predominant on the northern frontier of the Spanish Empire, the arid deserts of northern Mexico. Lowland extensive agriculturists were much more widespread, ranging from central Chile throughout most of interior Brazil to the whole of the Amazon Basin, including those portions now within the territorial borders of Bolivia, Peru, Ecuador, Colombia, Venezuela, and the Guianas. They also occupied the rest of Colombia and Venezuela and ranged northward through the whole of Central America and the Antilles. The third principal type was the highland intensive agriculturists, many of whom achieved state-level societies in the mountains and plateaus of Mexico, Guatemala, Ecuador, Peru, and Bolivia.

During the latter part of the twentieth century, a vigorous debate raged among historical demographers concerning the aboriginal population of the

41

Americas at the time of European discovery. Estimates range from 13 million to more than 100 million. For the Latin American region, however, an estimate of 80 million seems likely. Sixty million of these people belonged to the civilized states of Middle America and the central Andes. Most of the remaining, numbering about 18 million, were lowland agriculturists in the interior of South America, the northern coastal region, the Caribbean, and Central America. Hunting and gathering peoples accounted for no more than 2 million persons, and the figure was probably closer to 1 million.

European conquest radically disturbed the aboriginal societies. Perhaps the most drastic effect was a rapid and massive population decline, characterized by modern investigators as a "demographic disaster." The principal cause of the disaster was the introduction of several new diseases that decimated the native populations through repeated epidemic outbreaks. The wars of conquest also took their toll, as did slavery and other abuses of Indian labor, and there were ecological repercussions because of interference with the seasonal rhythm of native agriculture (by removing native labor for Spanish needs at critical periods in the agricultural calendar) and the introduction of livestock (which competed with natives for land and invaded their planted fields).

Estimates of the rate of depopulation differ, but the best calculations suggest an average decline of 95 percent in 130 years, leaving only about 4 million Indians south of what is now the United States in 1650. It must be remembered, however, that an unknown portion of this decline is represented by the mestizo offspring of European or African fathers and Indian mothers, who were treated as a class or caste apart from their parents and who often sought to "pass" into the higher-status European category.

The Caribbean population, which was conquered first, was wiped out in less than fifty years. African slaves were introduced to replace the Caribbean Indians as a labor force. Most of the continental hunters and gatherers also became extinct. The lowland agriculturists declined drastically, with many groups becoming extinct (some continue to disappear today); others, however, have survived and are today increasing in number. In the areas of highland civilization, there was also a drastic population decline, but the population reached its low of perhaps 3 million to 5 million around 1650. Thereafter, it grew slowly until around the beginning of the nineteenth century. Since that time, the Indian population of Middle America and the central Andes has been growing at an increasingly rapid rate.

Preconquest Societies

A moment's reflection about the areas occupied by these three major culture types helps one realize that these regions are still characterized by distinctive populations today. Elman Service has dubbed these areas Euro-America, Mestizo-America, and Indo-America, respectively.[2] Why are such differences of aboriginal culture type reflected in differences among the modern populations? Commonly, this is explained as resulting from differences in administrative policies of the European colonial powers. Not only did such policies differ among Spain, Portugal, and Great Britain, but there were differences in the way the policies were implemented in various parts of the colonial empires. Thus, it is frequently maintained that colonial policies were enforced more rigorously in the Antilles, Mexico, and Peru and that greater control was exerted over the colonists in those areas, both because these colonies were more valuable and because they contained greater numbers of colonists. In contrast, there was less interest in colonies like Venezuela and Buenos Aires, and consequently, crown control was much more lax in those areas.

There is, however, another way of looking at the question of contemporary differences. This approach begins by looking at the diversity of aboriginal cultures encountered by the white man and recognizing that the Europeans were forced to adjust differently in accordance with the basic differences in native cultures.[3]

The object of European conquest was to profit from these newly discovered areas. The preferred ways of doing so were to assess tribute from the native populations (by means of the *encomienda* and the *corregimiento*) or to exploit native labor in profit-making enterprises (through forced labor projects, or the *repartimiento*) such as construction, mining, ranching, and later, textiles.

In the highland areas of Mexico and Guatemala and in the central Andes, native societies had achieved a high level of cultural development, with complex state organization. The native peoples were integrated into complex economic, social, and political institutions and depended upon them to maintain their traditional way of life. It would not have been easy to survive on their own if they had been cut off from these state-level institutions. In addition, most of the natives had no easily accessible refuge areas to which they could flee from Spanish domination. Given the existence of well-defined state institutions, within which the native populations were accustomed to function, it was relatively easy for the European conquistadores to take these institutions over from the top and continue to control the population in much the same way as had the native elite. Such control was particularly effective because of the system of indirect administration that was worked out. Only minor modifications were made in most native institutions (except for religious ones), especially on the lower levels where native intermediaries continued to be employed in governing the mass of the population.[4]

Throughout the colonial period, there was a fair amount of racial mixture, and the native elites were gradually absorbed into the dominant Spanish ruling class. Among Indian commoners, local community and familial institutions retained strength in spite of racial mixture with the Spanish overlords and their African slaves. To this day, many Indian languages continue to be spoken throughout these areas, many rural communities have maintained their identification as Indian, and many aboriginal and/or ethnically distinct customs have been retained as central features of the local cultures. These are the areas Service characterizes as Indo-America.[5]

Lowland areas were occupied mostly by extensive agriculturists who were organized principally as independent localized tribes or villages.[6] Here there were no large organized communities or state-level institutions. It was much more difficult to control these small independent communities, for conquest of one did not give the victor authority over its neighbor. The European strategy was to capture single families and individuals and force them to become household servants or to work as agricultural slaves. The intimacy that existed between masters and household slaves or small numbers of agricultural slaves led to a rapid mestization of the native groups. Mestizos tended to identify with the dominant European population and to be absorbed into its lower levels. Thus, there was a continuing need to acquire additional slaves from the native groups. The Paulistas of Brazil are the best-known example of this type of exploitation. Their periodic expeditions ranged far and wide throughout the interior to capture Indian slaves. This type of exploitative relationship between the European colonists and native societies led to a breakdown of the more accessible Indian communities and the flight of many more to remote refuge areas where they might avoid the depredations of slavers. In some of these isolated locations, the Indians have been able to survive to the present day, particularly in southern Chile, parts of Amazonia, the interior of Venezuela, parts of Central America, and the extremely rugged and isolated regions of northern Mexico. These are the areas that Service identifies as Mestizo-America.[7]

Where plantation agriculture developed, there was need for large numbers of laborers. Because of the social and physical separation between owners and field laborers, the latter, which existed in large numbers, were treated impersonally. Under the rigors of the plantation system, Indian slaves often fled to the interior, which they could easily do because they were familiar with the environment and knew how to survive there. Even when they were unable to return to their own community, other native communities and social systems were similar enough that they were usually able to plug into them with relatively little difficulty. The very serious problem, for plantation owners, of runaway Indian slaves led to the introduction of African slaves, who were much easier to control. The Africans were in a wholly unfamiliar environment—an alien terrain filled with unknown plants and animals. They could not speak the native languages, and they did not know how to behave or participate in the aboriginal social systems. Consequently, African slaves were much more inhibited from fleeing the slave situation. These plantation areas developed principally in coastal Brazil, the Caribbean, and coastal Peru. In most of these areas, the African racial type remains predominant today, and I would therefore characterize this fourth category as Afro-America.

Where the European intruders found it impossible to control the native population, even as slaves over the short term, their only recourse was to exterminate the natives or to drive them from the areas of settlement. Hunters and gatherers lived a simple life, unburdened with abundant possessions or a complex technology. They were more or less nomadic and thus could readily flee areas of control. They also could survive quite well away from European control. In some cases, they found it possible to survive on the margins of European settlement. And in some instances, they actually developed a new and

highly successful adaptive strategy of attacking and living off the European settlements. Among such groups we may count the Tehuelche and Puelche of Argentina; the Pehuenche of Chile; the Argentine Araucanians; the Abipón,
Mbayá, and other Guaicuruan groups of the Gran Chaco in Paraguay; and the
Charrúa of Uruguay. At the northern limits of the Spanish colonies, in northern Mexico and New Mexico, similar groups developed; Apache, Ute, and Co-
manche raiders preyed on Spanish settlements for several hundred years. The
result in most of these cases of active raiding by native groups was chronic warfare between them and the Spanish colonists. The Spanish settlements grew
gradually over time and eventually reached the point at which the Spanish were
able to carry on intensive warfare against the native raiders, usually extermi-
nating them. These areas, where the native populations have been wholly eliminated, are what Service calls Euro-America,[8] and they include Argentina,
Uruguay, and Costa Rica.

One other point is worth emphasizing in this analysis of differential relations between the conquering Europeans and native societies. European culture was structurally complex, representing a state level of organization. In this
sense, it was most like the cultures of the highland state-organized peoples, less
like those of the lowland agriculturists, and most distinct from the cultures of
the marginal hunters and gatherers. It is clear that there was a more or less direct correlation between the cultural complexity of a native society and its survival after European conquest. It thus appears that the more alike the
conquerors and the conquered, the more simple and easy the adjustment to
conquest; the less difficult and disruptive the adjustment, the more likely the
survival of the conquered people and the preservation of at least the local basis
of their native social organization and cultural forms.

CONTEMPORARY LATIN AMERICA

Euro-America and Afro-America

Table 3.1 gives the current distribution of the Amerindian population in Latin
America according to the latest more or less complete data readily available,
which are centered on 2000.[9] It will be noted that in Euro-America and Afro-
America, the indigenous population generally accounts for 1 percent or less of
the total population. In Euro-America, it is just over 1 percent, and in Afro-
America it averages one fourth of that.

The principal exception is in the three Guianas, where population is sparse
and total population numbers are low. There, because of the limited population and the concentration of intrusive groups along the coast, the indigenous
groups who occupy the interior were not faced with as much direct competition as in Brazil or the Antilles. This situation is now changing because, since
independence, the Guianas have increasingly looked to development of the interior as integral to their goals of national economic development, although it
is likely that as the nonrenewable resources are depleted, the perceived usefulness of the indigenous population will diminish at the same time. In the case

TABLE 3.1   Amerindian Population of Latin America, ca. 2000

Country	Total Population	Indian Population	Indian Percent of Total
Euro-America (approx. 1 percent)	44,529,000	511,870	1.1
Argentina, Uruguay, Costa Rica			
Afro-America (< 1 percent)	185,058,000	489,066	0.26
Coastal Brazil	138,914,000	96,780	<0.1
Guianas	1,324,000	80,286	6.1
Coastal Colombia (est.)	7,095,000	306,700	4.3
Antilles	37,725,000	5,300	—
Mestizo-America (< 5 percent)	183,977,634	3,204,679	1.7
Northern Mexico	39,501,629	415,518	0.1
Central America (excl. Costa Rica)	21,229,469	1,063,000	5.0
Highland and Eastern Colombia (est.)	35,905,000	431,000	1.2
Venezuela (est.)	23,900,000	382,400	1.6
Braz. Amazonia	43,119,000	373,587	0.9
Paraguay	5,206,101	85,674	1.6
Chile	15,116,435	453,500	3.0
Indo-America (>10 percent)	108,433,219	27,798,844	25.6
Central and Southern Mexico	57,981,783	6,862,484	11.8
Belize	232,111	24,501	10.6
Guatemala	9,133,000	4,000,000	43.8
Ecuador	10,508,000	3,111,900	29.6
Peru	22,304,000	9,100,000	40.8
Bolivia	8,274,325	4,700,000	56.8

of Guyana, development of the interior is also a means of asserting and consolidating rights to territory claimed as well by neighboring Venezuela.[10] Coastal Colombia also has a larger indigenous population, but total population numbers of these areas is swamped by the much greater totals in the Antilles and coastal Brazil. Nonetheless, it is worth noting that except in the Antilles, the percentage of indigenous population has increased 1990.

In Euro-America population growth has been slow, although the indigenous population has increased by more than 130,000 between 1990 and 2000, growing more than twice as fast as the general population. Indigenous activism in Argentina led to legal recognition in 1989, the subsequent granting of land titles, and recognition of indigenous rights in the Constitution of 1994.[11] In Afro-America the indigenous population more than doubled in the same time period, increasing from less than 0.1 percent to 0.26 percent of the total population. Significant changes in coastal Brazil (from 34,165 in 1980 to 61,485 in 1990 and 96,780 in 2000) and northern Colombia (from 139,596 in 1980 to an estimated 306,700 in 2000) probably represent differences in the definition of an "Indian" as well as different methods of enumeration. Even the Guianas have seen an increase from 4.8 to 6.1 percent. There is increasing evidence, however, of significant numbers of people with indigenous ancestry who are systematically excluded from census enumeration and denied as "real Indians" for reasons of national pride and discrimination. Costa Rica, for example, considers itself "European," and campaigns of ethnocide are active in El Salvador and Guatemala. In Brazil it's felt that identification of Indians hinders development of the Interior. There may be a half million or more Indians in the Antilles and Central America alone.[12]

Mestizo-America

Most of the surviving indigenous populations of this region live in distinct communities, where they retain their aboriginal cultures and their identity as members of a traditional community, which is not integrated into national society. Instead they continue to function as members of distinct cultures within the modern state, thus leading some authorities to characterize them as "Fourth World" societies. But numerous native groups in this region are currently in the process of acculturating to the dominant national cultures, including significant numbers who are migrating to the cities.

There are more than 3 million Indians out of a total population of nearly 184 million. From the early 1980s to 1990 the indigenous population doubled, while the population as a whole grew only 27 percent. But from 1990 to 2000 the Indians barely increased at all, declining from 2.5 percent to 1.7 percent of the total. On a country-by-country basis, the Indians mostly represent from slightly less than 1 percent to about 7 percent of the total population (see Table 3.1). Their numbers have declined in northern Mexico and Chile, remained more or less stable in Central America and Paraguay, and grown dramatically in Brazilian Amazonia. Since the figures for Colombia and Venezuela are estimates, their significance is indeterminate at best.

In northern Mexico, the principal group is the Tarahumara—subsistence farmers widely scattered throughout their rugged mountain homeland. In Central America, interior Venezuela, and the vast Amazon Basin, the aboriginal populations were less dense at the time of European contact than in the Andean states. Disease, slavery, and European warfare against these highly divided groups led to their decimation and extinction in many localities. Nonetheless, a number of ethnically distinct groups persist in more isolated localities or on reserves protected by missionaries or national governments. Most of these populations are found in the lowland, tropical areas.

The economy of these lowland villages is based on subsistence slash-and-burn farming of tropical crops. The most important staples are manioc, bananas, and yams, but these are supplemented by a variety of other crops. Some groups, like the Karinya of Venezuela, cultivate nearly a hundred different crops. Fishing is also an important subsistence activity, providing the principal source of dietary protein. Hunting is generally less important, and even this activity is often oriented toward riverine and aquatic species (turtle, caiman, ducks, manatee, and so on). In some groups that lack ready access to the rivers—such as the Jivaro and the Yanomamö—hunting assumes greater importance. By exploiting the diverse resources of agriculture, fishing, and hunting, most of these groups have maintained a nutritionally balanced diet. Their crafts are generally simple, although many groups make excellent baskets and some, like the Jívaro, are known for their fine pottery.

Villages are politically independent, and ethnic identity is recognized only as a consequence of sharing a common language, common customs, and a mutual ethnic consciousness. Settlements generally number fewer than 300 inhabitants, although they may occasionally range up to as many as 1,000 to 2,000. Traditional residence was in communal houses, with one or more located in each settlement. Sociopolitical organization is based on kinship ties. Marriage tends to be endogamous within the local group. The headman or chief has limited authority over the group; he usually enjoys few, if any, special privileges. His influence is based on personal prestige and does not extend beyond the local village. The division of labor is based strictly on age and sex. With the exception of the shaman, there is no full-time specialization. Recent research has, however, uncovered evidence of earlier widespread multiethnic regional networks linking groups in trading and ritual exchanges.[13]

Warfare is frequent and often bitter, but it is never pursued for purposes of conquering territory or exacting tribute. Usually it is justified in terms of revenge, or sometimes to gain prestige or to acquire trophies that are supernaturally powerful. Many anthropologists subscribe to an ecological explanation for warfare among these communities—seeing it as a mechanism for acquiring and maintaining access to scarce resources, such as rivers, with their abundance of fish and game; good farmland, also mostly along the rivers; and, among the Yanomamö, women. Warfare may also serve to keep populations dispersed so as not to overexploit the limited resources of the tropical environment.

Except for marriage, which tends to be treated in a matter-of-fact way, life crisis rites are particularly emphasized among these peoples. Shamanism is also important and highly developed. The shaman works to cure illness, to affect the weather, and to ensure success in warfare. Often he organizes magical religious festivals and dances as well. He is generally the guardian of community religious tradition. The shaman may also practice witchcraft and sorcery, though he rarely admits to doing so unless it is directed against enemy groups. A wide variety of narcotics are used by the shamans, and sometimes by all adult men, in curing and other religious ceremonies. Although the concept of a high god may exist, it is relatively unimportant in religious belief and ritual. Instead, religion centers on culture heroes, who made the world as it is today, and on nature spirits who are closely associated with subsistence concerns, particularly fishing and hunting.

The Mapuche of southern Chile are somewhat distinct from the other groups being discussed here, since they have adopted European crops and farming techniques and participate, to a certain extent, in the national society. Crop surpluses are sold in the regional market, children receive formal schooling, and the Mapuche participate, at least marginally, in national political, legal, and judicial institutions. Under the Pinochet regime, however, they suffered severe discrimination and many communities lost their land.

All of the groups in Mestizo-America are under increasing pressure from national societies because the isolated areas they have occupied up to now are being opened up by the construction of highways, spontaneous colonization by peasant farmers, national development programs, and projects for the exploitation of natural resources by numerous multinational corporations. In Central America, the native groups seem to be holding their own so far, although there are concerns for the future. In Nicaragua the revolutionary Sandinista government was startled to find the 120,000 Miskito Indians living in the Caribbean lowlands resisting efforts to absorb them into national society. After several years of tense relations, the Mosquitia region was formally recognized as an autonomous region within the Nicaraguan state.

During the 1990s, in Venezuela the government attempted to protect Indian lands through legal action. The constitution of 1999 officially recognized indigenous languages and cultures and guaranteed their inalienable rights to occupy ancestral lands, to maintain their ethnic identity and cultural traditions, and to receive an education appropriate to their particular sociocultural traditions. Intellectual property rights are also guaranteed and protected.[14] Authorities in Colombia, Bolivia, and Paraguay have generally ignored the problems of the natives, but in Colombia indigenous peoples have suffered high levels of violence perpetrated by security forces, drug traffickers, leftist guerrillas, and paramilitary groups, as well as severe poverty. Efforts to legislate more rigorous paternalistic control over indigenous groups were defeated. Instead, indigenous groups contributed to the writing of a new constitution in the late 1980s that recognizes indigenous peoples as Colombian citizens with full rights. Indigenous representatives have also been elected to the Colombian congress.[15]

Brazil has vacillated between looking the other way while natives are pushed out or exterminated and attempting to resettle them on reserves. Brazil continues to have one of the worst human rights records with respect to its Indian population.[16] When faced with pressures from development interests, responsible officials have generally allowed these reserves to be fragmented or whittled down. For example, in spite of a vociferous international outcry, Brazil has made no concerted effort to keep thousands of prospectors, miners, and traders from intruding on Yanomamö territory. The democratic Constitution of 1988 includes a chapter on indigenous peoples that revises relations between them and the state, terminating five centuries of integrationist policy. On paper it increased enormously the rights of Indians, recognizing their right to land and the existence of collective (community) Indian rights. But Brazilian practice continues to be integrationist, while state and local governments ignore abuse of constitutionally guaranteed Indian rights.

Although most of these Indians have remained in distinct, small-scale communities, increasing numbers have also followed the general demographic trend in Latin America of rural-to-urban migration. While it has often been recognized that there are many Indians in Latin American cities, it has been nearly impossible to get a reliable estimate of their numbers. To judge from the available figures, more than 200,000 Indians are probably urban dwellers in Mestizo-America.

These traditional peoples cannot be ignored as human beings. Certainly, they are equal in importance to any other identifiable group in the countries of Mestizo-America. Many of their current difficulties arise from the fact that in terms of their numbers and the economic or political impact that they exercise, they represent a very small segment of the modern population.

Indo-America

By far the most significant indigenous populations, in terms both of numbers and of their place in national society, are the modern Indian types found in Indo-America, comprising most of Mexico, Guatemala, and the central Andean countries of Ecuador, Peru, and Bolivia. These Indians, most of whom live in the highland regions of those countries, must be included in any consideration of modern Latin America. Although their way of life differs from that of the non-Indians in the countries where they live, they share many patterns and institutions, mainly of European origin, with the other citizens. Numerically, they are an important segment of the population, constituting more than 10 percent in almost all of these countries. In some countries, such as Peru, Guatemala, and Bolivia, they make up from 40 percent to nearly 60 percent of the population, respectively (see Table 3.1).

Taking Indo-America as a whole, the indigenous population amounts to nearly 28 million, or 25.6 percent of the total population. This represents an increase of slightly more than 3 million, or 12 percent, since about 1990. Compare this to the growth in the general population of just under 3 million, or 2.8 percent. It is clear that while population growth has slowed in both groups, the indigenous population is still increasing much more rapidly than the general population.

During the colonial period, the Indians of these countries were taught Catholicism and often were concentrated into Spanish-type villages, where European forms of community organization were forced upon them. They borrowed freely from the European culture of the sixteenth and seventeenth centuries—a culture that in many respects contained as many "folk features" as their own. By at least the beginning of the eighteenth century, the fusion of the aboriginal and colonial Spanish patterns had formed a new culture among these peoples. This culture persists today, unchanged in its main outlines, and constitutes an important variant of national patterns in these highland countries. Because this culture is relatively unchanged from colonial times, it contrasts markedly with modern cultural patterns and is sometimes erroneously believed to represent a survival of aboriginal cultural practices.

Modern Indians in these countries generally speak an aboriginal language, although they frequently speak Spanish as well. Community cohesion tends to persist at a high level despite the encroaching power of the national states. The Indians of each community generally think of themselves as ethnic units, separate from other Indian groups and from non-Indian nationals of the country in which they reside. They are people of the village or town rather than Mexicans, Guatemalans, or Peruvians. Frequently, they wear a distinctive costume that identifies them as members of a particular pueblo. At the turn of the century, however, the global costume of Nikes, T-shirts, and blue jeans is increasingly favored by Indians and non-Indians alike.

Community structure is characteristically of the type known as the closed corporate peasant community. It is an organized communal structure with clearly defined social boundaries; in other words, it is very clear who does and who does not belong to the community. The community generally does not identify with the nation; its members find their personal and social satisfactions within the community by adhering to its traditional value system. The corporate peasant community is held together not by ties of kinship but by co-ownership of a landholding corporation. Members are not allowed to sell or rent land to outsiders, and this taboo severely limits the degree to which factors outside the community can affect the structure of private property or the development of class differences within the community. This is one of the most important ways of promoting and maintaining community integration.

Another common pattern, especially in the central Andes, is for the Indians to be clustered as peons on large hacienda estates. These Indians have no secure rights to property; instead, they provide labor to work the land belonging to a non-Indian owner. In exchange, they receive a plot of land on which to build a house and grow subsistence crops. Although a small wage may be paid, the plot of land serves in lieu of most wage income. The hacienda owner discourages community organization and tries to establish personal ties between himself and each laborer, thereby exercising greater control over his labor force. At the same time, by encouraging maintenance of the peons' native language and distinctive ethnic identity, with its own traditional customs, he ensures that the peonage community will remain isolated from the larger society.

These peasant communities depend on agriculture as their principal means of subsistence. Most of the land that the peasants possess for their own use is of marginal productivity. It is exploited by means of traditional technology, which involves continuous physical effort and much manual labor. Peasants rely on both the hoe and the plow drawn by draft animals, but there is little use of modern machinery. Their staple crops include the principal cereal grains (corn, wheat, barley), a variety of legumes (beans, broad beans, lentils, garbanzos, peas), chile peppers, and in the Andes, a variety of root crops, including potatoes. Most agriculture follows a short fallow cycle, with fields being rested for one year after several years of cropping. There is little use of fertilizers, although insecticides have become popular in recent years. In some areas irrigation is important.

Crafts are highly developed. The great variety of objects being manufactured includes textiles, pottery, baskets, wood carvings, jewelry, and toys, which often achieve a high degree of aesthetic creativity. The economy of the closed corporate community is closely linked to a peculiar sort of regional marketing system. Different villages specialize in different commodities, and these are brought together and exchanged in the market. For the same reason, the market brings together a much larger supply of articles than merchants in any one community could afford to keep continuously in their stores. Thus, there is much wider access to the products of each community. A shortage of money requires that sales and purchases in the market be small. The producer typically offers his or her goods for sale in order to obtain small amounts of cash, which can be used to purchase other needed goods. In recent years, increasing quantities of cheap manufactured goods have also been introduced into the regional market system and in some cases, they provide stiff competition for locally produced handicrafts. Another source of cash income is seasonal migration to work on plantations and *fincas* that produce sugar, coffee, or other goods for export. Typically, this migration involves movement from highland peasant communities to lowland areas. In Mexico increasing numbers of indigenous peasants are traveling to the northern part of the country or even further, into the United States, as migrant workers employed by agribusiness enterprises.

The basic social unit of these communities is the nuclear family. Households average about six persons. Marriage may be consecrated through formal religious ceremonies, but there is also a high incidence of marriages that are the result of elopement or abduction. Marriage is usually with an unrelated person, but it is preferentially endogamous within the village. This preference serves as another mechanism for local community integration. Fertility is high among these people, and although the rate of infant mortality has also been high, the mortality rate has been declining over the past several decades, leading to a rapid growth of population. The institution of *compadrazgo,* which establishes a special relationship between the parents and godparents of a child, is another important mechanism for social integration and mutual support.

Settlement patterns vary considerably. In some areas, such as central Mexico, residence is concentrated in a compact village. In others, such as southern Mexico or highland Ecuador, the preference is to scatter residences throughout the community's territory. In the organization of the local community, traditional native officials are often maintained alongside representatives of the national bureaucracy. The community's system of power embraces the male members of the community and makes achievement of power a matter of community decision rather than one of individually achieved status. This system of power is tied into a religious system or a series of interlocking religious systems. The politico-religious system as a whole tends to define the boundaries of the community and acts as a symbol of collective unity. Prestige within the community is largely related to rising from office to office within this system. Conspicuous consumption, principally by putting on elaborate fiesta celebrations, is geared to this communally approved system of power and religion, and it serves to level differences of wealth within the community. The system thus avoids the development of class divisions that might undermine the corporate structure of the community. Various psychic mechanisms of control, such as institutionalized envy and the concept of "limited good," serve as additional conservative factors that help in maintaining the traditional values and way of life.[17]

The modern Indian is nominally Catholic, but his religious beliefs and practices have incorporated a considerable amount of aboriginal belief as well. In addition, Catholic saints are endowed with local characteristics and powers. Fiestas are held to honor the patron saint and other locally important saints, and *cargos,* or religious offices, as well as magical practices, are assumed to preserve and promote these saint cults. Maintenance of traditional fiestas and associated ceremonies and celebrations is an important part of the traditional culture, and it serves as one more way of preserving a distinctive local identity. Some communities maintain folk priests—cantors, for example—who have contributed to the survival of folk beliefs and practices in the absence (sometimes for several generations) of Catholic priests. Since the 1970s, however, various evangelical Protestant sects have successfully recruited large numbers of indigenous adherents, particularly in Mexico and Guatemala. This often creates conflict between new converts and traditional segments of the community. *Evangélicos* typically abjure alcohol and dancing, refuse to participate in the traditional fiesta system, and tend to withdraw from customary practices of community reciprocity, thus creating factionalism and undermining community integration. In southern Mexico supporters of the Zapatista movement have tended to be Protestants who moved out of the traditional communities and who were often in conflict with the established indigenous leadership, which remained Roman Catholic.

Illness and disease are explained as resulting from an imbalance in the hot and cold humors that occur in the body, in the foods consumed, and in other objects with which the individual comes into contact. Certain psychological disorders are also explained as a result of *susto* or *espanto* ("fright"), in which the individual is frightened by an encounter with a supernatural entity, sometimes resulting in loss of the soul. The curing of these disorders is usually in the hands of local *curanderos* ("folk doctors") who may attempt to restore the hot-cold imbalance, call upon aboriginal supernaturals or Christian saints, or apply herbal remedies. Ethnographic reports suggest that many of the empirical remedies of these *curanderos* are effective and that their treatments are largely successful. If the family members of the sick person can afford it, however, they may try to hedge the probabilities of a successful cure by also consulting a medical doctor.

Adherence to the traditional culture validates membership in an existing society and acts as a passport to participation in the life of the community. The amount of wealth that can be gained by a typical peasant is enough to gain the prestige symbols of the Indian system, and thus, the individual is encouraged to maintain his identification with that system. The particular traits held by an Indian help him remain within the equilibrium of relationships that maintain the community. On the other hand, the non-Indian individual is attempting to gain wealth within the national system, where it is impossible to accumulate enough wealth through hard work to permit access to the prestige symbols of the upper sector. The non-Indian peasant is thus perpetually frustrated in his attempt to achieve meaningful goals.

These modern Indian populations are important elements of the national societies. Numerically, they represent a significant proportion of the total population. They participate, if only marginally, in the economic, political, and religious institutions of the nation, and they represent a large, inexpensive pool of labor that can be recruited whenever unskilled labor is required. There is a slow but constant interchange of ideas between the Indian subcultures on the one hand and the national culture on the other.

Since the 1990s, there has been increasing Indian activism, growth of grass roots organizations, and political participation. Not only is there a renaissance in indigenous languages and cultures, but these indigenous organizations have sought to maintain or reassert control over traditional lands and resources.

The Zapatista uprising of January 1994 in Chiapas is perhaps the most widely reported. It was motivated by limited access to land, a steep drop in coffee prices, the threat of increased economic disadvantage with the implementation of the North American Free Trade Agreement (NAFTA), long-standing abuse of the indigenous population by the dominant mestizo inhabitants, and government inaction in addressing these problems. Negotiations to resolve these complaints have continued for the past decade, long enough that one wonders how willing the Mexican government really is to deal with them.

In Guatemala the genocidal policies of the government in the 1970s and early 1980s were directed against suspected Mayan subversion. Over 400 villages were destroyed and their inhabitants massacred. By the late 1980s, massive oppression had abated, with new protections for "Indigenous Communities" being written into the 1985 constitution. Still, considerable tension exists between Maya and ladino in that country. The Maya community continues to be fragmented, but a new intellectual leadership is emerging, new forms of organization are being developed, and Mayan towns are defending themselves from government abuse. That the Maya themselves are taking an active role in defining their own identity may give hope for eventual development of a plurinational state in Guatemala.

Similar developments may be seen in growing Indian political participation in Bolivia, where the Aymara leader Víctor Hugo Cárdenas was elected vice president in 1993. Indigenous farmers have long demonstrated against U.S.-encouraged programs to control the growing of coca. Then in 2003 the government's proposal to sell Bolivia's gas reserves to an American company provoked massive demonstrations led by Aymara union leader Evo Morales. In the end the government abandoned the proposal and President Gonzalo Sánchez de Losada resigned.

Peru has long been the most conservative Andean nation, with strong biases against the two-fifths of the population that is indigenous. Yet in 2001, Alejandro Toledo, a man of Indian descent whose parents were speakers of Quechua, was elected president, albeit by a slim margin. To a considerable extent his electoral success was realized by his open identification with the Indian heritage of Peru. It remains to be seen, however, how much his government will benefit the Indian masses of the country.

In Ecuador the indigenous movement created a strong organizational base that is now an important actor in the national political arena. It has organized indigenous communities, established bilingual education, and resisted neoliberal economic policies. It has created a place in the political agenda where indigenous people are not merely subjects but active members of civil society. The cultural demands of the indigenous movement have allowed them to create a political force that came as a surprise to both the state and the left in Ecuador. Indigenous people were a major element in forcing the resignation of Ecuadorian President Jamil Mahuad in 2000.

With modernization, education, improved communication, and other developments, Indian interaction with the national culture is increasing all the time. The worldwide process of globalization is profoundly affecting the Indians of Latin America just as it is non-indigenous populations. Continuing population growth and resultant pressures on the land have led to a large-scale migration to the cities. Today, there are probably 5 million Indians or more living in the towns and cities of Indo-America. Once they arrive in the cities, there is rapid acculturation to urban life. But at the same time, they maintain their ties to and identification with the home community. Urban residents frequently return to visit their relatives or to attend major fiestas. There is also evidence that with increased incomes and greater sophistication, traditional customs and practices are being revived and even intensified in many of these communities. Thus, in spite of modernizing influences, there are indications that for the immediate future, many of these contemporary Indian communities will retain their ethnically distinctive subcultures, while the activism cited above may produce newer forms of nationwide indigenous identity.

NOTES

1. Herbert Barry III, "Regional and Worldwide Variations in Culture," *Ethnology* 7:2 (1968), pp. 207–217, and George Peter Murdock, "Ethnographic Atlas," *Ethnology* 6:2 (1967).

2. Elman R. Service, "Indian-European Relations in Colonial Latin America," *American Anthropologist* 57 (1955), pp. 411–412.

3. Ibid., p. 411.

4. Ibid., p. 418.

5. Ibid., pp. 411–412.

6. Some lowland societies were organized as chiefdoms—small, weakly centralized societies that were transitional between independent villages and strongly centralized states; in fact, they generally integrated a number of dependent villages. Chiefdoms were typically unstable, and with European conquest removal of the ruler usually resulted in social disintegration. The constituent villages then reverted to the level of independent communities (Karl H. Schwerin, "The Anthropological Antecedents: Caciques, Cacicazgos, and Caciquismo," in *The Caciques: Oligarchical Politics and the System of Caciquismo in the Luso-Hispano World,* ed. Robert Kern and Ronald Dolkart, pp. 5–17 [Albuquerque: University of New Mexico Press, 1973]).

7. Service, "Indian-European Relations," pp. 411–412, 418.

8. Ibid., pp. 411–412, 420.

9. Population figures are somewhat disparate. Some countries, such as Colombia and Venezuela, have not conducted a census since the early 1990s. In these cases I have estimated the indigenous population by using World Bank estimates for total population in 2000, and assuming the same rate of growth since 1990 for the indigenous groups. In other cases indigenous populations were either enumerated or estimated for the late 1990s or since 2000. And in some cases, like Mexico, Brazil, Ecuador, and Paraguay, not only has there been a recent census of indigenous populations, but the data is available on the Internet. See: http://www.inegi.gob.mx/est/contenidos/espanol/tematicos/mediano/med.asp?t=mlen01&c=3325; http://www.socioambiental.org/website/pib/english/whwhhow/table.asp; http://abyayala.nativeweb.org/ecuador/pueblos.php; http://www.dgeec.gov.py/Publicaciones/censo_indigena/Paraguay.pdf.

10. William Heningsgaard and Jason Clay, "The Upper Mazaruni Dam," *Cultural Survival Newsletter* 4:3 (1980), p. 103.

11. Gastón Gordillo and Silvia Hirsch, "Indigenous Struggles and Contested Identities in Argentina," *Journal of Latin American Anthropology* 8(3)(2003), pp. 4–30.

12. *Cultural Survival Quarterly* 13:3 (1989); for 1980 population figures, see table 3.1 in my chapter in Jan Knippers Black, *Latin America: Its Problems and Its Promise,* 2nd ed. (Boulder, Colo.: Westview, 1991). Population figures for 1990 may be found in table 3.1 of the 3rd ed. (1998).

13. Nelly Arvelo-Jiménez and Horacio Biord Castillo, "The Impact of Conquest on Contemporary Indigenous Peoples of the Guiana Shield. The System of Orinoco Regional Interdependence, in *Amazonian Indians from Prehistory to the Present: Anthropological Perspectives,* Anna Roosevelt, ed. (Tucson: University of Arizona Press, 1994), pp. 55–78; Silvia M. Vidal, "Kuwé Duwákalumi: The Arawak Sacred Routes of Migration, Trade, and Resistance," *Ethnohistory* 47(3–4):635–667 (2000), pp. 635–667; and Karl H. Schwerin, Carib Warfare and Slaving, *Antropológica* (in press).

14. See Domingo, Sánchez P., "A New Reality for Venezuela's Indigenous Peoples," Venezuelan National Foundation for Indigenous Studies. http://www.centrelink.org/SanchezEnglish.html

15. Donna Lee Van Cott, ed., *Indigenous Peoples and Democracy in Latin America* (New York: St. Martin's Press, 1994).

16. Amnesty International, *Brazil. "We Are the Land": Indigenous Peoples' Struggle for Human Rights* (New York: Amnesty International, 1992).

17. George M. Foster, *Tzintzuntzan: Mexican Peasants in a Changing World,* rev. ed. (New York: Elsevier, 1979), pp. 122–166.

Suggested Readings

Allen, Catherine J. *The Hold Life Has: Coca and Cultural Identity in an Andean Community.* Washington, D.C.: Smithsonian Institution, 1988. Discusses the social and ceremonial life of a highland community, emphasizing the ritual importance of mountain peaks and the socially and ceremonially integrative functions of coca use.

Amnesty International. *Brazil. "We Are the Land." Indigenous Peoples' Struggle for Human Rights.* New York: Amnesty International, 1992. Details abuses of indigenous human rights in Brazil.

Barry, Herbert, III. "Regional and Worldwide Variations in Culture." *Ethnology* 7:2 (1968), pp. 207–217. A cross-cultural statistical analysis, based on the *Ethnographic Atlas* (see Murdock 1967), of the distribution worldwide, and by continents, of the major types of subsistence economy, family customs, and social structure.

Brown, Michael F. *Tsewa's Gift: Magic and Meaning in an Amazonian Society.* Washington, D.C.: Smithsonian Institution Press, 1985. Explores how the private use of magic by the Aguaruna molds their transactions with nature as well as their practical activities such as hunting, gardening, and romantic relations.

Buechler, Hans C., and Judith-Maria Buechler. *The Bolivian Aymara: Case Studies in Cultural Anthropology.* New York: Holt, Rinehart and Winston, 1971. One of the few complete ethnographic descriptions of an Aymara community and the best short study available.

Cancian, Frank. *Economics and Prestige in a Maya Community: The Religious Cargo System in Zinacantan.* Stanford: Stanford University Press, 1965. Offers a thorough analysis of a typical religious *cargo* system and shows how traditional practices have been modified and elaborated in response to population growth and increasing wealth differentiation within the community.

Chagnon, Napoleon A. *Yanomamö: The Fierce People.* Case Studies in Cultural Anthropology. New York: Holt, Rinehart and Winston, 5th ed. 1995. The classic study of an extremely warlike people who inhabit an isolated area in the northern Amazon Basin.

Davis, Shelton H. *Victims of the Miracle: Development and the Indians of Brazil.* Cambridge: Cambridge University Press, 1977. Attempts to document the disruptive impact on the native peoples of the tropical forest of programs to develop the Amazon in Brazil.

Denevan, William M., ed. *The Native Population of the Americas in 1492.* Madison: University of Wisconsin, 1976. A collection of papers that treats the historical demography of the Americas. Each paper considers some aspect of the basic disagreement about the relative size of the aboriginal population of the New World.

Faron, Louis C. *The Mapuche Indians of Chile: Case Studies in Cultural Anthropology.* New York: Holt, Rinehart and Winston, 1968. An excellent summary of contemporary culture among the peasant Araucanian farmers of southern Chile.

Foster, George M. *Tzintzuntzan: Mexican Peasants in a Changing World.* Rev. ed. New York: Elsevier, 1979. The best general account of peasant society and worldview in Latin America. Although most inhabitants of Tzintzuntzan are mestizo, they share many characteristics with the modern Indian, or the closed corporate peasant communities of Indo-America.

Gregor, Thomas. *Mehinaku: The Drama of Daily Life in a Brazilian Indian Village.* Chicago: University of Chicago Press, 1977. The peaceful Mehinaku, who live in the southern Amazon Basin, contrast strikingly with the warlike Yanomamö (see Chagnon 1968).

Heningsgaard, William, and Jason Clay. "The Upper Mazaruni Dam." *Cultural Survival Newsletter* 4:3 (1980), p. 103. A brief account of the economic and political factors behind the construction of the dam and why this project means the Akawaio are being deprived of their land.

Hill, Jonathan D., ed. *Rethinking History and Myth: Indigenous South American Perspectives on the Past.* Urbana, Ill.: University of Illinois Press, 1988. Documents how South American indigenous peoples, in the highlands as well as the lowlands, have utilized both myth and history to develop dynamic interpretations of past and present interaction with colonial and national societies.

Isbell, Billie Jean. *To Defend Ourselves. Ecology and Ritual in an Andean Village.* Austin: University of Texas, 1978. Good analysis of a typical Andean community that treats both traditional culture and the processes of accommodating to a changing nation.

Murdock, George Peter. "Ethnographic Atlas." *Ethnology* 6:2 (1967). The culmination of Murdock's lifelong interest in tabulating the occurrence of cultural traits on a worldwide basis.

Murphy, Yolanda, and Robert F. Murphy. *Women of the Forest.* New York: Columbia University Press, 1974. An excellent account of a typical Amazonian society with an emphasis on the role of women and the woman's point of view.

Overing, Joanna, and Alan Passes, eds. *The Anthropology of Love and Anger: The Aesthetics of Conviviality in Native Amazonia*. London: Routledge, 2001. Reveals that indigenous South American thought and practice are fundamentally dissimilar from Western patterns. Conviviality or "sociality" is attained only through negotiation of the negative features of communal living to achieve positive harmony and sociability.

Schwerin, Karl H. *Oil and Steel: Processes of Karinya Culture Change in Response to Industrial Development*. Latin American Studies, 4. Los Angeles: UCLA, 1966. A comparison of social and cultural characteristics in two Venezuelan Indian communities with a theoretical analysis of the processes of culture change that occurred there during the twentieth century.

_____. "The Anthropological Antecedents: Caciques, Cacicazgos, and Caciquismo." In *The Caciques: Oligarchical Politics and the System of Caciquismo in the Luso-Hispano World*, ed. Robert Kern and Ronald Dolkart, pp. 5–17. Albuquerque: University of New Mexico Press, 1973. A summary statement on the general nature of chiefdoms, or *cacicazgos*, in pre-Columbian Latin America with discussion of their distribution and principal social and cultural characteristics.

Service, Elman R. "Indian-European Relations in Colonial Latin America." *American Anthropologist* 57 (1955), pp. 411–425. Presents the thesis that major differences in the character of modern Latin American states can be traced to European responses to differences in aboriginal cultural patterns, especially in relation to subsistence and sociopolitical complexity.

Stephen, Lynn. *Zapotec Women*. Austin: University of Texas Press, 1991. Explores how commercial weaving for export has altered the lives of Zapotec women in recent decades. Class, ethnicity, and gender determine women's roles and standing in the community. Yet, while the expansion of capitalism has produced class differentiation, it has also reinforced kin-based institutions supporting local ethnic identity.

Urban, Greg, and Joel Sherzer, eds. *Nation-States and Indians in Latin America*. Austin: University of Texas Press, 1991. Looks at the interaction between Amerindian cultures and the Europe-derived nation-states of Latin America.

Van Cott, Donna Lee, ed. *Indigenous Peoples and Democracy in Latin America*. New York: St. Martin's Press, 1994. Analyzes, within a broader theoretical framework, indigenous movements in eight Latin American countries: Bolivia, Colombia, Peru, and Ecuador; Mexico and Guatemala; Brazil and Paraguay.

Vogt, Evon Z. *The Zinacantecos of Mexico: A Modern Maya Way of Life*. Case Studies in Cultural Anthropology. New York: Holt, Rinehart and Winston, 1970. Beginning in 1955, Vogt directed the Harvard Chiapas Project in the *municipio* of Zinacantan in southern Mexico. This project has been dedicated to continuous observation and study in the same community in order to better understand the directional processes that are at work in social and cultural systems.

Warren, Kay B., and Jean E. Jackson, eds. *Indigenous Movements, Self-Representation, and the State in Latin America*. Austin: University of Texas Press, 2002. How indigenous movements in Latin America attempt to influence national agendas when governments articulate ambivalent attitudes about encouraging ethnic diversity.

Chapter 4

HARMONIZING AND DISHARMONIZING HUMAN AND NATURAL ENVIRONMENTS

DAVID STEA
G. SHANE LEWIS

TO ADDRESS CONTEMPORARY environmental issues of Latin America, it is first necessary to reach consensus on what constitutes *environment*. Such consensus is neither clear nor easy. As expressed succinctly by a former professor of philosophy in Mexico City, "*no me interesa el medio ambiente; me gusta vivir en la ciudad.*" ("I'm not interested in environment; I like living in the city.") For him, not only is the environment extra-human, it is also extra-urban.

This distinction between the city and the environment may be extreme, but even for those to whom "environment" is more inclusive, identification and prioritization of specific environmental issues varies widely around Latin America. "Environment" is much more than physical surroundings and cannot be dissociated from politics, poverty, insecure land tenure, human rights, and gender issues.

North Americans and many Latin Americans alike share bits of conventional wisdom, popularly held myths concerning the root causes of environmental problems. While containing certain partial truths, all are in the balance false, and this chapter attempts implicitly to debunk them. The text begins with some basic issues, proceeds to case studies, and concludes with a critique of a few suggested solutions. In this relatively brief treatment, we cannot consider all nations or all possible environmental issues, nor can we give more than a few lines to the islands of the Caribbean, whose environmental problems, exacerbated by poverty and widening gaps between rich and poor, include deforestation, water pollution, and loss of fisheries. For the same reason of space, specific citations are provided only for direct quotes.

BASIC ISSUES

The issues basic to defining and describing Latin American environmental problems are shared with the rest of the developing world. Central to these is the relationship of economic development to so-called *sustainable* development. Both forms of development imply efficiency:[1] The efficiency involved in sustainability, in particular, must exist in order that the present use of important resources not endanger the availability of such resources to future generations. In this, environmental issues are entwined not just with relative availability of natural resources, but with human beings—viewed as resources. Social, cultural, and political issues are, after all, intimately interrelated with economic development.

Economic development is a prime issue of the Southern tier, and environmental conservation is stressed by the North. While viewed as opposed by many participants in the 1992 Rio Declaration, these concerns—for both the economy and the environment—must be mutually reinforcing. The usual measure of economic development, standard of living as measured by increased gross national product, cannot be opposed to increased quality of life, including environmental improvement, however difficult that may be to index quantitatively. Truly *sustainable* development cannot take place unless socioeconomic development and environmental improvement proceed together, catalyzed by political action and will. Thus, of importance here is "political ecology," or, more inclusively, "sociopolitical ecology."

Central to the concerns of—and protest against—the 2002 World Summit on Sustainable Development were the prospects for and implementation of "globalization." Integration of economic and environmental concerns should involve internalizing and reducing externalities. However, in the opinion of many, one effect of globalization to date has been *increasing* negative externalities (Franko, 2003), which disproportionately impacts developing countries such as in Latin America and especially among destitute. The outstanding example of "free trade" agreements affecting Latin America is NAFTA, the North American Free Trade Agreement. Regardless of what it has done to or for the three national economies involved, there is substantial disagreement concerning whether NAFTA will contribute to environmental improvement (especially in Mexico) or further environmental degradation.

In sum, there is no single Latin American environmental problem; rather, there are multiple environmental problems that vary in importance based upon who you are, where you live, and what economic resources are available to you: whether you are rich or poor, urban or rural, male or female. A middle-class resident of Santiago, Chile, is likely to complain most about air quality, while someone living in a shack in São Paulo might be most affected by problems of water sanitation. A rubber tapper might ally with an international rain forest activist in arguing that tropical deforestation is the most pressing issue, but for very different reasons. Problems in maintaining fishing stocks off the coast of Argentina might seem a long way from the concerns of the Indians in Peru's Altiplano. Women might worry about the ways communities struggle to overcome deficits with water or sewage (Franko, 2003, 444–445).

Socioeconomic levels are intimately linked with levels of environmental quality, since poverty is both a cause and an effect of environmental degradation. In the absence of secure land tenure, the rural poor act rationally, in the short term, when they seek to extract as much from the land as possible. When excluded from the establishment and management of reserves, as in the case of the *Reserv Mariposa Monarca* (monarch butterfly reserve) in the Mexican states of Mexico and Michoacán, neighboring farmers understandably begin to nibble at the edges of the reserve. Land tenure is an issue in urban areas as well, where carefully planned irregular settlements, or "squatments," occupy often- precarious terrain such as denuding hillsides. These "squatments," too, represent a rational solution to the otherwise intractable problem of ultra-low-cost housing. Land tenure involves not just private *minifundia* or urban lots, but an understanding of how common areas are to be regulated, to avoid the so-called "tragedy of the commons."

URBANIZATION

Degrees of urbanization do not differentiate Latin American countries from the United States. Just over 77 percent of the U.S. population lived in cities in 2000, while almost 80 percent of Latin Americans lived in cities. Five Latin American countries are more than 81 percent urbanized: Argentina, Brazil, Chile, Uruguay, and Venezuela, with Uruguay at over 91 percent of the population living in metro areas. Recent estimates suggest that by the year 2025, South America will be the most urbanized of the world's continents, with 85 percent of its population living in cities. Any differences, therefore, in environmental problems of Latin America and the industrialized world are not related to *degree* of urbanization, but rather to the *nature* of that urbanization and to the way of life of rural peoples. Of the more than one-fifth of the U.S. population who live in rural areas, less than 1 percent is actively engaged in agriculture. Rural dwellers of Latin America are mostly farmers, with the vast majority living in poverty and some using technology unchanged in hundreds of years. None can compete in the market with expanding international agribusiness.

In contrast to the United States, where over 100 million people are spread over forty metropolitan areas of a million or more inhabitants each, Latin American urban places have evolved differently. In all but one country, a single megacity dwarfs all others.[2] Since the middle of the last century, these megalopolises have attracted immigrants from increasingly impoverished rural areas. Many move first to intermediate towns and then to the primate city, occupying land belonging to the government or the church or left undeveloped by private landowners. Such areas of irregular settlement, which characterize primate cities in Asia and Africa as well, often represent 20 percent or more of the urban population. For these people, the most pressing problems are water and sanitation. Due to the absence of any sewage facilities, fecal matter remains on the ground. In the case of Mexico City, it is desiccated during the dry season and carried as windblown dust from the periphery of the city into the center. The urban middle class, economizing by using slightly lower-priced leaded gas in their cars, reciprocates by filling the air with lead fumes, which then blow into areas inhabited by the poor and affect the mental capacity of their children.

The proportion of urbanized space devoted to green areas, such as parks and plazas, has decreased markedly over the past half-century. This is important not only in the reduction of opportunities for outdoor recreation, but also because trees and green plants can reduce certain forms of pollution. Mexico City, renowned for the amount of area devoted to parks in 1920, is now, as a result of unregulated sprawl, among the cities with the smallest proportion of its land areas devoted to green space. This lack has become so acute in recent years that Mexico City launched a program labeled *Cada Familia Un Arbol* ("each family a tree") and offered to provide trees for people to plant. Some citizens responded that there were already too many trees behind which street criminals could hide and proposed fewer, not more.

Each urban socioeconomic group perceives its problems from its own perspective, blames the others, and sees different solutions, mostly to be mediated by passively awaited governmental action. For dwellers in irregular settlements, the most pressing problem is usually insecure land tenure; urban environmental problems are perceived as absence of piped drinkable water and sewage disposal. People can upgrade their homes, and do so, but even with organization cannot provide the requisite infrastructure on their own. There are, however, hopeful signs. In Mexico's Colonia Miguel Hidalgo and Venezuela's Casalta II, two predominantly low-income neighborhoods with many irregularities, the residents, with the cooperation of faculty and students from neighboring universities, took environmental improvement into their own hands. Casalta II residents organized their work with the aid of donated computers, while Colonia Miguel Hidalgo solved the problem of dirt streets that flooded during rainy season by buying their own asphalt and threatening to do their own paving.[3] They designed *ecocalles* (ecological streets) where the rainwater runoff was to be channeled into drainage systems to irrigate the roots of trees they planned to install.

The urban middle class perceives environmental problems to be air pollution and choking traffic, whose solution is left to governmental entities. The wealthier perceive similar problems, but the causes are no better understood, and usually blamed upon the ignorance of the poor (Roberts, 1994). Bypassing this circle of blame, Jaime Lerner, mayor of the Brazilian City of Curitiba (population near two million), pursued an integrative approach to solving his city's environmental problems. He relieved floods by diverting rain water into park lakes, developed a trash-for-food/transport exchange system for squatters, designed a metrolike bus system, planned 150km of bicycle paths, and initiated tax breaks for developers who included green areas. Results included a decrease of 30 percent in gas consumption and, even more surprising, an equivalent reduction in use of private cars.

DEFORESTATION AND ASSOCIATED ISSUES

Mentioning "forests" in a Latin American context evokes the image of rain forests. Two countries immediately come to mind: Costa Rica and Brazil, the former as an exemplar of conservation, the latter as the apex of deforestation. The reality is more complex. Certainly, Brazil today has only 63 percent of its principal pre-conquest ecosystems intact, having lost 93 percent of the Atlantic Forest, 50 percent of the *cerrado*, and 15 percent of its Amazonian forest. The Amazon River Basin itself contains 20 percent of the world's fresh water. The Amazon forest is estimated to be the habitat of 50 percent of the world's species, although whether that number is two million or thirty million is still in question. In question as well is the number of indigenous peoples who call the forest home–somewhere between a quarter of a million and a million and a quarter. The current rate of destruction of the Brazilian Amazon ranges from 0.5 percent to 1.2 percent annually and represented a mean loss of *at least* three million hectares (8 million acres) a year between 1980 and 1995. Such conversion of land use has often been aided by loans received from the World Bank and other international organizations.

This Amazonian loss is deplorable. The fastest *rate* of deforestation, however, is represented by Central America. Tiny Costa Rica, which boasted just under two million hectares (5.3 million acres) of forest in 1980, was down to slightly more than 1.2 million hectares in 1995, a loss of about 50,000 hectares annually over that period. Although the raw numbers equal no more than one-sixtieth the *area* of deforestation in Amazonia, the *rate* of loss is at least two and a half times that of the Brazilian Amazon over the same fifteen-year period, and one of the highest in all Latin America.

What accounts for the paradox of the most environmentally conscious nation of Central America, a nation that has stressed low-impact ecotourism as a sustainable road to development, also exhibiting so high a rate of deforestation? Among the causes of deforestation in Latin America as a whole are, in order of importance, conversion of land use for agriculture, logging on a commercial scale, firewood gathering, and cattle raising. Of these, it is the last that has gotten most attention in the United States with the so-called "hamburger thesis" or "hamburger connection."

The "hamburger thesis" holds that forests are cleared for pasture to provide beef for U.S. fast-food chains. However, and not just in the case of Costa Rica, the "hamburger thesis" is only a partial explanation, in two senses. First, it represents just 8 percent of forest clearing, overall. Second, from the mid-1970s to the 1990s, U.S. consumption of Costa Rican beef decreased, while Costa Rican consumption increased; in fact, the Costa Rican cattle business experienced a severe crisis in the 1980s, as export taxes and interest rates increased, while beef prices dropped to 1950–1960 levels. As less affluent ranchers are forced to move further out, clearing still more forest, predatory animals, especially pumas, begin to take their toll on cattle. This further increases costs. Ranching may seem a relatively low-maintenance economic activity. However, all these factors taken together make ranching land-degrading and not necessarily profitable.

With regard to beef production in export and consumption, what has changed is domestic demand. In the United States, preference for tender steaks implies feedlot cattle; thus the tougher but tastier Central American beef is deemed suitable only for hamburgers. In much of Latin America, however, *carne asada* is the standard food product of range-fed cattle, and increasingly so. In those countries that are traditional exporters of beef, such as Brazil, El Salvador, Guatemala, Nicaragua, and Panama, domestic demand was growing faster by the 1980s than demand for export production.

Domestic demand has received insufficient attention in the "hamburger connection" literature, something that is particularly unfortunate in a period when it is of much greater weight as a stimulus to cattle production in Central America, Brazil, and elsewhere. It has long been recognized that meat is a product with a very high income elasticity of demand; small increases in income levels produce proportionately greater increases in demand. Population growth and urbanization are still producing rapidly rising demand for beef. (Edelman, 1995).

Lester Brown's *Who Will Feed China?* proposes that this elasticity is global and that increased affluence, as in the case of China's billion-and-a half people, inevitably produces rising domestic demand for beef.

In quantitative terms, conversion of forest to agricultural use is even more important. Some of this forest-clearing is accomplished by peasant farmers, many encouraged by ill-considered national subsidies for land-clearing, such as those offered in Brazil to settlers in Amazonia to reduce concentrations of the poor in other parts of the country. In lowland tropical rain forests, soil is generally nutrient-poor, while elsewhere, deforestation leads to loss of fertile topsoil. As increased ranching in other parts of Latin America forces small-scale farmers to move into often more precarious and less fertile areas, such as steep hillsides, deforestation and reduction or elimination of fallowing combines to lead to further loss of soil fertility (and of topsoil itself), reducing farm productivity, and further impoverishing farmers.

Of even more importance in deforestation is monocrop export agribusiness, such as melon-raising in Honduras. Such agriculture involves intensive irrigation and the input of large quantities of herbicides, pesticides, and chemical fertilizers.[4] Because the lower-level toxic chemicals formerly used left residues that impeded the passage of such products into the United States, producers switched to more toxic chemicals with a short half-life. Their impact has fallen mainly upon the agricultural workers themselves, especially in Mexico. Further, such toxic chemicals find their way into streams and rivers, and, eventually fish and even cattle, which graze on land once used for agriculture.

With the U.S.A. emphasizing the interception of drug traffic and industrialized countries increasing demand for high-quality timber, attention has been drawn to the impacts of both Andean coca cultivation and lumbering upon land use and deforestation. National and multinational lumber companies use heavy equipment to cut wide roads into forests to extract massive mahogany tree trunks. These roads provide access, first, for local timber cutters to extract wood of lower value, and later for colonists to enter the ravaged forest, clearing the area for cultivation. Farmers burn the remainder of the trees to prepare for cultivation. Where the soil is too exhausted to support agriculture, burning by ranchers allows grasses to grow that later feed cattle. In years past, smoke clouds that covered nearby towns and obscured the sun were visible from outer space, as reported by astronauts.

Older logging roads also enable coca farmers to gain access to potential new garden plots deep within forested areas. Coca production in Peru has deforested 700,000 hectares (1.9 million acres) over the past three decades, and since 1900, has accounted for 10 percent of deforestation in Amazonian Peru. Coca is the prime crop in certain areas, such as Bolivia's Chapare, but, while most profitable, it is not the only crop, for several reasons.

Coca leaf is the most difficult crop to accommodate within a production system based on family labor because the labor requirements are very high in comparison to other crops. Also, the use of insecticides on coca fields takes its toll in terms of toxic runoff and further contamination of waterways already degraded by deforestation-produced erosion. Farmers do not grow coca leaf because it is particularly attractive; they grow it because it is the only crop for which they know they will have a buyer (Painter, 1995, 156–158). However, land use may vary season to season, depending upon land ownership and consequently, insecure land tenure means indifferent land stewardship. It is not economically rational to expend much energy in the care of land that may be taken over by another after a short period of time, without warning. In the Amazon Basin of Peru, the rate of deforestation by squatters is twice that of legal tenants, for two possible reasons. First, squatters are likely to be more recent arrivals and therefore less familiar with the local ecology. Second, with insecure tenure, it makes better sense to plant annual rather than perennial crops. This argues as well, ironically, for longer-term timber concessions, such as those now favored not just by Conservation International, but by the World Bank. Such concessions do encourage replanting trees that mature over relatively short periods of time, but not mahogany, which requires eighty to one hundred years to maturity. Market unpredictability also affects the acceptability of long-term concessions.

ENERGY, EXTRACTIVE INDUSTRIES, AND ENVIRONMENT

Energy resource extraction and energy resource use both produce environmental impacts. Energy consumption varies greatly across Latin America. Mexico's energy consumption level was, on average, 15 percent of the United States's in 2000, and just 6 percent of Guatemala's. Examining *changes* in energy consumption levels, however, reveals a different picture. While per *capita* energy consumption increased 7 percent in the United States between 1970 and 2000, Brazil's and Mexico's more than doubled, Guatemala's more than tripled, and Paraguay's increased by almost six times. By contrast, Venezuela's use was just a quarter that of the United States, and its *per capita* consumption actually 4 percent *less* in 2000 than in 1970.

Contributors to increased Latin American energy consumption include increased urbanization, with concomitant substitution of fossil fuel energy for biomass energy, automobile acquisition and use, and expanded energy-intensive agribusiness (such as chemical fertilizers and heavy equipment). Energy efficiency has, as a rule, been poor. A combination of subsidized energy pricing in countries such as Mexico and profit-orientation elsewhere resulted in Brazil-marketed electrical appliances being only half as efficient as their U.S. equivalents. In fact, energy efficiency has decreased: In 2000, a unit of output required 7 percent more energy input than the same unit of output in 1980.

Along with energy consumption, air pollution has also grown proportionately. Carbon dioxide emission was more than a third higher in 2000 than in 1980, with the five years from 1995 to 2000 accounting for more than half this growth in Latin America. As a whole, Latin America produces just over 5 percent of the world's greenhouse gas emissions. While Mexico and Brazil account for more than half of this, the emissions of these two countries taken together account for only 12 percent of the emissions of the United States. Lower *per capita* energy consumption reflects lower mean incomes in the Latin American countries. But as income inequality is greater in Latin America than anywhere else in the world, so is *per capita* energy consumption—the consumption rates of the wealthy in Mexico and Brazil are greater than those of the same class in the United States, itself no paragon of conservation.

Electric power is generated by fossil fuels in some areas, and by hydroelectric facilities in others. Hydroelectric dams are true megaprojects, as a class the largest and most expensive construction projects in the world. Construction costs are so high that they inevitably involve large loans from transnational banks, such as the World Bank. In the 1980s, Brazil's "2010" Plan proposed a total of nearly eighty dams along the Amazon tributaries. A monumental set of projects was intended to provide electric power for the far-away megacities of São Paula and Rio de Janeiro. Environmental impacts, however, would fall upon Amazonia, including the flooding of farmland, loss of fertile silt, loss of species, and proliferation of disease. Further, the useful life span of such megadams as energy generators, often overestimated, is limited by eventual silt deposition.

Exploration, drilling, and transportation of fossil fuels, especially oil and gas, is of special concern in the major oil-producing nations of Latin America: Mexico, Venezuela, Ecuador, Colombia, and, to a lesser extent, Bolivia and Peru. Petroleum exploration has proceeded with little concern for the environment, whether carried out by such national oil companies as Mexico's Pemex or Ecuador's Petroecuador or such multinationals as Texaco and Conoco. Inadequate or absent monitoring of leaks has resulted in massive pollution of rivers and streams in Ecuador, which produces almost 400,000 barrels of crude daily. Toxic wastes discharged into waterways, including arsenic, lead, oil, and sulfates, kill fish and the cattle that come to drink. Refinery development on Mexico's Gulf Coast, spurred by drilling into massive offshore deposits, has completely changed the ecology of the state of Tabasco. Further, impacts of the petroleum industry are not limited to areas of sparse population. In Mexico, for example, the environment of Coatzácoálcos, Tabasco, has suffered greatly, while in Guadalajara a mid-1990s Pemex gas pipeline explosion killed 250 people along a seven-mile stretch of poor communities.

Extractive industries include, for example, tin mines in Bolivia and gold mines in Brazil. Rich silver mines in Guanajuato, Mexico, and Potosí, Bolivia, funded European wars of the eighteenth and nineteenth centuries. Potosí's silver-rich mountain became two, the second a hill of slag. The long-term cumulative effects of mercury used in silver refining in Guanajuato's *haciendas de beneficio* are still unknown. While mining of precious metals has declined in importance, other extractive industries, while volatile, continue to prosper and pollute.

IMPACTS ON INDIGENOUS PEOPLES:
ANOTHER HUMAN DIMENSION

While some people view the environment as "out there," others see "nature" as something nonhuman. This leads to criticisms of deforestation based upon the idea that various species of animals and curative properties of plants are as yet "undiscovered" and completely ignores the knowledge of those people who have dwelt in the forest for centuries. An extreme case in the tourism realm is the statement of a tour guide in northern Sumatra concerning an extraordinarily beautiful village: "We're going to make this a place nice for tourists. We're going to take away all the people."

From a more inclusive perspective, the environment is human as well as physical. As the environmental impacts of urban development in Latin America often fall disproportionately upon the urban poor, so the impacts of rural development often fall disproportionately upon the rural poor. A case in point is the Mexican state of Chiapas.

On New Year's Day 1994, the Zapatista Army of Liberation rose in revolt against the government of the State of Chiapas and the federal government. The rebels managed to occupy a number of *municipios* and several major towns in the eastern part of the state. Chiapas, on the Guatemalan border, was a part of Mexico untouched by the land reforms of the early twentieth-century revolution. Although many Mayan inhabitants of Chiapas were from other parts of Mexico or were refugees from Guatemala's genocidal civil war, and thus new to the territory, others had developed sustainable agricultural practices over centuries.

But the *mestizo* colonists dominated, and deforestation progressed until over 95 percent of Chiapas's tropical and montane rain forests had disappeared. In 1978, President José López Portillo created the Montes Azules Biosphere Reserve, in an attempt to preserve 1,250 square miles of the Lacandón forest. It was the first internal ecological reserve in Mexico, duly recognized as such by the United Nations. Inhabitants of the area were not involved in decisionmaking about the reserve, however, and were forcibly evicted. Relocated outside the reserve, they therefore felt little compunction about taking advantage of lax enforcement of the reserve's status (few funds were allotted to patrolling the area) to move the boundary posts at night, when no one was looking.

In prior years, as elsewhere in Mexico, the male members of many Chiapaneco families had become accustomed to spending large portions of each year elsewhere, such as in the United States, as laborers. Other Mayan farmers continued to suffer under the same regime that had brought about the revolution, many as landless peasants barely able to subsist under the yoke of exploitative ranchers and landlords. This, added to the governmentally declared end of land reform,[5] additional population pressures from the 22,000 or more Guatemalan refugees who remained in Chiapas, and, finally, the threat of NAFTA-style "free trade" affecting coffee and corn production, contributed to the Zapatista uprising and its subsequent short-lived success.

In contrast to the Mexican experience with Montes Azules was the creation of the Beni Biosphere Reserve and associated buffer areas in the Chiman forest by the Bolivian government, with the financial cooperation of Conservation International. More will be said about this later in this chapter.

CLASS, GENDER, AND TRANSNATIONAL IMPACTS

There are several class, gender, and transnational impacts to be discussed. First, the issue of gender, treated at much greater length by a number of Latin American writers and researchers, deserves more than brief mention here. "Women hold up half the sky," it is said, but they also till more than half the earth. They haul water and firewood, tasks that consume more of their time as they go greater distances each year due to the greater scarcity of these two vital resources. With increasing poverty, women are left to tend village gardens as men go to the cities (or to the United States) in search of wage labor, and the women live at a subsistence level with the aid of remittances sent from far away. In Mexico's *maquiladora* industries, women were, until recently, the principal employees. In addition, forced by inadequate incomes to seek scarcely livable housing near the plants in which they worked, they became the unwilling recipients of pollution and toxic wastes.

Second is the issue of so-called "natural" hazards. Women and children tend to be hit hardest by natural hazards, which also have unnatural, human-induced, dimensions. There is some suggestion, for example, that enormous reservoirs have the capacity to trigger earthquakes in seismic areas. Further, the impacts of these often fall disproportionately upon the poor. Mexico, Central America, and Andean countries are earthquake-prone, and in several Latin American countries, *terremotos* (earthquakes) are called *clasemotos*. The often callous and classist response of authorities exacerbates popular distrust of governments. Sometimes, paradoxically, this produces results favorable to reinforcing community. When the federal government refused outside aid following the horrific 1985 Mexico City earthquake, urban communities formed their own relief teams: Any reduction in loss of life from this disaster can be attributed largely to these informal groups. The government did act, however, when Mexico's volcano Popocatépetl resumed activity several years ago. The mountain peasants who were evacuated later returned to find their houses empty and sacked of all possessions. When Popo again spewed ash a year later, these same people, understandably, refused to move.

Third, there are the effects of the relief efforts that follow environmental disasters. In the case of Mexico City's 1985 earthquake, outside assistance might have helped, but in some cases disaster relief is almost as damaging as the disaster itself. Outside "experts" who arrive expecting all the comforts and conveniences of home occasionally contribute more to the confusion than to the solution. When the call goes out for earthquake relief from abroad, well-meaning people likely send powdered milk (water supplies are much more likely to be disrupted than the cattle) and canned food (but no can openers). Monetary contributions are as likely to end up in the hands of corrupt government officials as in the hands of those impacted by the disaster.

Fourth, complementing the environmental impacts of agriculture are the impacts of mariculture on the sea and its shores. The cultivation of shrimp for export in such countries as Honduras is a case in point. To increase the access to the shrimp, a quick-result strategy is decimation of the coastal mangroves.[6] The short-term productivity of the shrimp fisheries increases temporarily, along with long-term environmental degradation, which includes increased flooding and eventual long-term loss of seafood productivity. Further, the mangroves, which provide nurseries for fish and shellfish, as well as protecting the shoreline from storms and flooding, do not regenerate easily. There are, however, other approaches to improving shrimp fisheries that are not environmentally damaging, such as a project to assist the movement of shrimp from ocean to lagoon in coastal Oaxaca, Mexico.

A final, special, case is that of environmental problems straddling international borders. Latin American countries do not correspond to bioregions or ecoregions, and twentieth-century border wars have been ecological disasters. Amazonia, although usually identified with Brazil, actually extends into all the countries bordering Brazil to the north and west. Thus, the conservation of Amazonia, or the amelioration of damage to the region, is not a matter of national sovereignty, but of international cooperation. The U.S.–Mexican border region is more than 3,000 kilometers (1,865 miles) long, the largest part of it consisting of the Rio Grande/Rio Bravo. A mere trickle after making its way around the Big Bend, it is replenished by the Pecos River on the U.S. side and the Rio Conchos on the Mexican side. From Laredo/Nuevo Laredo on down, the lower Rio Grande is so depleted that it no longer reaches the Gulf of Mexico, but dies on the beach. *Maquiladoras* taking advantage of lax enforcement of Mexico's stringent environmental laws use the river as a sewer for the disposal of toxic wastes, damaging the health of the poor who inhabit both sides of the river. Pollution does not respect international boundaries, and, in spite of the existence of an International Boundary and Water Commission, jurisdictional confusion exacerbates the problem.

SOLUTIONS . . . OR ARE THEY?

Debt-for-Nature Swaps

Conservation organizations have come up with what some consider to be a perfect partial solution to environmental degradation: The organization in question offers to pay a part of the national debt of country "X" in return for a pledge from that country to spend an equivalent, in national currency, to establish, say, a national park. Another view is that the impact of debt-for-nature swaps upon either debts or nature is minimal. Ultimately, the question is "who benefits and who pays?"

There have been more than twenty debt-for-nature swaps worldwide: Latin American countries involved in such swaps include Bolivia, Costa Rica, and Ecuador. In Bolivia, Conservation International (CI) arranged the first "debt-for-nature" swap in the Americas in 1987. The arrangement was rushed (perhaps CI was in too much of a hurry to be the first to broker such a swap), as neither CI nor government agencies could exercise much control over rapacious lumber companies.

The logic of debt relief in exchange for conservation is flawed in Bolivia. This is because the poor bear the debt burden, not the political and economic elite, who contracted the debt in the first place. The elite feel no "relief," only an economic threat. They value debt-for-nature swaps only for the international respectability—and money—swaps attract (Jones, 1995, p. 202).

The experiences of the World Wildlife Fund in Costa Rica and Fundacion Natura in Ecuador are similar. In the latter case, funds were adequate to acquire land areas in Andean and Amazonian Ecuador and the Galapagos Islands, but not to protect these areas from poachers and illegal loggers.

Ecotourism

Ecotourism can be defined as "responsible travel to natural areas, which conserves the environment and sustains the well-being of local people" (Anon., 2003). As international tourism continues growing rapidly, ecotourism, low-impact tourism, and other alternative forms of tourism represent the largest areas of economic growth in much of the world, including Latin America. They promise to bring money and jobs into impoverished, ecologically or culturally sensitive areas, assuming that local residents can then develop their economies along lines that help protect resources attractive to tourists.

National and regional tourism promotion agencies tend to view tourism as a panacea. Environmental protection agencies are generally more guarded: The link between bringing additional people into a sensitive area and establishing greater protections for that area can be tenuous and indirect. The problems of alternative tourism development serve as examples of the broader conflicts and paradoxes present in all efforts at sustainable development: There are costs and benefits to different groups that should be, but rarely are, balanced.

Even small, isolated communities have independently begun to view ecotourism and alternative tourism as preferred development paths. Over the past decade, the managers of protected natural areas have begun seeking more input from locals over use of area resources. This is a critical step, because unlike the norm in the United States, many protected natural areas of Latin America already have long-established, if isolated, communities of residents. Cultural shifts are often required to make natural areas viable ecotourism destinations. Without consensus-building and a broad appreciation of how such industry could benefit the community, these changes can be impossible. State and local governments seldom have the political will or the personnel to enforce restrictions in designated park areas when these conflict with local needs or values. El Cielo Biosphere Reserve, in the Mexican State of Tamaulipas, is a positive example. There, women have established cooperatives dedicated to providing assistance to, and provisions for, ecotourism (Lewitsky, 2002). In the State of Coahuila, in northern Mexico, however, Cuatro Ciénegas, already identified as an extraordinary and unique ecosystem, experienced a political battle over whether or not area ranchers would be able to exploit water resources currently reserved for the lagoons. Risks to people's livelihoods in the ecotourism industry served to impede the extraction plan. Additional resources for resolving this battle were provided by an international community of scientists and non-governmental organizations (NGOs).

Advantages of ecotourism include the provision of rural employment opportunities that can allow people to remain on their ancestral lands and maintenance of urban water quality and quantity through preservation of natural areas. Augmented tourism is seen by people living in rural areas of Latin America as attracting increased government services, such as paved roads, water, sewage treatment, and electricity. Some of these services do increase the human "carrying capacity" of an area. Ecotourism can also assist local organizations in the direction of better land stewardship, such as less random garbage disposal. Finally, having an ecotourism "industry" provides a political counterweight to less sustainable industry. It can build international constituencies and money for the protection of special places and bring international pressure to bear on such domestic problems as polluted beaches.

Disadvantages and challenges of ecotourism include problems incident to the creation of parks and reserves: poaching, fire suppression, managing exotic flora and fauna, and plant epidemics. Lack of resources for enforcement has led to problems with fires, wildlife, and theft. Wilderness reserves are frequently administered under a confusing patchwork of jurisdictions, characterized by gaps and overlapping spheres of governmental responsibility, and all are chronically underfunded. A Brazilian television news reporter was once shown interviewing a federal guard in Araguaia National Park when a large boat roared past loaded with illegal tourists. The guard shrugged and said he stood powerless, being one man in a territory the size of Belgium (Harrington, 1993, p. 216).

When complicated by cumbersome bureaucracy, management of natural areas becomes excessively complex, especially so since there are few studies of carrying capacity of park regions. Residents of reserves, if not included in reserve management, may conflict with "free-ranging" tourists who disrupt traditional agriculture practices and livestock. Auto traffic degrades the natural environment that originally attracted tourists and causes additional erosion and associated damage, especially in fragile desert ecosystems. Commitment to ecotourism may imply cyclical livelihood, potentially subject to wild swings and possibly ending in obsolescence. U.S. consular information sheets warning of crime, promulgated by the Department of State, can impact an entire region economically; and crime does tend to invade popular tourist destinations.

CONCLUSIONS

On the surface, there seem to have been some improvements and promising initiatives on preservation of Latin American environments. These include experiments in innovative use of solar, hydro, and other forms of energy; popular movements for forest preservation; and creative involvement of the private sector, for example, through market-based instruments (MBIs) or even regional pacts, such as NAFTA. In the 1990s, Mexico City alone had more than three hundred (uncoordinated) environmental organizations. Universities have initiated environmental engineering programs, and primary schools give environmental education classes to young children.

Yet the impacts of these movements have thus far been scattered, and fairly minimal. Environmental engineering has invariably focused upon remedial rather than preventative action and omitted sociocultural considerations, while the effect of environmental education programs upon adults depends upon children educating their parents. But there are two larger factors. The first is the impact of *external* forces: the World Bank and regional development bank lending policies, the actions of multinational corporations, and the interests of industrialized countries. The preference of banks for ultra-large development projects (which vastly increase national debt) and neoliberal structural readjustment programs, for GNP and technological increments, have made certain that economic development and environmental concerns will conflict.

The second factor involves *internal* divisions within the Latin American countries themselves: the gap between incredible wealth and scarcely more credible poverty; between whites and *mestizos*, on the one hand, and indigenous peoples on the other; between urban modernity and rural traditionalism; and between female subservience and male hegemony. The rural poor are still, by and large, more concerned with subsistence and survival than with the preservation of endangered species, while the urban rich can buy themselves out of most environmental contingencies. On the other hand, the more democratic political regimes now in power in Latin America hold out promise in a number of realms: The environment, it is to be hoped, will be among these.[7]

NOTES

1. "Efficiency," as used here, has no scale implications. There are as many diseconomies of scale as economies of scale (Schumacher, 1973; Hawken, 1993).

2. The sole exception is Brazil, whose twin megacities, Rio de Janeiro and São Paulo, are among the world's most populous.

3. This was a threat to the then-reigning party, the PRI, which had traditionally manipulated votes and voters by (later unfulfilled) promises of community improvement. The idea of community empowerment, of people taking control of their future, was seen as having the potential to undermine this party prerogative. The local PRI *delegado* responded by lending road-paving equipment and operators to the *colonia* for several days, to help accomplish street improvement, and the *colonia* replied by staging a celebratory lunch, accompanied with speeches, for the *delegado*: a win-win situation.

4. The rate of increase in chemical fertilizer use in Latin America was eight times as high in 1990–1999 as it was in 1980–1989.

5. In 1992, the much publicized "reform" to Article 27 of the Mexican Constitution of 1917 ended land reform policies that had served to shape the relationship between government and peasants for three-quarters of a century.

6. Such coastal areas are called "wetlands" by those who appreciate their value, "swamps" by those who don't.

7. Sincere appreciation is extended to Silvia Elguea and Melissa Gray, whose edits and comments contributed to substantial improvement of successive drafts of this manuscript. Any errors of fact or interpretation are the sole responsibility of the authors.

SUGGESTED READINGS

Cummings, B. J. *Dam the Rivers, Damn the People: Development and Resistance in Amazonian Brazil*. London: Earthscan Publications, 1990.

Dogse, P., and B. van Droste. *Debt-for-Nature Exchanges and Biosphere Reserves: Experiences and Potential*. Paris: UNESCO, 1990.

Ganster, P. *The U.S.–Mexico Border Environment: A Road Map to a Sustainable 2020*. San Diego: San Diego State University Press, 2000.

Johnston, B. R., ed. *Who Pays the Price? The Sociocultural Context of Environmental Crisis*. Washington, D.C.: Island Press, 1994.

_____. *Life and Death Matters: Human Rights and the Environment at the End of the Millennium*. Walnut Creek, Calif.: Altamira Press, 1997.

Painter, M., and W. H. Durham, eds.. *The Social Causes of Environmental Destruction in Latin America*. Ann Arbor: University of Michigan Press, 1995.

Roberts, Bryan R. Urbanization and the environment in developing countries: Latin America in comparative perspective. In Arizpe, L., M. P. Stone, and D. C. Major. *Population and Environment: Rethinking the Debate*. Boulder, Colo.: Westview, 1994.

Simon, Joel. *Endangered Mexico: An Environment on the Edge*. San Francisco: Sierra Club Books, 1997.

Westerhoff, P. *The U.S.–Mexican Border Environment: Water Issues Along the U.S.–Mexican Border*. San Diego: San Diego State University Press, 2000.

BIBLIOGRAPHY

Bedoya Garland, E. "The social and economic causes of deforestation in the Peruvian Amazon basin: Natives and colonists." In Painter, M., and W. H. Durham, eds. *The Social Causes of Environmental Destruction in Latin America*. Ann Arbor: University of Michigan Press, 1995.

Brown, L. R. *Who Will Feed China? Wake-up Call for a Small Planet.* New York: W. W. Norton, 1995.

Cronon, W. *Changes in the Land.* New York: Hill and Wang, 1983.

Clark, J. G. "Economic development vs. sustainable societies: Reflections on the players in a crucial context." *Annual Review of Ecology and Systematics,* 1995, *26,* 225–48.

Cunningham, A. B. "Indigenous knowledge and biodiversity." In Place, S. E. (ed.) *Tropical Rainforests: Latin American Nature and Society in Transition.* Wilmington: Scholarly Resources, Inc., 1993, pp. 185–193.

Collett, M. "Bolivia blazes trail . . . to where?" *Christian Science Monitor,* July 10, 1989.

Czitrom Baus, S. *Sistema de Bombeo por Energía de Oleaje.* Mexico, D.F. Videoservicios Profesionales, 2000 (video film).

Díaz Romero, P. *Huicholes y Pesticidas.* Mexico, D. F.: Red de Acción sobre Plaguicidas y Alternativas en Mexico, 1994 (video film).

Dourojeanni, M. "Impactos ambientales de la coca y la producción de cocaína en la amazonia peruana." In Leonard, F., and R. Castro, eds., *Pasta Basica de Cocaína.* Lima, Peru: Centro de Información y Educación del Abuso de Drogas, 1989, pp. 281–299.

Edelman, M. "Rethinking the hamburger thesis: Deforestation and the crisis of Central America's beef." In Painter, M., and W. H. Durham, eds. *The Social Causes of Environmental Destruction in Latin America.* Ann Arbor: University of Michigan Press, 1995.

Elguea Vejar, S. Revisión sobre algunos aspectos que involucrán sustancias tóxicas. *Sociotam,* 2000, 10(1), 165–174.

Elguea Vejar, S. *La ética ecológica desde una perspective ecofeminista.* Masters thesis, Universidad Nacional Autonoma de Mexico, 2001.

Franko, P. *The Puzzle of Latin American Economic Development.* New York: Rowman & Littlefield, 2003.

Gebara, I. "Ecofeminism: A Latin American perspective." *Crosscurrents,* 2003 (Spring), *53*(1), 93–103.

Gedicks, A. *Resource Rebels: Native Challenges to Mining and Oil Corporations.* Cambridge, Mass.: South End Press, 2001.

Guillet, D. "Toward a cultural ecology of mountains: The central Andes and the Himalayas compared." *Current Anthropology,* 1983, *24*(5), 561–574.

Hardin, G. "The tragedy of the commons." *Science,* 1968, *162,* 1242–1248.

Harrington, T. "Tourism damages Amazon region." In Place, S. E., ed. *Tropical Rainforests: Latin American Nature and Society in Transition.* Wilmington, Del.: Scholarly Resources, Inc., 1993, pp. 185–193.

Hawken, P. *The Ecology of Commerce.* New York: Harper Collins, 1993.

Holl, K. D., G. C. Daily, and P. R. Ehrlich. "Knowledge and perceptions in Costa Rica regarding environment, population, and biodiversity issues." *Conservation Biology,* 1995, *9*(6), 1548–1558.

International Boundary and Water Commission (IBWC), U.S. Section/Texas Clean Rivers Program. *2003 Regional Assessment of Water Quality in the Rio Grande Basin.* IBWC, 2003.

Jarvis, L. S. *Livestock Development in Latin America.* Washington, D.C.: World Bank, 1986.

Jones, J. C. "Environmental destruction, ethnic discrimination, and international aid in Bolivia." In Painter, M., and W. H. Durham, eds. *The Social Causes of Environmental Destruction in Latin America.* Ann Arbor: University of Michigan Press, 1995.

Kenworthy, E. "Nature in Latin America: Images and issues." Chapter 11 in Black, J. K., ed., *Latin America: Its Problems and Its Promise* (3rd ed.)

Landa, R. J. Meave, and J. Carabias. "Environmental deterioration in rural Mexico: An examination of the concept." *Ecological Applications*, 1997(Feb.), *7*(1), 316–329.

Lewitsky, M. *Characteristics of a Successful Community Cooperative: A Case Study in the Community of Alta Cimas, El Cielo Biosphere, Tamaulipas, Mexico.* Masters thesis, Southwest Texas State University, 2002.

López, R. "The policy roots of socioeconomic stagnation and environmental implosion: Latin America, 1950–2000." *World Development*, 2003, *31*(2), 259–280.

Mahoney, R. "Debt-for-nature swaps: Who really benefits?" In Place, S. E., ed. *Tropical Rainforests: Latin American Nature and Society in Transition.* Wilmington, DL: Scholarly Resources, Inc., 1993, pp. 185–193.

Major, D. C., ed. *Population and Environment: Rethinking the Debate.* Boulder, Colo.: Westview Press, 1994.

Meadows, D. "The city of first priorities." *Whole Earth Review*, 1995 (Spring).

Painter, M. "Anthropological perspectives on environmental destruction." In Painter, M., and W. H. Durham, eds. *The Social Causes of Environmental Destruction in Latin America.* Ann Arbor: University of Michigan Press, 1995.

Painter, M. "Upland-lowland production linkages and land degradation in Bolivia." In Painter, M., and W. H. Durham, eds. *The Social Causes of Environmental Destruction in Latin America.* Ann Arbor: University of Michigan Press, 1995.

Pastor, R. "NAFTA's green opportunity." *Issues in Science and Technology*, 1993 (Summer), 47–54.

Price, D. *Before the Bulldozer.* Washington, D.C.: Seven Locks Press, 1989.

Rabinovitch, J., and J. Leitman. "Urban planning in Curitiba." *Scientific American*, March 1996.

Sanchez, E., K. Cronick, and E. Wiesenfeld. "Psychological variables in participation: A case study." In Canter, D., M. Krampen, and D. Stea, eds. *New Directions in Environmental Participation (Ethnoscapes* series). Aldershot, U.K.: Gower, 1988.

Sanderson, S. E. "Mexico's environmental future." *Current History*, February 1993.

Schumacher, E. F. *Small Is Beautiful: Economics as if People Mattered.* New York, Harper & Row, 1973.

Schwartz, N. B. "Colonization, development, and deforestation in Peten, northern Guatemala." In Painter, M., and W. H. Durham, eds. *The Social Causes of Environmental Destruction in Latin America.* Ann Arbor: University of Michigan Press, 1995.

Snell, M. B. "A fine balance: Cultivating smaller families and healthier farms in Ecuador's highlands." *Sierra*, 2004 (January/February), 27–29.

Stanley, D. "Demystifying the tragedy of the commons: The resin tappers of Honduras." In Place, S. E., ed. *Tropical Rainforests: Latin American Nature and Society in Transition.* Wilmington, Del.: Scholarly Resources, Inc., 1993, pp. 185–193.

Stea, D. "Human and cultural resources in the New World tropics." *Proceedings, New Jersey Academy of Sciences.* New Brunswick, N.J.: Rutgers University, 1993.

_____. "Debunking the myths: Indigenous settlements in tropical forests." (Centerstage lecture, Allegheny College, 1994). *Proceedings of the Seventh Annual Peter van Dresser Workshop on Village Development.* Albuquerque: Public Service Co. of New Mexico, 1994.

Stea, D., and V. Coreno. "Accion comunitaria, participación pública, y planificacion ambiental en una colonia mexicana." In Connor, D. M., ed. *Participación Pública: Un Manual.* Victoria, B.C.: CDS Ltd., 1997.

Stea, D., S. Elguea, and C. Pérez Bustillo. "Environment, Development, and Indigenous Revolution in Chiapas." In Johnston, B. R., ed. *Life and Death Matters: Human Rights and the*

Environment at the End of the Millennium. Walnut Creek, Calif.: Altamira Press, 1997, pp. 213–237.

Stonich, S. C. "Producing food for export: Environmental quality and social justice implications of shrimp mariculture in Honduras." In Johnston, B. R., ed. *Who Pays the Price? The Sociocultural Context of Environmental Crisis*. Washington, D.C.: Island Press, 1994.

_____. "Development, rural impoverishment, and environmental destruction in Honduras." In Painter, M., and W. H. Durham, eds. *The Social Causes of Environmental Destruction in Latin America*. Ann Arbor: University of Michigan Press, 1995.

Swinton, S., G. Escobar, and T. Reardon. "Poverty and environment in Latin America." *World Development*, 2003, *31*(11), 1865–1872.

Tropical Forest Management Trust. *Promising Approaches to Natural Forest Management in Latin America*. Gainesville, Fla.: Tropical Forest Management Trust, 1991 (video film).

Wasserman, E. "Environment, health, and gender in Latin America: Trends and research issues." *Environmental Research Section* A, 1999, 80, 253–273.

Williams, M. "Land invasions rising in Brazil. *Austin American-Statesman*," November 15, 2003, pp. A21–A22.

World Bank. *Energy Efficiency and Conservation in the Developing World: The World Bank's Role*. Washington, D.C.: World Bank, 1993.

PART II

HISTORICAL SETTING

Chapter 5

COLONIAL LATIN AMERICA

PETER BAKEWELL

THE COLONIAL PERIOD IN Latin America lasted just over 300 years. That is an impossible amount of history to describe even broadly in a few pages. So this chapter does not try to give a summary of events in colonial times. Rather, its aim is to examine two broad themes: What, in a quite practical way, is meant by "colonialism" in Latin America in the 1500s, 1600s, and 1700s? And, what features and influences of colonial times have carried over into, and helped to form, the Latin America of today?

CONQUEST AND SETTLEMENT

We begin with some basic dates and geographical data. The colonial period of Latin America began when Columbus sailed across the Atlantic from Spain in 1492 and claimed the lands he touched on for Spain. They were, on that first voyage of 1492–1493, the islands of Cuba and, as the Spaniards came to call it, Hispaniola (now divided between the Dominican Republic and Haiti). It is illogical to say that Columbus "discovered" the Americas, because, obviously, the true discoverers were the people who first entered and settled them. And people from Asia had done those things many tens of thousands of years before Columbus arrived, becoming in the course of time what are now referred to as "native Americans." From the point of view of Spain and Europe in general, however, Columbus did find the Americas, and more important, his "discovery" led to the establishment of a permanent link between the two sides of the Atlantic—something that the Norse expeditions to North America from Greenland, around A.D. 1000, had failed to do.

As soon as Columbus reported the existence of Cuba and Hispaniola to the Spanish crown, Spain claimed the right to settle and govern those islands and other lands that might be found in the same direction. The pope of the day, Alexander VI, who was a Spaniard, confirmed the claim. His confirmation was sought because, as the chief representative of God on Earth, he was the highest authority in the world known to Christian rulers. In any case, no other European state, with the possible exception of Portugal, was strong enough to challenge Spain's claim to possess and govern the lands Columbus had found.

The Portuguese had themselves been exploring westward and southward in the Atlantic for many decades before 1492 and were understandably disturbed by Spain's claim to all land on the west side of the Atlantic. Conflict was averted, however, by an agreement (the Treaty of Tordesillas), drawn up in 1494, that divided the tasks of exploring and settling the world between the two countries. To the west of an imaginary north–south line in the Atlantic, Spain should explore and settle, and to the east of that line, Portugal should do so. Although it was not realized at the time, that agreement was to give to Portugal a large section of eastern South America since, as defined in the treaty, the line passed down through the mouth of the Amazon, leaving the coastline again at about 30 degrees south latitude. Hence, the eastern "bulge" of South America, once it was discovered in 1500, became Portuguese territory, forming the basis of modern Brazil.

The colonial history of Spanish America, having begun in 1492 with Columbus, ended in the years 1810–1825. This was the period in which the various Spanish colonies in the Americas, with two small exceptions, fought for and gained their independence. The exceptions were Cuba and Puerto Rico, which did not become free of Spain, for various reasons, until 1898. Brazil broke from Portugal in 1822. So, in both the Spanish and Portuguese cases, the colonial period was long—almost twice as long, in fact, as the time that has elapsed between independence and the present.

Colonial Spanish America was much larger than Portuguese America. Even though the Portuguese did gradually push westward beyond the Tordesillas line, still Spanish America covered a greater area, extending ultimately from the southern tip of South America to well within the present limits of the United States. In the 1700s, Spain had settlements as far north as San Francisco in California, southern Arizona, most of New Mexico, and much of Texas—as well as in a substantial part of Florida. And all territory, with a few exceptions—by far the most notable being Brazil—between that northern frontier and the far tip of South America was Spanish. Spain also held the larger Caribbean islands and some of the smaller ones. The empire in the Americas—Las Indias (the Indies), as the Spanish called their possessions—was truly vast: some 9,000 miles (almost 14,500 kilometers) from north to south.

COLONIAL GOVERNMENTS AND ECONOMIES

What is meant by saying that these great areas explored and settled by Spain and Portugal were colonies? First, certainly, is the fact that the two home countries governed them. One of the remarkable features of Latin American colonial history is that governments were set up and actually worked. The difficulties of accomplishing this task were forbidding. For one thing, distances were enormous, not only within the Americas, but also between the Americas and Europe. The whole colonial period was, of course, a time of sailing ships, which were slow and unreliable. (Ships improved technically with time, but not until the 1700s were they good enough to allow regular sailings around Cape Horn to the colonies on the west coast of South America. Before then, communication between Spain and the west coast was by Atlantic shipping to the Isthmus of Panama, barge and mule across the isthmus, and Pacific ships to the various west coast ports.) Travel in the colonies themselves was difficult in most cases because of mountains, deserts, forests, and extremes of temperature. One basic necessity of effective government—communication—was therefore difficult to achieve from the start. Nevertheless, governments were installed, and their authority was extended into remarkably remote areas. A brief explanation of how this task was accomplished is necessary.

The Spanish had the greater problems because of the size and the distance from Spain of their colonies. (Brazil was quite easily reached by sea from Portugal.) The Spanish home government saw, once the size of the Americas began to be appreciated, that it would have to delegate a great deal of responsibility to administrators in the colonies, because it would be simply impossible to make all the necessary decisions in Spain. So two very powerful positions were created—those of viceroys who would live in Mexico City and Lima. The holders of these offices were usually Spanish noblemen of much experience, who were to act in their areas in place of the king (which is precisely the meaning of the word "viceroy"). They had authority to make all but the largest of decisions, and each was ultimately responsible for everything that happened in the area under his command. The first viceroy appointed to Mexico City arrived there in 1535. As the area of Spanish exploration expanded, this viceroy came to have control of the whole of Mexico, the Spanish islands of the Caribbean, and all of Central America except Panama. This area of authority, or jurisdiction, was known as the viceroyalty of New Spain. The first viceroy in South America reached Lima in 1544. The territory of this official eventually came to include everything from Panama in the north to Tierra del Fuego in the south, excluding, of course, Portuguese America. The jurisdiction centered on Lima was known as the viceroyalty of Peru. In the 1700s, for closer control, two further viceroyalties were created in South America: New Granada (corresponding roughly to modern Colombia) in 1739, and River Plate (roughly speaking, modern Argentina) in 1776.

It was obviously impossible for individuals to run these vast viceroyalties unassisted. So the Spanish government at home quickly created, in the 1500s, a series of councils to assist the viceroys and to carry their authority far from the two viceregal capitals of that time. These councils were called *audiencias*. Besides having the task of advising the viceroys and in many matters making executive decisions themselves, these councils also functioned as regional courts of appeal. By 1570, there were ten *audiencias,* each with authority over a large sub-area. At a lower administrative level than the *audiencias* were local governors, some of them in charge of large frontier regions and others, of lesser rank, administering towns and villages.

There was much wrong with this system. By modern administrative standards, it was certainly clumsy and corrupt. Many officials, for example, paid more attention to preventing other officials from intruding on their powers than they did to implementing the king's law. And nearly all officials, in the general manner of the times in Europe, saw their positions as means of enriching themselves far beyond the rewards of their salaries, which were often low. Nonetheless, in view of the difficulties, it is a near miracle that the system worked at all. Also very surprising was the speed with which the system was constructed. Generally speaking, within a few years of the conquest of a given region, there were royal administrators in place to enforce laws, collect taxes, and send reports home. Although Spanish America was a vast and rough place, the king's men made their presence felt throughout most of it, and they commanded respect.

The Portuguese set up a rather similar system in Brazil, centered on Bahia (until the mid-1700s, when Rio de Janeiro became the capital). They never, however, succeeded in achieving quite such a powerful grip on their colony as Spain did. There were various reasons for this difference. Two important ones were that Portugal, being a smaller and poorer country than Spain, simply did not have the resources of cash and men to create such a powerful administrative machine as Spain built in the Americas and that for many decades after locating Brazil, Portugal was far more attentive to its spice-yielding colonies in the Far East than it was to the apparently rather poorly endowed coast of Brazil.

The first outstanding feature of colonization, therefore, was government. The second was the extraction of wealth from the Americas—the Spanish themselves freely admitted that they had gone to and conquered the Americas for the sake of gold and God. One of the main tasks of the colonial governments was certainly to ensure that Spain and Portugal received as large an income as possible from the colonies. The main type of wealth that Spain received from its colonies was silver. We tend to think of Spanish gold, sunk perhaps in galleons off the coast of Florida, and the conquerors did seek, and find, large amounts of gold. But the more plentiful precious metal proved, in the long run, to be silver. One of the main reasons for Spain's very rapid exploration and settlement of the Americas (and hence, for the quick expansion of government) was that the conquerors ranged far and wide in search of mines. In a surprisingly large number of places, they found them, especially in the highlands of Mexico and what is now Bolivia. These mines were the greatest sources of silver in the world throughout the Latin American colonial period, and they made Spain the envy of its neighbors in Europe. Other profitable goods that Spain took from the Americas were red and blue dyes, chocolate beans, hides, sugar, and some spices.

The Portuguese also did well from their colony in Brazil. Before 1560 or so, the main export was a wood that yielded a red dye. From then until about 1700, a far more profitable export predominated: sugar, which the colonists produced on large plantations. For fifty years thereafter, gold and diamonds were the most spectacular products of the Brazilian economy, stimulating substantial population of the interior for the first time and an increase in immigration from Portugal. Finally, in the last half-century or so of colonial times, there was a recovery of the sugar trade and an increase in the cultivation of other crops, such as chocolate and rice.

The term "exploitation" is often applied to the extraction of wealth by Spain and Portugal from their American colonies. It is a term of criticism, signifying an unjust and greedy grasping by the colonizing powers of the natural riches of Latin America—a process that had the result, among others, of leaving the states of Latin America considerably poorer than they otherwise would have been after independence. But an unqualified charge of exploitation against the Spanish and Portuguese is too crude to be convincing. In some cases, the valuable export product was something that the colonizers had introduced into the Americas: sugar, for instance, in the case of Brazil, or hides from cattle introduced into Mexico by the Spanish. And even where the exported wealth was something already existing in the Americas, such as silver, that wealth was not merely lying on the ground waiting to be picked up and sent back to Europe. In all cases, and especially in that of mining, successful extraction of the product was the result of the application of new techniques, investment of capital, and use of freighting methods not known in the Americas before the Spanish and Portuguese arrived. The wealth of the Americas was great, but it did not come for nothing, even to the greatest of the conquerors or the most fortunate of settlers.

EXPLOITATION OF LABOR

That said, it cannot be denied that the term "exploitation" is a just description of the use Spaniards and Portuguese made of the native Americans for labor. Within a very few years of the conquest, the idea became firmly rooted among settlers, and even among some theologians and government officials, that the native Americans were by nature inferior to Europeans. It seemed, therefore, quite natural to both sets of colonists and both governments that the natives, once conquered, should work for their conquerors. Some enlightened Spaniards and Portuguese opposed this reasoning, but their views were far outweighed by Iberian public opinion. So the American native peoples were forced in one way or another to work for the colonists. Sometimes they were enslaved. This was particularly common in both Spanish and Portuguese America between the conquest and the mid-1500s. Also in the 1500s, many natives were distributed among Spanish settlers in a system called *encomienda* ("entrustment"). According to this system, the people who had been "entrusted" were to work for the settler, or to supply a tribute in goods or cash, in return for being taught Christianity and the Spanish way of life in general. Settlers were also charged with protecting the people entrusted to them from any enemies who might appear. On paper, this *encomienda* arrangement had strengths. The natives were not legally slaves of the settler in question, but free people. In return for services rendered, they were at least to receive physical security and what was for the Spanish, at least, the highest spiritual gift imaginable: Christianity. In fact, however, few Spaniards fulfilled their part of the bargain, and the *encomienda* often became an oppressive means of making the native people work for the settlers.

Because of its damaging effects and because it tended to direct disproportionate amounts of native tribute and labor toward the conquerors and early settlers at the expense of later Spanish immigrants, the *encomienda* soon ceased to be the home government's preferred arrangement for the supply of native labor to the colonists. Indeed, from the 1540s on, the home government actively opposed the *encomienda* and tried to take native people away from those settlers to whom they had been entrusted—much to the settlers' anger. Another system for obtaining native labor then became needed, and draft labor was introduced in many places from the 1550s on. Rather elaborate arrangements were made according to which a small proportion of the adult men from each Indian town would be assigned each year for a period of time—between a week and a month, generally—to a Spanish employer. The assignments were made by a Spanish official, and, at least in principle, workers were directed to tasks that were of public utility: agriculture, road and bridge building, and mining (because it was so central an economic activity).

When the system began, draft labor was probably less of a burden on the natives than *encomienda* had been. It also probably made more effective use of native labor than *encomienda* had, because the draft spread the available workers more evenly among Spanish employers. During the second half of the 1500s, however, the number of settlers wanting workers increased while the native population decreased, with the result that draft work also soon became a very great burden for the native people. Their solution to this problem was to offer themselves for hire to individual Spanish settlers, evading the draft as best they could. Since many employers were in great need of workers, the native volunteers could obtain much higher wages than they were paid under the draft system. Wage labor by volunteer workers naturally appeared first in situations in which the settlers were both very short of labor and able to pay high wages. Silver mining was one of these. By 1600, for example, three-quarters of all mining workers in Mexico were native people who had been drawn to that sort of labor by the high pay. After 1600, wage labor became increasingly common in many occupations in Spanish America. Broadly speaking, it gave the workers more freedom and better conditions than the previous labor arrangements had done. So it is generally true that the years of harshest exploitation of native workers by the Spanish were the 1500s.

Where, for one reason or another, there were not enough native people to do the Europeans' work, black slaves were imported from Africa. Exactly how many slaves were brought across the Atlantic to Latin America in colonial times is not known, but the number was certainly in excess of 3 million, with the main importing regions being Brazil and the Spanish Caribbean. Demand for black slaves was high in both of these regions because both produced sugar on plantations—a strenuous sort of labor that blacks proved more able to tolerate than native Americans. In the Spanish Caribbean, there was, in any case, little choice in the matter. Nearly all the native populations of the large islands were destroyed in the sixteenth century by maltreatment, enslavement, and above all, disease. In Brazil, the natives survived in larger numbers, but they proved too primitive to be easily adapted to plantation labor. The importation of blacks into Brazil was, furthermore, simplified and cheapened by the proximity of Brazil to the West African coast, which was the source of most slaves in colonial times, and by the fact that Portugal had several small colonies and bases on that coast in which slaves were traded.

The need for the labor of black slaves was greatly increased after the Spanish and Portuguese conquests in the Americas by the drastic decline in the native populations. There were several reasons for this decline. The battles of the conquest killed some natives. More serious, however, were the aftereffects of conquest: the seizure of good agricultural land by the Europeans; the disruption of families resulting from the imposition of labor burdens on the natives; and the fall of the birthrate of the native peoples as a result of poorer nutrition, dislocation of society, and above all, discouragement at finding themselves, their beliefs, and their gods so easily overcome.

Even more damaging to the native populations, however, were the diseases that the Europeans, quite unintentionally, brought with them. Many diseases common in Europe, Africa, and Asia were unknown in the Americas because of the geographical separation of the continents. Consequently, the American native peoples suffered very severely from diseases that today seem minor: the common cold and measles, for example. Other diseases that are still considered dangerous were also transmitted to the Americas by the conquest: plague and most damaging of all, smallpox. These sicknesses cut great swaths through the natives in conquered areas in the 1500s. In most regions settled by the Spanish, native populations had fallen, by the end of the 1500s, to one-tenth or less of what they had been just before the conquest. In Brazil, the drop may have been smaller. Because many native people there fled into the inland forests, it is not clear how many fled and how many died.

This terrible destruction of the native populations is one of the striking features of the social history of colonial Latin America, and its effects were equally striking. It made necessary a far larger importation of black slaves than would otherwise have taken place. It made the fate of the surviving Indians considerably harder since they were forced to do the work of those who had died (although some survivors at least received higher wages for their work if they chose to become wage laborers), and it reduced the difference in numbers between the native population and the white population, thus accelerating the rate of racial mixing between whites and natives. As a result, the present-day populations of Latin America are notably whiter and more European in culture than they would have been if the natives had survived in their original numbers.

ROMAN CATHOLIC EVANGELISM

In view of the work burden placed on the native Americans by the conquerors and the many very clear cases of harsh treatment, it might seem contradictory to say that Roman Catholic evangelism was one of the two main motives for the conquest and settlement of Latin America. But it was indeed so, especially for the Spanish. Spain was the most powerful Christian country in the world when Columbus crossed the Atlantic, and it continued to be strong for a century thereafter. The Spaniards were sure, for a variety of reasons, that it was not a matter of chance that their expedition, led by Columbus, had established the link between Europe and the Americas. They felt that Spain, as the leading Christian nation of the time, had been singled out by God to conquer and settle the Americas and to carry the Christian faith (for them, of course, the only true faith) to the native peoples of that region. Some Spaniards held an even more extreme belief. These were the believers in certain biblical prophecies that stated that once the whole world had been converted to Christianity, Christ would return and rule in justice and peace for a thousand years (the millennium). Clearly, the Americas made up a very large piece of the world, and until Christians knew of it and converted its peoples, the millennium could not begin. God, therefore, in apparently entrusting the Christianization of the Americas to Spaniards, had given Spain a central part to play in the history of the world. Spain's work in spreading the true faith was to be a large and direct contribution to the second coming of Christ. Only a small minority of Spaniards, mainly some rather mystically inclined Franciscan friars, truly believed in this prophecy, but the fact that even a few priests could see Spain's mission in the Americas as having such cosmic importance is some indication of the religious zeal of the Spanish as a whole.

That zeal resulted in great efforts to convert American native peoples during the first fifty years or so after the conquest in various regions of the Americas. Many remarkably tough and intelligent missionaries—drawn mainly from the Franciscan, Dominican, and Augustinian orders—set to work in Spain's expanding colonies. Their efforts were especially vigorous in Mexico, as manifested by the many church buildings that have survived from the 1500s. Millions of native people were baptized. Most of them did not understand Christianity very well and ended up with a faith consisting of elements of their pre-conquest religion mixed with elements of Christianity. The friars, however, generally took the view that it was better to convert many people partially than a few thoroughly.

After the mid-1500s, Spain's missionary zeal wore off considerably for many reasons. One was an understandable fatigue among the missionaries after many years of effort and after the newness of the challenge had gone. Another reason was that by then, many native people in the central areas of Spanish settlement had been converted up to a point and could be entrusted to the more humdrum care of parish priests. There were always missionaries active in some parts of the colonies, however—mainly in remote frontier areas where there were new peoples to convert. Among the best-known and longest-lasting of these later missionary enterprises were those of the Franciscans in New Mexico and the Jesuits in Paraguay.

The Portuguese were, on the whole, rather less concerned than the Spanish with making natives into Christians. From the start, the Portuguese had less religious zeal than the Spaniards, and their possession of colonies in Africa and Asia, as well as in the Americas, meant that the effort they made was spread rather thin. Precisely because of this lack of effort by the state, however, the Jesuits found in Brazil, from about 1550 onward, an open field for mission activity. The Jesuits, indeed, dominated the religious history of colonial Brazil as no single order managed to do in Spanish America. The spread of Jesuit missionary villages into the interior became, in fact, one of the means by which Portuguese America advanced westward beyond the Tordesillas line in the 1600s and 1700s.

CONCLUSION

Those, then, are some of the main features of colonization by Spain and Portugal in the Americas: rapid exploration and settlement (particularly by the Spanish), rapid installation of government (again more noticeable in the case of the Spanish than the Portuguese), economic employment of the settled lands for the profit of individual colonists as well as the home governments, exploitation of native labor, importation of black slaves, and the spreading of Christianity. Some of the processes, of course, took place only in the 1500s, though their influence persisted long after that time. Others—the utilization of land and other resources and the exploitation of native and black workers—continued through colonial times. They continued, though, in changing forms, as illustrated, for example, by the progression from slavery and *encomienda* to draft labor and finally to wage labor.

Similarly, there were changes, as time passed, in the strength of colonial governments. The initial, rapid formation of an administrative apparatus in Spanish America in the 1500s was a strenuous business, and there was a natural tendency toward a relaxation in the system once it had been built. This tendency was increased by the growth of Spain's problems in Europe in the late 1500s, which distracted the home government's attention from the colonies. As a result of these and other influences, colonial governments were less effective and disciplined in the 1600s than in the previous century. In the 1700s, Spain attempted, with some success, to remedy this weakness. The creation of the two new viceroyalties already mentioned was part of this effort (New Granada in 1739 and River Plate in 1776). Many other administrative reforms were introduced. The results were that the force of Spanish government was felt by the colonists in areas where it had never been strongly present before and that Spain's income from taxes on the colonies increased several times over. These were gains that Spain enjoyed only briefly, however, for the increasing pressure of government and taxation that the colonies felt in the late 1700s was resented by many colonists. Such pressures helped turn their thoughts toward greater self-determination and, in the end, toward outright independence from Spain.

Suggested Readings

Bakewell, Peter. *A History of Latin America.* 2nd ed. Oxford: Blackwell, 2003.

Bethell, Leslie. *The Cambridge History of Latin America.* Vols. 1 and 2. Cambridge: Cambridge University Press, 1984.

Chevalier, François. *Land and Society in Colonial Mexico.* Berkeley: University of California Press, 1963.

Gibson, Charles. *The Aztecs Under Spanish Rule: A History of the Indians of the Valley of Mexico.* Stanford: Stanford University Press, 1964.

Haring, Clarence H. *The Spanish Empire in America.* New York: Oxford University Press, 1947.

Hemming, John. *The Conquest of the Incas.* New York: Harcourt, Brace, Jovanovich, 1970.

Lockhart, James, and Enrique Otte, eds. *Letters and People of the Spanish Indies: The Sixteenth Century.* Cambridge: Cambridge University Press, 1976.

Lockhart, James, and Stuart B. Schwartz. *Early Latin America. A History of Colonial Spanish America and Brazil.* Cambridge: Cambridge University Press, 1983.

Lynch, John. *Spain Under the Hapsburgs.* 2 vols. Oxford: Oxford University Press, 1964–1969.

_____. *The Spanish-American Revolutions, 1808–1826.* New York: Norton, 1973.

Maclachlan, Colin M., and Jaime E. Rodríguez. *The Forging of the Cosmic Race: A Reinterpretation of Colonial Mexico.* Berkeley: University of California Press, 1980.

Parry, John H. *The Spanish Seaborne Empire.* New York: Knopf, 1966.

Phelan, John L. *The Kingdom of Quito in the Seventeenth Century: Bureaucratic Politics in the Spanish Empire.* Madison: University of Wisconsin Press, 1967.

Schwartz, Stuart B. *Sovereignty and Society in Colonial Brazil: The High Court of Bahia and Its Judges, 1609–1745.* Berkeley: University of California Press, 1973.

_____. *Sugar Plantations in the Formation of Brazilian Society. Bahia, 1550–1835.* Cambridge: Cambridge University Press, 1985.

Chapter 6

LATIN AMERICA SINCE INDEPENDENCE: AN OVERVIEW

MICHAEL CONNIFF

IN THE LAST TWO centuries, the region we know as Latin America has experienced immense changes, generally following the patterns of the rest of the Western world. These changes include the shift from colonial status to independence; from monarchy to democracy; from agricultural, pastoral, and mining economies to industrial ones; from rural to urban residency; from traditional cultures to multi-faceted ones; and from simple to complex societies. Historians usually emphasize continuities over long periods, but in the case of modern Latin America, the changes clearly overwhelmed lingering inheritances from the past.

This change has been all the more extraordinary because of the enormous diversity of peoples, geographies, resources, and ruling structures the region inherited from colonial times. The founders of new countries in this era faced greater difficulties in building institutions, citizenries, and national identities than did their counterparts in North America and Europe. Travel was difficult and costly. Large numbers, often majorities, of their people did not speak the national language nor identify with their leaders. Huge segments of some economies relied on massive imports of labor from abroad, mostly African slaves but also coerced workers from other parts of the world. Ethnically, religiously, culturally, the countries that emerged from independence were segmented, even disjointed.

Today, Latin America consists of nearly a half-billion persons organized into over thirty countries, ranging from the powerhouse of Brazil to tiny island-nations in the Caribbean. A few colonies persist—the Dutch and French territories—but they are mere reminders of a distant past. Most Latin American countries are democracies, largely presidential but with a few parliamentary systems, especially the former British dependencies. A rough tally shows that some 200 million persons participated in elections since the year 2000, a turnout rate that surpasses those of the United States and of many Western European countries. The economies of the larger countries, moreover, have become industrialized and sophisticated, and their workforces have organized into powerful unions and federations. Latin American women, who sometimes played exceptional leadership roles in the nineteenth century, have become respected actors in the political, economic, cultural, and social realms in the twenty-first.

These trends—generally, the "Westernization" of Latin America—seem about to give way to global forces that would sweep these people into a world-wide system of economic transactions, migration flows, power blocs or centers, climatic and meteorological vectors, and cultural transformations. Latin Americans themselves, however, show signs of rejecting such globalization, which would threaten their identities and perhaps their control over their own destinies.

POLITICAL GENERATIONS

For reasons not fully understood, leadership patterns in Latin America seemed to run in generations during the past two hundred years. Similar domestic situations, external pressures, foreign models, geographical determinants, broad economic cycles, and other factors probably brought about this patterned evolution.

The first identifiable generation of leaders in modern Latin America were the precursors of independence, the men and women who struggled against European rule in the Americas and the status deprivation brought on by colonialism. Most were socially well-to-do, though born in the New World and hence Creoles, and most received a good education. Most also had personal as well as political grievances against the colonial authorities and distant monarchies that ruled their lives. These leaders included Antonio Nariño, the Colombian firebrand; Tiradentes, the Brazilian revolutionary; Francisco Miranda, the Venezuelan adventurer; and Toussaint L'Ouverture, the African prince who began the overthrow of the French slave regime of St. Domingue, today Haiti. The precursors sacrificed their material well-being and eventually their lives, becoming martyrs to independence.

The next generation was the heroes of independence, those who succeeded in overthrowing European rule in the Americas during the 1810s and 1820s. Most were born in the 1780s and grew up with Enlightenment ideals. They tended to come from propertied families whose interests diverged from those of the colonial regime. The foremost hero of independence was Simón Bolívar, known as the Liberator of South America, followed closely by José de San Martín, who helped consolidate Argentina's independence and drove the Spanish from Chile and portions of Peru. Bernardo O'Higgins of Chile also figures in this group.

Several pseudo-heroes emerged in the era of independence, leaders who took advantage of the struggles of others and declared separation from Europe, but without the sacrifices and courage of the true heroes. This group includes General Agustín Iturbide of Mexico, Emperor Pedro I of Brazil, and President Francisco de Paula Santander of Colombia.

The conclusion of the wars of independence coincided with the onset of depression in Europe, bringing on a period of falling trade, prices, and incomes around the world. Latin Americans defaulted on loans and sought refuge in protectionism for domestic producers. The next leadership generation, the *caudillos*, rose to power in this setting. These leaders dominated the stage until the mid-nineteenth century and guided their young nations through perilous times. Foremost among the *caudillos* were José Antonio de Santa Anna of Mexico, Juan Manuel de Rosas of Argentina, Diego Portales of Chile, and José Antonio Páez of Venezuela. *Caudillos* are often referred to as men on horseback, and indeed most mounted while commanding troops. Yet their strength and authority also came from personal qualities such as fairness, intelligence, rectitude, and respect for hierarchy. They gathered followers and troops loyal to themselves and believed deeply in their legitimacy, regardless of the constitution. They cared for order and command, not for rule of law. *Caudillos* gave the outside world a negative impression of the region, yet they held their countries together, avoided warfare, reduced crime, and preserved a subsistence level of economic activity.

In the mid-nineteenth century, more principled leaders rose to power across the region, usually inspired by the promise of liberalism as practiced in Europe. These autocratic modernizers paid attention to constitutions and legislatures, enacted laws providing more freedom and equality for citizens, and tried to diminish the privileges of traditional institutions like the military, the Church, and landowners. Most of the reforms they introduced were aimed at unleashing the economic potential of land and labor, and at attracting foreign investment and technology. The best examples of the autocratic modernizer are Emperor Pedro II of Brazil, Benito Juárez of Mexico, and Bartolomé Mitre of Argentina. A second generation arose somewhat later, exemplified by Justo Rufino Barrios of Guatemala, Julio Roca of Argentina, Porfirio Díaz of Mexico, and Antonio Guzmán Blanco of Venezuela. The stability and incentives provided by these two generations led to construction of railroads and port facilities, urban modernization, distribution of public lands, growing efficiency in mining, ranching, agriculture, and industry, and booming export trade. For this reason, the last half of the nineteenth century is often called the era of the export economies. Their nations' economies boomed but their peoples suffered. Constitutional provisions for elections and representation languished. And the well-being of the workers and peasants, male and female, diminished due to punishing labor regimes and lack of protections.

After the turn of the twentieth century, fresh breezes blew over South America and awakened a very different sort of leader, the early populist. This generation was also principled but shifted goals from economic to social and political progress. The three outstanding examples of early populists were José Battle y Ordóñez in Uruguay, Hipólito Yrigoyen in Argentina, and Arturo Alessandri in Chile. These leaders championed workers' rights, public benefit over private privilege, restrictions on foreign capital, and open, clean elections. They campaigned among the common people and promised to defend their interests. And most of the early populists were reasonably honest and success-ful in fulfilling their campaign pledges. The appearance of this generation marked the beginning of democracy in the region.

About the same time, another generation arose, the dictators of the Caribbean Basin. What they lacked in principles they made up for in greed and self-indulgence. Guaranteed in power by corrupt military forces, the dic-tators went about the usual business of governing (building public works and utilities, hosting foreign corporations, expanding native enterprises, collecting taxes) but never consulted the common people nor concerned themselves with the general welfare. They also enriched themselves obscenely at the public's ex-pense. Among the best examples of this generation were Manuel Estrada Cabr-era of Guatemala and Mario García Menocal and Gerardo Machado of Cuba. Since their economies depended heavily on U.S. markets and Wall Street banks, the dictators maintained close relations with Washington, D.C. When necessary, they were capable of horrific violence and repression to protect the wealth and positions they and their families enjoyed.

Not all leaders sought power at the ballot box to institute needed reforms: almost simultaneously a generation of revolutionaries arose and led rebel armies against dictators and entrenched interests in government. Mexico's Rev-olution of 1910–1920 is the best known of these uprisings, led by famous or infamous *guerrilleros* like Emiliano Zapata and Pancho Villa, but others oc-curred in this period. Luís Carlos Prestes of Brazil pulled together several thou-sand rebel officers and recruits who had first protested in 1922 and led them on a great march through the backlands of his country. In Nicaragua, Augusto Sandino mounted a guerrilla action that stymied both his own country's forces and U.S. Marines sent to capture him. Few of these revolutionaries lived to take power and carry out their programs, but their courage and tactics inspired a later generation of revolutionaries who would be more successful.

A classic generation of dictators of the Caribbean Basin arose during and af-ter the Great Depression of the 1930s. As vain, corrupt, power-hungry, and ve-nal as its predecessor, this generation differed in its relation to and dependence on the United States. Because of a policy change during President Franklin Roosevelt's administration, the United States eschewed military intervention into Latin American countries. In the cases of Cuba, Nicaragua, the Domini-can Republic, and several other countries, however, instability led the United States to continue encouraging the formation of effective national guards, which could maintain order and protect U.S. interests. In each of these cases, the commander of the national guard gravitated to the presidency of his coun-try and assumed dictatorial powers, with the blessing of the United States. The best known of these classic dictators of the Caribbean Basin were Anastasio So-moza of Nicaragua, Fulgencio Batista of Cuba, and Rafael Trujillo of the Do-minican Republic. They ended up ruling for decades or passed along power to their children and cronies.

After the end of World War II, a new and much larger generation of pop-ulists appeared in Latin America, no longer limited to the Southern Cone. The return of peace and victory of the Western democracies strengthened the demands, internal as well as foreign, for elected governments in the region. The United States and the Soviet Union, in particular, pressured dictators to step aside in favor of duly-elected representatives. The mid-twentieth century classic populists, as they are called, revolutionized political campaigns, elections, media, and behavior. The best examples are Juan and Evita Perón of Argentina, Getúlio Vargas of Brazil (ruling from 1930, by election only 1950–1954), José María Velasco Ibarra of Ecuador, and Rómulo Betancourt of Venezuela. The classic populists posed as men of the people, protectors of the poor, defenders of the nation, and enemies of traditional corrupt politicians. Beyond that, they appealed to popular culture and used the print and electronic media expertly. They promised better lives for the worker and farmer, a helping hand and the vote to women, prosperity for business owners, in fact, something for practically everyone. They also traveled widely by car, bus, train, airplane, and even horseback, to visit every possible constituent. They were indefatigable campaigners, tireless speakers. They strove to create the impression of a personal connection to each and every voter.

The classic populists came from varied backgrounds and defy easy classification as to ideology. Their generation was defined more by how they got power—in competitive elections—than what they did in office. Some flirted with major structural changes in society, others drifted with little program. Some are remembered for major accomplishments, others were removed for incompetence or worse. One change they introduced across the board, however: the demand that direct, honest elections with the largest possible participation be the sole method of gaining high office. From World War II until the early twenty-first century, voter participation rose from under 20 million to over 200 million. Along the way populists and others extended the franchise to women, illiterates, immigrants, sixteen-year-olds, and soldiers in most countries. The advent of mass politics dates to the rise of the populists in mid-century.

A new generation of revolutionaries appeared in mid-twentieth century as well, inspiring many other rebel chieftains, both urban and rural. These leaders, exemplified by Fidel Castro and Ernesto "Ché" Guevara in Cuba and Daniel Ortega in Nicaragua, practiced an ancient form of warfare in contemporary settings—among the urban poor or in peasant regions. Just as importantly, they established revolutionary regimes in the context of the Cold War between the United States and the Soviet Union, thereby conceivably posing a security threat to the former. Latin America suddenly seemed a more dangerous, complex region in world affairs after the success of Castro.

The new revolutionaries demonstrated that small bands of *guerrilleros* with the right strategy could defeat vastly larger armed forces. They also showed that propaganda and psychological tactics play important parts in revolutionary struggle. Finally, they proved that a relatively small country could defy the will of the United States and survive. Once in power, the revolutionaries carried out major structural changes of a socialist nature, leading to huge exoduses of propertied and professional families. The revolutionaries nationalized most major enterprises and hence cut themselves off from trade and investment from the capitalist world and most international financial institutions. Throughout the region young leaders aspired to repeat the achievements of Fidel Castro in Cuba, who remained one of the last communist leaders in the world.

In the mid-1960s, a spate of right-wing coups brought to power a generation seldom before in the limelight, the military high command. At one point, a majority of the South American population lived under these military regimes. Unlike the earlier dictators, some of whom were military but took power as individuals, this generation of officers assumed control as institutional leaders who saw it as their duty to save their countries and clean up their politics and economies. Their regimes, sometimes characterized as the national security states, acted on the premise that the leaders who preceded them—populists, perhaps, or incompetents—could not be trusted with power. They would open their nations to leftist agitation or at least to collapse and disorder. In either case, the military leaders saw it as their institutional mission to prevent disintegration of public order and likely communist revolution. These leaders, best exemplified by Jorge Videla in Argentina, Humberto Castelo Branco in Brazil, and Augusto Pinochet in Chile, believed that the internal cohesion and competence of the military corps would save their nations, generate economic development, strengthen international ties, and bring about citizen solidarity. Of course they could also fight internal or external battles if necessary.

As the 1970s and 1980s wore on, many of the aims and promises of the military regimes failed to materialize; they grew unpopular and sometimes teetered on the brink of disaster. In order to extricate themselves from government, the military leaders found ways, sometimes gradual and other times abrupt, to return power to civilians. This process, at first called *apertura*, later *transition* and *democratization*, took place at various times in the 1980s. The last to exit power was Pinochet, who stepped down in 1990, ironically after losing a national plebiscite.

The generation of leaders that assumed control after the departure of the military proved heterogeneous. Veteran politicians, such as Fernando Belaúnde Terry in Peru, Raúl Alfonsín in Argentina, and José Sarney in Brazil generally failed to bring consensus and mission to their administrations. Insoluble economic and social problems plagued them, as well as generalized recessionary conditions. None was able to build a viable governing party.

A last identifiable generation in contemporary Latin America was made up of the neo-populists, dating from the 1990s. Like their predecessors, they strove to create loyalty and electoral participation among followers by appealing to nationalism and by promising improvements for the common people. They were unusually adept at using the latest media, public relations, and polling tools available. The biggest difference between this generation and the earlier populists was their abandonment of economic nationalism and pro-labor policies. Instead, they embraced neoliberal reforms, like lower tariffs, privatization, and a pro-business stance. The most prominent of the neo-populists have been Fernando Collor de Melo in Brazil, Alberto Fujimori in Peru, and

Carlos Menem in Argentina. The first stumbled badly in office and was impeached; the latter two had successful first terms and were reelected, but subsequently fell into disgrace.

The preceding account of the many generations of leaders in Latin America does not include all countries, of course—instead, it suggests broad political trends throughout the region. Mexico, in particular, has not followed this progression since the Revolution of 1910–1920, because of the enormous impact of that event on virtually all aspects of Mexican life. For one thing, the generals, especially Álvaro Obregón, Plutarco Elías Calles, and Lázaro Cárdenas, dominated politics for nearly twenty years and left in place an official party, the Partido Revolucionario Institutional (PRI), that governed the country for the next seventy years. Beginning with Miguel Alemán, elected in 1946, a long string of party leaders trained in the law occupied the presidency.

In 1982, however, partly in response to the economic crisis generated by a world recession, the PRI chose an economist, Miguel de la Madrid, as president. The next two presidents were also economists, which reflected the high priority the PRI placed on growth in GNP and jobs. In 1994, the economist presidents took a huge gamble by joining the United States and Canada in a North American Free Trade Agreement, or NAFTA. Mexico's economy stabilized in the 1990s, due largely to the economic prosperity of its northern trade partner. Still, the results of NAFTA were not positive enough to keep most Mexicans loyal to the party. In 2000, they rebelled and elected an opposition president, Vicente Fox, in a veritable political earthquake. A former businessman and state governor, Fox continued to emphasize the economy and tried to establish friendlier relations with the United States, in order to regularize the status of millions of Mexicans illegally living and working in the north. By 2004 it was not clear whether the PRI would return to power in the 2006 elections.

Economic Cycles

Similar to the generational succession in politics, the economic history of Latin America followed a series of global business cycles, overlaid by waves of immigration and imported technology and economic theory. Major expansions occurred in the periods 1816–1828, 1840–1869, 1880–1891, 1898–1914, 1920–1929, 1946–1972, and 1990–2000. By the same token, major recessions or depressions occurred in the 1830s, 1870s, 1890s, 1930s, 1980s, and the early years of the twenty-first century. Inevitably these expansions and retreats affected the quality of life and the nature of sociopolitical interactions.

The earliest economic boom in Latin America coincided with the last round of fighting for independence, and it was not experienced uniformly throughout the hemisphere. Countries that depended on exports of silver, especially Mexico and Bolivia, experienced major disruptions and spent the early years of nationhood struggling to subsist. Those where fighting was less intense and where production could revive found 1820s' market conditions for raw materials to be extremely favorable. This was especially true for Brazil's exports of sugar, cotton, coffee, and hides and skins. The boom was assisted by a general round of loans from British banks and by exuberant European and U.S. trading missions to the region. This cycle was ended by a general North Atlantic depression in the 1830s.

By the 1840s, Mexican silver production began to grow, and Brazil's new crops, coffee and cacao, found thirsty markets in Europe and the United States. Venezuela, Colombia, and Costa Rica expanded their coffee production, and Venezuela and Ecuador increased exports of cacao. Argentina began diversifying its exports to include wool produced by immigrant shepherds. Cuba, although still a Spanish colony, became the first Latin American country to employ the workhorses of the Industrial Revolution: railroads, steam engines, and iron milling equipment. Sadly, this decade also saw historic numbers of African slaves imported to Cuba and Brazil. This iniquitous trade would not end altogether until the 1860s.

The rise of the autocratic modernizers in the 1850s reinforced this expansion by modernizing corporate law, inviting foreign investors, welcoming immigrants, and subsidizing transportation infrastructure. Chilean exports surged with the advent of a new market in California and the revival of copper prices after mid-century. To a considerable degree, this economic growth was fueled by the second wave of industrialization in Europe and the occupation of the U.S. Midwest by millions of immigrants. Staples like sugar, coffee, cocoa, rum, cereals, and dried beef continued to enjoy high prices for the rest of the century. Huge amounts of guano from Peru and nitrates from Chile fertilized the farms of Europe and the U.S. East Coast. Meanwhile, industries in the north consumed growing inputs of hardwood, non-precious metal ores, cotton, hides, and nitrates.

Downturns in the Atlantic economies stifled demand for Latin American products in the 1870s and again in the 1890s, but the overall trend line sloped sharply upward. Argentina and Uruguay experienced a veritable revolution on the pampas, with the advent of meatpacking plants, grain exports, and wool production. Steam threshers and harvesters multiplied the land under cultivation. To the north, no matter how fast Brazilians expanded coffee plantings, they could not satisfy demand until the 1890s. European companies built railroads across South America, while U.S. firms built across Mexico. Port facilities were improved to accommodate a new generation of iron-hulled transatlantic steamers. Millions of Europeans flocked to South America, especially Argentina and Brazil, to participate in the agricultural revolution under way. So, despite down cycles, the golden age of the export economies in Latin America would not really end until the 1920s.

Although exports of raw materials and food commodities dominated Latin America's economies during this period, considerable industrial expansion also took place. Food and beverage processing led the way, followed by clothing and textiles, building materials, and consumer goods. Many of these manufacturing firms were owned by European and U.S. immigrants who joined the national elites through partnerships and marriages. Indeed, in some advanced economies—Mexico, Brazil, and Argentina especially—capital was increasingly transferred from primary production to industry as a way to hedge against declines in prices and demand. Moreover, some primary exports were processed before shipping: for example, refined sugar, cured tobacco leaf, rum, rope fibers, semi-refined metal ore, dried and cured cacao, and nitrates.

New and exotic products joined the flood of exports around the turn of the twentieth century. Bananas grown in Jamaica and later Central America were shipped in refrigeration for ripening in foreign markets. Rubber from the Amazon became a ubiquitous material in the age of electric appliances, bicycles, and automobiles. Copra from coconut palms cultivated on tropical beaches rendered comestible oil for northern food industries. Chicle from southern Mexico became chewing gum. Herbs, spices, and flavorings from tropical regions delighted the palates of northern consumers.

By the 1920s, most of Latin America was fully integrated into global trade and production systems. European and U.S. investors underwrote much of the heavy industrial growth, while light industry was financed by native capital. The technology and immigrants also came from abroad. Between 1880 and 1930, some 20 million foreigners moved to Latin America, literally changing the complexion of whole cities and regions.

World War I tentatively cut Latin America off from capital and markets, and the Great Depression did so more definitively. By 1945, the region's economies had changed in remarkable ways due to two world wars and the worst depression in modern times. For one, banking and finance had developed to the point that the economies were no longer as reliant on foreign investment as before. From their earliest efforts in the 1860s and 1870s, native and immigrant families developed banks and insurance firms capable of managing most local business. In the larger countries, manufacturers supplied a large proportion of the consumer goods and a considerable amount of the capital goods required. In some instances, immigrants actually developed new technologies in their shops and labs. Perhaps most strikingly, Latin Americans' willingness to believe orthodox economic theory from Europe virtually ended.

Throughout the nineteenth century, two theories had guided economic behavior, the traditional Spanish capitalist theory and the classic liberal theory derived from Enlightenment writers like David Ricardo and Adam Smith. The former valued capital in the form of land, machinery, animals, buildings, and cash that could be made to produce goods through the application of labor. Ownership of fixed assets and the ability to coerce labor were critical in the traditional economy. So too was the power to protect capital, create legislation, secure markets, and provide an orderly setting for business. Most successful nineteenth century businesses followed this traditional family-based pattern.

The newer ideas of liberalism found adherents from the generation of the precursors onward, until it became broadly accepted by the autocratic modernizers. In this view, the factors of production (land, labor, and capital—which came bundled with technology) had to be brought together in creative ways for profitable business. The government should do as little as possible to restrict the entrepreneurial efforts of its citizens, a policy known as laissez faire capitalism. Liberalism also held that each country should pursue its competitive advantage in world markets, the so-called international division of labor. If Europe produced cheap and reliable manufactures, Latin America ought to focus on tropical agriculture and mining. The terms of trade would reward both sides in their transactions.

If a limited number of powerful families or institutions monopolized land, labor, and political power, the vast majority of the population could never aspire to become productive citizens. In the particular case of Latin America, liberals saw as obstacles to economic growth the vast expanses of land held by the state, Amerindian reservations, and the Church; the prevalence of coerced labor (especially African and Amerindian) unavailable to new businesses; high tariffs; social and religious barriers against immigration; and restrictions on natural resource exploitation. Advocates of removing these obstacles undertook huge reform programs that awakened the wrath of those whose power was being diminished, especially the army and the Church. Benito Juárez carried out the boldest changes, collectively known as La Reforma, but others did so as well: Mariano Gálvez of Guatemala, the so-called Liberal Oligarchy in Venezuela, and General José Hilario López of Colombia. These programs provoked opposition and even civil war—known as the War of the Reform in Mexico—but in the end the liberals prevailed. Without these reforms, the economic boom that followed would likely not have occurred.

The liberal theories that prevailed after about the 1870s became dogma and reined until the Great Depression. They stressed low tariffs, private over public enterprise, international division of labor, protection of property rights, stable currencies (preferably tied to gold), borders open to foreign immigration and investment, and weak labor organization. As was seen above, this arrangement did not prevent Latin Americans from founding important industries in this era, either with tariff protection or because of costly international freight charges. And in the cases of Mexico and Brazil, government leaders often showed favoritism toward native producers while paying lip service to liberal ideals. They did this through subsidized transport systems, commodity price supports, tax advantages, low-cost credit, and protectionist tariffs.

The isolation of Latin America from the North Atlantic economies during World War I, and the sheer horror of death and destruction wrought by the fighting, shook Latin Americans' faith in European philosophies and models. True, in the 1920s many countries returned to trading in conventional products with traditional partners, but now the United States made a bid for economic leadership in the hemisphere. Communications, shipping, and finance also tended to shift toward the United States.

The Great Depression further eroded faith in the nineteenth century liberal economic model. Trading broke down, nations defaulted on loans, businesses failed, currencies collapsed, and the entire economic system seemed to crumble. National leaders looked to new ways to do business, like barter deals and cartelization of commodities. It was a dog-eat-dog situation that might one day lapse into world war again. John Maynard Keynes had already proposed major revisions to classic liberalism that promised relief from the ravages of depression. Franklin Roosevelt reversed U.S. policy and used federal money for public works and foreign aid and held bilateral trade talks to promote economic recovery and job creation.

Latin American leaders took unusual and sometimes creative steps to ameliorate the impact of the Depression in their nations. Mexico sped up the resettlement of Indians and peasants on communal lands, or *ejidos*, where they could at least subsist. Brazil experimented with alcohol-fueled engines and withheld coffee from the world market. Argentina struck a deal with England for preferential trade treatment. Chile created a national investment bank to promote economic recovery. Everywhere in the hemisphere domestic manufacturers moved boldly into consumer markets that had previously been served by imports. It was the end of an era.

After the war Latin Americans increasingly embraced an alternative theory of economics, with major domestic and external implications. This theory sprang from research conducted at the newly founded UN Economic Commission for Latin America (ECLA), based in Santiago, Chile. The basic tenet of this institute was that since the beginning of the twentieth century primary commodities had suffered declining terms of trade vis-à-vis manufactured goods. This meant that Latin America had to ship increasing amounts of goods to Europe and the United States to maintain the same level of import consumption. Further, the ECLA officials argued that adverse terms of trade would always favor the industrial countries, due to economies of scale, elasticity of demand for manufactures, oligopolistic pricing, and productivity gains from technological advances. The only way for Latin America to catch up was to industrialize also.

The strategy ECLA proposed was called import-substitution industrialization, or ISI. In this model, a country used tariffs to protect new industries until they could compete against imports. Eventually they would be as efficient as their competitors. Second, ECLA argued that most of the region's assets—land, labor, capital, natural resources—were tied up in unproductive arrangements, much as the liberals had claimed in the mid-nineteenth century. Structural reforms were needed to unleash their potential: land reform, housing, worker education, tax reform, health improvements, and so forth. Finally, ECLA proposed unorthodox ways to finance economic growth, through deficit spending and market-expanding customs unions. Remarkably, this new theory became an orthodoxy of its own and even served in part as the inspiration for John Kennedy's Alliance for Progress in the 1960s.

Most of the generation of the populists after World War II followed ECLA strategies to industrialize and gain a degree of economic independence from the already industrialized world. They adopted ISI, carried out land and tax reform, set up programs for literacy and public health, and invested in education at all levels. But deficit spending, carried too far, often led to chronic inflation. For a time, customs unions forged ahead—for example, the Central American

Common Market, the Latin American Free Trade Area, the Andean Pact, the Caribbean CARICOM—but in the long run they accomplished little.

The military regimes of the 1960s–1980s tended to adopt neoliberal policies as a way to clean up excesses of the populist era, yet circumstances did not favor their success. Only in Chile did a frankly laissez faire approach, led by economists associated with the University of Chicago, accomplish what was intended. In Brazil, Argentina, and Uruguay, early experiments with neoliberalism gave way to frenzied attempts to promote growth, deal with balance-of-payments crises, shore up currencies, and create jobs for the masses of young people joining the workforce each year. As neoliberalism was failing to produce results, what emerged was heterodoxy, or a jumble of whatever policies seemed capable of solving the problems of the moment. Nowhere was heterodoxy so pronounced as in Brazil during the ascendancy of Finance Minister Delfim Netto. In the end, failures of economic management by these regimes contributed heavily to the decisions by the military to return to the barracks.

The 1980s found most of Latin America in such financial trouble that it is often called the "lost decade." Stagflation and hyperinflation, energy crises, unemployment, debt defaults and serial rollovers, failed protectionism, capital flight, and general mismanagement plagued the region. Oil-rich countries like Mexico, Venezuela, and Ecuador found themselves unable to use their resources effectively. Those without oil resorted to extremes like alcohol fuel, nuclear plants, charcoal, and huge hydroelectric projects. In the end, the region did not emerge from these doldrums until the Atlantic economy began its recovery in the early 1990s.

Since that time, neoliberal policies have become the new orthodoxy in much of the region. Chile was taken as a model for export-led growth in the 1980s. The U.S.-trained economist presidents of Mexico, and certainly Vicente Fox, followed this line, as did the finance ministers of Argentina, Brazil, and Peru. For a time, Argentina and Brazil pegged their currencies to the U.S. dollar to gain price stability. El Salvador and Ecuador, joining Panama, actually adopted the U.S. dollar as currency. Even Cuba, when the collapse of the Soviet Union ended its subsidy, moved to attract investment and the U.S. dollar. The rest of the neoliberal recipe has been tried out in most countries: tariff reduction, direct foreign investment, elimination of subsidies and price controls, privatization, ending deficit spending, and curbing over-generous benefits for public employees. The pace of neoliberalization slowed in the early 2000s due to recession, and several countries, led by Brazil, have resisted the creation of a free trade area in the hemisphere, but official resistance to neoliberism has been cautious.

CONCLUSION

Latin America entered the twenty-first century by confronting global challenges, no longer using the hemisphere or West as a frame of reference. These challenges include trade competition against fierce rivals in Asia, first the so-called Tigers: Korea, Japan, Singapore, Taiwan, and now China. They also include an energy system groaning under the demands of the First World while trying to accommodate the development needs of the Third World. The superpower United States conducts business all around the globe, so Latin Americans need to be aware of developments on that scale. The threat of international terrorism, world crime and drug networks, unstable regions where war flares up, the spread of epidemic diseases, and the inevitable whiplashes of economic crises all must be monitored daily by Latin American leaders. Hemispheric organizations like the OAS, the School of the Americas, the Inter-American Defense Board, and the Pan American Health Organization are largely obsolete bodies today. Latin Americans must operate in the rarefied atmosphere of the United Nations, the World Bank, the IMF, the WTO, and other global entities.

Apart from these political and security challenges, Latin Americans must survive economically in a multi-polar world that becomes more integrated with each passing year. The region's best and brightest minds are devising their integration into this global economy, running some of the biggest companies in the world—petroleum, aviation, mining, manufacturing, entertainment, telecommunications, and services—and gambling that multinational corporate management is here to stay. How will individual workers and farmers operate in an informed way in this sort of world? The answer will perhaps dictate the success or failure of the integration process.

Less dramatic, yet perhaps just as threatening in the long run, will be the challenges of cultural erosion and the loss of social cohesion under the onslaught of global media. At the moment the media are dominated by U.S., European, and Japanese companies, which project leisure programming of all sorts to the rest of the world—cinema, drama, music, games, sports, and news. Whether Latin Americans can somehow domesticate or Latinize this programming remains to be seen. By the same token, Latin media, primarily in the United States but also coming from Mexico, Brazil, and Spain, are a growing presence in U.S. markets. The future of the arts, family life, spiritual worship, leisure activities, individual and group creativity, and the very core of Latin American-ness are at stake in this confrontation of cultures.

Suggested Readings

Bulmer-Thomas, Victor, *The Economic History of Latin America Since Independence* (Cambridge, England: Cambridge University Press, 1994).

Bushnell, David, and Neill Macaulay, *The Emergence of Latin America in the Nineteenth Century* (New York: Oxford University Press, 1988).

Clayton, Lawrence, and Michael L. Conniff, *A History of Modern Latin America*, 2nd ed. (Belmont, Calif.: Thompson-Wadsworth, 2004).

Conniff, Michael L., ed., *Populism in Latin America* (Tuscaloosa: University of Alabama Press, 1999).

Haber, Stephen, ed., *How Latin America Fell Behind* (Stanford: Stanford University Press, 1997).

PART III

ECONOMIC AND
SOCIAL STRUCTURES

THE LATIN AMERICAN ECONOMIES RESTRUCTURE, AGAIN

WILLIAM P. GLADE

RECENT YEARS HAVE BROUGHT a lively interest in Latin American economic restructuring, both on the part of the policy community in the countries involved and by scholars, development experts, and journalists who in their respective ways are concerned with studying and reporting on what is happening. If this literature does not yet amount to an equivalent of the Harvard five-foot shelf of books that decorated so many American homes earlier in the past century, it may soon exceed that number of linear feet—even if it never acquires the cachet of the older volumes as a documentation of household literacy.

It almost defies good judgment to try to compress into one short essay the complexity and variety that currently characterize the Latin American economies, which range from the semi-giant dimensions of an economically dynamic Brazil, the eighth largest GDP in the world, to tiny and deeply impoverished Haiti, which ranks among the poorest nations of the world and is of negligible importance to anyone but Haitians. Just about every combination of size and income level and, correspondingly, structure of national production can be found in between—along with an exceedingly complicated medley of geographical and climatic conditions. Nevertheless, with the exception of Haiti, Honduras, and Nicaragua, the countries of the region have at least made it out of the poorest category in the World Bank's four-category classification scheme and are more or less firmly ensconced in the lower-middle-income and upper-middle-income categories.[1]

Performance, recently as well as historically, has been no less varied, though since the 1970s, all the countries have been outdistanced in this respect by Asian "Tigers," both old and new. It might seem foolhardy to inject an historical dimension into what is unavoidably an already overly baroque narrative of development and backwardness, but since what one sees today is very much an accumulation of institutional overlays from consecutive episodes of systemic reorganization, a quick romp through the centuries may be the most effective

TABLE 7.1   Economic Dimensions of Selected Latin American Countries, 1994

	GDP (\$ million)	Population (millions)	GNP Per Capita (\$)
Brazil	555,000	159	2,970
Mexico	377,000	89	4,180
Argentina	282,000	34	8,110
Chile	52,000	14	3,520
Uruguay	16,000	3	4,660
Colombia	67,000	36	1,670
Peru	50,000	23	2,110
Venezuela	58,000	21	2,760
Ecuador	17,000	11	1,280
Guatemala	13,000	10	1,200
Costa Rica	8,000	3	2,400
Haiti	1,623	7	230
Honduras	3,333	6	600
Nicaragua	1,833	4	340

Source: World Bank, *World Development Report 1996.*

way to reach our central objective: that of understanding the problems that to-day vex the countries of the region, along with the exceptional opportunities that have led young investment bankers, perhaps rashly, to "enthuse" about Latin America's emerging—and reemerging—markets. Let us hope that Böhm Bawerk's faith that roundaboutness increases productivity applies to this short digression.[2]

THE PARADE OF RESTRUCTURINGS

The current episode—which the Inter-American Development Bank has rightly labeled a silent revolution in economic policy—is only the latest of five restructurings that have been visited on the region since the arrival of Columbus and his crew. Something remains of each of these in the contemporary economic landscape, and from the second restructuring onward, those advocating new policies have thoughtfully left us a diagnostic interpretation of what went before. Taken together, these recognizably edited versions of economic history are immensely helpful in piecing together a record of how the region got to where it is today.

The first "structural adjustment" began when the Spanish replaced sundry indigenous economic systems with one that was more in accord with imperial aspirations and European norms.[3] What emerged was a bureaucratically administered and intricately regulated system that brought under royal direction an ensemble of new local and regional economies, dispersed over a far vaster and more challenging territory than any European monarchy had previously tried to govern. It was in effect an integrated trading territory larger than any that has been cobbled together in more recent times in Latin America.

Agriculturally based, the economy was in time organized by a growing latifundism that defied stated royal objectives and was hastened in its expansion by demographic and other factors. These included a steep decline in the native population from exposure to European diseases; the regrouping of indigenous peoples for ease of governance; a limited acculturation, which vacated customary occupancies; a fundamental incompatibility between pre-Columbian land claims and those based on European custom; the need to devote much acreage to the production of food crops for the Spanish towns and cities and to pasturage for the draft animals on which the colonial transport system rested; and the ever-present attempts of settlers to lay hold of the huge expanse of land claimed by the crown and often poorly defended by the royal bureaucracy. Private estates of considerable size eventually became the basic unit in agriculture, displacing some of the community-held lands the crown had reassigned to the indigenous population, and over the centuries church institutions also became owners of extensive landholdings, often the best managed in the colonies. Inasmuch as land was the fundamental productive resource in an agrarian economy and the source of livelihood for the overwhelming majority of the labor force, the evolution of this pattern of land tenure in effect established an inequality system the vestiges of which have persisted to the present.[4]

Trade, among the urban centers of Spain's overseas kingdoms and between them and Spain itself, was a major activity, closely supervised by the crown to ensure the collection of the taxes that formed the bulk of the structure of public finance, and there grew up a considerable number of artisan manufactures, based on both indigenous and Spanish craft technologies. These, too, were regulated by royal and municipal ordinances and, in the case of the nonindigenous craftsmen, by guild regulations—except where larger workshops, known as *obrajes,* developed. Capital for settlement and other purposes was supplied by the public sector, merchant financiers, and, above all, ecclesiastical institutions. The technological stagnation that was perpetuated in agriculture, mining, and manufacture by this imperially sheltered system of production had its institutional counterpart in the astonishingly stunted development of the financial sector, where nothing remotely resembling the contemporary European developments could be found—leaving the region singularly ill-equipped to venture onto the territory of capitalist economic organization when Spain's empire came to an end.

The ambitious imperial enterprise was punctuated by the establishment and growth of important mining centers that supplied treasure for the Spanish crown and its never-ending dynastic wars in Europe, nourished an administrative machinery that grew in size and complexity as the centuries passed, and salted huge amounts of bullion amongst the European suppliers who furnished the New World its luxury imports. Even more important in many respects was the heavy and continuing investment of the New World economy's resources in the construction of urban centers and their linkage by costly transport networks, so that Spanish government, society, and culture—all of which could be considered analytically as produced public goods—could take root and prosper in the American setting.

A quadruple legacy, therefore, was bequeathed to Latin America from the colonial period. Local political organization was arrested by Spanish bureaucratic centralism, so that the insurgents who threw off Spanish rule had no real experience in self-government to draw on as they set about devising their new republics. Technological backwardness was pervasive, shielded as Spanish America had been from the exchanges of goods, services, and technologies that propelled the European economies toward modernity. Organizational or social capital remained little changed from the sixteenth and seventeenth centuries— at a time when the commercial revolution was reshaping the institutional architecture of Europe (and North America). And perhaps most nefarious of all, a foundational system of inequality came into being that was to continue to the present, so that a pronounced inequality in the distribution of wealth and income (and access to the opportunity structure) has been a dominant characteristic of Latin America ever since.

The second restructuring, which was launched in the eighteenth century by the Bourbons, sought a modest liberalization of trade, a revivification of the American production system, and greater efficiency in the administration of the imperial enterprise—objectives not too distant from those that are motivating today's structural adjustment programs. What is mainly interesting for our purposes, however, is that this second restructuring occasioned a considerable amount of analytical reflection on the conditions then prevailing in Spain's overseas kingdoms, both to diagnose ills and prescribe remedies. Indeed, from the economic writings of the Spanish mercantilists, who were surprisingly sophisticated in their understanding of economic processes, and the commissioned reports of special reconnaissance missions, of which the tour by Alexander von Humboldt may be the best known, we catch more than a passing glimpse of what needed to be done, and why, to remedy the accumulated weaknesses of the colonial economy.[5] Though the second restructuring program was only very partially implemented, it seems to have had a generally positive impact, as revealed by the quickening tempo of economic life as the eighteenth century drew to a close. The institutional architecture laid down by the first restructuring, however, remained very much in place.

A sidelight to this period, of more than passing interest, was the divergent growth path taken by Brazil, which virtually from the outset was conceived by the Portuguese as a commercial venture, supplementing the trading opportunities opened up by their earlier voyages along and around the African coast to Asia. There being no traded goods ready for the picking, however, commercial viability required the transfer to northeastern Brazil of the sugar plantation technology the Portuguese had developed on islands in the eastern Atlantic. When the native labor supply proved insufficient (the indigenous population was quite sparse compared with Mexico, Guatemala, and the Andean highlands), manpower, in the form of slaves from Africa, had to be imported to run the enterprise. The high initial fixed costs this entailed ensured that earning a return on the investment in labor supply would motivate plantation owners to extract an exportable surplus for sale to European markets.

Apart from northeastern Brazil, where the colonial capital was located, the rest of the colony served mainly to supply the plantation economy with a simple range of commodities, until the eighteenth century brought a mining boom in east central Brazil and pulled population southward, giving an additional impetus to growth in regions previously quite marginal, making Rio a more important port, and shifting the labor regime away from slave labor. The mining boom served also to reinforce the export orientation of the Brazilian economy and to consolidate its trading ties with the commercial network the Portuguese had constructed in Europe, including, not least, with Portugal's ally Great Britain.

The third restructuring, a much more ambitious enterprise than the second, arrived after the half-century hiatus of economic dislocation that beset the region with the arrival of independence, from which Brazil and Chile were the principal exceptions. The economic wreckage of the aftermath of independence—the wiping out of most artisan manufactures by cheap factory-made imports from Europe, the wholesale neglect of public investment in infrastructure, repeated defaults on external debt (both public and private), the chronic plundering of enfeebled fiscal systems by political adventurers, the removal of royal and clerical safeguards against exploitation of the indigenous population, the rape of the public domain, and the instability in the policy framework—all had composed a scenario very different from what the fighters for independence said they had in mind when they chased out Spanish bureaucrats. Public finances were a shambles, high risk levels undermined the investment environment, and a region now hitching its fortunes to the increasingly vibrant international economy did so bereft of even the rudimentary banking institutions needed to mobilize and allocate resources in the increasingly monetized capitalist system that was spreading out of Europe. In a sense, the third restructuring, launched when the political picture finally settled down a bit, was a bold remediation for this half century of failure.

To the disarray that prevailed in Spanish America up to the third restructuring, Brazil was again a contrast, providing a favorable climate for the germination of the new economic system that in time spread over the whole of Latin America, albeit unevenly. Owing to circumstances in Europe, the Portuguese court moved to Brazil to escape Napoleon and, when it finally returned to Lisbon, left behind an emperor to take charge of an independent Brazil that was governed from Rio, the city to which the court had fled under British protection. Thanks to the close commercial and political ties the new country inherited from its metropole with the center of the industrial revolution and to the effortless way it attained independence, Brazil was spared the turmoil that proved so costly elsewhere on the continent. And with the climate for economic modernization undisturbed by political change, the way was laid for a third dramatic export boom.[6] This time the product was coffee and the location was in the south of the country, so that the rapid spread of coffee cultivation on Brazilian-owned plantations around São Paulo triggered an explosion of economic expansion in this previously frontier region, based on a free labor force, the attraction of substantial capital and immigration from Europe, and the stimulation of capitalistic development throughout the south of the country.

From around 1870 to 1930, the third restructuring, which centered on the development of export economies, came to Spanish America and paid off handsomely for those not trapped by the inequality systems that had developed after 1492. As in Brazil for the whole of the nineteenth century, two engines of growth—the production and sale to world markets of a growing variety of primary commodities and the influx of foreign capital that made the export production system possible—propelled Latin America into the modern economic arena and transformed the economic dynamics of the region. Even more than the second restructuring, this project anticipated some of the main features of the so-called Washington consensus,[7] the chief difference being that there was no stable of deficit-generating public enterprises to privatize. Trade liberalization and the creation of a climate favorable to investment, both domestic and foreign, proved to be the foundations of the new economic order.

The third restructuring was an institution-building period par excellence as most of the organizational accoutrements of modern capitalism appeared around the continent, carried to all the principal urban centers, and in some cases beyond, by the vectors of modern transport and communications systems. Commercial banks, shipping companies, firms specialized in new legal and accounting transactions, engineering firms, portworks, new railway, street railway, and telecommunications companies, smelters, capitalistically organized mining companies, insurance companies, plantations using narrow-gauge railways and steam-engine-powered refineries, and a slew of other enterprises provided the social or organizational capital for Latin America to belatedly join the modern economy of the West and began to generate, or attract, the human capital needed to keep the ensemble in operation. Harbingers of a new age of factory production also sprang up here and there, following the needs of export-fed markets and new structures of production. Most of the new manufacturing was, naturally enough, of consumer goods, but foundries, smelters, and machine shops were indicative of the possibilities for industrial deepening, and around the turn of the century the first integrated iron- and steelworks appeared in Monterrey, Mexico.

Over much of the region, these new developments occurred in scattered enclaves, for growth was markedly uneven. Interregional disparities came to be immensely greater than they had been in earlier times, setting the stage for the notorious unevenness of development that characterizes most of Latin America today. Much of the area and population was thus left behind by the modernizing forces of international capitalism and its domestic offshoots, including substantial numbers of people trapped in subsistence cultivation.[8] Shorn of their communal holdings and proletarianized by the unrestricted expansion of large landholdings, the indigenous peoples in particular seemed destined for cultural obliteration in the liberal project that most governments pursued.[9] In the south of Brazil and the Rio de la Plata, however, the new economic influences spread untrammeled by colonial residues or sizable indigenous populations, with a transformative power that brought into being a region that today constitutes the economic heartland of South America (and the Mercosur, the Southern Common Market). Argentina even managed to reach the end of this era as one of the world's most prosperous economies, so that "rich as an Argentine" gained currency in Europe to describe vast wealth.[10]

As in the second restructuring, there was an abundance of new writing, this time mostly in the vein of the classical/neoclassical school of political economy and positivism, to reinterpret the past for its diagnostic value and prescribe ingredients for the policy armamentarium the governments of the day were putting together to ensure continued growth—and even progress, a term still very much in vogue in that pre-postmodern intellectual ambiance. It would be stretching a point to call this an age of unbridled laissez-faire, but it most certainly was one filled to overflowing with capitalist sentiments and language.

But beyond the Rio de la Plata and broad swatches of Chile and central and southern Brazil, the spottiness of the transformation made for glaring inequalities and a plethora of organizational and cultural disparities—contradictions of such severity as to delight the heart of a Marxist. In Mexico these were particularly acute, so that only a decade into the century, the ancien régime, as the nouveau régime soon came to be perceived, was cast aside and a kind of anticipatory glimpse of the next restructuring hove into view: one that would use a kind of economic nationalism to accelerate the process of industrialization. In Mexico, almost uniquely until the Bolivian revolution of the 1950s, agrarian reform was at first the dominant policy priority, but when the fourth restructuring set in, during the late 1930s and 1940s, it was manufacturing that was to call the tune.

ISI: The Fourth Restructuring

During the closing decades of the nineteenth century, the first modern factories appeared here and there in Latin America: in Argentina, Chile, Brazil, and Mexico especially, but with scattered outposts popping up elsewhere. Population growth, modest urbanization, the enrichment of the area's human resources by immigration (which brought entrepreneurs as well as skilled labor), and a rise in incomes, together with the knitting together of a greater area by railways and telecommunication lines, gradually expanded domestic markets and with them the number of local manufacturing establishments. As the twentieth century unfolded, these market-based trends produced a further widening of the industrial base—spurred on, briefly, by the interruption of European imports during World War I. In interpreting the record of growth in more recent decades, we need to remember that several of these factors—an accentuated population growth, more rapid urbanization, the filling in of national infrastructure, and the upward trend in per capita incomes—have continued to operate in ways supportive of manufacturing development, both broadening and deepening the industrial structure independently of the effects of policy.

When the Great Depression hit and export earnings collapsed, the depreciation of Latin American currencies favored the further expansion of domestic industry to replace the unavailable imports, while by this time tariffs originally designed for revenue had gradually been raised to levels according a measure of protection for competing local products. And while depression thus knocked out one of the props of the age of export-led expansion, the other engine of the region's third-restructuring growth, foreign investment, was likewise rendered hors de combat by the massive disorganization of capital markets in the centers of capitalism.[11] Import supplies and capital imports continued to be disrupted when World War II began, and while domestic manufacturing was spreading to meet the gap between domestic aggregate demand and imports, governments increasingly questioned the wisdom of continuing to rely on the external sector as the mainstay of economic growth. The conditioning of such circumstances lasted into the postwar era, as traditional sources of import supplies continued to be choked back by the reconstruction priorities that absorbed most of the capital Europe could generate and the United States could export.

It only remained for the new UN Economic Commission for Latin America (ECLA), based in Santiago, Chile, to fashion out of these circumstances a rationale for systematic promotion, under state leadership, of accelerated industrial development.[12] Thereafter, until the debt crisis struck in 1982, the policies that had evolved by ad hoc adaptation to circumstances in the 1930s and 1940s were reshaped into a well-articulated development program that justified a wide variety of interventionary measures and in time spawned the movement toward regional integration as an expedient to keep industrialization's momentum unabated. Protective tariffs, fiscal incentives, exchange-rate controls, parastatal financial and industrial enterprises, and a host of other policy instruments were deployed to push industrial development forward and, from the early 1960s, to promote such schemes as the Central American Common Market, the larger Latin American Free Trade Area, and the smaller Caribbean Free Trade Area. A bit later, the Andean Pact and the Caribbean Common Market were added. None of these regional associations lived up to the initial expectations, but in most there was a significant growth of intraregional trade—and, most likely, equally significant trade diversion effects.

Amid these changes there were also notable shifts in inter-American economic relations. The 1930s had brought the reciprocal trade agreements to build preferential commercial ties between the United States and Latin America, and the inauguration of the Export-Import Bank introduced government financing into the web of economic relationships. Technical assistance and additional intergovernmental financing for capital projects began during World War II, when the United States had need of increased Latin American production capacity. A trickle of economic aid of these types, especially technical assistance, continued through the 1950s, during which the World Bank became a significant external source of development financing and the Organization of American States, through such entities as the Pan American Health Organization, a modest supplier of economic counsel and technical assistance.[13] While the regional integration movement was reaching its heyday, the Inter-American Development Bank was instituted at the end of the 1950s as a multilateral regional supplier of development finance (and technical counsel), and soon thereafter the Alliance for Progress, sometimes misleadingly equated with the Marshall Plan, was introduced to mobilize public resources on a large scale for a concerted regional development push.[14] By the 1970s, however, these initiatives were playing out.

The strategy that was baptized "import-substituting industrialization (ISI)" came to be administered carelessly, distorted from the pristine ECLA vision by the tug of rent-seeking interest groups and by populist policies that have been characterized as macroeconomic populism.[15] Bedecked also with some of the trappings of the modern welfare state, to placate the crucial urban constituencies, the public sector came to exemplify a concept of the state as the great piñata. Inflation was rampant, balance-of-payments crises were frequent, agricultural and traditional export sectors were undermined, and in time the policy environment turned increasingly hostile to foreign direct investment.[16] To cap the mounting list of problems, Latin America's export market share was generally eroded in favor of other Third World exporters. Also, fiscal profligacy and excessive bureaucratization combined with the discouragement of foreign investment and the need to cover growing trade imbalances to produce an increasing reliance on commercial loans from money-center banks—while domestic savings rates were depressed by adverse policies and capital flight was even unintentionally stimulated. Meanwhile, it transpired that the industrialization that had been designed to replace imports had in fact made Latin America more dependent on imports than ever before.

The jig was up when the oil shocks of the 1970s worked their effects, and (on top of all the external-sector adjustments) the industrialized countries more or less simultaneously undertook to put an end to accelerating inflation, causing export prices and earnings to drop precipitously. The repercussions in Latin America produced the debt crisis, which struck all the countries save Colombia in the early 1980s and effectively ended the half century of accelerated industrialization and the policy framework that had sustained and nurtured it.[17] As the Inter-American Development Bank has noted, the longer-term effect of the crisis was to usher in a major shift in economic policy that gradually spread over the continent.[18]

THE FIFTH RESTRUCTURING AND WHAT IT REVEALS

Chile, Mexico, Argentina, and later Peru have been at the forefront of the new policy agenda, which has promoted macroeconomic stabilization, the ending of financial repression (the freeing of interest rates to find market-determined levels), and the removal of most exchange-rate controls so that the prices in the foreign exchange market would be anchored in supply-demand relationships. The deregulation of other prices and the withdrawal of subsidies have also furthered the marketization of economic decisionmaking, whereas trade liberalization has been relied on to widen the scope of contestable markets and intensify competitive pressures. This has brought about greater productive and allocative efficiency while aligning domestic price structures with those prevailing in the world market. In greater or lesser measure, deregulation has also been used to create a more favorable climate for capital formation, both domestic and foreign.

Privatization, once the most controversial of the new policies, has been employed for a variety of objectives: to strengthen the fiscal system by removing deficit-generating enterprises from the public portfolio and using the sales proceeds to reduce national debt; to link local production facilities more securely into the globalized production, financing, and marketing networks; to tap the more ample supplies of capital available in the private sector; and to pave the way for continuing technological upgrading. Secondary objectives have included the reduction of labor redundancy and making national capital markets more robust, both by spreading the ownership of shares and by enriching the options available to investors for portfolio diversification.

The recent peso crisis and its repercussions aside, the benefits of structural adjustment have been swifter to materialize than one might have expected, given all that has been said about the distortions and other shortcomings of the previous policy era—during which so many of the canons of orthodox economic theory were violated. No doubt it was indeed the flagrant character of these "violations" that led many to interpret the debt crisis as a well-deserved day of reckoning, in which policy sins of omission and policy sins of commission alike would finally be paid for. Yet, just as the three preceding restructuring episodes were the occasions for retrospective diagnoses of the economic orders that led into the restructurings, so also the present turnabout affords a useful vantage point from which to reflect on what legacy the twentieth century has left for the Latin American economies. A summing up of sorts, in other words, is plainly in order—not only for an accurate reading of the policies of the neoliberal model that critics have called the great restoration of capitalism but also to interpret the costs and benefits of the two most recent eras that have brought Latin America to this point.

It is clear that the foundations of growth were established in the 1870–1930 era, which, while it lasted, did so much to bring substantial parts of Latin America, finally, into the modern age, with a much-needed filling in of institutional deficits left over from the colonial age and repair of the damage inflicted in the first decades of independence. Amid the new organizational infrastructure through which Latin America was increasingly engaged with the world market, incipient industrialization appeared as the harbinger of the more sweeping changes that redrew the economic map of the region after 1930.

Notwithstanding the obvious costs of the ISI policies that followed the Great Depression and World War II, considerable strength was nevertheless added to the Latin American resource base, expanding the array of production options and creating the basis for considerably more production versatility than the region exhibited in, say, 1929. Not only was the structure of production totally transformed, and along with it the distribution of the labor force, but compared with the state of the region's economy at the close of the era of export-led growth, the Latin America of 1997 was richer by far in its human resources and in the organizational or social capital on which everything in the last analysis rests. The feverish pace of institution building that has characterized Latin America since the 1930s has been deeply flawed and often haphazard. Protectionism run riot most certainly contributed to both misallocations of resources among sectors and industries and suboptimal efficiency at the microlevel, just as it made rent-seeking pervasive and spread the opportunities for a socially corrosive corruption. Both no doubt contributed to the lopsided distribution of income for which Latin America has become notorious.

Yet, real-factor productivity has nonetheless chalked up impressive advances in most of the region, and there has been an enormous amount of learning by doing, in both public and private sectors. For all the problems and setbacks, per capita income for an awesomely larger population has reached levels far above those that prevailed before market-induced industrialization was joined by policy-induced industrialization.

In country after country, the comparative advantages based on natural endowments have thus been supplanted by comparative advantages derived from organizational growth and the accumulation of human capital. For example, Brazil, noted as late as the mid-1960s for its overwhelming export dependence on coffee, became, thanks to policy adaptations that began in the latter part of that decade, a country whose exports have consisted primarily of manufactures, including a range of sophisticated exports (to highly competitive markets) that extends from *telenovelas* and oil field services to aircraft and automobiles. Colombia, another coffee country, has learned to export coal, petroleum, flowers, and a considerable variety of other products, just as Chile has moved away from a lopsided dependence on copper into a varied basket of higher-value products and Mexican industrial products are eating into the commanding lead acquired in the 1970s by petroleum exports.[19]

The Chilean case is particularly instructive. Given the disruptive policy shifts introduced by the Allende regime of the early 1970s and the Pinochet regime that followed, one might have expected the Chilean industrial sector to vanish in the face of rapid trade liberalization and a deliberately overvalued currency, policies adopted as the cornerstones of restructuring—especially when the banking system, which was ruined under Allende, collapsed a second time in the midst of the restructuring. Nevertheless, the manufacturing sector managed to survive and grow stronger, in organizational capacity and efficiency if not in scale, and the economy as a whole eventually turned in a stellar performance year after year.

In short, behind the debt and peso crises and all the Sturm und Drang of the restructuring controversies, the evidence is unmistakable that the three consecutive policy regimes that began around 1870 have enabled the current restructuring to be carried out with considerable success. The new climate has also made the Mercosur, North American Free Trade Agreement (NAFTA), and the general economic opening effective catalysts for economic revival and renewal. In this, the reborn regional integration movement offers a notable contrast to the various experiments that characterized the 1960s: the Central American Common Market (CACM), the Latin American Free Trade Agreement (LAFTA), the Caribbean Free Trade Agreement (CARIFTA), and the Andean Pact, all of which petered out after their initial momentum—victims of economic nationalism, contradictory policies, feckless bureaucrats, and faulty design. Today, the Mercosur (which groups Brazil, Argentina, Uruguay, and Paraguay) has emerged as the largest and most successful example of regional economic cooperation in the Third World, and NAFTA, for all its stresses and strains, represents a boldly unique attempt to meld economies more disparate than any of those brought together in the European Union.[20]

There are, to be sure, a number of troubling accounts payable still remaining on the national ledger sheets: what has come to be called the social deficit. Environmental conditions have deteriorated over much of the continent, and the cities have patently exceeded the carrying capacity of their infrastructure, with consequent decay in the living conditions of all who dwell therein, even the rich, whose walled compounds nevertheless admit increasingly polluted air and who must from time to time sally forth to confront growing congestion and social disorder.[21]

Huge numbers of people and much of the rural sector have been left on the sidelines in the sweeping renovation effort, and the disparities among regions and income classes are greater than ever before.[22] Compared with the high-performance Asian economies, the most unequal Asian income distributions are more equitable than the least unequal of the Latin American cases. And the people Columbus encountered on his voyages live still in a state of economic and cultural anorexia, as powerless politically as they are deprived of assets and purchasing power in the economic arena.[23]

Much remains to be done, in other words, to make the current national projects credible as a path for general progress.[24] But it is hard to escape the conclusion that for all its ills, Latin America has more resources today than it has ever had before to enlist in the needed cleanup and social rectification efforts, which cannot be postponed much beyond the close of this millennium, and it has more social capability and institutional capacity as well. These assets, too, are products of development, albeit nonmeasured public-goods components that are not conventionally reckoned in the national accounts. But considering that they contribute importantly to future capacity to produce, one could reasonably conclude that the recorded growth figures for much of this century, high as they have been, have actually understated the rate of change—though a full and balanced accounting would have to tally the accumulated social costs as a major offset to this record of achievement. Perhaps only the outcomes in the new century will enable us to judge with some assurance of accuracy the net asset or liability position.

NOTES

1. The World Bank groups the economies into four categories. Low-income countries are found mostly in Africa and Asia and include the majority of the world's population. Most of Latin America has climbed into the lower-middle-income or upper-middle-income category, alongside Turkey, the central and Eastern European countries, and those spun off from the former Soviet Union, as well as the high-performance Asian economies. None has made it into the most prosperous group of countries, although Hong Kong and Singapore have reached those levels.

2. This literature on Latin American economic history is now enormous. Readers with an interest in examining it can conveniently begin with the relevant volumes in Leslie Bethell, ed., *The Cambridge History of Latin America* (New York: Cambridge University Press, 1984), or William Glade, *The Latin American Economies: A Study of Their Institutional Evolution* (New York: American Book Company, 1969). See also B. R. Mitchell, *International Historical Statistics: The Americas and Autralasia 1750–1988* (Detroit, Mich.: Gale Research Co., 1983).

3. The large city-state empires run by the Aztecs (in Mexico) and Incas (in Peru, Ecuador, and Bolivia) at the time of the conquest were agriculturally based and boasted extensive trade routes within them, partly to collect tribute and sacrificial victims from subjugated peoples. The Maya were by then in an advanced state of decline, and apart from a few other indigenous peoples, such as the Chibcha in Colombia, most of the other Amerindian groupings were still in the hunting and fishing stage of technological development—with scattered regions of sedentary agriculture. It should be noted that most long-distance traffic moved by human bearers over footpaths, there being no wheeled carts or draft animals (other than the llamas used as pack animals). Thus, two immense adjustments had to occur with European colonization: the shift of much cropland to pasturage to fuel the new transport technology based on pack and draft animals and a massive dedication of resources to road and bridge construction, an undertaking made immensely costly by the nature of the topography and distances involved.

4. It should be stressed that the latifundiary foundations of the New World order were not part of the original aims of the Spanish crown, which in principle was also committed to protection of the native population. A voluminous corpus of decrees, partly administered by royal officials and partly overseen by a parallel ecclesiastical bureaucracy, was designed to safeguard the social blueprint on which the empire was theoretically constructed. But the chronic hunger of the royal treasury had to be fed by all kinds of expedients, ranging from the sale of lower-level offices to payments by which land claims, even illegal ones, could be regularized, and problems of communication and bureaucratic oversight reduced the efficiency (and integrity) of administration. Thus, the collision between metropolitan ideals and New World realities left a deposit of institutions that shaped social relations in ways that were unintended but were foundational for what came afterward.

5. Had these economists had a better address, say, in England or France, they would undoubtedly have been credited with great contributions to the embryonic science of economics. But in Spain they worked beyond the intellectual pale defined by the upcoming liberal modernization movements of the Enlightenment and hence never figured much in any citation index of the day.

6. Neither the ending of the empire in exchange for republican government nor the abolition of slavery, both of which came at the dawning of the Belle Époque (1890–1914), occasioned serious conflict in Brazil.

7. The term is widely used today to refer to the standard policy package recommended by the IMF and the World Bank for countries in need of economic resuscitation: macroeconomic stabilization programs, trade liberalization, deregulation of prices (including interest rates) and general business activity (including foreign investment), market-based exchange-rate policies, and privatization, inter alia.

8. For a convenient introduction into the huge literature on agrarian development, see Robert G. Keith, *Haciendas and Plantations in Latin American History* (New York: Holmes and Meier, 1977).

9. The spread of latifundism, to dimensions unimagined even by the end of the colonial age, was fostered by factors both political and technological. In the political realm, the ownership of government was held by the class most interested in expanding its landholdings, and liberal ideology provided a cloak for self-aggrandizement of this group. In the technology realm, the spread of railways and telecommunications conferred value on parts of the public domain that had formerly held no interest for anyone save the native population that lived there.

10. In this region, where a relatively gentle topography and temperate climate facilitated agriculture and ranching, the cheap construction of roads and railways, supplemented by South America's most important inland waterway, spurred development and heightened the productivity of the immense amount of human capital that arrived through mass immigration from Europe.

11. The period is well covered in Rosemary Thorp, ed., *Latin America in the 1930's: The Role of the Periphery in World Crisis* (New York: St. Martin's Press, 1984).

12. The ECLA became in effect a graduate school for training a new generation of Latin American economists, the principal source of doctrinal inspiration for national industrial policies, a major purveyor of technical assistance for project and program planning, and the generator of a systematic strategy of development that was widely borrowed in other less developed parts of the world.

13. The International Labour Organisation, the Food and Agriculture Organization, and an assortment of other UN-related entities also came onto the Latin American stage in this era.

14. Smaller but important inter-American contributions were made by the Peace Corps and the Inter-American Development Foundation. Private U.S. foundations such as Kellogg, Rockefeller, and Ford were also enlisted on behalf of Latin American development, especially in institution building. The private foundations, however, had in some instances begun their Latin American programs before the 1960s, and by the end of that decade they were drawing back in favor of new programs in the United States. Significant advances in building Latin American intellectual capital resulted from their efforts as well as from the investments of others such as the Tinker Foundation, the Latin American Scholarship Program of American Universities, the U.S. Agency for International Development, a variety of church-related undertakings, and the Fulbright program.

15. Extremely effective analysis of the destabilizing patterns of policy that developed is contained in Rudiger Dornbusch and Sebastian Edwards, *The Macroeconomics of Populism in Latin America* (Chicago: University of Chicago Press, 1991).

16. An ever-increasing overburden of regulation was applied to foreign direct investment, and restrictive regulation was also applied to technology transfers. A culmination of sorts was

reached in the Andean Pact countries in the form of provisions to accelerate foreign disinvestment.

17. A different set of events had brought the Chilean economy to collapse in 1973, with the result that the fifth restructuring began there as a pioneering experiment in the mid-1970s, a decade before similar policies were introduced elsewhere in the region. For the Chilean case, see Dominique Hachette and Rolf Luders-Schwarzenburg, *Privatization in Chile: An Economic Appraisal* (San Francisco: ICSS press 1993), and Barry Bosworth, Rudiger Dornbush, and Raul Laban, eds., *The Chilean Economy: Policy Lessons and Challenges* (Washington, D.C.: Brookings Institution, 1994). For the debt crisis, see S. Griffith-Jones and Osvaldo Sunkel, *Debt and Development Crises in Latin America: The End of an Illusion* (New York: Oxford University Press, 1986), and Robert Devlin, *Debt and Crisis in Latin America: The Supply Side of the Story* (Princeton, N.J.: Princeton University Press, 1994).

18. Sebastian Edwards, *Crisis and Reform in Latin America: From Despair to Hope* (New York: Oxford University Press, 1995), provides an excellent review of the reform measures and their impacts.

19. Montague Lord, "Manufacturing Exports," in Inter-American Development Bank, *Economic and Social Progress in Latin America, 1992* (Washington, D.C.: Inter American Development Bank, 1992).

20. Greece and Portugal, the poorest members of the EU, were much, much smaller than Mexico and also relatively closer to European levels in per capita income—and therefore more readily "digestible." The closer counterpart to the NAFTA combination would have been the admission of Turkey into the European Community, a challenge the Europeans prudently declined.

21. Gordon J. MacDonald, Daniel L. Nielson, and Marc A. Stern, eds., *Latin American Environmental Policy in International Perspective* (Boulder, Colo.: Westview Press, 1997); Michael Painter and William H. Durham, eds., *The Social Causes of Environmental Destruction in Latin America* (Ann Arbor: University of Michigan Press, 1995).

22. Samuel A. Morley, *Poverty and Inequality in Latin America* (Baltimore: Johns Hopkins University Press, 1995); William Thiesenhusen, *Broken Promises: Agrarian Reform and the Latin American Campesino* (Boulder, Colo.: Westview Press, 1995).

23. George Psacharaopoulos and Harry A. Patrinos, eds., *Indigenous People and Poverty in Latin America* (Washington, D.C.: The World Bank, 1994), and Donna Lee Van Cott, ed., *Indigenous Peoples and Democracy in Latin America* (New York: St. Martin's Press, 1994).

24. Dagmar Raczynski, ed., *Strategies to Combat Poverty in Latin America* (Washington, D.C.: Inter-American Development Bank, 1996).

SUGGESTED READINGS

Agosín, Manuel R., ed. *Foreign Direct Investment in Latin America.* Washington, D.C.: Inter-American Development Bank, 1995. With its focus on the revival of capital inflows into a restructured region, this book is well paired with another book from the same publisher, José Antonio Ocampo and Roberto Steiner, eds., *Foreign Capital in Latin America* (1994). Both are strongly technical in their analysis.

Baer, Werner. *The Brazilian Economy: Growth and Development.* New York: Praeger, 1995. It is not hard to understand why this masterly analysis of Latin America's largest economy has gone through so many editions of which this is the latest.

Bethell, Leslie, ed. *The Cambridge History of Latin America.* New York: Cambridge University Press, 1984. This landmark work has chapters on economic aspects scattered among its multiple volumes.

Bresser Pereira, Luiz Carlos. *Economic Crisis and State Reform in Brazil: Toward a New Interpretation of Latin America.* Boulder, Colo.: Lynne Rienner, 1996. A noted specialist who grew to professional maturity under ISI speaks his piece on what has come to pass with the structural adjustment reforms, though Brazil has lagged notably on making many of these.

Glade, William. *The Latin American Economies: A Study of Their Institutional Evolution.* New York: American Book Company, 1969.

Gordon, Wendell. *The Political Economy of Latin America.* New York: Columbia University Press, 1966. The last edition of one of the best of the several textbooks written in the 1960s and 1970s on Latin American development.

Hachette, Dominique, and Rolf Luders-Schwarzenberg. *Privatization in Chile: An Economic Appraisal.* San Francisco: ICS Publishers, 1993. A magisterial analysis of this controversial policy in Latin America's trailblazing country.

Huber, Evelyn, and Frank Safford, eds. *Agrarian Structure and Political Power: Landlord and Peasant in the Making of Latin America.* Pittsburgh: University of Pittsburgh Press, 1995.

Inter-American Development Bank. *Economic and Social Progress in Latin America.* An annual report containing current economic information on the different countries, a useful set of time series data, and an extended analytical treatment of some particular aspects of Latin American development, such as fiscal decentralization, social security reform, manufacturing exports, and such. Earlier volumes have titles that vary slightly from the latest volumes.

Maddison, Angus, et al. *The Political Economy of Poverty, Equity, and Growth: Brazil and Mexico.* New York: Oxford University Press, 1992. One of a series of paired country studies by World Bank specialists, this one provides an intimate look at the two most important Latin American economies that for all their historical differences have gone through many of the same development policy hoops in recent years.

Ozorio de Almeida, Anna Luiza, and João S. Campari. *Sustainable Settlement in the Brazilian Amazon.* New York: Oxford University Press, 1995. A well-reasoned and well-documented analytical foray into one of the most controversial facets of Latin American development, for the problem explored is far wider than just Brazil. See also Charles H. Wood and Marianne Schmink, *Contested Frontiers in Amazonia* (New York: Columbia University Press, 1992), for an authoritative treatment of the demographic forces in environmental degradation.

Prebisch, Raúl. *Change and Development: Latin America's Great Task.* New York: Praeger, 1971. A rethinking of the Latin American predicament on the eve of the great borrowing spree and the oil shocks, by the man who, more than any other, shaped Latin American economic policy in the postwar period. The classical statement of the prevailing diagnosis of Latin American conditions and the policy that flowed from it is found in UN, ECLA, *The Economic Development of Latin America and Its Principal Problems* (Santiago: United Nations Economic Commission for Latin America, 1950). Ibid., *Development Problems of Latin America* (Austin: University of Texas Press, 1970), is a handy compilation of documents from the UN Economic Commission for Latin America that define the guiding vision of ISI policies.

Story, Dale. *Industry, the State, and Public Policy in Mexico.* Austin: University of Texas Press, 1986. See also, for Mexico, Roderic Ai Camp, *Entrepreneurs and Politics in Twentieth Century Mexico* (New York: Oxford University Press, 1989). For an equivalent glimpse of the policy process in Brazil, see Ben Ross Schneider, *Politics Within the State: Elite Bureaucrats and Industrial Policy in Authoritarian Brazil* (Pittsburgh: University of Pittsburgh Press, 1991). These three books, and their equivalents for several other countries, afford an insight into the dynamics that generated the economic outcomes analyzed by Maddison and associates. Although the neoliberal model has somewhat altered the institutional arrangements that these three studies examined, we would be rash to assume that the old order has altogether vanished in policy determination. In Latin America, as in the United States, policymakers listen selectively.

Thiesenhusen, William C. *Broken Promises: Agrarian Reform and the Latin American Campesino*. Boulder, Colo.: Westview Press, 1995. An important retrospective assessment by one who has followed the vagaries of agricultural policy for many years.

Tokman, Victor. *Beyond Regulation: The Informal Economy in Latin America*. Boulder, Colo.: Lynne Rienner, 1992. Although the informal sector, so baptized, was first spotted in Africa by ILO researchers, its Latin American twin has inspired a huge volume of studies, of which this is a good example. Hernando de Soto, *The Other Path: The Invisible Revolution in the Third World* (New York: Harper and Row, 1989), did much, in its earlier Spanish-language version, to stimulate scholarship on the Latin American phenomenon, though housing studies in squatter settlements during the early 1960s were perhaps the first to note the rise of the informal sector or the underground economy.

Urrutia, Miguel, ed. *Long-Term Trends in Latin American Economic Development*. Washington, D.C.: Inter-American Development Bank, 1991. Especially chapters 1 and 2.

Weeks, John. *The Economies of Central America*. New York: Holmes and Meier, 1985. Though written before this troubled region began to settle down, the survey is nonetheless useful for understanding what democratic governments will have to deal with today.

Chapter 8

SOCIAL STRUCTURE AND CHANGE IN LATIN AMERICA

HENRY VELTMEYER
JAMES PETRAS

For close to three decades, from the 1950s to the end of the 1970s, Latin America experienced historically unprecedented high rates of economic growth—more than 5 percent in the aggregate and 2.5 percent on a per capita basis. This growth, together with associated developments, was based on a model characterized by (1) state intervention in the economy, including regulation of private activity and restrictions on foreign investment; (2) an inward orientation—producing for the domestic rather than the world market; (3) import substitution—protecting and encouraging the growth of domestic industry; and (4) populism—the incorporation of the working and middle classes into the development process and politics.

In the 1970s, this process of development was arrested and reversed by governments in Chile and Argentina, both military dictatorships, acting in the interest of the economically dominant propertied class, which was deeply concerned about the mounting claims made by a restive working class and landless peasantry against their property. In the 1980s, under conditions of a region-wide debt crisis and a democratization process (the return to state power by elected regimes and the rule of law), a solution was found to both the growing power of the working class and the widespread economic imbalances. The Structural Adjustment Program (SAP), as it was called, was a series of economic stabilization measures and "structural" reforms designed by the economists at the World Bank and the International Monetary Fund, two international organizations set up to promote free-market capitalist development on a global scale.

Pioneered by Chile's military regime but eventually adopted by or imposed on the other governments, the SAP provides a standard recipe for curing a country's ills: (1) stabilization of the currency (adoption of a "realistic" exchange rate, that is, devaluation); (2) liberalization of trade and capital flows, eliminating or reducing trade barriers and favorable treatment of domestic capital; (3) reorientation of production toward the world market and opening up the economy to foreign competition; (4) deregulation of private activity; (5) privatization of public enterprises and all means of social production; (6) downsizing the state, reducing the scale and scope of its market intervention, eliminating subsidies and control of prices; and (7) fiscal austerity—a policy of fiscal discipline and balanced budgets. After a decade and more of such policies, Latin America today is a very different place from what it was in the 1970s and what it was becoming. In the process, a revolution—or rather a counterrevolution—has been wrought in the social structure of Latin American society.

It is of critical importance to understand the nature of this social structure. For one thing, the capacity for people to change this structure and thereby to improve the conditions of their social existence to some extent depends on this understanding. For another, it is not possible to understand the development of Latin American society in its critical dimensions (economic, social, political) without a solid grasp of the social structure that underlies this development.

THE SOCIAL STRUCTURE OF LATIN AMERICA

There are three basic levels to social analysis. One is in terms of the distribution or composition of a population's social characteristics. At this level, we can identify a number of ascribed or socially constructed features, such as gender, age, race, and ethnicity, and achieved characteristics such as level of education. A second form of analysis operates at a different (structural) level, identifying sets of positions occupied by groups of people and the social and economic conditions associated with these positions. Arguably, this is the most critical level of social analysis, requiring a combination of theoretical abstraction and empirical analysis. A third type of social analysis is based on the subjective and political conditions of people's behavior and experience, identifying the forms of their social awareness and the action associated with their shared position. In practice, the problem is how and where to combine these three forms of social analysis—to make the appropriate or necessary connections.

At the structural level, a number of critical factors and defining characteristics can be identified. One is spatial distribution and location. In these terms, Table 8.1 distinguishes between two groups of the population, one located in the region's urban centers and the other in the countryside, in the smaller communities and farms of rural society. Table 8.1 also points toward a fundamental change in the urban-rural distribution of the population as well as in the gender composition of the labor force since the 1970s.

Table 8.1 identifies significant country-by-country variations in the urban-rural distribution of the population. More than that, it highlights major changes in the structure of this distribution over the past two and a half decades. In most cases, the shift of the population toward the urban centers involves a change of at least ten percentage points. The table also identifies a trend toward the feminization of the labor force. This trend, identified in the relative shift of women and men in their labor force participation from 1975 to 2001, has accelerated

TABLE 8.1   The Population of Latin America and the Caribbean: Some Basic Distributions, 1994

| | *Population ('01)*[a] | | *% Urban*[b] | | *Participation Rate* [c] | | |
| | | | | | F/M | F/M | %F/M |
	Millions	%	'75	'00	'75	'01	'01
Argentina	37.5	7.5	78	90	30/69	36/67	47
Bolivia	8.5	1.6	41	65	26/69	48/68	58
Brazil	172.6	35.1	56	80	36/76	44/76	52
Chile	15.4	7.6	75	86	23/64	38/66	49
Colombia	43.0	3.1	57	75	29/64	49/67	61
Ecuador	12.9	2.1	45	63	21/70	31/72	39
Mexico	99.4	17.2	59	75	26/71	40/73	48
Uruguay	3.4	0.7	82	93	25/67	49/69	67
Venezuela	24.6	3.7	72	87	25/67	44/68	54
Central America/Cuba	56.8	9.9	42	56			
Caribbean, English Speaking	5.8	1.3	49	67			

Sources: (a) World Bank, World Development Report 2003; and UNDP, World Development Report, 2003: Table 5, p.251; (b) ECLAC, Statistical Yearbook, 2002; Demographic Bulletin, No. 69. Latin America and the Caribbean: Population Estimates and Projections, 2002.

over the past two decades, even though the participation rate of women in the urban labor force is still low relative to that of men as well as to women in other parts of the world. More significant, however, is that relative to men, women are generally integrated into the urban economy under conditions of sexist discrimination and a higher rate of exploitation. This is reflected in the fact that most employment growth over the past two decades has been in a sector characterized by low pay, poor working conditions, and irregularity; and women are disproportionately represented in jobs with these forms of employment and working conditions. Another indicator of sexism in the labor force can be found in the male/female ratio of average earned income by job in the urban labor force, which in economies and societies as diverse as Bolivia, Chile, Mexico, and Venezuela ranges from .38 to .45 (UNDP, 2003: Table 23). In many parts of the world over the past two decades the participation rate of women have begun to approach those of men, and the gender ratio of earned income is more in the range of .65 to .70. Clearly, women in these situations still have a long way to go in their protracted struggle for equality and equity.

But it is just as clear that in many Latin American societies and their economies that women have an even greater distance to travel in this struggle, which, it could be added, is an important part of a more general class struggle.

Even with a very preliminary and limited demographic analysis, it is possible to identify patterns in socioeconomic and working conditions that correspond to differences in a broader social structure. To some degree this is reflected in elements of this structure, such as the distribution of economic activities (Table 8.2) and the associated pattern of income distribution (Table 8.3). A cursory examination of these patterns indicates that the corresponding structures (institutionalized patterns or ways of doing things) are interconnected and form a system. That is,

TABLE 8.2   The Structure of Economic Activity, Selected Countries, Ranked (out of 132) in Reverse Order of Per Capita Income, 1994

	GDP per capita[a] ($US) 2001	% Share of Total Production[b]		
		Agriculture	Industry	Services
Bolivia	2,300	22	28	68
Ecuador	3,280	11	15	63
Peru	4,570	8	27	65
Venezuela	5,670	5	50	45
Colombia	7,040	13	30	57
Brazil	7,360	8	36	56
Mexico	8,430	4	27	69
Uruguay	8,400	6	27	67
Chile	9,190	11	34	56
Argentina	11,320	5	28	68

Source: (a) UNDP, Human Development Report, 2003; (b) World Bank, World Development Report (2003), pp. 238–39.

TABLE 8.3   Distribution of National Income, by Top/Bottom Quintiles (1-2) and Top Decile (3), for Selected Countries, Listed in Rank Reverse Order by Per-Capita Income Levels, 1993

HDI Rank[1]		Poorest		Richest		% Poor Households (1999)
		10%	20%	10%	20%	
34	Argentina[2]	2.3	6.0	36.7	51.6	16
40	Uruguay	2.1	7.2	31.7	41.5	6
43	Chile	1.3	4.4	45.6	54.9	17
55	Mexico	1.3	5.2	41.7	49.0	38
64	Colombia	1.1	3.9	46.1	54.8	49
65	Brazil	0.7	3.0	48.0	61.6	30
69	Venezuela	0.8	4.0	31.5	47.8	44
97	Ecuador	2.2	4.8	33.8	51.2	58
114	Bolivia	1.3	5.1	31.0	49.5	55

Sources: World Bank, World Development Report, 2003; ECLAC, Statistical Yearbook for Latin America and the Caribbean, 2002.
Notes:
1. The UNDP in its annual report (2002) ranks 175 countries according to their level of "human development," an index (HDI) that aggregates and weights the score of each country on (i) GDP (national income) per capita, measured in terms of 'purchasing power parity' (PPP) rather than official currency exchange rates; (ii) longevity, measured in terms of life expectancy; and (iii) level and quality of education, an indicator of a person's capacity of choice in their life.
2. By 2001, with an increase of the unemployment rate to over 20% under conditions of the country's worst economic crisis since the 1930s depression, Argentina's official poverty rate (% of households in poverty—below the poverty line) doubled from 18 to 36%. Across Latin America the poverty rate, which for the region in the mid 1980s was estimated by ECLAC at 44%, in most countries improved in the first half of the 1990s, an evident response to a mild recovery in the rate of economic growth in the region as well as efforts in many countries to implement a new social policy. In the second half of the decade, however, with a renewed region-wide propensity towards crisis, sluggish growth rates began to fall, income distributions worsened and rates of poverty resumed their upward climb, although nowhere as dramatically as in Argentina.

TABLE 8.4   Latin American Class Structure in the 1990s (% distribution of the EAP)

	Urban		*Rural*
Capitalist Class	4		2
Middle Class			
Professional/Bureaucratic	6		2
Business Operators	10		4
Independent producers (small/medium)			12
Working Class			
Formal	20		15
Informal	60	(Semiproletariat)	35
Agricultural Producers			
Small/Medium Size			12
Peasant			30

Source: These very rough estimates of the class distribution of the population in Latin America are based on official labor force data provided by ECLAC in its annual Statistical Yearbook (2002) and the ILO in its annual publication, World Employment Report (2002). It is not possible to accurately gauge the class structure because official labor force data distribute the population on the basis of an industrial and occupational classification that does not correspond to the structure of class relations.

an individual's economic activity and share of society's productive resources or wealth, as well as the income derived from ownership of or access to this wealth, is directly related to the individual's position within the social structure.

Within the economic and social system in place throughout Latin America and elsewhere, income is a critically important determinant of an individual's— and a household's—"life chances" (to use a term coined by Max Weber). Most people require money or income for meeting their basic needs, and the major source of this income is work, either for wages or a salary (employment) or on one's own account (self-employment) or commodity production (the direct production of goods and services for sale). In every Latin American society, with the exception of Cuba, there exists a class of individuals who receive income in the form of rent or profit derived from their ownership of property or some means of social production. Most people, however, have to work for a living. That is, they are part of the working class, dispossessed of land or any other means of production and thus dependent on the sale of their labor. Table 4 provides a graphic, if theoretical, representation of the class structure of Latin American society and of the position of workers and producers within this structure.

The Latin American Social Structure

To gauge the social and political forces that are generated in support of or in resistance to the neoliberal (market-oriented) economic reforms implemented in the 1980s, it is important to examine the underlying social structure. Changes in this structure since the reforms in the 1980s have had a significant impact on the politics of economic reform—on the forces that have been mobilized in support of or opposition to the SAPs. The restructuring has also produced changes in class relations and associated conditions, mobilizing social forces for change.

The major element of this structure is the relationship of capital to labor, which encompasses both those who own and control the means of production and those who have been dispossessed of all means of production except for the capacity to work, which they have to exchange for a wage. In addition to these two basic classes, several classes of individuals occupy a position somewhere in between or located entirely outside the structure of the wage-labor relation. The most important of these is composed of individuals who own some means of production, physical and tangible or mental and intangible, but who are not in a position to purchase the labor power of the direct producers. These individuals are generally viewed as part of the traditional "middle class" or strata, sharing this position with intellectuals, professionals, and low-level managers of capitalist or public enterprises.

The Capitalist Class

Members of the capitalist class are easy enough to identify by the size of their capital (big, medium, small) and by functional criteria (industrial, commercial, financial, rentier), as well as by the perquisites of their position, such as wealth and power. Estimates as to the size of the capitalist class range from a low of 3 percent in countries like Bolivia to 5–6 percent for Argentina, Brazil, Chile, and Mexico, and with a weighted regional average of under 5 percent of the "economically active population" (EAP). The category of "employer" in Table 4 provides a rough (and admittedly poor) proxy measure of this class, assuming that the capitalist sector is about two-thirds of all employers and that the vast majority of these employers dispose of very little capital. In fact, the core of the capitalist class is composed of people who derive most if not all of their "income" from investment. The population census lists these individuals—fewer than 1 percent of most national populations—in the category of financiers.

The core of this class is composed of individuals connected to the "big economic groups," a complex of banking, industrial, and agroexport conglomerates. In each country a core of such conglomerates can be identified, in addition to larger groupings (the new bourgeoisie) formed specifically as the result of the free market reforms implemented since the 1980s. It is possible in each country to identify various fractions and groupings within the dominant capitalist class on the basis of the source of their capital. For example, in Mexico and to various lesser degrees in other countries, there is a large and politically significant bureaucratic class formed on the basis of privileged access to state resources and its regulatory and other powers. This part of the Mexican bourgeoisie is internally divided into different factions and connected through ties of common interest to other fractions of the capitalist class, such as the industrialists, financiers, and bankers. In addition to these capitalists, there are groups of individuals who serve as CEOs of the transnational corporations that operate in each country or are connected to institutions such as the International Monetary Fund (IMF). They form a powerful faction of the capitalist class as a whole, with resources and connections that constitute a significant factor in the internal and political dynamics of the class struggle.

Policies instituted in the 1980s created the basis of several other elements of the dominant capitalist class. Of particular significance is the large-scale privatization of public enterprises undertaken by many regimes. In the case of Mexico, the privatization of over a thousand state enterprises under the administration of Carlos Salinas from 1989 to 1994 spawned a number of enormous private fortunes, which are reflected in the identification by *Forbes* in 1993 of twenty-four billionaires in Mexico, more than the number for all of Latin America just two years earlier. These billionaires, together with their not-quite-so-wealthy associates (the thousands of mere millionaires created in the economic reform process), form the core of the region's new bourgeoisie, a propertied and entrepreneurial class that is well connected to the local political establishments as well as to the international financial institutions (IFIs) and multinational corporations that dominate the global economy. This bourgeoisie forms a part, albeit subordinate, of what the sociologist Leslie Sklair has termed the "transnational capitalist class."

The Middle Class

Important sources of the middle class have been the holding of land for the purpose of agricultural production and the operation of small businesses, mostly in the urban centers. Although these two components of the middle class vary significantly by country and have been subject to forces that have tended to decimate them, they remain numerically—and politically—important in most countries. The expansion of corporate capital has had a negative impact on the conditions of existence and survival of both the independent smallholders of land and urban-centered businesses. The specific impact of the government's economic policies on their enterprises and activities is more difficult to gauge. What is clear is that in every country a large number of small businesses and landholdings—over 50 percent in many cases—involve very marginal economic operations, microenterprises, the owners of which are barely able to survive in what is called "the informal sector." In this connection it is possible to distinguish between the formal petite bourgeoisie (the traditional middle class) and an informal petite bourgeoisie, which, it has been estimated, composes 10 percent or so of the region's economically active population (EAP).

Another element of the middle class is often self-identified as "professionals." These individuals provide a broad range of intellectual services, from the semiprofessional services of teachers, technicians, social workers, bureaucrats, and managers of office work to the professional and high-level management and business services provided by the legion of well-paid functionaries (of capital as well as government). A number of sociologists view these high-level functionaries and managers of capitalist and state enterprise as a distinct class (professional-technical/bureaucratic) that, it is estimated, constitutes an estimated 6–8 percent of the EAP in most countries. This is probably a fair estimate if restricted to the upper stratum of paid functionaries and distinguished from the two other major elements of the middle class—small proprietors (independent producers and business operators) and lower-level paid functionaries (salaried employees in public and private enterprises, semiprofessionals, and intellectuals).

The size of this social category in different societies is difficult to measure, largely because of the ambiguity of their position in the class structure. As salaried employees, they can also be regarded as part of the working class—as its white-collar element concerned with some form of mental or nonphysical labor. In any case, whether viewed as a stratum of the middle class or of the working class, these individuals probably make up 10–15 percent of the economically active population. In Table 4 they are subsumed under the formal working class, with no attempt to differentiate among different categories of stratification or possible political divisions—manual and mental, waged and salaried, urban and rural, private and public sector, male and female, organized and unorganized.

Whether or not any of these categories relate to political differences is a matter of empirical analysis. A cursory look at the political responses to SAPs suggests that there is a strong element of resistance and opposition from groups tied to the education system, state enterprises, and the bureaucracy. Individuals and groups in this public sector have been seriously affected by policies of privatization and the cutback of the state apparatus. To a considerable but varying degree in different countries, neoliberal policies have produced a bifurcation of this class, with some elements doing well and accommodated to the neoliberal agenda and other elements doing poorly and disposed toward resistance. In a number of contexts, like Argentina and Mexico, this class constitutes an important if not critical factor in the dynamics of social change.

The Working Classes

The working class comprises the vast majority of the population, but it takes diverse forms and in many countries it has been substantially restructured as a result of policy-induced and political conditions associated with SAPs. A sharp distinction has traditionally been made between wage laborers and those who work on their own account or without pay (housewives and unpaid family members). In the context of developments since the 1980s, the latter has assumed a growing proportion of the working class in all countries.

The Formal Sector.   Together with the big and the petite bourgeoisie, these workers make up the so-called modern sector of the economy, which accounts for an estimated 30 percent of the regional EAP. Estimates as to the size of this class fluctuate widely but essentially define three categories of countries: the Southern Cone (Argentina, Chile, Uruguay), where the formal proletariat represents a clear majority of the EAP; an intermediate grouping of countries (Brazil, Costa Rica, Panama, Peru) in which this class amounts to at least one-fourth of the EAP; and the rest of Latin America, where it represents on average barely 10 percent of the population.

In the 1960s and 1970s, these workers formed the social base of organized labor, which in each country led the struggle against capital for better wages and conditions of work. And in the 1970s, in the context of a region-wide (indeed worldwide) counteroffensive by capital, this class was also the chief target of state repression, of the "dirty war" against subversives waged by the "national security" military regimes that took state power all over the region. In the 1980s' context of a region-wide debt crisis, the institution of market-friendly reforms, and a re-democratization process, the formal proletariat also bore the brunt of efforts to restructure the economy and the society. In this process, the industrial proletariat in the private sector, the backbone of the labor movement, was severely retrenched and in some cases decimated. From 1988 to 1992, these industries lost 1.3 million workers, a trend that continued throughout the 1990s. As a result of these developments, the industrial proletariat was reduced to but a shadow of what it had once been—decimated numerically, weakened organizationally, and everywhere on the defensive, with a weak leadership accommodated to tripartite or corporatist arrangements, unable to mount any effective campaign or to mobilize the significant potential political forces of labor against capital.

By the end of the 1980s, public sector employees and workers constituted an important part of both the working class and the labor movement. This was the result of a several-decades-long process of state-led development in infrastructure and social services as well as of the nationalization of enterprises in strategic industries such as oil. However, a key element of the "new economic model" of structural adjustment to the requirements of a single global economy (globalization) was a policy of privatization—turning over (or returning) public enterprises to the private sector (profit-making). Carlos Salinas Gortari, president of Mexico from 1988 to 1994, turned over 1,100 public enterprises to the private sector, effectively privatizing all of the public enterprises in the key sectors of the economy—with the exception of electric power generation and the extraction and processing of oil. In the 1990s, the other political regimes in the region, notably in Argentina and Brazil, the two other biggest economies in the region (with Mexico, accounting for up to 75 percent of the gross regional product), followed suit. By the end of the decade, the privatization agenda was so advanced as to considerably weaken the public sector of the labor movement both numerically and politically.

The Informal Sector. The largest component of the working class, representing in many countries up to 40 percent of the labor force and as much as 70 percent of workers, the informal proletariat is characterized by a diverse mix of production relations: irregular and nonstandard forms of wage labor for operators of small and unstable enterprises; part-time or casual labor without the benefit and protection of a legal contract; wage labor for subcontractors; self-employment (namely, the operation of unregulated micro-enterprises producing or selling goods and services from the home, in makeshift workplaces, and in the streets); domestic services to middle-class and bourgeois households; and an array of illegal activities ranging from petty thievery, burglary, and smuggling to the manufacture, distribution, and sale of drugs. By all accounts the size of this class, combined with the small-firm sector, has been on the rise, increasing its share of the EAP from less than a third in the early 1980s to over half of the occupied labor force in the late 1990s. According to Alejandro Portes, et al. (1989) and studies by the International Labor Organization, in a number of countries the informal sector accounted for up to 80 percent of job and employment growth over the past decade and a half.

The Peasantry and the Rural Proletariat

As a region, Latin America is highly urbanized, overly so in relation to the capacity of industry to absorb the large numbers of individuals dispossessed of productive land or otherwise led to migrate to the rapidly growing towns and cities. In the postwar period, a large part of the rural population was pushed into the towns and cities and converted into an urban proletariat. This process also led to the formation of a huge sector of informal enterprises and activities.

At the same time, in the countryside, an even more complex structure of economic activities and relations of production evolved. This sector incorporated various classes of producers and workers, including both middle-class and capitalist operators of farms and businesses; a rural proletariat composed of wageworkers in these sectors; a large class of smallholders, composed of individuals and households involved in farming or work under diverse relations of subsistence, independent commodity production, sharecropping, and other forms of tenancy (including, as in the case of indigenous communities in Bolivia, Ecuador, Guatemala, and Mexico, various forms of communal tenure); the semi-proletariat, who make up the majority of direct producers in most countries; and large numbers of landless workers, in the case of Brazil totaling up to 4.2 million families.

Although the EAP includes large numbers of children under working age, elders, retirees, the disabled, and other dependents, it also includes an equally large number of individuals, mostly women, whose contribution to either or both domestic and social production is not accounted for and whose labor is not remunerated at all. The majority of rural households have at least one member in this position, accounting for a significant number—perhaps 25 percent of the entire rural population.

The expansion of capitalism in the countryside has resulted in variations of this class structure. In addition, it has generated various processes of change within this structure: the transformation of the hacienda system of tenant farming into capitalist farming and agribusiness—what the Inter-American Development Bank (IDB) defines as "the entrepreneurial sector of commercial enterprises"; the growth of temporary, casual, and seasonal forms of wage labor; the feminization of rural wage labor; and the urbanization of this labor.

THE SOCIAL IMPACTS OF ECONOMIC REFORMS

The announcement by the Mexican government in the summer of 1982 that it was unable to pay the interest on its accumulated external debt sent shock waves throughout the community of international finance. Mexico was not alone. Widespread structural conditions of extraordinarily high interest rates and plummeting export commodity prices threatened the entire fabric of global capital. However, the international financial institutions, under the guardianship of the IMF, rallied in defense of the system.

The solution, imposed on or adopted by country after country in the region (most often imposed as a condition of renegotiation of their debts or of accessing new capital in the form of loans, aid or investment), was a program of market-oriented economic reforms or structural adjustments. The stated goal of this program was growth and macroeconomic equilibrium (restoration of growth in the total output of goods and services under conditions of balanced budgets, the control of price inflation). There are, however, major unstated goals of these sweeping reforms, including making sure of the capacity of countries in the region to "service" (make payments on) their external debts. But the major internal adjustment has been a restructuring of labor, particularly in regard to its share of national income and increased "flexibility." As to labor's share of national income (as opposed to the share that goes to capital, that is, that is invested rather than consumed or used to purchase goods and services), most countries in the region have experienced a significant reduction—from 30 percent and greater (up to 40 percent in some cases) down to 20 percent and less. These declines in the share of labor in national income signify a corresponding increase in the share given to or appropriated by capital—presumably in the interest of increasing the rate of national investment, deemed to be the most critical factor in a process of economic activation.

The social cost of this process of structural adjustment has been exceedingly high: a deepening and extension of poverty, the conditions of which (unemployment, informalization of work, economic insecurity, falling wages, low income, homelessness, malnutrition, disease, illiteracy) have been borne mainly by the working class. A large part of this class has been impoverished in the process, as has a part of the middle class. In addition, there are significant gender as well as class and national ethnic dimensions to poverty and other conditions of structural adjustment. In terms of the basic indicators of social development, Cuba, the one Latin American country that has pursued a socialist rather than a capitalist path, stands out as a striking anomaly, with levels of education, health, and welfare comparable to the most industrially developed countries in the world. The UNDP's *Human Development Report* (2003) provides a clear testament to this.

By the early 1980s, after three and a half decades of sustained economic and social change, the material conditions of social existence for the majority of the Latin American population had substantially improved. In the 1980s, however, under conditions of a widespread debt crisis and structural adjustment, these gains were wiped out. With a fall of up to 60 percent in the value of wages or purchasing power in a matter of just a few years, the life situation of most people in the region seriously deteriorated.

Despite a minimal and fragile "recovery" after close to a decade of sweeping economic reforms, in many countries the average level of income and standard of living in the 1990s was lower than it was in 1970. Under conditions that include growth in unemployment, informalization of labor relations, a drastic decline in the value of wages, and cutbacks in government services and social programs, the structural adjustment to which the economies in the region were subjected led to a substantial worsening in the distribution of wealth and income, already among the most unequal and inequitable in the world. The gap between the incomes of the poorest households and the richest widened and deepened, in some cases dramatically. Today in every country in the region the top decile of income earners receive over 30 percent of the national income— 48 percent in the case of Brazil, which, according to the World Bank, exhibits one of the most skewed distributions of income in the world. Worldwide, only Sierra Leone is disgraced by a greater maldistrbution of income, although in Sierra Leone's case, unlike developments in Brazil (see Petras and Veltmeyer, 2003), government policies cannot be held responsible. Also, the decline in both the share of labor in national income and the purchasing power of workers' wages over the years, as well as the loss of employment opportunities in most countries, had a particularly strong impact on those at the bottom of the income pyramid and class structure. The overall result has been a significant increase in income inequalities for most countries in the region.

These inequalities have produced striking differences in social situations for different groups and classes of the population. At one extreme they have spawned a small number of billionaires, whose combined wealth exceeds that of half of the population and whose conditions of social existence are almost unimaginable and certainly obscene. At the other extreme, the grossly unequal distribution of wealth and income is reflected in a widening and deepening poverty. The population living in poverty substantially increased over the course of the 1980s, declined somewhat in the early 1990s, but as of 1995, with the beginnings of another "decade lost to development," has moved steadily upward. By the end of the decade, according to some estimates (see Table 8.3), over a third of all households—58 percent in the case of Ecuador— were impoverished to the point of their members being unable to meet their basic needs. Most of these households are located in the urban centers, although the incidence of poverty is higher in the rural areas, home to the landless and near landless, masses of marginal small landholders and producers, and most indigenous peoples, who form 10 percent or so of the population in the region (up to and more than 50 percent in countries like Ecuador, Bolivia, and

Guatemala). Typically, this element of the population suffers the most blatant forms of exploitation and oppression and the resulting conditions of abject poverty.

THE DYNAMICS OF CLASS STRUGGLE: POLITICAL RESPONSES TO NEOLIBERAL REFORM

Over the years, there has been a recurring debate as to the social base and political dynamics of social movements for change in the region. However, the policies and conditions of structural adjustment have recast some of the issues involved, especially as they relate to the popular sector of civil society. But two important questions remain. One is whether the objective and subjective conditions of struggle, resistance, and protest are structural and class-based or are based on localized issues and the politics of "identity," defined by gender, ethnicity, and other culturally specific struggles. A second contested area has to do with the specific structural source of the conditions that have given rise to social movements and the politics of resistance and social protest.

Apart from the problem of determining how relations of exploitation and social exclusion fit in the social structure of Latin American societies, the political conditions of these relations—the social and political forces that have been generated—are not clear. Forms of popular resistance and political protest and the conditions that produced them need further study. Some preliminary results of such a study are briefly summarized below.

Work on One's Own Account
The dramatic growth of the informal sector reflects decisions made by members of income-poor households (often recent rural emigrants) in the failed search for income-generating employment. These decisions are generally shaped by conditions over which their agents have absolutely no control and that provide few if any options. In other words, they represent a survival strategy, a defensive response to the economic and social conditions of poverty—the deprivation of basic needs. Household members are generally constrained to provide labor power, or the products of their self-organized labor, at a level of remuneration well below its value. As for the women in these households, their rate of exploitation tends to be considerably higher than that for men, given their general responsibility for housework and childcare, which, when added to their compensated labor, often leads to working days of twelve to sixteen hours, or seventy to eighty work-hour weeks.

However, as a household "strategy," self-exploitative informal economic activities, even with all members participating, generally have not enabled the household to meet its basic needs for food, nutrition, shelter, clothing, education, and human development. As a result, in the context of deepening economic crisis and adjustment, the female heads of some of these income-poor urban households in the 1980s came together to pool their limited resources and cooperate in the provision for these needs. Such inter-household forms of cooperation and association can be found in most shantytowns in cities such as Lima, Mexico City, Sao Paulo, Rio de Janeiro, Santiago, and Guayaquil. According to some theorists these households have created a new form of economy—a "social economy" that does not make use of, or rely on, money, but on barter, free labor, and relations of solidarity.

The Popular Economy: Community-Based Cooperation

In Lima in 1979, a number of *comedores populares* (popular canteens/dining halls/soup kitchens) were set up and cooperatively run by a group of around fifty women from income-poor shantytown households. By 1982 there were already an estimated 1,500 such organizations, in addition to 6,500 or so "glass of milk" committees that brought together and serviced over 100,000 households. In Santiago similar forms of popular economic organization (PEO), the *ollas comunes* (communal soup pots) and community soup kitchens, were formed on the basis of various associations of women in *las poblaciones,* as they are called in Chile (each country describes them in the same way but in different words—*ranchos, favelas, villas de miseria,* and so on), the shantytowns that surrounded the city. Such associations existed in Chile in the early 1970s, but under conditions created by the sweeping free-market reforms of the Pinochet regime and the worst economic crisis in the region, they proliferated. In 1982, when the country was in the throes of another economic crisis, there were thirty-four *ollas comunes* in Santiago; by 1988, fifteen years into the Pinochet regime, there were 232 of them. In the 1980s, entire networks of such popular organizations, based on associations of women, were formed throughout the shantytowns. In addition to the *ollas comunes,* they included self-help groups, production workshops (small units with three to fifteen people producing and selling goods and services such as bread, clothing, laundry, carpentry), organizations for the unemployed, housing committees, committees for the homeless, and organizations related to housing problems such as water and electricity.

Similar women's organizations of the urban poor were formed in Brazil, Mexico, and other countries in the region subject to the same conditions of crisis and adjustment or austerity measures. By taking charge in this manner, the women of poor working-class households have come to feel collectively stronger and more self-reliant. In a number of cases, the civil society organizations (CSOs) have also provided a grassroots base for mobilizing resistance to the austerity and repressive policies of military regimes in the 1970s and the equally repressive economic policies of many neoliberal governments in the 1980s and 1990s. In this context, these CSOs represent the transition made by some associations of the urban poor from community action to collective protest. However, they also form the social base of an option, an alternative to collective protest and the formation of social movements, made available and presented to the poor by the "overseas development associations" (ODAs) and governments. The option: participatory development in the form of local development—projects implemented in the community by a growing army of nongovernmental organizations (NGOs) enlisted in the cause of turning popular organizations away from a confrontationalist politics (direct action) to a new politics of dialogue, consultation, and participation in public policy.

From Community Development to Street Protest

It is difficult to distinguish between forms of community-based cooperative actions and collective forms of resistance and to see where the former end and the latter begin. But in the context of spreading reforms, worsening socioeconomic conditions, and military rule, the urban poor took to the streets and moved from collective community action to collective forms of protest, including rioting and demonstrations. There is no question about the effectiveness and political impact of these collective acts of protest. In the outburst of political protest from 1983 to 1986, the urban poor were center stage, and working women were among the first to protest the regressive and repressive free-market policies. Unionized workers, in contrast, were slow to respond and took their cue from the urban poor. And the intellectuals and politicos associated with the traditional parties were even slower to react and were manifestly ineffective in attempts to direct the self-mobilized forces of the urban poor, who in specific situations were joined in their struggles by unionized workers, students, teachers, public employees, shopkeepers, and other elements of an impoverished middle class.

A widely documented form of overt resistance and protest against neoliberal policies of stabilization and structural adjustment is the *riot*—the spontaneous outbreak of street protests against publicly announced increases in the price of food, gasoline, kerosene, or means of transportation. In the contemporary context of debt and adjustment, the first recorded street riots occurred as early as 1976 in Peru. In subsequent years there were sporadic outbreaks in various countries and a veritable wave of riots in 1982–1983 in Argentina, Bolivia, Brazil, Chile, Ecuador, and Panama. The forty-nine recorded riots in these years (fifty-two if we add the riots of 1984 in the Dominican Republic) represented more than one-third of all recorded riots worldwide at the time. A second wave of rioting hit the region in 1985–1986, followed by a series of riots in Venezuela in 1989 that left over 300 dead.

The immediate trigger of these riots both initially in the 1980s, and more generally in the 1990s and into the twenty-first century, is beyond dispute: They are invariably in response to policy measures attributed by the rioters themselves to the IMF, often the symbolic if not immediate target of protest. In this connection, rioters and protesters tend to be manifestly unsympathetic to the efforts of various Latin American governments "to get prices right" by cutting or eliminating subsidies and price controls or other such austerity measures. In some countries, including Ecuador (January 2001) and Argentina (December 2001) rioting and protests against such policies have brought down governments; in other cases the government was forced to retreat from the neoliberal agenda, which included both austerity measures (eliminating subsidies, cutting social programs), liberalization of trade (opening up local markets to overseas competitors), and the privatization of public enterprises.

Riots are but one of a number of politically overt forms of resistance and acts of street protest against austerity measures. They have often been combined with other tactics, such as mass demonstrations, marches on public buildings, encampments, land occupations, roadblocks, hunger strikes, boycotts, work stoppages, nonattendance at work or school, and labor strikes (the traditional and well-tried tactic of organized labor), as well as civic strikes. A most effective tactic used by indigenous peasant farmers in Bolivia and Ecuador, and more recently by unemployed workers in Argentina, has been *cortas de ruta*— cutting off and barricading highway and other transportation access to economic activity.

These acts of resistance and protest are significant in that they bring together diverse groups and classes in the popular sector, and lead to concerted action. An example of such concerted action took place in Ecuador in 1994, when an association of urban women, the Federation of Trade Unions, and the National Association of Indigenous Peoples took to the streets in a carefully orchestrated and scheduled series of marches, mass demonstrations, and strikes. Similar associations were formed in other countries in response to the same conditions. For example, after the devaluation of the Mexican peso in December 1994, more than 1,200 demonstrations and 550 marches—a daily average of five acts of protest—were organized in Mexico City in the space of a year. On one day alone (March 10, 1995), there were over 100 separate acts of protest. This wave of street protests was followed by the formation of a huge coalition of diverse social movements and organizations of farmers, peasants, independent business operators, workers, and nongovernmental organizations (NGOs) that came together to reject the government's economic model, which has generated only misery and unemployment. For the past five years in Argentina the streets in popular neighborhoods have been veritable cauldrons of protest, bringing together families of unemployed workers with other workers and groups in the popular sector in a common struggle against the source of their oppression— most often neoliberal policies of structural adjustment and globalization.

Workplace Protest and Resistance

In the context of widespread economic restructuring, the Latin American working class no longer is what it once was. A traditional stratum of full-time workers remains in place, strategically situated in various expanding industries, well organized to defend and advance their collective interests, able to negotiate collective contracts with managers of capitalist enterprises and to engage in effective workplace strike action. However, in the 1990s, such workers were in the minority. Where found they tended to be very much on the defensive, with a weakened capacity for collective action in an inhospitable if not hostile environment and with an accommodating and compromised leadership, disposed to engage in tripartite pacts with business and government.

Under these conditions, the politics of resistance by workers in the formal sector of capitalist firms, public institutions, and remaining state enterprises tends to take different forms than before. Class struggle still involves strikes and electoral activity, but resistance to and protest against government policies of structural adjustment are now more likely to take the form of street demonstrations, mass rallies, and marches on government buildings, as well as takeover of factories. Currently up to 200 factories have been occupied and taken over by the workers in the industrial cities of Argentina.

It is clear that many workers remain opposed to the neoliberal agenda, as evident in the mass actions of workers all across the region throughout the 1990s. In Bolivia, almost every year since 1995, public sector workers and other workers organized by the powerful Workers' Central, the Central de Obreros de Bolivia (COB), have orchestrated multiple mass actions, including declarations of a general strike, with the *cocaleros* and other indigenous peasant organizations, with major popular mobilizations against efforts of the political class to extend the privatization agenda. Despite the understanding reached between the COB and the government in 1995, which led among other things to the end of a fifty-day teachers' strike, organizations of affiliated workers affirmed their commitment "to continue the struggle against neoliberal policies." In the same year similar commitment was expressed by over 150,000 workers in Mexico City on May Day in a massive rally against the government's privatization policy as well as an announced 50 percent increase in the value-added tax (VAT), and other elements of the government's neoliberal program. If anything, protest actions by workers and direct producers in different sectors over the years in Bolivia, Ecuador, Mexico, and elsewhere have increased in number if not in intensity. Such protest brought down the Bolivian government in 2003. The Confederation of Indigenous Nationalities of Ecuador (CONAIE) planned for January 2004 a massive mobilization of the most diverse social and political forces of resistance against the government's neoliberal policies. Key sectors of organized labor were involved in this exercise in popular democracy

No government in the region adopted the neoliberal program of policy reforms with such avidity as Carlos Menem's regime in Argentina in the 1990s. By 1998, however, Menem's policies, regarded by the World Bank as a model for other countries in the region to follow, brought about an economic crisis of momentous proportions, reflected in the official unemployment rate that grew from under 7 percent early in the decade to over 20 percent in 2002—up to 60 percent in some areas. Another consequence of the crisis was the impoverishment not only of the working class but of one half of what had once been the most powerful middle class in Latin America—"the new poor." In December 19–20, 2001, the growing economic crisis reached explosive proportions, bringing together a growing movement of unemployed workers and the pot-banging, income-impoverished middle-class employees, service professionals and para-professionals, and business operators. In a matter of weeks up to four governments were brought down, workers took over and occupied hundreds of factories, and unemployed workers and their families increased the pace of their *cortas de ruta*, cutting off and blockading major transportation routes in an effort to force the governments to institute short-term work projects and deal with a variety of demands by an increasingly restive population. The country was caught up in what could be seen as a "pre-revolutionary situation"—somewhere between the worst recession in Argentina's history and the rapid growth and mobilization of a new community-based movement of unemployed workers.

Protest and Resistance in the Countryside

The penetration of capitalism into the countryside has been associated with a number of developments, including the transformation of the hacienda system of tenant labor into a wage-labor-based system of agroexport production; a crisis in peasant agriculture based on communal forms of land tenure; the expulsion of many proletarianized producers from the land, leading to a massive out-migration from the countryside to the urban centers; and a marked increase in temporary and seasonal forms of wage labor in the agricultural sector, with a significant gender dimension.

The combination of these developments has had a decided impact on the political capacity of workers and producers in the countryside and on the form of their organized resistance. For one thing, noted changes in employment practices toward more casual, precarious, and feminized forms of "flexible" labor have tended to increase the control of capital and the bargaining power of employers vis-à-vis labor. For another, the casualization of rural labor has contributed to the fracturing of a well-established and at times militant peasant movement. Although seasonal and casual laborers can be highly militant, they are notoriously difficult to organize, in part because of their mixed composition and shifting residence. As for the mass of landless workers that has been generated, the pressures to migrate and the possibilities of doing so have also undercut their capacity to organize and fight in the countryside.

At the same time, throughout the countryside conditions of capital accumulation and policies of structural adjustment have spawned numerous associations of producers and workers, organized with the objective of resistance and political protest. The central issue for these organizations has been to agree on a form of struggle appropriate to their conditions and for which resources and cross-class support can be generated. The internal debates on this issue have been long and were relatively inconsequential until the January 1994 outbreak of armed insurrection in Chiapas. Among the highland peoples in the area, such uprisings have not been unusual, this one having been in the works since the early 1980s. But in Chiapas on January 1, 1994, a number of distinct but interrelated processes led to the formation of the Zapatista Army of National Liberation.

The demands of the Zapatistas relate to conditions generated by economic and political structures that are deeply embedded in the history of the state's indigenous peoples, but a subsequent declaration by subcomandante Marcos, the official spokesperson for the Clandestine Revolutionary Indigenous Committee, points to the right of rebellion against the inhumane and unjust policies of neoliberalism. In this declaration, the Zapatistas threatened to march on Mexico to press their demands, a similar approach to that taken by indigenous peoples in both Bolivia and Ecuador. In Bolivia the blockade of highways and mass marches on La Paz in 1993 and again in 1995 came in response to the call by the federation of organized urban workers for support of their struggle. However, in Mexico, as in Ecuador, there was no such call. It was the action of indigenous peoples that provoked the response of urban workers, leading to widespread mobilization and the creation of a social movement in solidarity with the Zapatista struggle in Chiapas and with similar struggles waged by indigenous peoples and peasant producers elsewhere. In January 2001 the indigenous uprising in Ecuador not only brought down the government but managed to take it over, holding all the reins of state power via a triumvirate that represented the rebellious indigenous peasants of the country, a coalition of organized workers and social groups led by the state oil workers, and the armed forces. This popular government only lasted a matter of hours, but the message resounded in all of the corridors of political power across Latin America: Workers and peasants in the popular sector were on the march—a long march toward liberation, democracy, and state power.

Conclusion

The social structure of Latin American society is fraught with problems that bear most heavily on the working class. The nature of these problems can best be understood in terms of economic policies that governments in the region have instituted at the behest of "capital," that is, a U.S.-dominated "transnational capitalist class." These policies, packaged and presented as the "structural adjustment program," relate to an agenda of this class to create a single global capitalist economy and to integrate countries across the world into it.

Widespread implementation of this agenda over the past two decades has brought about a radically different Latin America from the one that had been in the works. The resulting society is characterized by class divisions that need to be analyzed in both economic and political terms. In economic terms we can identify conditions of economic exploitation and social exclusion that have led to a serious regression in the life chances of most people. At issue in these life chances is the growth of poverty and deepening social inequalities in access to society's productive resources and in the distribution of the incomes generated by these resources.

However, the same process that generated these conditions has also generated forces of opposition and resistance to the agenda of the dominant and ruling class. In political terms it is possible to discern the emergence of social movements designed to mobilize the forces of opposition and resistance. These movements take diverse forms and require further study. However, it is clear enough that their political dynamics derive from conditions of class relations and not from the localized politics of gender and ethnic identity, as some would argue. In the context of these conditions found in most countries in Latin America, the widespread and multiform politics of protest and social movements of opposition and resistance respond to the social costs of structural adjustment, the conditions of which have been catastrophic for the majority of the working population. This is clear enough. However, what needs further study are the dynamics of political opposition to these conditions—the dynamics of class struggle. This is where sociology comes in. Or it should do so.

Suggested Readings

ECLAC—United Nations' Economic Commission for Latin America and the Caribbean. *Statistical Yearbook of Latin America and the Caribbean.* Santiago, 2002.

Petras, James, and Henry Veltmeyer. *Cardoso's Brazil: A Land for Sale.* Boulder, Colo: Rowman & Littlefield, 2003.

_____. *System in Crisis: The Dynamics of Free Market Capitalism.* London: Zed Books/Halifax: Fernwood Books, 2003.

Portes, Alejandro et al., eds. *The Informal Economy: Studies in Advanced and Less Developed Countries.* Baltimore: John Hopkins University Press, 1989.

Saney, Isaac. *Cuba: A Revolution in Motion.* London: Zed Books/Halifax: Fernwood Books, 2003.

Sklair, Leslie. "Social Movements for Global Capitalism: The Transnational Capitalist Class in Action." *Review of International Political Economy,"* 2, 3 (1997).

UNDP—United Nations Development Programme. *Human Development Report.* New York: Oxford University Press, 2003.

Veltmeyer, Henry, and James Petras. *The Dynamics of Social Change in Latin America.* London: Macmillan Press, 2000.

World Bank. *World Development Report.* New York: Oxford University Press, 2003.

Chapter 9

EMERGING SOCIAL MOVEMENTS AND GRASSROOTS CHANGE

WENDY MUSE SINEK

POPULAR PROTEST HAS EXPLODED in Latin America at the beginning of the twenty-first century. Since 2000, social movements in Brazil and Venezuela have been instrumental in electing leftist presidents to office, while presidents in Peru, Ecuador, Argentina, and Bolivia were unseated in part due to massive outpourings of grassroots discontent. Yet despite increased activism, traditional structures that facilitate popular sector political participation, most notably unions and labor-based parties, have weakened. Some analysts claim that this erosion demonstrates that ordinary people are alienated from the political process, but others take a different view, contending that community associations and social movements are becoming important actors in the political arena, supplementing more traditional structures of representation.

This chapter will expand on the latter perspective, introducing the reader to the many social movements that have emerged and crystallized as important political actors in Latin America since the 1990s. First, I discuss how changes in the region's economic models have weakened traditional structures of interest intermediation, creating political space that some social movements have attempted to fill. Then, I illustrate four issue areas around which emerging social movements in Latin America have coalesced and consider some of their most prominent expressions. Finally, to understand possible future trajectories of these movements, I outline some common predicaments that may be useful in thinking about the dynamics of change within social movements as they evolve.

ECONOMIC CHANGES AND GRASSROOTS REACTIONS

The question of popular representation arose in the twentieth century in Latin America as the new working classes sought to make their voices heard in the political arena. Two new institutions were created as a means of incorporating labor into the political system: unions and union-affiliated populist parties.[1] Albeit imperfectly, the working classes were in many respects able to express their demands through these structures. However, Latin America's economic context has changed markedly since the 1970s, and this has engendered profound social and political changes. Many of these effects are discussed elsewhere in this volume; here, I draw out the implications of these changes for social movements in Latin America. In short, links among unions, populist parties, and the lower classes do not function as well as they used to in representing the interests of ordinary people in the political sphere.

After World War II, many countries in Latin America followed an Import Substitution Industrialization (ISI) economic model, in which the economy was oriented toward producing goods for the domestic market to reduce dependence on foreign imports. Within this model, the goals of creating economic growth and meeting the demands of labor were not in conflict. Because workers were also consumers, it was in the interest of both labor and business to raise wages. As a result, there was space for class compromise, and labor-based parties, as well as business interests, were quite successful in gaining political and economic concessions from the state.

However, the onset of the debt crisis, along with problems inherent in this model of production, made ISI difficult to sustain. In 1973, members of the Organization of the Petroleum Exporting Countries (OPEC) increased the price of oil fourfold and deposited their rapidly expanded revenues in Western banks. In turn, the banks made numerous loans with extremely low interest rates to developing countries, especially those in Latin America, a region considered to be a low investment risk with great potential. For their part, Latin American countries borrowed heavily—not only to invest in domestic development projects, but also to fuel the ISI model with capital. However, OPEC raised oil prices again during the 1980s, and borrowing increased yet again, since countries needed to purchase oil and make payments on their debt. As the demand for loans increased, creditors became more cautious, and banks began making shorter-term loans at ever-higher interest rates. By 1982, this cycle of debt had snowballed into a crisis situation, and when Mexico announced that it could not meet the payments on its debt, lending throughout Latin America came to an abrupt halt.

As developing countries struggled to manage their debt burdens, international lending institutions often demanded liberal economic reforms, such as open markets, increased exports, and privatization, in exchange for debt restructuring. These economic transformations in Latin America have had some positive results: Short-term capital flows to the region have increased, competition is prevalent, and both production and consumption have become more efficient. Concurrently, aggregate measures of income have also increased.

Yet this wealth has not been widely shared. As of 2002, over 43 percent of all Latin American people were living in poverty, with nearly half that number considered extremely poor, and these levels are projected to rise as per capita GDP stagnates. Latin America also features the most unequal distribution of wealth and income in the world, and inequality rose in most South American countries during the 1990s. Moreover, the 2003 *Panorama Laboral* report from the International Labor Organization finds that working conditions in Latin

America have been deteriorating, and for the first time, there are slightly more workers in the informal labor sector (51 percent) than in the formal arena. Of every ten new jobs created since 1990, seven were located in the informal sector, and the vast majority of all new jobs lacked social benefits such as pensions and health care. Clearly, the region's economic recovery during the 1990s did not affect all Latin Americans in the same way.

One outcome of this economic shift has been the erosion of populist coalitions and union influence. When a nation's customers are located in the international arena instead of the domestic market, the state no longer needs to strengthen its national consumer base to facilitate economic growth. At the same time, as states increasingly rely on the international market for capital, greater attention is paid to protecting stable capital flows from international sources than to consolidating national economic markets. Moreover, states are encouraged by international lending organizations to become fiscally responsible by curtailing social spending, thus diminishing their capacity to implement and expand domestic benefits. As a result, the state no longer has the same incentives—or the same financial ability—to make concessions that benefit working class interests, and the space available for class compromise diminishes.

Relatedly, neoliberal reforms, such as privatization, have meant that, as firms downsize and gain in efficiency, the number of workers employed by the formal sector shrinks. With fewer workers in the formal economy, the potential membership pool for unions is decreasing, thereby diminishing organized labor's bargaining power. At the same time, informal workers and the unemployed—groups increasing in numbers—have their own grievances that are not often included in the demands of unionized workers. These changes have made labor-based parties less effective in representing the concerns of the working class.

In sum, the momentum in Latin America has shifted. The organizations that represented popular interests in the past hold less influence today. Yet the working classes, the unemployed, and the poor still want their voices heard within the political system. Moreover, economic policies of structural adjustment undertaken by states have negatively affected the economic well-being of many. Therefore, members of these less well-represented groups have taken matters into their own hands, and a resurgence of social-movement activity has been the result. Ordinary people have begun to organize, finding new ways of not only meeting their collective survival needs, but also advancing their interests within the political sphere. The following section gives an overview of four issues around which social movements have coalesced in the region: agrarian reform, urban community revitalization, unemployment, and indigenous and ethnic rights.

EMERGING SOCIAL MOVEMENTS IN LATIN AMERICA

Agrarian Reform

Highly unequal patterns of land tenure have existed in Latin America since colonial times, and small farmers have faced significant obstacles in terms of access to credit, capital, and markets for their agricultural products. However, agricultural modernization programs undertaken in the 1970s and 1980s have heightened these barriers. Abundant subsidized credit was often provided to large producers of export crops, and small farmers were slowly crowded out of the market. Moreover, most export products, such as soybeans and beef cattle, are generally much less labor-intensive than previous crops, and this reduction in the labor force left many agricultural laborers without steady employment. Also, since land was rapidly increasing in value, a greater percentage of land was left fallow for speculative purposes. These policy changes succeeded in modernizing the agricultural sector, but they also separated small farmers from resources and decisionmaking processes, and in some countries created a large contingent of impoverished landless rural workers.

In response, many peasants pressured their governments to dismantle large, unproductive landholdings and sell them for a nominal fee to those willing to farm them. Peasants also claim that a rural sector geared overwhelmingly toward the international export market increases Latin America's dependence on multinational corporations, raising the issue of "food sovereignty": the right of a nation to manage its domestic food production not only to meet the subsistence needs of its population, but also to allow the rural population a voice in making decisions about how food is produced. This perspective emphasizes preserving the livelihood of small farmers, engaging in environmentally sustainable cultivation methods, and selectively entering into trade agreements that promote these values, while opposing those that do not.

One of the largest, and arguably most influential, social movements in Latin America was organized in support of these goals: the Landless Rural Workers' Movement (MST) in Brazil. The social impact of agricultural modernization generated a crisis among Brazil's rural population, and the members of the MST—currently over one million strong—have been struggling since the 1980s to achieve agrarian reform. The organization's members have traditionally come from peasant communities, but within recent years the MST has increasingly drawn "second-generation" peasants: individuals who have migrated to the urban sector, but wish to return to their rural roots.

Since its founding in 1984, the MST, through engaging in land invasions, has pressured successive administrations to enact redistributive land reform. The MST organizes groups of landless peasants who enter large, unproductive estates and set up an encampment on or around the unused land. Conditions within the encampments are quite harsh; settlers live in makeshift tents of plastic and bamboo and sometimes raise crops for food with nothing more than their bare hands. Landowners have often resisted the MST's invasions, and in some cases have raised private militias to force the settlers to leave. Over 1,000 rural activists have died as a result of these confrontations, and recent data indicate that violence in the countryside is on the rise.[2] However, in many cases the landless remain encamped, and this has pressured the government to enact agrarian reform, distributing, as of August 2003, over 20 million acres of land to approximately 350,000 Brazilian families.

The movement for agrarian reform is active not only in Brazil; it has spread throughout Latin America, with organizations flourishing in Bolivia, Chile, Ecuador, Nicaragua, and Peru. Many of these local movements also participate in two international social movement organizations, the Latin American Co-ordinating Body of Peasant Organizations (CLOC) and *Vía Campesina*. These organizations provide a structure through which peasant activists can exchange ideas, strategies, and information. One of their main activities is coordinating events to commemorate the International Day of Farmers' Struggle on April 17 of each year.[3] In 2003, landless peasants in Brazil marched on state capital cities, peasant farmers in Colombia held an Agrarian Congress, indigenous activists in Ecuador launched a National Campaign for Food Sovereignty, farmers in El Salvador organized a forum with over 100 mayors to discuss environmentally sustainable agriculture, and Chilean farmers held activist training camps under the slogan "In Chile the Countryside Cannot Take it Any Longer." Many of these movements also seek to connect local agrarian interests with the international movement against the World Trade Organization and the expansion of free trade agreements that call for aggressive trade liberalization and privatization around the developing world.

Urban Community Revitalization

Social movements are also coalescing around issues of concern for impoverished urban communities. The wave of migration from rural areas to cities that could not support the population influx has led to hundreds of thousands of people settling in shantytowns on the edges of urban areas. At the same time, governments have often been persuaded to reduce domestic spending to meet their financial obligations to lending institutions. These fiscal constraints reduce or eliminate some public services on which many people have come to rely, such as regular garbage collection, transportation, health care, and public schools. As a result, in many Latin American cities, water supplies are erratic, sewage treatment is nonexistent, roads are in poor condition, and housing is scarce. Public safety is also a concern; the World Health Organization claims that as of late 2003, Latin America became the most violent region in the world. In response to these problems, grassroots activists have pressured governments at all levels to improve the quality of life in urban communities.

One urban movement attempting to address these issues is the Homeless Workers' Movement (*Movimento dos Trabalhadores Sem Teto*, MTST) in Brazil. Their members, nearly 300,000 poor urban families and growing, state on their website that they are "unemployed, homeless, and hungry, but most of all, we are excluded from political decisions that determine the course of our lives." The MTST asserts that about 74 million Brazilians, or 43 percent of the population, are either homeless or living in buildings that lack running water, electricity, and sanitation. To demonstrate the need for affordable housing and city services, the MTST occupies vacant and abandoned buildings. During the summer of 2003, MTST occupations took place throughout the country: in Recife, a former children's hospital was turned into makeshift apartments for eighty families, and in the state of São Paulo, 3,500 individuals created a shantytown in a vacant lot owned by Volkswagen. Although the police forced the homeless to evacuate on each occasion, in October 2003 the president of Brazil stated that he intended to transform unoccupied city buildings in São Paulo, Rio, and Belo Horizonte into affordable public housing.[4]

A similar movement is also active in Peru, and to a lesser extent Ecuador and Venezuela. Though they lack a formal unifying organization like the MTST, many poor families in the Andes have illegally seized land on the outskirts of major cities since the 1950s. Thousands of people might invade a site in the middle of the night, using scrap metal, lumber, and cardboard to build shelters and create a "squatter settlement" community. The following day, local authorities often bulldoze the settlement and evict the squatters, but determined families persist in setting up camp night after night until municipal governments finally capitulate. Over time, residents make improvements to their homes and employ a variety of strategies to pressure the municipal government to provide their community with city services, such as running water, garbage collection, and electricity.

Massive urban protests have also erupted over high prices for public services. In Bolivia, a condition of debt relief from the IMF required that the country privatize municipal water systems, and Bechtel Corporation purchased the water monopoly. However, this action tripled consumer prices for water within weeks, and continuous demonstrations were held for four months, from January to April 2000. Cities were shut down as roadblocks were erected and workers went on strike until the Bolivian government finally agreed to restore state control over the water system.

Grassroots activists are also attempting to curb widespread urban violence. The Brazilian NGO Viva Rio has been at the forefront of combating trafficking in small arms and improving life in the country's shantytowns. In August 2003, members of Viva Rio organized a public destruction of over 4,000 firearms confiscated from criminals, crushing some with a steamroller and destroying others in a pyre, termed the "Flame of Peace." Actions continued throughout the next two months, as tens of thousands of people held demonstrations in most of Brazil's major cities to show their support for a nationwide Disarmament Statute to create strong restrictions on firearms ownership. The statute was ultimately approved by the Brazilian legislature in December 2003.

As urban populations in Latin America expand while governments simultaneously reduce the scope of social services, the popular sectors have responded with vigor. They are pressuring their governments to provide housing and public services at prices that workers can afford to pay, and to improve safety within urban areas. It appears that as these concerns increase in urban communities, social movements are likely to grow in size and in influence.

Unemployment and the Argentine Piqueteros

As the formal labor sector has shrunk in Latin America, the issue of persistent unemployment has increasingly affected the lives of many. According to the International Labor Organization, over 19 million individuals in Latin America were unemployed during 2003. Argentina has arguably suffered the brunt of this current trend, and the *piqueteros*, or picketing unemployed workers, have become an increasingly influential social movement with a growing political voice.

Although Argentina's economy had been relatively stable throughout the twentieth century—the annual unemployment rate had rarely surpassed 4 percent—it underwent substantial restructuring during the 1990s.[5] Deindustrialization led to a marked decrease in the number of workers employed in the formal sector, and unemployment increased, reaching 18.5 percent by the middle of the decade. At the same time, Argentina lacked a social safety net for unemployed persons, and as government support for education, health care, and pension plans declined, the ranks of the informal labor sector and the poor swelled. Unable to rely on unions, these workers turned to neighborhood associations to advance their interests, and the unemployed workers' movement began at the local level.

One of the first labor actions took place in the province of Neuquén, in an oil-producing enclave that had been privatized in 1991, resulting in massive layoffs. Over 7,000 unemployed workers set up roadblocks with sticks to prevent vehicles from entering or leaving the area. The police attempted to clear the roads, but the unemployed stood their ground, and the matter was resolved when the provincial governor offered the protesters work through the *Plan Trabajar*. Within the following months, unemployed workers began organizing in different communities around the country, especially Greater Buenos Aires, Mar del Plata, and Cordoba. They became known as *piqueteros*, or "picketers," due to their primary tactic of setting up roadblocks to press for their demands. These include not only increased jobs and labor programs, but also widespread national reforms to address poverty and hardship in the provinces.

In this way, collective action against poverty in Argentina has become centered within local, community-based organizations instead of traditional workplace-based unions. This sentiment is expressed in one of the *piquetero* movement's main slogans: "the new factory is the territory," calling for unemployed workers to come together in their own neighborhoods, just as they did in the factories, to establish social links and become relevant political actors. Although unemployment and poverty remain major issues of concern, the *piquetero* movement has succeeded in many endeavors, sparking the creation of new labor programs or preventing their subsequent retrenchment. Most notably, however, the unemployed are now recognized as a significant political actor in Argentina. Local communities have become a space in which the popular sectors have been able to organize and articulate their interests, and the issue of providing jobs for all who want to work has been placed on the national agenda.

Indigenous and Ethnic Rights

Indigenous mobilizations also emerged in Latin America throughout the last few decades of the early twenty-first century. While indigenous peoples have been active for some time as members of leftist political parties, women's associations, and peasant unions, only recently have they organized around a shared indigenous identity to promote an agenda of ethnic rights.

Because indigenous communities exist within diverse cultural contexts, the goals of indigenous organizations are equally heterogeneous. However, most organizations want to secure some degree of individual and collective rights for their members. In many countries, indigenous people often face discrimination, lacking opportunities and rights enjoyed by members of the dominant ethnic group. For this reason, organizations seek to ensure that individual indigenous people be treated equally under national law. At the same time, indigenous populations comprise a distinct cultural group and want the state to legally recognize their collective autonomy. In practice, different groups define collective rights in many ways, ranging from input into school curricula, state recognition of collective land ownership, and consensus forms of decisionmaking to official recognition of customary laws and the right to govern themselves within a specified territory. In this way, individual and collective rights often intertwine as indigenous movements seek to obtain rights for their members as a distinct cultural group, while also protecting their full rights as individual citizens.

One of the largest indigenous organizations is the Pan-Mayan movement, which spans Southern Mexico, Guatemala, Belize, and Honduras. The members' activism grew rapidly in 1991, as planned celebrations of the 500th anniversary of Columbus' "discovery" of the Americas inspired Mayan groups to organize transnational activities commemorating "500 Years of Indigenous and Popular Resistance." The movement seeks to protect diverse Mayan cultural practices in order to preserve and revitalize traditional languages and customs, while also adapting to modernity on their own terms.

Indigenous groups are also increasingly organizing in response to the detrimental effects of neoliberal economic policies. For example, the Zapatista rebellion in Mexico not only sought indigenous rights, land reform, and democratization, but also called for a halt to neoliberal reform due to its negative effects, which were particularly felt in the countryside. In fact, the first day of the uprising, January 1, 1994, when thousands of indigenous Mayans took control of seven towns in Chiapas, intentionally coincided with the first day that the North American Free Trade Agreement (NAFTA) among Canada, the United States, and Mexico went into effect. Ten years after the rebellion, economic reform remained a salient issue for many Zapatistas who continue to struggle for the implementation of the San Andrés Peace Accords.

In Ecuador, the National Confederation of Indigenous Peoples (CONAIE) advocates not only for ethnic rights, especially bilingual education at the elementary level, but also for economic reform. CONAIE believes that Ecuador's export-oriented economic model has resulted in widespread poverty, inequality, and environmental degradation, and the group has organized nationwide strikes and roadblocks to protest dollarization and other neoliberal policies. CONAIE's director of communications explained, "Petroleum and mines are supposed to help exports and the development of the people. But after 30 years of exports, we've seen no development at all. No education, no nothing. That makes us think that the only beneficiaries are multinationals and the individuals that carry out their interests. And so we say '*Ya no mas*' (No more.)"[6]

Indigenous mobilizations have achieved some tangible results. CONAIE's actions have been notable not only for their pacifist character, but also for their success: The movement has gained control over two million acres of land from the Ecuadorian government, and was instrumental in toppling two presidents who attempted to enact neoliberal reforms in 1997 and 2000. During the 1990s, Ecuador, Bolivia, Mexico, and Colombia inserted language into their constitutions that described these countries as "multiethnic" and included some degree of recognition of indigenous rights.

However, in many cases, even minimal reforms have not been robustly implemented, and as structures of economic inequality persist, ethnic discrimination perpetuates economic disadvantage. For example, most indigenous groups in Ecuador speak a language other than Spanish, usually a variant of Quichua. However, few elementary schools offer bilingual teachers or educational materials, and many indigenous children cease attending classes at a young age, which in turn reduces their prospects for economic advancement. Trends like these suggest that future indigenous activism in the region may include efforts not only to preserve traditional cultural identity, but also to promote an agenda of expanded social and economic rights.

COMMON PREDICAMENTS: STRATEGIC CHOICES FOR SUCCESS

The four areas just discussed—agrarian reform, urban community revitalization, unemployment, and indigenous rights—are some of the most prominent issues around which social movements have coalesced in Latin America. As historical events unfold, how might these movements respond to the challenges that will undoubtedly arise? Each movement has its own individual characteristics and will necessarily undergo change in ways that are unique in some respects. Nevertheless, by considering some general dynamics of social movement organizations and identifying common patterns, it is possible to gain some insight into decisions taken by movement leaders and activists. Throughout its life cycle, a social movement experiences certain defining moments at which it must make particular choices with respect to achieving its goals. These "common predicaments" represent a similar set of decisionmaking areas, basic questions such as: "Who are we?" "What do we want?" and "How are we going to get it?"

"Who Are We?" Selecting Movement Members

Movements do not usually confront each predicament at the same time; there are particular instances at which each becomes important. One of the first choices for emerging movements centers on questions of membership: determining who can qualify as a movement participant. One dimension of this decision revolves around clarifying how *narrow* versus *broad* the organization should be in its outreach efforts. If the movement is open to all who sympathize with the group's goals, even if they are not part of the movement's targeted beneficiaries, this can result in a larger organization. The benefits to this are clear: Additional members may give the movement more power to voice its concerns as well as expanded public recognition. Yet at the same time, there is power to be gained through exclusivity, if membership is carefully limited to certain individuals or groups.

Paul Dosh describes a salient example of this common predicament. In 1995, a group of 300 Ecuadorian families, the "Cooperative of San Juan Bosco," organized an illegal land invasion of Itchimbía Park in metropolitan Quito, which had become a dumping ground for refuse and waste.[7] The cooperative defined their identity in environmental terms, and intended not only to settle in the park, but also to act as its ecological custodians. However, when 3,000 additional squatters arrived the night after the invasion, the cooperative had to make a choice: either allow the newcomers to join, and possibly gain political strength in numbers, or refuse to admit them, restricting membership to those with a proven commitment to environmental conservation. The group decided on the latter course of action, and as of January 2004, the settlers of San Juan Bosco had legally built high-quality condominiums and had initiated the task of park management.

An additional example from the United States is César Chávez's efforts to organize an agricultural workers' union in California's Central Valley during the 1960s. When Chávez decided to limit membership to only dues-paying individuals, some criticized this decision, claiming that it placed an undue burden on already impoverished farm workers. However, Chávez was convinced that the organization would be stronger if it were composed only of those who demonstrated their firm support by making a financial commitment. Ultimately, this strategy created a strong union that won improved working conditions and fair pay for many of California's farm laborers. These examples demonstrate how a smaller organization, but one in which every member is committed to the group's goals, might ultimately be more effective than a larger group composed of marginally affiliated individuals.

In selecting movement members, leaders also need to clarify whether membership should be primarily *identity-based* or *goal-based*. In other words, must supporters share a common identity as well as common goals? While no movement organization is solely based on identity, movements generally focus on substantive issues to a greater or lesser degree. Defining a movement's identity is also important because the way the movement sees itself, and wants to be seen by others, affects what it will do to achieve its goals. For example, if a movement's goal centers on winning *acknowledgment* of a particular cultural identity and preserving its uniqueness, as in the case of Pan-Mayan indigenous movements, it might be most practical to limit membership to those who share this identity. However, if the movement emphasizes gaining *rights* for a particular identity, such as CONAIE's efforts to expand bilingual education in Ecuador, then it may be strengthened by allowing all ideological sympathizers to join, even if they do not share the identity of the group in question.

"What Do We Want?" Determining Movement Goals

Social movements also face the task of deciding what they hope to achieve through collective action. This is an ongoing predicament for social movements— it is a concern not only in the initial stages of movement formation, but it can arise repeatedly if limited goals are realized, or if more expansive goals prove too difficult to attain.

First, it is necessary to clarify the movement's scope: whether to pursue a narrow agenda or a broader one. If a movement decides to focus on fewer issues, it may be easier to attract a unified base of supporters who have a common vision, as well as to minimize internal conflict. However, more limited goals might also narrow the range of potential participants, and defining a movement's aims too specifically risks leaving some aspects of the movement's agenda unaddressed. Conversely, there might be "something for everyone" in a movement with a wide array of goals, and this variety has the potential to attract a larger base of supporters. Yet an inclusive agenda is likely to attract a more diverse membership, one that may have conflicting priorities. This variation can render overall consensus difficult to attain, and the movement may find itself fragmenting into contradictory factions.

The Brazilian MST is currently struggling with this predicament. During the 1990s, the movement's goals broadened to encompass overall social and economic issues, such as the international campaign against genetically modified food and opposing the creation of a Free Trade Area of the Americas. However, there is an incipient disconnect between these expanded ideological goals and those of local grassroots activists, especially among new urban entrants who are eager to obtain land for themselves and their families. Since the movement's leaders do not want to narrow the current agenda, they are attempting to make these broader concerns relevant to their newest members.

A second aspect of determining movement goals includes clarifying the degree to which the movement aims for *overall systemic* or *more delimited change*. The movement might choose a delimited approach if it seeks to implement or revoke specific laws, procedures, and policies within the current system. At the other end of the spectrum, a movement might opt for overhauling existing institutional structures if it seeks comprehensive systemic change. Actions oriented toward delimited change may earn greater public legitimacy and generate relatively less social conflict. However, the movement must navigate within existing institutional structures, which may or may not be well-suited to implementing the movement's agenda. Successful systemic change, on the other hand, would allow institutions to be crafted in a way that meets the group's goals over the long term. Yet achieving systemic change is often fraught with risk and social upheaval, since efforts to transform entrenched institutions often meet with a great deal of resistance.

The decision to aim for more delimited or systemic change is closely tied to the distinction between narrow and broad goals mentioned above. Narrower goals can often be achieved by changing specific parts of the existing system, while broader goals may require transforming social, economic, and political institutions. However, this relationship does not always hold. A narrow goal, such as land redistribution or wage increases, might threaten powerful, entrenched interests within the system, and therefore have little chance of being implemented unless systemic change occurs. Conversely, a broader goal, such as societal recognition of indigenous rights, might be addressed within the scope of the current system, such as through enactment of a constitutional amendment.

Finally, movements also need to determine if their goals, once achieved, will be *collective* or *private:* Will everyone in society be entitled to reap the benefits, or will they be limited in some way? If the benefits are available to everyone, this raises the "free-rider" dilemma that Mancur Olson (1971) described: There will be little incentive for individuals to work in support of the movement's goals if the benefits are not contingent on participation. Olson's solution to the collective action problem is to provide selective incentives—benefits that are linked to one's participation in the movement.[8] This strategy has been successfully employed by many organizations; for example, it was arguably one important factor that allowed the MST to expand rapidly. Shortly after the organization was officially formed in 1984, a group of landless families that had been encamped at Erval Seco finally gained official title to a nearby government-owned farm. Families who initially joined the occupation but left during the ensuing months received nothing, but those who endured until the end acquired land of their own. This provided a powerful selective incentive for individual landless workers to join the MST and remain on the encampments despite years of hardship, and the number and size of occupations increased throughout Brazil over the next few years.

At the same time, selective incentives are not always necessary for high levels of participation. The desire to collaborate with one's friends, rectify an injustice, and/or overcome hardship in pursuit of a collective goal are just some of the factors that can motivate individuals to participate in collective endeavors even when individual gain is unlikely. Also, it can be quite difficult to translate a movement's goals into private benefits. Some intangible goals, such as expanded political and social rights, may be nearly impossible to privatize. What is more, exclusive benefits are often contrary to the underlying ideological framework of the movement itself. Consider the various movements that aim to recognize the rights of the indigenous by formally amending constitutions. It would be antithetical to the movement's purpose, as well as impractical, to prevent indigenous persons who had not participated in the movement from enjoying equal and expanded rights if they are achieved. While offering private goods to participants can be a powerful tool for member recruitment and retention, such as approach is difficult to implement in practice and may not always be necessary in order to attract movement participants.

"How Are We Going to Get It?" Choosing Movement Strategies

Once a movement has determined who can qualify as a member and clarified the nature of its goals, the question of strategy becomes salient: What should the movement actually do to achieve its ends? One important strategic dimension involves coalitional choice—the extent to which the movement forms alliances with other organizations or pursues an autonomous course. The question of *autonomy* versus *alliances* is a recurring, long-term predicament that social movements face not only at their formative stages, but also throughout their life cycle.

A coalitional strategy based on alliances occurs when a social movement forms partnerships with outside actors in order to combine resources, knowledge, and capabilities. Allies can provide an infusion of resources, both financial and organizational, and this can be especially welcome during the process of movement formation. Grassroots movements comprised primarily of poor and working-class individuals often find that networks, skilled leadership, and financial assistance provided by alliance partners can help the movement address its goals more effectively.

However, external organizations often have their own interests and agenda in mind. Groups that contribute resources may believe that doing so gives them authority to drive the local movement's ideological and tactical agendas. If the degree of difference between the movement's goals and their allies' agenda is small, this is not a significant drawback. When a large discrepancy exists, however, grassroots members might not be included in leadership and decisionmaking roles. Conversely, if a movement chooses an autonomous course, it is free to determine its own agenda and priorities without external influence. However, an important trade-off is that an autonomous movement is solely dependent on its own resources to organize and implement collective action.

The Argentine *piquetero* movement has recently faced this common predicament. Since 1999, clientelistic ties between the movement and political parties have eroded, as subsidies have been provided directly to unemployed individuals instead of local party bosses.[9] This new autonomy enabled the movement to respond more directly to its members' needs and gave leaders increased freedom to choose their own strategies. However, by the beginning of 2000, the newly elected Alianza administration let existing labor programs expire and reduced federal funding for new initiatives. Garay (2003) argues that this new policy direction, combined with a sharp increase in poverty, encouraged the *piqueteros* to ally with one of the main Argentine unions, the CTA, as the movement realized that negotiations needed to take place at the national level if they were to have any lasting effects. The movement's current degree of autonomy versus alliances remains a matter of some debate; what is clear is that the *piquetero* movement is in the process of addressing this coalitional predicament.

Another dimension of strategy involves determining whether the movement should pursue its goals through *legal* or *extralegal means*. This question arises less frequently than others presented here, but when it arises, it is often quite intense. Most movements find that employing legal methods works well when pursuing narrowly defined goals within a context of delimited change. However, after legal strategies have been undertaken for an extended period without success, movements might consider extralegal means to advance their cause. These methods can encompass nonviolent, passive resistance strategies of refusing to comply with existing laws, as well as acts of civil disobedience such as sit-ins, protest marches, and boycotts. At another level, violence may or may not be present if movement participants engage in strikes, roadblocks, building takeovers, and land invasions in order to have their voices heard. In their most extreme form, extralegal methods can also include strategies centered around violence, such as mass riots and armed rebellion.

Clearly, strategies that are within the boundaries of the law present a lower degree of personal risk. However, effort must be expended in building a wide social coalition that can support the movement's goals within the boundaries of the legal system. This effort may take a great deal of time, if it is possible at all. For this reason, some movements eventually choose to incorporate some extralegal means within their strategic plan. Yet illegal methods are often risky, as many governments willingly detain, arrest, imprison, and occasionally harm activists. Prolonged use of extralegal activities—especially those that include violence—might also significantly disrupt social stability, bringing about civil conflict and a repressive backlash.

Social movements sometimes shift between employing legal and extralegal means. In his analysis of land invasion organizations, Dosh (2004) explains that when municipal services were publicly owned in Peru and Ecuador, settlers had two options: They could go through legal channels to solicit services, and/or pressure the government through extralegal, militant protests. As city services were increasingly privatized, however, land invasion organizations altered both their legal and illegal strategies in response to the change in ownership. For example, after electricity was privatized in Lima, Peru, settlers in many districts first illegally tapped into the electrical grid to obtain power, and then attempted to raise funds to purchase the service legally. However, those settlers who could not afford the cost simply continued to steal electricity, illegally hooking up their homes to local power lines.

A more dramatic transformation is exemplified by the Zapatistas (EZLN) in Mexico. Indigenous activism in Chiapas is rooted in various peasant union organizations, created during the 1970s and 1980s to protest the dismantling of the traditional *ejido* system of land tenure, corruption of public officials, widespread poverty in the countryside, and general lack of indigenous political representation. However, in some instances the Mexican authorities ignored their demands, while in other cases they pledged reforms, but implemented them minimally, if at all. Finally, when peaceful protests were met with violent repression, this was seen as the last straw for many indigenous activists, and they took up arms in resistance. However, by 1996, two years after their initial uprising, the Zapatistas were already expressing an eagerness to revert to legal means; the *Fourth Declaration of the Lacandon Jungle* outlines a thirteen-point plan to transform the EZLN into a national grassroots opposition movement that "does not struggle to take political power, but for a democracy where those who govern, govern by obeying."[10] As these examples show, as social movements evolve, they may shift between legal and extralegal strategies in response to new political and economic contexts.

CONCLUSION

Individuals at the grassroots level in Latin America are engaging in collective action with renewed vitality, and this chapter has introduced some of the social movements that are organizing and channeling their demands. As economic transformations across the region have rendered political parties and unions less effective advocates for the working classes, social movements have become additional vehicles through which ordinary people can express their interests within the political sphere.

Admittedly, social movements can be imperfect vehicles for interest intermediation. Most notably, a movement cannot elect representatives to public office to craft public policy as political parties do—though some social movements have resolved this dilemma by sponsoring a political party, such as CONAIE has in forming *Pachakutik*, its political arm. Despite this limitation, as parties and unions remain flawed in their ability to accurately express the public will, it is reasonable to expect that the popular sectors in Latin America will continue to voice their concerns in the political arena through social movement activity. The common predicaments identified here may be a useful way to gain insight into the strategic choices that these movements make as events unfold.

NOTES

1. Ruth Berins Collier and David Collier, *Shaping the Political Arena* (Princeton: Princeton University Press, 1991).

2. Eighty-four individuals died as a result of rural confrontations between January and November 2003, a 40 percent increase in mortality rates from the previous year. From "Brazil's Rural Struggle" in *The Economist*, January 8, 2004.

3. On April 17, 1996, the Brazilian military police attacked a group of encamped rural workers in Eldorado dos Carajás, killing 19 and severely wounding 69. The case was finally brought to trial in 2002, but only 2 of 146 soldiers were convicted for their role in the massacre. The delay in bringing the perpetrators to justice, combined with the weak sentences meted out, has energized many rural activists to commemorate April 17 as an annual day of struggle for agrarian reform.

4. *Correio Brasiliense*, October 4, 2003.

5. This discussion primarily draws from the research of Gabriela Delamata, "The Organizations of Unemployed Workers in Greater Buenos Aires: The Erosion of Clientelistic Practices," a working paper presented at the UC–Berkeley Center for Latin American Studies,

October 2003, and M. Candelaria Garay, "Origins of the Unemployed Movement in Argentina: Government Policy Initiatives as a Trigger for Contention," May 2002, unpublished M.A. essay, UC–Berkeley.

6. "Latin America: Local Resistance," *Energy Intelligence Group–Energy Compass*, January 2, 2004.

7. Paul Dosh, "Demanding the Land: Urban Social Movements and Local Politics in Peru and Ecuador," Ph.D. dissertation, UC–Berkeley, 2004.

8. Mancur Olson, "The Logic of Collective Action," Harvard University Press, Cambridge, Mass.: 1971.

9. Gabriela Delamata, "The Organizations of Unemployed Workers in Greater Buenos Aires," Center for Latin American Studies Working Papers (Paper 8), UC–Berkeley, March 2004.

10. EZLN, *Fourth Declaration of the Lacandon Jungle*, 1 January 1996. Available as of January 2004 at: http://www.ezln.org/documentos/1996/19960101.en.htm

Suggested Readings

Collier, Ruth Berins. "Political Participation in the Age of Neoliberalism." *Center for Latin American Studies Newsletter,* UC–Berkeley: Winter 2002.

Collier, Ruth Berins and David Collier. *Shaping the Political Arena.* Princeton, N.J.: Princeton University Press, 1991.

Domínguez, Jorge I., ed. *Social Movements in Latin America: The Experience of Peasants, Workers, Women, the Urban Poor, and the Middle Sectors.* New York: Garland Publishing, Inc., 1994.

Eckstein, Susan Eva, and Timothy P. Wickham-Crowley, eds. *Struggles for Social Rights in Latin America.* New York: Routledge, 2003.

_____. *What Justice? Whose Justice? Fighting for Fairness in Latin America.* Berkeley, Calif.: University of California Press, 2003.

González, Victoria, and Karen Kampwirth, eds. *Radical Women in Latin America: Left and Right.* University Park, Pa.: Pennsylvania State University Press, 2001.

Harvey, Neil. *The Chiapas Rebellion: The Struggle for Land and Democracy.* Durham, N.C.: Duke University Press, 1998.

Keck, Margaret E., and Kathryn Sikkink. *Activists Beyond Borders: Advocacy Networks in International Politics.* Ithaca, N.Y.: Cornell University Press, 1998.

Maybury-Lewis, David. *The Politics of Ethnicity: Indigenous Peoples in Latin American States.* Cambridge, Mass.: Harvard University Press, 2002.

Sinclair, Minor, ed. *The New Politics of Survival: Grassroots Movements in Central America.* Washington, D.C.: EPICA/Monthly Review Press, 1995.

Smith, Jackie, Charles Chatfield, and Ron Pagnucco, eds. *Transnational Social Movements and Global Politics: Solidarity Beyond the State.* Syracuse, N.Y.: Syracuse University Press, 1997.

Tarrow, Sidney. *Power in Movement: Social Movements and Contentious Politics.* New York: Cambridge University Press, 1998.

Warren, Kay B., and Jean E. Jackson, eds. *Indigenous Movements, Self-Representation, and the State in Latin America.* Austin: University of Texas Press, 2002.

Wright, Angus, and Wendy Wolford. *To Inherit the Earth: The Landless Movement and the Struggle for a New Brazil.* Oakland, Calif.: Food First Books, 2003.

Yashar, Deborah J. *Contesting Citizenship: Indigenous Movements and the Postliberal Challenge in Latin America.* New York: Cambridge University Press, 2005 (forthcoming).

Suggested Internet Resources

Some of the emerging movements discussed in this chapter have their own websites; those that have some information available in English are presented below.

Choike: a Portal on Southern Civil Societies
http://www.choike.org/nuevo_eng/
This site provides globally Southern NGOs and social movements a platform for sharing information on their activities, and also includes a searchable directory of NGOs.

CONAIE (National Confederation of Indigenous Peoples)
http://conaie.nativeweb.org/index.html
CONAIE's site in English. Contains a history of the movement, related news, and information on Ecuador's indigenous culture.

Food First: Institute for Food and Development Policy
http://www.foodfirst.org/index.html
Food First is a nonprofit think-tank that investigates solutions to worldwide hunger and poverty and advocates for establishing the right to sustenance as a fundamental human right.

Homeless Workers' Movement (Movimento dos Trabalhadores Sem Teto–MTST)
http://www.mtst.org/
Official site of the MTST; mostly in Portuguese but with some resources in English.

Landless Workers' Movement (Movimento dos Trabalhadores Rurais Sem Terra–MST)
http://www.mst.org.br/
Official site of the MST. Contains almost daily updates on the movement's activities in Portuguese; most resources are translated into English.

Viva Rio
http://www.vivario.org.br/
Official site for Viva Rio. Updated weekly in Portuguese, monthly in English.

Zapatista Network
http://www.zapatistas.org/
A site in English dedicated to supporting the Zapatistas. Contains historical information, current political positions, and an e-mail discussion group.

PART IV

POLITICAL PROCESSES
AND TRENDS

PARTICIPATION AND POLITICAL PROCESS: THE COLLAPSIBLE PYRAMID

JAN KNIPPERS BLACK

ALL POLITICAL SYSTEMS ARE systems of limited participation. Even the societies we might call primitive—societies in which essential tasks and rewards are shared more or less equally among families—generally limit participation on the basis of sex and age; that is, women and minors are excluded. Such systems of exclusion may enjoy "legitimacy," or acceptance, even by the excluded, but they are ultimately based on physical prowess. Exclusion in more-complex societies, like the modern nation-state, typically follows the lines of class, often reinforced by racial or ethnic divisions. Exclusion may also be based on political ideology.

In the United States, for example, the franchise was generally limited to property-holding white males until the 1830s, when the populist movement headed by Andrew Jackson led to the elimination of property-holding requirements. The franchise was extended to women in 1920 only after years of struggle on the part of the suffragettes. Suffrage for blacks in the South did not become effective until the issue was forced by the civil rights movement, led by Dr. Martin Luther King Jr., in the early 1960s. It was only after university students were mobilized in opposition to the Vietnam War that the voting age was lowered from twenty-one to eighteen. In parts of the country, poor blacks or Hispanics are still turned away from the polls by one device or another.

Furthermore, as suffrage has been extended, the vote, which is only one of many forms of political participation, has become devalued as a consequence of the preponderant role of money in the U.S. electoral system. As campaigns have become outrageously costly media events, the candidate or elected official has become far more attentive to the wishes of major campaign contributors than to those of an amorphous electorate. The low level of voter turnout in the United States suggests, among other things, that a great many eligible voters see campaign promises as hollow and electoral choices as meaningless.

Likewise in Latin America, participation takes many forms, and effective participation is by no means automatic. For all but the wealthiest it must be earned or won, often through protracted struggle and great sacrifice.

INEQUALITY AND THE BID FOR PARTICIPATION

Most complex, highly stratified social and political systems can be traced to armed conquest, and the national systems of Latin America as we know them today are no exception. The subjugation upon which contemporary social inequality in Latin America is based included not only the conquest and enslavement by Spaniards, Portuguese, and other Europeans of native American populations, but also the kidnapping, by European merchants of flesh, of Africans and their subsequent enslavement in the New World.

The preponderance of brute force thus led to wealth, as the conquistadores acquired land and slaves or serfs and passed them on to their legitimate offspring. Over time, this system of exploitation acquired a measure of legitimacy, as it was moderated and condoned by the religious system imposed by the conquerors. In Latin America as elsewhere, the violent roots of such systems of inequality have been progressively obscured from subsequent generations of the conquered populations, and the myth has been established that differential reward and punishment and limitations of access to wealth and power rest somehow on divine purpose or merit. Those who would challenge that interpretation of the social reality are branded subversive and dealt with accordingly.

Through miscegenation, immigration, and an increase in the categories of tasks to be performed, classes of intermediate social and economic rank—that is, between the masters and the "slaves"—have come into being. It is quite possible, as social and political systems become more complex, for individuals, through accepting the social myth and incorporating the values of the conquering class, to rise above the status of their birth. The masters, however, do not voluntarily relinquish a share of their authority to a lower stratum on the social pyramid. Such a sharing of power across class lines comes about only when organization and the potential for the use of force on the part of a lower social stratum are such that the masters conclude that they must share their wealth and power or risk losing it all.

The great political theorists, at least since Aristotle, have noted that power systems and the distribution of wealth and opportunity are interdependent. Thus, the concepts of social class and class struggle introduced by Karl Marx are crucial to an understanding of the political process in its broadest implications. These concepts are, however, abstractions. Social classes do not compete as such. Individual competitors for political power act through or on behalf of groups, which, in turn, represent more or less limited sectors of society. Such groups may represent one or more social classes, or a sector within a single class. They may act on behalf of one class at one time and on behalf of another at a later date. They may act on behalf of very narrowly construed organizational or institutional interests, which only indirectly impinge upon the class struggle. They may represent interests fundamentally alien to their own societies. Or they may represent a combination of national and foreign, class and institutional interests.

Political parties constitute only one of many categories of group actors in politics. The alignment of groups that participate or seek to participate in political competition in a particular national system depends to a large extent on the level of differentiation, or complexity, of the socioeconomic system. In any system based on marked inequality, those in power will maintain armed bodies (vigilante squads, police, and/or military units) to keep the have-nots from going after what the haves have and to ensure that the labor force fulfills the role to which it has been assigned.

A ruling class cannot perpetually maintain its position through the use or threat of brute force alone, however. Thus, it will seek to fortify itself by propagating a religion or ideology that sanctions the existing order. The groups or institutions that provide force (for example, the military) and legitimacy (the Church or, more recently, the media), since they are essential to the maintenance of the power position of the ruling class, will soon acquire a measure of power in their own right. In fact, at any level of development ruling elites must stabilize their own power positions by balancing the enforcers, or wielders of force, against the bestowers of legitimacy.

In an international system characterized by colonialism or hegemony (dominance by a foreign power), the ruling class of a colony or client state may be highly dependent on a foreign power. In most of Latin America, the conquering class remained Spanish or Portuguese, protected and legitimized by Spanish or Portuguese troops and clergymen for some 300 years.

Typically, in Latin America, participants in the political system at the time independence was achieved were the *hacendados*—or members of the landowning class—the military, and the Roman Catholic Church. The hegemony that had been exercised by Spain and Portugal during the colonial period was soon assumed by the United States in Mexico, Central America, and the Caribbean and by Great Britain (with lesser participation by other European powers) in South America. The United States gave strong competition to the British and other European powers in South America during the first half of the twentieth century and, by the end of World War II, had consolidated its position of dominance over the whole of Latin America.

The pace and order of the admission of new groups and classes to political participation have varied from country to country, having proceeded most rapidly in the Southern Cone countries and most slowly in the Andean and Central American highlands. In general, a commercial sector, associated with export-import operations, was admitted during the last half of the nineteenth century, and industrial elites and middle classes began participating in the first decades of the twentieth century. By the 1920s and 1930s, labor was organizing and making its bid, but in few countries was it admitted to participation before the 1940s and 1950s. The admission of peasants, by nonrevolutionary means, was scarcely even at issue until the 1960s, and it was not until 1979 in Ecuador and 1980 in Peru that new constitutions gave illiterates—that is, the Indian peasants—the vote for the first time in those countries. Peasant participation has been rare and tenuous, and the peasants' gains, like those of organized labor, were reversed in several countries in the 1960s and 1970s through counter-revolution. In politics, there is no "final analysis"; as far as we know, participation and its perquisites may be won and lost and won again ad infinitum.

POLITICAL ACTORS AND ARENAS

The means of seeking entry into, or control of, a political system depends upon the strengths of the particular group, or political actor, and the openness of the system. In general, however, elections and other processes associated with the democratic system become available to groups previously excluded only *after* they have become organized and have demonstrated, through illegal or extralegal means, their ability to disrupt the system and to threaten seriously the interests of the power elite. Furthermore, as Charles Anderson has noted, election results are by no means considered sacred by all participants; elections are but one of the many means of garnering and demonstrating power.[1]

Anderson has pointed out that there are certain resources, or "power capabilities," without which governments would find it difficult or even impossible to function. These resources include, for example, a cooperative labor force, agricultural or industrial production, control over the use of armed force, moral sanction, popular support, and the support of a dominant foreign power. In order to secure participation in or control over the political process, political groups, or "power contenders," must demonstrate control of a power capability.

In most contemporary Latin American countries, these power contenders would include landowners, industrial and commercial elites, religious leaders, military factions, labor unions, political parties, students and intellectual leaders, foreign corporations, and agencies of foreign governments. In distinguishing between power contenders and power capabilities, Anderson notes that within the military establishment, the business community, the labor movement, or even the Catholic Church, there are generally various factions seeking to speak for the institution or the community. (One might add that even agencies of the U.S. government have been seen marching to different drummers. Civilian politicians in several countries have found, to their dismay, that the support of the U.S. ambassador did not assure the support of the Pentagon and the CIA as well.) In order to be "taken into account" by those groups that are already participants in the system, a new power contender must flex its muscles. A military faction might demonstrate control of a power capability without firing a shot by establishing a credible claim to the loyalty of a few important garrisons. A labor federation might demonstrate such control by calling a successful general strike; a peasant group, by seizing a significant amount of land; a student group, by amassing a large turnout for a march; a political party, by receiving a sizable vote. Traditional participants, feeling threatened, might in turn demonstrate their own capabilities; disinvestment and capital flight are among the many ways economic elites may respond to threat.

When a new power contender demonstrates its capabilities, the power elite must decide whether the greater risk lies in admitting the new group to participation in the system or in attempting to suppress it. The new group may be admitted if the risk of suppression appears to be as great as the risk of recognition, and if groups that are already participating believe that the new group will be willing to abide by the rules of the game—that is, to respect the perquisites of the other players. Thus, what Anderson calls the normal rule of Latin American political change, and what we shall call the defining principle of the evolutionary process, is that new power contenders may be added to the system but old ones may not be eliminated.

Political conflict, as Martin C. Needler notes, takes place simultaneously in various "arenas," differing in accessibility to social groups, in methods or "weapons" of competition, and in visibility to the public.[2] In the least-developed political systems, the dominant arena is the private one, where family pressures, personal contacts, bribery, blackmail, and graft determine the outcome of political conflict. In the most highly developed polities, decisions are reached through popular election, parliamentary debate, and judicial review. Between the development levels of court intrigue and constitutional mediation of conflict is a level in which conflict takes place in the streets—in which demonstrations, strikes, and riots determine the outcome of the conflict.

Merging the models of Needler and Anderson, we might say that the "street arena" holds sway while the political elite is unwilling to admit new participants to the system but unable to repress them fully. It might be added that the street arena is employed not only by nonelites on the way up but by elites who fear that they are on the way down. When elites in a more highly developed constitutional system begin to feel that their interests are threatened by electoral and other constitutional processes, they will use the street arena—the provocation of highly visible "instability"—along with other arenas in preparing the way for counterrevolution.

SOCIAL CHANGE AND POLITICAL PROCESS

What factors, then, determine when and how participation will be won or lost by various groups and classes of Latin American societies? Many of the factors that contribute to pressure for social change fall into the category Karl Deutsch has labeled "social mobilization"—that is, urbanization, education, mass communication and the consequent "revolution of rising expectations."[3] The transistor radio has been called the greatest force for change in the twentieth century.

The circulation of new ideas or ideologies imported from other societies (liberalism at the turn of the nineteenth century, Marxism at the turn of the twentieth) or revived from earlier eras of pre-conquest or national experience (Mexican and Andean *indigenismo* or "nativism," Nicaraguan *sandinismo*) may give momentum and a sense of direction to otherwise sporadic or unfocused social unrest. Likewise, hope may be aroused and organization promoted by the appearance of agents of change. These agents may be foreigners with new ideas and ambitions, such as labor leaders who immigrated from Europe at the turn of the century or representatives of foreign or international development

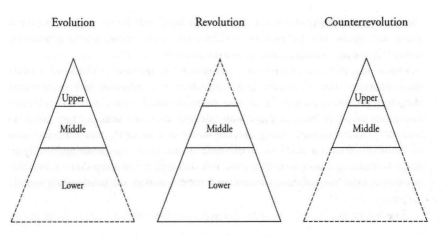

FIGURE 10.1   Political Participation by Social Strata: The Collapsible Pyramid

agencies who have descended on Latin America since the 1960s. Or they may be Latin Americans associated with new institutions or with old institutions that are assuming new roles. Students, for example, became agents of change after national universities came into being in the early twentieth century, and Catholic clergymen and nuns, inspired by liberation theology, became powerful agents of change in the 1970s and 1980s. Pressure for change may also be generated by natural or manmade disasters, such as earthquakes or wars, by an abrupt downturn in the economy, or by a particularly greedy or brutal move on the part of the ruling classes—a paranoid overreaction, for example, to some minor incident of protest or insubordination.

The factors that contribute to pressure for social change do not, however, in themselves determine what the nature of that change will be. The nature of the change that comes in response to social mobilization is a product of the interaction of the forces of change and the forces of resistance. If the political elite is willing and able to share power, incorporating new groups into the polity, change will follow the evolutionary pattern. If the elite is unwilling to share, determined instead to repress would-be participants, change may take the form of revolution, of counterrevolution, or of a holding operation (indecisive cycles of insurrection and repression) we shall call "boundary maintenance." The outcome will depend largely upon the relative strength, unity, and determination of the opposing forces.

Thus, the major political processes that may flow from social change or pressure for additional social change will be labeled, for the purposes of a model that we shall call "the collapsible pyramid," as evolution, revolution, and counterrevolution (Figure 10.1). Political evolution implies the incorporation of new political actors, representing previously unrepresented social strata, without the displacement of previous participants in the system. Revolution is defined as the displacement or disestablishment of groups representing one or more strata from the upper reaches of the social pyramid. Our definition of counterrevolution is implied in that of revolution. It is the displacement, or elimination from effective participation, of groups representing strata from the base of the social pyramid.

Evolution

The experiences of Latin American countries suggest that limitations on a client state's links to the dominant foreign power and racial or ethnic homogeneity are among the factors that make it more likely that change will follow the evolutionary pattern. Each of these two factors has independent explanatory power, but in Latin America, the two are also related historically.

Limitations on colonial or neocolonial control may be a consequence of, among other things, physical distance, competition among prospective hegemonic powers, or the relative absence of strategic or material assets. The political significance of such limitations is that, unable to rely on the backing of the dominant foreign power, the political elite may find it necessary to come to terms with new groups seeking participation. The first Latin American states in which the middle class, and to a lesser extent the working class, gained access to political power were those of the Southern Cone—Argentina, Uruguay, and, somewhat later, Chile. This area, which offered neither the gold and silver nor the exploitable Indian civilizations of the Andean and Middle American highlands, was of little interest to the Spanish crown. The Río de la Plata Basin was among the last areas of the New World to be settled by Europeans and among the first to declare and win independence.

Relative to the rigid hierarchical systems of Mexico, Peru, and other early centers of royal domination, the social systems of the Southern Cone were loosely stratified, and their political systems were fluid. The nomadic Indians of the pampas were gradually exterminated, while those across the Andes in Chile—fewer than 100,000 in the late nineteenth century—were confined on reservations. Most of the African captives who were delivered to the Rio de la Plata Basin were subsequently transshipped north to zones where plantations were dominant. Argentina and Uruguay, predominantly mestizo at the time of independence, became overwhelmingly European as a consequence of large-scale immigration in the late nineteenth century. Chile's predominantly mestizo population was also relatively homogeneous. Thus, the social distance to be bridged in those countries in the incorporation of new groups into the polity was not nearly so great as in the countries of predominant Indian population, presided over by a tiny Hispanic elite.

From the late colonial period until the end of World War II, the Southern Cone countries were subjects of competition among hegemonic powers. Great Britain had competed very successfully with Spain for dominance in matters of trade even before the struggle for independence was undertaken. Britain then remained the dominant, though not unchallenged, foreign power in the area until World War II. The rise of the middle classes and the beginnings of labor organization occurred long before the United States acquired dominance over the area.

Other areas that have experienced evolutionary change have displayed some of the same characteristics. Venezuela and Costa Rica, for example, had sparse native American populations and were of little interest to the Spanish. Both have relatively homogeneous populations. Both were among the last areas to be settled by Europeans, and Venezuela, along with Argentina, was one of the first settlement areas to develop important trade ties with Britain and to rise in revolt against Spain. Representative government has been the rule rather than the exception in Costa Rica since the 1880s. In abolishing its army in 1948, Costa Rica eliminated a major threat to participation.[4]

The bid of the middle classes for participation has generally come about in conjunction with urbanization and the expansion of national institutions and government services. Spearheaded by merchants, bureaucrats, or students and intellectuals, middle-class movements have often led to the organization of new parties advocating social reform and appealing to incipient labor organizations. Victory at the ballot box, however, has generally been the confirmation, rather than the means, of middle-class ascent. The strength of the movement or party has had to be demonstrated first in the street arena, and its initial assumption of power has often been assisted by "young Turks" within the military.

As middle-class parties have generally needed the support of organized labor, and to a lesser extent of peasants, to confront the traditional political elite, the assumption of power by such parties has meant at least limited participation for the working classes as well—participation expressed, for example, in the right of collective bargaining as well as in the vote. Working-class groups may also be admitted prematurely to the political system, before their capabilities for disruption are fully developed, through the initiatives of one sector of the political elite that is seeking to enhance its position over another or by power holders seeking to maintain some degree of control over the development of labor's capabilities. Brazilian *caudillo* Getúlio Vargas cultivated labor as a counterpoise to the economic elite, but he kept it under the firm control of the labor ministry. In Colombia, the preemptive admission of organized labor and its incorporation into the pyramidal structures of the traditional parties delayed labor organization along horizontal lines of class interest.

The redistribution of power implied in the evolutionary process should be reflected in the long term in a redistribution of goods and services toward the newly participant groups. But this does not necessarily imply a redistribution toward all disadvantaged classes. For example, the economic position of a participating organized labor force may be enhanced while that of unorganized peasants or of unemployed and underemployed urban workers deteriorates. In the case of Venezuela, the middle-class parties gained admittance to the system by incorporating the strength of organized labor into their own. Nevertheless, while organized labor has reaped the benefits of political participation, there is a large and growing class of unorganized poor in Venezuela for whom the resultant inflation has only made things worse.

Effective working-class participation and thoroughgoing redistribution have been known to come about, even in Latin America, through the evolutionary process. In the early twentieth century, Uruguay, without suffering the devastation of social revolution, came to enjoy one of the most fully democratic systems and most highly developed welfare states in the world. In 1973, however, Uruguay's social and political advantages were erased by a brutal counterrevolution that brought the military to power until 1984.

While economies were expanding (in Uruguay, for example, from early to mid-twentieth century), the demands of newly participant social strata, such as urban labor, could be met without undue threat to the perquisites of traditional elites and middle classes; a concession to one pressure group was not necessarily at the expense of another. Moreover, the illusion of economic expansion could be maintained for a while by artificial means such as inflation or foreign borrowing. But when economies began to decline, the upper and middle classes came to fear that the gains of labor could only be at their expense. Moreover, in highly dependent economies, like those of Latin America, foreign businesses that feel threatened may appeal to their home governments and to public and private lending institutions to initiate measures, such as credit freezes and trade embargoes, that damage all economic interests in the client state.

Thus, the economic elites, both foreign and domestic, with substantial middle-class support, backed by the dominant foreign power and fronted for by the armed forces, move to silence lower-class demands and to regain control of the processes whereby wealth and power are allocated. Such was the fate of Brazil and the Southern Cone.

Costa Rica and Venezuela, the countries that most successfully maintained their evolutionary systems through the 1970s, were blessed with relatively healthy economies. But Costa Rica's economy, disabled by a drop in coffee prices, took a nosedive in the early 1980s. That country's democratic system was made more vulnerable by the efforts of the Reagan administration to transform its nonprofessional civil guard into a professional military establishment, and its social welfare system has been stripped in the 1990s to meet the conditions of creditors.

Petrodollars have freed the Venezuelan government to meet the most urgent demands of lower and middle classes without seriously taxing the rich. But petroleum wealth has not been converted into agricultural development and industrial diversification fast enough to alleviate the effects of oil-induced inflation and to bridge the gap between rich and poor. Rather, its social welfare system was stripped in the 1990s to meet the conditions of creditors, and the oil bonanza has served, for the most part, to bloat the bureaucracy. The global oil glut of the 1980s, coupled with the foreign debt and the austerity measures imposed by creditors, brought social tensions closer to the surface. Those tensions erupted in early 1989 in a popular rampage that left more than 300 dead and demonstrated the fragility of Venezuela's democracy.

Revolution

The displacement of a social stratum through revolution does not necessarily mean the physical elimination of individuals or the blocking of their participation, as individuals, in the political system. Rather, it means the removal of the resources (material or institutional) that have enabled them to exercise power as a class.

The revolutionary process is likely to involve violence both in the initial phase of insurgency and repression and in the secondary phase of struggle among insurgent groups. If the redistributional phase is delayed, renewed violence is likely to accompany that phase as well. But politics is the process whereby power relationships are established, so violence—or the threat of it— is implicit in all political processes. The violence accompanying revolution is not necessarily greater than that which accompanies other political processes.

The Cuban Revolution claimed several thousand lives, but considerably fewer than the Chilean counterrevolution, now believed to have claimed up to 10,000. About 50,000 people were killed in the course of the Nicaraguan Revolution, and another 30,000 or so were killed in postrevolutionary struggles against the U.S.-sponsored "contras," or counterrevolutionary forces, but an even greater number of Guatemalans have been killed, mainly by vigilantes and official security forces, in the "boundary-maintenance" effort—the effort, essentially, to keep the Indians "in their place"—that characterized Guatemalan politics from 1954 at least until 1997. The Colombian *violencia*, suggestive of the pattern whereby elites maintain their position while nonelites fight only among themselves, claimed more than 200,000 lives over more than a decade (mainly 1948–1958) of sporadic, nonpurposeful fighting. Revolution is only one—and perhaps the least likely—of many possible outcomes of violent confrontation.

The term "revolution" has been used very loosely, especially since the success of the Cuban Revolution in 1959 spread hope or fear, depending on one's point of view, throughout the Americas. It has been used as a synonym for violence, for social change, or for regime change; it has even been appropriated by rightist military rulers, like those who seized the Brazilian government in 1964, in vain attempts to legitimize their own counterrevolutions. In fact, however, successful revolutions are most rare.

In the Western Hemisphere, the only society to dismantle an entire ruling class (the French planters) in the process of ousting the colonial power was that of Haiti. Haiti was not only the first Latin American country to gain independence (1804) and to undergo a successful revolution, but the first state in the modern world to be born of a slave revolt.

The other Latin American countries that have experienced successful revolutions are Mexico (1911), Bolivia (1952), Cuba (1959), and Nicaragua (1979). Insurrectionary forces showed great strength in El Salvador in the 1980s and remarkable tenacity, at least, in Guatemala, but counterrevolutionary forces, backed by the United States, also remained strong, as conflict surged and ebbed and surged again without resolution (see Chapter 16).

Facilitating Factors. Reams have been written on the causes of revolution in Latin America. Most of the causal factors cited fall into the category we have labeled "social mobilization." Such factors may rightly be viewed as causing pressure for political change, but they do not in themselves cause violent revolution. A necessary, though not sufficient, cause of violent revolution is the violent suppression of the nonviolent pursuit of change—that is, the blocking of the evolutionary process.

Factors that have facilitated or contributed to the perpetual blockage of the evolutionary process, and thus to the maintenance of a very low level of political participation, have included great social distance between elites and masses and proximity to the hegemonic power. The importance of the social distance factor lies in part in paranoia. The small elites of European origin who preside over a different racial group with an alien culture tend to feel exceedingly vulnerable and to fear that the slightest break in the traditional system of authority will unleash the contained wrath of centuries. Rather than welcoming the development of an incipient middle class that might serve a brokerage role and accepting the marginal political changes that might allow "things to go on as they are," the elites systematically eradicate would-be political brokers and strive to maintain a vacuum in the political center. This pattern has been particularly clear in recent decades in El Salvador and Guatemala.

The significance of close ties between dominant and client states has several facets. The most obvious is that, bulwarked by the might of the colonial or hegemonic power, colonial or client-state oligarchies are under little pressure to offer incremental concessions to middle or lower classes. But, as previously noted, there is also a historical connection between the factors of social distance and external control. European civilization in the New World was built quite literally on the ruins of Indian ones, and figuratively on the backs of Indians and transplanted Africans; so it is not coincidental that the areas of earliest and deepest penetration by the colonial powers are also the areas of least racial homogeneity and greatest social distance. Those are also the areas in which landed aristocracies, with the long-term backing of colonial military, religious, and bureaucratic authority, became most firmly entrenched.

Furthermore, even after routing the Spanish, the supposedly free states of Middle America and the Caribbean had little respite from foreign domination. After seizing half of Mexico's territory, the United States, devastated by its own Civil War, had to suffer competition from the French in Mexico and from the British in Central America in the latter half of the nineteenth century—but by the turn of the twentieth century, U.S. control over that area was virtually complete. In the Dominican Republic, Hispanic elites, frightened by Haiti's successful slave revolt and a subsequent period of Haitian occupation of their end of the island, scrambled to exchange national sovereignty for security under the flag of some stronger country. They succeeded in persuading the Spanish to return for a brief sojourn. Cuba, after the Spanish American War, merely exchanged one foreign master for another.

Thus, there was rarely a time when middle-class pretenders, sporting reformist ideas, could pose a credible threat to ruling aristocracies. As major U.S. corporations became an integral part of the power elite of those countries, the U.S. government made it clear that it would intervene militarily, if necessary, to protect the economic order from the greed and depredations of hungry natives. In fact, the United States did intervene extensively in the area and established constabularies in several countries that, in time, replaced the original landholding oligarchy at the pinnacle of power.

Finally, the greater the economic and political dominance or penetration of a foreign power, the fewer will be the nationals with a major stake in the old order. By the mid-twentieth century, the extent of U.S. economic holdings in much of Middle America and the Caribbean, and the fact that ruling constabularies answered to the United States rather than to any sector of local society, meant that relatively few families had extensive economic interests to protect and fewer still had a stake in the political order. Furthermore, the crudeness of U.S. power plays enhanced the importance of nationalism as a unifying theme. All of these factors facilitated the construction of a multiclass alliance in opposition to the ruling groups, particularly in Cuba and Nicaragua and to varying extents in Mexico, Guatemala, and the Dominican Republic. In the last two countries, reformist, potentially revolutionary, movements were crushed in 1954 and 1965, respectively, by U.S. military intervention.

Another social phenomenon that has correlated with insurgency and, in some cases, with successful revolution in Latin America has been the physical uprooting of subject populations. In the case of the Chaco War between Bolivia and Paraguay (1932–1935), peasants on both sides of the border, mobilized for the war, were not prepared to be demobilized when the fighting was over. In Paraguay, they contributed to the rise of a new party, which seized power in 1936. In Bolivia, they organized other Indian peasants, who ultimately seized the land and disestablished the Hispanic landholding aristocracy.

Throughout Middle America in the late nineteenth and early twentieth centuries, Indians were driven from their traditional communally held lands by Hispanic planters or by U.S. corporations intent upon cashing in on the expanding market for export crops, particularly coffee. Many of the peasant uprisings of the period, including that led by Zapata in Mexico, represented efforts to take back land that had been seized.

In Central America, the cycle of planter encroachment, peasant uprising, and government reprisal that gave rise, for example, to El Salvador's notorious *matanza* of 1932—the massacre of some 30,000 Indian peasants—has continued up to the present. The creeping uprootedness of Salvadorans was exacerbated suddenly in 1969 when the Soccer War, fought against Honduras, resulted in the displacement of some 300,000 Salvadoran peasants who had settled on uncrowded land across the Honduran border. These peasants were thrust back upon a rural society in which a majority of the peasants were already landless migrants in desperate competition for seasonal labor at meager wages. In northern Guatemala, the pace of seizure of Indian land by non-Indians was accelerated in the 1970s as a consequence of the discovery of oil in the region.

The Phases of Revolution.   The phases of a successful revolution that runs its full course—that is, without falling prey to counterrevolution—might be described as (1) power transfer, (2) redistribution, (3) institutionalization, and (4) reconcentration.

Power Transfer. The political, or power transfer, phase is a twofold one, comprising the toppling of the offending regime and the consolidation of the new power structure. The first step of a revolution, the displacement of the old regime, calls for the launching of insurrectionary movements on different social levels, either independently or in coalition. Intra-elite political conflict is not, in itself, revolutionary. On the other hand, uprisings of workers or peasants stand little chance of success unless there are important pockets of alienation in the middle class as well or unless the ruling class is sharply divided.

The dethroning, however, is only the beginning of the reallocation of political power. The affluent and the indigent, who might agree on the kind of government they do not want, cannot be expected to agree on the kind they want in its place. The struggle then continues within the coalition itself. As has often been noted, revolutions consume many of their authors.

In Mexico, after the demise of the dictatorship of Porfirio Díaz in 1911, armed struggle continued intermittently for another ten years; yet another decade was to pass before power was consolidated in a predominantly middle-class party representing predominantly middle-class interests. In Bolivia, the middle-class party, the National Revolutionary Movement (MNR), which took power in 1952, chose to embrace the rampaging Indian peasants rather than attempt to suppress them. Nevertheless, the brevity of the tenure of the Bolivian Revolution may be attributed in part to the facts that the competing interests of the three elements of the revolutionary triad—the MNR, the miners, and the peasants—were never reconciled and that no element of the triad was able to gain control over the others.

In the Cuban case, the consolidation of power in the hands of Castro and his rebel army, who favored, in particular, the rural poor, was facilitated by the mass exodus of middle- and upper-class Cubans to the United States. In Nicaragua, the multi-class coalition that strained to project unity when Somoza fled with the national treasury in 1979 began to unravel within the year. Anti-Somoza businessmen, overwhelmed in their bid for power by workers and peasants mobilized in support of the Sandinistas, turned to subversion in league with exiled national guardsmen and the U.S. government.

Class Demolition and Redistribution. The fate of the various upper-level social strata, and of the organizations and institutions representing them in political competition, has varied greatly from country to country in the aftermath of revolution. In general, however, a successful revolution requires the displacement of the colonial or hegemonic power that has backed the ruling elite and underwritten the old order. Such displacement does not imply that the external power is stripped of influence over the client state; rather, it means that that power is deprived of some of its prerevolutionary points of access or of its means of participating directly and overtly in domestic power struggles and policymaking. (It is not uncommon, for example, in Latin American countries that have not undergone revolution, for U.S. officials to exercise a veto over presidential candidacies or cabinet appointments.)

In the case of Haiti, the colonial power and the landowning aristocracy were one and the same. French officials and planters were expelled (or killed) in the course of the fighting, along with the military and religious institutions that protected and legitimized the rejected social order. Fifty years were to pass before Catholic priests again appeared on the scene.

In the Mexican case, the revolution disestablished the landowning aristocracy and the Church, which, until the reforms of the late 1860s, had itself been a major landowner. The revolution also displaced that sector of the business elite whose wealth and power were based on export-import operations and other external ties and weakened the role of the United States in the manipulation of domestic power relationships. The national industrial sector was not a casualty of the revolution, but rather a product of it; that sector was nurtured by the strengthened postrevolutionary state while the state itself began to fill the vacuum left by the displacement of foreign business interests from infrastructure (such as transportation and utilities) and the primary production sector.

Bolivia's landowning aristocracy was displaced in 1952 along with the private interests controlling the country's major industry, the tin mines. The Church, which had never been strong in Bolivia, was relatively unaffected, but the military officer corps was purged of the protectors of the prerevolutionary order. Although the United States had previously sought to suppress the MNR, the country had little visibility in Bolivia and thus was not a major target of the revolutionary process. Consequently, the new MNR government accepted U.S. economic and military assistance under conditions that contributed to the disintegration of the revolutionary coalition, the nurturing of a new military elite, and, ultimately, to counterrevolution. Hernán Siles Suazo, president from 1956 to 1960, commenting later on the strings attached to U.S. assistance, said that the United States had given him just enough rope to hang himself.

Prerevolutionary Cuba was so thoroughly penetrated by U.S. businesses that its patriarchal landholding elite and its nationally oriented industrialist class were relatively small and weak. Thus, the most important displacements of the revolution were those of the hegemonic power (the United States) and the military establishment that served it and of the businesses based in or linked to the United States. Ultimately, however, almost all owners of income-producing property were deprived, as the economy was thoroughly socialized.

The initial targets of the Nicaraguan Revolution were the Somocistas—that is, the dictator, his relatives and cronies, and the national guard that propped up the Somoza dynasty on the local level—and the United States, which had been the ultimate benefactor and protector of the dynasty. The removal of the Somocistas provided the first fruits of victory for the purpose of redistribution. The economic squeeze imposed by the United States and the counterrevolutionary stance adopted by much of the remaining commercial elite led to some additional nationalizations. Nevertheless, some 60 percent of the economy remained in private hands.

The role of the Catholic Church in the Nicaraguan Revolution represents a first. Whereas in revolutions past the stance of the Church had ranged from moderate opposition to outright hostility to insurrectionary groups and revolutionary goals, the Nicaraguan Church was among the most potent and committed elements of the revolutionary coalition. In the aftermath of the revolution, however, while most parish-level priests and nuns continued to support the Sandinista leadership, the bishops withdrew their support or made it highly conditional.

Just as there has been considerable variation in the extent of displacement and deprivation suffered by the upper classes in the aftermath of revolution, there has been great variation in the extent of redistribution of wealth and power and in the actual benefits reaped by lower social strata. The revolutionary process may be a protracted one. In the case of the Mexican revolution, the constitution that set forth the principles of the new social order did not appear until six years after the overthrow of Porfirio Díaz in 1911, and the participation of workers and peasants was not reflected in significant redistribution until the 1920s, under the presidency of Alvaro Obregón. It was not until the administration of Lázaro Cárdenas (1934–1940) that the most far-reaching redistribution was undertaken. During that period, some 20 million hectares (49 million acres) of land were distributed to peasant communities (*ejidos*), workers' rights were expanded and wages raised, and the very important petroleum industry was nationalized.

The extent of redistribution, and thus the success of a revolution, depends, in large part, on how much wealth there is to redistribute. Cuba, at the time of its revolution, was a relatively prosperous country as measured in GDP or per capita income. Redistribution took the form, primarily, of the extension of services, and within a few years, Cuba's public health and educational systems were among the most comprehensive in the hemisphere. In Bolivia and Nicaragua, by contrast, there was relatively little wealth to redistribute. Haiti, where prerevolutionary wealth evaporated with the abolition of slavery, presents the starkest proof that successful revolution does not necessarily mean living happily ever after.

Institutionalization. The process of institutionalizing a revolution includes the creation of an entirely new set of political support groups as well as new constitutions, laws, and behavior patterns. The process is complete when a mechanism for regulating succession to power is functioning more or less smoothly. The most important umbrella organization for the new support groups is usually a political party. The Mexican revolutionary party took shape in 1929. It was reorganized in the 1930s and again in the 1940s, when it was renamed the Institutional Revolutionary Party (PRI). Presidential elections take place every six years, and until 2000 the revolutionary party never acknowledged defeat, though the 1988 margin was the closest ever.

The institutionalizing vehicle of the Bolivian revolution was to have been the MNR. The MNR's first president, Victor Paz Estenssoro, attributed the survival of the revolution in its early years to the creation of armed peasant militias.[5] But the party did not succeed in fully incorporating or co-opting the miners or in institutionalizing succession by prohibiting reelection; thus, the uninstitutionalized revolution succumbed, within twelve years, to counterrevolution.

In the Cuban case, the dominant vehicles of institutionalization on the national level have been the Communist Party and the Revolutionary Armed Forces. However, the levers of power in both organizations have remained in the hands of Castro and his rebels of the Sierra Maestra campaign. The national political superstructure is built upon an extensive base of popular organizations. Although the mechanisms for succession at the pinnacle of power remain untested, local representation has been regulated by direct election since 1975 and members of the national legislative assembly have been chosen by direct election since 1992.

In Nicaragua, the Sandinista National Liberation Front (FSLN), which began in 1959 as a tiny insurrectionary group composed largely of university students, was already in a clearly dominant position at the time of the triumph of the revolution. Groups mobilized for fighting Somoza and his national guard were quickly expanded and converted into vehicles for reconstruction and political support. Prerevolutionary political parties continued to operate after the revolution, but without numerical significance.

In the first elections of the postrevolutionary period, in November 1984, the Sandinistas won 67 percent of the vote. Under pressure from the United States, a coalition of prerevolutionary parties and factions withdrew from the race, but several other small parties participated and claimed seats in the National Assembly. Elections were held again in February 1990. This time, after a decade of suffering economic strangulation and proxy war mounted by the United States, the Sandinistas succumbed to defeat. The National Opposition Union (UNO), a U.S.-funded coalition of fourteen organizations, won about 55 percent of the vote. Elements of the same coalition prevailed again in 1996, though the Sandinistas, as before, remained the largest party in the National Assembly, with about 40 percent of the seats.

Reconcentration.   Twenty years. There is no "happily ever after" in politics. Revolutions, like other secular readjustments of power relationships, are impermanent. Wealth and power tend to reconcentrate.

Reconcentration is akin to evolution in reverse. It refers to a gradual weakening of the power and income positions of political participants from the lower echelons of the social pyramid. If a revolution is not subsequently undermined by counterrevolution, a period of reconcentration may be expected to follow the institutionalization of the revolution.

Revolutionary leaders may themselves become a "new class"—an economic as well as a power elite, as happened in Mexico. Or the new class may derive from the bureaucrats who inherit power when the revolutionary generation passes from the scene. In the Cuban case, although Castro and his rebel cohorts have conspicuously avoided the material trappings of elite status, rank differentiation, with accompanying privileges, has already crept into what was once a people's army.

Nevertheless, countries that have undergone successful revolutions tend to be far more stable than those in which progressive movements have been thwarted. And countries in which revolutions have been aborted, or reversed by counterrevolution, are the least stable of all. The redistribution that generally takes place within the first few years following the consolidation of a revolution gives most citizens a stake in the new government. That loyalty is likely to last at least for a couple of decades, until the passing of the revolutionary generation, and may, in fact, last long after the redistributional phase has given way to the reconcentration of wealth and power in a new class. On the other hand, where reform has been thwarted or revolution aborted, a vicious cycle of insurgency and repression generally sets in, a cycle that likewise may last for several decades.

Counterrevolution

Counterrevolution has been defined, for the purposes of this model, as the displacement of one or more strata of political participants from the base of the social pyramid. It may take place in response to an incomplete revolution or to rational or irrational fear of revolution. But it may reflect simply the recognition by economic elites that the logical long-term consequence of a political process that allows for the effective participation of nonelites will be redistribution of wealth as well as of power. In fact, since counterrevolution requires a military and paramilitary establishment at the service of an elite and/or of foreign interests, it is more likely to take place in countries in which political development has been evolutionary than in countries that have undergone successful revolution. It is precisely because the power bases of the economic elites and the connections of those elites with the military and the dominant foreign power have remained intact that a minority is able to override the apparent will of the majority—as imperfectly expressed, for example, in elections—and reverse the tide of redistribution. (The crushing of a political order through direct foreign occupation is not encompassed in this concept of counterrevolution.)

Although dictatorship has been the rule rather than the exception in the history of most Latin American countries, counterrevolution, as such, is largely a phenomenon of the latter half of the twentieth century; in earlier eras, there were rarely "participant" lower classes to be displaced. Among the first clear cases of counterrevolution was the overthrow of Guatemala's President Jacobo Arbenz in 1954, followed by the withdrawal of rights recently won by labor and the recovery by non-Indian *hacendados* of land that had been distributed to Indian peasants. Both Brazil and Bolivia underwent counterrevolution beginning in 1964, as did Chile and Uruguay in 1973. Argentina has experienced counterrevolutionary episodes periodically since 1930, the most dramatic having been those accompanying the military coups of 1966 and 1976.

Facilitating Factors.   Deterioration of an economy, expressed particularly by runaway inflation, is among the most obvious factors that contribute to counterrevolution. In the face of a shrinking economic pie, middle-class elements, generally dependent and insecure, begin to see the demands of the working classes as a threat to their own precarious positions. Thus, a major portion of the middle class, anxious perhaps because of popular agitation and/or elite-inspired scare propaganda, aligns itself with the upper classes in a bid to reverse the trend toward redistribution.

Since the proponents of counterrevolution are a minority element of the population (were they not in a minority, their interests would not be threatened by democratic processes), counterrevolution can only be successful if that minority can rely upon military and paramilitary forces that are alienated from the majority of the population. Furthermore, as the military role is central, the ultimate provocation leading to the overthrow of a reformist president and his replacement by a military government—typically, the first overt step of a counterrevolution—is often a threat to the military itself: rank-and-file insubordination, a military budget cut, or a threat of suspension of foreign military aid.

Even so, national economic elites and military establishments are not likely to undertake counterrevolution unless they can rely upon the help, or, at the very least, the benign neutrality, of the dominant foreign power. With the possible exception of some of Argentina's counterrevolutionary episodes, all successful counterrevolutions in Latin America since the middle of the twentieth century have had the direct or indirect support of the United States. In some cases, economic deterioration, military alienation, middle-class fear, and other facilitating factors have been intentionally exacerbated by the actions of U.S. government agencies. The complicity of the United States was particularly apparent in the Guatemalan, Brazilian, and Chilean cases.

The Phases of Counterrevolution. The initial phases of counterrevolution are related to those of revolution in that the struggle between proponents and opponents of counterrevolution is immediately followed by struggle among the counterrevolutionary conspirators themselves. Counterrevolution, like revolution, calls for a multi-class alliance—in this case, of upper and middle classes. It also requires a coalition of military and civilian elements. Even within the military, there are various factions with differing perspectives and objectives. In the Chilean case, the counterrevolution began with a bloody purge of the military itself.

Initial agreement among military conspirators to topple the incumbent president and to assume power in the name of the armed forces by no means assures agreement on longer-term objectives. Thus, simultaneously with the process of demobilizing the nonelites—the disarming of opponents in the street and constitutional arenas—the conspirators engage in fierce competition among themselves in the private arena. In general, power is first consolidated in the hands of the military faction favored by the dominant foreign power, though rivalry within the military is perpetual and the balance of power among factions may shift over time. Meanwhile, civilian parties and political leaders who expected to profit from the demise of their civilian opponents soon find themselves stripped of their power bases and vulnerable to the whims of the new military authorities.

Political Demobilization.   The most immediate and dramatic manifestations of counterrevolution are political. The street arena is the first to be closed down. Labor, peasants, and student leaders, for example, are killed or arrested, and their organizations are dissolved or "intervened" (taken over) by the new government. The constitutional arena is the next victim. Congress is dissolved or its less malleable members are purged. Courts and local governments are purged of uncooperative individuals. Some or all political parties are dissolved, and government ministries, university faculties, and communications media that might be obstructive or critical are purged and brought under government control. The political process moves back into the private arena, which is now centered in the military establishment but continues to embrace economic elites and representatives of the dominant foreign power.

The extent of violence involved and of government control required is dependent, of course, upon the country's level of political development: The greater the proportion of the population that had come to participate in the political system, the greater the violence required, at least initially, to demobilize it. In the cases of Argentina, Uruguay, Chile, and to a lesser extent, of Brazil and Bolivia, counterrevolution called for overt executions; disappearances (usually unacknowledged executions); the establishment of concentration camps; and systematic, highly modern, and sophisticated techniques of torture. In the case of less-developed Guatemala, counterrevolution was manifested in a reversion, so to speak, to the campaign of conquest and the Indian wars.

Although the Catholic Church, like most middle-class or nonclass national institutions, is subject to marked factionalism in the face of either revolution or counterrevolution, the severity of the violation of human rights in the course of modern counterrevolution has made the Church the primary bastion against the excesses of counterrevolutionary regimes. As the only national institution that cannot be crushed outright by military authorities, the Church becomes the refuge of last resort for the dissident and the devastated.

Once power has been consolidated in a dominant military faction and effective opposition to counterrevolution has been crushed, authorities are free to move ahead with the transformation of the economy.

Economic Transformation.   Counterrevolutions do not merely freeze socioeconomic relationships or maintain the status quo. The expulsion of lower social strata, such as workers and peasants, from the political arena results in redistribution of wealth from the bottom up. This may be accomplished through a combination of tax, tariff, budget, wage, and land tenure policies. Land reform measures may be revoked, or squatters may be expelled. Graduated personal and corporate income taxes may be diminished or abandoned in favor of regressive taxes. Social services may be cut, and wages may be frozen in the face of inflation.

The central role of the military and paramilitary forces dictates that their budgets will be expanded. The involvement of the hegemonic power and/or the requirement of external aid and investment dictate acceleration of the denationalization of resources and the adoption of policies that favor foreign enterprises over national ones. Thus, the national industrialist class, which supported counterrevolution as a means of containing the demands of labor, finds itself crippled by tariff and credit policies and foreign competition. And the middle class, having lost free expression and political participation, suffers also the shrinkage of its economic mainstay—government employment.

Institutionalization.   Institutionalization does not come easily to counterrevolutionary regimes, partly because of the difficulty of achieving legitimacy. Establishing procedures to routinize policymaking and the succession to power in a manner that does not threaten the power position of the ruling faction or of the counterrevolutionary elite also proves difficult.

Counterrevolutionary regimes have often sought the support, or at least the acceptance, of certain sectors or institutions by labeling themselves "revolutionary" or "Christian." Such regimes in Bolivia were able to court, or at least to neutralize, most peasant groups for the better part of the decade by waving the revolutionary banner while crushing the miners and other elements of organized labor. The revolutionary label adopted by Brazil's military rulers in 1964, however, did not appear to impress anyone.

Regimes claiming to be bastions of "Western Christian values confronting atheistic communism" often succeeded initially in attracting support from some element of the Church hierarchy. But as the oppressed tend to cast their lot with any institution that dares to speak for them, the weight of the Church's influence has shifted to those members of the hierarchy who have defied the government. In defending the poor and other victims of government oppression, the Church itself becomes liable to government reprisal. Once clergymen and nuns have been added to the ranks of those subjected to imprisonment, torture, and execution, it becomes more difficult for any element of the Church hierarchy to continue to serve as apologist for the regime. Thus, appeals to the pious soon lose their credibility, and counterrevolutionary regimes fall back upon the slogans of "national security" and "free enterprise" that appeal to their own limited constituencies.

Counterrevolutionary regimes, like other ruling elites, have sometimes attempted to co-opt or to establish political movements or parties on the supposition that such movements or parties could be controlled from the top and grassroots initiatives could be blocked. But they have generally found that organizational initiatives carry unwarranted risks and may prove counterproductive.

Military governments are not necessarily counterrevolutionary, but counterrevolutionary governments are necessarily military, generally with considerable paramilitary support (police, vigilantes, "death squads," and so on) as well, because the abrupt reconcentration of wealth and power can be carried out only by armed force. Such regimes have begun their tenure as institutional ones, or what we shall call "militocracies." Power is seized and exercised in the name of the armed forces, as such, rather than by a *caudillo,* and the military establishment as a whole becomes the first-line political base of the government. The nominal president may be civilian, as was the case in Uruguay from 1973 to 1981, and a congress may be allowed to convene, as was usually the case in Brazil between 1964 and 1985, but such officials hold their posts for the convenience and at the sufferance of the military. Elections and plebiscites, held with varying degrees of regularity and under varying degrees and techniques of control, are the rule rather than the exception.

The failure of such regimes to achieve legitimacy may be compensated for by the maintenance of a high level of repression and coercion, but the failure to routinize succession to power means continual instability and vulnerability. The process whereby the most powerful position, be it the presidency or the highest military or army post, changes hands among individuals and factions is generally one or another form of palace coup, although it may be bloodless and may be sanctified by "elections."

In the Brazilian case, probably the most successful institutionalization of a counterrevolutionary regime, the succession process generally involved an "election" or polling process carried out among the highest-ranking officers— for example, four-star generals. The victor of that process was then "nominated" by the official party and duly elected by an electoral college including members of the national congress and representatives of state legislative assemblies. Military elections—formal or informal polling among upper-echelon officers—are not simulations of democratic process; rather, they are simulated battles, as votes are weighted in accordance with command of firepower.

Decompression.   Decompression (in Portuguese, *distensão*) is one of the terms used by Brazilians in reference to the process that got under way in their country about 1978. The term will be used here in the same sense, but to refer to the process in other countries as well—a process of attenuation of the power and control of the military and other counterrevolutionary forces, resulting in a lessening of repression and an increase in political participation, particularly by the middle class.

The factors that tend to weaken the grip of a counterrevolutionary elite are not unlike those that undermine other elites and other systems. They include division within the ruling group or between that group and its constituencies, economic stress, and external pressure. Commonly, all of these factors come into play simultaneously and reinforce each other.

The headiness of power and the spoils of office, not to mention the occasionally genuine conflicts of ideologies, are just as conducive to competition within a military caste as within a ruling civilian elite. If power becomes highly concentrated in the hands of an individual or a clique, other factions that have ceased to profit adequately from military rule may garner support from civilian groups in order to unseat the offending individual or clique. The price of civilian support will be a commitment to some degree of political opening.

Economic stress is likely to exacerbate divisions within the military as well as to alienate some elements of its constituency. The support of the dominant foreign power may be weakened or even withdrawn as a consequence of the regime's economic mismanagement. Also the level of repression may reach such proportions as to embarrass the hegemonic power. Such was the case in the mid-1970s when human rights policies adopted by the U.S. Congress and highlighted briefly by the Carter administration served to weaken, at least temporarily, some of Latin America's counterrevolutionary regimes.

In the Brazilian case, all of these factors were apparent in the 1970s. But Brazil's decompression gained additional impetus as the façade of democracy—the apparatus of parties, elections, and representative bodies that had served the regime well in the process of institutionalization—blossomed into a reality beyond the facile control of the still-dominant military. In Bolivia, neither revolution nor counterrevolution has gained any semblance of institutionalization; instability has reigned supreme. When the military abandoned power in 1982 to the government of Hernán Siles Suazo—elected, but suppressed, in 1980—it was primarily because the economy had collapsed under the weight of military corruption. Economic collapse was also a major factor in the disintegration of the Argentine regime that occurred in early 1983, but the disintegration had been accelerated by a humiliating defeat in the Falklands/Malvinas War of 1982.

From Aristocracy to Militocracy

In general, the constitutional and legal systems of Latin American countries were borrowed from France and the United States and, at least until the twentieth century, served merely to legitimize political arrangements that had been reached in private—in the smoke-filled rooms of men's clubs and other gathering places of the wealthy. In such arenas, competition among landholding families, and later between landholders and representatives of new wealth based on international commerce and industry, could be regulated. Such competition was not necessarily peaceful; it often led to clashes among armed hirelings of families or sectors of the economic elite. But electoral and parliamentary systems were little more than a ritualistic adjunct to a process based on wealth, force, and interpersonal intrigue.

It was only with the successful bid for participation by the middle classes that electoral and parliamentary systems came to have a serious function. In general, however, Latin America's middle classes have not constituted an intermediate level of property holders. Nor have they represented other independent sources of wealth. Rather, they have been a salaried class, derived from and dependent upon the expansion of commerce and government. Their bid for effective participation, beginning in the late nineteenth century in Argentina and continuing into the early twenty-first century in Central America and the Andean highlands, could not (and cannot) rest upon their own numbers and resources alone. They found it necessary to incorporate the numbers and the potential disruptiveness of lower social strata, particularly the incipient labor movement, into their power bases. Middle-class bids for political power have generally been spearheaded by university students and intellectuals and carried to fruition by political parties, but they have rarely been successful unless they were believed to have the backing of organized labor. Thus, the effectiveness of the ballot box has been preceded by an effective demonstration of power on the streets and in the factories.

Where, for reasons of social distance based on racial and ethnic difference, the original postconquest aristocracy has concluded that it *dare* not expand political participation, and/or, for reasons of powerful external support, the economic elite has concluded that it *need* not expand political participation, the upshot has been either revolution or "boundary maintenance" depending on the relative strengths of contending forces.

Where aristocracies have felt constrained to give in to middle-class demands for effective political participation, democratic processes have acquired substance—for a time and to a point. But middle-class leaders have generally proved unable or unwilling to extend fully effective participation, through the electoral system, to urban workers and peasants, particularly when economic decline has sharpened competition between middle and lower classes.

Uruguay's felicitous early experience with the evolutionary process does not seem likely to be repeated in Latin America in the near future. Although a middle class may rise to the full exercise of political power through the evolutionary process, recent developments in Latin America suggest that, at least for the time being, there is a high threshold of participation that manual workers and peasants will not be allowed to cross.

Once middle-class parties and labor organizations have been incorporated into the system, political conflict may come to be centered in the constitutional arena. But, at least in Latin America and perhaps in most dependent states, limited participatory democracy contains the seeds of its own destruction. The greater the level of effective participation and the longer the unbroken tenure of constitutional rule, the more policy will incline toward nationalism, nonalignment, and egalitarianism. Thus, the middle class, dependent upon salaries from the government or the property-holding upper class and insecure in its status, begins to align itself with the upper class. These classes, seeing their power slipping away and their economic interests threatened, abandon the constitutional arena. They enlist the military establishment and the United States in their defense against the perceived threat—until recently "the menace of communism." Thus, counterrevolution is most likely and most violent precisely in those systems that have achieved the highest levels of political development through the evolutionary process.

The destabilized constitutional system is then replaced by a militocracy—a system in which the military establishment as a whole serves as a ruling elite. Competition for power within this system assumes the form of simulated battles, as command of firepower confers political power. Civilian instigators and supporters of counterrevolution soon find that military rulers are not content to become their pawns. Although economic policy initially reflects the interests of the counterrevolutionary coalition, over time it increasingly reflects the institutional and personal interests of military officers themselves.

Counterrevolutionary systems, like evolutionary and revolutionary ones, and the political and economic gains and losses they represent, are impermanent. But the praetorianism, or militarism, that facilitates counterrevolution and is, in turn, strengthened by it appears more durable. The Argentine military has often withdrawn in the period since the overthrow of Perón in 1955, but never to a safe enough distance to allow labor a free rein. Even though the military establishments of Chile and Uruguay have withdrawn from the direct exercise of power, it is most unlikely that those countries will return in the early twenty-first century to the freewheeling democracies that flourished before the counterrevolutions of the 1970s. Even if elections are unfettered, it will remain clear that full powers are not vested in the electorate. The experiences of Latin American countries suggest that nothing short of revolution would be likely to bring those military establishments under civilian control. And, as Bolivia can attest, even revolution offers no long-term guarantees against militarism. At any rate, in countries having acquired a large middle class, revolution is no longer an option. And in the post–Cold War global village, where economic policymaking is globally controlled by a creditor cartel, conquest of the state would no longer be much of a prize.

Transitions and Illusions

The end of the Cold War, and with it the end of the dialogue as to optimal and feasible means of organizing a new order, coincided with the end of militocracy in Latin America and the spread of democracy—at least the input, or electoral, side of it—over much of the globe. This welcome development may have become possible, however, precisely because those whose interests would be most threatened by egalitarianism do not feel threatened by the U.S.-marketed election-as-spectacle approach to democracy, with its soaring costs and sinking value.

By the end of the 1980s—particularly after the elections in Paraguay and Chile in 1989—all of the South American countries had acquired a facade, at least, of civilian, constitutional rule. The "redemocratization" of Central America responded to a somewhat different set of pressures and dynamics, including greater sensitivity to the peculiarities of foreign policy decisionmaking in Washington. The Reagan administration, seeking to roll back the revolution in Nicaragua and to crush rebellion in El Salvador and Guatemala, had found that scheduling elections throughout the region would persuade a recalcitrant Democratic Congress to continue appropriating military assistance. It was only in the 1990s, when U.S. interests and priorities changed, that the process of pacific settlement, initiated by Latin American leaders and supported by the United Nations, bore fruit and elections acquired a meaningful role in the political process. Even then, however, elected leaders generally operated within parameters narrowly drawn by military and paramilitary bodies and domestic and foreign economic elites.

Redemocratization has been accompanied by increasing indebtedness and surrender of economic sovereignty, the discrediting of reformist leaders and programs, and a return to economic elitism, albeit buffered by parties and parliaments and the ritual of elections. Civilian leaders have sometimes appeared to be virtual prisoners in their own presidential palaces, and violence, particularly against the poor, continues unabated. A Brazilian social worker commented that the military dictatorship had "democratized" the violation of human rights, in that many among the usually untouchable rich were also abused. The subsequent redemocratization has meant that violations have once again been restricted to the poor, who have always been vulnerable.

In the first decade of the twenty-first century, as in the early 1960s, most Latin American governments are considered democratic because elections have taken place. Now, as then, there is less to such democracy than meets the eye. The obstacles and deceits are, however, of a different order. In the early 1960s, "democracy" was being discredited in Central America and the Caribbean by fraud and in the Southern Cone by vulnerability to military intervention. Now democracy is being discredited by irrelevance—by the absence of options and expectations. The democracy of the 1960s was unstable precisely because there was hope—hope that political democracy might lead in the direction of economic democracy. The democracy of the mid-2000s is more nearly stable because there is little such hope (and consequently little fear). More than ever, electoral politics is the moral equivalent of sport. Military force is no longer required to hold the line. The politically articulate are kept in check by the lack of options—and the lack of an alternate theoretical paradigm; and the desperate are distanced from the comfortable by gated communities and new categories of police.

CHALLENGES FOR A NEW MILLENNIUM

The problems now facing the continent's old and new democratic regimes are staggering, but they are not the same problems that most preoccupied national leaders during the last interlude of civilian rule a generation ago. That earlier generation of civilian leaders sought means of modernizing their economies at minimal cost to traditional and marginal sectors. As it happened, the cost has been scandalous, but modernization has indeed taken place. The overriding problems now are not those associated with traditionalism but rather with the flotsam of modernization: inflation and unemployment, urbanization and population growth, migration and displaced persons, crumbling cities, crime, pollution, and dwindling resources.

Those Latin Americans who had dared to hope that the end of militocracy would bring economic development and social justice have been sadly disillusioned. In fact, the retreat of the generals has been only partial. And inequitable socioeconomic systems have been reinforced by the demands of foreign creditors and international financial institutions. Civilian elites who can no longer blame the military for policies that serve to line their own pockets at the expense of the impoverished masses can now pass the buck to the seemingly omnipotent International Monetary Fund.

The resurgence of electoral politics since the 1980s has come about in part because both military and civilian elites had come to recognize the need for an institutional buffer zone between management and labor, or between haves and have-nots. That is, elites had become willing to share their power—or at least their stage—so long as their new partners also shared the blame for inequitable policies. Even so, in many cases Latin America's return to democracy was instigated in large part by genuinely popular movements, parties, and leaders. Particularly in those cases, however, organization charts notwithstanding, the elected leaders have lacked the full powers normally associated with the office: most important, control over military and paramilitary forces, including the police, and over resource allocation.

Potemkin Democracy

After a run of just over a dozen years, the redemocratization trend in Latin America began to be challenged. The overthrow in September 1991 of Haiti's civilian president, Father Jean-Bertrand Aristide, elected in 1990 by an impressive 68 percent majority, unleashed a savage assault on the Haitian people and prompted an exodus of refugees toward an unwelcoming United States. Less than a year later, in April 1992, Peru's elected president, Alberto Fujimori, in league with the country's military high command, staged a coup of his own, dissolving the congress and detaining many of its members, particularly leaders of the dominant party, APRA.

In Venezuela, characterized for more than three decades by high per capita income and stable civilian rule, the debt crisis of the late 1980s forced incoming president Carlos Andrés Pérez of the social democratic party, Acción Democrática, to adopt extreme austerity measures. The upshot was rioting and police countermeasures that resulted in some 300 deaths by official count, 1,000 or more by unofficial count. The instability and discontent that followed generated a climate propitious for military conspiracy, which expressed itself in two abortive coup attempts in 1992.

Much of Latin America may be settling once again for a system relatively open but heavily compromised, a midpoint on the spectrum of political possibilities long known as *dictablanda* or *democradura* ("soft dictatorship" or "hard democracy"). New forms of authoritarianism have not been widely recognized as such, however, because in most cases repression has been selective or subtle, and elections, complete with hoopla and foreign observers, continue to take place regularly. In that regard, the Peruvian case appears to be a harbinger. New elections several months after the 1992 coup restored credit and international respectability even though they were boycotted by the major parties.

Staging regular elections in Latin America without eliminating fraud or expanding effective participation may also serve to legitimate older authoritarian systems, thus giving them a new lease on life. The Paraguayan elections of May 9, 1993, are a case in point. They aroused international interest in that they offered the prospect that after almost a half century of military dictatorship Paraguay might at last undergo a transition to democracy. Paraguay had indeed come a long way since the corrupt and brutal thirty-five-year rule of General Alfredo Stoessner was ended by a coup d'état in 1989. But in 1993, the ruling triad of military, bureaucracy, and official party (the Colorados) still had control of most of the money, all of the weapons, and all of the electoral machinery. Even so, a new generation mobilized to force a democratic opening. Freedom of expression and of assembly gradually came to be generally respected; and the electoral process, flawed as it was, gave the opposition a leverage point from which to extract concessions. By 1996, the judiciary and the electoral tribunal had undergone major reform.

Meanwhile, in the 1990s, elections in Mexico were becoming more competitive in partisan terms, as the business-oriented National Action Party (PAN) and the left-leaning Revolutionary Democratic Party (PRD) wrested major provincial and municipal posts as well as congressional seats from the control of the PRI, seriously weakened by assassination, increasingly blatant corruption, and ever bolder narco-traffickers. A presidential victory for the PAN's Vicente Fox in 2000 was widely seen as a democratic breakthrough. However, Mexico's economy, now linked with those of the United States and Canada in the North American Free Trade Agreement (NAFTA), remained a crap game for the high rollers and a downward escalator for the majority, whose frustrations were expressed in strikes and demonstrations as well as in a rash of new guerrilla movements.

Renewed or continuing momentum toward redemocratization in the late 1990s took the form of U.S. intervention in Haiti to restore civilian rule; the ratification of accords ending a struggle of more than thirty years between the Guatemalan government and the Guatemalan National Revolutionary Unity (URNG), a rebel coalition that has sought to represent the Mayan community; and serious attempts on the part of the Honduran government to prosecute military and intelligence agents accused of human rights abuse.

On the other hand, even Haiti, one of the world's poorest countries, responded to creditors' demands for austerity measures; and availability of the weapons used so freely by political adversaries in Central America in the 1980s gave rise in the 1990s to a rash of routine street muggings. By 2004, Haiti's President Aristide, reelected in 2000, had once again been overthrown by many of the same military and paramilitary operatives who removed him in 1991. And the political climate in Guatemala had become increasingly tense. Meanwhile, guerrilla activity, along with narco-trafficking, continued in Peru and Colombia, provoking extralegal and often brutal military and paramilitary responses.

The bad news in Ecuador in early 1997 was that the imposition of austerity measures generated a crisis that deposed a president and left the country at one time with three claimants to the office. The good news was that the crisis did not—at least in the short term—give rise to a direct military takeover. The colonel soon to assume the presidency did so by election—elected, in fact, as a populist and nationalist.

For the most part, contemporary manifestations of authoritarianism take the form of police power, its relevance to politics shrouded as unrest degenerates into anomic street crime and as economic problems giving rise to it become increasingly untreatable at the national level. Still, to say that democracy is failing to live up to its promise is not to say that parties and elections and parliaments are likely to be abandoned. In many countries, though progress in demilitarization has been halting and exasperatingly slow, military power has continued to ebb. Few other than would-be autocrats see promise, at this point, in autocracy. And only those having very short memories could fail to find hope in an increased measure of respect for human and civil rights.

Getting Out of Control

At the turn of the twentieth century, in some of the most populous and most rapidly modernizing countries—Brazil, Argentina, and Mexico, for example—spurts of export-driven growth gave rise to illusions of economic progress. But the wealth so accumulated did not trickle down. And hard-working people tired of waiting to be trickled on. They also tired of waiting for the nonperforming seeds of democracy to take root. The upshot in Brazil was a halting but relatively peaceful and ultimately successful independence movement. In Argentina, it was a breakthrough from oligarchic to middle-class rule, underpinned by a broadly based political party. In Mexico, the upshot was all-consuming revolution that for a time brought peasants and workers to the bargaining table and that enabled a party of egalitarian roots to rule for some three-quarters of a century.

As before in Latin America, at the turn of the twenty-first century, spurts of economic growth bouncing from country to country, generated now by the draw of a broader range of resources, including cheap labor, offered the illusion of economic recovery. Economists' number-crunching captured the tide of globalized free market successes but failed to record the gathering of a powerful undertow of anger and desperation. Likewise, as before, the illusion of democracy heightened frustration and opened crevices in carefully crafted control systems, giving rise to open agitation for the real thing.

What may come to be seen as a new phase of Latin American populism was heralded by the election of Hugo Chávez to the presidency of Venezuela in 1998. The election, by a strong margin, of the colonel who had led the first of two abortive coup attempts in the 1990s was generally viewed as a strong repudiation of the country's political establishment. Chávez's election on a nationalist, populist platform was to be followed in 2002 by that of Ecuador's Colonel Lucio Gutiérrez, leader of the military-indigenous rebellion of 2000.

As will be elaborated in succeeding chapters, the undertow of nationalism and populism, deriving from new deprivations and expressed in new forms of organization and of street theater or direct action, has unseated more-or-less-elected governments in Peru, Ecuador, Argentina, and Bolivia. The same kinds of organizations, lacking the ambitions of revolutionary movements and the elaborated ideologies or programs of political parties, but strong in numbers, in solidarity, and in determination, have underwritten governments in Venezuela, Argentina, and Brazil.

The Brazilian government of Luiz Inacio da Silva, universally known as Lula, elected in 2002, was also based on the extraordinarily strong and broadly based Workers Party (PT), which grew out of the struggle against dictatorship. In Uruguay in 2004, Tabaré Vazquez of the leftist coalition Broad Front-Progressive Encounter was elected president. In Mexico, Manuel López Obrador of the Revolutionary Democratic Party (PRD) was leading in opinion polls, and the Socialist Party heading Chile's governing coalition was showing surprising strength.

The appearance that Latin America was getting out of control had become a source of some consternation to the administration of President George W. Bush, which had intervened openly and unapologetically, through "diplomatic" threats and assertions, to influence the outcome of elections in Nicaragua, El Salvador, and Bolivia as well as through poorly disguised attempts—successful in Haiti, unsuccessful to date in Venezuela—to bring about regime change by other old-fashioned means. Of greater concern to democratic leaders in the more developed states was the enhanced leverage available to those who would squelch any move toward expanded political participation and enhanced accountability through promoting market jitters and capital flight as well as through manipulation of electoral processes.

Other sources of unease were new U.S. funding agencies, like the Endowment for Democracy, for political operations; new technological exports, like voting machines of dubious security; and new means of information gathering. The Mexican government had opened an investigation into the collection of extensive and intimate data on its citizens by the U.S. Department of Justice through a long-term contract with the same company that in 2000 overhauled Florida's voter registration records so as to erroneously disenfranchise thousands of mainly black voters in a presidential election decided by a few hundred votes.

How unfortunate it is that, when confronted by demands from Latin America's disadvantaged masses for greater participation, U.S. leaders who speak fervently of promoting democracy in Latin America pull ever tighter the leash of hemispheric hegemony. In so doing, those U.S. leaders make it ever more clear to Latin Americans that achieving democracy must mean "getting out of control," that there can be no democracy without national sovereignty.

NOTES

1. Charles W. Anderson, *Politics and Economic Change in Latin America* (Princeton, N.J.: Van Nostrand, 1967).

2. Martin C. Needler, *An Introduction to Latin American Politics: The Structure of Conflict* (Englewood Cliffs, N.J.: Prentice-Hall, 1977).

3. Karl Deutsch, "Social Mobilization and Political Development," *American Political Science Review* 55:4 (September 1961).

4. Some scholars have viewed the outcome of Costa Rica's civil strife of 1948 as revolutionary. Others have viewed it as counterrevolutionary. The outcome, in this author's view,

was a mixed one, with gains and losses for elements of both upper and lower social strata, but one that did not fundamentally alter the evolutionary course of change.

5. Conversations with Paz Estenssoro, Albuquerque, spring 1978. Paz told of a visit during his presidency by a delegation of peasants from a village on the Altiplano. They had come to plead for a telephone for the village and for a bridge to connect the village with a road leading to La Paz. Paz Estenssoro responded that the demands on his administration were enormous and the treasury was bare. Thereupon, the spokesman of the delegation said: "Mr. President, I'm sure you remember that an angry mob hanged President Villarroel from a lamppost. When the counterrevolutionaries come for you, you can call us on our telephone and we'll come running across our bridge and save you!" Paz said they got their telephone and their bridge.

SUGGESTED READINGS

From the perspective of development theory, Charles W. Anderson, *Politics and Economic Change in Latin America* (Princeton, N.J.: Van Nostrand, 1967), has provided a useful model of political actors—who they are and how they go about seeking participation and power. Martin C. Needler, *Political Development in Latin America: Instability, Violence, and Evolutionary Change* (New York: Random House, 1968), foreshadowed more recent work on the relationships between economic and political development.

The paradigm that has had greatest currency for dealing with the counterrevolutionary trends of the 1970s was provided by Guillermo O'Donnell in *Modernization and Bureaucratic-Authoritarianism: Studies in South American Politics* (Berkeley: Institute of International Studies, University of California, 1973). Penny Lernoux, *Cry of the People* (New York: Doubleday, 1980), depicts the changing role of the Church in the face of revolution and counterrevolution. The roles of Latin America's modern military establishments are treated in Philippe C. Schmitter, ed., *Military Rule in Latin America: Function, Consequences, and Perspectives* (Beverly Hills, Calif.: Sage Publications, 1973). Military withdrawal and the trend to "redemocratization" during the 1980s are covered in James M. Malloy and Mitchell A. Seligson, eds., *Authoritarians and Democrats: Regime Transition in Latin America* (Pittsburgh: University of Pittsburgh Press, 1987); Larry Diamond, Juan J. Linz, and Seymour Martin Lipset, eds., *Democracy in Developing Countries*, vol. 4, *Latin America* (Boulder, Colo.: Lynne Rienner Publishers, 1989); and Robert A. Pastor, ed. (with a foreword by Jimmy Carter and Raul Alfonsin), *Democracy in the Americas: Stopping the Pendulum* (New York: Holmes and Meier, 1989).

Cole Blasier, *The Hovering Giant: U.S. Responses to Revolutionary Change in Latin America* (Pittsburgh: University of Pittsburgh Press, 1976), deals with the U.S. stance vis-à-vis revolution, and Jan Knippers Black, *United States Penetration of Brazil* (Philadelphia: University of Pennsylvania Press, 1977), outlines the U.S. role in destabilizing democratic governments and promoting counterrevolution. More general coverage of U.S. involvement in the politics of Latin American and other Third World countries is found in Noam Chomsky and Edward S. Herman, *The Political Economy of Human Rights,* vol. 1, *The Washington Connection and Third World Fascism* (Boston: South End Press, 1979).

Among the many noteworthy books on mature and fledgling revolutionary regimes are Martin C. Needler, *Mexican Politics: The Containment of Conflict*, 3rd ed. (New York: Praeger, 1995); Jorge Domínguez, *Cuba* (New Haven, Conn.: Yale University Press, 1979); and Thomas W. Walker, *Nicaragua: The Land of Sandino* (Boulder, Colo.: Westview Press, 1981). Late-developing Andean countries receive good coverage in David Scott Palmer, *Peru: The Authoritarian Tradition* (New York: Praeger, 1981), and Osvaldo Hurtado, *Political Power in Ecuador,* trans. Nick Mills (Albuquerque: University of New Mexico Press, 1980).

Roots and branches of counterrevolutionary regimes are covered in Alfred Stepan, ed., *Authoritarian Brazil: Origins, Policies, and Future* (New Haven, Conn.: Yale University Press, 1973); Arturo Valenzuela, *The Breakdown of Democracy in Chile* (Baltimore: Johns Hopkins University Press, 1978); and Peter G. Snow, *Political Forces in Argentina* (New York: Praeger, 1979). Previous classified documents on the period of military rule in Chile are laid out and interpreted by Peter Kornbluh in *The Pinochet File: A Declassified Dossier on Atrocity and Accountability* (New York: The New Press, 2003).

Among the many outstanding books on tumultuous Central America are Stephen Schlesinger and Stephen Kinzer, *Bitter Fruit: The Untold Story of the American Coup in Guatemala* (New York: Doubleday, 1982); Cynthia Arnson, *El Salvador: A Revolution Confronts the United States* (Washington, D.C.: Institute for Policy Studies, 1982); Peter Calvert, ed., *The Central American Security System: North-South or East-West?* (Cambridge: Cambridge University Press, 1988); Peter Kornbluh and Malcolm Byrne, *The Iran-Contra Scandal: The Declassified History* (New York: New Press, 1993).

More recent assessments of the political potential of the military are found in Alfred Stepan, *Rethinking Military Politics: Brazil and the Southern Cone* (Princeton, N.J.: Princeton University Press, 1988), and Brian Loveman and Thomas M. Davies Jr., eds., *The Politics of Antipolitics: The Military in Latin America,* 3rd ed. (Wilmington, Del.: Scholarly Resources, 1996).

Post–Cold War works on the Caribbean and Central America include Anthony Payne and Paul Sutton, *Modern Caribbean Politics* (Baltimore: Johns Hopkins University Press, 1993), and Thomas W. Walker, ed., *Nicaragua Without Illusions: Regime Transition and Structural Adjustment in the 1990s* (Wilmington, Del.: Scholarly Resources, 1997).

Chapter 11

Women in Latin American Politics: Progress Toward Gender Equity

JANE S. JAQUETTE

Any attempt to address gender equity in Latin America must acknowledge the complexity of the region as well as the explosion of information and writing by and about women—in literature and the arts, as economic as well as political actors, and as women confronting a range of challenges, from structural adjustment to HIV/AIDS. This essay looks at women's political mobilization over the past three decades; it also addresses the concern that women's movements have been largely pushed to the margins of politics and that the promises of grassroots democracy have gone largely unfulfilled. The positive results of the recent wave of women's organizing far outweigh the disappointments, however. More women are entering leadership positions, both elected and appointed, and women's issues, although often contested, have made their way into national debates and public policy. Legal and cultural supports for male domination in the family have been challenged.

This essay focuses particularly on the period since 1975, when the first UN conference on women was held in Mexico City. By 1975, the trend toward "bureaucratic authoritarian" governments was consolidated in the Southern Cone, while the countries of Central America, except for Costa Rica, were ruled by military dictatorships. The status quo in Central America would soon be challenged by the successful revolution in Nicaragua in 1979, followed by U.S. attempts to overthrow the Sandinistas and prevent further revolutions in El Salvador and Guatemala. These events polarized the Central American countries most directly involved, but also mobilized women.[1]

The essay looks at women's politicization using three different frames. The first is an *historical* frame, which shows that, counter to the image that women are victimized by machismo and the Church, they have long been politically and economically active—during the colonial period, as fighters in the independence movements of the early nineteenth century, and in the twentieth

189

century demanding women's rights. The Cuban revolution brought new attention to "the woman question" in Marxist theory and practice, and women became increasingly visible as guerrilla fighters and political leaders as revolutionary challenges multiplied in the region in the 1960s.

The period from the mid-1970s to the late 1980s was the era of women's mobilization through *social movements*, from the marches of the Mothers of the Plaza de Mayo in Argentina in 1977 to the women who worked together to defeat Chile's authoritarian government of Augusto Pinochet in 1988. In the Southern Cone and Peru, women's organizations from many sectors of society joined broader coalitions calling for an end to military rule. As a result, women came to be recognized as political actors in their own right; they demanded space for women and women's issues in the new democratic governments that were coming to power in the 1980s and in Central America by the 1990s.

As democratization changed the rules of the game, social movements weakened and solidarity gave way to debates over *political representation*. How effective were bureaucratic strategies to create women's ministries and incorporate women's issues into the state? Would gender quotas work to increase women's power in national legislatures? Were women's nongovernmental organizations losing their ties to the grassroots and moving away from political advocacy to providing services that the neoliberal state could no longer afford?

I conclude by looking at the politics of the new millennium, which has been marked by fragmentation and self-reflection. There is a growing awareness that women's politicization is not only a factor on the left, but also on the right; that feminist agendas are encountering serious backlash; and that the Church, an early supporter of women's organizations, is actively opposed to reforms that can be construed to attack the traditional family or to extend reproductive rights to women. The costs of globalization have been disproportionately borne by women, but it has been difficult for women's groups to mount a challenge to the neoliberal model. Indigenous movements have grown in size and influence, revitalizing the social movement cause. These groups promote pluralist ideas of citizenship and are strong environmentalists, but their efforts to restore traditional cultural practices have contradictory implications for gender equity.

These concerns are valid, but they cannot diminish the remarkable successes—nationally, regionally, and internationally—of Latin American women's movements over the last thirty years, or the continuing effects of women's political mobilization on women's lives. Latin American states have signed and ratified the UN Convention on the Elimination of Discrimination Against Women (CEDAW). Women's movements have actively pushed reform on a variety of issues ranging from violence against women to the rights of illegitimate children and from labor laws to reproductive rights. Women's active engagement in public life is now seen as legitimate, and even male politicians have declared it desirable on the grounds that women bring new perspectives into policymaking. There is widespread acceptance of the feminist position that women should have a greater voice in the family as well as the state.

THE HISTORICAL FRAME

Women can more easily be excluded from politics when their history of political activism is forgotten or erased. Contemporary women's movements and feminist scholarship have greatly increased the knowledge we have of women's lives from the pre-colonial period to the present. Much of that history, as Francesca Miller demonstrates, is an integral part of the wider struggle for social justice in the region.[2]

Assessments of women's roles during the colonial period are an important dimension of the "encounter" between indigenous groups and their European conquerors. The symbolism of La Malinche, a Tabascan slave who was both translator and lover to conquistador Hernan Cortes, and to whom some commentators attribute Cortes's dramatic defeat of the Aztecs, has helped shape the view of the conquest as rape.[3] On the other hand, many European women who came to the "New World" helped establish settlements and even "managed expeditions on their own," challenging the view that European women were pampered elites.[4] The slave trade brought women from Africa, providing a further element to the complex mix of races that has characterized Latin America since the colonial period.

A growing number of studies explore family, legal, and church records to trace the lives of colonial women; these show evidence of resistance and revolt by indigenous women as well as men and challenge the view that women were powerless in the family.[5] Perhaps the brightest star of Latin American intellectual life in the colonial period was a woman, Sor Juana de la Cruz (1648–1695), who chose to live as a nun rather than marry. A great lyric poet, and a favorite of the vice regal court in Mexico City, Sor Juana saw her "plays performed and her poems published," and "transform[ed] her convent into a literary and intellectual salon."[6] Sor Juana was eventually disciplined by the Church for her writing, retreated to a life of self-abnegation, and died of a disease contracted while caring for her fellow nuns who had been stricken by an epidemic.

Sor Juana's story is an example of genius and courage; it is often cited as evidence of the strength of patriarchal constraints on colonial women who had to choose between marriage and the convent and were expected to know their place. Research increasingly shows, however, that the situation of women does not lend itself to easy generalizations and that a woman's status and power depended on many factors, including her class, race, education, marital status, and urban or rural residence.

The wars of independence in the first quarter of the nineteenth century (1804–1823) are replete with stories of heroic women who inspired the rebelling armies and became nationalist icons in the new republics. However, as Rebecca Earle has observed, even the most heroic women revolutionaries were turned into "passive symbols" after the Spanish granted independence. Perhaps the most famous example is Policarpa Salavarrieta ("La Pola") of Colombia, who was publicly executed by the Spanish in 1817, at the age of twenty. She was later portrayed "not [for] her valiant attempt to undermine the royalist garrison, but rather her beauty, her virtuous female character, and her unswerving determination to die for the fatherland," although eyewitnesses say she fought her executioners to the last.[7] In general, women were cast as "quintessential victims of war" and their most important patriotic duty was to send their sons to battle.[8]

Simón Bolívar recognized the valor of women "amazons" who fought side by side with men, but it did not alter his view that "women should not mix in public business" and that a woman's "family and her domestic duties are her first obligation." Nonetheless, Miller believes that the "iconography of women participating in the wars of independence" has had the effect of "inscrib[ing] women in history." These early heroines were "precursors of latter-day female political activists."[9]

During much of the nineteenth century, as the states of Latin America struggled to form themselves as nations in the shadow of British and then U.S. power, women virtually disappeared from view. Against the usual interpretation that the century was a period of gradual progress and liberalization, Elizabeth Dore maintains that women were increasingly displaced by capitalist property relations and disadvantaged by secularization, because the Church had defended women's property rights and officially backed "sexual equality within marriage."[10] From her case study of Diriomo, an Indian community in Nicaragua, Dore takes the position that during the nineteenth century local governments "modernized" patriarchy, using their "ample powers of regulation and surveillance" to "regulate matters of domestic life." The local government of Diriomo reinforced the patriarchal family, although nearly half of the households in the community were headed by women.[11]

In the twentieth century, there were two important challenges to this confluence of capitalism, patriarchy, and state power. The first was the rise of women's organizations promoting changes in the social conditions and the legal status of women. The second was the emergence of revolutionary movements. Although women were involved in the Mexican Revolution of 1910, they had little impact on the Mexican constitution of 1917. But women's visible roles in the Cuban (1959) and Nicaraguan (1979) revolutions helped ensure that the new leadership paid more than lip service to the Marxist ideal of women's equality.

Women in Latin America had begun to organize at the end of the nineteenth century, publishing journals that linked women's emancipation with the freeing of slaves and the progressive drive toward modernity. The first International Feminist Congress was held in Argentina in 1910. The women who attended were largely from the Southern Cone (along with Mexico the most industrialized and cosmopolitan countries in the region) and from sectors ranging from women in labor movements to professional women and volunteers. In 1916, North American and Latin American women joined together to form what became the Pan-American Women's International Committee; its members were also part of a wider international effort to bring suffrage and other women's issues to bear on the design of the League of Nations.

The Pan-American League for the Advancement of Women, founded in 1922, was the first international group to make the vote for Latin American woman a key issue. Although such "feminist" agendas were not met with enthusiastic support at home, where conservative attitudes about women's roles prevailed, Latin American women leaders drew on their international networks and continued to press for reform.[12] Their strategies anticipated the mutually reinforcing connections between the "local" and the "global" that have been an important factor in the success of contemporary social movements.[13] Latin American women took leadership roles in international forums, and women from Brazil, the Dominican Republic, and Mexico are responsible for the fact that the words "equal rights for men *and women*" appear in the first paragraph of the UN Charter.[14]

In the 1960s, the fact that women were combatants, and among the top revolutionary leadership, drew global attention. In Cuba after 1959, the Marxist leadership took women's issues seriously, leading the many guerrilla groups who took the field during the 1960s to publish platforms that addressed women's equality,[15] as did the Zapatista movement in Chiapas in the 1990s.[16] Some saw Castro's emphasis on women as instrumental to increasing Cuba's economic production. But many "second wave" feminists in the North were inspired by the Cuban example, particularly the revolutionary government's willingness to confront powerful cultural traditions and its efforts to incorporate women politically as well as economically.[17] Twenty years later, the "woman question" remained an important issue for the Sandinistas in Nicaragua.[18]

WOMEN'S MOVEMENTS OF THE 1970S AND 1980S

Initially, Latin American reactions to second wave feminism in the North were negative. Feminists were dismissed as "hedonistic" and self-serving, hostile to men and the family. In Mexico City in 1975, Latin American representatives rejected the feminist argument that male domination was the issue, arguing instead that "dependency"—the economic exploitation of the South by the North—was the main cause of women's oppression. Feminism was criticized by the orthodox left as a diversion from the necessary focus on class, and it was rejected as inappropriate to Latin American realities.

The events of the next decade substantially altered, but did not fully displace, that assessment. The term "feminist" remained controversial in the region, and economic and social rights were top priorities for the newly mobilizing "women's movements." As women's groups began to play an increasingly visible role in civil societies opposed to military rule, feminist issues such as women's representation, violence against women, and women's legal rights became a part of the debate over what kind of democracies would emerge from the transition process.

The women's movements of the 1980s were loosely knit coalitions of women's groups drawn from different classes and with different agendas, brought together by their shared opposition to military rule. Urban poor women had organized for decades in response to specific needs: for clinics, daycare centers, and urban services or to organize consumer boycotts. The economic decline that began after the first "oil shock" of 1973 and deepened into the "lost decade" of the 1980s propelled new forms of neighborhood organizing and injected grassroots energy into the struggle for democracy.

The case of Brazil offers a good example. As Sonia Alvarez writes, when the UN declared 1975 the International Year of the Woman, it inspired "women who had been concerned with issues of gender inequality in Brazilian society . . . to organize for the first time." Their meetings "provided the still politically repressed left-wing opposition with a new forum for political action." The early Brazilian feminists saw themselves as a "vanguard" who would head a "united, cross-class, mass based women's movement."[19] Meanwhile women of the popular organizations in the urban periphery (including some formed under the auspices of the Church's "Christian base communities") who had organized to address immediate issues, like daycare and the cost of living, began to discuss problems that arose in their personal lives, including their relations with their husbands and their desire to control their fertility, issues the feminists thought would be considered taboo. For their part, the feminists were torn between their growing movement involvement and their ties to political parties, particularly on the left; many opted for "double militancy," trying to maintain their activism on both fronts.

In addition to popular women's groups and feminist activists, women organized groups seeking amnesty for political prisoners, and trade union women began calling for women's departments within the unions. As the transition moved forward, and previously repressed groups were allowed to meet, women's groups were increasingly able to focus more narrowly on gender issues, while remaining active participants in the opposition to military rule.

Women's human rights groups were among the most visible forms of women's organizing in both Central and South America. In Argentina in 1977 (a year after the military coup), a group of fourteen women began to march silently in front of the presidential palace, demanding the return of their children who had been "disappeared" by the junta.[20] The Madres of the Plaza de Mayo would soon become the most internationally recognized women's movement in the region, providing a model and inspiration to groups in many other countries who were fighting for the release of political prisoners and for the military governments to admit responsibility for using state terror against suspected leftists.

The Madres were notable not only because of their cause and their courage, which helped advance human rights organizing around the world, but also for making a strength out of what had previously been viewed as a political weakness: their private role as mothers. The Madres "used traditionalism as a daring gesture" in a way that denied that motherhood meant passivity and submission; they challenged the cynicism and militarization of Argentine society, creating their own organization "based upon equality, ties of affection, and the promotion of radical goals."[21]

The politicization of motherhood blurred the line between public and private, taking issues like "reproduction, domestic tasks, the socialization of children . . . and sexuality" out of the realm of the "natural" into the world of the "political," as Mexican sociologist Gloria Bonder put it.[22] The Madres created a new practice of citizenship, showing how women could "*hacer política*" (do politics) in groups that emphasized solidarity over self-interest, while bringing about broad political change through nonviolence in the tradition of Gandhi and Martin Luther King Jr.

"Militant motherhood" allowed women to mobilize politically in the name of the family, rather than in opposition to it, turning the high value Latin Americans place on motherhood into a political asset rather than a barrier. In turn, Latin American women's groups, representing "collective citizenry of political motherhood," served as real-world examples for Northern feminists who wanted to argue that women's political participation should be based on women's differences from, rather than their equality with, men and that women's participation would change not only the content but also the style of politics.[23]

Women's popular organizations were also experimenting with new forms of political mobilization. In Peru, women's organizations were critical to family survival in the urban shantytowns hit hard by the debt crisis and structural adjustment. "In 1986, the municipal Vaso de Leche program distributed milk every day to a million children in Lima," according to Maruja Barrig, and "although there is no hard data, about 600 communal dining halls were organized by poor women in 1988 . . . ."[24] Vaso de Leche and the communal kitchens movement provided women with economic management and political organizing skills, with support from the municipal government, nongovernmental organizations, and the Church; both programs made use of the "cheap food" that was available through U.S. food aid.[25]

The neighborhood base of these organizations, their relative lack of hierarchy, and their collective goals led many observers to argue that, like the Madres, popular women's groups were part of a new kind of political mobilization; "militant mothers" were changing the parameters of the political. Along with environmental and human rights groups, women's groups fit the global rise of what some have called "new social movements" in the 1980s. The new social movements were different from political parties and interest groups in that they were not interested in gaining control of the state and that they "target the social domain of civil society" by focusing on cultural and ethical rather than strictly economic or survival issues.[26]

The idea that women should define their citizenship through their role as mothers and the belief that women's mobilization has had a substantial effect on politics have not been accepted uncritically, however. According to Maruja Barrig, "the communal kitchens . . . did not succeed in changing the way women valued their potential as citizens or as dynamic agents of change in their own communities." She concludes that, "lacking consistent links to the public sphere, the political dimension of everyday life remained separate from local and municipal politics, further accentuating false [gender] dichotomies."[27] Maria del Carmen Feijoo observed that the traditional gender division of labor, which had its ethical justification in Church doctrine, had acquired a new, secular rationale as a result of the example of the Madres, although she also recognized that political motherhood had opened an avenue to political participation for many women who would otherwise have felt uncomfortable taking an activist role.[28]

In Mexico, which underwent a long process of democratic transition from the mid-1980s to the electoral defeat of the PRI (Institutionalized Revolutionary Party) in 2000, Victoria Rodríguez finds women's politicization strongly linked to economic factors.[29] Rodríguez's analysis is also relevant to the region as a whole, although attention has been drawn away from economic factors by the primary focus on women in revolutionary movements in Central America and in democratic transitions in South America.[30]

The debt crisis and structural adjustment policies of the 1980s pushed more women into the labor force, including work in *maquiladoras* and the informal sector. Rodríguez argues that women's gains are "irreversible," although women earn only half of what men do and many women returned to the household when economic conditions improved. "Men have become exposed to female decisionmaking and household democracy, and women have come to demand the more powerful household role that accompanies this more democratic environment."[31]

The growth in the number of women heading households has been seen by many as a social and economic failure, but, based on her work in Mexico, Sylvia Chant argues that women in female-headed households have more options, that daughters who work are more likely to send money back to their families when they are headed by women, and (as has been shown in a number of studies worldwide) that women spend more of their income on their families than men do.[32] Chant's defense of female-headed households (which are among the poorest) subverts patriarchal definitions of the family and makes a strong case for increasing women's access to economic resources.

MOBILIZATION WITHOUT EMANCIPATION? WOMEN'S ORGANIZATIONS AND WOMEN'S INTERESTS

Observing the impact of the revolution in Nicaragua on women, Maxine Molyneux[33] suggested that analysts should distinguish between "practical" and "strategic" gender interests, touching off a heated debate about whether organizing to meet everyday needs without overtly challenging patriarchal institutions serves feminist goals. Along with class and race, the strategic/practical distinction became a central issue for the women who began to meet biannually in regional feminist "Encuentros" or "Encounters."[34]

The first, held in Bogotá in 1981, drew 200 feminists from fifty organizations in eleven countries, and debated the relationship between socialism and feminism. The 1983 meeting in Peru drew three times as many participants and concluded that there could be "many feminisms." The 1985 meeting in Brazil is remembered for the conflict that emerged when the organizers refused to allow a busload of poor women from a Rio *favela* to participate in the meeting.

The fourth *Encuentro* in 1987 in Taxco, Mexico, marked the first time a large number of Central American women and women from organizations of the urban poor attended; the result was a debate about what kinds of goals and organizations could truly be called feminist. Were women's groups who worked on survival issues only interested in "practical" outcomes, and not in "strategic" challenges to patriarchy? Should the issues of addressing urban poverty be left to the popular women's organizations, while feminists concentrated on issues like women's human and reproductive rights?

These divisions arose from regional as well as class differences. The women's movements in Central American had formed during the civil wars of the 1980s, in a very different context from the transitions to democracy that had shaped the South American movements. Few of the Central American participants considered themselves "feminist," and most had come to discuss the issues arising from their roles within revolutionary movements, political parties, unions, and peasant and human rights organizations.[35] In the end, the Taxco *Encuentro* opened the way for greater inclusivity and flexibility on the ways in which feminist goals could be pursued.

Race was an important focus of the fifth *Encuentro*, held in Argentina in 1990, with three thousand women attending; new networks were formed, including one of black women and indigenous women, who met separately for the first time. The next meeting was to be held in El Salvador, but was nearly shut down by the Salvadoran right on the grounds that the organizers had close ties with the international supporters of the revolutionary opposition (the FMLN) and that the meeting had invited the open participation of lesbians. Although the organizers received death threats, the meeting was held as scheduled, with 1,300 in attendance. The diversity of the participants and the range of panel topics showed that the movement had broadened to include the range of organizations and strategies that marked an extraordinary period of political change for women in the region.

DEMOCRACY AND THE CHALLENGE OF REPRESENTATION

In the 1990s, the emphasis began to shift from social movements, which were being displaced from the central roles they had played in the transitions by the return of political parties and legislative politics, toward questions of how women and women's issues could most effectively be represented through democratic institutions that were shaped by neoliberal economic policies, permeated by persistent authoritarian tendencies, and weakened by the lack of an effective and modernized judicial system.

Three initiatives seem particularly useful to illustrate the challenges of Latin American democratization for women. First, efforts to institutionalize women's "space" in the state by establishing women's councils and ministries to review legislation and initiate policy change fell far short of expectations. Second is the open question of whether quotas that ensure that parties reserve a percentage (usually 30 percent) of their nominations for women can succeed in creating a critical mass of women in national legislatures and, if that can be achieved, whether this will produce feminist outcomes. The third is what Sonia Alvarez has labeled the problem of "NGO-ization": Were NGOs becoming too professionalized and losing touch with grassroots movements? Were they losing control of their own agendas due to their dependence on outside funding?[36]

These questions emerged as key issues in the 1990s as women's movements seemed to have lost their earlier momentum and there was growing disenchantment with democratic practices and outcomes. Political science tells us that social movements arise during crises, and decline when the crisis is over and political participation becomes routinized. In democracies, political parties, not social movements, are the gatekeepers of the policymaking process and the conduits for popular concerns. When the military was in charge, women's movements—although not all women—were part of the opposition, united in purpose, and able to engage in collective politics. Their subsequent marginalization is distressing though not surprising, but it has fed growing popular cynicism as the new democracies veered between gridlock and "soft" authoritarianism and were repeatedly shaken by corruption scandals. Environmental and human rights movements also lost leverage during the 1990s.

Women have been disproportionately affected, however, by the loss of political space that has occurred under democracy. This is the case in part because, once the goal of removing the military was achieved, women were again made aware that they are divided by class and race and by their degree of commitment to feminist goals. Because the state's ability to mount social programs was sharply curtailed by neoliberal reforms, the differences among activist women could not be bridged by forming new coalitions to lobby the state to resolve social problems or provide better safety nets. Legal reforms, another arena focused on by women's organizations, were limited by the weaknesses and inequities of the justice system in every country of the region, and by the loss of support for universal human rights.[37]

Indigenous movements did gain new ground in the 1990s; their demands for relative autonomy had implications for citizenship and sovereignty, but did not make demands on state economic resources. In general, however, indigenous gender norms emphasize male/female complementarity rather than equality, which conflicts with the universalist view of human rights on which both feminists and human rights activists base their claims. Many women's groups found they were able to receive funding for providing services but not for advocacy, a result of their dependence on government funding or on foreign donors.

State Feminism: Brazil and Chile

Brazilian feminists were innovators in seeking representation in the state. Women of the opposition PMDB (Party of the Brazilian Democratic Movement) were experimenting with the idea of a "Council on Woman's Condition" when their party won control of the state of São Paulo in 1982. When it was established by decree in 1983, the council had "broad advisory powers," but "no executive or implementation powers" and no independent budget.[38]

According to Sonia Alvarez, the council "remobilized" the women's movement and led to a "two-pronged" strategy. Some women lobbied for specific policies, using the council as a point of access. Others thought the council had been co-opted and chose to work for change outside the state structure. An issue that brought women together was the prospect that the military government (still in power at the national level) might institute a top-down policy of population control. In the end, the São Paulo Women's Health Organization was able to work with the São Paulo Department of Health to administer contraceptive programs. The council pressured the Ministry of Health to create a commission on reproductive rights "to help promote a safe, accessible, and non-coercive federal family planning policy."[39]

In addition, in 1985 the Council's Commission on Violence against Women was able to get the state of São Paulo to establish the first *delegacia da mulher,* a women's police station staffed to deal with cases of violence against women. *Delegacias* were later established in other cities in Brazil and imitated by other countries in Latin America and elsewhere.

The São Paulo Council was a model for a National Council on Women's Rights (CNDM), which was established in the Ministry of Justice by President Jose Sarney in 1985. The CNDM had considerable policy influence from 1985–1988, including working with independent women's organizations to get its agenda incorporated into the new constitution passed in 1988, although many of the provisions never came into effect due to lack of enabling legislation.[40] Despite active lobbying, women's groups did not succeed in legalizing abortion, but they did prevent a statement that protected life "beginning at conception" from being inserted in the constitution.[41]

It is argued that the CNDM was successful because it worked with independent women's organizations to lobby policymakers and bureaucrats for CNDM's policy agenda.[42] However, many felt that the CNDM was too partisan and that it was better to work autonomously. In 1989, Jacqueline Pitanguy, head of the CNDM, and several other feminists resigned from the council when the Ministry of Justice cut its budget and President Sarney appointed new members with no connections to the feminist movement. Feminists were again appointed to the council under the next president, but the ties between the council and the feminist movement were never fully restored. NGOs, women's studies centers in universities, and journals became platforms for influencing public policy from outside, rather than within, the state.[43]

Chile's Servicio Nacional de La Mujer (SERNAM) provides another example of the difficulties feminists encounter with the state-based approach. One of the demands put forward by the women's movement in Chile in 1988 was for a women's ministry with cabinet status. When the center-left opposition came to power, it established SERNAM in 1990.[44] From the beginning, SERNAM was caught between the demands of its feminist constituency and the resistance on the right, which felt that the feminist agenda was anti-family. Because the governing coalition included the Christian Democratic party, it was sensitive to an increasingly active effort by the Church under Pope John

Paul II to promote "pro-life" and "pro-family" agendas. The first director of SERNAM did not come from the feminist movement and was appointed to calm conservatives rather than to champion feminist causes.[45] And it is striking that, although Chilean women are among the best educated in a country with one of the highest per capita incomes in the region, and despite pressures from a sophisticated women's movement and SERNAM itself, the Chilean legislature did not pass a law legalizing divorce until 2004.[46]

As the women's movement weakened, SERNAM became the main conduit between women's organizations and the state. María Elena Valenzuela (who was on the staff of SERNAM) maintains that "women lost the pluralist ideological space in which they had been working out their own issues" as SERNAM came to play a "defacto leadership role by default." Other critics have been harsher, charging that, because SERNAM occupied a privileged place, it co-opted women's groups and weakened the movement as a whole. SERNAM did support specific initiatives (many paid for by international donors) to educate women on their rights, address teenage pregnancy and women in poverty, and advocate legal reforms.

The right responded that many of SERNAM's initiatives amounted to an attack on traditional religious and family values. SERNAM's effort to have the needs of single mothers recognized in public policy was considered controversial because it challenged the conventional definition of the family. SERNAM was successful in developing a five-year "Equal Opportunity Plan" for women, but its attempts to get an equal rights amendment through congress failed in 1992 and 1995. An increasing number of women have been appointed or elected to public office, however, and all of the parties have recognized the importance of women's issues.

In Valenzuela's view, despite its apparent strength in the late 1980s, the women's movement declined in the democratic environment of the 1990s, unable to push for new policies or provide independent support, and that reduced SERNAM's ability to negotiate effectively for feminist reforms within the state. SERNAM raises the question of whether it is necessarily a good strategy to have a women's ministry, even one that is demonstrably doing good things for women, if it is seen to compete with feminist organizations outside the state[47] and is forced by its position within the state to become the mediator between feminist and anti-feminist agendas, rather than being able to pursue openly feminist goals.

Gender Quotas

Argentina led the way in experimenting with gender quotas by passing a law in 1991 that required all parties to nominate women to at least a third of the positions on their party lists (in proportional representation systems, parties gain a share of seats in the legislature depending on the percentage of votes they win) and required that women be placed in winnable positions on those lists.[48] As a result, women went from 4 percent in the congress to nearly 30 percent by 1995.[49] Since then eleven other countries have adopted quotas although, as Mala Htun and Mark Jones argue, their effectiveness in actually electing women increases when the electoral system uses a closed list system in a relatively large electoral district with multiple candidates.[50] Only Argentina and Costa Rica stipulate that women must be placed high enough on the list to have a reasonable chance of winning. The appeal of political motherhood has meant that both equality and difference arguments have been used to support gender quotas. Quotas are egalitarian because they increase the number of women in elected positions, but they are also defended on the grounds that "women's voice" must be brought into policymaking.[51]

Quotas have their critics. Some argue that they ensure that the responsibility for legislation on women falls to women, letting men off the hook. Quota systems can be abused for partisan purposes or when women stand as proxies for others. Feminists are concerned that the women who are elected under quota systems may have little or no commitment to women's issues, much less to feminist positions. As Virginia Vargas put it, commenting on the large number of women in the administration of President Alberto Fujimori (1990–2000), "authoritarian women do not represent [me] any better than authoritarian men."[52]

Quotas allow political parties to say they are "doing something" for women, without having to go out on a limb on feminist platforms that may divide their supporters. One test of whether quotas make a difference is whether women's representation affects public policy. Evidence from Europe and North America suggests that the presence of women, whatever their political affiliations, does make a difference, but in Latin America it is still too early to tell. Women legislators are more likely to act on women's issues when independent women's groups take an active role in lobbying for legislation and monitoring results. There is also some evidence that women representatives are more likely to introduce legislation for women when they are part of a "critical mass" and feel they will not be isolated as a result. In general, feminists have supported quotas on the grounds that they can have a cumulative effect over time, as the experiences of the Nordic countries (with high levels of women's representation and strong legislation on women's issues) show.

Women's Organizations and NGO-ization

A third issue is "NGO-ization." Although there is good evidence that membership in women's organizations is seen as empowering by the participants themselves, and there is no doubt that neighborhood organizations to address shared problems have had positive material effects while enriching civil society, questions have been raised about whether NGOs truly represent the larger populations for whom they claim to speak. Many NGOs fit the profile of "NGO-ization."[53] They are professionalized, have gone from more democratic to more hierarchical leadership structures, and are highly dependent on foreign and/or government funding. This has deepened the distinction between NGOs and grassroots or popular movements and has raised the question of whether NGOs can maintain their independence and their critical stance. Northern-based foundations, including groups engaged in human rights work or in promoting development, may prefer funding projects that deliver services rather than support advocacy, especially when that advocacy involves resistance to globalization.

Conclusions

The issues outlined suggest several concerns for future efforts to promote gender equity. Feminist agendas are under attack from both the left and the right. Women's "strategic" issues in Latin America are part of a cultural debate that has "gone global." The Vatican and several Muslim countries coordinated strategies at the Fourth World Conference in Beijing in 1995 to exclude the term "gender" from the conference document, with support from conservative groups and some Latin American states that did so under pressure from the Church.[54] They did not succeed, but it is clear that conservative groups are not going to be absent from future UN conferences, as they were in the 1970s and 1980s.[55]

The fact that the United States has used the "liberation of women" as a justification for its invasions in Afghanistan and Iraq, without regard for the backlash this will cause, is another sign that the international environment is changing in ways that are not promising for future advances in international norms or local practices. The last three decades of women's mobilization have greatly advanced women's legal, economic, and cultural status in the region, but it is increasingly obvious that women can mobilize women on the right as well as the left.[56] Anti-globalization and indigenous movements, which are on the upswing in the region today, are not likely to put gender equity or even women's leadership high on their agendas, although they do bring women into the streets.

The critique from the left comes in the form of an attack on civil society as a support for the neoliberal state. Although the expectations that social movements would radically democratize Latin American politics was never realistic, the more cautious hope—that women's organizations supporting democracy by representing formerly marginalized groups, monitoring implementation of laws and programs, and acting as a curb on corruption—now seems the product of a more idealistic moment. Some critics feel that the organizations of civil society have not represented the poor but instead have made it possible for the state to implement neoliberal policies, which have produced increased inequalities and loss of national sovereignty.[57] Veronica Schild's critique of SERNAM is that it has helped "integrate" women into a system that emphasizes individual improvement over collective action, and promotes "self help" rather than asking that states take responsibility for the welfare of their citizens. From this perspective, the very institutions that have been praised as pluralist, "popular" (meaning "of the people" in Spanish), and democratic have also enabled neoliberal policies to continue, despite their unacceptable human costs.

This does not mean that globalization would be halted if women's groups and other social movements had made different choices. It does mean, however, that women's groups are losing legitimacy on the left and with their grassroots base, along with their sense of purpose and moral legitimacy. One result may be a further retreat into autonomy; for those groups who are the most opposed to globalization, there is new unity in resistance. This would be consistent with recent data from a UN study that finds democracy in the region suffering from a "deep crisis of confidence" and that only 50 percent of Latin Americans today prefer democracy to authoritarianism.[58]

Nikki Craske has observed, "Latin American women have demonstrated a deep antipathy to formal politics and an attachment to their social roles."[59] Women remain more alienated than men from formal politics despite the fact that they are disadvantaged in markets (and therefore more dependent on the state to regulate market outcomes and provide social safety nets); they are also more concerned that the state invest in social infrastructure (especially education and health) and provide adequate safety nets.

But democratic politics has eroded movement solidarity and has not provided the economic policies and social programs that are high on women's agendas. Feminists will find disheartening the results of a study by Mala Htun showing that, contrary to the conventional wisdom, earlier authoritarian governments in Brazil, Chile, and Argentina were more able to make reforms in the areas of family law and divorce than are the new democracies.

Yet women have a stake in democracy, which has given them access to the public arena and representation in the state. And they have a stake in the state, which is the only institution that can regulate markets, provide security, and improve the performance of the judiciary, conditions on which women's agendas and gender equity ultimately depend. It is not yet clear how women will mobilize to confront these and future challenges, but it is clear that they will have a major part to play.

Notes

1. This essay focuses primarily on the Southern Cone, Peru, and Mexico. For an excellent study of women in Venezuela, see Friedman; for more on women in Central America, particularly women's experience going from revolution to democracy, see Luciak; M (forthcoming), and X and Y (forthcoming).

2. In *Latin American Women and the Search for Social Justice* (Hanover, N.H.: University Press of New England, 1991).

3. See Octavio Paz, *Labyrinth of Solitude*. Carmén Ramós Escandon suggests that a gender perspective on the conquest would look at how this affected the power relations among men, the relations between indigenous men and women, and the development of Latin American masculinity in "Reading Gender in History," Elizabeth Dore, ed., *Gender Politics in Latin America: Debates in Theory and Practice* (New York: Monthly Review Press, 1997). For a very different interpretation of La Malinche, see Tzevtan Todorov, *The Conquest of America: The Question of the Other* (New York: Harper and Row, 1984).

4. Miller, 21.

5. E.g. Asunción Lavrin, ed., *Sexuality and Marriage in Colonial Latin America* (Lincoln: University of Nebraska Press, 1989) and Lavrin, ed., *Latin American Women: Historical Perspectives* (Westport, Conn.: Greenwood Press, 1978).

6. Octavio Paz, quoted by Miller, 26.

7. Rebecca Earle, "Rape and the Anxious Public: Revolutionary Colombia, 1810–1830," in Elizabeth Dore and Maxine Molyneux, eds., *Hidden Histories of Gender and the State in Latin America* (Durham, N.C.: Duke University Press, 2000), pp. 139–140.

8. Ibid.

9. Quoted in Miller, pp. 34, 32.

10. Elizabeth Dore, "One Step Forward, Two Steps Back: Gender and the State in the Long Nineteenth Century," in Dore and Molyneux, op.cit., pp. 16–17.

11. Elizabeth Dore, "Property, Households and the Public Regulation of Domestic Life," in Dore and Molyneux, op.cit., p. 166.

12. The previous paragraphs draw on Miller, op.cit., chapter 4.

13. See Margaret Keck and Katherine Sikkink, *Activists Beyond Borders* (Ithaca, N.Y.: Cornell University Press, 1998).

14. Jane S. Jaquette, "Introduction" to Jaquette, ed., *The Women's Movement in Latin America: Participation and Democracy* (Boulder, Colo.: Westview Press, 1994), p. 3.

15. See Jane S. Jaquette, "Women's Role in Revolutionary Movements in Latin America," *Journal of Marriage and the Family*, 1973.

16. Lynn Stephen, *Women and Social Movements in Latin America* (Austin: University of Texas Press, 1997), p. 14.

17. According to *Women in the Americas*, a 1995 report by the Inter-American Development Bank, Cuba's 1975 Family Code was "ground-breaking." It "stipulated that men and women were to share equally the tasks related to the household and child rearing" and gave women "equal rights over the family's assets and participation in the country's economic and political activities." In addition, "the Cuban state implemented polices to provide women with birth control, daycare, education and job training" (Inter-American Development Bank, *Women in the Americas,* 1995, p. 105). For a recent assessment, see Maxine Molyneux, "State, Gender and Institutional Change: The Federacion de Mujeres Cubanas," in Dore and Molyneux, op.cit., pp. 291–321.

18. See Norma Stoltz Chinchilla, "Feminism, Revolutions and the Democratic Transition in Nicaragua," in Jane S. Jaquette, ed., op.cit., pp. 177–198.

19. Sonia Alvarez, "The (Trans)formation of Feminism(s) and Gender Politics in Democratizing Brazil," In Jaquette, ed., op.cit., pp. 21–23.

20. Marguerite Guzmán Bouvard, *Revolutionizing Motherhood: The Mothers of the Plaza de Mayo* (Wilmington, Del.: Scholarly Resources, 1994), p. 69.

21. Maria del Carmen Feijoo and Marcela Maria Alejandra Nari, "Women and Democracy in Argentina," in Jaquette, ed., op.cit., p. 113; Bouvard, op.cit., p. 15.

22. Gloria Bonder, "The Study of Politics from the Standpoint of Women," quoted in Jaquette, "Conclusion," in Jaquette, ed., op. cit., p. 224.

23. The quote is from Jennifer Schirmer, ""The Seeking of Truth and the Gendering of Consciousness: The COMADRES of El Salvador and the CONAVIGUA Widows of Guatemala," in Sarah A. Radcliffe and Sallie Westwood, eds., *"Viva": Women and Popular Protest in Latin America* (London: Routledge, 1993). On equality and difference feminism, see Anne Phillips, *Democracy and Difference* (London: Polity Press, 1993).

24. "The Difficult Equilibrium Between Bread and Roses: Women's Organizations and Democracy in Peru," in Jaquette, ed., op.cit., p. 165

25. Barrig, p. 164. U.S. food aid programs were stimulated by the need to deal with U.S. agricultural surpluses, not solely out of generosity, and have been blamed for lowering agricultural prices and undermining local agricultural production.

26. Jean L. Cohen, "Strategy or Identity: New Theoretical Paradigms and Contemporary Social Movements," *Social Research* 52:4 (Winter 1985), 667.

27. Barrig, op.cit., p. 155.

28. Feijoo and Nari, op.cit., p. 115

29. Victoria E. Rodríguez, *Women in Contemporary Mexican Politics* (Austin: University of Texas Press, 2003), especially Chapter 2.

30. An important study of a country that underwent democratic transition much earlier, in 1958, is Elizabeth J. Friedman, *Unfinished Transitions: Women and the Gendered Development of Democracy in Venezuela* (University Park, Pa.: Pennsylvania State University Press, 2000).

31. Ibid., p. 58.

32. Sylvia Chant, "Gender, Families and Households" and "Conclusion," in Sylvia Chant and Nikki Craske, *Gender in Latin America* (New Brunswick, N.J.: Rutgers University Press, 2003).

33. Maxine Molyneux, "Mobilization Without Emancipation? Women's Interests, the State and Revolution in Nicaragua," *Feminist Studies* 11:2 (1985), pp. 227–254.

34. In what follows I draw on summaries by Stephen and by Nikki Craske, *Women & Politics in Latin America* (New Brunswick, N.J.: Rutgers University Press, 1999); and on the discussion in *Women in the Americas* (Washington, D.C.: Inter-American Development Bank, 1995).

35. Stephen, op.cit., pp. 16–17; Miller, op.cit., pp. 235–237.

36. Sonia Alvarez, "Advocating Feminism: The Latin American NGO 'Boom,'" *International Feminist Journal of Politics* 1:2, 181–209.

37. Teresa P. R. Caldeira, "Justice and Individual Rights: Challenges for Women's Movements and Democratization in Brazil," in Jane S. Jaquette and Sharon L. Wolchik, eds., *Women and Democracy: Latin America and Central and Eastern Europe* (Baltimore: Johns Hopkins Press, 1998), pp. 75–103.

38. Alvarez, op.cit., p. 35. See also Alvarez, "Contradictions of a Woman's Space in a Male-Dominant State: The Political Role of the Commissions on the Status of Women in Postauthoritarian Brazil," in Kathleen Staudt, ed., *Women, International Development, and Politics: The Bureaucratic Mire* (Philadelphia: Temple University Press, 1990), pp. 37–78.

39. Alvarez, "(Trans)formation . . . ," op.cit., p. 40.

40. Caldeira, op.cit., p. 93.

41. Alvarez, "(Trans)formation," op.cit., p. 43.

42. Alvarez, "Contradictions . . . ," op.cit., p. 66.

43. Caldeira, op.cit., p. 78.

44. This account draws on María Elena Valenzuela, "Women and the Democratization Process in Chile," in Jaquette and Wolchik, eds., op.cit., pp. 47–73, and Veronica Schild, "New Subjects of Rights? Women's Movements and the Construction of Citizenship in the 'New Democracies'" in Sonia E. Alvarez, Evelina Dagnino, and Arturo Escobar, eds., *Cultures of Politics/Politics of Cultures: Revisioning Latin American Social Movements* (Boulder, Colo.: Westview Press, 1998), pp. 93–117.

45. Lisa Baldez (2002) points out that few of the women from the grassroots organizations in Chile were Christian Democrats (they had been supporters of the leftist government of Salvador Allende, the socialist president who was elected in 1970 and who died when the military attacked the presidential palace in the 1973 coup led by Pinochet). She comments: "Conservatives tend to view the women's movement, and feminism in particular, as a cultural cover for the traditional Marxist-Leninist left, and an unacceptable threat to the social order." *Why Women Protest: Women's Movements in Chile* (Cambridge: Cambridge University Press, 2002), pp. 193–194.

46. For a detailed examination of family law, divorce, and abortion in Argentina, Chile, and Brazil, see Htun (2003).

47. Schild, op.cit., p. 105.

48. This was largely on the initiative of Peronist President Carlos Menem, and in the tradition of the Peronist support for a women's section of the party in the late 1940s, under the influence of Eva Peron.

49. Jane S. Jaquette, "Woman and Power: From Tokenism to Critical Mass?" *Foreign Policy* (1997) 33.

50. Quoted in Craske, op.cit., p. 40.

51. Craske, p. 22. On quota laws in Central America, see Ilja A. Luciak, *After the Revolution: Gender and Democracy in El Salvador, Nicaragua and Guatemala* (Baltimore: Johns Hopkins Press, 2001).

52. Quoted by Craske, op.cit., p. 21.

53. Alvarez, "Advocating Feminism . . . ."

54. Sally Baden and Anne Marie Goetz, "Who Needs [Sex] When You Can Have [Gender]? Conflicting Discourses on Gender in Beijing," in Cecile Jackson and Ruth Pearson, eds., *Feminist Visions of Development: Gender Analysis and Policy* (London: Routledge, 1998).

55. On the advances made in UN conferences toward progressive international norms for women, see Mary K. Meyer and Elisabeth Prugl, eds., *Gender Politics and Global Governance* (Lanham, Md.: Rowman and Littlefield, 1999), and essays in Anne Winslow, ed., *Women, Politics and the United Nations* (Westport, Conn.: Greenwood Press, 1995).

56. For example, see Lisa Baldez, op.cit; Victoria Gonzalez and Karen Kampwirth, eds., *Radical Women in Latin America: Left and Right* (University Park, Pa.: Pennsylvania State University Press, 2001).

57. See, for example, George Yudice, "The Globalization of Culture and the New Civil Society," in Alvarez, Dagnino, and Escobar, op.cit., p. 372.

58. UNDP, "Democracy in America: Towards a Citizens' Democracy," April 2004. Available at http://www.undp.org/dpa/pressrelease/releases/2004/April/0421prodal.html.

59. Quoted in Craske, op.cit., p. 40.

Suggested Readings

Alvarez, Sonia E. *Engendering Democracy in Brazil: Women's Movements and Transition Politics.* Princeton, N.J.: Princeton University Press, 1990.

Chant, Sylvia, with Nikki Craske. *Gender in Latin America.* New Brunswick, N.J.: Rutgers University Press, 2003.

Craske, Nikki. *Women & Politics in Latin America.* New Brunswick, N.J.: Rutgers University Press, 1999.

Dore, Elizabeth, and Maxine Molyneux, eds. *Hidden Histories of Gender and the State in Latin America.* Durham, N.C.: Duke University Press, 2000.

Htun, Mala. *Sex and the State: Abortion, Divorce and the Family Under Latin American Dictatorships and Democracy.* Cambridge: Cambridge University Press, 2003

Inter-American Development Bank. *Women in the Americas: Bridging the Gender Gap.* Washington, D.C.: 1998.

Jaquette, Jane S., ed. *Women's Movements in Latin America: Participation and Democracy.* Boulder, Colo.: Westview Press, 1994.

Miller, Francesca. *Latin American Women and the Search for Social Justice.* Hanover, N.H.: University Press of New England, 1991.

Stephen, Lynn. *Women and Social Movements in Latin America: Power from Below.* Austin: University of Texas Press, 1997.

Chapter 12

GLOBALIZATION AND INSECURITY
IN THE AMERICAS

JORGE NEF

By most statistical accounts and with very few exceptions (Haiti, Honduras, Bolivia, Nicaragua), Latin America comprises the "upper layer" of the Third World. Unlike the Middle East, Africa, and especially Asia, the balance and diversity of resources to population is most favorable. In this sense, Latin America and the Caribbean, other than by virtue of their proximity to the overdeveloped "North," appear to have overcome the condition of critical poverty. Moreover, business confidence in the post "lost decade" recovery (3.3 percent average growth throughout the 1990s), which made investments profitable again, has fueled occasionally bullish waves of optimism among Western economic and political elites. However, distributional inequity, rooted in powerlessness and exclusion, has remained and even become more pronounced than in other regions of the world. Most of the Latin American population lives under very precarious and vulnerable circumstances. Even when economic recovery is factored in, the overall income levels are still below those of 1980.[1] As is the case throughout the globe, slow economic improvements have failed to translate themselves into social well-being. Nor are there signs of extreme inequalities being arrested, let alone reversed. Paraphrasing Brazilian dictator General Emilio Garrastazú-Medici's unintended irony in 1975, even in times of economic bonanza "the economy is doing well, people aren't."

THE PROBLEM OF INSECURITY IN THE AMERICAS

Despite the fact that all-out revolutions look unlikely for the moment, the long and deep social antagonisms under the seemingly democratic veneer have not vanished. Rather, they have resurfaced in the familiar spiral of poverty and institutional, repressive, and insurgent violence. The weak civilian governments that replaced the military dictatorships of the past and the few election-based regimes that survived the authoritarian 1970s are paralyzed by ineffectiveness and low legitimacy. A careful look at the emerging literature and the mass of statistical and qualitative data renders a view that is far from optimistic. The alleged business and official confidence has little to do with social equity, political democracy, or even the state of real economic well-being, nor with actual security for the region's inhabitants. Rather, it rests on the ideological illusion that a felicitous correspondence between market politics and market economics has finally emerged, preventing turbulent social change from below.

Two central propositions are advanced. The first is that the repressive military regimes of the 1970s and today's limited democracies exhibit a greater degree of continuity than the proponents of transition theory and the popular media suggest. Despite the normalization supposedly taking place, persistent violence and political turmoil are not things of the past. The underlying social, economic, and international forces, which have enjoyed extraterritorial power and privilege, still prevail. Contrary to myth, the Americas as a whole and with few and reversible exemptions have not undergone profound social revolutions. Their social and economic systems are mostly conservative and elitist. Regime stability has been maintained with significant levels of exclusion and systemic violence. The second proposition is that this kind of stability in the long run has hampered sustainable, equitable, and democratic development. In fact, the current style of modernization hinders real democracy and increases, rather than decreases, poverty and insecurity for most people in the hemisphere. As the current style of unipolar, imperial globalization[2] deepens, so do de-democratization, widespread insecurity, and mutual vulnerability.

The Roots of Underdevelopment

Since the sixteenth century, the region has been subordinated to one or another more highly developed part of the world. The patterns of production, trade, and finance have reflected an enduring satellite-metropolis international division of labor. The insertion of Latin America and the Caribbean in the global economy, with their boom-and-bust cycles, was firmly established by the latter part of the nineteenth century. The export economy was based on the overseas marketing of raw materials, the import of manufacture, and the super-exploitation of labor. The "modernization" of these commodity (and *rentier*) states has been largely anti-developmental, as endogenous development has been overdetermined and distorted by external factors, has been undermined by flights of local capital, and has resulted in the marginalization and exclusion of most of the population. Nearly two centuries after formal independence, structural underdevelopment persists.

Under the above conditions, social underdevelopment has predictably endured, creating conditions favorable to the perpetuation of outward-looking and parasitic commercial elites and facilitating the emergence of a patrimonial system of labor relations based upon indenture, paternalism, and servitude. Class and racial barriers have been intertwined in highly hierarchical, rigid, and exploitative social structures. The very existence of privilege has been largely a function of elites' linkages with external constituencies. Local oligarchies have objectively benefited from social inequities and foreign domination. These structural circumstances have been imbedded into the national states and the system of inter-American relations, bringing about a vicious cycle: The key function of the regional and local political systems has been largely the maintenance of a hemispheric socioeconomic order based on inequality and de-development.

After decades of frequent civil strife following independence, the prosperity brought about by increased demand for raw materials in industrial economies facilitated intra-elite compromise and the cessation of intra-elite conflict. Toward the end of the century most countries had evolved into various forms of stable oligarchic rule: "gentlemen politics." Generally, for as long as there was enough surplus to distribute among the elites, the dangers of regional fracturing and civil wars remained subdued. Meanwhile, repression, by the newly professionalized military and police forces, was effectively directed against the lower strata. The transformation of a peasantry into a working class was also a byproduct of the modernization and internationalization of the economy. While the military establishment acted as an insurance policy against popular challenges to the status quo, intra-elite consensus was maintained by regulating and facilitating private accumulation of the export bonanza. In a few instances (Uruguay, Argentina, Chile, Costa Rica, Mexico), the process of economic modernization gave rise to a greater degree of social differentiation, above and beyond the "butler" strata of officers and patrimonial clients in the public payroll. Instead, a middle class of sorts, constituted of professionals, employees, schoolteachers, bureaucrats, small retailers, and the like, emerged as a "buffer" between the oligarchy and the mass of workers and peasants.

The Great Depression of the 1930s shattered the old oligarchic arrangement. With the collapse of markets, the tenuous system of accommodation that had sustained the republics crumbled. As intra-elite tensions increased, so did the challenges to the existing order coming from labor, the peasantry, and the dispossessed. In the aftermath of economic collapse, the "Dictator of the Thirties" became a dominant feature practically everywhere.[3] Yet, depending upon the previous modality of socioeconomic development and institutional consolidation, the long-term effects of the crisis varied from country to country. In the relatively more industrialized South American nations and in Mexico, where middle-class reformism had evolved in the previous decades and where republican practices had become institutionalized, import-substitution industrialization (ISI) with populism became the dominant form. Under the leadership of a middle-class-controlled state, an uneasy alliance with national entrepreneurs and unionized labor was constructed. Their program was one of reactivation, employment, and national development. In the lesser developed societies in Central America and the Caribbean, where, with the exception of Costa Rica, neither a constitutional order had emerged (nor a professional and bureaucratic middle class played a meaningful role), the populist alternative was impossible. The political pattern there was one of strict exclusion of the non-elite sectors. For the next thirty or forty years dictatorial rule with U.S. support became further entrenched.

Both patterns of conflict-management began to fall apart between the mid-1940s and early 1950s. Riots, revolts, and generalized political turmoil exploded in Colombia, Costa Rica, Guatemala, El Salvador, Argentina, Venezuela, Peru, Bolivia, Cuba, and Puerto Rico. U.S. administrations, mesmerized by the Cold War, the Truman Doctrine, a newly established Rio Treaty for the collective defense of the Americas (1947), and the hysteria of McCarthyism at home responded to these domestic events in their backyard as threats to American national security. Local oligarchies, besieged by social unrest and unable to withstand popular mobilization and pressures for democratization, took advantage of the new international environment by playing with the anticommunist fears of their extraterritorial allies. Entangling transnational alliances between Northern and Southern business, political, and military elites were built. The East–West conflict created the conditions for both a new North–South and elite-mass confrontation. It also marked the return of an active interventionism reminiscent of the "Big Stick" and "gunboat diplomacy" of Theodore Roosevelt and William Howard Taft that preceded the 1934 Good Neighbor Policy of President Franklin D. Roosevelt. The rationale for interventionism was justified by a new and compelling ideological motif: the struggle between the "free world" and "communism".

The CIA-orchestrated overthrow of the elected government of Guatemala in 1954 was paradigmatic of the new mood. The long-term effects of interventionism were destructive for the region's institutional and democratic development. Washington became, in the eyes of many, the principal force for the preservation of oppressive regimes and an unabashed supporter of military dictatorships. Yet, even this support proved insufficient to prevent the popular uprisings that precipitated a crisis of domination in Venezuela and Cuba. Cuba in the 1960s appeared as the vanguard of a wave of national revolutionary movements backed by a wide array of popular forces. Its revolution was one of the most significant developments in the region since the Mexican revolution four decades earlier. It set into motion a fateful chain of events involving a confrontational escalation and a growing internationalization of domestic conflicts. Attempts to destabilize and subsequently overthrow Castro and reverse the revolution culminated in both the calamitous effort to undo the regime and President John Kennedy's Alliance for Progress, launched in 1961. Washington's main purpose was to prevent "another Cuba" by encouraging social and economic reforms in the region. Economic and social development was perceived as the antidote to insurgency.[4] It was to be accomplished by propping up middle-class, progressive reformist and democratic governments. But the alliance failed. Import substitution industrialization had already come to a dead end, populism had run its course, social tensions were mounting, and a profound fiscal crisis had set in. The inability of the reformist governments to deliver and quell social unrest rendered the initiative virtually useless.

Though ineffectual for the region's long-run democratic development, the other side of the alliance, as a containment strategy,[5] met with more verifiable success. It involved the isolation of Cuba as well as a massive effort to give the collective defense of the Americas encoded in the Rio Treaty a new meaning: the introduction of counterinsurgency and civic action as the central preoccupation of the region's security forces.[6] A radical reorganization of the Latin American military ensued. The change in military mission and doctrine from the defense of territorial security (external aggression) by conventional forces to fighting the "internal enemy" by special forces was a blow to the already precarious sovereignty of the Latin American countries. It transformed the U.S. security establishment into the head of a vertically integrated regional counterrevolutionary system, giving the local military a new self-justifying and professional mission: fighting "subversion," however loosely defined.[7] In a relatively brief period and irrespective of declared intentions, the local military and police forces (the latter through public safety programs) were turned into the dominant internal linkage groups, operating the lower rungs of the hemispheric security regime. With the reformist and preventive side of the Alliance for Progress marred by internal and external inconsistencies, the counterinsurgency and containment elements took precedence over democratic concerns. This reorientation became manifest as early as 1964, with the Johnson administration's encouragement and promotion of the Brazilian counterrevolution of 1964.

In the more institutionalized democracies, the exhaustion of import substitution and populism led to a breakdown of consensus and civic confidence. ISI with national-populism failed to bring long-term, sustainable development and political stability. In the 1960s, wage and price spirals became a muted and protracted form of civil strife in many countries. Political deadlock eroded both the legitimacy and the effectiveness of these regimes. Labor practices inherited from the populist years reproduced and accelerated the "push-up" effect of institutionalized social conflict. The rules of the pluralistic game decomposed in the midst of rapid mass mobilization. In these countries, the existing socioeconomic order, both domestic and international, ended up being maintained by resorting to naked, yet highly bureaucratized, repression under a new political alliance. The latter involved a coalition between the externally linked business elites, which gave content to a conservative economic package, and the security establishments, transnationalized by the ideological "professionalism" of the Cold War. The military, representing a unique externally trained, indoctrinated, and financed fraction of the middle class, provided the force required for keeping the population at bay. Its ideological-professional software was—and continues to be—the National Security Doctrine.[8]

Authoritarian Capitalism and the Repressive State

The above-mentioned doctrine, also referred to as "Pentagonism" by Juan Bosch,[9] was constructed on three notions: an internal and external enemy ("subversion"), an external "friend" (the regional security regime), and ideological frontiers. Its effect was to erode the national character of the local military institutions and decisively transnationalize the state. The explicit articulation of this strategic posture was the Nixon Doctrine, outlined in the Rockefeller

Report of 1969. The document clearly showed a shift in the normative ideal of political development, from democracy and participation to authoritarianism and order. Between 1969 and 1973, with a few notable exceptions,[10] the number of military dictatorships steadily climbed: ten in 1969, twelve in 1970, fourteen in 1972, and fifteen in 1973.

The liberal-authoritarian projects that unfolded in the 1970s rejected the nationalist and protectionist premises of import substitution and other induced development policies. Instead, economic growth was seen as a function of a re-insertion of the countries' economies into the international division of labor as exporters of raw materials: a return to a widened export economy. With the exception of Brazil in the late 1960s and the 1970s, economic modernization, far from "deepening industrialization," meant increased reliance on both the natural resource sector and heavy borrowing. The aggregate foreign debt, which in 1960 amounted to about one-third of the regional annual exports, had grown by 1970 to 1.7 times the total value of exports. Just before the oil crisis in 1973, it had climbed to 1.9 times that value. By 1993, the gap had grown to over 2.7 times,[11] and finally became stable at about 1.8 times in 2002.[12] The strategy of hyper-accumulation also involved the creation of favorable conditions, through deregulation, denationalization, and the disarticulation of labor organizations, for domestic and transnational elites to increase their share of profits.

The era of national security was not extreme only in its persistent abuses of human rights; the early neoliberal design of its economic strategies implied the tearing down of the welfare state and import substitution industrialization policies and of social safety nets developed since the 1930s. Authoritarian capitalism rejected the demand-side implications of the early Cold War liberalism of the Alliance for Progress and was more concerned with direct containment and the protection of the status quo than with development.[13] Other than offering "economic miracles" financed by illusive foreign investment, the orthodox policies imposed monetarism (later identified with the Chicago School) over the structuralist, Keynesian doctrine of the UN Economic Commission for Latin America (ECLA). These deflationary measures were far more effective as a shock therapy—by atomizing labor, freezing wages, letting prices float to world levels, and privatizing the economies—than in raising living standards. They were much more effective in the short run as weapons in a social war, defining "friends" and "foes," than as instruments of national development. On the contrary, the long-term socioeconomic consequences of these policies were, by and large, disastrous and persistent for the region. So were their social, environmental, and financial implications. In fact, far from generating stability and bringing prosperity, the combination of dictatorial rule with unrestricted free-market policies created a serious governability problem. The formula of authoritarian politics with free markets also set the conditions for the subsequent debt crisis and recession of the 1980s.

The bureaucratic-authoritarian states that emerged in South America, patterned on the example of post–1964 Brazil, were attempts at modernizations from the top, with strong external inducement. The benefits of this new order accrued to a small alliance of domestic entrepreneurs and speculators supported by a technocratic-military middle class and their business, political, and military associates in the center. Its narrow base generated a persistent crisis of legitimacy that was managed by three instruments. One was military force, through strengthening the alliance between officers and the domestic socioeconomic elites. The other was the inclusion of external constituencies—military, business, political, and diplomatic—to compensate for lost internal support. The third was the demobilization and exclusion of the bulk of the population. Dictatorship became an intrinsic component of economic freedom.[14] The social cost for the majorities was enormous, since overall living conditions declined and the gap between haves and have-nots widened. Nor did these regimes succeed in unleashing real counterrevolutions. At best the national security regimes provided a repressive brake against social mobilization, economic nationalism, regional integration, and a perceived threat from the left. The effective operation of their neoliberal policies required large amounts of external financing, which was facilitated in the 1970s and early 1980s by massive deposits of recycled petrodollars in Western private banks.

Foreign Debt and Regime Crisis

Indebtedness, fueled by the illusion of prosperity, ensued. As both the governments and especially the private sector in the region increased their financial obligations, the failures of production and exports to keep pace with borrowing, and, most importantly, with swelling interest rates, resulted in huge debt burdens. Despite diverse ideological discourses, the hard-line military regimes in Brazil, Argentina, Chile, Uruguay, and Bolivia did not behave very differently from the more populist ones in Peru, Panama, or Ecuador, or those in civilian-controlled oil-producing countries (Mexico and Venezuela), or in the microstates of the Caribbean. The policies may have had different intentions, yet their effects were similar: unmanageable indebtedness and de-development throughout the region.

The crisis of the dictatorships in Brazil, Argentina, Uruguay, and Chile involved the erosion of the political alliances that had permitted the implementation of the repressive socioeconomic projects. Other populist military regimes, like those of Peru, Ecuador, and Panama, quietly faded away. The main political limitations of the national security regimes were threefold. One was that government by force was ultimately untenable; the other was that the pretended security was based upon the insecurity of most of the population; and finally that national security was not national. The Nicaraguan uprising of 1979 and the protracted civil wars in El Salvador and Guatemala signaled another form of transition: popular, radical, and potentially anti-liberal. From a Northern optic, these endogenous developments posed a more serious threat to the maintenance of the hemispheric order than the erosion of the bureaucratic-authoritarian regimes in South America. The combined impact of economic crises, a growing inability to manage conflict among internal factions, and a new "post-Watergate" political coalition in Washington concerned about the long-run effects of authoritarian solutions created the conditions for military withdrawal. The Linowitz Report outlined a transitional strategy in 1975.[15] This document was heavily influenced by the views of the Trilateral Commission[16] and was critical of the previous "Pentagonist" policy toward Latin America. It constituted the blueprint for President Jimmy Carter's initiative on democratization.

Intra-Elite Alliances and "Democratic" Transition[17]

Democratic transition for most of Latin America was largely the result of intra-elite negotiation superintended by external actors. Rather than regime transition, this meant the consolidation of a non-democratic socioeconomic order under a formally democratic façade. The orderly retreat of the national security regimes preserved many authoritarian traits. In this, the re-emerging democracies shared some of the political characteristics of older "managed democracies," such as those in Colombia, Venezuela, or Mexico, which did not experience direct military rule. Such closely watched transition to democracy had strict limits. Although authoritarian capitalism proved to be largely a developmental failure, the radical restructuring of the economies along free-market lines by means of political repression had been profound enough to prevent a return to economic nationalism. Likewise, the restructuring and transnationalization of the security establishment made the pursuit of nationalist and nonaligned foreign policies impossible. In this sense, the political arrangements that emerged in Latin America as a result of re-democratization, while possessing the formal trappings of sovereignty and democracy, have been neither truly sovereign nor democratic. They have produced precariously balanced civilian regimes, based on negotiations within the elites, with exclusionary political agendas and narrow internal support. In these, the popular sectors are effectively maintained outside the political arena, while external actors, both economic and military, enjoy de facto veto power over the state. In addition, the countries have remained saddled with cumbersome, and in some cases unmanageable, foreign debts (see Tables 12.1 and 12.2), not to mention the debt-management conditionalities of IMF-inspired structural adjustment policies (SAPs).

The ultimate effects of these policies has been the perpetuation of both dependence and underdevelopment. The latter express themselves in a vicious cycle of built-in vulnerability to external economic and political influences, requiring ever increasing doses of external supports. This vulnerability can be dramatically illustrated by the inability of the countries to extricate themselves from chronic indebtedness: the "debt-trap."[18] Debt-management became the number one political concern in the regional agenda in the early 1980s. The service, both principal and interest, grew from slightly over 40 percent of the total value of annual exports in 1979 to over 65 percent in 1983. The total indebtedness figure for 1988 was over $400 billion, with the higher sums being those incurred by Brazil, Mexico, Argentina, Chile, Venezuela, and Peru.

TABLE 12.1   Indebtedness: Selected Countries 1970–1985 and 1985–2000

	1970	1982	1985	2000	1970–85 growth %	1970–2000 growth %	% Annual growth to '85	% Annual growth to '00
Argentina	1.9	15.8	50.8	146.2	2674	7693	178.3	256
Brazil	13.2	47.6	107.3	238.0	3353	1802	223.5	60
Chile	2.1	5.2	21.0	37.0	1000	1760	66.7	59
Mexico	3.2	50.4	99.0	150.3	3094	4696	206.3	156
Venezuela	0.7	12.1	33.6	38.2	4800	13966	320.0	465

Source: Louis Lefever, "The Problem of Debt," International Viewpoints, Supplement of the *York Gazette*, York University (March 2, 1987), p. 2; also in the 2002 World Bank electronic publication: www.worldbank. org/data/wdi2002/.

TABLE 12.2   Latin America: Foreign Debt 1990, 1992, and 2000 Figures

	Debt/GDP Per capita			Debt Service as % of Exports		
	1990	1992	1999	1990	1992	2000
Argentina	79.9	30.3	51.2	34.1	34.4	71.3
Bolivia	94.3	61.2	65.9	39.8	39.0	39.1
Brazil	28.8	31.2	40.0	20.8	23.1	90.7
Chile	74.7	48.9	50.7	25.9	20.9	26.0
Colombia	42.4	36.9	44.7	36.4	38.9	28.6
Costa Rica	70.9	58.7	33.6	24.5	20.6	8.2
Dominican R.	74.7	57.0	28.7	10.3	13.5	4.8
Ecuador	119.9	99.9	107.3	33.2	27.1	17.3
El Salvador	36.9	25.5	17.4	17.1	13.2	6.7
Guatemala	33.6	24.2	28.6	13.3	24.0	9.4
Haiti	37.0	*	30.6	9.5	*	8.0
Honduras	116.3	92.0	83.3	40.4	33.7	19.3
Mexico	44.5	34.1	33.5	27.8	44.4	30.2
Nicaragua	199.4	750.3	231.0	14.7	21.8	23.0
Panama	152.0	107.2	55.7	9.7	12.6	10.0
Paraguay	44.7	24.6	22.6	11.0	40.3	10.4
Peru	83.9	92.7	50.9	11.0	23.0	42.8
Uruguay	46.7	46.7	40.1	41.8	23.2	29.2
Venezuela	66.1	61.1	71.1	20.7	19.5	15.7

Source: World Bank, World Development Report, 1990, 1991 and 1992, passim. and 1994, pp. 206–207. Figures were calculated from data contained in The International Bank of Reconstruction and Development/The World Bank, World Development Report 1989 and World Development Report 1992. Development and the Environment, (New York: Oxford University Press, 1989 and 1992). Tables used include Table 1 Basic Indicators, table 21, Total external Debt, Table 24, Total External Debt Ratios, Table 26 Population Growth and Projections. The 1990 GNP figure for Nicaragua was estimated on the basis of the 1987 figure and an average decline of 2.5 % per year. 2000 figures came from the United Nations Development Program, Human Development Report 2002, p. 203–205.

Despite the fact that about one half of the countries had reduced their liabilities by 1990–1991, the over-all debt had grown to $421 billion: a 3.5 percent annual increase. By 2001, it reached $787 billion, expanding at an average annual rate of 8.7 percent. In fact, out of the seventeen most indebted countries in the world in 1992, twelve were in the Latin American region. On average the annual interest rate payments fell from 33 percent of all exports in 1987 to 22 percent in 1991, as the "lost decade" came to an end. Between 1992 and 1999, the burden was reduced even further: Countries like Brazil and Mexico decelerated their rate of indebtedness respectively from staggering annual rates of 223 percent to 60 percent for Brazil and 206 percent to 156 percent for Mexico. These figures are mind-boggling and unsustainable by any stretch of imagination. Argentina accelerated its already huge rate of indebtedness from a fifteen-year average annual growth of 178 percent to rate of 256 percent annually in the thirty years between 1970 and 2000. Venezuela, in turn, went from a yearly increase of 320 percent between 1970 and 1985 to a whopping 465 percent from 1970 to 2000. If the debt problem is measured as inability to pay, an analysis of the ratio between exports and debt service shows figures that are equally dramatic. For instance, the ratio of debt service to exports for Argentina moved from an already high 34 percent in 1990 to over 71 percent in 2000. For Brazil, the jump was from 23 percent to near 91 percent. So far, and despite economic disasters in Mexico (1994), Ecuador (1999), Argentina (2001), Brazil (2002), and Bolivia (2003), most countries in the region did not default on their debt, nor resort to a strategy of "debtors' cartels." This policy of fiscal responsibility has been extremely hard for the civil society, which had to absorb its full impact, especially after a number of governments have "nationalized" corporate debts.

The end of the cycle of national security in the 1980s was a direct consequence of the insoluble contradictions between and within the nature of the reactionary coalitions in power and the centrality of external supports for the authoritarian regime. Given limited resources, there was a long-run impossibility of reconciling the interests of the national security bureaucracies with those of domestic and foreign business. There was also the additional problem emerging from the extreme vulnerability of the countries to external factors (for example, the unmanageable debt burden and deteriorating terms of trade) and constituencies. As power conflicts intensified in Washington in the post–Nixon era, opposition from liberal political sectors against authoritarian regimes grew. Furthermore, the shrinkage of crucial support from international business compounded the internal erosion of power suffered by the Latin American dictatorships. Democratic transition became the alternative to popular revolt. The conversion from dictatorship to limited democracy has to be seen in the context of the previous transition to national security, both in the bureaucratic-authoritarian context of the Southern Cone and in the less institutionalized setting of Central America. Growing participation and dependent development could coexist only under conditions of economic expansion and for as long as such participation did not threaten the perceived interests of the local and regional elites.

The Nature of the Receiver State

The mounting debt crisis set the parameters for the emergence throughout the Americas in the mid-1980s of a new political formula: a *"receiver state,"* blending limited democracy and neoliberal economics. The result was a highly transnationalized and weak state, acting in partnership with foreign creditors and international financial institutions as manager, executor, and liquidator of national bankruptcy. The central function of this arrangement has been the administration of the debt combined with the implementation of structural adjustment policies geared to massive privatization and de-nationalization of the economy. This state reflects the nature of the transnationalized political alliances and the narrow spaces for political participation, where economic and fiscal policies have been effectively left out of the political debate. Yet these policies define the rules of the game and set the limits for social policies.

Pacts of Elites and Exclusionary Socioeconomic Agendas

The various national incarnations of receivership exhibit important differences. These depend upon the nature of the transition processes, as well as on the particular coloration of the civilian management, to appear in the post-authoritarian period and in the early adjustment phase. At close scrutiny, irrespective of the elected nature of the government in charge, the economic agenda has a striking resemblance with that imposed under authoritarian rule. These arrangements are not a mere transitional phase, from elite domination to genuine democracy: free and participatory politics, with effective popular control. Rather, the repressive state of the 1970s and the receiver state of the 1990s and 2000s are two different manifestations of a similar cluster of elite interests.

The receiver state expresses the consensus of a mostly transnational and conservative coalition, though at times managed by tamed center-left governments. Limited democracy with narrow mobility opportunities and exclusionary agendas provides a thin cushion to confront the deep structural problems once controlled by repression. The current modality of conflict management, while reducing the most blatant (and uglier) human rights abuses, has left the most pressing and fundamental socioeconomic and political problems largely unresolved. The combination of the transnational integration of the domestic elites (economic, military, technocratic, and bureaucratic) with the demobilization and marginalization of the popular sectors does not provide a formula for stable governance, let alone democracy. In the absence of tangible rewards to buy legitimacy, insurgent, repressive, institutionalized (as well as criminal) violence has become a common expression. State failure—as in 1999 Ecuador, or Argentina in 2001 and Colombia—has also emerged as a distinct possibility.

Despite the phasing out of the "old" national security regimes, contemporary Latin America is not undergoing a change toward substantial democratization. Formal demilitarization and return to limited democracy are not synonymous with an alteration of the status quo. Nor is democracy nowadays any more real in those countries in the hemisphere where civilian governments have remained in control. On the contrary, the prevailing discourse on democracy among the official intelligentsia throughout the Americas involves a juxtaposition of a substantially domesticated democracy with neoliberal economics.[19] The above model amounts to a plutocracy with popular support, occasionally resorting to electoral rituals. While this "low-intensity democracy" may appeal to the consumption-intensive, high-income core groups in the hemisphere, it is not majority rule. It is basically the same elitist formula articulated by the Trilateral Commission in the mid-1970s that considers the root cause of the crisis of democracy to be democracy itself. Under a legal façade, this mode of conflict management entrenches a corporatist pact of elites representing basically the same economic, social, and political alliances that sustained the antidemocratic regimes: the power elite at the core, the military, the local bourgeoisie, and upper segments of the middle classes. Democratic development, with the qualified exception of Costa Rica, is weak and fragile at best throughout the hemisphere.

The regressive socioeconomic policies implemented under authoritarian rule have been enshrined both in the pacts of transition and in ad-hoc constitutional mechanisms. The re-democratized regimes are constrained by other factors too. One is the weakness of the governing political alliances, since the transition arrangements effectively excluded most left-of-center and populist political forces from holding power. Another is the crucial, autonomous role played by the transnationalized security forces, as a parallel state to maintain the status quo and prevent exposure of past and present human rights abuses. Then, there are the odious massive debt obligations incurred mostly under the previous repressive regimes. They severely limit the rendering of services to those in need, while fiscal austerity inevitably leads to confrontation and increasingly repressive governmental responses. The impact of the debt service on already exiguous fiscal resources is compounded by the strict conditionalities imposed by the international financial institutions (the IMF, the World Bank, the IDB, and private banks). Structural adjustments resulting from such conditions have gravitated against demands for reform, equity, and social justice, already frozen by the previous dictatorships.

The Biophysical and Environmental Effects of Public Policies

Since the 1980s, the Latin American and Caribbean countries have experienced an expanding and converging set of problems, whose common denominator is a fiscal crisis of the state. These affect employment, purchasing power, housing, the safety of drinking water, the quality of sanitation, the growing incidence of old and new diseases of epidemic proportions, a deteriorating ecosystem, and a profound inability to meet health challenges. A regional health crisis is unfolding as life-threatening ailments that were considered eradicated (such as malaria, Chagas, tuberculosis) are making a dramatic comeback, and new morbidity and mortality factors (such as HIV/AIDS) are on the rise. This has happened at a time when social safety nets and health delivery mechanisms are collapsing as a consequence of structural adjustment policies. The 1990 cholera epidemic was paradigmatic of extreme mutual vulnerability. A poverty-driven disease, multiplied by the dismantling of the institutional mechanisms for disease containment and treatment, increased generalized insecurity across class and national boundaries.

Environmental threats are another example of policy-driven dysfunction. These include sewage, waste, and air pollution, but also encompass a broader complexity of and multiplicity of reciprocating issues. In an earlier study[20] we sketched a calamitous situation in which retro-feeding and destructive processes create a vicious cycle of vulnerabilities. Current industrial, mining, and agricultural practices, mixed with uncontrolled urbanization,[21] create an interwoven pattern of biophysical and social stress upon the ecosystem and human populations. For instance, deforestation, with its sequel of health-related consequences, accounts annually for over 40 percent of the global loss of forests. On a per capita basis, this makes Latin America the number one contributor to green depletion and loss of biodiversity. Furthermore, in the midst of an expansion of agricultural production for export, food insecurity still remains a major threat to large segments of the population, even in the statistically "rich" countries. Once again, the pressure to manage the debt and its conditionalities put a premium upon cash crops and the merciless exploitation of natural and human resources.

Structural Poverty and Inequality

Since 1980, those living below the poverty line in Latin America and the Caribbean *increased* from above 120 million to over 200 million and from 41 percent to 46 percent of the population.[22] The most affected have been those already vulnerable: women, children, the elderly, ethnic minorities. Though poverty and indigence have gone down to 1996 levels in most countries, overall deprivation is still higher than two decades ago, and rural poverty has increased steadily. Central America has been the most seriously affected by the double impact of concentration of wealth and the spread of poverty: Reportedly nearly 80 percent of its inhabitants were unable to access a basic food basket and half of these were destitute. According to the same report, between 1977 and 1994, Guatemala witnessed an accelerated concentration of wealth and resources[23] with fewer than 2 percent of the landowners owning more than 65 percent of the total farmland. Between 1990 and 1993, after just two years of structural adjustment, the poverty rate in Honduras increased from 68 percent of the total population to 78 percent. In Nicaragua, as a result of the contra war and the implementation of the post-war austerity package, 71.3 percent of the economically active population was either unemployed, or underemployed. Illiteracy, which had been effectively reduced to 12 percent between 1979 and 1989, actually *increased* in 1993 in absolute and relative terms. The same was the case with infant mortality, from 50 per 1,000 in the 1980s to 71 per 1,000 in 1991 and 83 per 1,000 in 1993. Although the acuteness of these figures has been less pronounced in recent years, the legacy of a catastrophic decade of manmade and natural catastrophes has left its deep imprint.

TABLE 12.3   Growth of the Estimated % of Population in Poverty and Indigence in 19 Countries in Latin America, 1980–1990

	Poverty			Indigence		
	1980–86	1986–90	% Annual	1980–86	1986–90	% Annual
Nationwide	4.9	7.0	10.5	4.8	1.3	1.5
Urban	20.0	8.3	27.3	7.1	2.7	1.5
Rural	0.0	1.7	9.1	2.8	0.1	1.1

Note: The figures are calculated from Oscar Altimir, "Income Distribution and Poverty Through Crisis and Adjustment," *CEPAL Review*, No. 52 (April 1994), p. 12.

Even the much-hailed economic "miracles" have not produced lasting development. The combination of entrenched elite interests, extreme free-market agendas, and structural adjustment policies left a lasting burden of poverty and despair. The areas of health, education, and community development have suffered continuously, impacting precisely those less protected in society. Since the end of the boom of the 1970s, Brazil's only enduring feature has been the most unequal income distribution in the Western hemisphere, and one of the worst in the world. Chile's "success story" does not fare any better under close scrutiny. Between 1970 and 1987, the proportion of Chileans defined as poor increased by an average yearly rate of 7.2 percent. Meanwhile, real income per capita grew at an annual average rate of 0.3 percent. Since 1990, with a democratic government and despite the fact that the speed of impoverishment has been arrested, widespread privation persists. Despite impressive GNP annual growth rates between 4.5 percent and 10 percent, after Brazil, Chile has the second worst income distribution in a region.

Pauperization and expanding inequity are not limited to the cases mentioned above. They are present all over the hemisphere: throughout the Caribbean, in Argentina, Uruguay, Paraguay, Venezuela, Colombia, Peru, Bolivia, Ecuador, Panama, Costa Rica, the Dominican Republic, Haiti, and particularly Mexico. As mentioned, the most affected are the rural and urban poor; but also white-collar, middle-class sectors have seen their economic opportunities and social safety nets dramatically eroded. In fact, in Latin America, as in Canada and the United States today, the middle classes are disintegrating in the growing gap between the extremities of wealth and poverty. [24]

Civil-Military Relations

Beneath the civilian mantle, praetorianism has a lingering presence. Given the polarized and violent nature of political conflicts, militarization has been a long-standing feature of the Latin American state. It has also been a constant in the United States. With few exceptions, the military establishment has played a disproportionately large role in most of the countries, whether under civilian executives or not. Even in the supposedly exceptional cases, a careful examination reveals that direct military rule or militarized repression have always been present. This is abundantly clear in the deepening conflict in Colombia. Although with the withering of the Cold War the military appeared less conspicuously pre-

TABLE 12.4   Regional Military Balance

Country	Defense as % of GDP/GNP			Numbers in Armed Forces per 100		
	1985	2000	Change	1985	2002	Change
Argentina	2.9	1.3	-55.0	108.0	69.9	-35.0
Bolivia	2.0	1.5	-25.0	27.6	31.5	14.1
Brazil	0.8	1.3	62.5	276.0	287.0	4.0
Chile	7.8	4.0	-49.0	101.0	80.5	-8.4
Colombia	0.8	2.3	187.0	66.2	158.0	138.0
Costa Rica	0.7	1.0	42.9	*	*	*
Cuba	9.6	5.0	-47.9	161.5	46.0	-72.0
Dominican Republic	1.1	0.5	-54.5	22.2	24.5	10.0
Ecuador	1.8	2.2	22.2	52.5	95.5	82.0
El Salvador	4.4	0.7	-98.0	41.7	16.8	-59.7
Guatemala	1.8	0.8	-53.6	31.7	41.4	-1.0
Haiti	1.5	1.1	-26.7	6.9	0.0	100.0
Honduras	2.1	0.6	-71.4	16.6	8.3	-50.0
Mexico	0.7	0.5	-28.6	129.1	192.8	49.0
Nicaragua	14.2	1.1	-92.3	62.9	14.0	-77.7
Panama	2.0	1.2	-40.0	12.0	11.8	-2.5
Paraguay	1.3	n.k	n.k	14.4	14.9	3.5
Peru	4.5	3.8	-15.6	128.0	110.0	-14.0
Uruguay	2.5	1.1	-56.0	31.9	23.9	-25.0
Venezuela	1.3	1.2	-7.7	49.0	82.3	68.0
Bahamas	*	1.6	*	0.5	0.9	44.4
Belize	1.8	2.6	44.0	0.6	1.5	150.0
Guyana	9.7	1.9	-80.4	6.0	1.6	-73.3
Jamaica	0.9	0.7	-22.2	2.1	2.8	33.3
Trinidad-Tobago	1.0	1.3	30.0	2.1	2.7	28.6
Suriname	2.4	3.4	41.7	2.0	1.8	10.0
United States	6.5	3.1	-52.3	2,151.6	1,414.0	-34.0
Canada	2.1	1.2	-42.9	83.0	52.3	-37.0

Sources: IISS, *The Military Balance*, several issues 1989–2003; *World Resources*, 1994–95 and *SIPRI Yearbook 1993.*

sent in politics than in the recent past, a closer scrutiny reveals a more complex picture. True, the ending of the civil conflicts in El Salvador and Nicaragua, declining insurgent threats in Peru, and the effects of structural adjustment packages upon defense budgets suggest a trend toward demilitarization.[25] Yet, over-all budget reductions have not been necessarily matched by personnel reductions. Rather, a small increase in personnel has taken place. But average figures are deceiving: Downturns in countries with large establishments, such as Argentina (–39.8 percent), Chile (–9.1 percent), Nicaragua (–76.6 percent), and Peru

(–12.5 percent) reduce the incidence of significant upturns in most other countries. Twelve out of twenty of the countries actually increased the size of their defense forces between 1985 and 1991. Colombia topped the list with 76.7 percent, followed by Venezuela (53.1 percent), Guatemala (40.7 percent), and Mexico (35.6 percent). The largest establishment, that of Brazil's, with nearly 270,000, grew 7 percent between 1988 and 1993 (IISS 1087–1992).

Though in comparison with the G–8 nations and the Middle East, the size of the Latin American forces is relatively modest, the impact, influence, and transnationalization of the security establishment, especially of its officer corps, remain extensive. Not including some 760,000 paramilitary, and an indeterminate number of reserves, Latin America has over 1.3 million individuals under arms and spends close to $9 billion in defense. Given its economic base, Latin America remains overly militarized; the externally controlled security sector is still a voracious competitor for the scarce resources needed for development. It constitutes a persistent obstacle to the sovereignty of, and the cooperation among, nations and continues to be the single most serious threat to political stability, integration, sustainable democracy, and human rights.

With the end of the Cold War and with the threat of regional insurgency reduced, a fundamental security issue in the Americas is not so much how to protect society from external and internal "enemies" but still how to safeguard the population in most countries from their security forces. In this context, we must reconsider civil-military relations and the nature of the prevailing civil-military regimes in the emerging Inter-American order, especially in light of new strategic factors. One is the increasingly conservative, interventionist, and apocalyptic mood in American politics, and the extensive post–September 11 resurgence of "Pentagonism." Another is the lingering of often-construed border tensions, exemplified by flare-ups like the 1995 Ecuadorian-Peruvian war. A third factor is the growing militarization of social conflicts, as in Chiapas, or in the expansion of Colombia's civil strife, narco-wars in the Andean region, the re-emergence of Haiti's security establishment, the ongoing confrontation in Venezuela, and the involvement of Latin American forces in the Middle East conflict.

Limited Democracy and Elected Plutocracies

Current political developments in Latin America, while conveying a less repressive picture, especially by contrast with a somber record of the 1970s, present at best mixed signs. In the positive side, most of the region is ruled nowadays by governments generated through formally free and competitive elections: what former Guyana's President Cheddi Jagan sarcastically called "five-minute democracy."[26] In various instances, some sort of consolidation has taken place, as a second and even a third generation of elected governments have been inaugurated. There have been also sporadic, yet significant attempts to hold governments accountable to the electorate. Instances of torture, disappearances, and blatant state terrorism have become less frequent, with notable exceptions, such as Colombia. However, there are also disturbing signs. One is the persistence, and even revival, of authoritarian and oligarchic traditions.

TABLE 12.5   Electoral Participation (as percentage of those registered)

	High Turnout			Low Turnout	
Country	*1988–1991*	*1998–2001*	*Country*	*1988–1991*	*1998–2000*
Uruguay	96.9	94.6	Peru	56.9	78.6
Argentina	89.4	78.1	Paraguay	56.3	59.4
Chile	88.3	83.1	Haiti	52.7	60.5
Costa Rica	85.1	73.7	Bolivia	51.0	64.5
Brazil	76.6	81.0	Mexico	50.0	48.2
Honduras	75.7	78.0	Dominican R.	45.8	45.6
Nicaragua	73.3	76.2	El Salvador	44.0	31.1
Venezuela	72.3	46.5	Colombia	40.1	40.5
Panama	70.1	76.1	United States	36.5	46.5
Canada	68.3	54.6			
Ecuador	64.7	48.5			

Source: "International Institute for Democracy and Electoral Assistance (IDEA), Voter Turnout from 1945 to Date," Stockholm, Sweden, 2003, www.idea.int/vt/analysis.

Power remains highly concentrated. Other less tangible but basic values, such as respect for human life, honest government, and the reduction of discrimination and official abuse, are not widely adhered to. Corruption in both parts of the hemisphere is widespread, deep, and fast-growing.

Limited democracies based upon pacts of elites are distinctively exclusionary. Electoral processes, though a common sight throughout the Americas, are increasingly void of choice and even meaning. Fraud and manipulation still persist. Voters can cast the ballot but the menus and policy options are roughly the same. The socioeconomic and institutional pillars of the former national security regimes (landowners, business, foreign investors and authoritarian preserves within the military, the judiciary, and the technocracy) are also those of the new democratic orchestrations. The large majority of those who perpetrated crimes against humanity are still at large, and have gone unpunished. Thus, it is hardly surprising that public apathy and cynicism throughout the hemisphere are at an all-time high, while governmental legitimacy is shrinking. Despite the unfolding of formally contested elections during the 1990s in all of the countries and apparently normal constitutional reforms in a good number of others, these processes failed to provide real alternatives. The alienation of the population from the political process has resulted in extremely high rates of electoral abstention.[27] For instance, 84 percent abstained in the Guatemalan referendum of 1994 and 50 percent in El Salvador's general election of March 1994. In the Colombian parliamentary elections of 1994, over 70 percent did not vote, while in the Ecuadorian congressional competition the same year, spoiled ballots received the second largest plurality. Colombia tops the list of electoral abstention, with roughly 40 percent of the voters casing their ballots in 2000, followed closely by the United States.[28] In addition, many of these contests have been tainted with serious irregularities.

Beyond ceremonial transfers of offices by electoral means and the absence of direct military rule, democracy in the Americas has not been consolidated in this decade. Transition remains incomplete and in some cases de-democratization has been the dominant trend. Oligarchies throughout the continent have shown a remarkable continuity. The old practice of executive *continuismo* and dynastic-type succession (the elimination of which was central to the region's past democratic agenda) has resurfaced. There is also a remarkable continuity of policy. Neoliberal recipes have become entrenched in the conditionalities attached to debt-alleviation, regional trade agreements (such as NAFTA or MERCOSUR), and the so-called macroeconomic equilibrium policies, which effectively remove fiscal, monetary, and credit matters from national political debate. In addition, the "new" cold war in the context of unipolarism, with its pseudo-moralistic and messianic discourse, has debilitated democracy, development, and security.

Conclusions: The Fires Within

A profound structural contradiction has emerged in the region's governance. If elected governments stress *democracy*, equity, majority rule, and the interests of the public (the civil society), they would face relentless opposition and sabotage from domestic and international elites, leading to eventual ineffectiveness, if not outright destabilization. Thus, the more common course is to stress *liberalism* and ignore the civil society and rule on behalf of the profit sector. This is what in the North American context Ralph Nader has labeled a *plutocracy*. The political cost of this option is very high in the long run: loss of legitimacy, loss of sovereignty, and an erosion of the trust between elected officials and the electorate, a central tenet of both governance and pluralist institutionalization.

Given the level of political alienation, it is not surprising that there have been popular insurrections where angered communities confronted threats to their livelihood: Chiapas (1993), Quito (2000), Buenos Aires (2001), La Paz (2003). These mobilizations and insurrections have had broad domestic and international implications. They are a specific Latin American expression of the anti-globalization movement, re-creating a civil society where popular organizations had been crushed by the double squeeze of military rule in the 1970s and economic restructuring in the 1990s. These developments suggest that popular movements and rebellions are present in the new globalized regional order.[29] They have re-emerged as political options and it is likely that we may witness more such manifestations in the near future. Instability, even under the illusion of the NAFTA and FTAA umbrella, is more than skin-deep. On the other hand, by challenging the legitimacy of the new intra-elite and transnational arrangements, the new modes of resistance reveal the intrinsic weakness of the current regimes.

Thus, from a long-range structural perspective, violent upheavals have not withered away altogether in the region, although their manifestations have changed. Our analysis strongly suggests that the politics of limited democratization with neoliberal economics, while an improvement over the human rights record of the military dictatorships, imposes built-in constraints upon the realization of a truly stable and sustainable democratic project for and by the populace. Nor is the combination of limited democracy with neoliberalism a guarantee against expanding corruption or popular alienation. In fact, the opposite seems to be the case. If economic recovery fails to produce a better standard of living for the majorities (as it is currently the case), or should the structural crisis deepen, it is likely that these weak and "pragmatic" civilian regimes could be overturned by equally weak, yet violently repressive civil-military regimes. After all, the national security doctrine is still the ideological "software" (or culture) of the security establishments and a regular staple in the training of special forces in the hemisphere. The "communist" subversion of yore is being replaced by a new definition of the internal enemy: "terrorism," "anarchy," or "war on drugs," or more broadly anything that threatens the investment climate or core elites' interests. Growing military and U.S. involvement, as in the case of Plan Colombia, is a case in point. Certainly, the post–September 11 atmosphere may have a most destabilizing effect by reviving a hard "counter-terrorist" posture to justify elite rule.

As the entire region becomes more closely integrated, a potentially dysfunctional system of mutual vulnerability is taking shape. Its impact on the life of millions throughout the Americas can be catastrophic. The present course points toward scenarios where unemployment, poverty, violence, criminality, health hazards, addiction, refugee flows, massive population displacements, repression, and environmental decay feed upon each other. The drug-trading regime is a dramatic illustration of this interconnectedness. The ties that link the drug trade begin with peasant producers in the depressed Andean region and continue with crime syndicates in both producing and importing areas, corrupt officials (as well as rabid "patriots"), retailers, and users, ranging from the destitute to those in high social standing. Being an essentially consumer-driven market, and operating on pure market logic, containment of drugs requires addressing its social-psychological end economic causes—including the roots of addiction—rather than exclusively its symptoms.

Under these circumstances, the dysfunctional linkages of mutual vulnerability between North and South, and their multiple accelerators, create a spiraling lose-lose situation: a negative-score game. Without profound changes in both the South and the North of the hemisphere, the possibility of arresting or reversing serious threats to human security will remain doubtful. Short of a radical reorganization of the pattern of governance throughout the Americas, including decisionmaking, accountability, and regional cooperation—for instance, the largely dysfunctional Organization of American States system— multiple and critical dysfunctions are likely to increase.

Regional security cannot be equated with short-term business confidence, or with a messianic vision of "Manifest Destiny", or "wars" on terrorism or drugs, or more recently, fending off the "Hispanic threat."[30] A breakdown of democratic development, prosperity, and equity and the increase of tensions in the

TABLE 12.6   Comparative Indicators for Latin American and the Caribbean

Country	A Corrupt (CPI) 2001	B GDP p. capita 1999	C Growth/ GDP 1999	D Debt/ GDP 1999	E Inflation (annual) 1999	F GINI Index 1999	G Defense exp/GDP 1999	H Forces per 1000 1997	I Human Dev. Index 1999	J Population in 1000s 1999	K Urbanize Index 1999	L Education Index 1999
Mexico	3.7	8,200	3.7	33.5	16.6	53.7	0.9	1.9	0.786	104,087	73.8	0.83
Cuba	—	2,400	6.2	80.0	7.0	—	5.0	5.1	0.765e	11,003	—	—
Dominican R.	3.1	5,500	8.2	28.7	3.0	—	0.5	2.0	0.726	7,582	—	0.79b
Haiti	—	1,100	2.5	30.6	8.7	—	0.1a	0.7a	0.430	7,019	35.1b	0.50b
Jamaica	3.8**	3,500	-1.0	57.6	5.9	36.4	0.1	1.1	0.734	2,512	63.5	0.78
Guatemala	2.9	4,000	3.5	28.6	4.9	59.6	7.8	2.6	0.624	12,224	39.4	0.60
Honduras	2.7	2,200	-1.9	83.3	11.6	53.7	0.2	1.2	0.644	6,795	45.0	0.66
El Salvador	3.6	2,900	2.6	17.4	0.5	52.3	1.1	2.7	0.674	6,179	45.6	0.73
Nicaragua	2.4	2,200	4.0	231.0	10.9	50.3	0.9	3.3	0.616	4,816	63.2	0.63
Costa Rica	4.5	7,500	8.3	33.6	10.0	47.0	0.5a	2.3a	0.801	3,722	50.3	0.85
Panama	3.7	6,900	3.2	55.7	1.3	48.5	0.5a	4.1a	0.791	2,880	56.0b	0.86
Colombia	3.8	5,800	-5.0	44.7	11.2	57.1	2.9	3.6	0.768	42,400	73.6	0.84
Venezuela	2.8	8,000	-7.2	71.1	23.6	48.8	0.5	3.3	0.792	24,238	88.5	0.84
Brazil	4.0	6,300	0.5	40.0	4.9	60.0	2.7	1.8	0.739	164,000	86.5	0.83
Paraguay	2.0**	3,700	0.0	22.6	6.8	59.1	1.4	3.6	0.730	5,639	65.0	0.83
Uruguay	5.1	9,100	-2.5	40.1	5.6	42.3	2.6	9.8	0.826	3,264	90.7	0.91
Argentina	3.5	10,100	-3.0	51.2	-1.2	49.0	1.9	1.9	0.827	37,300	88.6	0.91
Chile	7.5	12,200	-1.1	50.7	3.3	56.5	4.0	5.8	0.844	15,088	84.2	0.89
Bolivia	2.0	3,100	1.1	65.9	2.1	42.0	1.7	4.0	0.652	8,140	62.3	0.79
Peru	4.1	4,500	3.8	50.9	3.5	46.2	1.6	4.4	0.739	25,916	77.9	0.85
Ecuador	3.3	4,300	-7.0	107.3	52.3	43.7	2.3	4.5	0.747	12,884	60.4	0.85

Sources: IISS, The Military Balance 2000–2001 and The Military Balance 2002–2003, Volume 102 (London: Oxford University Press for the International Institute of Strategic Studies: 2003) ; PNUD World Development Report 1999. a = No military forces; only police and other security forces. * PPP= Parity equivalent in US $. ** Ranking and score for 1999. b= data for 1999. c= Transparency International's 1999 and 2001 Corruption Perception Index (CPI). d= UNDP's Human Development Index (HDI). e= HDI values are for 1997, unreported in 2001.

For comparative purposes, the figures for North America, for all the above variables (A to L) were the following:

Country	A Corrupt (CPI) 2001	B GDP p. capita 1999	C Growth/ GDP 1999	D Debt/ GDP 1999	E Inflation (annual) 1999	F GINI Index 1999	G Defense exp/GDP 1999	H Forces per 1000 1997	I Human Dev. Index 1999	J Population in 1000s 1999	K Urbanize Index 1999	L Education Index 1999
Canada	8.9	24,800	3.7	93.0*	1.7	31.5	1.6	2.0	0.932	29,512	77.0	0.98
United States	7.6	33,100	4.2	59.3*	2.1	40.8	3..3	5.0	0.927	275,636	77.0	0.98

Note 1: The bulk of the U.S.—and to a lesser extent Canadian—debt is internal debt, unlike that of the LAC countries, which is foreign debt.

Note 2: This table was calculated by the author on the basis of individual country data provided in the International Institute of Strategic Studies (IISS), The Military Balance 2000–2001, (London: Oxford University Press, 2001), pp. 25, 54, 227–251; also from the United Nations', PNUD, Informe Sobre Desarrollo Humano 1999 (Madrid: Mundi Prensa Libros, 1999), pp. 134–241. The IISS figures for the GNP in Latin America and the Caribbean presented in this table, unlike that of the World Bank used to calculate debt/GNP ratio on Table 2 above, are higher than those prepared by U.N. agencies, like the World Bank and the UNDP.

more volatile countries of the region would have a direct and most deleterious effect upon the well-being and security of both Americas. The weakness of democratic institutions and their inability to traverse from democratic transition and elected plutocracies to consolidation of popular rule is a critical structural flaw in the security of the hemisphere. It is becoming painfully obvious elsewhere that the end of the Cold War did not automatically translate into a Fukuyama-type scenario of the "end of History," with global prosperity, peace, and democracy.[31] The nearly two-decade old democratic transition in the region cannot be made synonymous with either the entrenchment of participatory practices, nor with responsible government, let alone the enhancement of human dignity. The "safe," "limited," "low-intensity," and meaningless democracy, peddled by transition theorists and the neoauthoritarians, impedes more than facilitates the emergence of a sustainable security community in the Americas. So does the persistence of economic dogmatism and the rebirth of National Security doctrines designed to fight elusive and perpetual global conflicts. Regime change throughout the hemisphere is a necessary condition for human security.

Notes

1. United Nations, *World Economic and Social Survey 1994* (New York: United Nations), p. 42.

2. Terry-Lynn Karl and Richard Fagen, "The Logic of Hegemony: The United States as a Superpower in Central America," in Jan Triska, ed., *Dominant Powers and Subordinate States. The United States in Latin America ad the Soviet Union in Eastern Europe* (Durham, N.C.: Duke University Press, 1986), pp. 218–238.

3. These include General Uriburu in Argentina, General Ibáñez in Chile, Getulio Vargas in Brazil, President Terra in Uruguay, General Somoza in Nicaragua, General Hernández-Martínez in El Salvador, General Trujillo in the Dominican Republic, General Carías in Honduras, General Ubico in Guatemala, General Sánchez-Cerro in Peru, and Colonel Busch in Bolivia.

4. Eugene Stanley, *The Future of Underdeveloped Countries. Political Implications of Economic Development* (New York: Praeger, 1961), pp. 3–4.

5. U.S. Senate Committee on Foreign Relations, Subcommittee on Western Hemisphere Affairs, Hearing (June 24–July 8, 1969), pp. 62–64, 57–61; also Yale Ferguson, "The Departments of Defense and State and Governor Rockefeller on U.S. Military Policies and Programs in Latin America," in Ferguson, ed., *Contemporary Inter-American Relations: A Reader in Theory and Issues* (Englewood Cliffs, N.J.: Prentice-Hall, 1972), pp. 327–328.

6. John Lovell, "Military-dominated Regimes and Political Development: A Critique of Some Prominent Views," in Monte Palmer and Larry Stern, eds., *Political Development in Changing Societies: An Analysis of Modernization* (Levington: Heath Lexington Books, 1971), pp. 159–179.

7. Charles D. Corbett (Col., U.S. Army), *The Latin American Military as a Socio-Political Force. Case Studies of Bolivia and Argentina*, Monographs in International Affairs, (Center for Advanced International Studies, University of Miami, 1972), pp. 13–19; also see "Appendix F: Précis of the Counterinsurgency Course (1963), the Special Warfare School Fort Bragg, North Carolina," in Willard Barber and Neale Ronning, *Internal Security and Military Power. Counterinsurgency and Civic Action in Latin America* (Columbus, Ohio: Ohio State University Press, 1966), pp. 275–276, 217–245; as well as U.S. Army Special Warfare School, *Counterinsurgency Planning Guide*, Special Text No. 31–176 (NC: May 1964).

8. Jean-Louis Weil, Joseph Comblin, and Judge Senese, "The Repressive State: The Brazilian National Security Doctrine and Latin America," *LARU Studies*, Doc. No.3 (Toronto: LARU, 1979), pp. 36–73; also see Robinson Rojas, 2003. "Notes on the Doctrine of National Security": *rrojasdatabank.org/natsec1.*

9. Juan Bosch, *El Pentagonismo sustituto del imperialismo,* third edition (Santo Domingo: Editora Alfa y Omega, 2000), pp. 5–14.

10. Mexico, Venezuela, Colombia, Costa Rica, and communist Cuba.

11. Our calculation is based upon ECLA *Anuario Estadístico* data between 1970–1985.

12. According to ECLAC's *Anuario Estadístico 2001,* the figures for disbursed foreign debt were $22,256 million US (1980) and $739,930 million US (2000).

13. For a direct view of the "developmental deontology" of counter-insurgency, see U.S. Army Special Warfare School, *Counterinsurgency Planning Guide,* Special Text No. 31–176 (Raleigh, N.C.: May 1964).

14. Orlando Letelier, "The 'Chicago Boys' in Chile: Economic Freedom's Awful Toll," *The Nation,* August 28, 1976, pp. 138, 142.

15. Sol Linowitz, Commission on United States–Latin American Relations (Sol Linowitz, chairman), *The Americas in a Changing World* (New York: Quadrangle Books 1975).

16. Holly Sklar, "Managing Dependence and Democracy—An Overview," in Sklar, ed., *Trilateralism: The Trilateral Commission and Elite Planning for World Management* (Montreal: Black Rose, 1980), pp. 1–55.

17. Arturo Siat and Gregorio Iriarte, "De la Seguridad Nacional al Trilateralismo", *Cuadernos de Cristianismo y Sociedad* (Buenos Aires, May 1979), pp. 23–24.

18. Osvaldo Martínez, "Debt and Foreign Capital. The Origins of the Crisis," *Latin American Perspectives,* Issue 76, Vol. 20, No. 1, (Winter 1992), p. 65; also World Bank, *World Development Report,* 1990, 1991 and 1992, and 1994, pp. 206–207; and *World Debt Tables. External Debt of Developing Countries,* 1987–1988, 1989–1990, and 1991–1992 editions, Vol. II, Country Tables (Washington, D.C.: The World Bank, 1988, 1989, 1992).

19. Verónica Montecinos and John Markoff, "Democrats and Technocrats: Professional Economists and Regime Transition in Latin America," *Canadian Journal of Development Studies,* Vol. XIV, No. 1 (1993), pp. 7–22.

20. Jorge Nef and Wilder Robles, "Environmental Issues, Politics, and Administration in Latin America: An Overview," in Joseph Jabbra and Onkar Dwivedi, eds., *Governmental Response to Environmental Challenges in Global Perspective* (Amsterdam: IOS Press, 1998), pp. 42–62.

21. Urban population has expanded exponentially in the region, at nearly twice the average rate of population growth. While in 1950, only one city (Buenos Aires) was among the ten most populated cities in the world (at number eight, with 5 million), by 2000 there were three cities among the world's largest, respectively ranking number two, four, and ten: Mexico City (18.5 million), Saõ Paulo (17.8 million), and Buenos Aires (12.6 million). While this expansion of megalopolis has been dramatic, even more pronounced is the growth of large metropolitan (Santiago, Bogotá, Caracas, Lima) and secondary cities (Medellín, Curitiba, Córdoba, Concepción, Guadalajara, for example). This phenomenon is the tip of the iceberg of a looming urban crisis, resulting from migration rooted on rural poverty (see Table 12.1). It has been estimated that by 2050 Latin America will double the population of North America.

22. William Robinson, "Central America: Which Way After the Cold War?," *NotiSur,* Vol. 4, No. 8, February 25, 1994, pp. 1–9, especially p. 5; also Oscar Altimir, "Income Distribution and Poverty Through Crisis and Adjustment," *CEPAL Review,* No. 52, (April 1994), passim.

23. *NotiSur,* January 14, 1994, p. 9.

24. William Robinson, citing the 1993 UNDP *Human Development Report,* notes that the wealthiest 20 percent of humanity receives 82.7 percent of the world's income. They also control 80 percent of world trade, 95 percent of all loans, 80 percent of all domestic savings, 80.5 percent of world investments. They consume 70 percent of world energy, 75 percent of all metals, 85 percent of its timbers, and 60 percent of its food supplies. He noted that in this

context the middle classes are tending to shrink considerably, since the 20 percent of what could be called the world's middle class only receives 11.7 percent of the world's wealth. *NotiSur*, February 18, 1994, p.7. A U.S. study by the Levy Institute, based on the 1998 Federal Reserve's Survey of Consumer Finances indicated that while the top 1 percent of the population controlled 38 percent of the country's net worth, the poorest 40 percent controlled 0.26 percent of it. In the period between 1983 and 1998, the net worth of that top 1 percent increased 42.3 percent, while the bottom 40 percent of the population was 76.5 percent worse off. See Edward Wolff, "Recent Trends in Wealth Ownership, 1983–1998," *Levy Institute Working Paper No. 300*, Tables 2 and 3 (2003). All indications are that income concentration has worsened since 1998.

25. Between 1985 and 1991, the region's defense budgets declined on the average 24.6 percent, or 4.1 percent per year, and twelve out of twenty countries cut defense expenditures ranging between 59 percent (Chile) and 4.8 percent (Honduras). On the other hand, two rather large countries, Venezuela and Colombia, dramatically increased such expenditures: respectively 23 percent and 275 percent. When the number of troops is examined, the trend is a seemingly modest increase of 4.2 percent for the region, or 0.7 percent per year.

26. Cheddi Jagan, "Sustainable Development in the Americas," keynote address to the XXVII Annual Congress of the Canadian Association of Latin American and Caribbean Studies, York University, October 31, 1996.

27. *NotiSur*, Vol. 4, No. 5, February 1994, p. 8.

28. For purposes of comparison, the rate in the United States for 2002 was 46.6 percent and in Canada, about 55 percent (2000). An examination of voting turnout in parliamentary elections held in both Latin and North America in the decade between 1988–1991 and 1998–2001 shows a declining trend in half of the countries and also low voting turnout in nearly half of the nations, by comparison to most European democracies.

29. *Latin America Weekly Report*, January 13, 1994, p. 2; February 17, 1994, p. 62.

30. Samuel Huntington, "The Hispanic Threat," *Foreign Policy*, electronic version (March–April 2004), *http://www.keepmedia.com/pubs/ForeignPolicy/2004/03/01/387925*.

31. Francis Fukuyama, "The End of History?" *The National Interest*, No. 16 (Summer 1989), pp. 3–18.

PART V

EXTERNAL RELATIONS

Chapter 13

International Relations in Latin America: Conflict and Cooperation

JAMES LEE RAY

THE BATTLE OF AYACUCHO in 1824 traditionally marks the end of Spanish rule in South America; Brazil broke its ties with Portugal a couple of years earlier. This chapter will focus on the relationship among the states that emerged from the ruins of Spanish and Portuguese empires in Latin America. The United States has played an important role in those relationships, of course, but the foreign policy of the United States vis-à-vis its southern neighbors will be treated only tangentially (U.S. policy in Latin America is dealt with in Chapter 15). The United States will enter the discussion here, however, to the extent that it has presented challenges and problems with which Latin American states have tried to deal in their foreign policies and in their dealings with each other.

Dreams of Unity, Realities of Strife

The Early Years

The Spanish colonies achieved their independence in three more or less separate movements. The first movement originated in Mexico and was joined by Central America. Mexico emerged as an empire under Agustín de Iturbide, who annexed Central America. But that empire lasted only briefly. Central America went its own way in 1823, and by 1824, Iturbide had been kicked out of Mexico by General Antonio López de Santa Anna. Mexico, of course, evolved into a solitary independent nation, but the United Provinces of Central America fell apart by 1838, with Guatemala, Honduras, El Salvador, Nicaragua, and Costa Rica emerging as independent nations.

Simón Bolívar led the campaign for independence in the northern part of Spanish America while José de San Martín fought against the Spanish colonialists in the southern part of the continent. The two revolutionary leaders met in 1822 and discussed the possible coordination of their liberation efforts. For reasons that to this day are rather mysterious, they parted company without an agreement. So this early step toward the unification of Spanish America met the same fate as all the numerous succeeding ones to date. It failed.

When Buenos Aires revolted against Spain, the leaders of that movement tried to bring the territory that became known as Paraguay along with them. But a Paraguayan army defeated troops from Buenos Aires who aimed to persuade Paraguayan leaders of the wisdom of unity against the Spanish. Buenos Aires, of course, provided the core of what became Argentina. Chile and Argentina, one can reasonably surmise, were fated to emerge as two countries because of the Andes Mountains, which separate them.

If Simón Bolívar had had his way, the territory that obtained freedom under his leadership would have emerged as two large republics. But Upper Peru, led by Antonio José de Sucre, wanted freedom from both Spain and Peru, and the first great republic of Bolívar's dreams was split into the independent countries of Bolivia and Peru. Bolívar did manage to bring the republic of Gran Colombia into the world in 1819, but by 1830, this republic had also fallen prey to geographical barriers, regional antagonisms, and the ambitions of quarreling political leaders. Gran Colombia dissolved ultimately into the separate countries of Venezuela, Colombia, and Ecuador. Bolívar's death occurred soon after that of "his" republic. Shortly before he died, he mourned the demise of his dreams: "America is ungovernable. Those who have served the revolution have plowed the sea."

Nineteenth-Century Conflicts

Nineteenth-century relations among the newly independent countries in Latin America involved a series of important conflicts and wars, and the impact of those struggles is still visible in the twenty-first century. Conflicts between Brazil and Argentina, for example, evoked the mediation of Great Britain, which managed to arrange the creation of the buffer state of Uruguay in 1830. Peru and Colombia agreed to settle a dispute between them in a process that resulted in the birth of another buffer state at about the same time, that is, Ecuador. By 1835, General Andrés de Santa Cruz in Bolivia established the Peru–Bolivia Confederation as part of an effort to enlarge his domain. Both Chile and Argentina objected to this confederation for the classical balance-of-power reason that it represented a concentration of power that was dangerous to their continued independence. Argentina declared war against the confederation, but it was the intervention of Chile that effectively brought about its dissolution in 1838.

The 1840s and 1850s were marked by subtle, more or less independent balance-of-power maneuverings among two sets of states: Chile and the other western states constituted the first set; Argentina, Uruguay, Paraguay, and Brazil on the eastern half of the continent made up the second. Major warfare was avoided until a very bloody conflict occurred among the latter set of states beginning in 1864, with Uruguay serving as the pawn over which the other states fought. Both Brazil and Argentina had made repeated attempts to influence the frequently violent political conflict in Uruguay in ways that would benefit their interests. Left to their own devices, it seems likely that Brazil and Argentina might have become involved in a war against each other over Uruguay. But Paraguay managed to get all three of these states into a war against it.

Until the 1860s, Paraguay had been a rather isolated state, ruled by dictators since the days of liberation. The second of these dictators, Carlos Antonio López, did modify this isolation somewhat, but perhaps his most fateful decision was to put his son, Francisco Solano López, in charge of Paraguay's army. In that role, the younger López traveled to England, France, Germany, Italy, and Spain in the early 1850s, picking up a large amount of arms and ammunition, ideas of grandeur from Napoleon III in France, and an Irish mistress, Elisa Lynch (whom he met in Paris), along the way.[1] Solano López became president of Paraguay upon the death of his father in 1862. In the ensuing years, he grew increasingly suspicious of the motives of both Brazilian and Argentine leaders with respect to Uruguay. In 1864, he became so certain of Brazil's imperialistic ambitions vis-à-vis Uruguay that he decided to thwart them forcefully. (This is not to deny that he had imperialistic ambitions of his own.) To do so, he requested permission for his troops to cross part of Argentina en route to Uruguay. Argentina refused to allow this. When Solano López sent his troops into Argentina anyway, he soon found himself at war with Brazil, Argentina, and Uruguay.

Whether little Paraguay had any chance of winning the war is an interesting historical question. During the war, the provisions of a secret treaty signed by Brazil, Uruguay, and Argentina became known. It was obvious that Brazil and Argentina meant to destroy the government of Paraguay and to help themselves to ample slices of Paraguayan territory. It is commonly asserted in standard historical sources that the Paraguayans fought so desperately that something on the order of nine out of ten males, or roughly half the population of the country, perished in the struggle. However, at least one contemporary historical-demographic analysis indicates that "the War of the Triple Alliance actually cost Paraguay between 8.7 and 19.5 percent of its prewar population. . . . The evidence demonstrates that the Paraguayan population casualties due to the war have been enormously exaggerated."[2]

Interestingly, both during and after the war, the nations of western Latin America objected to Brazilian and Argentine plans to dismember Paraguay and limit its sovereignty. This was an important step toward the integration of the two more or less independent balance-of-power systems on the continent.[3] That process was reinforced by rivalries among the western states that culminated in the War of the Pacific between Chile on one side and Bolivia and Peru on the other. They fought over the bleak Atacama Desert and the rich nitrates it contained. By 1870, Chileans, Peruvians, and Bolivians were all exploiting the mineral resources of the area. The Chileans were the most energetic and successful in these ventures. Unfortunately, from their point of view, many of their successes occurred in territories that belonged to Bolivia or Peru. When the Bolivians tried to increase taxes on Chilean operations in their territory and the Peruvians nationalized Chilean nitrate works in theirs, the Chilean government decided to resist these steps by military means.

Chile was eminently successful in this war, which began in February 1879. By 1883, Chile had won, taking over Antofagasta from Bolivia and the provinces of Tarapacá, Tacna, and Arica from Peru. With the addition of that territory, "Chile entered . . . upon an era of unequaled prosperity from the sale of nitrates, copper and other minerals."[4] Bolivia and Peru, on the other hand, got nothing from the war but grievances, which survived for decades. Bolivia lost its only seaport, at Antofagasta, and despite consistent efforts for the last 120 years, has yet to regain it. Chile promised Peru that a plebiscite would be held ten years after the war in the provinces of Tacna and Arica to determine their permanent status, but that plebiscite was continually postponed. The dispute was finally resolved in 1929, with the help of the U.S. government; as a result of the Washington Protocol of that year, Chile retained Arica while Peru reclaimed Tacna.

THE CHANGING OF THE GUARD

The United States Edges Out Great Britain

The remainder of the nineteenth century in Latin America was most notable, perhaps, for the culmination of a long-term trend. The United States had issued its Monroe Doctrine in 1823, warning other states to refrain from colonizing efforts in the Western Hemisphere. It is widely agreed that the United States lacked the power to enforce the doctrine through most of the nineteenth century. Latin America was not, however, subjected to serious or sustained colonizing efforts for most of that century because Great Britain, in effect, enforced the Monroe Doctrine for the United States. (The most obvious exception to this rule occurred when France set up the empire of Maximilian in Mexico from 1864 to 1867.) Throughout most of the nineteenth century, Great Britain and the United States shared a common interest in keeping other powers out of Latin America. Long-range ambitions by the United States to replace Great Britain as the most influential power in the Western Hemisphere added a measure of conflict to the relationship. In fact, "from the War of 1812 to the Venezuela boundary crisis of 1895, there was scarcely an administration or a decade in which the United States and Great Britain did not face a crisis or war scare in their tense and turbulent relations."[5]

In 1895, a crisis resulted from the culmination of a dispute between Great Britain and Venezuela over the boundary of British Guiana. President Grover Cleveland insisted on arbitration, and the British ultimately gave in, partly because they were more concerned at the time about the apparent inclination of the German kaiser to stir up trouble for them in South Africa.

Thus, the year 1895 marks the point at which British hegemony in South America began to be challenged seriously by the United States. Further indications of this "changing of the guard" were soon to follow. For example, in 1850, the United States and Great Britain had signed the Clayton-Bulwer Treaty, in which both agreed that neither would attempt to build or exclusively control any canal through Central America. But in 1901, the Clayton-Bulwer Treaty was superseded by the Hay-Pauncefote Treaty, which gave the United States exclusive rights to build and control such an interoceanic canal.

The Era of U.S. Military Interventions

In between the boundary dispute involving Great Britain and Venezuela and the Hay-Pauncefote Treaty, of course, the United States took on and defeated Spain in the Spanish American War of 1898, acquiring Cuba, Puerto Rico, and the Philippines. By 1903, the United States had helped arrange the independence of Panama from Colombia and had signed a treaty with the new Panamanian republic granting to the United States, in perpetuity, a zone in which a trans-isthmus canal was to be built. A year later, Theodore Roosevelt proclaimed his famous corollary to the Monroe Doctrine, in which he claimed the right to intervene in the internal affairs of other nations in the Western Hemisphere that through "flagrant . . . wrongdoing or impotence" give rise to a need for an "international police power." The United States used this corollary as a rationale for a lengthy series of armed interventions in the ensuing years. For example, the United States militarily occupied Haiti from 1915 to 1934, the Dominican Republic from 1916 to 1924, and Nicaragua from 1912 to 1925 and again from 1927 to 1932. Since these were only the most-prolonged examples among a longer list of interventions, it is not surprising that for the first decades of the twentieth century, one of the primary foreign policy concerns of the Latin American states was to find means of restraining "the colossus of the North."

It is, perhaps, a revealing indication of the desperate and vulnerable position in which the Latin American states found themselves vis-à-vis the United States that the first line of defense to which they resorted was international law. As early as 1868, the Argentine jurist Carlos Calvo had argued that intervention by foreign governments to enforce claims of their citizens residing abroad was illegal because it violated the principle of national sovereignty. In 1902, when Venezuela was the target of a blockade by Britain, Germany, and Italy, the Argentine foreign minister Luis Drago argued that it was also illegal for foreign governments to intervene in attempts to collect public debts (which is what Britain, Germany, and Italy were doing).

The Calvo Doctrine and the Drago Doctrine were originally designed to counter interventions by European states, but the "Roosevelt Corollary . . . and the subsequent U.S. interventions in the Caribbean area based on it, definitely shifted Latin American fears from Europe to the United States."6 For the first three decades of the twentieth century, Latin American states tried repeatedly, and unsuccessfully, to get the United States to accept the international principle of nonintervention embodied in the doctrines espoused by Calvo and Drago.

Latin American states were only tangentially involved in World War I. Eight declared war, but only Brazil and Cuba played an active role. Five other states severed diplomatic relations with Germany, while such important states as Argentina, Chile, and Mexico remained neutral. Since the war cut Latin American countries off from their hitherto major trading partners in Europe, it dramatically reinforced the paramount role of the United States in the Western Hemisphere, and U.S. political pretensions were further reinforced by a burgeoning economic ascendancy. This made the Latin American states even more anxious, of course, to curb the interventionist tendencies of the U.S. government, and many thought they had found a useful instrument in the League of Nations. That organization emphasized the principle of nonintervention and might have provided allies for the Latin American states against any interventionist moves by the United States. It is not surprising, then, that most Latin American countries were disappointed when the United States refused to join the league, even though its covenant explicitly recognized the legitimacy of the Monroe Doctrine.

Since the Latin American states had not been successful in their efforts to restrain the United States within the framework of the League of Nations, they pressed even harder to construct such restraints within the inter-American system. The Pan-American movement had begun with a meeting in Washington in 1889. From that year to 1928, there were six international conferences of American states. Those meetings adhered to a definite pattern. The United States was primarily interested in measures that would facilitate international trade, while the Latin American states preferred to dwell on measures that would secure them against intervention by the United States.

The official attitude of the U.S. government began to change perceptibly in 1929. The new president, Herbert Hoover, ordered a study of the Monroe Doctrine in that year, and by 1930, he had publicly endorsed the results of that study in a move that amounted to a rejection of the Roosevelt Corollary. Franklin D. Roosevelt, of course, adopted the Good Neighbor Policy toward Latin America, the highlight of which was a nonintervention pledge made tentatively at the Seventh Inter-American Conference in Montevideo in 1933 and reaffirmed, with significantly smaller loopholes, in 1936 at the Inter-American Conference for the Maintenance of Peace at Buenos Aires. The sincerity with which the Roosevelt administration adopted this new policy was given two significant tests when Bolivia nationalized foreign oil companies in that country in 1937 and Mexico nationalized its oil industry in 1938. Roosevelt resisted pressures to intervene in both cases.

TERRITORIAL CONFLICT IN SOUTH AMERICA

The Chaco War

As the Latin American states were in the midst of their successful effort (albeit only temporarily) to deal with U.S. interventions, two of those states fought each other in the only major war between Latin American states in this century. This war was fought between the two big losers of the most important South American wars in the nineteenth century, perhaps not coincidentally. After Bolivia lost its outlet to the sea during the War of the Pacific, some historians argue, its leaders began to look to the Rio de la Plata system and possible ports on the Atlantic. This meant that Bolivia needed access to the Paraguay River, and early in the twentieth century, Bolivia began building forts in the area of that river to ensure access to it. Paraguay, in the meantime, according to several accounts, was looking for some way to recover its national honor after its humiliating defeat in the war against Brazil, Uruguay, and Argentina. The emotions evoked in this manner soon focused on the Chaco Boreal, a desolate area near the border between Paraguay and Bolivia. Both countries had made claims to this area as early as the mid-1500s, during the colonial era, and border clashes between the two states occurred as early as 1927. Then rumors of vast oil deposits in the Chaco added fuel to the controversy, so to speak. War finally broke out in 1932.

Bolivia's population at the time was roughly three times that of Paraguay, but Bolivia suffered disadvantages that, in the end, turned out to be more important. Perhaps the most important was the composition of its army. Most Bolivian soldiers were Indians who had been drafted into the army off the two-mile-high (three-kilometer) plain known as the Altiplano. They were not accustomed to the tropical heat of the Chaco and had no understanding of the conflict (which is not to say that they would have been enthusiastic if they *had* understood the reasons for the war). Paraguayan soldiers, in contrast, were more comfortable in the climate of the area and felt they were defending their homeland.

Even so, the war dragged on for three years, with both sides suffering heavy losses. Estimates of these losses vary widely, of course: One apparently authoritative source concludes that 50,000 Paraguayan soldiers died in the conflict while 80,000 Bolivian soldiers met the same fate.[7] A truce was finally arranged in 1938. In the treaty, Paraguay was awarded most of the disputed Chaco area; Bolivia's reward was further frustration of its quest for an outlet to the sea.

Further Disputes

Two serious border disputes between Latin American states surfaced during the 1930s and 1940s. Both involved Peru. Peruvian troops seized the Amazon River town of Leticia in 1932. Since that town had been awarded to Colombia in 1930, the Colombian government sent troops to Leticia to make its objections known. There was some brief but bloody fighting. After a change of government in Peru, serious negotiations began. It took two years, but an amicable settlement was achieved, with Colombia retaining its hold on Leticia.

Peru was more successful in a dispute with Ecuador, which reached a crisis stage in 1941. Peruvian troops occupied territory claimed by Ecuador north of the Marañón River. That river is important because it allows access to the Amazon River. The dispute did escalate into actual military combat, with each side losing several hundred troops, but a wider war was averted, probably, by the Japanese attack on Pearl Harbor in December 1941. That catastrophe made the United States in particular unwilling to let its neighbors engage in such disruptive activities. So the United States, in cooperation with Argentina, Brazil, and Chile, imposed a peace through the Rio Protocol of 1942. The protocol forced Ecuador to relinquish control over the disputed territory, some 77,000 square miles (199,000 square kilometers), to Peru. Understandably, Ecuador has never been happy with this solution. In 1960, the Ecuadorian Senate renounced the Rio Protocol. Open border clashes between Ecuador and Peru occurred in 1981, and even more serious military conflict broke out between Ecuador and Peru in early 1995.

World War II and Its Aftermath

Latin American countries played a minor role in World War II. With the onset of the conflict, the United States tried to get the Western Hemisphere organized, but this project met with more problems than might have been anticipated. Argentina was least enthusiastic about unification against the Axis powers. The government of Argentina, in fact, did not break relations with Germany until 1944 and did not declare war until 1945. Brazil, on the other hand, sent a significant number of troops to Italy, while Mexican troops served in the Pacific theater. Generally speaking, the effect of World War II on inter-American relations was to reinforce trends set in motion by World War I. Once again, the Latin American states were cut off from the world outside the Western Hemisphere and became more closely tied to the United States. The United States, of course, emerged from World War II as the most powerful state in the world, regardless of how the controversial concept of power might be defined or measured.

In the years after the war, a controversy about the agenda of relations between the United States and Latin American countries surfaced in a shape that was to remain consistent in the postwar decades. For the United States, the primary issue was communist subversion; the Latin American states, on the other hand, were almost always more interested in policies and strategies that would foster their economic development.

One of the first indications of concern about international economic issues on the part of Latin American states was their proposal to form the Economic Commission for Latin America (ECLA) as a part of the new United Nations organization. The United States was opposed to the idea, but ECLA was created in 1948 in spite of that opposition. In the early 1950s, ECLA proposed the creation of a new inter-American bank and a Latin American common market (the Inter-American Development Bank was established in 1959). The United States was more interested in a collective defense treaty, that is, the Inter-American Treaty of Reciprocal Assistance (Rio Treaty) signed on September 2, 1947, and the establishment of the Organization of American States (OAS) in 1948. Latin Americans preferred that economic issues be dealt with in ECLA, but "for years, the United States favored the OAS Inter-American Economic and Social Council and regarded the efforts of the competitor ECLA with political disapproval as well as deep distrust."[8]

REGIONAL APPROACHES TO DEVELOPMENT

Economic Integration as a Tool

One of the proposed solutions to the problems of underdevelopment seized on by ECLA and several Latin American economists was economic integration.[9] Integration might provide markets sufficiently large, for example, to make it feasible for Latin American states to manufacture their own capital goods, thus reducing their dependence on the imports of such heavy equipment. Large markets created by the elimination of intraregional tariff barriers, and the construction of common external tariffs that would be part of the economic integration processes, might also allow industries to benefit from economies of scale, which, in turn, could evoke efficiency at levels competitive on the world market.

With these ideas in mind, ECLA and national officials worked toward the creation of two regional integration organizations: the Central American Common Market (CACM) and the Latin American Free Trade Association (LAFTA). The former organization was launched in 1960 with Guatemala, El Salvador, Honduras, Nicaragua, and later, Costa Rica as its members. Ten South American countries, later joined by Mexico, formed LAFTA in the same year. Both organizations were inspired to some extent by the success enjoyed by the European Economic Community (EEC) at the time. Furthermore, both were based on a philosophy of economic integration similar to that utilized in Europe. That is, CACM and LAFTA both sought economic integration on the basis of the functional (or neofunctional) theory of integration. According to that theory, the benefits that accrue to the member states as a result of the activities of the central organization of the integration organization mean that the member states, little by little, become willing to allow that central organization much broader authority until someday (in theory), it is running virtually everything.[10]

Such ideas had seemed to work reasonably well in Europe, and they seemed to work for a time in Latin America. The CACM promoted a marked increase in intraregional trade, and the rate of economic growth of the Central American countries increased. Similarly, the members of LAFTA managed to negotiate numerous reductions of tariffs, and intraregional trade increased 100 percent from 1961 to 1968.[11] But the two organizations soon ran into problems, at least one of which plagued both.

That problem involved the distribution of the benefits of integration among the member states. The founders of both the CACM and LAFTA had anticipated this problem by initially giving special concessions to the poorer member states. In the CACM, for example, special incentives were adopted in order to lure new industries into the relatively poor states (such as Honduras and Nicaragua). Members of LAFTA divided themselves into three categories according to levels of development and size of domestic markets. The countries in the lower categories were given trade concessions and the right to protect some infant industries from competition with similar industries in such relatively developed countries as Brazil, Argentina, and Mexico. Nevertheless, by the end of the 1960s, both organizations were showing signs of strain resulting in part from suspicions by the less-developed members that they were receiving an unequal share of the benefits of integration.

Problems for CACM and LAFTA

In 1969, the CACM was plagued by an even more dramatic problem. Two of its member states, Honduras and El Salvador, fought a war against each other. El Salvador is densely populated, whereas Honduras is relatively underpopulated. Throughout the 1960s, unemployed workers from El Salvador poured into the empty fertile valleys in Honduras. By 1969, the military government of Honduras was faced with considerable internal unrest, and it decided to deal with that discontent with a land reform program that, not accidentally, deprived many Salvadoran squatters of their recently acquired property.

The government of El Salvador responded with a surprise attack in July 1969. The attack failed, and a bloody stalemate resulted. The OAS managed to arrange a truce, which was broken in January 1970. A prolonged kind of "cold war" between Honduras and El Salvador ensued. Trade between them stopped, and Honduras put an embargo on trade between El Salvador on the one hand and Nicaragua and Costa Rica on the other. All in all, the war was a devastating blow to the CACM.

In the process of resolving the conflict between Honduras and El Salvador, CACM officials and government leaders discovered that other fissures in the organization threatened its existence. Honduras had been dissatisfied with the Common Market in any case, for an eminently predictable reason. Honduras, along with Nicaragua the least-developed country in that area, felt itself the victim of unfair competition. Relief from the burdens of such competition was difficult to arrange in the face of continued antagonism between El Salvador and Honduras. By the end of the 1970s, of course, the CACM faced a new set of problems. The overthrow of Somoza in Nicaragua and serious civil unrest elsewhere, especially in El Salvador, threatened to destroy what was left of the organization.

In the late 1960s, LAFTA also began to fall apart. Bolivia, Chile, Colombia, Ecuador, and Peru made plans to form a common market among themselves, excluding Argentina, Brazil, and Mexico. These five countries, later joined by Venezuela, formed what became known as the Andean Common Market

(ANCOM). The members of ANCOM hoped to achieve sufficient economic progress to be able to compete successfully with the larger, more economically developed countries in LAFTA. Then, according to the plan, the ANCOM countries would rejoin LAFTA, able to share more equally in the benefits of economic integration provided by that organization.

ANCOM aroused a lot of interest in the Third World because of its approach toward foreign investment. By the late 1960s, the evidence arising out of the experience of the European Common Market made it obvious that multinational corporations (particularly U.S.-based ones) could benefit enormously from the new, enlarged, and protected markets resulting from the process of economic integration. There was fear that integration among Latin American states might make them even more vulnerable to penetration and domination by foreign investors than they had been in the past. It was this fear, in part, that led ANCOM to adopt regulations aimed at controlling foreign investment within the boundaries of its member states.

There were rules, for example, concerning which sectors of the economies were open to investors. There were limits on the amount of capital that could be repatriated. Parent companies were forbidden to restrict exports by their subsidiaries. Provisions were also made to ensure that subsidiaries of foreign corporations would become locally owned in time. "Foreign enterprises already established in the Andean region must within three years of the code's adoption work out gradual divestment plans that would give local investors . . . majority control (51%) of the total shares within 15 years. New foreign investors must adopt similar 15-year fade-out schedules two years after production begins."[12]

How well these rules aimed at controlling foreign investments worked is a controversial question. Some corporations managed to obtain exceptions to them in important cases. And there are ways in which these kinds of rules can be subverted even if they are ostensibly enforced.[13] Furthermore, there were obvious differences in the manner in which the rules were enforced by the members. Chile provided the most spectacular example of these differences. Under Allende, of course, the Chilean government was an enthusiastic supporter of strict controls on foreign investment. The post-Allende government, however, was so desperate to attract foreign investment that it pushed hard for a relaxation of those controls. Even though the other members of ANCOM gave Chile much of what it wanted in this regard, the Pinochet regime withdrew Chile from the organization in 1976.

Peru, in the meantime, underwent a political transformation of its own. The Peruvian "revolution" in 1968 served as an inspiration for many of the innovations adopted by ANCOM with respect to foreign investment. But the new regime experienced a series of economic disasters that helped bring about a change of government and a change of attitude about foreign investment. As a result of this transition, Peru became a less-enthusiastic supporter of some of the innovations adopted by ANCOM. This increased skepticism about the extent to which rules on paper were being enforced in fact. As the end of the

1970s approached, ANCOM could hardly be written off as a failure, but even sympathetic observers admitted that its future was uncertain.[14]

INTER-AMERICAN RELATIONS AFTER THE COLD WAR IN THE ERA OF GLOBALIZATION

Emerging from the end of the Cold War in the early 1990s, Latin America appeared to be poised on the threshold of an era of unprecedented political progress, stability, and democracy, as well as economic growth based on free trade, foreign investment, and domestic economic policies based on market principles. In 1991, for example, an important economic integration organization, MERCOSUR, was formed by Argentina, Brazil, Paraguay, and Uruguay. By 1994, the *New York Times* declared that "On Rio's bay, two huge Brazilian cannons have been waiting for Argentine warships for decades, monuments to the long enmity between South America's two regional powers. But today the guns are frozen with rust, visited by tourists, many of them Argentines." The story goes on to attribute the decrease in tension between Brazil and Argentina, as well as similar improvements in bilateral relationships around the South American continent, to increased interdependence among these countries, primarily in the form of international trade.[15] As economic integration made important strides in the southern part of the Western Hemisphere in the early 1990s, it also enjoyed substantial progress in the northern part. The North American Free Trade Agreement, or NAFTA, was launched in 1994.

In the meantime, there was political instability of a seemingly rather traditional type when the democratically elected president of Haiti was ousted in an old-fashioned military coup in 1991.These apparently anachronistic events appeared to continue when the U.S. military intervened, once again, in the internal affairs of Haiti in 1994. There were important differences between this intervention, however, and dozens of American military interventions that had preceded it in the previous decades not only in Haiti, but also in the rest of the Caribbean and Central America. For one thing, the intervention resulted in the restoration to power of a democratically elected leader. For another, this intervention was sanctioned by both the Organization of American States (OAS) and the Security Council of the United Nations. So, by 1994, not only did democracy seem more firmly entrenched throughout the Western Hemisphere than ever before in its history. Economic integration, economic growth, democracy, and political stability also seemed quite firmly in place.

But appearances were deceiving. In retrospect, 1994 seems a high water mark in the inter-American system for democracy, economic integration, and progress and for interstate relations based on respect for international law and regional international organizations such as the OAS. It was about that time, it seems, that things began to fall apart.

For example, the launching of NAFTA coincided with the onset of a rebellion in the Mexican province of Chiapas, and an "economic shock, the Tequila crisis of 1994–95. Huge capital inflows into the country in the early 1990s were followed by rapid outflows toward the end of 1994, causing the peso to plunge."[16] NAFTA was associated with significant increases in trade between its members during the 1990s. And it may even have had something to do with the first peaceful transition of executive power in Mexico from one independent political party to another since the Revolution, with the election of Vicente Fox in 2000. But by 2004, "politically, the skeptics, ten years on, can fairly claim victory. NAFTA is unpopular in all three countries."[17]

And Mexico is certainly not the only place in Latin America where there was apparent increasing skepticism about and growing antagonism toward "liberal," market-oriented economic models, along with serious economic problems that seemed to augment at least some doubts about democratic political systems. Argentina, for example, in 1991, adopted a Convertibility Law, which pegged the Argentine peso to the dollar at a one-to-one rate. Argentina in general adopted a neoliberal economic approach apparently based on the "Washington Consensus," featuring strategies and tactics advocated by the United States. These policies were soon associated with economic disaster in Argentina. By 1995, the unemployment rate, which had been very low for most of the twentieth century, had skyrocketed to 18.6 percent.[18] By 2001–2002 Argentina was in the grips of a "wrenching depression," with a GDP shrunk to the level of 1993, unemployment at 22 percent, and a soaring poverty rate.[19] The ensuing political crisis led to the election of a Peronist president, Néstor Kirchner, who was notably suspicious of American advice and the supposed virtues of globalization.

But Kirchner is rather pro-American compared to the current president of Venezuela, Hugo Chávez. Chávez came to power in 1999, and soon made headlines with warm, praising statements about and friendly meetings with Fidel Castro and Saddam Hussein and with the institution of increasingly leftist, and, according to his critics, autocratic policies. He was thrown out of power, briefly, it turned out, by a coup in 2002. "The Bush Administration's . . . mishandled response to the April 2002 military coup . . . —failing to show any concern and instead expressing undisguised glee—eroded the administration's credibility on the democracy question."[20]

In Bolivia, in 2003, a long-time liberal and friend to the United States, Gonzalo Sánchez de Lozada, was driven from office by street protests. These were organized to some important extent by a long-time leftist leader, Evo Morales. Sánchez de Losada was replaced by Carlos Mesa. President Mesa, in a nationwide speech in 2004, criticized U.S.-sponsored economic policies during the 1990s that made Bolivia one of the most open economies in Latin America. These, he claimed, had done grievous damage to local producers and failed to reduce poverty. He called for the Bolivian state to serve as an "engine of economic growth."[21]

Perhaps the most significant harbinger of future trends in Latin America was the election in 2002 of a long-time leftist leader as Brazil's president: Luiz Inacio (Lula) da Silva, a member of Brazil's "Workers Party." It is probably safe to say that the election of Lula at almost any point in the Cold War era would have resulted in full-fledged panic in Washington, D.C. (and, quite likely, some subversive plot against him). Lula promised to be a major roadblock for American plans, for example, to create a Free Trade for the Americas (FTAA) by the end of 2005.

In short, throughout much of Latin America in the first half decade of the twenty-first century, there were substantial trends away from market-oriented policies favored in Washington, D.C., toward anti-Americanism, and perhaps away from democracy. "There is clearly a major backlash in much of Latin America. . . . The common language of open democracies and free markets used in the past decade by reform-minded opinion leaders throughout the hemisphere has less and less resonance."[22]

So, current trends in place in inter-American relations are worrisome for supporters of democracy and market-oriented economic policies, as well as for those who hope for friendly, supportive relationships between the United States and its neighbors to the south. There was very little by way of indications of concern about these trends in Washington, D.C. Political leaders in the United States are far too distracted by the war on terrorism, and dealing with the ramifications of September 11, 2001, to worry much about what is happening in their "backyard" (an obnoxious way for U.S. citizens to refer to Latin America, since it implies ownership and that what occurs there is nobody's business but their own). Ultimately, if these trends are unchecked, they will surely produce crises and concerns for the United States at a very high level.

This is not to say that Latin America is inexorably sinking into an abyss of ever-increasing poverty, misery, and political chaos. On the contrary, despite the fact that it is very easy to get the opposite impression from recent trends and daily headlines, there are very encouraging long-term economic and social trends in place throughout Latin America. According to World Bank figures, for example, the percentage of the citizens of Argentina with access to safe water increased from 51 percent in 1960 to 58 percent in 1980 and to 94 percent in 2001. The analogous figures for Brazil are 32 percent, 56 percent, and 87 percent, and for Mexico, 38 percent, 50 percent, and 88 percent. The proportion of the population of all of Latin America with access to safe water increased from 35 percent in 1960 to 53 percent in 1980 and 86 percent in 2001. Infant mortality in Latin America decreased dramatically in the forty years after 1960, in Argentina, Brazil, and Mexico, separately, and in Latin America as a whole, from 154 deaths per 1,000 live births in 1960 to 34 deaths per 1,000 live births in 2001. And in terms of what is arguably the most comprehensive indicator of the quality of life, throughout the whole of Latin America (as well as in Argentina, Brazil, and Mexico separately), life expectancy increased from 56.5 in 1960 to 70.6 in 2001.[23] All these improvements occurred during a period of increasingly intensive integration of Latin America with the world's economic processes, and of Latin American states with each other. Perhaps globalization is not responsible for these dramatic improvements in the lives of millions of people in Latin America. But at the very least, one must acknowledge that it obviously did not prevent the improvements from taking place.

NOTES

1. Mention of the last acquisition might seem out of place in an otherwise somber and proper discussion, but Elisa Lynch reputedly had a significant impact on the policies of Solano López. Pelham H. Box, for example, asserts that "the nature of the influence that for sixteen years the 'lorette parisienne' expressed over the mind of Francisco Solano López has not been adequately investigated. That it was considerable admits of no doubt" (Box, *The Origins of the Paraguayan War* [Urbana: University of Illinois Press, 1927], pp. 181–182).

2. Vera Blinn Reber, "The Demographics of Paraguay: A Reinterpretation of the Great War, 1864–1970," *Hispanic American Historical Review* 68 (May 1988), p. 290. For a standard source making the higher estimate of the Paraguayan casualties of the kind referred to by Reber, see Charles J. Kolinski, *Independence or Death: The Story of the Paraguayan War* (Gainesville, Fla.: University of Florida Press, 1965), p. 198.

3. Robert N. Burr, "The Balance of Power in Nineteenth-Century South America: An Exploratory Essay," *Hispanic American Historical Review* 25 (February 1955), pp. 40–41.

4. Hubert Herring, *A History of Latin America*, 3rd ed. (New York: Alfred A. Knopf, 1972), p. 655.

5. Walter Russell Mead, *Special Providence* (New York: Alfred A. Knopf, 2001), p. 19.

6. G. Pope Atkins, *Latin America in the International Political System* (New York: Free Press, 1977), p. 323.

7. J. David Singer and Melvin Small, *The Wages of War 1816–1965: A Statistical Handbook* (New York: Wiley and Jones, 1972), p. 67.

8. Minerva M. Etzioni, *The Majority of One: Towards a Theory of Regional Compatibility* (Beverly Hills, Calif.: Sage Publications, 1970), pp. 118–119.

9. This section relies heavily on my earlier discussion of integration in Latin America in James Lee Ray, *Global Politics,* 4th ed. (Boston: Houghton Mifflin, 1990), pp. 429–440, as well as on an updated analysis in James Lee Ray, *Global Politics,* 6th ed. (Boston: Houghton Mifflin, 1995), pp. 392–397.

10. David Mitrany, *A Working Peace System* (London: Royal Institute of International Affairs, 1943), and Ernst Haas, *The Uniting of Europe* (Stanford, Calif.: Stanford University Press, 1958).

11. Joseph Grunwald, Miguel S. Wionczek, and Martin Carnoy, *Latin American Economic Integration and U.S. Policy* (Washington, D.C.: Brookings Institution, 1972), p. 51.

12. Roger W. Fontaine, *The Andean Pact: A Political Analysis* (Beverly Hills, Calif.: Sage Publications, 1977), p. 19.

13. Thomas J. Biersteker, "The Illusion of State Power: Transnational Corporations and the Neutralization of Host-Country Legislation," *Journal of Peace Research 17* (1980), pp. 207–221.

14. Ricardo French-Davis, "The Andean Pact: A Model of Economic Integration for Developing Countries," in Joseph Grunwald, ed., *Latin America and the World Economy* (Beverly Hills, Calif.: Sage Publications, 1978), pp. 165–194.

15. James Brooke, "The New South Americans: Friends and Partners," *New York Times,* April 8, 1994, p. A3.

16. "Free Trade on Trial," *Economist,* January 3, 2004, p. 14.

17. Ibid., p. 13.

18. Steven Levitsky and María Victoria Murillo, "Argentina Weathers the Storm," *Journal of Democracy* 14 (2003), p. 153.

19. Enrique Peruzzotte, "Argentina After the Crash: Pride and Disillusion," *Current History* 103 (2004), p. 86.

20. Michael Shifter, "The U.S. and Latin America Through the Lens of Empire," *Current History* 103 (2004), pp. 64–65.

21. Kevin G. Hall, "New President Struggles to Control Chaotic Nation," *Miami Herald.com*, February 7, 2004. http://www.miami.com/mld/miamiherald/7898001.htm

22. Shifter, op.cit., p. 65.

23. "Wanted: A New Regional Agenda for Economic Growth," *Economist*, April 26, 2003, p. 29.

Suggested Readings

Atkins, G. Pope. *Latin America in the International Political System.* 2d ed. New York: Free Press, 1989. A good broad and basic introduction to inter-American relations, as well as to the relationship of the Latin American region with the rest of the world.

Burr, Robert N. "The Balance of Power in Nineteenth-Century South America: An Exploratory Essay." *Hispanic American Historical Review* 25 (February 1955), pp. 37–60. An informative discussion of relations among the South American states in the nineteenth century, with a focus on the impact of the interstate wars in that time period.

Casteñeda, Jorge. "The Forgotten Relationship," *Foreign Affairs* 82 (2003), pp. 67–81. A plea from a former minister of foreign affairs from Mexico for the United States to recommit to Latin America in the wake of September 11, 2001, and in the midst of its war on terrorism.

Connell-Smith, Gordon. *The United States and Latin America.* New York: John Wiley and Sons, 1974. One of the liveliest historical accounts on U.S. foreign policy toward Latin America.

Davis, Harold Eugene, and Larman C. Wilson, eds. *Latin American Foreign Policies: An Analysis.* Baltimore: Johns Hopkins University Press, 1975. Concentrates on a country-by-country analysis of the foreign policies of Latin American states. Emphasizes recent foreign policy problems and approaches.

de Soto, Hernando. *The Other Path.* New York: Harper and Row, 1989. An English translation of this Peruvian work, which has apparently become a kind of "bible" of advocates of neoclassical reforms in Latin America. There is a rather lengthy introduction by Mario Vargas Llosa.

Domínguez, Jorge. "Consensus and Divergence: The State of the Literature in Interamerican Relations in the 1970s." *Latin American Research Review* 13:1 (1978), pp. 87–126. Interesting discussion of the current trends and competing viewpoints in the academic literature on inter-American relations.

Herring, Hubert. *A History of Latin America.* 3rd ed. New York: Alfred A. Knopf, 1972. A very comprehensive, authoritative history of the region with each country discussed in some detail.

Levinson, Jerome, and Juan de Onis. *The Alliance That Lost Its Way.* Chicago: Quadrangle Books, 1970. A penetrating analysis of the Alliance for Progress. Especially good on the problems faced by the United States in its attempts to mold the internal political systems of Latin American states.

Malloy, James M., and Mitchell A. Seligson, eds. *Authoritarians and Democrats: Regime Transition in Latin America.* Pittsburgh: University of Pittsburgh Press, 1987. An analysis of the transition to democracy in several Latin American countries with a general, theoretical discussion of the phenomenon in both the introduction and a concluding chapter.

Mora, Frank O., and Jeanne A.K. Hey, eds. *Latin American and Caribbean Foreign Policy.* Lanham, Md.: Rowman and Littlefield, 2003. A state-by-state analysis of the foreign policies of most the countries of Latin America.

Smith, Peter H. *Talons of the Eagle: Dynamics of U.S.–Latin American Relations.* New York: Oxford University Press, 1996. An analysis of U.S.–Latin American relations broken down into three periods, from the 1790s to the 1920s, the Cold War era, and the contemporary era.

Szulc, Tad. *Fidel: A Critical Portrait.* New York: Avon, 1986. A very readable biography with lots of interesting tidbits about, for example, how the CIA helped Fidel financially in the 1950s and how Fidel contacted and developed a close relationship with the traditional Communist Party in Havana almost from the moment he came to town in 1959.

Chapter 14

THE UNITED STATES AND LATIN AMERICA: INTO A NEW ERA

WAYNE S. SMITH

U.S.–LATIN AMERICAN RELATIONS are at a historic turning point. It is not simply that the Cold War is over: That, after all, was a phenomenon of only the past half century. Rather, it is that the basic strategic calculations that shaped U.S. policy over the past 200 years or more—or virtually since the birth of the republic—are now suddenly obsolete.

The most central of these was what has been called the concept of strategic denial.[1] Simply put, this was the response of U.S. leaders to the calculation that while no state or potential state to the south was powerful enough to threaten the security of the United States, their very weakness rendered them vulnerable to the control of outside powers. The United States had first the Atlantic, and later the Pacific, the two great oceans, between it and those who might intend it harm. The latter, however, might overcome those natural barriers by positioning themselves to the south of the United States. Thus, one of the earliest and most enduring U.S. objectives was to keep other powers out of the Western Hemisphere.

At first, of course, two European powers, Spain and Portugal, were already positioned to the south. But Portugal was never viewed as a threat, and by the beginning of the nineteenth century Spain also had come to be seen as the weakling of Europe. So long as the colonies were in their hands, there was little cause for concern. Transfer to a more powerful state, however, was unacceptable. Obviously, it was this concern also that underlay Secretary of State Henry Clay's assertion in 1825 that "we could not consent to the occupation of those islands [Cuba and Puerto Rico] by any European power other than Spain under any contingency whatever."[2] It was a warning repeated several times over the next few decades.

Indeed, with the Louisiana Purchase, Cuba had come to be seen as the most strategically vital piece of territory outside the continental limits of the United States itself. From 1803 forward, the Port of New Orleans was the window onto the rest of the world for the vast interior of the United States. All trade and communications funneled through that window and out through the Gulf of Mexico. And what sat in the entrance to the gulf, like a cork in a bottle? The island of Cuba. That Cuba not be allowed to fall into the hands of a powerful enemy, which might thus block vital U.S. trade routes, became a maxim for U.S. leaders.

The second basic calculation was that the United States must assert hegemony over the lands to its south. The second in effect flowed from the first, for keeping other powers out obviously required some degree of control on the United States part. As Gaddis Smith has put it, the Monroe Doctrine was an assertion of a U.S. sphere of influence.[3] Ideas as to the form that might take changed over time. Early leaders tended to assume the U.S. flag was destined eventually to fly over the entire continent, that is, the United States would exercise outright sovereignty. By the end of the nineteenth century, however, it was seen that control was more important—and cheaper—than sovereignty. Thus, Secretary of State Richard Olney could say with satisfaction in 1895 that the United States "is practically sovereign on this continent, and its fiat is law upon the subjects to which it confines its interposition."[4]

One may smile at Olney's statement and others like it (though at the time few Latin Americans found them amusing), for they certainly exaggerated the degree of control actually enjoyed by the United States. It was in fact never "practically sovereign" in the hemisphere (though it came close to it for a time in Central America and the Caribbean). The point, however, is that Americans tended to believe it was and, more important, to believe that their very security required that it be so.

Obviously, that is no longer the case. With the collapse of the Soviet Union, there are now no powers in the world that have the capability to position themselves in Latin America so as to threaten U.S. security. In today's world, a far more realistic danger lies in the possible clandestine introduction of a nuclear device by terrorists—or some other terrorist act on the magnitude of the attacks on September 11, 2001. But no Latin American base would be required for that. There are various terrorist organizations against which the United States must be alert, and there are still a few adversary nations which perhaps wish us harm—countries such as North Korea. But none has the capability—or the need—to mount a threat from the south. Nor do the terrorist organizations.

And indeed the nature of warfare has so changed that the old concepts are now obsolete. One thinks today in terms of terrorist bombs or of intercontinental missiles that reach their targets from the other side of the world in less than forty minutes. The great oceans are no longer much protection and have not been for decades. Having nearby naval bases so as to position a fleet off American shores is a tactic of the past, not of today.

Thus, the entire concept of strategic denial has become invalid. So, too, has the rationale for the Monroe Doctrine, and with it any need for the United States to assert hegemony over the rest of the hemisphere. The problems that face the United States today require a cooperative relationship, not the exercise of hegemony. The United States needs to rethink its entire position and to base its policies on today's realities, not yesterday's. But old habits die hard. Whether U.S. policymakers can make the necessary mental adjustment and fashion an effective policy for today remains to be seen. Certainly the administration of George W. Bush has not made that adjustment. On the contrary, it reflects a unilateralist trend and a do-it-our-way-or-else approach that has alienated other countries around the world—and in Latin America. This is not the place to comment on Bush's march to war in Iraq in virtual defiance of the UN Security Council, because, he said, Iraq had weapons of mass destruction ready to fire and we could not wait. But then no weapons of mass destruction were found. It *is* the place to note that U.S. standing in Latin America is at its lowest point in many years. This is little short of tragic.

Why has it turned out that way? Mexico is a perfect example. It had been expected that President Bush and President Vicente Fox of Mexico would forge a warm personal relationship and bring relations between the two countries into a period of unprecedented friendship and cooperation. President Bush had promised to negotiate a comprehensive agreement on immigration matters that was of key importance to Fox. But then Mexico voted against the United States in the UN Security Council on the matter of the war in Iraq. That was the end of the special relationship—and so far, of a comprehensive agreement on immigration. Fox was left holding the bag .

Before turning to an analysis of the post–Cold War and post–September 11 situation, however, a historical review would seem to be in order. The future of U.S.–Latin American relations is uncertain. Rationale even for today's policies is confused. To put it in literary terms: The United States is uncertain where it is going or even of the ground on which it now stands; all the more important that we at least be clear as to how it got here.

MANIFEST DESTINY, 1823–1898

Since for over a century the Monroe Doctrine has been described as the "great American shibboleth," one would imagine that it was issued with great fanfare and comment. That was not at all the case. Europeans were momentarily irritated by its brashness, but, realizing that the United States had little means of enforcing it, they paid it little heed. And even in the United States itself for over two decades there was little further reference to Monroe's statement. If European powers were dissuaded from adventures in the Caribbean Basin, it was largely because of the presence of a powerful British naval squadron, not because of anything the United States said or did. The United States had to grow into the role of protector, had first to become strong. U.S. leaders expected the Stars and Stripes to fly over the rest of the hemisphere, yes, but that was for the future. For the moment, they were focused on consolidating their hold over the vast territory already within U.S. borders.

By 1845, however, the United States was looking beyond those borders. It not only had decided to bring Texas into the Union but was also casting covetous eyes at California and Oregon, areas on which Great Britain and perhaps other European powers had designs as well. President James Polk therefore saw fit to revive the Monroe Doctrine, restating it twenty-two years to the day, December 2, 1845, after President Monroe's famous message to the Congress. The Western Hemisphere, Polk emphasized again, was not open to colonization by outside powers, though because of the focus of U.S. attention at that point (that is, Texas, California, and Oregon), he added that this was especially true of North America.

In early 1846, war broke out with Mexico, a short-lived conflict that ended with U.S. troops occupying Mexico City and the United States seizing half of Mexico's territory, including California. The country thus became a continental power, with shores on both the Atlantic and Pacific Oceans. Manifest Destiny was on the march. As cargo and passengers bound from one coast to the other now more often than not moved across the Central American isthmus, control of that area took on new importance. It was no coincidence that the United States encouraged William Walker's filibustering expeditions to Central America and his successful efforts to establish himself (briefly) as the ruler of Nicaragua.

As early as 1823, John Quincy Adams had described Cuba as a ripening fruit destined inevitably to fall into the lap of the Union. Guarding as it did one of the approaches to the isthmus, the island took on even greater strategic importance after 1848, and U.S. administrations began a series of efforts to acquire it, beginning with President Polk's attempted purchase that year. Over the next half century, four other U.S. presidents tried to buy Cuba outright. There were also a number of abortive and certainly less-straightforward schemes to transfer the island to U.S. ownership.[5] In addition, there were three major filibustering expeditions against the island. One of these, led by a Venezuelan-born former Spanish army officer named Narciso López, came in 1850 and in many ways was a preview of the Bay of Pigs disaster more than a century later. Just as did the CIA in 1961, López assured his little band of invaders that as soon as they landed, the Cuban people would rise in arms against their government. That turned out to be as wild a dream in 1850 as in 1961.

The acquisitive tendencies that were so much a part of Manifest Destiny were interrupted by the Civil War, that great and bloody conflict that tested the very survival of the nation. Further, while the United States was locked in its own mortal combat, the Monroe Doctrine was challenged more clearly than ever before. Louis Napoleon of France occupied Mexico and imposed an emperor, Maximilian of Hapsburg, to rule it—on the points of French bayonets. Maximilian's reign came to a tragic end, however, as the Civil War ended and the United States warned Louis Napoleon to withdraw his troops. He did, leaving Maximilian defenseless. An honorable man, the latter would not abandon his few Mexican supporters. He fought on and was captured and shot by Mexican patriots led by Benito Juárez. The Monroe Doctrine and Mexican sovereignty (not always easy traveling companions) had been preserved.

At mid-century, it had seemed that more and more territory in Latin America was destined to come under the U.S. flag, but by the end of the century U.S. perceptions of its security needs were changing. Washington wished to assert hegemony and to turn a profit financially, especially in the areas nearest to it, that is, in Central America and the Caribbean, but it had growing reservations about the need, or even the desirability, of bringing these areas into the Union or in some other way incorporating them into the U.S. system. That would require permanent occupying forces and be expensive. That was one objection. Probably a more important one was chauvinistic. As E. L. Godkin, editor of *Nation* magazine put it, "semi-civilized Catholic states" had no place in the American system.[6]

As the other states were to remain independent, there might even be something to be gained by developing a hemispheric grouping of nations, though with the United States clearly to be primus inter pares. Thus, in 1889 the first Pan-American Conference was held in Washington under the stewardship of Secretary of State James G. Blaine. All independent states attended except for the Dominican Republic. With the Argentine delegation taking the lead, the majority of Latin Americans present made it clear that they were not to be dictated to by the United States, and a number of U.S. proposals were rejected. Even so, a permanent secretariat was established in Washington that eventually became the Pan-American Union, and a system of arbitration was set up for handling disputes between nations—a system, however, that was all too rarely used. The governments apparently were not prepared to go as far as the delegates to the congress.

Even long-standing U.S. designs on Cuba were altered by this new reluctance to incorporate territories into the U.S. system. Despite all its past efforts to acquire the island, in 1898, just as Cuba's war of independence against Spain was reaching its climax and the United States was on the verge of entering the conflict on Cuba's side, that is, just as conditions seemed most favorable for annexation, the United States stepped back. Under the famous Teller Amendment attached to the declaration of hostilities, the United States vowed not to acquire Cuba as the result of those hostilities. Nothing was said about the Philippines or Guam or Puerto Rico. As a result of the war with Spain, the United States took them all, and in the process became a global power. But Cuba was left with its independence—not fully independent, to be sure; rather, under the Platt Amendment, which the United States forced Cuba to attach to its constitution, Cuba became virtually a U.S. protectorate.

The United States in effect supervised Cuba's foreign affairs, including foreign loans, and had the right to intervene whenever it saw fit to preserve peace and stability. "It is not the absolute independence we had dreamed about," mused the embittered old Cuban military leader Máximo Gómez.[7] He nonetheless urged his fellow countrymen to accept the amendment as the price of U.S. withdrawal. It was better to accept limited sovereignty and be rid of the occupying forces, he reasoned. Perhaps in the future, the dream of the republic might be realized. (In 1959 it was.)

Gunboat Diplomacy, 1898–1929

This was the pattern followed over the next thirty-four years. The United States considered everything to the south to be its sphere of influence, and it often exercised outright control in Central America and the Caribbean Basin. U.S. capital flooded into those same nearby regions. Banks, utility enterprises, and companies, such as United Fruit, soon virtually controlled the economies of several countries. By 1929, for example, over 65 percent of the Cuban economy was in the hands of U.S. owners. It was an age of dollar diplomacy backed up by U.S. gunboats.

The United States did, however, continue to meet periodically with the other governments at Pan-American conferences. The fiction of juridical equality was maintained, and, most important, the United States did not seize outright any more territory, not even to build a canal in Panama, one of President Theodore Roosevelt's overriding priorities. The United States first negotiated with Colombia, of which Panama was a province. When those negotiations did not prosper, Washington engineered a rebellion in the province, immediately recognized the breakaway rebels as the government of a new Panamanian state, and in 1903 signed an agreement with them to build a canal. U.S. forces made certain Colombia did not intervene. But the new state remained independent (though with a circumscribed form of independence, as in the case of Cuba) and almost eight decades later would itself assume control of the canal.

Elsewhere, U.S. insistence that extra-hemispheric states not meddle in its sphere of influence raised difficulties. It was all well and good for the United States to say that other powers could not intervene, but what, then, if the states of the hemisphere defaulted on their debts or in some other way (in the parlance of the times in the United States) "behaved irresponsibly"? Who was to police them? In his annual message to Congress in 1904, President Theodore Roosevelt gave the answer: The United States would become the policeman of the Western Hemisphere. "Chronic wrongdoing," he said, "or an impotence which results in a general loosening of the ties of civilized society, may in America, as elsewhere, ultimately require intervention by some civilized nation, and in the Western Hemisphere the adherence of the United States to the Monroe Doctrine may force the United States, however reluctantly, in flagrant cases of such wrongdoing or impotence, to the exercise of an international police power."[8]

This became known as the Roosevelt Corollary to the Monroe Doctrine. The United States wasted no time in implementing it. In 1905, it intervened in the Dominican Republic to set up a customs collection operation to pay off that country's debt to several European creditors. It did the same thing in Nicaragua in 1912 and in Haiti in 1915, with marines remaining in occupation of those countries off and on for many years. On various other grounds, it intervened at least twenty-six times in other states of Central America and the Caribbean. Even President Woodrow Wilson landed marines in Veracruz and sent U.S. troops under General John Pershing into northern Mexico. By

1927, U.S. hegemony over Central America was so complete that Undersecretary of State Robert Olds could say, "Central America has always understood that governments we recognize and support stay in power, while those we do not recognize and support fail."[9]

Old's statement was as direct an assertion of hegemony as one can imagine. Perhaps in part it was the very brazenness of the attitudes behind such statements—a brazenness that clashed painfully with U.S. idealism—that caused opinion in the United States to begin to swing toward a more cooperative relationship. Shifting opinions were pushed also by the growing resistance of Latin America. Offended by the condescending paternalism of the Roosevelt Corollary, Latin American countries increasingly protested U.S. interventions and high-handed actions. By the Pan-American Conference held in Havana in 1928, the other states were demanding a rectification of U.S. policy. Perhaps to their surprise, the United States listened. There was a greater spirit of equality and cooperation than ever before, and issues such as intervention in the internal affairs of the member states were discussed frankly. In the past, they had not even been on the agenda. As the conference broke up, it was understood that at the next meeting, an anti-intervention resolution would be on the agenda. The stage was set for the Good Neighbor Policy.

The Good Neighbor Policy, 1929–1953

Many chronologies mark the beginning of the Good Neighbor Policy in 1933, with the inauguration of President Franklin Delano Roosevelt. In fact, however, it was begun under President Herbert Hoover. He deplored U.S. interventionism, and during his presidency, 1929–1933, U.S. marines were pulled out of every country in Latin America except Haiti. Hoover also ordered a review of the historical rationale for interventionism. In response, a memorandum prepared by Undersecretary of State J. Reuben Clark and published in 1930 held that nothing in the Monroe Doctrine had ever given the United States the right to intervene in the internal affairs of its neighbors. This removed the underpinning from the Roosevelt Corollary, and the corollary was never again cited as the basis for U.S. policy.[10]

The trend away from interventionism was given new impetus during the presidency of Franklin Roosevelt. He stressed strong economic ties with Latin America, not political domination, and favored collective security over unilateral actions by the United States. He abrogated the Platt Amendment, thus removing the protectorate infringement of Cuban sovereignty. And, as promised at Havana in 1928, at the 1933 Pan-American Conference in Montevideo, Uruguay, the United States pledged itself to the principle of nonintervention. The following year, Roosevelt pulled the last marines out of Haiti and, true to his word, did not send them again into any Latin American country during his long presidency (1933–1945).

Good relations were further spurred by World War II. With the exception of Argentina, which tended to sympathize with the Axis powers (until a last-minute change of sides in 1945), all the Latin American states were allies of the United States and made no small contribution to the war effort, assuring natural resources and other needed commodities, providing air and naval bases, and, in the case of Mexico and Brazil, even sending troops. A Brazilian army division fought in Italy, a squadron of Mexican fighter aircraft in the Pacific. As the war ended, U.S.–Latin American relations were more harmonious than they had ever been.

Even warmer, more cooperative relations seemed to lie ahead. Roosevelt's successor, President Harry S. Truman, continued Roosevelt's noninterventionist policy and in 1947 also helped bring into being the so-called Rio Pact, a collective security treaty that made defense of the Western Hemisphere the responsibility of all member states. This was followed in 1948 by the creation of the Organization of American States (OAS), which provided for the adjudication of disputes among members and for collective peacekeeping measures. The OAS, in effect, took the old Pan-American Union to a new level of cooperation and organizational cohesion.

If the hemisphere still had to be defended from outside powers, it was clear that those who had framed the OAS charter and the Rio Pact did not think that was any longer the responsibility of the United States alone. Rather, it now became the duty of all member states. As U.S. political leaders and scholars commented at the time, the Monroe Doctrine was thus to become a multilateral instrument.[11] And so it might have. Unfortunately, as the OAS was being formed, the Cold War between the United States and the Soviet Union was heating up. Soon it was to become an all-consuming struggle to which all other considerations and objectives were sacrificed.

THE COLD WAR, 1953–1989

In the same year that the Rio Pact was signed, 1949, China fell to the Communists and the Soviet Union exploded its own atomic bomb. The next year, 1950, saw the outbreak of the Korean War. The Cold War was on in earnest. That had little immediate effect on U.S.–Latin American relations, however. Latin America was perceived to be far removed from the Soviet Union and safely within the U.S. sphere of influence. Indeed, Latin American states were perceived as important allies on whose votes in the UN General Assembly the United States could always count. The Truman administration continued its noninterventionist policies. Thus, despite the growing Cold War hysteria in the United States as reflected by McCarthyism, and despite some rumblings in the Policy Planning Bureau of the State Department that a harder line might be in order, it can be said that the Good Neighbor Policy toward Latin America continued until 1953.

In that year, however, with the inauguration of Dwight Eisenhower as president and the appointment of John Foster Dulles as secretary of state, the Cold War came to Latin America full force. The concept of strategic denial now had but one focus: the Soviet Union. Thus, Dulles, on the basis of no hard evidence, immediately warned of increasing Communist influence in the hemisphere that the Soviet Union was determined to exploit. He pointed to Guatemala as a case in point. At the meeting of OAS foreign ministers in Caracas in 1954, he presented a resolution that stipulated that any hemispheric government under Communist influence represented a threat to peace and security against which the other states would take multilateral action. Dulles made it clear that the other states could either accept the resolution and cooperate with the United States or risk a return to unilateral interventions. The resolution was accepted, but only after it had been changed to provide for "consultations" rather than immediate multilateral action.

Undaunted, the Eisenhower administration moved ahead with plans to oust the "Communist-controlled" government of Jacobo Arbenz with a coup clandestinely organized by the CIA. In June 1954, Colonel Castillo Armas, a disaffected Guatemalan officer, led a group of several hundred armed men in an uprising against Arbenz.[12] The United States could maintain that it was not intervening, that this was a Guatemalan reaction. Few believed it, but all that was needed was a fig leaf. As the Guatemalan army would not fight for the government, the coup quickly succeeded. The Guatemalan Revolution, which might best be described as a liberal reform movement begun in 1944, ended. What followed, thanks to the U.S. intervention, was a long series of bloody military dictatorships, occasionally interrupted by elected governments—governments, however, that served at the sufferance of the military and were rarely allowed even to serve out their terms. Repression was massive. Tens of thousands of Guatemalans were slaughtered by the army in the next fifty years. Only recently has there been encouraging movement toward democracy and an end to the bloody guerrilla warfare that has plagued the country since the early 1960s.

In retrospect, it is clear that there was no Communist—let alone Soviet—threat in Guatemala. Arbenz himself was not a Communist. On the contrary, though elected by the people, he was a colonel in the Guatemalan army. There were no Communist cabinet ministers in his government and only four Communist Party members in the National Assembly. The Soviet Union had not even bothered to establish diplomatic relations with Guatemala and certainly was providing no assistance of any kind. The government was progressive, however, and was carrying out an agrarian reform. In the process, it nationalized some land belonging to United Fruit. That may have been what really triggered Arbenz's overthrow, especially when we consider that John Foster Dulles's law firm had handled the United Fruit account and that his brother, CIA director Allen Dulles, Henry Cabot Lodge, the United States' UN ambassador, and a series of other senior government officials had all been members of the United Fruit board.

The Eisenhower administration also adopted a policy of supporting any right-wing dictatorship, no matter how repressive, so long as they professed themselves to be "anti-Communist." For eight years, from 1953 until 1961, the United States forgot all about the pursuit of democracy. It seemed to see dictators as more reliable allies. Secretary of State Dulles at one point even described Venezuela under Pérez Jiménez, that country's comic-opera military dictator, as pursuing the kind of political and economic policies the United States would wish to see emulated by every Latin American country.[13]

In the Guatemalan case and in most other U.S. interventions in Latin America during the Cold War, the perceived threats of Communist takeovers were more figments of the imaginations of U.S. leaders, fed by Cold War hysteria, than real. Only in the Cuban case was there legitimate cause for concern. Not that Fidel Castro was a Communist when he took power in 1959. But his objectives of sharply reducing U.S. influence in the hemisphere and encouraging the emergence of a series of other revolutionary regimes seemed likely to carry him toward an alliance with the Soviet Union. They were objectives, after all, that he could not achieve on his own. By early 1960, the United States concluded that such an alliance was in formation and began preparations to overthrow the Castro government. That effort was made at the Bay of Pigs in April 1961, with disastrous results. The idea that the 1,200 men of the Cuban exile brigade could defeat Castro's army of over 60,000 armed with tanks and artillery was preposterous. They could have succeeded only had they been supported by U.S. troops. President John F. Kennedy, who had taken office in January 1961 and inherited the invasion plan from the Eisenhower administration, had stated flatly that no U.S. forces would be used, but the CIA counted on a change of orders once it became clear that the brigade could not hold the beach. The CIA was wrong. Kennedy stuck by his determination not to commit U.S. forces, and the invasion failed. Its two principal results were the destruction of any internal opposition to Castro and the consolidation of a Cuban-Soviet alliance.

The latter led, in October 1962, to the Cuban missile crisis. Suddenly the worst nightmare U.S. policymakers could imagine in Latin America was upon them. For almost 150 years, the Monroe Doctrine had been intended to keep other powers out of the hemisphere and thus prevent them from threatening U.S. security from the nation's southern frontier. Now the United States's principal global adversary, the Soviet Union, was doing just that, and threatening in a most fearsome way, with nuclear missiles. The crisis was eventually resolved through the Kennedy-Khrushchev Understanding, under which the Soviet Union agreed to withdraw its missiles in return for a U.S. pledge not to invade Cuba. Even so, it is fair to say that U.S. policymakers were badly traumatized by the missile crisis and that from 1962 onward they were absolutely determined that there would be no more Cubas.

The Kennedy administration itself followed a two-track policy toward that objective: (1) It moved to contain Castroism by trying to isolate him in the hemisphere and by giving military assistance to the other governments to defend themselves against Castro-backed guerrillas. But (2), to its credit, it also launched the Alliance for Progress, a program of economic and technical assistance. This recognized that revolutionary conditions resulted from economic and social distress and that addressing these problems was as important as military aid. For the same reason, the Kennedy administration also gave greater emphasis to supporting democratic regimes rather than dictatorships.

With Kennedy's death, however, the Alliance for Progress was for all practical purposes abandoned by the harder-line administration of Lyndon Johnson. In 1964, Johnson also made it clear to the Brazilian generals that the United States would endorse their overthrow of the democratically elected government of Jango Goulart, who was regarded by the United States as much too far to the left. The generals proceeded to do just that, thus aborting the democratic process in Brazil and ushering in two decades of military rule.

Johnson also sent troops into the Dominican Republic in 1965 when it seemed that political instability there might open the way to "a Castroite takeover." Johnson was able to get OAS cover for the intervention (the grateful Brazilian generals providing many of the troops). What he was unable to do was to come up with any evidence of a Communist conspiracy.[14]

Eight years later, Richard Nixon and Henry Kissinger played a role in Chile similar to that of the Johnson administration in Brazil. Regarding the Popular Front government of Salvador Allende to be under the influence of the Communists, they at the very least indicated to the Chilean military that they would welcome his overthrow, if indeed they did not actively encourage it. True, Allende was a Socialist and the Communist Party was part of the ruling Popular Front. On the other hand, Allende had been democratically elected (in 1970). All Chile's political institutions were intact and functioning. Thus, he had either to play within the constitutional parameters or face impeachment. There was no need to overthrow him. He could have been voted out at the polls in the next elections. But neither the Chilean military nor the Nixon administration wanted to wait. On September 11, 1973, the coup was launched—and not in the cause of democracy. On the contrary, what followed were seventeen years of the bloodiest military dictatorship in Chile's history, a period during which tens of thousands of Chilean citizens were tortured and murdered, often because they simply looked like leftists. Not until 1990 did democracy return to Chile. To its credit, the United States, which must bear some responsibility for those seventeen years of horror in Chile, under the administration of George H. W. Bush encouraged Chile's return to democracy.

The last significant Cold War chapter in the hemisphere was played out in Central America—with one small sideshow in Grenada. In Nicaragua, where the Somozas had ruled the country since 1936, the administration of Jimmy Carter found itself in an uncomfortable position. It was glad to see the Somoza dictatorship end in 1979 but concerned that the Sandinista guerrillas who had ousted him were avowedly Marxist and friendly to Fidel Castro, although they quickly vowed to move toward elections and to address U.S. security concerns. The Carter administration, albeit nervously, was prepared to meet them halfway, to handle differences through negotiations and even to provide limited economic assistance as an incentive. Not to the administration of Ronald Reagan, which took office in January 1981. It regarded the Sandinistas as nothing less than instruments of Soviet aggression and was determined to get rid of them one way or another.

Meanwhile, encouraged perhaps by the Sandinista victory in Nicaragua, left-wing guerrillas in El Salvador had launched an all-out effort to topple the government in that country, and with it the traditional control of the landowning elite. The Carter administration focused as much on the need for economic and social reforms as on the need to contain the guerrillas, and the U.S. ambassador, Robert E. White, insisted that the government curb the right-wing death squads (which had been responsible for the murder of Archbishop Romero) as a condition for U.S. assistance.

The Reagan administration had no such qualms. As it came into office in 1981, it in effect told the government and the military to do whatever they deemed necessary to defeat the guerrillas. Atrocities on the government's side shot up at an appalling rate, often carried out by troops or death squads trained by the United States. Equally determined to win in Nicaragua, the Reagan administration eschewed negotiations and other efforts at peaceful solutions. Instead, it armed former Somoza national guardsmen and other anti-Sandinista elements, organized them into a force called the Contras, and launched them as a guerrilla force against the government in Managua. The ensuing conflict raged from 1982 until 1989. During that time, the United States pulled Honduras into the conflict by having the Contras operate from its territory and by training Honduran death squads to go after suspected leftists. In 1984, it also mined Nicaraguan harbors, an act that resulted in a 14–3 decision by the International Court of Justice (ICJ) declaring the United States to be in violation of international law. The United States, having already taken the position that the ICJ did not have jurisdiction in the matter, simply ignored the decision.

In its frantic efforts to do away with the Sandinistas, officials of the Reagan administration also lied to the Congress and then, in their efforts to circumvent congressional restrictions on aid to the Contras, initiated what became known as Iran-Contragate, a bizarre operation that began with efforts to divert to the Contras "profits" made by overcharging for arms the United States illegally sold Iran as part of a deal to bring about the release of Americans held hostage by Islamic groups in Lebanon. Eventually, the operation involved secret donations made by a whole series of governments and shady individuals, and all in direct violation of congressional directives.[15] The U.S. Army even trained Central American officers in methods of torture and assassination and wrote manuals advocating those methods that were used in the infamous School of the Americas.[16]

In short, the last chapter of the Cold War was one in which the United States seemed to lose its way or to forget the values on which the country had been founded. As Gaddis Smith has so well put it:

James Monroe in 1823 had contrasted American principles of candor, self-government, and respect for national independence with the devious, autocratic, imperial ways of Europe. The [Monroe] doctrine was proclaimed as protection of the first against the second. The abandonment after 1945 of its original ideals made the last years of the Monroe Doctrine a history of moral degradation. Sometimes the words and principles of the Monroe Doctrine were embraced openly, enthusiastically, and with complete candor. More often they were muffled in secrecy, tainted by lies, and in conflict with the public creed of democracy and human rights.[17]

In the end, the Central Americans ended the conflict through their own peace process, with little encouragement or support from the United States. Indeed, it would be more accurate to say that until quite late in the day, the United States opposed the peace negotiations. Certainly, it was U.S. opposition that frustrated the so-called Contadora process, an effort on the part of the Central American and Mexican presidents begun in 1983 to work out solutions to the region's conflicts. As this stood near the verge of collapse, however, it was followed by a new effort begun in 1987 at a meeting of presidents in Esquipulas, Guatemala. The prime mover of this new negotiating effort was Oscar Arias, the new president of Costa Rica and a man of great determination. Over the next two years, agreements were hammered out that eventually led to an end to the civil war in El Salvador, the phasing-out of fighting between the Contras and the Sandinistas in Nicaragua, and the holding of elections in that country in 1990. When the Sandinistas lost, they peacefully turned power over to the opposition.

And so the conflict ended in Central America—no thanks to the United States. Oscar Arias won the Nobel Peace Prize, much to the disgust of some in the Reagan administration who had thought his plan for negotiations simply a means of appeasing "the Communists." Meanwhile, back in 1983, in something of a sideshow performance, the Reagan administration had used U.S. forces to invade the island of Grenada. Relations with Grenada had deteriorated steadily after the New Jewel Movement took power there in 1979. It was led by Maurice Bishop, a friend of Castro's who was considered by both the Carter and Reagan administrations as being much too far to the left. On the other hand, Grenada was a tiny island that threatened no one. Even so, in October 1983, the Reagan administration took advantage of internecine political strife on the island to send in U.S. forces and remove the New Jewel Movement from power. The specific pretexts for the invasion were to assure the safety of U.S. students at a medical school on the island and to prevent the completion of an airfield that President Reagan himself warned was probably intended for use by the Soviets.

In fact, subsequent investigations made clear that the students were in no danger and in any event could have been peacefully evacuated had it not been for the invasion. It also turned out that the UN Development Program had recommended construction of the airfield as part of an effort to expand tourism on the island. And once the invasion was over, the U.S. taxpayers forked over $19 million to help the new Grenadian government complete that same airfield—to expand tourism. In other words, the pretexts were phony.

The United States did at least have a legal fig leaf for its invasion, however. The other governments of the eastern Caribbean said they had urged the United States to step in. They said it only after the fact, however, and that was the case also of the alleged invitation from the British governor-general, which no one remembered to mention until the invasion was over. No one was fooled by these after-the-fact invitations. Certainly the British government was not. Prime Minister Margaret Thatcher, friend though she was of President Reagan's, roundly condemned the invasion. Still, by holding to its fig leaf, the United States was at least suggesting that it cared about the diplomatic and legal niceties, and it was sticking to the pattern that had existed since the withdrawal of the last marines from Haiti in 1934 of not intervening unilaterally with its own forces—without, that is, at least some shred of multilateral endorsement.

Strangely, with the Cold War virtually over, President George H. W. Bush broke that pattern, sending U.S. forces to invade Panama in December 1989 without any invitation from the OAS, the Central American countries, or anyone else. And unlike all other U.S.–organized interventions since 1954, the invasion of Panama was not aimed at thwarting some thrust on the part of the Soviet Union or Cuba. Indeed, it had nothing to do with the dwindling Cold War. Rather, Panama was invaded in order to arrest its president, Manuel Noriega, who was said to be involved in major drug trafficking. Noriega, once a paid asset of the CIA, had made the mistake of courting Cuba's Castro and of thumbing his nose at the United States. He paid the price. In blatant violation of international norms, U.S. forces stormed into Panama, arrested Noriega, and brought him back to the United States to stand trial, much as conquering Roman legions once brought their prisoners back to Rome in chains.

Few shed any tears for Noriega, who had indeed won election by fraud and was something of a thug. The U.S. invasion was nonetheless illegal and was so condemned by near unanimous vote in the OAS. For the first time since 1934, U.S. troops had intervened in Latin America without even an effort to win multilateral approval. Some wondered if the end of the Cold War meant a return to U.S. gunboat diplomacy.

Meanwhile, the Soviet Union was in the throes of cataclysmic change. Mikhail Gorbachev had taken power there in 1985 and tried to revive the sputtering Soviet economy by introducing liberalizing reforms. In effect, he tried to fashion a socialist system with a more democratic face. Some said he went too far too fast. Others held that the system depended on coercion and ground to a halt when Gorbachev removed the coercion. Whatever the case, the Soviet system began to collapse.

Gorbachev had also changed dramatically the thrust of Soviet foreign policy. In the past, it had been geared to the Marxist tenet that worldwide revolution was a historical inevitability. In other words, it had been geared to expanding the socialist system to every extent possible. Quite understandably, the West had perceived this to be aggressive and threatening. But Gorbachev abandoned the whole concept. No more would the Soviet Union try to extend the reach of socialism; rather, it was now strictly up to each country to determine its internal arrangements without outside interference. With that, the Cold War began to wind down.

When an abortive coup by hard-liners in late 1991 failed, the almost seventy-five years of Communist Party rule was swept aside in reaction. The other republics then quickly pulled out of the Soviet Union, and by 1992, the latter had disappeared, replaced by the Russian Republic and a loose grouping of the former union republics. The Cold War was over.

THE POST–COLD WAR PERIOD, 1992 TO THE PRESENT

As stated at the outset, with the end of the Cold War, the imperatives that had driven U.S. policy for almost 200 years were suddenly rendered obsolete. If the United States had treated the Caribbean as an American lake so as to protect the approaches to the Panama Canal, there was now no other power that wished to hinder those approaches; the canal passed into the hands of Panama and in any event was no longer of vital importance to the United States. The factors that had once riveted U.S. attention to the Caribbean had gone the way of the three-mile limit to territorial waters (because that had once been the range of a cannon shot). There was no need to treat the Caribbean as an American lake. There was no need either to assert U.S. hegemony, in the Caribbean or Central America and certainly not in the rest of the hemisphere. The kinds of interests and objectives the United States has in the hemisphere today require the cooperation of the other governments, not their subservience. A new approach geared to vastly changed circumstances is required. This was true under the first post–Cold War presidency of William Clinton (1993–2001), and it is especially so under the administration of George W. Bush (beginning in 2001) given the terrorist attacks on the World Trade Center and the Pentagon on September 11, 2001. This in effect opened a whole new chapter in U.S. foreign policy, one in which U.S. efforts and attention will be focused on the struggle against a series of terrorist forces in the world (Al Qaeda, the Taliban, and several others) intent on destroying U.S.—and Western—influence and values in the world at large.

What are U.S. interests and objectives in the hemisphere? The most pressing ones, not necessarily in order of priority, are: (1) to engage other countries in a cooperative struggle against terrorism, but in a balanced way, so as not to lose sight of other U.S. objectives in the hemisphere; (2) to halt or at least sharply reduce the flow of drugs into the United States; (3) to encourage the economic development of the countries to our south, both to keep the populations in place (the United States does not want to receive vast flows of illegal immigrants or refugees from the south), and to increase trade, especially U.S. exports; and (4) to help protect the environment on which we all depend.

Is the United States developing a new and more cooperative approach to address these interests? Let us examine them case by case.

THE STRUGGLE AGAINST TERRORISM

Following the September 11 attacks against the United States, virtually all the countries of the Western Hemisphere, including Cuba, condemned the acts themselves and terrorism in general, indicating at the same time their solidarity and willingness to cooperate with the people of the United States. That has not changed over the more than three years since. Indeed, on October 28, 2003, the Organization of American States approved a new multifaceted security agreement to "fight terrorism in all its forms," and to expand the hemisphere's "traditional concept and approach . . . to encompass new and nontraditional threats, which include political, economic, social, health, and environmental aspects."[18]

The other countries have been willing to cooperate in the struggle against terrorism. That has not been the problem; rather, the problem has been the tendency of the United States to so concentrate on efforts against the Al Qaeda and against Saddam Hussein that Latin America has virtually dropped off the radar screens. The other countries complain that efforts to address other pressing problems, such as economic development and the health of their populations, receive scant attention and even less support from the United States. It was for that reason that they insisted on the "multifaceted" nature of the new security agreement, though few believe that will bring the attention of the United States back to Latin America.

Another problem has been with the "with-us-or-against-us" attitude of the Bush administration. Countries that opposed the U.S. war in Iraq, such as Mexico, were, in effect, sent to stand in the corner. But in fact, most of the OAS countries disagreed with the war in Iraq, and certainly their populations did. They took a dim view indeed of the fact that the United States went in virtual defiance of the UN Security Council, thus weakening the United Nations. And when no weapons of mass destruction were found, the foray was seen as unjustified, irresponsible, and a blatant violation of the UN Charter. As a result of all this and other factors, U.S. prestige in Latin America has fallen to its lowest point in many years, perhaps ever, as reflected by the fact that at a meeting of the OAS in Santiago, Chile, in June 2003, the other countries for the first time ever voted to exclude the United States from membership on the Inter-American Human Rights Commission.

As always, Cuba has been a special problem, not so much because of Cuban attitudes, but because of the almost fanatical determination of the Bush administration not to see or say anything positive about the Castro government. Immediately after the September 11 attacks, Cuba expressed its solidarity with the American people and opened Cuban airspace to any American planes caught in the air when U.S. space was closed. Subsequently, it offered to cooperate with the United Nations and with all governments, including the United States, in the fight against terrorism. It signed all twelve UN anti-terrorist resolutions and offered to sign an agreement with the United States on cooperation in fighting international terrorism, an offer that the State Department almost insultingly rejected.

Meanwhile, the State Department continued to include Cuba on the list of "terrorist nations." The evidence for its inclusion, however, ranged from totally false to irrelevant. The department maintained, for example, that Cuba had harbored Chilean terrorists wanted for murder in Chile. It pointedly neglected to report the findings of the Chilean government itself, which had thoroughly investigated the case, even sending a delegation to Cuba, and concluded that Cuba had in fact not harbored or assisted the Chileans at all.[19]

The State Department report also alleged that Cuba had given safe haven and support to terrorist groups in Colombia. But the Colombian government itself, in the person of General Fernando Tapias, the commander of the Colombian armed forces, testifying before the House Committee on International Affairs on April 24, 2002, said there was no information "that Cuba is in any way linked to terrorist activities in Colombia today. Indeed, Cuban authorities are buttressing the peace movement."

If one is serious about the struggle against terrorism, surely one should not diminish the importance of the list by keeping Cuba on it without convincing evidence. To do so calls into question our seriousness of purpose, as does refusing even to consider cooperation with Cuba in what we say is this all-important struggle.

Drug Interdiction

The United States cannot reduce the flow of drugs over its borders by sending battleships and marines to the Caribbean and Central American states, and certainly not by landing troops in South America. Further, the drug problem is in fact two-sided: consumption and production, with the former centered in the United States. It is up to the United States to address the matter of demand, for so long as there is a market for any product, it will be produced, no matter how energetic the efforts to turn it off. So far, the United States has done very little to reduce consumption. That would require a major effort and outlay of funds, for which U.S. political leaders have simply not had the stomach. Unless they do make such a commitment, however, their seriousness of purpose is in question, their vows to come to grips with the drug problem not really credible.

As to the second side, neither the United States nor the Latin American governments can eradicate production through legislation and police action, though those are of course necessary components. The result of those efforts over past years has been but to contain production to a 10-percent-per-year increase.[20] The cartels are in fact only part of the problem. By and large, the coca and other narcotics are grown by poor peasants in Bolivia, Peru, Colombia, and other countries. They depend upon their crops of coca leaves, poppies, and marijuana to eke out a meager existence. They have raised these plants for centuries and have little concept of the havoc they cause elsewhere. They are not likely to give up their major source of income just because the United States and their own governments demand it. (This was certainly a factor in the

October 2003 overthrow of Bolivian President Gonzalo Sánchez de Losada (see Chapter 25). They must find alternative crops and sources of income, and this will occur only as the result of a major cooperative effort among the United States, individual Latin American governments, and international organizations. Such an effort would require a large-scale input of resources, most of which would have to come from the United States. It would be a small price to pay, however, if, as President George H. W. Bush told Americans some years back, drugs are the principal threat to national security.[21] So far, the United States has shown not the slightest interest.

Most important of all, the fight against drugs must be a cooperative one, one in which the United States and its Latin American neighbors join as equal partners. That has not yet been the case. At a summit conference of the presidents of Colombia, Peru, Bolivia, and the United States held in Cartagena, Colombia, in February 1990 to discuss the drug problem, President George H. W. Bush did indeed stress the need for a broad multilateral campaign, but he was woefully short on specifics. In fact, he offered no plan at all. Meanwhile, the United States has done all too little to reduce consumption, has put few resources into the fight to reduce production, and instead has tended simply to shift the blame to the Latin American governments. The system of certification imposed by the United States in 1987 was, as many Latin American governments saw it, confirmation that the United States saw itself as judge and jury of whether the efforts of Latin American governments to interdict drugs were adequate. If it deemed them inadequate, then that government was no longer eligible for certain economic benefits. Never mind what the Latin American governments might think of the inadequacy of U.S. efforts and its failure to commit resources. Clearly, this was not a cooperative effort among equal partners.

Moreover, that the administration of George W. Bush was willing to put narrow ideological objectives ahead of curbing the flow of drugs was seen in its outright refusal to take up Cuban offers to increase cooperation in interdiction efforts. The Cubans offered to sign agreements to increase the degree of cooperation, and on several occasions showed their good faith by assisting in the arrest of smugglers. The Bush Administration responded to none of these overtures. To have done so might have offended a few hard-line Cuban exiles and that was a risk the Bush administration would not take—even if it meant passing up opportunities to reduce the flow of drugs into the United States.

The major U.S. effort in the drug war has been, and still is, in Colombia. With Plan Colombia, President George W. Bush promised to reduce coca production in Colombia by 50 percent by the year 2005. As a recent Senate Appropriation's Committee report indicated, however: ". . . the amount of coca and poppy under cultivation has increased. In addition, peace negotiations have collapsed, the armed conflict has intensified, and the country is preparing for a wider war, which few observers believe can be won on the battlefield."[22]

In short, U.S. efforts to reduce the flow of drugs coming into the country from Latin America are failing. The flow is not being reduced. And as for consumption in the United States, no concerted effort at all is being made to reduce that.

PROTECTION OF THE ENVIRONMENT

The United States also needs the cooperation of the Latin American governments in the protection of the environment, or the habitat in which we all live. Yet it has yet to provide the leadership and resources that are required. The so-called Earth Summit in Rio in June 1992 (or, more formally, the United Nations Conference on the Environment and Development) offered a perfect opportunity at least to provide leadership. Rather than that, the administration of President George H. W. Bush raised objections to the two major treaties to be signed at the conference even before it opened. In the event, it refused to sign the treaty to preserve the world's plants, animals, and natural resources, much to the disgust of the other delegates and even of many in the U.S. delegation. It signed the other major treaty, dealing with the problem of global warming, but only on the condition that the strict timetable for curbing harmful emissions was deleted. Rather than leading and encouraging cooperation, the Bush administration played an obstructionist role and was almost completely isolated in its position.[23]

The intentions at least of the administration of Bill Clinton were an improvement over those of the first Bush administration. In 1993, Clinton called for "a new covenant for environmental progress." His administration then negotiated a multilateral agreement aimed at halting the depletion of the ozone layer in the upper atmosphere, and in 1996 it began massive negotiations for a worldwide effort to address the critical problem of global climate change. These were steps in the right direction, but they were never funded, Congress refusing to come up with the money. The United States was not even able to come up with seed money for the project to reduce chloroflourocarbons (CFCs) worldwide and thus reduce the depletion of the ozone layer. Even under Clinton, the United States was the biggest debtor in the Global Environmental Facility, the principal international funding mechanism for the effort called for by the Climate Change Convention.[24]

The heart of the matter in the Western Hemisphere is the need to halt the destruction of the Amazon rain forest, often described as the lungs of the world. But halting deforestation is linked to responsible economic development. Alternatives must be offered so that destruction of the forest is no longer profitable, but that requires a carefully coordinated developmental effort and, again, the outlay of resources. As one Brazilian official put it: "We of course want to protect the environment. In the best of all possible worlds, we'd like to preserve the rain forest. On the other hand, we must develop, must offer our people a better way of life. We can't afford to be the lungs of the world if we are also to pay off our foreign debt and finance our development plans."[25] As one might imagine, Congress has shown no interest whatever in funding any projects related to saving the rain forests. By 2003, the

Brazilian government was moving in the opposite direction, toward increased development in the Amazon.

Worse, with the inauguration of George W. Bush in 2001, any pretense that the United States was interested in the Amazon or even took seriously the protection of the environment as a whole went out the window. From undercutting the Clean Air Act to proposals promoting wholesale clear-cutting of national forests in the United States in the guise of "fire prevention," the administration moved almost across the board to weaken measures to protect the environment. Perhaps the worst was its announcement in March 2003 that the United States would not cooperate with the Kyoto treaty aimed at reducing greenhouse gas emissions in order to slow global warming. Under George W. Bush, any interest in cooperating with the other nations of the hemisphere to protect the environment is a dead letter.

ECONOMIC DEVELOPMENT

During the Cold War, U.S. representatives often answered Latin American requests for economic assistance by pointing to the United States's huge defense expenditures. Were it not for the need to defend the rest of the world against the aggressive intentions of the Soviet Union, politicians said, the United States would have ample resources to assist the economic development efforts of its neighbors. As it was, those resources had to be diverted to defense. But in the decade between the end of the Cold War and the September 11 attacks, there was virtually no change of attitude on the part of the United States, no appreciable decrease in military spending, and no increased willingness even to consider economic development programs of a magnitude required to get the Latin American nations on the road to prosperity. And with its attention on the struggle against terrorism since the September 11 attacks, it is even less willing.

This U.S. cold shoulder is difficult to understand given that the interests of the United States would be advanced by such developmental efforts. It is not simply that an economically imbalanced hemisphere is unhealthy and morally unsustainable; it is that such a situation fuels one of Washington's major headaches: the influx of illegal immigrants from the south. There is only one way to encourage these unstable populations to remain in place (that is, not to head for the United States), and that is by giving them some hope of a better future in their own countries. Clearly, this was the reason for the U.S. intervention in Haiti in 1994. It had been noticed that during Aristide's brief period in power, after his election in 1990, the flow of boat people from Haiti had dried up. But once he was overthrown in 1992 and the military again began its repression of the Haitian people, the flood resumed. And so, in 1994, the United States returned Aristide to power, arranged for elections, and began some efforts toward economic development. This worked, at least temporarily. The number of boat people dropped off dramatically. Typically, however, while willing to commit troops, at least for a time, the United States was unwilling to commit more than token financial and material resources and within two years the troops also were withdrawn.

Haiti, a country with over two centuries of political instability, acute poverty, and social disparity, was left to make it on its own. Aristide was re-elected in 2000 in a process that most considered fraudulent. He went the way of all Haitian political flesh without international supervision. He became as corrupt and undemocratic as all past Haitian governments. In 2002, the Bush administration made matters worse by cutting off all forms of assistance to Haiti and even blocking international loans. In early 2004, Aristide was overthrown by the same corrupt elements who had forced him from power in the first place. Haiti is an extreme case, yes, but one that serves to make the point. Without a sustained and concerted effort on the part of the international community, led by the United States, to bring about economic development and a more socially just socioeconomic system, there can be no hope for political stability in Haiti. A society in which the 2 percent at the top control the overwhelming majority of all the wealth in the country, while the vast majority of its people live in the most abject misery, poverty, and hopelessness, cannot be the basis for political stability. And a politically unstable Haiti will always be the possible source of floods of impoverished refugees, exactly what the United States does not want. But as of March 2004, there is no indication that the United States has absorbed this lesson and will act upon it; rather, the Bush administration seems poised to make all the mistakes of the past, that is, to introduce a peacekeeping force for a brief period and then wash its hands and withdraw. If so, the pattern will repeat itself yet again.

Elsewhere, rather than developmental programs involving even small-scale transfer of public resources, the United States has urged the countries to its south to privatize and to depend upon private investment, both local and foreign. In short, it has urged a neoliberal approach. This was accompanied during the administration of George H. W. Bush by a good deal of rhetoric centering around the "Enterprise for the Americas," a vague program of trade preferences, incentives for private investment, calls for limited debt reduction, and promises of movement toward a hemispheric free-trade zone. While praiseworthy in its concept, very little came of it. Few of the necessary legislative packages were ever even presented. One of the few concrete achievements was that the Bush administration did succeed in negotiating and winning congressional approval for a free-trade agreement with Canada, the first step in putting in place a North American Free Trade Agreement (NAFTA). It initiated the process with Mexico, but it was left to the Clinton administration to complete it. In 1994, at the urging of the Clinton administration, NAFTA was extended to Mexico as well.

Much hoopla attended the so-called Summit of the Americas held in Miami in December 1994. The heads of thirty-four governments met and signed a Declaration of Principles and Plan of Action involving twenty-three separate initiatives on everything from efforts to end corruption to the extension of the free-trade zone to virtually all states of the hemisphere by the year 2005. The

Clinton administration did little to push the initiative. Even so, by November 2003, a new meeting would be held in Miami, supposedly to follow on the work of the Miami Summit and form the Free Trade Association for the Americas—with disappointing results.

Meanwhile, the results of the new economic policies advocated by Washington were decidedly mixed. Over the first five years of the 1990s, most countries succeeded, with their new neoliberal economic measures, in controlling inflation, reducing budget deficits, attracting foreign investment, and getting growth rates up around a respectable 3 percent (after a near-stagnant decade during the 1980s). The downside, however, was that the reforms produced higher unemployment, more people living in poverty, a greater disparity between rich and poor, and declining standards of living for the majority. According to the World Bank, income distribution in Latin America "approaches the most unequal in the developing world."[26]

This was exacerbated by the neoliberal policy of reducing social welfare programs whenever possible. The poor not only got poorer but found even less of a safety net than there might otherwise have been to ease their suffering. Even in Argentina, once one of the bread baskets of the world, the poor simply went hungry. Social injustice in Brazil is perhaps the most glaring in the world.

Mexico went through a dramatic economic crisis during the Clinton presidency. Shortly after becoming part of the NAFTA and as a direct result of mistakes in adjusting to the agreement, in December 1994 Mexico's economy virtually collapsed. Only a massive bailout led by the U.S. Treasury kept Mexico from going under. By late 1996, it had begun to recover. That is, growth rates were back in the black and foreign investment was again beginning to flow into the country. But the disparities were worse than ever. Mexico could boast of fifteen billionaires (only four other countries had more), but 50 percent of the Mexican population was living in abject misery, and more were falling beneath the poverty line every day.[27] Social and political tensions rose, as evidenced by the peasant uprisings in Mexico's southern states. These were muted by the election of Vicente Fox of the opposition PAN party in July 2000, and, as indicated above, an era of warm relations with the United States was supposed to ensue. The problem of illegal aliens coming in from Mexico was to have been addressed in a comprehensive way. But the warm relationship broke down quickly and the migratory problems were not addressed. The flow of illegal aliens from Mexico has, if anything, continued to increase.

Meanwhile, whether NAFTA has been of benefit—or harm—to Mexico is increasingly debated. A study by the Carnegie Endowment for International Peace in November 2003, for example, concluded that real wages in Mexico are lower now than when the agreement was adopted, and that income disparity (as suggested above) has increased. A World Bank study also issued in 2003, on the other hand, contended that Mexico would have been worse off without the agreement as it struggled to recover from its financial crisis in the mid-1990s. That, however, left aside the argument of many that the crisis was caused precisely by Mexico's entry into NAFTA. The argument will doubtless sharpen in the months and years ahead. [28]

As for the administration of George W. Bush, it has done even less than that of Clinton to address economic problems in Latin America. The Argentine economy collapsed on its watch and, unlike the reaction of Clinton in Mexico, the Bush administration did nothing to rescue it. It stood aside. The Argentine problem was, by and large, caused by the mismanagement and corruption of Argentina's political leaders. Some part, however, was the result of the neoliberal economic model urged by the United States, one that the Bush administration continued to favor until the end.

With the election of Néstor Kirchner in 2003, Argentina began to recover, both economically and politically. It remains deeply resentful of U.S. neglect, however, and suspicious of U.S. intentions. U.S.–Argentine relations are likely to remain distant for some time to come.

Rather than supporting economic development programs, there has been a tendency on the part of the Bush administration to offer the Latin American nations free trade agreements—but free trade agreements on decidedly unequal terms. The United States does not want agriculture or non-tariff barriers to be on the table. At the same time, it wants the Latin American states to compromise their national sovereignties by agreeing to investor "protections." It has already signed such agreements with Chile (in June 2003) and with the Central American states, except for Costa Rica, in December 2003. Costa Rica finally signed in January of 2004.

As part of that same tendency, the Bush administration has pressed for all countries to support an agreement for Free Trade Area for the Americas (FTAA), and it hosted a hemispheric meeting in Miami in November 2003 to sign agreements that would then lead to the formation of the FTAA by 2005. There was strong opposition, however, led by Brazil, but seconded by Argentina, Venezuela, Bolivia, and a number of other states, in part over U.S. agricultural subsidies and other trade barriers, which the other countries say are unfair and would neutralize any positive effects of the agreement. Sentiment against free trade agreements has also come to be linked to growing rejection of neoliberal economic policies. In any event, the Miami meeting could be called a standoff. The United States refused to give up its agricultural subsidies, and Brazil refused to agree to rules on intellectual property rights or investment and government procurement. The meeting was adjourned early with a call for continued discussions. Perhaps there will be an FTAA by 2005, perhaps not. An editorial in the *New York Times* on November 22, 2003, said the whole effort "runs the risk of being downsized to a point of near irrelevance."

Referring to the resentments in the Latin American states resulting from U.S. insistence on agreements with such unequal terms, Joseph Stiglitz, a Nobel Prize–winning economist, said in a commentary piece in the *New York Times* on January 6, 2004: "If these trade agreements do no better for them than NAFTA has done for Mexico, then both peace and prosperity in the hemisphere will be at risk."

In sum, the United States has made few efforts to stimulate economic development in Latin America. The flow of illegal aliens continues unabated. Economic underdevelopment continues to affect U.S. interests in another area: trade. Countries with growing numbers of impoverished masses are not good markets. Thus, rather than booming trade, with balances in favor of the United States, trade has increased little at all, and the balances against the United States continue to escalate. In 1992, the balance against the United States was only $991 million. By 1995, it was almost $9 billion, and by 2003 over $10 billion.[29]

Failure of U.S. Policy

What is clear is that the United States has failed to formulate a policy that works in the changed post–Cold War world. What is needed is the cooperation of the other governments in combating the drug problem and protecting the environment. But the United States provided little leadership and little in the way of resources under the first Bush and Clinton administrations, and even less under that of George W. Bush. Hence, the problems of drugs and a deteriorating environment have not even been reduced, let alone resolved.

The neoliberal approach to economic development advocated by the United States has fared little better. Growth rates improved somewhat overall but were accompanied by worsening poverty and social instability, exactly the conditions that can be expected to produce an increased flow of illegal immigrants to the United States. Further, the market for U.S. products shrinks as more and more Latin Americans fall below the poverty line.

Obviously, the key to the achievement of all four major U.S. objectives would be a large-scale developmental effort, counting with significant resource inputs from the United States. An economically healthy Latin America would be a far more effective partner in stopping drug trafficking and protecting the environment. Its populations would be more likely to remain in place and would be able to buy more U.S. products.

Unfortunately, the United States seems unwilling to mount such a joint developmental effort, and certainly unwilling to transfer resources. On the contrary, its leaders now seem so wholly consumed by the war on terrorism that Latin America has largely disappeared from their priorities.

Return to Unilateralism

Worse, the United States gives evidence of moving back toward a kind of unilateralism more appropriate to the days of gunboat diplomacy than to the post–Cold War world. During the Cold War, the United States often spoke of committing itself to abide strictly by the United Nations Charter and international law if the Soviet Union would but do so also.[30] With the Soviet Union having collapsed and its successor state, the Russian Republic, indeed having committed itself to adhere to the charter, it had been hoped that the United

States might now go back to the spirit of multilateralism that had so briefly prevailed with the formation of the Rio Pact in 1947 and the Organization of American States in 1948. That spirit had been undermined by the anti-Communist hysteria of the Cold War. Might it now be possible to resuscitate it and to construct a hemispheric system based on rule of law?

As of mid-2004, the answer seems to be a decided "no." For one thing, the United States continues to behave as though the Cold War is not over, at least with respect to Cuba. During the 1980s, the U.S. position was that there could be a significant improvement in relations with Cuba if the latter would but (1) remove its troops from Africa, (2) stop fueling revolutionary situations in Central America and elsewhere, and (3) reduce its military ties with the Soviet Union. But as of 1992, all those conditions had been met. Yet rather than moving to relax tensions and improve relations with the island, the United States did exactly the opposite. With passage of the Cuban Democracy Act of that year, it actually tightened the embargo against the island. Congressman Robert Torricelli (D–New Jersey), the act's principal proponent, assured one and all in a television debate in December 1992 that as the result of his legislation Castro would be gone within months.[31]

But a decade later, Castro is still in power and the Cuban economy has not collapsed. Meanwhile, ultraconservative forces in the U.S. Congress came up with even more draconian legislation aimed at forcing other countries to reduce trade with and investments in Cuba. The Helms-Burton Act, signed into law in March 1996, is extraterritorial in nature and violates international law and various international agreements to which the United States is a party, including the NAFTA. It represents nothing less than an effort on the part of the United States unilaterally to dictate to the rest of the world without regard to the rules of the international system.

Not surprisingly, Helms-Burton has been roundly condemned by the international community. At its General Assembly in June 1996, the Organization of American States rejected it by unanimous vote and called on the Inter-American Juridical Committee (IAJC) to rule on the legislation's legality. In a unanimous ruling handed down on August 23, the IAJC found Helms-Burton to be in violation of international law on at least eight counts. In November 1996, the United Nations General Assembly condemned the U.S. embargo, including Helms-Burton, by a vote of 138–3. Only Israel and Uzbekistan voted with the United States that year, and they both trade with Cuba. The vote has followed that pattern every year since, with only two countries—sometimes Uzbekistan, sometimes the Marshall Islands, and always Israel, voting with the United States, everyone else against. In other words, no one supports U.S. policy.

Canada, Mexico, and the European Union have all drafted retaliatory legislation under which their companies can sue U.S. entities if the latter take action against them under Helms-Burton. This could lead to disruptions of the whole international commercial system, to say nothing of chaos in the courts. And meanwhile, on October 4, 1996, the European Union also filed an official request for the Dispute Settlement Body of the World Trade Organization (WTO) to rule on whether Helms-Burton conforms to the WTO's rules of conduct.

One cannot be certain what all this will produce. It points up, however, that Helms-Burton is an irrational act on the part of the United States. With the Cold War over, Cuba no longer represents even a potential threat to U.S. security and certainly not to U.S. economic interests. In fact, in terms of U.S. interests, Cuba is of little importance at all. U.S. commercial ties with Canada, Europe, and Mexico, on the other hand, are vital. That the United States is willing to place at risk that which is important over that which is not is simply illogical.

Unfortunately, Helms-Burton seems to be part of a pattern. If some see the end of the Cold War as providing an opportunity to construct a more stable international system based on international law and adherence to rules of conduct agreed to by all in such international fora as the United Nations and the WTO, others, such as former Senator Jesse Helms (R–North Carolina) (let us call them the unilateralists), see it in quite another light. To them it means that the United States is the only remaining superpower and so can and should order things to suit its own purposes, paying less attention to such abstractions as international law and international organizations. The United States wants to bring down the Castro government and so insists that other governments cooperate with it or face the consequences. It wanted to get rid of Boutros Boutros-Ghali as UN secretary-general, and so, acting against the will of the other countries, it forced his resignation. Senator Helms made it clear that as far as he was concerned, the United Nations must either carry out the reforms the United States wanted (whether or not the rest of the world community agreed with them) or the United States would simply pull out.

Senator Helms is gone, but the administration of George W. Bush has moved even further in the direction of trashing the United Nations and the system of international law than he would have. Almost immediately after taking office, Bush announced that the United States would withdraw from the Anti-Ballistic Missile Treaty of 1972, one of the foundation stones of the international arms-control system that had functioned well for many years. He then issued a thirty-three-page report, *The National Security Strategy of the United States,* which discarded the policy of détente and containment and, rather, endorsed preemptive or preventive military actions against states with which we are at peace, with or without the approval of the United Nations Security Council.[32]

In March 2003, in defiance of the Security Council, which did not vote to approve the U.S. action, the Bush administration launched its war against Iraq, claiming the latter had weapons of mass destruction virtually ready to fire and that it had to take immediate and preemptive measures. No weapons of mass destruction were found, but the Bush administration was not in the least apologetic. The fact that its actions had seriously undermined the United Nations system founded by earlier American presidents and supported by all until George W. Bush seemed not to concern it in the least.

The Bush administration has also become even more threatening toward Cuba, claiming that it is somehow a "potential threat" to U.S. security, thus raising the possibility of some preemptive strike against it as well. Indeed, in October 2003, the Bush administration confirmed that the objective of U.S. policy toward Cuba is to get rid of the Castro government. As Assistant Secretary of State Roger Noriega put it to the Senate Foreign Relations Committee on October 2, 2003: "The president is determined to see the end of the Castro regime and the dismantling of the apparatus that has kept him in office for so long."

Cuba took this threatening attitude most seriously. The day that the United States invaded Iraq, it launched a massive crackdown against dissidents on the island, fearing, apparently, that it might be next on the list for a preemptive attack and that it had to batten down the hatches. If this was indeed the thinking, it was an overreaction. The United States in fact appeared to have no intention of attacking Cuba—certainly not at that point—and the arrest of some seventy-five dissidents and the execution of three hijackers (even though their hijacking effort failed) turned international public opinion massively against Cuba. That, in effect, played into the hands of the Bush administration, which hardened its line against the island still more and redoubled efforts to gain international support for sanctions against the Castro government. As of the early months of 2004, U.S.–Cuban relations were even more strained than they had been during most of the years of the Cold War.

None of this bodes well for the kind of international system many Americans had hoped would emerge in the wake of the Cold War. The imperatives that brought forth the Monroe Doctrine are now but a memory. Rather than grasping the opportunity thus presented to fashion a more cooperative and productive hemispheric system, however, the United States is going in the opposite direction. The policies it is now following seem aimed at undermining any international system based on rule of law.

NOTES

1. See Lars Schoultz, University of North Carolina, "Inter-American Security: The Changing Perceptions of U.S. Policymakers," a paper dated April 1990. See also Wayne S. Smith, "The United States and South America: Beyond the Monroe Doctrine," in *Current History*, February 1991.

2. Quoted in Julius W. Pratt, *A History of U.S. Foreign Policy* (Englewood Cliffs, N.J.: Prentice-Hall, 1955), p. 165.

3. Gaddis Smith, *Last Years of the Monroe Doctrine* (New York: Hill and Wang, 1994), p. 8.

4. Pratt, *History of U.S. Foreign Policy*, p. 348.

5. Wayne S. Smith, *Portrait of Cuba* (Atlanta, Ga.: Turner Publishing, 1991); see footnote on p. 41.

6. George Black, *The Good Neighbor* (New York: Pantheon Books, 1988), p. 16.

7. Louis A. Perez, Jr., *Cuba Between Empires* (Pittsburgh: University of Pittsburgh Press, 1983), p. 327.

8. Quoted in Black, *The Good Neighbor*, p. 23.

9. Quoted in Wayne S. Smith, "Will the U.S. Again Send in the Marines?" in *World Paper*, November 1983.

10. J. Reuben Clark, *Memorandum on the Monroe Doctrine* (Washington, D.C.: U.S. Government Printing Office, 1930).

11. Ann Van Wynen Thomas and A. J. Thomas Jr., in *The Organization of American States* (Dallas: Southern Methodist University Press, 1963), p. 356, conclude that "the Rio Treaty is the final step to date in the multilateralization of the Monroe Doctrine." See also Samuel Guy Inman's account of Republican senator Arthur Vandenberg's conclusion that this would be the effect of the OAS, in *Inter-American Conferences, 1826–1954: History and Problems* (Washington, D.C.: University Press of Washington, 1965), pp. 221–222.

12. See Smith, *Last Years,* pp. 78–84. For perhaps the most penetrating study of the U.S. intervention in Guatemala, see Piero Gleijeses, *Shattered Hope* (Princeton, N.J.: Princeton University Press, 1991).

13. See Stephen G. Rabe, *Eisenhower and Latin America* (Chapel Hill, N.C.: University of North Carolina Press, 1988), p. 94.

14. Smith, *Last Years,* pp. 122–129.

15. Ibid., pp. 196–199.

16. Dana Priest, "U.S. Instructed Latinos on Executions, Torture," *Washington Post,* September 21, 1996.

17. Smith, *Last Years,* p. 7.

18. Associated Press, Mexico City, October 28, 2003.

19. *Cuba on the Terrorist List,* International Policy Report of the Center for International Policy, November 2000.

20. James Brooke, "Peru Suggests U.S. Rethink Eradication in Land Where Coca Is Still King," *New York Times,* November 18, 1990, p. 3.

21. Ibid.

22. See "The 'War on Drugs' Meets the 'War on Terror,' The United States' military involvement in Colombia climbs to the next level. An International Policy Report of the Center for International Policy," February 2003.

23. See discussion in the following articles in the *New York Times:* Sanjoy Hazarika, "India Is Facing Ecological Quandary in Plans to Dam River," April 11, 1992, p. 8; Gwen Ifill, "Clinton Links Ecology with Jobs," April 23, 1992, p. 22; Keith Schneider, "U.S. to Reject Pact on Protection of Wildlife and Global Resources," May 30, 1992, p. 1; James Brooke, "U.S. Has a Starring Role at Rio Summit as Villain," June 2, 1992, p. A10.

24. See article by Deputy Secretary of State Strobe Talbott, "Our Mission and the Global Environment," *State Magazine,* December 31, 1996, pp. 15–32.

25. Interview with a senior Brazilian diplomat who requested anonymity, Washington, D.C., May 1990.

26. Molly Moore, "Three Years After Mexico Embraced Free Trade, Rural Poor Still Flock to the Capital," *Washington Post,* December 31, 1996, pp. A12–13.

27. Ibid.

28. See "Report Finds Few Benefits for Mexico in NAFTA," *New York Times,* November 19, 2003.

29. Figures are taken from tables 6 and 8 of *U.S. Foreign Trade Highlights, 1995* (U.S. Department of Commerce, International Trade Administration, Office of Trade and Economic Analysis, August 1996) and from table 8 of a Trade and Economy: Data and Analysis report issued by the Department of Commerce's International Trade Administration on August 25, 2003.

30. See the interesting debate in Council on Foreign Relations, ed., *Might vs. Right* (New York: Council on Foreign Relations, 1989). See especially the presentation by Jeane Kirkpatrick and Allan Gerson, "The Reagan Doctrine, Human Rights, and International Law," pp. 37–71, in which they make the point that respect for international law is based on reciprocity, that is, if I respect it, so must you.

31. See the transcript of *Crossfire* on CNN, December 30, 1992.

32. See *National Security Strategy of the United States,* Office of the President, Washington, D.C.; September 2002. See also comments under *Bush League Diplomacy: How the Neoconservatives Are Putting the World at Risk* by Melvin A. Goodman and Craig Eisendrath (Amhurst, N.Y.: Prometheus Books, 2004), pp. 125–145.

Suggested Readings

Langley, Lester. *America and the Americans.* Athens: University of Georgia Press, 1989.

Munro, Dana. *Intervention and Dollar Diplomacy.* Princeton, N.J.: Princeton University Press, 1964.

Prins, Gwyn, ed. *Understanding Unilateralism in American Foreign Relations.* London: The Royal Institute of International Affairs, 2000.

Smith, Gaddis. *Last Years of the Monroe Doctrine.* New York: Hill and Wang, 1994.

Smith, Peter. *Talons of the Eagle: Dynamics of U.S.–Latin American Relations.* New York: Oxford University Press, 1996.

Whitaker, Arthur. *The Western Hemisphere Idea.* Ithaca, N.Y.: Cornell University Press, 1954.

Wood, Bryce. *The Dismantling of the Good Neighbor Policy.* Austin: University of Texas Press, 1985.

_____. *The Making of the Good Neighbor Policy.* Austin: University of Texas Press, 1961.

PART VI

MEXICO AND
CENTRAL AMERICA

Chapter 15

MEXICO: A REVOLUTION
LAID TO REST?

FRED R. HARRIS

MARTIN C. NEEDLER [1]

ALL NATIONS AND PEOPLES are, more or less, products of their own history. Mexico and Mexicans are more so than most. Mexican sociologist Raúl Béjar Navarro has shown that studies seeking to prove that there is a unique Mexican "character" are largely impressionistic and unscientific.[2] But there certainly is, in Mexico, such a thing as national experience, a shared history.

History is not only a chronological recording of past events but also an attempt to explain the events. In order to understand a country and a people, then, we must know not only what has happened to them but also what they choose to remember and what they choose to make of what they remember—what they teach.

HISTORICAL FOUNDATIONS

"To say Benito Juárez is to say Mexico. To say Mexico is to say sovereign nation." Those were the beginning words of a patriotic speaker at the annual Mexico City ceremony on Benito Juárez Day, March 21, 1982—the 176th anniversary of the birth of the Zapotecan Indian who rose to be president of Mexico. Virtually every Mexican town and city has a monument to Juárez or a principal street named for him—this stern "man of law" who stripped the Catholic Church of its property and privileges; reformed Mexican politics; instituted public education; ended the rule of the Mexican dictator Santa Anna; and later, drove the French from Mexico.

Reform. Respect for law. Nationalism and resistance to foreign aggression. Civilian control of the government. The importance of "great leaders." Public morality. Separation of church and state. Pride in Indian history. These are some of the concepts that the memory of Benito Juárez evokes for Mexicans— and is used to evoke. To Mexicans, Juárez was an Indian who became a Mexican, as Mexico was an Indian nation that became a Mexican nation. But it was Indian first.

THE PRE-CORTÉS PERIOD

Within the great sweep of Middle America lies the Valley of Mexico (in which present-day Mexico City is situated). It is 7,000 feet (2,134 meters) above sea level and encompasses some 5,000 square miles (12,950 square kilometers). The valley is bounded on all sides by snowy volcano mountains. In prehistoric times, much of the valley floor was covered by large shallow lakes. By around 8000 B.C., people had begun farming in the valley. After 1500 B.C., population centers began to develop. Stratifications of power and wealth evolved. Trade flourished over wide areas. Agriculture became highly advanced.

Civilization was already ancient—great cities, like Teotihuacán and Tula, had already risen and then fallen—by the time the Aztecs came into the Valley of Mexico in the thirteenth century. They were an especially industrious, vigorous, and expansionist people. By 1425, they had subjugated, or made alliances with, all the other peoples of the valley. Eventually, their influence reached from the Mexican highlands to the coasts on either side and as far south as present Guatemala. Only the Tlaxcalans to the east, the Tarascans to the west, and some of the Mixtecs to the south remained apart.

By the time Moctezuma II became its principal lord in 1502, the capital city of the Aztecs, Tenochtitlán, was a clean, healthy, bustling metropolis, one of the largest cities of the world, with a population as high as 200,000 people. (By contrast, Seville, the Spanish city from which the conquistadores were later to sail, had a population of around 40,000, and only four European cities—Paris, Venice, Milan, and Naples—had populations of 100,000 or more.) There were some fifty other cities in the Valley of Mexico. Millions and millions of people lived in an area of one of the greatest population concentrations in the world.

THE SPANISH CONQUEST

When Hernán Cortés and the conquistadores came over the snowy pass to the east and first saw Tenochtitlán and the other cities in and around the lake, they could hardly believe their eyes. Bernal Díaz del Castillo, who was in the party, later wrote that "we were amazed and said that it was like the enchantment they tell of in the legend of Amadis, on account of the great towers and cues and buildings rising from the water, and all built of masonry." Within three years thereafter, Cortés was the ruler of all he had at first surveyed—except that, by then, the great city was in ruins.

Why did Moctezuma II, the Aztec ruler, let the Spaniards come freely into Tenochtitlán? Cortés's monstrous use of terrorism as a tactic must have been puzzlingly and terrifyingly different from any kind of war that Moctezuma II had known. Why destroy a huge tribute city like Cholula and the income one could derive from it, as Cortés did? Why kill such great numbers of people for no useful purpose? Moctezuma II must also have let the Spaniards come because he was certain that at any later moment when he wanted to, he could easily defeat and capture Cortés and his army. Moctezuma must have been influenced, too, by Cortés's continued and effusive expressions of friendly intention. And, philosopher and thinker that he was, intellectually curious, Moctezuma must have been intrigued by these strange white men and anxious to know more about their identity and their place of origin.

In any event, Cortés did indeed come in. Once inside Tenochtitlán, he seized Moctezuma and held him prisoner. But Cortés soon had to leave for the Gulf Coast to defeat a rival Spanish army sent by the governor of Cuba. While he was away, the Aztecs at last rose up and attacked the Spaniards. Moctezuma was killed in the bloody fighting. Cortés, with his Tlaxcalan allies, marched back to Tenochtitlán to relieve the embattled Spanish garrison there. But the Aztecs had had enough, and they drove Cortés and the Spaniards from the city.

Then came into play one of the most terrible factors in the success of the conquest—European disease, in this case, smallpox. The European plagues—smallpox, influenza, typhus, typhoid, diphtheria, measles, whooping cough, and others—were unknown in the New World. The native peoples of the Western Hemisphere had built up no immunities to them. Time after time, then, with first contact, one or another of the European diseases decimated whole populations in the Americas. Such was now the fate of Tenochtitlán. Smallpox swept through the city with devastating effect, throwing social and political organization into disarray and shaking religious beliefs. Thousands upon thousands died within the span of a week. Bodies piled up and could not be disposed of rapidly enough. Cuitlahuac, the nephew of Moctezuma who succeeded him, was one of those who died. Cuauhtémoc assumed the leadership. As one historian has written, "Clearly, if smallpox had not come when it did, the Spanish victory could not have been achieved in Mexico."[3] Another historian concurs, writing that "the glorious victories attributed to Spanish arms would not have been possible without the devastation wrought by Spanish disease."[4] Cortés had time to regroup. When he attacked, he fought a weakened enemy. Still, Cuauhtémoc and the Aztecs resisted fiercely until, at last, they were defeated—and Cuauhtémoc captured—in the suburb of Tlatelolco on August 21, 1521. By that time, Tenochtitlán had been destroyed.

As Robert E. Quirk and others have written, one can tell a great deal about a country by the monuments it chooses to erect—and by the monuments it chooses *not* to erect. There are no monuments in Mexico to Cortés. Neither are there monuments to Malinche, the collaborating Indian woman who became mistress of and interpreter for Cortés (indeed, in Mexico today, *malinchismo* is the act of selling out one's country to foreigners). There are no monuments to Moctezuma. Cuauhtémoc is the Indian hero of Mexico history.

SPANISH COLONIALISM

Cortés had cut off the head of the Aztec Empire. In the next years, the body followed. The Spanish captain rewarded his men—and himself—as richly as he had promised. There were great quantities of gold. Cortés took for himself vast estates of rich land and huge *encomiendas* (entrustments or grants of Indians) to work them. He gave land and *encomiendas* to his followers, also.

The first year, Cortés began growing sugar cane. With this and other crops, the plow was also introduced. Soon, great herds of sheep and cattle were imported and set to graze. Slave labor built *ingenios,* or sugar mills. Forests were felled to provide fuel, lumber for building, and charcoal for cooking. Thus began, from the first year of Spanish colonialism, the overplowing, overgrazing, deforestation, and desertification that have continued to plague Mexico to this day.

Gold and silver mines were established, expanded, and worked, under incredibly brutal conditions, by Indian slave labor. *Obrajes,* or sweatshops, were everywhere set up to produce the coarse cloth and other products needed for domestic consumption. When the *encomienda* system and slavery were later made illegal, these monarchical edicts were often ignored, or were replaced by debt peonage, which was just as bad. Brutal treatment and European diseases wiped out more than two-thirds of the native population in the Valley of Mexico between 1519 and 1650.

Spanish colonialism, then, was characterized by exploitation of people and natural resources. It was also characterized by mercantilism—the crown's practice of keeping Mexico a producer of raw materials only and a purchaser of Spain's manufactured goods. Education was a privilege in colonial Mexico, not a right. The Roman Catholic Church was the established church. After a first period of missionary zeal, the Church fell, in many instances, into dissolution. The Church, itself, became a great landholder and exploiter of Indian labor. There were wholesale conversions to Catholicism, but the Indian converts still held on to much of their old religion. The Spaniards built churches on sacred Indian sites. The Virgin of Guadalupe appeared to an Indian convert, Juan Diego, at a site where there had previously been a shrine to an Aztec goddess.

After 1700, the Mexican and Spanish economies, both of which had been depressed, began to revive. The population in Mexico began to grow—mostly among the mestizos. The numbers of the *criollos* (Spaniards born in the New World) also grew, and they began to develop a pride in Mexicanness, which paralleled their increasing resentment of the privileged position of the *peninsulares,* who had been born in Spain.

Spain's wars in Europe meant more taxes in Mexico, more "forced loans" to the crown, and confiscation of Church charitable funds. Then, Napoleon Bonaparte imposed his brother on Spain as its ruler. At this, some *criollos* in Mexico attempted a revolt against the *peninsulares,* but this revolt was put down. Political dissatisfaction was soon joined by economic troubles.

Independence and Empire

Throughout Mexico, groups of dissidents began to meet in 1809, some to plot. One such group met regularly in Querétaro. Among its members were a young cavalry captain, Ignacio Allende, thirty-five, and a fifty-seven-year-old priest, Miguel Hidalgo y Costilla, whose parish was in the small nearby village of Dolores. Hidalgo, a *criollo,* had been investigated twice by the Inquisition for his political views. When word leaked out about the conspiracy in Querétaro, its members were warned by the wife of the local *corregidor,* or governor (she is celebrated in Mexican history as *la corregidora*). In Dolores, with Allende by his side, Father Hidalgo rang his church bell to summon his parishioners and issued what came to be called the *grito de Dolores,* a call to rebellion, on September 16, 1810. Many *criollos* were alarmed by the excesses of the mestizos and Indians who fought for Hidalgo and independence. Government forces rallied. Hidalgo and Allende were defeated, captured, and killed.

A mestizo priest, José María Morelos y Pavón, took up the sword of leadership, and in the congress that he called in 1813, he made clear by his stirring speech to the delegates that the sword he carried was meant to cut the *criollo,* as well as the *peninsular,* bonds that had for so long held down the mestizos and Indians of Mexico. The constitution adopted by this congress was a liberal document. Principles could not stand up to guns, however. *Criollos* and *peninsulares* joined together in opposition to this rebellion, and by 1815, Morelos, too, had been captured and killed. Still, the war—or wars—for independence sputtered on for another five years.

In Spain, Ferdinand VII had been restored to the throne in 1814, but the *criollos* of Mexico felt increasingly separate from Spain. In 1823, led by a conservative military man, Agustín de Iturbide, the *criollos,* backed by the Church, declared Mexican independence—a conservative independence, much different from that for which Morelos and Hidalgo had fought and died. Spain, after years of war, had no alternative but to agree to Mexican independence. The Mexican economy was in shambles. And after all the fighting, the lives of the great mass of the Mexican people had not changed. The identity of their oppressors had changed, but the nature of the oppression remained the same. Iturbide had himself declared emperor of Mexico—the first of its *caudillo,* or strongman, rulers. But the imperial grandeur in which Iturbide lived and ruled lasted only ten months.

Now, there rode onto the Mexican scene one of the most flamboyant and most enduring *caudillos* of Mexican history, the Veracruz military commander, a twenty-nine-year-old *criollo,* Antonio López de Santa Anna. Santa Anna had switched from the Spanish army to support Iturbide. After Iturbide dissolved the Mexican congress, Santa Anna switched and led the forces that unseated Iturbide. He could be a monarchist or an antimonarchist. He could be a liberal or a conservative. He could be a defender of his country, or he could sell it out. For him, expediency and self-interest were the first principles. In February

1823, Iturbide was driven into European exile, and his rule was replaced by that of a provisional government, run by a three-man military junta.

Needless to say, there are no statues in Mexico honoring Iturbide. By contrast, both Hidalgo and Morelos had states named after them, and there are many monuments to them. On each anniversary of the *grito de Dolores,* the president of the Mexican republic rings the old bell, now at the National Palace, in commemoration of that important event.

THE MEXICAN REPUBLIC

A new Mexican constitution was promulgated in 1824. It established the Estados Unidos Mexicanos, which consisted of nineteen states and four territories. Patterned after the constitution of the United States and influenced by the writings of the French philosopher Montesquieu, the Mexican constitution established a national government of three branches—executive, legislative, and judicial—a bicameral legislature, and a president to be elected by nationwide popular vote. Roman Catholicism was continued as the established religion. Military men and priests were guaranteed their special privilege of the *fuero*—that is, the right to be tried for any offense not by the civil courts but by military or Church courts.

After Manuel Félix Fernández Guadalupe Victoria was elected as the first president, poor Iturbide mistakenly thought he heard a call of the Mexican people—all the way over in Italy. He unwisely returned home, where he was arrested and executed. In 1827, Santa Anna put down another attempted revolt. In 1830, he was called on to defend the country and the government once more. When the second republican president had pushed through legislation expelling all Spaniards from Mexico, Spain had invaded Mexico at Tampico. Santa Anna laid siege to the Spanish forces and eventually forced their surrender. By then, he was easily the most popular figure in Mexico. The president of Mexico was then thrown out of office and executed by his vice president. Santa Anna rose up and threw this usurper out of office. He was then elected president of Mexico in 1833.

It turned out that Santa Anna was not very much interested in governing. His vice president, though, began to push through liberal reforms. So the army, the Church, and other conservatives banded together to overthrow the constitutional government and rescind the reforms. And who should lead this revolt but the president of the republic himself, Antonio López de Santa Anna. Now the foremost conservative, Santa Anna abolished the Constitution of 1824 and made the states into military districts. He required that he be addressed as Your Serene Highness. He was to occupy the presidency again and again, off and on, until 1855. During those years, the army became larger and larger, the bureaucracy became ever more bloated, taxes became higher and higher, the economy stagnated, bribery and corruption of officials became outrageous, and there were conflicts with foreign governments—first with the

Republic of Texas, then with France, and finally, and disastrously, with the United States.

For years, Mexico had encouraged emigration from the United States to the sparsely settled, vast lands of Texas—provided only that the new emigrants were Catholics, would be loyal to the Mexican government, and would use Spanish as their official language. As the years passed, little was done to enforce these requirements. The flood of emigration swelled. Eventually, people from the United States greatly outnumbered Mexicans in Texas, and they became increasingly critical of the central government, until, at last, they rebelled and declared the establishment of the Lone Star republic in 1836. Santa Anna took personal command of the Mexican army and marched to San Antonio, where, at the Alamo on March 6, 1836, he defeated the 150 Texas defenders there and killed them all. Another part of the Mexican army captured the small town of Goliad, taking 365 prisoners, all of whom Santa Anna had executed. Then, on April 21 of that same year, Santa Anna was himself defeated at the San Jacinto River and was taken captive.

To save himself, Santa Anna promised the Texans that Mexico would not again fight against Texas and that the Mexican cabinet would receive a formal mission from the Lone Star republic. When the cabinet heard of these agreements, they immediately repudiated them and sent Santa Anna back to his estate near Veracruz. Soon, however, the trumpets sounded again for Santa Anna. Provoked by Mexico's refusal—actually an inability—to pay its French debts, France ordered a shelling and invasion of Veracruz. Santa Anna led the Mexican forces that eventually drove the French away.

WAR WITH THE UNITED STATES

Then came the war between the United States and Mexico (1846–1848). U.S. attitudes toward Mexico and Mexicans were highly derogatory, even racist— especially after the war with Texas. Furthermore, the people and government of the United States felt that it was their Manifest Destiny to stretch their country's boundaries westward, all the way to the Pacific. The United States annexed Texas as a state in 1845. Mexican officials seethed, but were largely powerless to do anything else. Then, without any discoverable basis in law or fact, Texas claimed that its border went, not just to the Nueces River, but much past it to the Rio Grande (which the Mexicans call the Rio Bravo). Not only had Mexico suffered the loss of Texas, but it was now expected to accept the doubling of Texas territory—to include additionally, for example, San Antonio, Nacogdoches, and Galveston in Texas as well as Albuquerque, Santa Fe, and Taos in present New Mexico.

It is known from President James K. Polk's diary that he had made up his mind early to engage in a war with Mexico and was only waiting for a provocation. He sent U.S. troops into the area between the Nueces and the Rio Grande. When they skirmished with Mexican cavalry, Polk went before Congress, declared that he had made every effort at reconciliation, that the Mexicans had invaded U.S. territory and "shed American blood on American soil," and asked for a declaration of war. Congress complied.

The U.S. Army of the West was divided into three attack groups, which rapidly took New Mexico, California, and Chihuahua. The Army of the Center attacked Monterrey, where it was stopped by none other than Santa Anna. The main U.S. attack came from the Army of Occupation at Veracruz, which eventually marched all the way to Mexico City. The last battle there was on September 13, 1837, at Chapultepec Castle, the site of a military academy. Young Mexican cadets fought alongside the Mexican regulars, many preferring death to surrender. Mexico was defeated.

Peace was even more humiliating for Mexico than the war had been. According to the Treaty of Guadalupe Hidalgo, Mexico lost half of its territory in return for a payment of a little over $18 million—all of California, some of present-day Colorado, and most of the present states of New Mexico and Arizona. More humiliation was to come. When Santa Anna again came to power in 1853, needing money, he sold the rest of present New Mexico and Arizona (in the so-called Gadsden Purchase) to the United States for $10 million.

Today, one of Mexico's principal national monuments is located in Chapultepec Park. It is dedicated to the *niños héroes* ("boy heroes") of the war with the United States. Similar national monuments commemorating the patriotism and courage of the young cadets have been erected in villages and towns throughout Mexico. There are no monuments to Santa Anna.

THE REFORM

By 1854, the liberals of Mexico had had enough of dictatorial government. Among them was Benito Juárez, the lawyer of Zapotec Indian origin who had been governor of his home state, Oaxaca. They rose up in arms behind the liberal Plan of Ayutla. Santa Anna was driven into exile in 1855. Thus began what is called La Reforma (the Reform). Benito Juárez, as secretary of justice in the new government, was instrumental in having promulgated three important new reform laws: *ley Juárez, ley Lerdo,* and *ley Iglesias.* The first law abolished the *fuero,* the right of priests and military men to be tried in their own courts. The second law prohibited the Church and public units (including *ejidos,* the communal landholdings of Indian villages) from owning more property than was necessary for Church or governmental functions. The extra lands were not divided among the people. They were put up for sale. The unfortunate result was that large landholdings went to those who had the money. The third law struck again at the Church—making registration of births, deaths, marriages, and adoptions a civil, not a Church, responsibility; giving control of cemeteries to civil authorities; and prohibiting priests from charging high fees for administering the sacraments.

The Constitution of 1857 incorporated these and other reforms. Pope Pius IX declared any who followed the constitution heretics. The lines were sharply and bitterly drawn between the liberals on one side and the conservatives and supporters of the Church on the other. The War of the Reform broke out in 1858. Conservative forces overran the capital. Benito Juárez, who had earlier been elected chief justice and was, therefore, next in line for succession to the presidency, took over that office when its occupant resigned. Juárez eventually made his capital in Veracruz.

The conservative government in Mexico City renounced the reform laws and swore allegiance to the pope. The Juárez government, on the other hand, issued even stronger decrees against the Church. The Church and the state were formally separated. Monastic orders were outlawed. All Church properties and assets were nationalized. Taking advantage of dissension within conservative circles, the liberal forces began to win some battles. Finally, on January 1, 1861, Mexico City fell to them.

French Intervention

Juárez entered Mexico triumphantly in March and was officially elected president. But before 1861 was over, foreign troops invaded. Mexico owed debts to France, Spain, and Great Britain that it had not been able to pay. Napoleon III of France persuaded the other powers to join with him in an invasion of Mexico. The Spanish and British withdrew after they learned that Napoleon III was bent on conquest. The French troops were then reinforced, and they began to march toward Mexico City. On the *cinco de mayo* (the fifth of May), the French troops were defeated near Puebla by the Mexican army. After this victory, Juárez, incensed by the fact that many priests had urged their parishioners to support the French, issued a decree prohibiting priests and nuns from wearing distinguishing garments and from speaking against the government.

The *cinco de mayo* victory was short-lived. Juárez retreated northward, eventually all the way to El Paso del Norte (later to be renamed Ciudad Juárez). Now began one of the most bizarre and tragic episodes in Mexico's political history—the imposition in 1864 by Napoleon III of the Hapsburg prince from Austria, Ferdinand Maximilian, as emperor of Mexico. Poor Maximilian and his wife, Carlota, believed the Mexican conservative, monarchist, and pro-Church emissaries who came to urge Maximilian to accept the Mexican throne. They were told that the people would welcome them with warm enthusiasm. They also believed Napoleon III when he said he would finance Maximilian's rule and sustain him on the Mexican throne with French troops as long as necessary. They also believed their Mexican advisers who told them that Juárez was defeated and had fled to the United States. These things were not true.

When the U.S. Civil War ended, the United States again turned its attention to Mexico and began to pressure France to withdraw. At the same time, the U.S. government began to furnish munitions and other supplies to Juárez. In late 1865 and early 1866, the French troops were called home, and Napoleon III announced that he could no longer pay the costs of Maximilian's government. Carlota went to Rome to secure the pope's help; when this effort was unsuccessful, she lost her mind. Maximilian began a final and hopeless resistance to the republican army—being soundly defeated and captured in Querétaro on May 15, 1867. Despite a great number of petitions by numerous heads of state, Juárez denied clemency for Maximilian and had him executed. Juárez entered Mexico City once more, reinstituted the Constitution of 1857, and in December 1867 was elected to a third term as president. During this "restored republic," Juárez reduced the size of the army, instituted economic and educational reforms, and began construction of a railroad system to pull Mexico together as one nation.

Mexico had developed a strong sense of nationalism—and significantly, this nationalism had flowered in struggles against foreign powers. There are, of course, no monuments in Mexico to Maximilian. There are many monuments dedicated to Juárez, and Mexico City's principal boulevard is named the Paseo de la Reforma.

THE PORFIRIATO

Perhaps Juárez stayed in office too long. There were complaints that he centralized too much authority in the presidency, manipulated and dominated the Congress, caused the alienation of *ejido* land, and increased the power of the national government, to the detriment of state and local governments. Nevertheless, Juárez announced for election to a fourth term in 1871. There was a three-way contest, and no candidate received a majority of the vote. The election was thrown into the congress, which chose Juárez. One of the other candidates, a military hero of the battles with the French, Porfirio Díaz, attempted a revolt under the slogan of No Reelection. The attempt failed. The revolt was quashed. But, in July of 1872, before he could take office, Juárez died.

The chief justice, one of the other candidates, Sebastián Lerdo de Tejada, succeeded to the office and in special elections in October of that year, was elected president. Lerdo continued the basic policies of Juárez and then announced for reelection to a second term. Porfirio Díaz took to the field with his military supporters again. This time, his No Reelection slogan caught fire. By force of arms and general support among those who counted, Díaz took over the presidency in 1876. This Mexican *caudillo* was to rule Mexico for over a third of a century. True to his No Reelection theme, Díaz did not seek reelection in 1880. After the undistinguished administration of his successor, Díaz became president again in the election of 1884. Thereafter, he remained in office until he was forced out in 1911.

The Porfiriato, as the Díaz reign is called, was a time of stability, law and order, and overall economic growth. It was dominated by men whom detractors later came to call *científicos*—followers of French positivism (a belief in progress through scientific knowledge and the scientific method), pragmatism, and social Darwinism. Chief among the *científicos* was the son of a French immigrant, José Ives Limantour, who became secretary of the treasury. Porfirio Díaz and his backers believed, among other things, that Mexico needed a period of "administrative power"—a nice way to say dictatorship—if the country was to be transformed from a backward nation into a modern one.

Díaz created a powerful political machine, run from the top. He practiced a shrewd politics of conciliation and coalition. There were great political and economic benefits for those who joined up—jobs and positions, land, subsidies, concessions. Constitutional local government continued in theory, but real local power was vested in some 300 *jefes políticos* (political chiefs), named by Díaz. The military was also a part of the Díaz coalition. Key generals were allowed to dominate their states. Government policies encouraged bigness in agriculture, as in everything else. New laws allowed surveying companies to keep a portion of any idle, unclaimed, or public lands they surveyed. Great land grabs resulted. Four surveying companies, for example, were able to obtain two-thirds of all the land in the northern state of Sonora, territory equal to the size of England and Wales combined.

The *científicos* believed that Mexico's economic development depended upon attracting foreign capital through special subsidies and concessions. By 1910, U.S. interests controlled 75 percent of Mexican mines, 72 percent of the metal industry, 68 percent of the rubber business, and 58 percent of oil production. Other foreigners—mostly British, French, German, and Dutch—controlled 80 percent of the rest of Mexico's industry.

The theme of the Porfiriato was "peace, order, and progress." A modern railroad network was built. This helped to double cotton production. Mining flourished; so did industrialization. Some ports were modernized and others opened. Exports mushroomed—and Mexico became dependent upon them. Mexico's population doubled.

But the costs were exorbitant. The great majority of Mexicans lived in misery or in otherwise intolerable conditions. The Indians, who Limantour believed were biologically inferior, were considerably worse off by 1910 than they had been a hundred years earlier, prior to independence. The rural *peones,* or laborers, were also worse off. The *peones,* as well as the miners, were paid, not in money, but in scrip or special coins, which could only be spent at the *tienda de raya,* the company store, and they were perpetually behind in what they owed. *Rurales* (rural police) hunted down and brought back anyone who tried to escape. Debts were passed on from one generation to another. Because Mexico's agriculture had increasingly been converted to cash crops and to the cattle and sheep business, especially for export, Mexico was producing less corn and beans in 1910 than it had produced in 1867—and was a large importer of food.

Railroad, mining, and industrial workers became increasingly hostile to the owners, to foreigners, and to their own government. Labor agitation and attempts at organization began in the 1880s—some of it encouraged by the Catholic Church following the issuance of a papal encyclical in 1891 that called for greater recognition of the rights of labor. Between 1881 and 1911, there were 250 strikes. In the worst of these, against French- and U.S.-owned companies, federal troops were used to break the strikes.

A growing Mexican middle class was also increasingly unhappy with the government. The economic policies and the educational programs of the Díaz regime had helped to create this middle class. But, as Porfirio Díaz and his administration aged, they turned more and more to a politics of exclusion. Liberal intellectuals began to speak out against the undemocratic practices of the government and the exploitation of Mexican labor. Two Flores Magón brothers, Jesus and Ricardo, started a liberal publication, *Regeneración,* to call for change. The publication was closed down by the government, and the Flores Magón brothers fled to the United States, where their writings and calls for action became increasingly radical.

On top of all this came bad economic times. The year 1907 was one of both severe drought in Mexico and severe economic problems in the world. A financial panic in the United States cut off credit to Mexico. The worldwide economic problems deprived Mexico of its export market, upon which it had come to depend so heavily. Mines were shut down. The economy stagnated. The prices of food and clothing rose rapidly—the costs of flour, beans, wheat, corn, and chile nearly doubling.

Then, in an interview with a U.S. magazine in 1908, Porfirio Díaz announced—and this was widely publicized in Mexico—that he felt the time had come for Mexico to choose its own president in the elections of 1910. Díaz himself eventually became a candidate for reelection. In the meantime, Francisco Ignacio Madero, the son of a Coahuila *hacendado* who had studied for five years in France and eight months at the University of California in Berkeley, wrote a very important book, *The Presidential Succession of 1910,* in which he called for political reform (although he said virtually nothing in regard to land, labor, or other economic or social reforms). Madero formed an Anti-Reelection Party and began to expound his views in well-attended meetings around the country. Actually doubtful that Díaz would really allow a free election, Madero nevertheless announced as a candidate for president. Madero's doubts were well founded. He was arrested and jailed. Díaz was declared the winner in the 1910 elections; Madero went into exile in San Antonio, Texas.

The Revolution

With this latest usurpation of power by Porfirio Díaz, Madero's frustrations at last rose to a level that matched Mexico's. In October 1910, he issued his Plan of San Luís Potosí, reiterating his call for political reform and asking Mexicans to rise up in arms against the Díaz regime on November 20. Rise up they did. This moderate man, with his moderate plan, became the lightning rod that attracted all of the dissident elements of the country. Some who joined him were more conservative than Madero; many were more radical. Some joined him to secure a share of the power and wealth, others to fight for social and economic, as well as political, reforms.

There was an uprising in Yucatán. The Flores Magón brothers led an uprising in Baja California. In Chihuahua, Pascual Orozco Jr., a muleteer disgruntled by the political and economic stranglehold of the *hacendados,* raised an army and began to achieve significant victories over the federal forces. Among his lieutenants was a man who called himself Francisco "Pancho" Villa. Born Doroteo Arango into a poor family living on a hacienda, Villa had spent most of his life as a bandit and a cattle rustler.

In February 1911, Madero returned to Mexico and took command of the revolutionary army. In the state of Morelos, Emiliano Zapata, a charismatic and dedicated leader for land reform, announced his support for the Madero revolution. It turned out that the federal army had become as debilitated by power and corruption as the government itself. It could not stop Zapata in the state of Morelos nor Orozco and Villa in the northern states. Zapata took Cuautla; Orozco and Villa captured Ciudad Juárez. It became clear to Díaz and those around him that after a third of a century, his government had lost its legitimacy and, with it, control of the country. Limantour went to Ciudad Juárez and negotiated a transfer of power. Díaz abdicated on May 25 and left for Europe, never to return. The Porfiriato had ended. Madero thought that the Revolution had also ended, but it had only begun.

The war was to continue for another decade. Countless Mexicans, including Madero himself, were to be killed by other Mexicans. The country was to be ravished, the economy devastated. The population of Mexico, which had been rapidly growing, was to suffer a decline of nearly 1 million people between 1910 and 1920. But all that was somewhere in the future when a triumphant Madero boarded the train for Mexico City. The troubles to come were presaged, though, by a harsh confrontation Madero had with Orozco and Villa just before he left Ciudad Juárez. In Mexico City, Madero made a strategic mistake. A stickler for legality, he allowed an interim president to serve until Madero could be formally elected in October 1911. By then, perhaps, his moment had passed. Madero was to govern for only thirteen months. His meager and timid reforms did nothing to satisfy labor and land-reform demands. He continued the fiscal policies of Díaz and retained many of the Porfiriato's high officials.

Orozco took to the battlefield again. Zapata issued his Plan of Ayala, which demanded immediate land reform; denounced Madero; and recognized Orozco as the true leader of the Revolution. Now, Madero made another mistake, this one literally a fatal mistake. He called upon a Porfiriato general, Victoriano Huerta, a mestizo from the state of Jalisco, to head the federal army against Orozco and Zapata. Huerta was successful against Orozco (who later, opportunistically, joined forces with him), and he began to put pressure upon Zapata. Then came another challenge—from the right. Felix Díaz, a nephew of the former president, rose in arms in Veracruz against the Madero government. Again, Huerta was successful. This rebellion, too, was quashed, and Felix Díaz was brought to Mexico City and jailed. Soon, however, other conservative forces freed Díaz and threatened the government again. There then ensued what is called in Mexican history the decena trágica ("the ten tragic days"). The killing and destruction wrought by the Díaz and the Huerta forces, fighting against each other, were horrible. It appears now that Huerta might have been going through a sham in order, purposely, to cause the decimation of his own government army, because he was, at the same time, opening secret negotiations with Díaz. These negotiations culminated in an agreement, reached under the direction and guidance of the U.S. ambassador, Henry Lane Wilson. Huerta switched sides and the U.S. ambassador supported him. Herta immediately took over the government, arrested Madero, and had the president's brother killed. Madero was imprisoned. Despite the pleas for help by Madero's wife to Wilson, the ambassador did nothing, and Madero and his vice president were taken out and cruelly murdered.

In the United States, President Woodrow Wilson refused to recognize the Huerta regime. But, in Mexico, most state governors did. Zapata, of course, did not recognize Huerta. Neither did Villa, and he was joined in arms by Alvaro Obregón, a former schoolteacher and *cacique* (political boss) in Sonora, and a former revolutionary commander. The leadership of these constitutionalist forces was assumed by Venustiano Carranza, nearly sixty years old, the governor of Coahuila, and the patriarch of a distinguished *criollo* family there. Carranza took as his title first chief. He issued his Plan of Guadalupe, a moderate plan, promising, again, only political reforms. As the fighting worsened and widened, as villages were taken first by one side and then another, many people began to wonder what it was all about. Even the soldiers—in both the federal and constitutionalist armies—were not agreed among themselves on what they were fighting for.

Although, interestingly, Huerta probably achieved more in the way of reforms and in support of education than did Madero, he also severely suppressed the press, jailed opponents, countenanced the use of assassination as a political tool, and practiced harsh repression generally. Huerta also initiated forced conscription to supply his army with soldiers—producing an inferior army and depleting the Mexican work force, adding injury to the Mexican economy. President Wilson possessed a moralistic zeal for democracy. He replaced Henry Lane Wilson and, using the pretext of a Mexican affront to some U.S. sailors, sent an armed force to capture the port of Veracruz in 1914. This caused a new wave of severely anti-U.S. feeling in Mexico. The vigor and successes of the constitutionalist army, augmented by the facts that Huerta had to divert troops to Veracruz and that his outside sources of supply had been cut off by the U.S. occupation of that port, brought down the Huerta government in July of that same year. Huerta resigned, blaming the United States for his fall (he later died in a Texas jail in 1916, still plotting to return to Mexico).

The first chief, Venustiano Carranza, took control of the Mexican government. Partisans of social and economic reform soon found out that he was not one of them. To consolidate his position, Carranza called a military convention in Aguascalientes in 1914. *Carrancistas, Villistas,* and *Zapatistas* met to pull the country together and to decide upon a provisional president until elections could be held. But the convention soon got out of hand. Led by the *Zapatistas,* a majority of the delegates, in a burst of revolutionary fervor, elected a provisional president who was opposed by Carranza. The first chief disowned the convention and called for his representatives to withdraw from it. Fatefully, as time would show, one of those who decided to obey this order was Alvaro Obregón.

The troops of Villa and Zapata marched on Mexico City. Carranza withdrew his headquarters to Veracruz (from which, incidentally, the U.S. occupation forces were eventually evacuated). The provisional president chosen by the Aguascalientes Convention was installed in office. But Obregón was a student of the new tactics of war being used at the time in Europe. At Celaya, in April 1915, he met an old-style massed cavalry charge with a deadly stationary defense. Thousands of Villa's men were killed and wounded, and Villa himself withdrew northward. Zapata thereafter confined himself and his forces to the state of Morelos.

Carranza returned to power in Mexico City. His government was recognized by President Woodrow Wilson. The first chief then called another convention, this one a constitutional convention in Querétaro. To avoid his earlier mistake, he decreed that none of the delegates to be elected could include anyone who had fought with Huerta, Villa, or Zapata. But when the convention met, these restrictions proved unavailing. A majority of the delegates quickly rejected the moderate model constitution that Carranza had sent them. Instead, they wrote an organic law—still in effect in Mexico—that was a radical document for its day. It limited the president to one four-year term. Its Article 3 was vigorously anti-Church, incorporating all such earlier restrictions and prohibitions and, further, taking primary education away from the Church (making education purely secular as well as mandatory and free). Article 27 incorporated the basic philosophy and provisions of the Plan of Ayala in regard to land reform, made private ownership a privilege subject to the public interest as the government might define it, and restricted the right to exploit Mexico's water and mineral resources to Mexican nationals. Article 123 mandated extensive labor reforms—an eight-hour day, a six-day week, equal pay regardless of sex or nationality, and a minimum wage. The right of labor to organize and to strike was guaranteed.

Shocked as he was by the product of this second runaway convention, Carranza nevertheless accepted the constitution, although he made it clear that he had no intention of following it. He was elected president in March 1917. Carranza distributed very little land. His labor reforms were also minor, although he did permit the organization of Mexico's first nationwide union, the Regional Confederation of Mexican Labor (CROM). In the north, Villa was relatively quiet—and wealthy—on his hacienda. But from Morelos, Zapata wrote a defiant open letter to Carranza, calling on him to resign and charging that Carranza and his friends had only fought in the Revolution for "riches, honors, businesses, banquets, sumptuous feasts, bacchanals, orgies." Carranza had tried direct military action against Zapata, to no avail. Now he decided upon treachery. On Carranza's orders, an officer of the federal army in Morelos, indicating that he wanted to defect to Zapata, led Zapata into a trap and killed him in 1919. Carranza rewarded the assassin with an army promotion and a generous cash prize.

But things were far from settled in Mexico, and the battered country had not seen the last of political violence—nor of political assassinations. General Obregón, the one-armed hero of the constitutionalist forces, had gone back to his native Sonora after Carranza's government had been firmly put in place. As a *hacendado*, a grower and "merchant of garbanzos," a cattleman and an exporter of beef and hides, and an all-around entrepreneur, Obregón had grown very wealthy. But power interested him as much as wealth. So, when he thought Carranza had passed over him in choosing the "approved" presidential candidate for 1920, Obregón led a military revolt against Carranza—a successful one. Sadly, Carranza was killed while retreating toward Veracruz. Obregón's subsequent election as president in 1920 was not the last time a presidential election would ratify a result earlier achieved by military means. But Obregón's revolt was the last successful revolt against the government.

The Mexican Revolution was over, and it was soon enshrined forever—with a capital *R*—in Mexican history. With time, the Mexican constitution came to be regarded as a nearly sacred document—though it was a long way from actually being implemented. Time did not improve the image of Huerta, whom Mexican history remembers as "the bloody usurper." No Mexican monuments were erected in memory of Porfirio Díaz (although, ironically, a street in El Paso, Texas, still bears his name). But plenty of Mexican monuments and street names, today, pay homage to Madero, Carranza, and Zapata. Mexican history makes Madero "the apostle" of the Revolution and of Mexican democracy, Carranza "the father of the constitution," and Zapata the heroic fighter for the Mexican masses.

THE NORTHERN DYNASTY

Alvaro Obregón and his fellow Sonoran, Plutarco Elías Calles, who had fought with Obregón, apparently soon worked out an arrangement by which they agreed to pass the presidency back and forth between them in the years that were to follow. Obregón was elected president in 1920. He was a charismatic leader and a dynamic orator, and he gathered power into the presidency. Obregón was also a conciliator. He made a kind of peace with the Church and with his former foes. He had another rich hacienda bought for Pancho Villa, and the mellowing revolutionary of the North settled down (and was assassinated in 1923). The economy recovered. Mexico became the world's third largest producer of oil. The first national system of education was established, and rural schools were built. Obregón allowed some cautious labor advances to be made and endorsed some cautious land reform. A sense of what came to be called revolutionary nationalism began to develop in the country—in its writings, in its music, and in its art. In the United States, Warren G. Harding, a friend of big oil, became president in 1921. He pressured Mexico to recognize the U.S. oil holdings there, and Obregón yielded.

Calles became president in 1924—after an attempted rightist rebellion was put down by military force. Taking office, Calles became the strongest—and, as it turned out, the longest-lived—president and *caudillo* since Díaz. He put down his enemies without mercy. He built up Mexico's economy, pushed health programs, expanded education, helped make labor more powerful, and established a cooperative relationship with CROM. He also vigorously enforced, as Obregón had not, the anti-Church provisions of the constitution. Militant Catholics rose up in a bloody rebellion, their cry being "Viva Cristo Rey!" ("Long live Christ, the King!"). Calles dealt very harshly with this *cristero* rebellion and, after much shedding of blood on both sides, eventually suppressed it.

Calles also confronted the United States in regard to oil. It was decreed that all interests that predated the Constitution of 1917 would have to be renegotiated with the government—and these new concessions were to be limited in duration. The United States sent a Wall Street investment banker, Dwight Morrow, to Mexico as its ambassador. His quiet negotiations eventually worked out a compromise. The oil interests were allowed to continue their concessions without the duration lid.

Calles caused the presidential term to be changed from four years to six years. He then prepared to turn the government back over to Obregón in the 1928 presidential election. There was a rebellion, again, and it was again put down. The election ratified the earlier military victory. But before Obregón could take office, he was killed by a religious mystic. Calles assumed power again—ruling through puppets as the *jefe máximo* (maximum chief) until 1934. During this period, called in Mexican history the *maximato,* Calles established Mexico's ruling party in order to institutionalize his political control, since he was not charismatic or dynamic enough to rule by power of personality. Calles shifted the Revolution to the right. Powerful leaders of labor, business, and government became immensely wealthy during the Calles *maximato.* Calles, himself, seemed to own property almost everywhere.

The Cárdenas *Sexenio*

With the end of the 1928–1934 *sexenio,* the *maximato* had run its course. Calles was the last survivor of the great revolutionary *caudillos*—Madero, Zapata, Villa, Carranza, and Obregón had all been assassinated—and he was now to lose control. But Calles did not know that that was about to happen when he chose the populist and popular governor of Michoacán and his former minister of war, Lázaro Cárdenas, as the National Revolutionary Party (PNR) presidential candidate in the elections of 1934. Elected, Cárdenas turned out to have a mind of his own. Once he had cut down the strength and influence of the military and had bolstered his own political position with labor, the peasants, and other elements in the country, he confronted Calles and exiled him from the country.

Cárdenas undertook more land reform—mostly by delivering land to *ejidos*—than all of his predecessors put together. He instituted "socialist" education in the schools and expanded education generally. He reorganized the national labor union into the Confederation of Mexican Workers (CTM) and made this organization a much more aggressive and representative body. The minimum wage was raised. The old hacienda system was broken. A limited peace was achieved with the Church. The railroads were nearly all nationalized. Nationalistic artists were encouraged. A cultural nationalism blossomed. The ruling party, PNR, was reorganized to make it much more broad based and more truly representative of the people to the government, rather than, as it had been, from the government to the people. The name of the party was changed to Mexican Revolutionary Party (PRM).

Then, in 1938, came the major decision of the Cárdenas *sexenio,* the confrontation with big oil. Oil workers had gone on strike. By modern standards, their demands in regard to wages, hours, and working conditions were modest. But the oil interests, chiefly based in the United States and Great Britain, were adamant in their rejection of the demands and in their intention to crush the strike. When the companies showed their arrogance toward the president himself and, thus, toward Mexican sovereignty, Cárdenas invoked Article 27 of the constitution and nationalized the oil industry. He did not turn the industry over to the workers as they wanted, but he did create a public corporation, Petróleos Mexicanos (PEMEX), to run it. He saw to it that this public company dealt generously with the *petroleros,* or oil workers, as it has done ever since.

In the United States, the powerful oil industry called upon the United States to take action—from economic sanctions to outright invasion—to protect their oil holdings and businesses. The U.S. government, and the government of Great Britain, were only too happy to back the companies. They boycotted Mexican oil and sought to isolate PEMEX from oil-production and exploration technology and technical assistance (thus, it turned out, forcing Mexico to build what is today a first-rate oil industry of its own).

Cárdenas had spent a great part of his term walking among the ordinary people of Mexico. Unannounced, he would visit small villages and, on the spot, sign orders for irrigation projects, for distribution of land, for clinics, and for other responses to local petitions that were humbly presented to him. The people of the country saw Cárdenas as one of their own. Now, with the expropriation of oil, the people—including even leaders of the Church and many conservatives—stood up with Cárdenas and with their country against the "greedy" oil companies and against foreign powers—particularly *el coloso del norte* (the colossus of the North), the United States. Never had there been such an outpouring of popular support for a president and his government.

Today, Cárdenas remains the greatest hero of Mexico's modern history. The anniversary of his birth and the anniversary of his expropriation of Mexico's oil are national holidays (by contrast, Calles is not considered to have been one of the "revolutionary family"). Under Cárdenas, Mexico's political system became more firmly institutionalized—in the presidency and in the official party (later renamed Institutional Revolutionary Party, PRI).

Mexico Since 1940

Mexico's history since 1940 can best be capsulized by considering a series of "lasts" and "firsts" among its presidents during that period and earlier. Calles was the last presidential exemplar of *continuismo,* continued control past one term. Cárdenas (1934–1940) was the last of the openly and consistently leftist and populist presidents. After his *sexenio,* the Mexican government increasingly focused its attention and efforts on rapid economic growth—the *milagro mexicano* (Mexican miracle)—to the detriment of economic equity.

Avila Camacho (1940–1946), chosen by Cárdenas to succeed him, was the last military man to serve as president. Interestingly, it was he who disbanded the military arm of the official party (though this action by no means eliminated the influence of the military on government and policy). Miguel Alemán Valdés (1946–1952) was the first civilian president popularly elected for a full term. He allowed new parties to form (some had formed earlier, too). But the PRI's monopoly was not seriously challenged. Alemán was the first Mexican president to exchange visits with a U.S. president. Trade with the United States flourished, as did U.S. private investment in Mexico. Alemán was the last president to devote a substantial portion of Mexican public investment to agriculture. After his term, the trends toward rapid industrialization and urbanization were accelerated, and Mexico eventually became an urban nation and a net importer of food.

Gustavo Díaz Ordáz (1964–1970) was the last Mexican president to come from outside the metropolis of Mexico City, and he was the last president to have held prior elective office. His political experience did not protect his popularity, though, when economic conditions worsened. The legitimacy of the Mexican political system was seriously strained when students at the national university and other protesters mounted huge demonstrations against government policies and were brutally attacked, with many killed and imprisoned, at Tlatelolco. Still, Díaz Ordáz was the last president under whom Mexico's foreign debt was below double-digit billions of dollars. He was the last president, too, during whose administration the rate of inflation remained at tolerable levels and the value of the peso continued to be stable.

Luís Echeverría Alvarez (1970–1976) was the first of four "insider" presidents—Echeverría, José López Portillo, Miguel de la Madrid Hurtado, and Carlos Salinas de Gortari; each came from the Federal District, had built his career in federal-government positions, and had served in the cabinet of his predecessor. Echeverría was also the first president since 1954 to devalue the peso. He was the first president to lead Mexico into an activist role in foreign affairs, particularly in regard to its own region and Third World countries, and this role increasingly diverged from U.S. policy. Echeverría was the first Mexican president to institute government-backed family planning—none too soon, since Mexico's population had gone from 16.5 million in the 1930s to around 51 million by 1970 (and over 80 million and growing by 1987).

José López Portillo (1976–1982) was the first Mexican president to expropriate Mexican private banks. He did so after hopes had soared at the beginning of his term, when new oil was discovered, only to plummet with a drop in world oil prices. This drop in prices, coupled with skyrocketing federal deficits, inflation, foreign borrowing, and two devaluations, as well as reports of widespread corruption, produced a crisis of confidence for his government.

Miguel de la Madrid Hurtado (1982–1988) was the first president to institute a *sexenio*-long austerity program, causing increased Mexican unemployment and poverty. Pressured to follow this course by the International Monetary Fund and the foreign banks that held Mexico's mammoth $100 billion foreign debt, he was the object of increasing public criticism and opposition during his term.

Carlos Salinas de Gortari (1988–1994) was the first recent president to take office with questioned legitimacy, his victory having been clouded by serious charges of widespread election fraud, as were previous PRI-claimed victories in certain northern state elections. He was the first president to face heavy parliamentary opposition and the first president whose inaugural ceremony in the great hall of the Chamber of Deputies was marred by a raucous demonstration and a protest walkout. Improvement in economic conditions and restoration of the legitimacy of the Mexican system—these were the fundamental challenges Salinas de Gortari had to confront. The economy was at first restored, and Salinas de Gortari signed the North American Free Trade Agreement. But after a *Zapatista* rebellion in Chiapas exploded and the handpicked PRI presidential candidate, Luis Donaldo Colosio, was assassinated, a severe financial crisis and economic depression ensued.

The succeeding PRI nominee and president, Ernesto Zedillo (1994–2000), was truly elected but took office at a time when the legitimacy of the system and the hegemony of PRI were being challenged as never before. The brother of Carlos Salinas de Gortari was imprisoned for complicity in political assassination and for unlawful enrichment, and the former president himself fled into exile. President Zedillo struggled to restore political and economic stability.

The Legacy of Revolution

Mexican politics and government are products of—and are to some degree constrained by—Mexican history. The role of the "great leader" is still highly important. Authority is still concentrated in the national government and, within it, in the president. Mexicans have a justified cynicism about government and a skepticism about the revolutionary rhetoric of candidates and officials. Still, candidates and officials know that they must make the obligatory obeisance toward the principles of the Revolution and the constitution. They would act in substantial and open opposition to these principles at their peril—although, obviously, they can fail to act in pursuance of these principles. And at the beginning of each *sexenio*, there is hope anew (tinged, of course, with some skepticism). Each new president becomes the symbolic leader of the country as well as its official leader, the repository of national authority and national honor, and the focus of Mexican aspirations. For more than fifty years, the Mexican system was stable, and the country's governmental system generally was seen as legitimate by Mexicans—despite gross inequities that have existed, and still exist, and a good deal of misery. The "institutionalization" of the Revolution and the legitimacy of the "official" PRI government have faced serious questioning and challenge, however, since the 1980s.

A New Beginning

The present time—the first years of the twenty-first century—is a difficult time in which to try to understand Mexican politics and economics. Today is a time of fundamental shift in the system's parameters, and it is not clear, even to the major participants themselves, what directions change will take.

The system that is undergoing change might have been difficult to characterize, but it was not hard to understand. It was established after the Mexican Revolution had stabilized. Behind the façade of a constitutional democratic system similar to that of the United States, it was dominated by a hegemonic political party growing out of the coalition of those who had fought successfully for the Revolution. In this respect it was similar to other dominant parties that claimed origins in a national revolution, such as those in the developing countries of Africa and Asia, and even those in the Communist countries of Eastern Europe. Like them, its social and economic policies reflected in part its revolutionary and nationalist rhetoric. But after a period of experimentation the ruling elite had come to terms with the facts of the world capitalist system and Mexico's position as a neighbor of the dominant country in that system: Although the economy was mixed, with some government ownership of basic utilities and major industries and with central government guidance and planning, the bulk of the economy was in private hands, and foreign investment was encouraged.

The rules that were supposed to protect Mexico's independence from foreign control by carefully stipulating the areas in which foreign investment was allowed, and the circumstances in which only state investment or investment by private Mexican nationals was to be tolerated, could often be evaded. Indeed, evasion of the law was widespread, political figures became wealthy by one means or another, and the various police forces of the republic were notorious more as a cause of crime than as a deterrent to it. But Mexico was not simply a kleptocracy, a government that existed only so that its rulers could steal; the ideals of the Revolution lived on and were frequently embodied in policy, and many government officials were capable and progressive servants of the public interest.

The Political System

The formal political system resembles that of the United States in its major structural features, but it was modified in major respects to meet objections raised by opposition parties to the fact that the same party, the Institutional

Revolutionary Party, or PRI, occupied the presidency and dominated the legislature and the state governments from its founding in 1929 until the year 2000.

There is a constitutional separation between the president and the two houses of the legislature, that is, they are elected independently of each other and each has powers specified in the constitution. The president is directly elected by the voters for a single six-year term and can never be reelected. Members of the Senate, now four from each state—the number increased from two to make it easier for the opposition parties to elect senators—are now not elected for staggered terms, as formerly, but all at the same time as the president. Members of the Chamber of Deputies are elected for three-year terms by a method similar to that pioneered by the German Federal Republic but increasingly adopted elsewhere; under it 300 members represent individual districts, but another 200 are chosen by proportional representation on party lists—again, so that opposition parties have a better chance of electing representatives.

It is a federal system, with each state having its own constitutional structure and elections for governor and a single-chamber legislature. During the years of PRI dominance of the system, governors' normal autonomy was often overridden by high-handed presidential acts. President Carlos Salinas (1988–1994), especially, used to treat governors as though they were his political appointees, moving them into cabinet or party positions or ordering them to resign if he thought the local political situation required it.

President Ernesto Zedillo (1994–2000) found himself in a much weaker political position than Salinas, however. Not the most popular or politically able of the possible successors to Salinas, Salinas picked him—behind the formal procedures, the outgoing PRI president in effect designated his successor—after the popular nominee, Luis Donaldo Colosio, was assassinated in a crime that has still not been satisfactorily explained. Zedillo was not able to impose his authority on a disciplined PRI, and local party machines resisted his attempts to comply with promises to fully democratize and constitutionalize Mexican political life by guaranteeing honest elections, impartial media, and an uncorrupt police and judiciary.

Nevertheless, a 1996 reform eliminated the possibility of political manipulation of election results by establishing an electoral tribunal independent of the executive branch (along with providing for the direct election of the governor of the Federal District, which includes Mexico City) and paved the way for an opposition victory in the 2000 presidential election.

The second strongest party is the PAN, the Party of National Action. Its leadership core has traditionally consisted of those educated in Catholic secondary schools and active in Catholic lay organizations, working in the professions and small business, but as its access to local- and state-level political power grew, it attracted some big-business support and the votes of opponents of the regime from across the class and income structure. Its national organization is uneven, being stronger in the northern border states and some other specific regions, such as Yucatán, but its presidential candidate Vicente Fox, governor of Guanajuato, finally won the presidency in 2000.

This meant less of a change in policy than might have been expected, since the policy positions of the PRI had shifted to the center-right of the political spectrum, with acceptance of neoliberal economic theory. Thus the PRI and the PAN had already formed an implicit alliance on some policy issues in the legislature, especially when two-thirds of the votes were required to pass a constitutional amendment, more than the PRI could muster on its own.

Such cooperation was made necessary by the growth of the third party in strength, the PRD, or Democratic Revolutionary Party. The PRD developed out of a secessionist movement from the left of the PRI loyal to the nationalism, agrarianism (support of land reform), and semisocialism that had characterized the PRI's rhetoric, and to some extent its policy, before the shift to the right that began under President Miguel de la Madrid (1982–1988) and was carried further by Carlos Salinas. That movement managed to attract substantial support for its 1988 presidential candidate, Cuauhtémoc Cárdenas, the decidedly uncharismatic son of the leftist revolutionary general who served from 1934 to 1940 as probably the most popular president of Mexico ever. While Salinas may well have received more votes than Cárdenas, the actual official results announced were universally regarded with skepticism. Cárdenas's incompetent campaigning and indecision on policy questions, however, together with the apparent success of Salinas's economic policies and a strong showing by a dynamic PAN candidate, put the PRD in a weak third place in the 1994 presidential elections. The disgrace into which Salinas fell after the end of his term, however, led to an upswing in support for the PRD and the election of Cárdenas, then vindicated, as governor of the Federal District.

The PRD has held the governorship of the D.F.—essentially the mayoralty of Mexico City—since then, and the mayor who took office in 2000, Manuel López Obrador, proved able, popular and a strong future candidate for the presidency.

With electoral reforms making for a multiparty system—essentially of three major parties and a few much smaller ones—with weak party discipline, President Fox was unable to register any significant departures in policy, especially since control of the bureaucracy also eluded him. In historical retrospect, his achievement will simply be to have been elected, and thus finally to have broken the political monopoly of the PRI. However, the PRI remains the largest party until the PRD is able to extend its reach beyond its areas of strength in the South and the capital, or the PAN can impose some organizational and policy coherence on its miscellany of personalist and anachronistic militants. But to return to power and govern effectively, the PRI has to find a new identity that can transcend the debris of corrupt machine politics, compromise of principle, and bureaucratic inertia that characterized the party in power.

Extra-System Opposition

The movement of the PRI to the right, and especially its abandonment of the principles of the land reform, under which land expropriated from large owners was owned in common (but usually farmed individually) by *ejido* collectivities, provided the occasion for a revolt of rural workers who had been mobilized through Catholic liberation theology grassroots organizations by activists left over from the student movements of the late 1960s. Taking the name of the great agrarian reformer of revolutionary days, Emiliano Zapata, the movement was catalyzed in the southern border state of Chiapas by the collapse in coffee prices and competition from immigrant Guatemalan agricultural workers. As notoriously mistreated people espousing noble goals, the Chiapas Indians who made up the Zapatista forces that took up arms on January 1, 1995, and especially their ironic and quotable leader, Marcos, aroused general sympathy among the Mexican public. Although the Zapatista forces were too weak to win any military victories, the government correctly perceived that a straightforward military attempt to wipe them out would create an endless Vietnam War in southern Mexico, with all the political costs that would entail, and instead settled down to an indefinite process of negotiating, making agreements that were never fully implemented, and continuing tactics of local repression that fell below the radar of the major international media.

The mountainous state of Guerrero, which lies west and south of Mexico City, has always been home to bandit and even guerrilla forces. From time to time, guerrilla movements appear there, and sometimes in other mountainous states, but it is out of the question that guerrilla movements of this kind could come to power by force. The country is too big, too complicated, and too sophisticated; as weak as the government may be, it is stronger by many orders of magnitude than any conceivable guerrilla army.

Economic Structure and Performance Until 1980

The economic performance of the country was very impressive until the early 1980s. The long-term rate of growth in the gross national product between 1940 and 1980 was 7 or 8 percent annually. Industry grew, producing both for the domestic market and, under special tariff arrangements, for export; but today about 8 million Mexicans still work on the land. Commercial farmers in the north of Mexico grow a great many specialty crops, such as winter vegetables, which are exported to the United States and are a valuable source of foreign exchange.

Since the middle of the 1970s, Mexico's major industry and major export has been petroleum. Early in the century, before the coming of the automobile era, when demand for the product was small, Mexico was the world's leading producer of petroleum. The international oil companies were active in Mexico until 1938. They played the obstreperous role they have often played elsewhere, mixing in the country's politics to try to keep down their tax payments and labor costs and making themselves generally disliked. The 1938 expropriation of the oil companies by Lázaro Cárdenas was thus very popular in Mexico and was looked upon as a kind of economic declaration of independence. After the expropriation, the international corporations got their crude elsewhere, however, and Mexican production declined to the level necessary simply to supply the domestic market. The state oil corporation, now called Petróleos Mexicanos (PEMEX), contented itself with producing mostly from already established wells, lacking the incentive or the funds for serious exploration.

However, over the years, PEMEX built up the technical capabilities necessary for all phases of the industry—exploration, production, refining, and marketing—except for offshore drilling. With the development of an adverse balance of payments and the sharp rise in world petroleum prices that took place in the early 1970s, PEMEX undertook explorations that established Mexico's possession of huge reserves; in mid-1997 proved and potential reserves exceeded 300 billion barrels. Yet this figure represents the exploration of only a fraction of the sedimentary basins that could contain hydrocarbon deposits. Mexico advanced to fourth place among the world's petroleum producers and became the third largest exporter after Saudi Arabia and Venezuela.

The ambiguity of the economic system, which combined capitalism with a strong dose of nationalism and socialism, paralleled the ambiguity of the political system, whose democratic institutions were belied by its underlying authoritarian character. In foreign policy, similarly, Mexico combined a wariness of its giant neighbor that reflected a long history of intervention, insult, and loss of territory, with a lively appreciation of the relative political and economic power of the two countries, which meant that defiant confrontation was not a viable option. Thus, equally well-informed observers believed that Mexico had a nationalist foreign policy behind a façade of cooperation with the United States or that it had a policy of subservience to the United States behind a nationalist façade.

Despite its revolutionary rhetoric and the many social welfare and economic projects undertaken by the government, twentieth-century Mexico fell a long way short of meeting the goals of the Revolution. Although Mexico's economic growth was undeniable, the benefits of that growth were concentrated in the upper and middle ranges of the income distribution. Moreover, privilege and corruption were widespread, and the country never came close to achieving full employment. Nevertheless, by the relative standards appropriate to an imperfect world, on the whole most observers accounted the Mexican experiment a success until late in the century.

Political stability was underwritten by economic growth. For most of the period, the economy grew steadily—indeed Mexico had more years of continuous uninterrupted economic growth than any other country. The political system remained stable, and since 1920 the constitutional succession has been unbroken, although perhaps bent a few times. The possibility of a military seizure of power, a daily worry in many of the Latin American countries, has long been a thing of the past in Mexico.

There was room for steady expansion of the domestic market as remote rural areas and indigenous populations that had been self-sufficient were progressively incorporated into the national market. In a country that lacked so much, government expenditure on infrastructure—communications, social investment, or the provision of basic utilities—was bound to generate a substantial return. Mexico's geographic position next to the United States guaranteed a constant inflow of capital and income from tourism and border transactions, providing a steady stream of convertible currency that normally made unnecessary the fiscal austerity to avoid inflation that put brakes on economic growth elsewhere.

THE INEVITABILITY OF CHANGE

When democracy triumphed with the collapse of the Soviet Union, so did the world capitalist system, which flexed its muscles and decided it no longer needed to tolerate socialist- or nationalist-inspired restrictions on its ability to seek maximum profits across state boundaries. So the classic Mexican-mixed economy would have been under pressure to change in any case. However, the change in the Mexican economic model, like most major events in history, was overdetermined—that is, several factors were working in the same direction to make it happen.

It had been clear to students of development that the political and economic model that characterized the middle years of the century could not last indefinitely. For one thing, the social changes that were occurring would clearly put intolerable strains, sooner or later, on the single-party system. As the country developed socially, more students went to the university, more illiterates learned to read, more peasants moved to the city. A nation of illiterate peasants may believe that their government always does everything right and public officials are invariably competent and public-spirited. A nation of sophisticated urban dwellers led by a large university-trained elite is likely to be more skeptical. A growing managerial class is likely to chafe at government controls, and it is not possible to provide comfortable, well-paying positions for all members of a rapidly growing educated elite.

Mexico's steady economic growth was based on the gradual incorporation into the market of hitherto marginalized Indian peasants, gradually growing foreign earnings, and a stable exchange rate of the peso to the dollar. In the late 1970s, however, a volatile new factor was introduced into this equation when the rise in international petroleum prices made it worthwhile for PEMEX, the national oil monopoly, to incur the costs involved in exploring for new sources of petroleum. The tremendous reserves that were then found made it possible for Mexico to earn huge amounts of money on the international oil market. But the sudden affluence brought by oil exports, like the touch of King Midas, proved in the long run a curse rather than a blessing.

Corruption grew to new levels; the ready availability of foreign exchange made it easier to import everything than to produce it in Mexico, and Mexico's own factories closed down; government employment mushroomed; and growing inflation hurt the standard of living of everyone not in a position to benefit from oil revenues.

When the inevitable downturn in oil prices came, the government of President José López Portillo (1976–1982) refused to adjust and instead borrowed abroad to cover the government's inflated expenses, hoping that prices would quickly rebound. When that didn't happen, Mexico's international creditors forced a drastic retrenchment in expenditures, so that all available resources could be devoted to paying down the debt. The result was that it was precisely those who had benefited least from the oil boom who were forced to bear the brunt of the policies of austerity that became necessary in its wake.

The abandonment by the governments of de la Madrid and Salinas of the distinctive Mexican mixed economic model, as they moved to align Mexico with the norms of the world capitalist economy, was thus presented as a painful but necessary process of adjustment that would get the economy on a sound footing and make renewed growth possible. During Salinas's presidential term, it appeared that the formula was successful. The value of the currency stabilized, economic growth resumed, and for a while the ruling PRI seemed to have regained the legitimacy it had lost with the economic crisis.

The shift in the economic model was drastic, involving not only changes in the laws governing the freedom of action of foreign capital but also a colossal sell-off of industries that had been in the public sector and the introduction of private-enterprise norms into the reformed sector of agriculture, whose collectivist principles had until then been viewed as sacred cows of revolutionary ideology. Out of the profits of the privatization program (which would have been greater if state property had not been sold to the president's friends and family at bargain prices), Salinas managed to mount a significant poverty-reduction program, called Solidarity, which softened the blow that structural reform dealt to Mexicans of lower income. It also contributed to the president's popularity and looked for a time as though it could provide a new generation of political activists Salinas would use to replace the "dinosaurs" of the PRI party organization.

However, the economic stabilization successes of the Salinas administration were based in part on a sort of confidence trick. Long-term monetary stability and economic growth were financed by short-term and potentially volatile investment funds, much of them attracted into high-interest government bonds. Not wanting to damage his image as a financial wizard, which he thought would help him win the post of secretary-general of the new World Trade Organization, Salinas did not devalue the peso when it would have been appropriate to do so. His successor, Ernesto Zedillo, then mishandled the overdue devaluation, when it finally came, with the result that capital fled the country, the value of the peso dropped, and a new wave of foreign borrowing, "structural reform," and decline in standards of living ensued.

Much was hoped for from the North American Free Trade Agreement (NAFTA), which went into effect in 1995, and which purported to integrate the economies of Mexico and Canada with that of the United States. Mexico had already had a partially integrated zone along the border with the United States, where *maquiladoras,* or assembly plants, could import raw materials and components from the United States, and export finished products, without being subject to tariffs and other restrictions. As is the case with such arrangements, some interests benefited and some were disadvantaged, though the overall balance was supposed to be advantageous on both sides of the frontier. But a stronger power can be expected to bias the arrangement in its own favor—for example, NAFTA allowed the free movement of capital but not that of labor—and although provisions were added to the agreement embodying anti-pollution rules and fair labor practices, enforcement mechanisms were weakened so as to make them ineffective. Meanwhile, capitalism's relentless pursuit of lower costs and higher profits meant that the jobs that had left the United States often did not stay long in Mexico before moving on to China.

Social Structure and Problems

During the years of steady economic growth, before the borrowing, inflation, and austerity of the 1980s and 1990s, things gradually got better for most Mexicans. Life expectancy at birth, a good general measure of well-being, increased from forty-eight years in 1950 to sixty-eight years in 1986. Literacy climbed during the same period from about 66 percent to about 90 percent of the population. The high rate of annual population increase—which made social problems more difficult to resolve—dropped from 3.2 percent in the 1960s to 2.9 percent in the 1970s and 2.4 percent in the 1980s.

Thereafter, however, social indicators stopped improving and indicators of economic well-being deteriorated as gains in income were nullified and the average standard of living in the mid-1990s dropped back to about where it was in the 1960s. Income inequality increased. By 1995, the top 10 percent of Mexicans received 41 percent of national income, while 3.2 percent went to the 20 percent at the bottom of the scale. As many as half of the urban population lacks regular paid employment and makes do with occasional temporary work, street vending, or marginal and dubiously legal activity. In the rural areas, about half of those engaged in agriculture are landless laborers, while most of the rest have small plots that provide hardly more than a subsistence living.

Problems of Mexico City

Even if the rate of population increase should decline further, however, it will come too late to avoid the onset of some major problems. The combination of population growth and migration to the cities has made Mexico City the largest urban agglomeration in the world. This has meant the loosing of an avalanche of problems—in the areas of housing, employment, transportation, sanitation, and so on. Government performance has fallen short of a satisfactory resolution of these problems, which were worsened by the effects of the 1985 earthquake. Unemployment and underemployment are acute; standards of housing are uneven, ranging down to very poor in the satellite city of Netzahualcoyótl; and pollution sometimes reaches health-threatening proportions. Surface transportation can be an ordeal; a worker may have to travel as much as two hours each way to get to work and back each day. Construction of a subway system has alleviated the situation somewhat, however, and the energetic PRD mayor, Manuel López Obrador, is generally credited with sincere efforts, at least, to attack the city's other problems.

CHANGE IN THE POLITICAL SYSTEM

The political effects of these economic developments reinforced tendencies in the political arena that grew out of other causes. The general strategy adopted by the ruling PRI for dealing with the political pressures arising from the changes going forward in Mexican society was to negotiate a long drawn-out strategic retreat that kept opposition political forces engaged in the political game and willing to channel their opposition into constitutional means within the system, by delivering a phased series of concessions. These, it was thought, were enough to enable the opposition parties to feel they were gaining ground but not enough to affect the substance of power at the national level. From time to time, electoral laws were reformed so as to enable opposition parties to win a few more legislative seats; some opposition victories in municipal elections were recognized. Over time, the concessions became greater: Opposition victories were recognized for governorships, and senators from opposition parties were seated. Finally, all of the little changes coalesced into one big change, and political life in Mexico began to approximate the façade it had always had, that of a constitutional democracy.

Mexico, that is, after so many years of distinctiveness, faces the future of a "normal" country. Today, however, that means a country in which money influences the media and the political process; and Mexico is still next door to a preponderant country dominated by powerful economic interests and is embedded in an unforgiving international financial system. Will it make any difference, in years to come, that Mexico was the locus of one of the great social revolutions of the twentieth century?

NOTES

1. The "Historical Foundations" portion of this chapter was written by Fred R. Harris, the portion titled "A New Beginning" by Martin C. Needler.

2. Raúl Béjar Navarro, *El Mexicano: Aspectos culturales y psicosociales* (Mexico City: Univérsidad Nacional Autónoma de México, 1979).

3. William C. McNeill, *Plagues and People* (Garden City, N.Y.: Doubleday, Anchor Press, 1976), p. 207.

4. John Duffy, "Smallpox and the Indians in the American Colonies," in Roger L. Nichols, ed., *The American Indian, Past and Present,* 2nd ed. (New York: John Wiley and Sons, 1981), p. 64.

Suggested Readings

Barry, Tom, ed., *Mexico: A Country Guide.* Albuquerque, N.M.: Inter-Hemispheric Education Resource Center, 1992. A detailed and very good report and analysis of Mexico's politics, government, and economy.

Basáñez, Miguel. *El Pulso de los Sexenios: 20 años de crisis en México.* 2nd ed. Mexico City: Siglo XXI, 1991. An account of the shifts in popular attitudes as revealed in opinion polls.

Collier, Ruth Berins. *The Contradictory Alliance: State-Labor Relations and Regime Change in Mexico.* Berkeley, Calif.: International and Area Studies, 1992.

Grayson, George W. *The United States and Mexico: Patterns of Influence.* New York: Praeger, 1984. This is an excellent history and assessment of relations between Mexico and the United States, with particular emphasis on key issues, including marketing of oil and gas, policy toward Central America and Cuba, and illegal immigration of Mexicans to the United States.

Hellman, Judith Adler. *Mexico in Crisis, 2nd ed.* New York: Holmes and Meier, 1983. An important study of Mexican politics from a leftist perspective, this book is also very useful because of its treatment of the history of the Mexican Revolution, its institutionalization, and the formation of the ruling political party.

Informe. This annual report by Mexico's president is one of the most valuable sources on Mexican politics and policies. It consists of a compendium of figures, a review of the previous year's performance (hardly an impartial one, of course), and a prognosis of what is to come. The report is reproduced in the major newspapers, and it is usually made available as a separate document by the office of the president (and sometimes in translation by the U.S. embassy).

Levy, Daniel, and Gabriel Székely. *Mexico: Paradoxes of Stability and Change.* 2nd ed. Boulder, Colo.: Westview Press, 1987. An outstanding brief text, this book discusses Mexican politics and government from precolonial days to the time of President de la Madrid.

Lustig, Nora. *Mexico: The Remaking of an Economy.* Washington, D.C.: Brookings Institution, 1992.

Meyer, Michael C., and William L. Sherman. *The Course of Mexican History.* New York: Oxford University Press, 1979. This is a highly readable and well-researched history of Mexico from pre-Cortés times to the election of President José López Portillo.

Needler, Martin C. *Mexican Politics: The Containment of Conflict.* 3rd edition. New York: Praeger, 1995. This general book covers the country's history, geography, economy, and social structure—as well as its politics—from the same point of view as this chapter.

_____. *Politics and Society in Mexico.* Albuquerque: University of New Mexico Press, 1971. Interpretive essays, generally optimistic and favorable in tone.

Pastor, Robert A., and Jorge Castañeda. *Limits to Friendship: The United States and Mexico.* New York: Knopf, 1988. A U.S. and a Mexican authority have written alternating chapters in this illuminating book about U.S.–Mexican relations and the misperceptions that have hampered their greater cooperation.

Paz, Octavio. *The Labyrinth of Solitude.* Translated by Lysander Kemp. New York: Grove Press, 1961. A brilliant discussion of the national character of Mexico by one of the country's leading men of letters.

Philip, George. *The Presidency in Mexico.* New York: St. Martin's Press, 1992. Examination of the terms of the recent presidents that takes into account psychological as well as political and economic factors.

Raat, W. Dirk, and William H. Beezley. *Twentieth Century Mexico*. Lincoln: University of Nebraska Press, 1986. This highly worthwhile anthology contains chapters that usefully explain Mexico "from Porfirio Díaz to petrodollars."

Ruíz, Ramón Eduardo. *The Great Rebellion: Mexico, 1905–1924*. New York: W. W. Norton,
1980. This is a well-researched and fully footnoted study of the events, conditions, and
leaders that made the Mexican Revolution. It concludes that the Revolution was a bourgeois revolt, led by middle-class dissidents, that did not produce the social and economic
justice some of its rhetoric promised.

Selee, Andrew D., ed. *Mexico in Transition*, Washington, D.C.: Woodrow Wilson Center,
2003. Summary reports on various aspects of Mexico's society, economics, and politics by
leading commentators.

Wilkie, James W., and Albert L. Michaels. *Revolution in Mexico: Years of Upheaval,
1910–1940*. New York: Knopf, 1969. This excellent sourcebook reprints a large number of
works of various authors, as well as some original documents, and contains several useful
chronologies.

Wolf, Eric. *Sons of the Shaking Earth*. Chicago: University of Chicago Press, 1959. Written by
an anthropologist, this history of Mexico is particularly useful in regard to the pre-Cortés
and colonial periods.

Womack, John, Jr. *Zapata and the Mexican Revolution*. New York: Random House, 1970. This
is a detailed, step-by-step account of the Mexican Revolution and the part played in it by
the heroic fighter for agrarian reform.

Chapter 16

Central America: From Revolution to Neoliberal "Reform"

THOMAS W. WALKER
CHRISTINE J. WADE

THE QUARTER CENTURY FOLLOWING the victory of the Sandinista Front for National Liberation (FSLN) in Nicaragua in 1979 was a time of truly kaleidoscopic change for Central America. In the realm of politics, Nicaragua experienced revolutionary rule and a bloody and costly U.S.-orchestrated counterrevolution for almost eleven years before its people elected a conservative government more compatible with the whims of Washington. Prolonged armed struggle between revolutionary insurgents and elite-dominated regimes led eventually to a comprehensive peace settlement in El Salvador (1992) and protracted negotiations and a peace settlement in Guatemala (1996). Although they avoided armed struggle, Honduras and Costa Rica were strongly buffeted by events taking place in neighboring countries.

Political debate spilled over into religion. Progressive priests, nuns, and Catholic laypersons were moved to action on behalf of the poor through their understanding of Jesus's original message and example as a cry for social justice. These were the practitioners of liberation theology.[1] Conservative forces in Central America and elsewhere were alarmed by this progressive approach to religion, which they saw as playing into the hands of an international "Communist" conspiracy. Government troops and right-wing death squads in El Salvador and Guatemala killed progressive priests and nuns (including Archbishop Oscar Romero of El Salvador in 1980) or, particularly in Guatemala, drove them out of rural parishes where conservative Protestants then became the only religious personnel present. By the mid-1990s, liberation theology was largely in eclipse; the Catholic Church itself had become increasingly conservative, extraworldly, and, some would say, out of touch with the impoverished majority; and there were Protestant temples and chapels in even the poorest urban neighborhoods and most remote villages throughout the region.

Equally important, in most of these countries in the same short period, national economic policy based on a belief in the government's responsibility to manage the economy to ensure social justice gave way to a more market-driven approach in which the impoverished majority would be asked to wait to receive their "fair share" until some ill-defined future after the national economic pie had been allowed to grow "naturally." When the period began, Costa Rica could already boast a viable welfare state dating from the 1940s, Nicaragua was embarking on sweeping social reform orchestrated by a revolutionary government, and U.S. advisers were pushing state-run social and economic reform in El Salvador as a counterinsurgency technique. By the dawn of the twenty-first century, however, countries in the region had implemented structural reforms in varying degrees. Cuts in government bureaucracy and social services, the privatization of former government enterprises, the redirection of credit away from the peasantry into large private export activities, and a variety of other socially regressive policies designed to stimulate export were implemented to earn foreign exchange and ultimately service the region's enormous foreign debt. Many of these neoliberal policies were reminiscent of the laissez-faire, agro-export measures promoted by the region's liberal politicians of the late nineteenth and early twentieth centuries.

CONTEMPORARY DIFFERENCES AND THEIR HISTORICAL DETERMINANTS

Within this matrix of sweeping change, however, there were significant differences among the countries that deserve examination and explanation. Why, for instance, did Nicaragua, El Salvador, and Guatemala experience violent upheaval while Costa Rica and Honduras remained relatively peaceful? The answer, as John Booth and Thomas Walker suggest elsewhere,[2] probably lies in five centuries of historical formation. Put in very simple terms, the large native populations of what would become Guatemala, Nicaragua, and El Salvador were quickly conquered by invading Spaniards at the beginning of the sixteenth century, thus forming a vast, racially distinct underclass that could be exploited for the enrichment of a small European ruling class. In those countries the foundations of very inegalitarian societies were already firmly set within decades of the arrival of the conquistadors. In Costa Rica, in contrast, the native population resisted fiercely and, for their troubles, were largely exterminated or driven out of the fertile highlands where the Spanish eventually settled. With no racially distinct underclass to exploit, the society created by the Spanish settlers in Costa Rica was always relatively more egalitarian. For its part, Honduras until the twentieth century was so underpopulated and such an economic backwater that a self-confident and exploitative ruling class was slow in developing.

By the 1970s, as a result of these distinct social histories, Costa Rica had developed a functioning democracy and welfare state; Honduran governments, though not always democratic, were normally willing at least to pay lip service to grassroots demands; and the dictatorships in the other three countries had become accustomed to responding with violence to growing demands for social justice from the impoverished majority. While social problems existed throughout the region, they had been allowed to build to explosive levels only in Nicaragua, Guatemala, and El Salvador. It was primarily this built-up pressure rather than some sort of sinister "Communist" conspiracy—as the U.S. government would claim[3]—that led to the armed revolts of the 1970s and 1980s.

THE REVOLUTIONARY THREE

Though Nicaragua, El Salvador, and Guatemala share the experience of prolonged armed revolt, only in Nicaragua did the insurgents actually seize power. It is interesting to ask why insurgents succeeded there and not in the other two countries. Perhaps the best explanation is given by Timothy Wickham-Crowley.[4] Rejecting single-factor theories, he argues that four conditions were met in Nicaragua that were not fully met elsewhere in Latin America except Cuba two decades earlier: Nicaragua (and Cuba) had the right social conditions (an impoverished and exploited rural population living in very precarious circumstances); an intelligent and flexible guerrilla movement; a target regime so despicable that it had alienated most of its political base; and the right international environment (that is, a temporary lapse in U.S. support for the local dictator).

Guatemala and El Salvador met only the first two conditions. In both of the latter countries, military and eventually civilian presidents succeeded each other at relatively short intervals. Though brutal and certainly not democratic, these governments were hardly *caudillo*-dominated "mafiacracies" of the type run by Fulgencio Batista in Cuba or Anastasio Somoza in Nicaragua. As a result, much of the Salvadoran and Guatemalan upper and middle classes remained loyal to their respective regimes. In addition, alarmed by the Sandinista victory in Nicaragua, the United States—which had been immobilized by the contradictions inherent in trying to promote human rights in Somoza's Nicaragua—now focused on preventing leftist victories in the other two countries, often with little regard to human rights.

Therefore, with the backing of the United States and privileged domestic groupings, Salvadoran and Guatemalan regimes were able to ward off rebel takeovers. But their victories and the rebels' failures were certainly not absolute. Even though they did not come to power, the rebels in both countries achieved some measure of success in that they eventually forced their foes to accept major changes in historically repressive systems as their price for peace.

Nicaragua

The Sandinista Period. From July 19, 1979, to April 25, 1990, Nicaragua had an avowedly revolutionary government. However, sobered by an awareness of the weakness of the socialist model of the Soviet Union and the Eastern

European countries[5] and some obvious excesses of the Cuban experiment (for example, the cult of personality and overnationalization of the economy), the Sandinistas developed policies that were actually quite moderate and pragmatic.

The Sandinista revolution can be divided into two periods: transition and reconstruction (1979–1984) and the constitutional period (1985–1990). The first was a time of innovation, experimentation, some excesses, yet a number of successes. In the second, the U.S.-orchestrated Contra war, though never a military threat, inflicted such heavy economic and human damage that the revolution began to unravel and was eventually voted out of office.

The Period of Transition.   The economic policy adopted during the period of transition and maintained thereafter was one of a mixed economy. Confiscation of property was confined mainly to land and enterprises owned by ousted dictator Anastasio Somoza and his henchmen. Though these were turned into public enterprises or cooperatives or parceled out to the poor, around 60 percent of the productive capacity of the country remained in private hands throughout the revolution. Indeed, though very nervous about the intent of the Sandinistas, the private sector was actually encouraged, through favorable exchange rates and other measures, to remain productive.

Complementing these domestic economic policies, the Sandinistas pursued international policies—renegotiating and servicing the national debt and writing liberal foreign investment laws—designed to maintain Nicaragua's credit in Western circles. These policies paid off. From 1979 through 1983, Nicaragua's gross domestic product per capita grew 7 percent, while Central America as a whole suffered a decline of 14.7 percent.[6] It was only in the wake of the full impact of the Contra war and a U.S.-orchestrated international credit boycott that the Nicaraguan economy began to decline (1984) and then plummet (1985 onward).

The new government also oversaw innovative and highly successful social projects during this period. Inexpensive, grassroots-based programs for literacy (1980) and health (beginning in 1981) brought such positive change that by 1984 even President Reagan's Kissinger Commission had to admit that "Nicaragua's government has made significant gains against illiteracy and disease."[7]

There was also much innovation and some success in the area of politics and government. First, the government encouraged the creation or strengthening of massive grassroots organizations representing neighborhoods, women, youth, urban and rural workers, and peasants. These groupings in turn were given the responsibility of articulating the interests of their constituencies and delegated the task of implementing programs designed to help the people (the literacy crusade, health work days, neighborhood watches). By 1984, an in-house U.S. embassy report placed membership in these organizations at 700,000 to 800,000, the equivalent of about half of the population aged sixteen or over.[8]

The revolution also moved during this time from transitional to elected constitutional government. The first institutions of government were a multiperson executive, or junta; a corporative legislature (Council of State); and a judiciary composed of the usual lower and higher courts plus People's Anti-Somoza Tribunals set up to process Somoza-era war criminals but later used to deal with Contras. By 1983, however, the Council of State was writing election and party laws (designed with the advice of the Swedish Electoral Commission and modeled after Western European practices) that would enable the holding of a clean, competitive, internationally monitored[9] election in November 1984 and the swearing-in of a Constituent Assembly and an elected president, Daniel Ortega, in 1985.

Finally, in the area of human rights, Sandinista performance, though not perfect, was better than that of most other contemporary Latin American governments—and strikingly good compared with that of U.S. client regimes in northern Central America. There were restrictions of civil liberties, as take place almost anywhere when a country is under siege, but freedom of religion was generally respected, there were no death squads, and extralegal deprivation of life was relatively infrequent.[10]

The worst problems Nicaragua encountered during the early 1980s were in foreign affairs, particularly with the United States. Though the Sandinistas repeatedly expressed their interest in having good relations with the superpower to the north, the victory of revolutionaries in Nicaragua—and the specter of a "second Cuba"—had alarmed Washington from the very beginning.[11] While the Carter administration was frigid but correct in its relations with the new government in Nicaragua, the Reagan administration, inaugurated in January 1981, set out immediately to destroy what it portrayed as a dangerous extension of Soviet and Cuban influence into Central America. Almost immediately, it began training, equipping, and directing a Nicaraguan exile counterrevolutionary ("Contra") army to fight against its own government; used its influence to block normal World Bank and Inter-American Development Bank loans to the upstart state; and orchestrated a massive propaganda campaign and program of dirty tricks to discredit the Sandinistas.[12]

The Constitutional Period.   The second half of the Sandinista period was marked both by significant achievements and serious economic, social, and political setbacks. Respect for human rights continued at a relatively high level. New governmental institutions were created by the Constituent Assembly elected in 1984. After much open public debate, a new constitution was promulgated in 1987. That same year, an innovative autonomy law for the peoples of the Atlantic Coast was formalized. Later, new parties and electoral laws were passed (1988) and amended (1989), laying the groundwork for a second clean, internationally supervised election in February 1990. Two months later, the losing FSLN turned over the reins of power to the victorious opposition.

But this was also a time of hardship that ultimately led to the defeat of the FSLN at the polls. The cost of the Contra war, U.S.-orchestrated international economic strangulation, and some Sandinista mismanagement combined to produce such a collapse of the economy that by 1988, hyperinflation had reached over 33,000 percent annually. Though the Sandinistas implemented structural reforms that year and the next that would cut inflation to 1,690 percent by 1989,[13] the unemployment and social pain these early neoliberal policies caused was enormous. Added to this, cutbacks in government social programs and the tremendous human cost of the war (almost 31,000 dead[14] and many more wounded and maimed) created an environment in which the U.S.-organized, -managed, and -funded National Opposition Union (UNO) was able to defeat the Sandinistas handily in the 1990 election.[15]

The Post-Sandinista Period.[16]   Violeta Barrios de Chamorro, elected president with 55 percent of the vote, was inaugurated in April 1990 for a term of office that would expire almost seven years later. Though a political novice with only a high school education, Chamorro would eventually score some important successes. Her economic policies cut inflation to relatively low levels and by the mid-1990s actually led to modest overall growth for the first time in over a decade.

Her greatest achievements, however, lay in the area of peacemaking and reconciliation. After months of negotiation, the Contra war was brought to an end in mid-1990. By cleverly allowing Sandinista general Humberto Ortega to oversee that otherwise difficult task, Chamorro was able to bring the size of the Sandinista People's Army down from over 80,000 to under 15,000. Finally, Chamorro steadfastly eschewed pressure from the United States (until 1993) and right-wing members of UNO to engage in a vengeful "desandinization" program for the country. As a result, a new political normalcy gradually developed. Negotiations in the National Assembly led to the promulgation of a new Military Code (1994) and some revisions in the 1987 Constitution (1995). Elections on the Atlantic Coast (1994) and nationwide (1996) were carried out without a major hitch. In January 1997, Chamorro passed the reins of office to Arnoldo Alemán of the National Liberal Alliance.

There were also notable failures in this period. The most glaring were in the social area. The neoliberal economic policies urged on Nicaragua by Washington and the international financial community and enthusiastically implemented by the Chamorro administration pummeled the poor majority. The downsizing of government, cutbacks in social services, privatization of state enterprises, credit emphasis on agro-export rather than peasant production of domestic foodstuffs, and so on combined to exacerbate the misery of ordinary people. Unemployment, underemployment, crime rates, drug addiction, domestic violence, homelessness (especially among children) all soared.

This was accompanied by a growing sense of cynicism about politicians and government institutions. In ethically dubious, self-serving legislation, some top Sandinista leaders had appropriated large amounts of property in the last months of their administration. Also, it soon appeared that both Arnoldo Alemán and Antonio Lacayo (Chamorro's son-in-law) had increased their fortunes through corruption while serving, respectively, as mayor of Managua and minister of the presidency before launching their presidential campaigns in

1996. Thus, ironically, while Nicaraguans retained faith in elections and the electoral process, many by the mid-1990s were bitterly skeptical about politicians, parties, and most institutions of government.

The unprecedented corruption of the Alemán administration further depleted funds that might have been available to help impoverished Nicaraguans. This corruption, combined with the further destruction of the social service infrastructure, defined Alemán's presidency. Such corruption was dramatically illustrated in the wake of Hurricane Mitch in October 1998, which left 2,400 Nicaraguans dead and another 700,000 displaced. Spending cuts in social services and the armed forces left the Nicaraguan government incapable of responding to the crisis in any meaningful way. Instead, Nicaragua relied heavily on international aid. When Alemán tried to channel relief funds through departments where the Liberal Party was in control or through Liberal Party headquarters where it was not, international donors resorted to the unusual practice of channeling assistance through nongovernmental organizations rather than the government.

Negotiations between Alemán and Daniel Ortega hurt Nicaragua's democracy in late 1999 with the Ortega-Alemán Pact, which sought to consolidate the emerging two-party system. The electoral laws passed in early 2000 by the FSLN/PLC* legislative majority, represented an effort to eliminate third parties. Additionally, the Supreme Court, the Office of the Comptroller General, and the Supreme Electoral Council were all packed with FSLN/PLC partisans. Finally, former presidents were made legislators for life, hence making them immune to prosecution.

The 2001 elections were relatively clean procedurally despite being designed to favor the two major parties. Enrique Bolaños, Alemán's Vice President, defeated the FSLN's Ortega by pledging to battle corruption and impunity in Nicaraguan politics. For his part, Ortega argued, with justification, that the United States had actively worked to prevent his reelection. As in 1990 and 1996, U.S. pressure shaped the outcome of the 2001 elections. Playing on the events of September 11, 2001, the U.S.-alleged connections between Ortega and "terrorists," while actively supporting Bolaños' candidacy. When Bolaños entered office in 2002, he appealed to the National Assembly to repeal Alemán's legislative immunity and used the legal system to pursue him and other individuals in his corrupt administration. At the time of this writing, Alemán was in prison awaiting trial on charges of laundering and embezzling more than $100 million.

El Salvador

Insurgency and Counterinsurgency: 1979–1992. The 1970s had been a time of tremendous mobilization in Salvadoran society. Social democratic and Christian democratic parties, as well as segments of the Catholic Church and

---

*Sandinista Front for National Liberation (FSLN)
Liberal Constitutionalist Party (PLC)

even the U.S. Agency for International Development and the U.S. Peace Corps had promoted development projects and grassroots participation. Salvadoran elites and the military regimes they supported, however, viewed this phenomenon with alarm and responded to it with repression. Apparent opposition victories in both the 1972 and 1977 elections were overturned as increasingly brutal military regimes used security forces and associated death squads to kill party, interest group, and religious leaders working with the masses. Responding to this repression, groups of various political affiliations fielded small guerrilla armies that in 1980 would unite into the Farabundo Martí National Liberation Front (FMLN).

The Sandinista victory in Nicaragua alarmed defenders of the status quo and heartened popular organizations in El Salvador. Convinced that it was now possible to topple the dictatorship, the FMLN began preparing for its (unsuccessful) "final offensive" of early 1981. At the same time, sobered by events in Nicaragua, the Salvadoran elite and the U.S. government took measures to prevent a repetition. Within days of the Nicaraguan victory, planners in Washington had decided that in order to justify beefing up the Salvadoran military, the existing regime would have to be replaced with a cosmetically more acceptable government run by a junta combining both progressive military and civilian members.[17] On October 15, 1979, a military coup by "moderates" essentially implemented this objective.

For the following twelve years, the forces of the status quo would pursue a two-pronged strategy for containing revolution. On the one hand, until the end of the Cold War, Washington would insist on military victory over the insurgents. In these years it would give its ally in the war against "communism" over $6 billion in aid—much of it military aid to security forces that were responsible for killing most of the 75,000 people (mainly civilians) who died during the conflict. Though Salvadoran regimes, especially in the late 1980s, would occasionally go through the motions of negotiating, no serious effort to arrive at a peace accord was made.

On the other hand, in order to get a reluctant U.S. Congress to provide the arms necessary to implement the overall military strategy, it was also necessary for Salvadoran governments to appear both democratic and progressive. Accordingly, after several years of civilian-military juntas in which civilians had no real power, elections for a Constituent Assembly (1982) and then president (1984) were held. Staged against a background of state-sponsored terror and in the absence of a free press, these elections—in which voting was obligatory and the sequentially numbered, translucent ballots were deposited in clear plastic ballot boxes—produced the presidencies of conservative Christian Democrat José Napoleón Duarte in 1984 and right-wing Nationalist Republican Alliance (ARENA) Party member Alfredo Cristiani in 1989.

At the same time, government social policy took an apparently more humane turn. Immediately after the Sandinista victory in Nicaragua, Salvadoran regimes (under tremendous U.S. pressure) actually seemed to be competing in the social realm with the Nicaraguan revolution.[18] The first junta, like the Sandinista government, implemented sweeping agrarian reform programs and nationalized the banking industry. Though some of this reform was stillborn and much of the rest was reversed after a right-wing victory in the 1982 Constituent Assembly elections, heavy aid from the United States allowed various civic action and other programs to continue throughout the period.

Meanwhile, responding to international reality, the FMLN modified its objectives in the early 1980s. By 1982, the guerrillas had come to realize that an all-out victory would, in the words of their civilian ally Rubén Zamora, "be ashes in our mouths."[19] They had seen what the United States was already doing to the Nicaraguan revolution. And, though they still had confidence that they could win militarily, they had decided instead to fight only until the regime agreed to a peace treaty instituting major changes in the military, political, and social character of the system.

The war dragged on, with Washington and the Salvadoran military pushing for all-out victory and the guerrillas fighting to achieve a negotiated settlement. By the end of 1989, it looked as if the stalemate was beginning to break. Early that year the government refused an opposition request to delay the national election in order to institute democratic safeguards so that FMLN candidates might participate. That November, in response, the FMLN staged a massive assault on the city of San Salvador, taking over and holding whole neighborhoods for weeks at a time. In addition, under the cover of the turmoil of that period, the U.S.-trained Atlacatl Battalion (under orders of the Army High Command) entered the grounds of the Central American University and executed six prominent Jesuit intellectuals, their maid, and her daughter.

As a result of all this, it was now very clear that (1) the FMLN was still alive and effective, and (2) the regime was still badly in need of reform. Thus, when the Soviet Union collapsed a little over a year later, the first Bush administration decided to cut its losses in El Salvador by reversing its position on negotiations. As a major report on El Salvador prepared for the U.S. Defense Department put it, with the end of the Cold War, "'Winning' in El Salvador no longer matters much. A negotiated solution, or even 'losing,' would no longer carry the same ominous significance."[20] Now, with the full backing of Washington and even such right-wing Salvadorans as Roberto D'Aubuisson, the United Nations could move ahead and broker a formal peace.

The Imperfect Peace: 1992 Onward. The peace accords of January 1992 encompassed most of the reforms and changes the FMLN had proposed almost a decade earlier. Under UN supervision, the government was to depoliticize and drastically reduce the size of its army. It was obliged to abolish "rapid deployment" forces (such as the Atlacatl Battalion), the Treasury Police, and the National Guard. The hated National Police would be replaced by a Civil Police in which veterans of the conflict would be drawn equally from both sides and, together, would constitute less than half of the force. An ad hoc commission was to be named to provide a list of war criminals to be purged from the armed forces. Once that purging had taken place, a truth commission was to make a report on war crimes committed by both sides and by civilians. On another plane, there were to be significant reforms of electoral mechanisms and of the judiciary. And land and resources were to be set aside to resettle former combatants from both sides. In return, the FMLN was to demobilize.

The peace accords were in fact implemented, if imperfectly and slowly. The FMLN demobilized, if a bit behind schedule, and turned over most—but apparently not all[21]—of its weapons. The ad hoc and truth commissions performed their duties bravely. The armed forces were reduced, reorganized, and purged, though at a slow pace and not as originally stipulated. Sweeping changes were made in the police forces, though not to the extent envisioned in the accords. Limited changes were made in the corrupt judicial system. In 1994, a much-observed national election took place in which the FMLN was allowed to participate—but on a far-from-level playing field.[22] As a result of the 1994 election, the candidate of the ruling ARENA Party, Armando Calderón Sol, was inaugurated president on June 1. Though ARENA won the largest block of seats in the Legislative Assembly, the FMLN came in second ahead of the Christian Democrats, who had been discredited by corruption and ineffective rule.

Calderón Sol deepened the neoliberal program by reducing tariffs, increasing the already regressive value-added tax from 10 to 13 percent, privatizing the Salvadoran telecommunications and electrical industries, and establishing a convertability plan that pegged the Salvadoran colon to the U.S. dollar. This uncompromising pursuit of neoliberal policies was the source of great tension within ARENA, pitting the industrialists against the traditional agricultural elites. While the early 1990s were a period of economic growth, averaging 6 percent annually between 1990 and 1995, economic growth averaged only 3 percent from 1996 to 2000.[23] Despite overall economic growth, poverty remained rampant, with nearly one-half of Salvadorans living below the poverty line.[24]

The FMLN was able to capitalize on ARENA's internal troubles and increasing public dissatisfaction with neoliberal policies in the 1997 legislative and municipal elections, winning twenty-seven legislative seats and forty-eight mayoral contests, including the one in the capital. While ARENA maintained a majority of the seats in the Legislative Assembly and mayoralities, the FMLN clearly demonstrated its fortitude as a political party. The FMLN's electoral success at the legislative and municipal levels failed to translate into a presidential win in the 1999 presidential elections. FMLN candidate Facundo Guardado was easily defeated by ARENA's Francisco Flores.

The Flores administration continued the neoliberal thrust of his predecessors, overseeing conversion to the U.S. dollar in 2001. The plan to privatize the segments of the health care sector resulted in two prolonged and bitter strikes, which occurred against the backdrop of the 2000 and 2003 elections. Like his predecessors, Flores's application of the neoliberal model was resolute. However, El Salvador managed to avoid any significant popular opposition to the neoliberal model due to the influx of remittances from Salvadorans living abroad, which were $2 billion in 2002.[25]

In the 2000 elections the FMLN became the largest political party and secured some of the largest municipalities, gaining four seats in the Legislative Assembly and winning seventy-seven (ten in coalition races) mayoralities. While the FMLN did not make significant gains in the 2003 legislative and municipal elections, the party was able to maintain its thirty-one seats in the Legislative Assembly while ARENA lost two seats. Additionally, the FMLN retained its mayoral post in San Salvador despite losing very popular two-time mayor Hector Silva as a candidate. Little more than a decade after the signing of the peace accords, the FMLN had clearly demonstrated its potency as a political party. Such potency caught the attention of the United States, whereupon the former U.S. ambassador and other officials publicly expressed their "concern" over the prospect of a FMLN presidential victory in 2004. As was the case in Nicaragua in 2001, U.S. diplomats engaged in the undiplomatic practice of favoring (or disparaging) candidates in an effort to manipulate the outcome of the elections.

Guatemala

The Guatemalan experience in the same period bore both striking similarities to and important differences from that of El Salvador. There, too, bloody civil war raged throughout the late 1970s and 1980s, and the possibility for real peace emerged only after the end of the Cold War and a change in policy in Washington. And as in El Salvador, the guerrilla strategy of fighting to force reform of a previously brutal system seemed by 1996 to pay off. However, unlike the case in El Salvador, the U.S. role in the conflict—though very real—was somewhat less visible, and the Guatemalan military appeared to be a bit more autonomous. In addition, the peace settlement would be negotiated (and implemented) in a step-by-step fashion over a period of more than half a decade rather than all at once as in El Salvador.

By the late 1970s, Guatemala had already experienced almost two decades of bloody civil war. Frustrated by the destruction of the democratic revolution in 1954 and by a U.S.-approved military coup that blocked the return to elected civilian rule in 1963, some Guatemalans had turned to armed insurrection. In response, the United States had trained the Guatemalan army and security forces in the methods of counterinsurgency and "counterterror." By 1966, death squads had begun to operate and the term "disappeared" was first used as a noun to refer to victims of these tactics. By 1979, thousands of people— mainly civilians—had already been killed and a long series of military dictatorships had ruled the country.

As in El Salvador, U.S. policy toward Guatemala was often two-tracked.[26] On the one hand, there was the primordial need to "stop communism." On the other, it was always important to appear concerned with human rights and democracy. Early in his administration, Jimmy Carter's criticism of Guatemalan human rights violations had led to a rupture in the flow of open military aid. Though Washington obviously hoped for a Salvador-type coup that would justify a resumption of such aid, the military clung to power until the mid-1980s, thus making it impossible to get such assistance approved by Congress. To some extent, the Reagan administration got around the problem by relabeling as "civilian" such obviously military items as helicopters; by successfully pressuring Israel—the world's leading recipient of U.S. assistance—to increase arms assistance to Guatemala;[27] and by continuing both covert CIA assistance and the U.S. military's counterinsurgency advisory role.

But by the early 1980s, things seemed to be getting out of hand. President/General Lucas García (1978–1982) sharply increased already high levels of repression. As a result, the divided guerrilla opposition came together in one organization, the Guatemalan National Revolutionary Unity (URNG), in 1982. Replacing Lucas in a coup d'état that same year, President/General Efrain Ríos Montt increased the repression even more. Altogether, in a scorched-earth war that lasted from 1981 through 1983, between 100,000 and 150,000 civilians were killed, hundreds of villages were destroyed, and over 1 million persons were displaced.[28]

Though the United States had approved of Guatemala's dirty war, it eventually became the better part of wisdom to push for the emergence of a more cosmetically acceptable system. The vehicle for this policy was General Oscar Humberto Mejía Victores, who overthrew Ríos Montt in 1983. Though the brutality did not cease, a new constitution was written, an election was held, and a civilian president, Christian Democrat Vinicio Cerezo, was inaugurated in 1986.

It would be hard to argue that democracy in Guatemala was born again in 1986. Though the constitution was a reasonably good one and the elections were fairly clean from a procedural standpoint, the fact that the former was frequently violated, that the latter had been held against a background of state-sponsored terror, and that the military, rather than the new president, continued to hold real power obviated such claims. Nevertheless an atmosphere of "possibility" began to emerge. For its part, the URNG—by now convinced that outright military victory was neither possible nor desirable for the guerrillas—began calling for a negotiated settlement. In August of the following year, President Cerezo and the other four presidents of Central America signed the Esquipulas Peace Accord, which, after the end of the Cold War four years later, would serve as a rough framework for peacemaking in Guatemala.

With its ally's surface "democratization" in the mid-1980s, the Reagan administration was able to get Congress to approve military aid for Guatemala. The war dragged on, and not much was done to promote a general settlement throughout the rest of the Cerezo administration. However, as the Cold War was winding down, the Catholic Church and then important civilian groups began to establish a dialogue with the URNG. Finally, in 1991, newly inaugurated, conservative president Jorge Serrano began negotiating directly with the guerrillas. In 1992, an agreement on democratization and some discussion of human rights took place. The following year, after Serrano tried (and failed) to seize dictatorial powers, he was removed from office by the military and replaced with former human rights ombudsman Ramiro de León Carpio. Though negotiations stalled for a while, they picked up again in January 1994 and resulted in a framework accord for the negotiation of a settlement to be brokered by the United Nations. This was followed in rapid succession by a global human rights accord in March and two accords in June, one dealing with the resettlement of displaced populations and the other with the creation of a truth commission. In March 1995, a landmark identity and rights of indigenous peoples accord was signed—very important for a country in which over 60 percent of the population is indigenous.

In November 1995, the possibilities of a comprehensive peace moved forward even farther as Alvaro Arzú, a conservative who understood that civil war is bad for business, was elected president. Negotiations were accelerated. In March 1996, the URNG declared an open-ended cessation of hostilities, and the army soon followed suit. This was followed in September by the landmark Accord on the Strengthening of Civilian Power and the Function of the Army. Finally, in December, the two sides signed a definitive ceasefire, an Accord on Constitutional and Electoral Reforms, Bases for the Incorporation of the URNG into Legality, and, at the end of the month, the final comprehensive peace settlement. All said, these appeared to constitute a truly revolutionary end to the war.

The revelry of the Guatemalan peace process was short-lived. The April 1998 assassination of Bishop Juan Gerardi shortly after his presentation of the Recovery of Historical Memory (REMHI) report revealed atrocities committed during the war, most of them attributed to the armed forces, was a sober reminder that the road to peace would not be smooth.[29] This atmosphere was reinforced when the truth commission's report was unveiled in 1999. President Arzú downplayed the report and openly rejected the commission's recommendations. The peace accords received another blow in May 1999 when a referendum on constitutional reforms (including judicial and military reform) required to implement some provisions of the accords was defeated at the polls.

Arzú's failure to address the socioeconomic concerns of the Guatemalan people was a far greater factor in the 1999 elections than issues surrounding the peace accords. Alfonso Portillo, candidate of a rival conservative party, the Guatemalan Republican Front (FRG), easily defeated the PAN candidate in the second round. The FRG, comprised of numerous former army officers, dominated the Congress—with former dictator Ríos Montt presiding.[30] Portillo fared no better than his predecessors in battling corruption, improving social conditions, or furthering the peace accords. His administration was plagued by corruption and stagnation.

Guatemala's peace process had not been as successful as El Salvador's. The lack of political will was the most persistent problem in ensuring their successful implementation. Additionally, the URNG did not hold the political clout or support that the FMLN continued to enjoy in El Salvador. As such, many important terms of the peace accords were ignored or delayed. Additionally, human rights abuses and intimidation of human rights workers persisted in Guatemala. Maneuvers by Ríos Montt, whose candidacy the U.S. outwardly shunned, to insert himself into the 2003 presidential race further demonstrated that Guatemala's peace was imperfect.

Although he came in a distant third, Ríos Montt won nearly 20 percent of the vote.[31] His presence was enough to force a second round of voting between National Unity of Hope (UNE) candidate Alvaro Colom and Great Alliance (GANA) candidate Oscar Berger. Former Guatemala City mayor Berger defeated Colom in the second round, promising jobs and a renewed focus on peace accords.

THE "TRANQUIL TWO"

Honduras

Having experienced decades of military rule, Honduras was certainly no democracy as it entered the period examined in this chapter. However, its military was different from that of the three neighboring republics in that it believed in responding to grassroots mobilization with reform and co-optation rather than with repression.[32] As a result, tiny guerrilla groups that appeared in the 1960s and 1970s never gained legitimacy or support.

In the late 1970s, as part of its policy of promoting human rights, the Carter administration began pressuring Honduras to return to democratic forms. The regime of President/General Policarpio Paz García responded by holding Constituent Assembly elections in 1980 and full national elections in 1981. The winner of the presidential race, Liberal candidate Roberto Suazo Córdova, was inaugurated early in 1982.

As it turns out, Suazo Córdova would be president in name only. By the time he donned the sash of office, the United States was deeply involved in containing "communism" in El Salvador and programming the Contra war in Nicaragua. Nestled between the two, Honduras was seen as an ideal base of operation for many aspects of these two projects. Salvadoran military personnel would be trained in Honduras to circumvent a ceiling Congress had placed on the number of U.S. military advisers to be sent to El Salvador. Honduran and Salvadoran forces would perform pincer operations on the border to annihilate Salvadoran civilian populations thought loyal to the guerrillas. Nearly continuous joint U.S.-Honduran military "training" exercises—designed to intimidate the Sandinistas—would be conducted on Honduran territory close to the Nicaraguan border. Several U.S. military bases would be built. And Honduran troops and civilians would be moved out of some territory bordering Nicaragua to allow the Nicaraguan Contras sanctuaries out of which to operate against their own government.

To do all of these things, the United States worked closely with the Honduran military while essentially ignoring the weak civilian government. In the early 1980s, Honduras received hundreds of millions of dollars in U.S. aid, much of it military. CIA asset General Gustavo Alvarez became the head of the military and virtual dictator of the country in 1982. For the first time in Honduran history, death squads became active, as opponents to the military were murdered or disappeared by the hundreds. Meanwhile, Alvarez and his clique reportedly "embezzled over $30 million of public funds."[33]

By 1984, Alvarez, who had gone beyond bounds acceptable even to the military, was replaced in an internal military coup by another general with CIA connections, Walter López Reyes. From then until the end of the Cold War, a growing segment in Honduran society would call for a return to real civilian rule, an end to human rights abuses, and greater U.S. respect for their country's sovereignty. Nominal civilian presidents came and went as Suazo Córdova was succeeded in 1986 by fellow Liberal José Azcona Hoyos, who in turn passed the presidential sash to Nationalist Leonardo Callejas in 1990.

In August 1987, Honduras agreed to the Esquipulas peace framework for Central America. However, under pressure from the United States (which was still pursuing the dream of military victory over the "communists" in Nicaragua and El Salvador), it failed to fulfill its obligations—most important, that of not allowing its territory to be used by irregular troops (the Contras) attacking the government of a neighboring country (Nicaragua). Widespread dissatisfaction with U.S. and Contra troop presence in Honduras simmered throughout the 1980s. On April 7, 1988, after the United States engineered the illegal extradition of an accused drug trafficker from Honduras, thousands of enraged students set fire to the U.S. consulate building in Tegucigalpa. It is probably significant that the Honduran police took over two hours to respond to calls for assistance from the embassy.

In the long run, the Honduran people would have to wait until the end of the Cold War and the demobilization of the Contras for their country to return to some form of normalcy. Even then, Rafael Leonardo Callejas in the early 1990s would refuse to reform the military, and human rights abuses, a legacy of the early 1980s, would continue at high levels. To make matters worse, as part of an overall package of neoliberal reforms, an Agricultural Modernization Act would be passed in 1992 that would partially dismantle Honduras's earlier agrarian reform laws, thus threatening the interests of members of agricultural cooperatives.

Understandably, the inauguration of human rights lawyer Carlos Roberto Reina of the Liberal Party as president in 1994 was cause for hope for many Hondurans. The new president, while pursuing generally neoliberal economic policies, was at least willing to negotiate with those sectors of society (peasants, workers, and so on) upon which these policies had the biggest negative impact. In addition, he moved decisively to curb the inordinate power of the military. The secret police were abolished. Obligatory military service was ended in 1994. In 1997, military control of police was transferred to civilian authority, and a civilian police force was created. Trials of military officers charged with atrocities during the early 1980s were held and their outcomes were upheld by the Supreme Court—despite three amnesty laws passed during previous, more subservient administrations. The administration also ended the military's control of various nonmilitary entities such as the telecommunications industry and immigration services.

In 1997, Carlos Flores Facussé of the Partido Liberal (PLH) defeated former Tegucigalpa mayor Nora Gunera de Malgar of the Partido Nacional (PN).[34] Flores's economic plan proposed to strengthen the neoliberal model through the expansion of the maquila industry, increasing tourism, and strengthening the agro-export sector. The neoliberal reforms of the 1990s exacerbated decades of environmental devastation, including deforestation, soil erosion, and urban migration.[35] Many peasants displaced by agribusiness settled on the unstable hillsides of Tegucigalpa and Choluteca. The results would be horrific.

In October 1998, Hurricane Mitch devastated Honduras. The human toll was immense. Official records indicate 5,657 dead, 8,058 missing, 12,272 injured, and 1.5 million displaced. Many of those affected were migrants who had settled on the crowded hillsides surrounding Tegucigalpa. Some 35,000 homes were destroyed and another 50,000 damaged. The hurricane caused nearly $4 billion in economic losses. The costs of Hurricane Mitch forced Honduras to seek relief under the World Bank's Heavily Indebted Poor Countries (HIPC) initiative, permitting the suspension of payments on its $4.4 billion debt until 2007 and cancellation of $768 million of its debt balance.[36] The incompetence of the military demonstrated by its lack of preparedness in responding to Hurricane Mitch resulted in action by Congress to further demilitarize the country. In 1999, the military was placed under civilian rule, the president was given direct command of the armed forces, and the first civilian defense minister with any real power was appointed.

As in other Central American countries, Honduras experienced a prolonged crime wave. Gang activity, extrajudicial killings, and common street crime became all too common in Honduras's two major cities, Tegucigalpa (the capital) and San Pedro Sula (the business center). More than 100,000 members belonged to 500 gangs (or *Maras*), primarily in the two cities. Much of the crime wave was blamed on gang activity, a belief promulgated by the media despite the fact that only a small portion of the murders committed in Honduras were attributed to gangs.

One of the most disturbing trends of the crime wave was the extrajudicial killings of Honduran youth, portayed in the media as gang members. Between 1998 and 2002, more than 1,500 youths were murdered, more than 40 percent of whom were under the age of 18. Casa Alianza, a human rights organization working with street children, attributes some of these deaths to state police and private security forces. Similar reports by other groups, including Amnesty International, suggest that police and security forces engaged in "social cleansing" to combat crime. Equally disturbing is the impunity with which these murders were committed.[37]

Crime was a major theme of the 2001 presidential elections. Ricardo Maduro (National Party), former central bank president and successful businessman, promised a crackdown on crime, corruption, and inequality. Maduro, whose own son was killed in a bungled kidnapping, defeated Liberal

Party candidate Rafael Pineda. Maduro enlisted 10,000 officers to wage his war against crime and appointed a military official as the head of security, which led to concerns of a regression toward the militarization of the police force.[38]

The socioeconomic realities of Honduras complicated efforts to reverse the crime wave. More than one-half of the Honduran population lived in poverty. Unemployment and income inequality persist at high levels. All of these conditions were exacerbated by Hurricane Mitch and the subsequent drought. Additionally, Honduras's ability to address such vital issues is hindered by its debt burden and implementation of neoliberal reforms. Honduras was spending more servicing its debt than on health care and education combined. Thus, Honduras's transition to democracy was far more precarious than those of its revolutionary neighbors.

Costa Rica

Costa Rica remained the country with the strongest democratic traditions and most egalitarian society in Central America. Its formal democratic system continued to function without a major hitch, although increasing voter abstention was cause for concern. Conservative Unity (Unidad) president Rodrigo Carazo (1978–1982) was followed in office by Party of National Liberation (PLN) presidents Luis Alberto Monge (1982–1986) and Oscar Arias (1986–1990), Social Christian Unity Party (PUSC) president Rafael Angel Calderón (1990–1994), PLN president José María Figueres (1994–1998), PUSC president Miguel Angel Rodríguez (1998–2002), and PUSC president Abel Pacheco (2002-onward).

Similarly, Costa Rica's relatively more egalitarian social structures appeared to be holding their own. In the period 1980 to 1990, even though population grew from slightly less than 2.3 million to over 3 million and gross domestic product per capita declined slightly from $2,032 to $1,829, the frequency of households in poverty stayed constant at 19 percent, infant mortality actually dropped from nineteen per thousand to fifteen, and life expectancy increased from 72.6 to 75.6 years.[39] Costa Rica's economy was strong throughout the 1990s, averaging 5 percent growth throughout the decade. Economic growth slowed significantly in 2000, dropping from 8.4 in 1998 to 1.7 in 1000 and 1.1 in 2001. Despite this, life expectancy increased to 77.6 and the infant mortality rate dropped to nine per thousand in 2001.[40]

But even for Costa Rica, all was not well in this period. First, the Cold War struggles to the north during the 1980s inevitably had their impact on the region's most democratic republic. Attempts by the Reagan administration to involve Costa Rica in the U.S. crusade against Sandinista Nicaragua caused serious problems. During the presidencies of Rodrigo Carazo and Luis Alberto Monge, the United States operated a Contra "southern front"[41] out of Costa Rica. At the same time, it built a military airstrip and subverted Costa Rica's tradition of not having a military by pouring tens of millions of dollars into that country's "civil guard." Meanwhile, the CIA carried out dirty tricks and disseminated anti-Sandinista propaganda via segments of the

Costa Rican media that it came to influence. There were even credible charges that CIA planes carrying weapons for the Contras were off-loading in Costa Rica and returning to the United States with drugs to help pay for the Contra war.[42]

All of this offended the national sensibilities of many Costa Ricans and led to the February 1986 electoral victory of Oscar Arias, who had promised to bring such affronts to his country's sovereignty to an end. Almost immediately the airstrip was shut down for fear that "it was being used by counterrevolutionaries or by drug traffickers."[43] Arias also defied the will of the United States—at the time still bent on outright military victory over its chosen enemies—by working on a comprehensive peace plan for Central America. The Esquipulas Peace Accord of August 1987 won Arias that year's Nobel Peace Prize. Apparently annoyed by Arias's disloyalty, the United States would subsequently channel large sums of money through the National Endowment for Democracy into the conservative Costa Rican Association for the Defense of Democracy and Liberty, whose executive director, Rafael Calderón Fournier, would win the 1990 presidential election.

Though Costa Rica's Contra war–related problems would fade by the late 1980s, economic difficulties quickly took their place. A growing government deficit and foreign debt, combined with intensified pressures from international lenders, would cause the country's leaders to implement neoliberal economic reforms in the late 1980s and 1990s that would threaten the relatively egalitarian nature of the country's social system. Social spending would drop in 1989 to 1992 from slightly under 22 percent to slightly under 19 percent of gross domestic product.[44] By the mid-1990s, neoliberal policies were in play as José María Figueres was downsizing the government payroll and reducing social services, selling state enterprises, lowering tariffs, raising taxes, and "reforming" Costa Rica's unique state pension system.

The PUSC and PLN continued to dominate Costa Rican politics throughout the 1990s. In 1998, PUSC candidate Miguel Angel Rodríguez defeated PLN candidate Jose Miguel Corrales. Voter abstention, typically 20 percent, was 30 percent in the 1998 elections. While Costa Rica had been more successful than its neighbors in offsetting the costs of adjustment, opposition to neoliberal policies and public displeasure at corruption scandals began to emerge. In fact, increasing evidence suggested that Costa Ricans' confidence in political parties and government was only marginally better (and sometimes worse) than in other Central America countries.[45]

Costa Rica's traditional two-party dominant system was challenged in the 2002 elections when a coalition dedicated to transparency, accountability, and citizen participation entered the race. The Citizen's Action Party (PAC) was founded in 2001 by Ottón Solís Fallas, formerly of the PLN and the minister of planning under Oscar Arias. The PAC's platform was anti-neoliberal and opposed the privatization of the remaining state enterprises–telecommunications, electricity, oil processing, and social security among others. Its campaign against corruption and neoliberal policies was particularly appealing to the urban middle class, which had been become poorer as a result of neoliberal policies.[46]

The PAC's presence forced a runoff in the presidential election, a first in Costa Rican history.[47] In it Abel Pacheco (PUSC) defeated Rolando Araya (PLN), 58 percent to 42 percent. The election was also notable because it was the first time that the PUSC held the presidency for two successive terms. As evidence of increasing public displeasure with politics as usual, the abstention rate for the second round was 39 percent. The PAC also prevented the PUSC and PLN from holding a majority in the Legislative Assembly.[48]

Thus, even Costa Rica had not emerged from the neoliberal onslaught unscathed. While its social structures were measurably better than those of its neighbors, implementation of the neoliberal model had significant consequences for Costa Rica's political structures.

CENTRAL AMERICA IN THE TWENTY-FIRST CENTURY

It is clear that the previous quarter century under review had brought advances as well as tragedy and problems to Central America. The insurrectionary wars, and especially the U.S.-coordinated reaction to them, cost the lives of well over 300,000 people, mainly innocent civilians. Yet the political landscape of Central America was radically transformed. The political systems in Nicaragua, El Salvador, and Guatemala, though not perfect, were far more democratic than they were in the 1970s. The militaristic political culture of Honduras was transformed into one dominated by civilian control. Costa Rica remained resilient despite emerging difficulties.

However, all is not well. Neoliberalism had a significant impact on the region. Increasing disparities in wealth had led to rising levels of disenchantment among the new democracies in the region and in Costa Rica as well. The social violence of peace replaced the political violence of war, contributing to increased levels of insecurity and disillusionment with the democratic process. Despite economic growth throughout the 1990s, poverty continued to plague the region and to threaten its fragile peace. Additionally, U.S. attempts to manipulate elections in Nicaragua and El Salvador posed a serious threat to the democratic process and threatened to undermine the hard-won peace in both countries. Central America thus faced the twenty-first century with great opportunities but with tremendous challenges as well.

NOTES

1. See Edward L. Cleary, *Crisis and Change: The Church in Latin America Today* (Maryknoll, N.Y.: Orbis Books, 1985).

2. John A. Booth and Thomas W. Walker, *Understanding Central America* (Boulder, Colo.: Westview Press, 1999).

3. Washington's point of view was articulated in the Kissinger Commission Report of 1984: National Bipartisan Commission on Central America, *Report of the National Bipartisan*

Commission on Central America (Washington, D.C.: Government Printing Office, 1984). While mentioning social injustice, the report stresses the Communist conspiracy explanation.

4. Timothy P. Wickham-Crowley, *Guerrillas and Revolution in Latin America: A Comparative Study of Insurgents and Regimes Since 1956* (Princeton, N.J.: Princeton University Press, 1992).

5. In fact, Daniel Ortega once argued, if immodestly, that "it is the Sandinista Revolution which invented perestroika." In his first meeting with Mikhail Gorbachev in April 1985, he claims to have informed the new Soviet leader—who had not yet gone public with his reformist ideas—that Nicaragua was following a path very different from that of the Soviet Union with its command economy. To his surprise, Gorbachev had responded with approval. (From an Ortega interview with Pierre Hurel, "Ortega ne rend pas les armes," *Paris Match*, March 22, 1990, pp. 78–81).

6. Michael E. Conroy, "Economic Legacy and Policies: Performance and Critique," in Thomas W. Walker, ed., *Nicaragua: The First Five Years* (New York: Praeger, 1985), pp. 219–244.

7. National Bipartisan Commission on Central America, *Report of the National Bipartisan Commission*, p. 30.

8. This information was revealed by an official of the U.S. embassy to a group of which Thomas Walker was part on June 25, 1985.

9. For a discussion of that election and citation of the pertinent British Parliament and House of Lords, Irish Parliament, Dutch government, and other observer reports, see Thomas W. Walker, *Nicaragua: Living in the Shadow of the Eagle* (Boulder, Colo.: Westview Press, 1991), pp. 52 and 53, and footnotes 23 and 25 on pp. 71 and 72.

10. Michael Linfield, "Human Rights," in Thomas W. Walker, ed., *Revolution and Counterrevolution in Nicaragua* (Boulder, Colo.: Westview Press, 1996), pp. 275–294.

11. On August 2, 1979, less than two weeks after the Sandinista victory, co-author Walker had the unusual experience of being one of three academics to deliver short presentations at a dinner seminar on Central America hosted by CIA director Admiral Stansfield Turner in his executive dining room. (By prior agreement, Walker's presentation consisted of a sharp criticism of U.S. policy in Central America.) Turner, who had just left a long meeting with President Carter, set the tone of the evening with his first six words: "There can be no more Nicaraguas."

12. See Thomas W. Walker, ed., *Reagan Versus the Sandinistas: The Undeclared War on Nicaragua* (Boulder, Colo.: Westview Press, 1987).

13. Both inflation figures are from United Nations ECLAC, "Balance Preliminar de la Economía de la América Latina y el Caribe, 1990," *Notas Sobre la Economía y el Desarrollo* 500/501 (December 1990), p. 27.

14. This figure is from eight pages of charts on the human cost of the war provided Walker by the Ministry of the Presidency in January 1990.

15. William I. Robinson, *A Faustian Bargain: The U.S. Involvement in the Nicaraguan Elections and American Foreign Policy in the Post–Cold War Era* (Boulder, Colo.: Westview Press, 1992).

16. For coverage of this period, see Thomas W. Walker, ed., *Nicaragua Without Illusions: Regime Transition and Structural Adjustment in the 1990s* (Wilmington, Del.: Scholarly Resources, 1997).

17. In fact, that solution was openly discussed at the August 2, 1979, CIA dinner seminar mentioned in note 11.

18. Indeed, State Department official James Cheek, addressing a plenary session of the Latin American Studies Association congress in Washington on October 18, 1980, argued passionately—if unconvincingly—that Salvador's was the "real" revolution.

19. As part of the Presbyterian Task Force on Central America, co-author Walker had the opportunity to interview both Rubén Zamora (once) and several official spokespersons of the FMLN (twice) in Managua in November 1982.

20. Benjamin C. Schwarz, *American Counterinsurgency Doctrine and El Salvador: The Frustration of Reform and the Illusion of Nation Building* (Santa Monica, Calif.: Rand Corporation, 1991), p. xii.

21. A large cache of FMLN weapons exploded in Managua in March 1993.

22. For good coverage of the implementation of the Salvadoran peace accords, see Hemisphere Initiatives, *Justice Impugned: The Salvadoran Peace Accords and the Problem of Impunity* (Cambridge, Mass.: Hemisphere Initiatives, 1993); Jack Spence and George Vickers, with Margaret Popkin, Philip Williams, and Kevin Murray, *A Negotiated Revolution: A Two Year Progress Report on the Salvadoran Peace Accords* (Cambridge, Mass.: Hemisphere Initiatives, 1994); and Jack Spence, David R. Dye, and George Vickers, with Garth David Cheff, Carol Lynne D'Arcangelis, Pablo Galarce, and Ken Ward, *El Salvador: Elections of the Century: Results, Recommendations, Analysis* (Cambridge, Mass.: Hemisphere Initiatives, 1994).

23. El Salvador Central Bank (BCR).

24. CEPAL (2001). Total poverty in 1997 was 48 percent, while rural poverty was 62 percent and urban poverty was 26 percent.

25. In 2002, remittances accounted for 10 percent of El Salvador's GDP and were largely responsible for bolstering consumerism and managing inflation.

26. See Susanne Jonas, "Dangerous Liaisons: The U.S. in Guatemala," *Foreign Policy* 103 (Summer 1996), pp. 144–160.

27. For lengthy documentation, see Booth and Walker, *Understanding Central America*, pp. 224, 225, note 27.

28. Jonas, "Dangerous Liaisons," p. 147.

29. In June 2001, three members of the military were convicted in his death. The convictions, however, are on appeal.

30. On a positive note, the URNG coalition had a better-than-expected showing, winning 13 percent of the vote.

31. URNG candidate Rodrigo Asturias garnered less than 3 percent of the vote.

32. Rachel Sieder, "Honduras: The Politics of Exception and Military Reformism (1912–1978)," *Journal of Latin American Studies* 27, part 1 (February 1995), pp. 99–127.

33. James D. Cockcroft, *Latin America: History Politics, and U.S. Policy* (Chicago: Nelson Hall, 1996), p. 191.

34. The Liberals continued to hold a majority in congress as well as mayoral posts.

35. Jeff Boyer and Aaron Pell, "Mitch in Honduras: A Disaster Waiting to Happen," *NACLA Report on the Americas*, (September/October 1999), pp. 36–43.

36. Debt servicing consumed 46 percent of the annual budget, or nearly 23 percent of GDP.

37. United Nations Report of the Special Rapporteur, *Civil and Political Rights, Including the Question of Disappearances and Summary Executions* (United Nations Economic and Social Council Commission on Human Rights, 2003).

38. Ismael Moreno, SJ, "A New President and Cracks in the Two-Party Structure," *Envio* (January–February 2002), pp. 37–43.

39. Proyecto Estado de la Nación, *Estado de la nacion en desarrollo humano sostenible* (San Jose, Costa Rica: Estado de la Nación, 1996), p. 4.

40. World Bank Development Report 2001.

41. Former U.S. ambassador Lewis Tambs, as quoted in Cockcroft, *Latin America,* p. 240.

42. Martha Honey, *Hostile Acts: U.S. Policy in Costa Rica in the 1980s* (Gainesville, Fla.: University of Florida Press, 1993).

43. Costa Rican minister of public safety Hernán Garrón Salazar, as quoted in Cockcroft, *Latin America,* p. 240.

44. Proyecto Estado de la Nación, *Estado de la Nación,* p. 68.

45. Amaru Barahona, "Costa Rican Democracy on the Edge," *Envio* (May 2002), pp. 22–29.

46. Barahona, "Costa Rican Democracy on the Edge."

47. The PAC won 26 percent of the vote. The PUSC won 38.5 percent and PLN won 31 percent.

48. The PUSC won nineteen of the fifty-seven seats, while the PLN won seventeen and the PAC won fourteen. Two smaller parties, the PML and PRC, won six and one respectively.

Suggested Readings

Booth, John A. *Costa Rican Democracy.* Boulder, Colo.: Westview Press, 1997.

Booth, John A., and Thomas W. Walker. *Understanding Central America.* Boulder, Colo.: Westview Press, 1999.

Robinson, William I. *Transnational Conflicts: Central America, Social Change and Globalization.* London: Verso, 2003.

Sanford, Victoria. *Buried Secrets: Truth and Human Rights in Guatemala.* New York: Palgrave MacMillan, 2003.

Williams, Philip J. and Knut Walter, eds. *Militarization and Demilitarization in El Salvador's Transition to Democracy.* Pittsburgh, Pa.: University Pittsburgh Press, 1997.

Chapter 17

PANAMA AND THE CANAL

STEVE C. ROPP

PANAMA IS A COUNTRY that should be well known to every citizen of the United States because the United States was literally present at the creation. Panama gained its independence from Columbia in 1903 largely because the United States, under President Theodore Roosevelt, was interested in constructing a canal across the isthmus. After independence, U.S. citizens in large numbers journeyed to Panama to dig "the big ditch." Upon completion of the canal in 1914, many chose to stay, becoming permanent residents of the Canal Zone. In subsequent decades, the U.S. political and economic presence on the isthmus was massive, and it was not until the 1978 signing of the Torrijos-Carter treaties that the United States recognized Panama's sovereign rights in the Canal Zone.

During the 1980s, Panama remained in the public eye because of the confrontation between the U.S. government and General Manuel Antonio Noriega. The administration of President Ronald Reagan at first supported Noriega and the Panamanian Defense Forces (PDF) in exchange for the help Noriega provided in dealing with the crisis in Central America. But a policy shift began to occur in 1986 for a number of reasons, including increasing national concern about the drug problem. Beginning in 1987, both the Reagan and Bush administrations used economic sanctions and other means in an attempt to unseat Noriega. When these policies failed to remove him, President Bush launched a military invasion in December 1989 that resulted in Noriega's capture and transport to the United States to face drug trafficking charges.

And yet in spite of our deep historical involvement in isthmian affairs, there is little understanding today in the United States of Panama and its people. This problem of understanding has been compounded by the fact that those U.S. leaders and citizens who were historically interested in Panama remained so primarily because of the strategic importance of the Panama Canal and our associated large civilian and military presence in the Canal Zone. Even such interest as did exist in Panama, due to the canal's strategic importance, had evaporated by the year 2000. As a result of the Torrijos-Carter treaties, the canal was turned over to Panama, and the country subsequently dropped off the U.S. "radar screen" when the last U.S. troops left in the year 2000.

With these thoughts in mind, we turn to a closer examination of the country called Panama. This chapter consists of four parts. In the first, we examine the historical setting. In the second, we look more closely at some of the specific ways in which Panama's socioeconomic structures have been shaped by the country's unique development as a transit area. The third section focuses on the changes in government structure and policy substance that have taken place during the past fifteen years following two decades of military rule. Finally, we take note of Panama's relationship with the United States and its changing place in the world.

HISTORICAL SETTING

Although geography is not always destiny, Panama has been influenced more than most countries by its location. Panama is an isthmus, a narrow strip of land 420 miles (676 kilometers) long, which joins Central and South America. As both the narrowest and the lowest point in the Southern Hemisphere, the isthmus has historically served as a transit route from the Atlantic Ocean to the Pacific. The first Europeans to take advantage of Panama's location were the Spaniards, who occupied the isthmus soon after Vasco Núñez de Balboa discovered in 1513 that it linked the Atlantic to the great "south sea." With the Spanish discovery and conquest of the Incan Empire after 1532, Panama became a major transit route for treasure shipped back to Spain and for slaves and foodstuffs flowing to Peru.

The social and economic system that emerged on the isthmus during colonial times reflected Panama's importance as a strategic "bridge." A small urban elite developed that derived its influence from the ability to control isthmian trade. The political and economic position of this urban elite was quite strong until the middle of the eighteenth century because the Spanish crown had made Panama City one of only three ports in all of Latin America through which trade with the home country could be conducted. However, Panama City (and hence the urban elite) lost its favored position in the Spanish Empire during the seventeenth and eighteenth centuries, when the Spanish trade monopoly in Latin America began to erode. By 1655, the British had established a military and trading base in Jamaica from which they began rapidly to expand their reach. The final blow to Panama's favored economic position came in 1739, when the British destroyed the forts protecting the isthmian trade route.

Termination of Panama's port monopoly seriously undermined the economic base of the urban commercial and bureaucratic elite. Some members of this elite managed to maintain their power positions, but on greatly reduced sources of income. Although they no longer controlled the port, they were able to turn to contraband trade with the British or to provisioning military garrisons that continued to occupy the isthmus under Spanish, and later Colombian, rule. Most important, termination of Panama's port monopoly led to diversification within the social and economic system. Although many of the high-ranking Spanish-born administrators returned to the metropole or found bureaucratic posts elsewhere in Latin America, the locally born Creoles were forced to find other local sources of income, particularly in the countryside. There they could invest in cheap rural land. Because there was no large indigenous labor force like that found in the Andes, the major rural activity became cattle-raising. Termination of the port monopoly and the attendant decline in trade thus led to the creation of a new economic class of small property owners in the interior.[1]

During the nineteenth century, those who remained on the isthmus had to adjust to a new set of relationships with outside powers. On November 28, 1821, Panama declared its independence from Spain. After considerable debate, a decision was made to affiliate with the former viceroyalty of New Granada. This led in turn to Panama's becoming a province of Colombia when Colombia went its separate way.

As a small but strategically important province of a weak Latin American country, Panama was tugged in a number of directions. Lacking any strong historical allegiance to Colombia, Panamanians made numerous attempts to achieve either outright independence or increased autonomy within the Colombian political system. Both Great Britain and the United States were interested in the isthmus because of its central importance to the existing and potential hemispheric transportation network. As the United States expanded across the North American continent, the isthmus came to be viewed as a major component of the "domestic" transportation system, linking the industrialized cities of the East Coast to the rapidly expanding settlements in the West.[2] In 1851, U.S. financiers underwrote the construction of a railroad across the isthmus. To forestall any possible conflict over future canal rights, the United States and Great Britain had signed the Clayton-Bulwer Treaty in 1850. This treaty guaranteed that any canal constructed by either country anywhere in Central America would not be exclusively fortified or controlled.

The social and economic consequences of Panama's new relationship with these outside powers during the nineteenth century cannot be overestimated. Renewed attention to the transit function restored the economic vitality of the urban transit area and even led to the creation of an entirely new city, called Colón, on the Atlantic side of the isthmus. Panama City once again became an economic magnet, drawing workers from the interior to construct the railroad and later to work on the canal project undertaken by the French in 1878. A second major effect of these new external relationships was to change the composition of Panama's urban lower class. Until the middle of the nineteenth century, the urban lower class consisted largely of Hispanicized blacks who had come to Panama as slaves during the colonial period to work in the transit area. Beginning with construction of the railroad, English-speaking black workers were imported in great numbers from the Caribbean islands. At the height of the U.S. canal-building efforts in 1910, the Panama Canal Company employed over

35,000 such workers. Many remained in urban Panama after the canal was completed in 1914. Their English language and Protestant religion set them apart from preexisting Panamanian culture and society.

Growing U.S. interest in constructing a canal across the isthmus led to Panama's independence from Colombia in 1903. President Theodore Roosevelt gave tacit encouragement to Panamanian nationalists intent on liberating the isthmus from Colombian rule. The result was an uprising on November 3, 1903, that led to the creation of the Republic of Panama.

It is not surprising that U.S. influence in early Panamanian politics was extensive. Article 136 of the new constitution granted the United States the right to "intervene in any part of Panama, to reestablish peace and constitutional order if it has been disturbed."[3] Panamanian politicians frequently called upon U.S. officials in the Canal Zone for help in restoring order when it suited their purposes. Additionally, many high-level positions in the Panamanian bureaucracy were held by U.S. citizens. The United States also exercised overwhelming economic influence in the new republic. The primary source of such influence was the Canal Zone, the ten-mile-wide (sixteen-kilometer strip of U.S.-controlled land that cut the isthmus in half. Employing a large number of U.S. and Panamanian workers, it was both a major source of jobs and a market for Panamanian products. Furthermore, large banana plantations established by the U.S.-owned United Fruit Company in the interior employed many Panamanians and served as a primary source of export income for the new nation.

As in a number of other Latin American nations, the highly visible U.S. political and economic presence eventually caused a strong national reaction, particularly in the 1920s and 1930s. During this period, a number of factors worked to seriously undermine the economy. There was a massive reduction of the canal workforce after completion of the locks in 1914, and heavy debts were incurred by the national government, leading to a cutback in public-sector employment after 1916.

On August 19, 1923, a semisecret nationalist group was formed that embodied much of the resentment Panamanians felt toward the United States as well as toward the Antillean blacks who held many of the jobs in the Canal Zone. Called Community Action, it espoused Hispanic nationalism. Although not the founder of Community Action, Arnulfo Arias soon became its natural leader. Born on a small cattle ranch in the interior in 1901, Arias graduated from Harvard Medical School and returned to Panama, where he practiced medicine and began to dabble in politics. Elected president on three separate occasions (1940, 1949, and 1968), he was never allowed to complete a full term.

The popular political movement led by Arias was partially displaced by another emerging political force beginning in the 1950s. After Panama achieved independence in 1903, the army was disbanded because of the threat it posed to the political elite and to the United States. Only a small police force was retained. However, during the 1930s, the National Police gradually began to gain political influence under the guidance of José Antonio Remón. By the late 1940s, Colonel Remón and his police organization had become important arbiters in the feuds among leaders of the traditional political parties. Using the police as a springboard, Remón won the presidential election in 1952. Several years later, the National Police was converted into a National Guard and given a new, expanded military role.

With the rise in the power and influence of the National Guard in the 1950s, the base was laid for several subsequent decades of military government. Although the government returned to civilian hands after Remón's assassination in 1955, the National Guard retained much of its political influence. During this period, the guard became increasingly professionalized as more officers with academy training entered it. Because of the Cold War, the United States greatly expanded its military assistance programs during the 1950s, and many Panamanian soldiers were trained at U.S. installations.

On October 11, 1968, the civilian government of President Arnulfo Arias was overthrown by a military coup. The young lieutenant colonel who soon emerged as the central figure in the National Guard was Omar Torrijos. He quickly moved Panamanian policy in a symbolically anti-U.S. direction and restored diplomatic relations with Castro's Cuba. Although Torrijos and the National Guard never displayed the same degree of anti-U.S. sentiment that existed in the early days of Community Action, the restoration of the armed forces to a central position in Panamanian politics created an important new institutional base from which nationalist sentiments could be voiced.

Transit Area Growth and Socioeconomic Structures

Panama's social and economic structures are largely the product of its unique development as a transit area. The perceived need by the United States for hegemonic control of this transit area led to the creation in 1903 of an enclave (the Canal Zone) in the heart of urban Panama. Although foreign-controlled enclaves have been common elsewhere in Latin America, the economic importance and geographic centrality of the Canal Zone were such that it largely determined not only the rate and direction of national economic growth but also the nature of the domestic class structure. Urban commercial groups and rural cattlemen depended heavily on the Canal Zone as a market for their products. Perhaps most important, the existence of the zone played a determining role in the evolution of Panama's urban working class.

In many Latin American countries, the urban working class has served as an important base of support for political leaders intent on restructuring internal relations between elites and masses or relations between the nation and outside powers. However, in Panama the working class has remained quite dormant except for a brief spurt of activity while the military governed during the 1970s. This dormancy has come about because workers have operated within the context of an alliance between Canal Zone and Panamanian elites that actively worked to limit the workers' influence since 1903. During the

early years of the republic, repression of working-class interests was often brutal and exercised through the direct use of military force. For example, when
canal workers living in Panama City went on strike in 1925 to keep rents
from being raised, Panamanian slumlords called on U.S. troops from the zone
to quell the rioting.

The ease with which working-class demands were historically repressed was
also due to the fact that the Canal Zone workforce was largely composed of
English-speaking blacks who enjoyed little sympathy among the Spanish-
speaking Panamanian population. That Canal Zone workers historically received higher wages by national standards led to the general perception that
they were a "labor elite," privileged and culturally distinct from Panamanians
elsewhere in the republic.

Rapid growth of economic activities in the transit area during the 1960s and
1970s led to the mass migration of people from the interior provinces. As in
many other Latin American countries, Panama's urban population grew very
rapidly, increasing from 36 percent of the national total in 1950 to 48 percent
by 1970.[4] The result of this massive internal migration was the creation of a
large, culturally and economically heterogeneous class of urban poor living in
numerous squatter settlements around Panama City.

The magnetic attraction of the transit area during the 1960s and 1970s
served, in turn, to reinforce the historic marginality of the countryside. The interior provinces continued to be neglected by urban civilian politicians representing the interests of commercial elites, so that neither the rural cattlemen
nor the peasants prospered. However, the structure of the rural economy was
significantly altered during these two decades. Traditionally, the Panamanian
peasant engaged in subsistence farming on small plots of land that were owned
by the government. The expansion of commercial cattle-raising activities
greatly reduced the amount of land available to peasants. In addition to forcing many of them off the land and into the cities, this development increased
the tension between cattlemen and peasants.

The military regime that controlled politics from 1968 until 1989 came to
power partly because of the above-mentioned marginality of those living in the
countryside and because of related changes in the structure of the rural economy. Power was taken from the hands of the urban economic elite who had
held sway since 1903. In contrast to members of this elite, General Torrijos
was born and raised in the interior. And although his anti-urban biases were
not as strong as the smoldering antagonism of the marginalized cattlemen who
had supported Arnulfo Arias, his concern for the culture and economy of rural
Panama was just as real.

Industrial growth after World War II created an economy that consisted by
the 1960s of three major parts. Supplementing the traditional service and agricultural activities was an expanded industrial light manufacturing sector,
which led to growth of the industrial working class. The most important economic development in the 1970s and 1980s was the dramatic change in the
overall importance of these three sectors. Although the service economy con-

tinued to expand at a rapid rate, industrial manufacturing activities began to level off. The same was true for the agricultural sector, which experienced a number of problems related to international competitiveness, marketing, and farm technology.

Panama's transit area and related service sector continued to play a central role in the economy following the transition to civilian rule in the 1990s and also following the U.S. departure from Panama in the year 2000. Growth of this sector is primarily driven not by domestic political factors or by external relations with Great Powers like the United States, but rather by Panama's continuing importance in the twenty-first century as a strategic "bridge." During the 1970s and 1980s, global multinational corporations used Panama as a location for servicing their regional financial transactions with a minimum of red tape, as well as for a variety of transportation, communication, and warehousing activities. More recently, large corporations in the United States, Europe, Japan, as well as in newly industrialized countries of East Asia (South Korea, Taiwan, Singapore) have been using the transit area for service-related activities associated with continuing growth of free trade regimes in the region. These include the North American Free Trade Area (NAFTA), the Central American Free Trade Area (CAFTA), and the proposed Free Trade Area of the Americas (FTAA)

The importance of this continued rapid growth of the service sector for Panamanian social and political development is difficult to assess. However, it may result in a further reduction in the political influence of urban laborers engaged in manufacturing activities. Not only has the growth of the industrial labor force slowed, but the nature of the new service sector (with its close ties to the multinational corporations) would seem to suggest impediments to the further organization of the urban workforce. One of the attractive features of service-sector workers, as perceived by multinational corporations, is their current lack of organization.[5]

GOVERNMENT AND POLITICAL DYNAMICS

For some two decades (1968–1989), Panama was dominated by the military.[6] During these years, government structures were altered to give the military more of a role in policy formulation and implementation. The substance of policy also changed because military officers viewed themselves as representing previously marginalized rural and urban working-class groups. Military leaders used heavy state intervention in the economy and enlarged governmental structures to pursue economic development strategies aimed at improving the lot of their class allies.

Following the U.S. military invasion of 1989, there were major changes in government structure associated with Panama's return to civilian rule, although the constitution adopted by the former military government remained in place. Just as important, there were changes in the substance of policy. Two successive civilian administrations, one dominated by the old urban commercial elite

(1989–1994) and the other by civilian allies of the military (1994–1999) both moved in the direction of reducing the role of government and implementing neoliberal economic reforms. The third and most recent administration to complete a full term (1999–2004) was controlled by interests associated with former populist President Arnulfo Arias, who had been overthrown by the military coup in 1968.

Although there was considerable modification of the Panamanian government structure after the military seized power in 1968, it is important to note that the fundamental characteristics of government under *both* military and civilian leaders have been heavily influenced by the nation's Iberian political heritage.[7] When Panama declared its independence from Colombia in 1903, a new constitution was drafted that was based on Colombian law. Provision was made for a centralized unitary government composed of three branches: executive, legislative, and judicial. The president was to be elected for a four-year term and to be ineligible for immediate reelection.

The legislative branch historically centered around a unicameral National Assembly, whose members were elected for four-year terms at the same time as the president. Assembly representatives were elected from circuits corresponding to the nine provinces into which the country was divided. This traditional political system was eminently "presidential," since the chief executive normally dominated both the legislative and judicial branches. Through his power to appoint provincial governors, the president's authority extended into the countryside and influenced administration on the local level. Although the municipalities theoretically possessed more autonomy than the provinces, this autonomy was seldom manifest in practice.

After the military coup in 1968, the dominance of the executive branch became even more pronounced, but power was concentrated in military rather than civilian hands. A new constitution promulgated in 1972 made General Omar Torrijos "maximum leader of the Panamanian Revolution." As for the legislative branch, this new constitution substituted a system of representation for the National Assembly based on the nation's 505 municipal subdistricts. Members of this reconfigured legislature were elected for longer terms in a process that was tightly controlled by the executive branch, and traditional parties played no role.

The military's domination of these civilian political institutions remained contingent upon its ability to both circumvent legal mechanisms designed to curb military power and maintain strict discipline within the military institution itself. Prior to the 1968 coup, the president of the republic was commander in chief of the armed forces as specified by the 1946 Constitution. As such, the president had the right—if not always the power—to appoint and remove military personnel. Under provisions of the 1972 constitution, the president (appointed, in fact, by the military) had no such powers. Furthermore, Article 2 stated that government agencies were to act in "harmonic collaboration" with the armed forces.

General Torrijos and his successor, General Noriega, maintained control of the military through a highly centralized administrative apparatus. Lines of authority ran directly from the commander in chief to all military units without being channeled through the general staff. Torrijos maintained direct control over all seven of Panama's infantry companies, and no officer assignments were made, even at the lieutenant level, without his express approval.

One important additional change following the 1968 coup was that the traditional political parties were banned, largely because they were perceived as representing the interests of the traditional elites. In 1978, the Democratic Revolutionary Party (PRD) was formed to incorporate and guide the various groups that supported the military regime. According to its declaration of principles, the PRD was to be democratic, multiclass, unitary, nationalistic, revolutionary, popular, and independent.[8] In many respects, it resembled other Latin American political parties historically established by military leaders to give civilian institutional form to their ideas. As with Mexico's existing Institutional Revolutionary Party (PRI), the PRD attempted to ensure, through close collaboration among military, government, and party leaders, that participation of opposition groups would be carefully channeled.

In sum, a form of "guided democracy" existed in Panama for two decades. Military leaders adopted economic policies that were tailored to improving the lot of their multiclass popular constituency and relied on heavy state intervention to implement them. During this period, the government bureaucracy experienced considerable growth, organized labor gained more influence, and the social safety net was expanded to include a large number of new and previously marginalized social groups.

When civilians returned to power in Panama following the U.S. invasion, most of the country's traditional democratic institutions were reestablished, including the unicameral National Assembly. At the same time, problems of democratic governability soon emerged that related to three major factors. First, some Panamanians remained unconvinced that the urban commercial elite that had been returned to power on the backs of U.S. tanks was fully legitimate and that it would govern in the best interests of all the people. Second, there were serious political divisions within this elite governing coalition. And finally, changes in the global economy forced civilian governments to undertake neoliberal economic reforms that were perceived as possibly having a negative impact on certain social groups and classes.

Guillermo Endara, Panama's first post-invasion civilian president, was sworn into office on a U.S. military base. A longtime supporter of Arnulfo Arias, he headed an alliance of political parties that had been kept from assuming power by General Noriega following fraudulent 1989 elections. From the very beginning, this alliance was plagued by internal disagreements and bickering. The roots of this problem can be traced to the fact that General Noriega had not permitted Endara's political party to participate in the 1989 elections. This forced many of the party's numerous supporters to vote for the candidates of several smaller, elite-based coalition parties, giving these smaller parties an exaggerated impression of their post-election importance.

With regard to the economy, Endara's administration initially focused its attention on efforts to restore the government's credibility in international financial circles. As a consequence, it made some rather halfhearted and unsuccessful attempts to reduce the size of the public sector in order to allow for larger payments on the country's substantial national debt. More important, his administration began reacting to the sea change in global economic thinking that had taken place during the late 1980s with regard to the most appropriate national strategies for promoting growth. The new neoliberal economic model that gained ascendancy following the collapse of Soviet Communism emphasized the lowering of national tariff barriers, reduction in the size of the public sector through the privatization of state-owned companies, and a shift from the traditional import-substitution growth strategy to one that emphasized promotion of industrial exports.

While Endara was president of post-invasion Panama, the nation made some headway with regard to making major policy changes that would be required for genuine productive restructuring. However, it was only following the election of Ernesto Pérez Balladares in 1994 that the government began to make serious and sustained efforts to implement economic reform. The curious aspect of this situation was that Pérez Balladares represented the old party of military rule, the Democratic Revolutionary Party. As the party that had been largely responsible in previous decades for doubling the size of the government bureaucracy and calling for increased state economic intervention, it seemed a most unlikely candidate to lead such neoliberal reform efforts.

When Pérez Balladares took office in fall 1994, he moved quickly toward the pursuit of his major economic goals. These included joining the General Agreement on Tariffs and Trade (GATT) and reducing the size of the public sector. Another centerpiece of this neoliberal reform process was the effort to alter the progressive labor legislation that had been enacted in 1972 during the early years of military rule. Economics minister Guillermo Chapman argued that some changes in the labor code would be necessary to create a more modern and efficient state.

Panama's next president rode to victory in 1999 on the crest of a popular backlash against neoliberal economic reforms. Mireya Moscoso, the first woman president in the country's history, was the daughter of a schoolteacher who lived in a rural and impoverished part of the interior. After joining the political party led by Arnulfo Arias, she eventually married him and they lived together in exile following the 1968 military coup. Following Arias's death in 1988, Moscoso became the standard bearer for the Arnulfista Party (PA) and ran unsuccessfully for the presidency in 1994. A tireless campaigner, she finally succeeded in donning the presidential sash five years later.

President Moscoso's years in office were dominated by attempts to soften the impact on Panama's poorest citizens of the neoliberal economic reform policies that had been adopted by the two previous administrations. However, her ambitious populist agenda, which included attempts to protect the interests of the urban working class, small farmers, and teachers, fell prey to a combination of economic difficulties, personal ineptitude, nepotism, and more generalized corruption. By the fourth year of her five-year term, a public opinion poll indicated that two-thirds of Panamanians viewed her performance as president as either "poor" or "very poor."[9] [10]

PANAMA'S CHANGING PLACE IN THE WORLD

Because of Panama's small size and unique geographical position, its foreign relations have been heavily influenced by outside powers. [11] By 1903, the United States had emerged as the dominant outside power, with multiple sources of influence over Panama's foreign initiatives. The large U.S. troop presence in the Canal Zone and the strategic importance of the isthmus to the United States limited the contacts the Panamanian government was allowed to develop with global adversaries of the United States, such as the Soviet Union. In addition to this military presence, U.S. dominance of the economy meant that independent foreign policy initiatives had to be cautiously pursued. During the Cold War, Panama's economic reliance on the U.S. government and private companies was probably greater than that of any other country in the world.[12]

Because of the dominant position of the United States throughout most of the twentieth century, Panama's foreign policy was largely bilateral. The commercial elites who controlled the foreign ministry were primarily interested in extracting the maximum economic benefits from their relationship with the United States. A secondary concern was to modify the worst colonial aspects of the U.S.-Panamanian relationship, particularly as it related to the Canal Zone. According to terms of the original 1903 treaty, the United States could act "in perpetuity" in the Canal Zone "as if it were the sovereign of the territory . . . to the entire exclusion of the exercise by the Republic of Panama of any such sovereign rights, power, and authority."[13] Numerous attempts were made over the years by leaders of various political persuasions to negotiate treaties that did not so egregiously violate the country's sense of sovereignty.

In spite of these attempts, the major provisions of the 1903 treaty remained unchanged until the 1970s, when perceptions of the diminished strategic importance of the canal led to new thinking during the presidency of Jimmy Carter. In 1978, the U.S. Congress ratified two completely new treaties, the Panama Canal Treaty and the Treaty of Neutrality. The former recognized Panamanian sovereignty over the Canal Zone and specified that U.S. troops would be withdrawn completely from this area by the year 2000; the latter guaranteed that the waterway would remain permanently neutral in time of peace or war.

It would be hard to overstate the degree of change that occurred in U.S.-Panamanian relations when Panama assumed control of the canal in the year 2000 as a result of the 1978 treaties. Before the year 2000, Panama had been a major seat of U.S. diplomatic and military power in the Western Hemisphere—

a place from which power could be reliably projected, whether it be to deal with a growing threat of guerrilla insurgency or a looming humanitarian crisis. Following the transfer of the canal, Panama became more of a problem than a solution in the eyes of the U.S. diplomatic and military planners, requiring special attention because of the canal's vulnerability to potential terrorist attacks, the country's logistical importance to regional drug and arms smugglers, and its potential vulnerability to the rapidly escalating crisis in the northern part of South America.

More specifically, Panama has become deeply entangled in the combined civil and drug wars that have engulfed large parts of the neighboring country of Columbia. For many years, this war has spilled over the border and created numerous problems for Panama, including increased drug trafficking, floods of refugees, and increased crime. As if all of this were not bad enough, Panama has also been affected by the U.S. War on Terrorism, initiated in 2001 after attacks on New York City and Washington, D.C. A climate of concern surrounds alleged threats by members of Al-Quaeda to interrupt canal boat traffic, and security measures have been tightened in port facilities and surrounding waters.

As a result of these recent and dramatic changes in Panama's traditional bilateral relationship with the United States and the country's more generalized place in the world, Panamanians have had to think long and hard about their future. This has resulted in the emergence (or perhaps reemergence) of two quite different views concerning Panama's fundamental nature as a global entity, views that predominate among different segments of the population. The first is the belief that Panama is really more of a transnational global city than a true nation-state. This view is deeply rooted in the historical memory of the white ruling classes. It stresses Panama's unique place in the world as a result of its geographical location and attendant role as a strategic "bridge" within the global transportation network.

The second view, long dominant among the followers of Arnulfo Arias as well as among followers of the old military regime, suggests that Panama is just another normal nation-state, a rather small one that must learn to survive on its own in a harsh global political and economic environment. From this perspective, Panamanians need to stop looking back nostalgically to the "good old days" of a close relationship with the United States or forward to playing a new role as a transglobal city. Rather, Panamanians need to focus on strengthening domestic institutions and building inter-state alliances in a way that will protect vital national interests.

In sum, while it is clear that Panama's dramatically changed relationship with the United States has altered the context in which Panamanian leaders must think about their future place in the world, there is as yet no fundamental agreement with regard to what this place should be. The country is becoming more deeply entangled in regional crises and conflicts, but without either the old sense of certainty that came from a historically close relationship with the United States or a post–2000 elite consensus to guide foreign policy.

Conclusions

Panama's geographical location has played a critical role in determining the country's global function as a transit area, in shaping domestic socioeconomic structures, and in defining and redefining its place in the world. Because Panama has long served as a strategic "bridge," it has historically attracted the attention of great powers, such as Spain, Great Britain, France, and the United States, that were intent on enhancing their geostrategic position. This continues to be the case today as Panama struggles to define a role for itself in the world following the U.S. withdrawal from the isthmus.

With the return to democratic government in the 1990s, four successive presidents and their administrations have struggled with the question of how best to balance the need for neoliberal economic reforms in order to remain competitive within the global economy with the need to protect Panamanians from the threat of growing unemployment, increasing class inequality, and the like. This has not proved to be an easy task, and is surely one with which future Panamanian presidents will continue to struggle.

As mentioned at the onset of this chapter, people in the United States have a short memory when it comes to thinking about our deep historical relationship with Panama. However, since we were present at the creation and thus are particularly responsible for the birth of the Republic, we have a moral obligation to help ensure the people of Panama's continued welfare in the future. Panama played a critical role as a trusted regional ally during most of "The American Century"—a role that we should never forget.

Notes

1. Omar Jaén Suárez, *La Población del Istmo de Panamá del siglo XVI al siglo XX* (Panama City: Impresora de la Nación, 1978), pp. 187–190, 301.

2. Walter LaFeber, *The Panama Canal: The Crisis in Historical Perspective* (New York: Oxford University Press, 1979), p. 8.

3. Juan Materno Vásquez, *Teoría del estado Panameño* (Panama City: Ediciones Olga Elena, 1980), p. 122.

4. Panamá, Dirección de Estadística y Censo, Contraloría General, *Panamá en cifras: 1973–1977* (Panama City), p. 38.

5. Steve C. Ropp, *Panamanian Politics: From Guarded Nation to National Guard* (New York: Praeger, 1982), pp. 60–61.

6. For an attempt to explain this long period of military rule, see Steve C. Ropp, "Explaining the Long-Term Maintenance of a Military Regime: Panama Before the U.S. Invasion," *World Politics* 44, January 1992, pp. 210–234.

7. For a discussion of this tradition as it relates to Iberian corporate practices in Central America, see Steve C. Ropp, "What About Corporatism in Central America?" in Howard Wiarda, ed., *Authoritarianism and Corporatism in Latin America—Revisited* (Gainesville, Fla.: The University Press, 2004).

8. Partido Revolucionario Democrático, "Documentos fundamentales" (Panama City, 1979), pp. 16–17.

9. Survey conducted by Dichter and Neira for *La Prensa* (July 2003).

10. Martín Torrijos, Panama's latest president and son of General Omar Torrijos, faces a different set of domestic challenges. Most importantly, a free trade agreement with the United States that was initiated by the Moscoso administration needs to be completed and the growing public debt brought under control.

11. Jan Knippers Black, "The Canal and the Caribbean," in Richard Millett and W. Marvin Will, eds., *The Restless Caribbean: Changing Patterns of International Relations* (New York: Praeger, 1979), pp. 90–91.

12. Neil R. Richardson, *Foreign Policy and Economic Dependence* (Austin: University of Texas Press, 1978), pp. 103–106.

13. U.S. Congress, Senate Committee on Foreign Relations, *Hearings on the Panama Canal Treaties*, 95th Congress, 1st Session, September 1977, pt. 1, p. 588.

Suggested Readings

Biesanz, John, and Mavis Biesanz. *The People of Panama*. New York: Columbia University Press, 1995. This is a classic book on Panamanian politics and society. It offers insights that are still valuable.

Conniff, Michael L. *Panama and the United States: The Forced Alliance*. Athens, Ga.: The University of Georgia Press, 1992. A concise account of the relationships between Panama and the United States during the twentieth century.

McCullough, David. *The Path Between the Seas: The Creation of the Panama Canal, 1870–1914*. New York: Simon and Schuster, 1977. An epic book dealing with the French and U.S. efforts to build the Panama Canal.

Pearcy, Thomas L. *We Answer Only to God: Politics and the Military in Panama, 1903–1947*. Albuquerque: The University of New Mexico Press, 1998. A well-researched study of the historical role of the military in Panamanian politics.

Perez, Orlando J., ed. *Post-Invasion Panama: The Challenges of Democratization in the New World Order*. Landham, Md.: Lexington Books, 2000. An excellent collection of essays concerning political developments following the U.S. military invasion of 1989.

Ward, Christopher. *Imperial Panama: Commerce and Conflict in Isthmian America, 1550–1800*. Albuquerque: The University of New Mexico Press, 1993. Solid account of developments in Panama during the colonial period.

PART VII

CUBA AND
THE CARIBBEAN

Chapter 18

THE CUBAN REVOLUTION

NELSON P. VALDÉS

A SOCIAL REVOLUTION IS a radical, abrupt, thorough, and systematic alteration of the social relations, the patterns of behavior, and the institutional structures that exist in the economic, political, cultural, and social life of a country. By definition, a social revolution touches every facet of interaction in society. It often attempts a total break with tradition. But even revolutionaries cannot escape their material and historical contexts.

The agendas of social revolutions have changed through time. From the seventeenth century on, Western Europe dealt with a series of critical problems, ranging from nation-building (the creation of national institutions, a central system of authority, and a national economy) to the creation of representative political institutions and industrialization. This process of becoming modern capitalist nation states took centuries to unfold and was often plagued with social conflict at home and war abroad. During this century, the countries of the Third World (including most of those in Latin America) have confronted some of the same difficulties (nation-building, economic development, the problems of citizenship) as well as new ones (national self-determination and ending foreign control and neocolonial institutions and practices).

In general, revolutionaries have defined their tasks in such a manner that their aims are, to say the least, awesome. Social revolutions are supposed to bring about the full blossoming of national sovereignty, fight foreign influence, develop national resources, distribute the economic benefits of growth, centralize political power while increasing the sense of citizenship and the degree of political participation, and carry out a total transformation in the major institutions of the country. And all of these tasks are to be done in a short time with the few resources the country may have at its command.

The Cuban Revolution is worthy of study because it presents us with an example of what a revolutionary state has tried to do, how it has gone about it, and what has resulted from the effort. Also, this revolution, although multifaceted and complex, has been a unique phenomenon that a number of countries have attempted to emulate. Finally, the very fact of the revolution placed this small island in the center of the struggle between the superpowers. The impact of the Cuban Revolution, in other words, has been felt not only within its own borders but beyond its shores.

THE HISTORICAL CONTEXT

Social revolutions occur in particular places and times. They cannot escape either of the two. The fact that Cuba is an island in a very strategic location has made it a crossroads of trade and cultures. And the fact that it lies only 90 miles (145 kilometers) from the U.S. mainland has preoccupied U.S. as well as Cuban authorities, particularly since 1959.

Yet the islanders have been somewhat isolated from most of Latin America. There is a certain attitude of self-containment and self-sufficiency in the culture. Moreover, Cubans are not sufficiently aware of the dramatic differences between a country that developed a plantation economy very early in its history and the agrarian, peasant, and other traditional forms of social interaction found elsewhere in the hemisphere. This has led some Cubans to consider their experience a model that could be emulated elsewhere—a vanguard rather than an exception.

Social revolutions do not occur in a historical vacuum; they are shaped and bound by history. History, as such, is a dynamic, ever-changing process. How that process unfolds and how it is interpreted do not have to coincide. Yet the interpretation that a society or a portion of a population gives to that process may have a power all its own. Historical interpretation may be a tool for understanding as well as a call to action. Revolutionaries know this well.

SPANISH COLONIAL PERIOD

The history of Cuba has been quite different in its basic pattern from that of most of Latin America. From the onset of the Spanish conquest, the island became a springboard for the conquest of Mexico, Central America, and even portions of South America. Lacking mineral wealth and a large native labor force, Cuba offered little incentive for settlement. The population was fairly small, and the economy was geared toward servicing the fleet system that visited the port of Havana once or twice a year. Most of the population tended to concentrate in the small towns. Colonial institutions were not as strong as in Peru or Mexico, and the Catholic Church held sway only in the urban milieu.

From the 1760s on, Cuba experienced dramatic changes in its economic, social, and political organization. These changes were initiated by the development of the sugar plantation economy and, with it, of a cohesive class of sugar planters (referred to in Cuba as the *sucarocracia*). As sugar production rose, the demand for labor also increased. Since this shift in production occurred just as the British began their industrial revolution, the steam engine was soon introduced into the refining of sugar. This generated a greater demand for sugar cane and thus for the labor force that cut it. Hence, with the sugar plantation and the modernization of production, black slaves arrived in ever-larger numbers.

Sugar production was essentially for profit, although dependent on slave-master relations. The sugar economy dominated the western part of the island, particularly around Havana. In the eastern region, however, a small farming class, mainly white, produced coffee, tobacco, and cattle—a significant portion for barter or direct use.

The sugar areas were held by people born in Spain (*peninsulares*), and the rest of the land was essentially in the hands of poor farmers who had little contact with the Spanish colonial system. The latter were, in a sense, the early *criollos*; the first indications of a Cuban national identity would be found in the eastern part of the island. The differences between the two economic regions, with their distinct modes of production, gave rise to tensions between the Spaniards and the Cubans. The latter, of course, were barred from political power.

The early nineteenth century witnessed independence struggles throughout most of Latin America. Cuba, however, remained under Spanish control. This was due to three factors. First, economic prosperity brought about by sugar cultivation kept much of the population contented. Second, the defeats suffered by the Spanish military forces throughout the hemisphere meant that a large proportion of the defeated personnel ended up in Cuba—thus fortifying colonial rule there. Finally, the sugar planters, as well as many other whites who were not directly connected to the sugar economy, were afraid that a war of independence would be transformed into a slave revolt, as had been the case in Haiti after 1791.

In 1868, Cuba began a war of independence led by the independent, small, white farming class of eastern Cuba. The war went on for ten years but ended in defeat for the rebels as well as in the total destruction of the non-sugar economy. The plantation became ever more powerful and began to expand to the east. The class system, at the same time, was simplified: A basic tension surfaced between the slave owners and the slaves. In this confrontation, the Catholic Church sided with the plantation and the colonial system. Thus, sugar-plantation slaves and colonial rule became one side of the equation, while the emancipation of the slaves, the reduction of the dominance exerted by the plantation, and Cuban independence became united themes. It is in this period that one begins to find the anti-sugar mentality that has dominated the thinking of Cuban revolutionists ever since.

In 1895, the war of independence broke out again, this time led by the Cuban Revolutionary Party (PRC) under the guidance of Cuba's most important poet, national hero, and thinker: José Martí. The PRC was a unique development. No other independence war in Latin America was organized by a political party. The party had political and military control of the entire struggle. This was new as well. But the PRC went even further. José Martí had studied the conditions of Latin America and concluded that even though many countries had attained political independence, the laws, traditions, practices, and institutions of colonialism had survived. The PRC therefore had a decolonization program. In that respect, the party foretold a process that would take root throughout the Third World in the second half of the twentieth century.

THE AMERICAN PROTECTORATE

But the war of independence did not achieve its goal. The international situation was far different from what it had been when the rest of Latin America became free of Spain. Late in the nineteenth century, the United States was emerging as a major power in the hemisphere. Manifest Destiny had numerous adherents in Washington, D.C., and the Caribbean was considered an American lake. The Cuban war of independence was lost when the United States and Spain went to war in 1898. U.S. military intervention in the island brought to an end Spanish colonial rule, but only to initiate a new period of U.S. hegemony.

The island became an integral part of the U.S. economy. The culture and education of the Cubans became ever more Americanized. The United States imposed a new economic arrangement, new trade partners, and a new political system. The U.S. dollar became the main currency. From 1899 to 1902, the U.S. military ruled over Cuba, restructuring its socioeconomic system so as to meet U.S. needs. U.S. investors began to control the strategic sectors of the Cuban economy (sugar, transportation, utilities, trade). All communal lands were lost, passing into U.S. ownership.

An amendment to the Cuban constitution, dictated by U.S. military authorities, allowed the U.S. government to pass judgment on the acceptability of Cuban public policy. And should that judgment be negative, the United States asserted, through the Platt Amendment, the right to intervene militarily to ensure that its dictates were honored.

A new regime in Cuba, ushered in by the so-called sergeants' revolt, unilaterally repudiated the Platt Amendment in 1933. Other progressive and nationalistic reforms that had followed the sergeants' revolt were soon undermined as the leader of that revolt, Fulgencio Batista, assumed dictatorial powers and curried favor with the United States. But that revolt, which elevated noncommissioned officers of lower-class background to command positions, had severed the tie between the traditional Cuban elite and the officer corps, a factor that later worked to the disadvantage of the military.

The Cuban Revolutionary Party, which had spearheaded the struggle for independence from Spain, had disintegrated after the death of its leader, Martí. But in 1944, a new populist party, of the same name and inspiration, was elected and allowed to rule until 1952, when Batista displaced it and again established a dictatorship.

From 1953 to 1958, the opposition to Batista clustered around the 26th of July Revolutionary Movement. This was a movement formed by ex-members of the Cuban People's Party (PPC), a splinter of the PRC, many of whom remained committed to populism, nationalism, and general concepts of social justice. Under the leadership of a young lawyer, Fidel Castro, they successfully carried out a guerrilla war that managed, for the first time in Latin America, to overthrow a military regime. The United States apparently misunderstood the degree to which these revolutionaries were committed to thorough and rapid social change. But it soon became obvious.

FROM NATIONALISM TO SOCIALISM

The young revolutionaries sought control over the major economic decisions affecting their country in order to redistribute wealth and promote development. There is no evidence that they had envisioned either a complete break with the United States or a thorough socialization of the economy. But the U.S. government and business community equated the nationalist policies of the revolution in regard to foreign investments and the reformist policies, beginning with land reform, with communism. U.S. countermeasures, including the slashing of Cuba's sugar quota and, later, the economic embargo, pushed the Cubans to further expropriations.

By late 1960, the state owned a significant portion of the means of production in Cuba. No one had planned this. Through a process of confrontation and nationalist actions and reactions, the capitalist economy of Cuba had been socialized, even though the Cuban state did not have the personnel to run all the enterprises. At issue had been the right of Cuba to make decisions within its own borders, and failure to reply to the U.S. challenge would have amounted to forfeiting sovereignty.

It was the identification with, and the defense of, nationalism that led the Cuban revolutionaries, in practice, to socialism. The United States had come to represent capitalism as well as imperial power, and Cuban nationalism and socialized property were integrated into the new revolutionary ideology. The Bay of Pigs invasion, organized and financed by the CIA, captured the dichotomy well.

On April 15, 1961, airplanes piloted by Cubans hired by the CIA bombarded the airports at Santiago de Cuba and Havana. This was the softening-up period prior to a Cuban-exile invasion. Seven persons died. Speaking at the burial ceremony the next day, Fidel Castro said that a counterrevolutionary invasion, seeking to return capitalism, was imminent. And on that day, he characterized the Cuban Revolution as socialist. The invasion began on April 17, but within two days it had been defeated. Again, just as the cutting of the sugar quota led to the socialization of the basic means of production, the Bay of Pigs invasion made Cuba's identification with socialism the only possible reaction that a radical nationalist movement could take.

This turn of the revolution surprised the United States as well as the Soviet Union. In fact, the Cuban experience defied some basic tenets of orthodox Marxist theory. Communists, following the views of Lenin, had believed for quite some time that without a revolutionary theory (that is, Marxism-Leninism), there could be no revolutionary party or movement. And without the party, there could be no revolutionary practice—seizing political power and socializing the means of production. In Cuba, the formula was reversed. Power was seized without a revolutionary theory or party. The state took over a significant part of the economy and months later called the outcome socialism. Only much later, on December 2, 1961, was there a formal adoption of Marxism-Leninism. It was only in early 1962 that a revolutionary party began to be formed, and it held its first party congress thirteen years later. Thus, the Cuban experience has been unique in many ways.

THE POLITICAL SYSTEM

During the first sixteen years of revolutionary rule, Cuba's leaders successfully merged charisma with patrimonialism and a high degree of mass mobilization. The Communist Party did not play an important role during that first phase of the revolution because the very nature of a political party runs counter to charismatic authority. Until 1970, political and organizational work was concentrated on the growth and development of mass organizations (Cuba has six mass organizations: Cuban Confederation of Labor, Federation of Cuban Women, National Association of Small Farmers, Federation of Secondary School Students, the Union of Young Pioneers, and the Committees for the Defense of the Revolution).

The institutionalization of the revolution, after 1975, redefined the role of the Communist Party. It was to coordinate, control, lead, and supervise the tasks of the state and the mass organizations, without administering. But to assume such roles, the party had to grow, train its cadres, develop efficient methods of leadership, establish internal discipline, and improve its political training as well as the educational level of its members.

In 1965, the Communist Party had just 45,000 members; ten years later, the number had increased to 211,642, and in 1980, the membership numbered 434,143. The educational level changed as well. In 1970, 33.6 percent of the members did not have a sixth-grade education; nine years later, that proportion had declined to 11.4 percent. The proportion of members with higher education rapidly increased, from 2.8 percent in 1970 to 6.2 percent in 1979. Party cadres showed an even greater improvement, with 16 percent having had a high school education in 1975 and 75.5 percent five years later. Meanwhile, membership in the mass organizations ceased to grow. Since the 1970s, the revolutionary leadership prepared the party to play the "leading role" that Marxist-Leninist theory had claimed for it.

COMMUNIST PARTY ORGANS

The present system of government is characterized by a complex web of interlocking power relations. The Communist Party, the state, and the government are functionally differentiated, although some individuals occupy more than one post in each of these three centers of power. The Communist Party, at present the locus of political power, is highly structured. At the base, the party membership is organized in cells, or *nucleos,* 26,500 of them in 1980. The party is organized on a territorial basis (local, municipal, provincial, and national).

On the national level, the party congress is the highest authority, but only in a formal sense since it meets only once every five years. Delegates to the party congress, elected from subordinate territorial levels, in turn elect (really ratify) from among themselves the members of the Central Committee (CC). Because of its size, and the fact that its members have other responsibilities, the CC has only about two one-day plenums annually. At these meetings, the CC selects the members of the Political Bureau (PB) and the Secretariat.

The PB makes policy between congresses and plenums on behalf of the CC and the party. Its task consists of translating general principles and aims into more precise policy, and its decisions are binding. The Secretariat is also a powerful institution. To some it has appeared that the PB is much more powerful than the Secretariat because the latter has to answer to the former (just as the PB answers to the CC, and it, in turn, responds to the party congress). However, it would be more useful to see the PB and the Secretariat as functioning in different arenas.

The Secretariat is responsible for the maintenance of the party apparatus. It decides who may join or who is expelled. It also takes care of internal political education and promotion within party ranks. The Secretariat also transmits to the institutions of the state, government, and mass organizations the guidelines of the PB.

The internal organization of the Communist Party parallels that of the administrative and political divisions of the island, with fourteen committees representing the provinces and 179 representing municipalities. Below the municipal committees are the party cells, organized at work centers, schools, and military barracks. At the base, then, the party is organized by function rather than by territory (which discriminates against people who are not employed, do not study, or are not in the military).

The functions and hierarchical lines of the CC, the PB, and the Secretariat are clearly demarcated, but in practice, the demarcations seem to be insignificant. Many of the same individuals can be found in all three bodies. The Secretariat has nine members—five are full members of the PB, and two are alternates. Political power is interlocked for the simple reason that the same person can have two entirely different statuses and roles. On the basis of that web, it can be stated that in 1982, thirty men and one woman comprised the core of revolutionary power in Cuba (what in Mexico has been called "the revolutionary family").

The Communist Party makes decisions but does not execute them, guides but does not administer. The implementation of policy—that is, practical day-to-day decisionmaking and policy formulation—is carried out by a different set of institutions. From 1959 to 1975, the people who had political power and those who held key government posts were the same; there was no distinction of roles. In 1976, however, a constitution was adopted proclaiming the socialist nature of the Cuban state and establishing the rules of government. Executive, legislative, and judicial powers were separated. Granted, the executive still had some legislative prerogatives, but nothing similar to those of the 1959–1975 period.

In the 1980s, a number of changes took place within the Communist Party. Some of these were due to the internal dynamics of the revolution itself. The party grew from just 50,000 persons in 1965 to 523,639 members in 1986. There was some fluctuation in the growth; however as a whole, party recruitment increased faster than population increase. In the period 1975–1980, it grew almost 21 percent; in the 1980s, it dropped to 4.1 percent (1980–1986). After 1986 there was a greater effort to gain members again, particularly young ones. Tied to the reduction in membership age was an improvement in educational level. In 1975, 19.6 percent of the members had a ninth-grade education or more; in 1986, the figure was 72.4 percent. This shift reflects the overall improvement in the educational level of the population at large.

There have been some changes in the internal organization of the party over the years. The Central Committee membership can be divided into full members (who actually participate in decisionmaking) and alternates (who may take the place of full members due to death, promotion, and so forth). There were 100 full members in the CC in 1965. As the PCC membership grew, new members were incorporated into leadership positions. The PCC avoided demoting CC full members, however, by inventing the concept of alternates. By 1986, the Central Committee had 146 members and 79 alternates.

The Political Bureau had also expanded. Whereas it had eight members when the party was organized in 1965, it had thirteen full members and fourteen alternates in early 1990. Eleven of the fourteen alternates had assumed their positions since 1986.

At the 1986 Party Congress, Fidel Castro noted that "we had to renew or die." Thus, he went on, "we must trust our youth." Indeed a policy of affirmative action that targeted women, the young, and blacks began from the 1986 Congress on. At previous congresses the party stressed the recruitment of workers and peasants. In other words, class had priority. By 1980, special attention was being given to having more women in the PCC. The same theme was repeated at the Third Congress, but the PCC went further this time, enunciating a policy of affirmative action for women, blacks, and the young. The Main Report read by Fidel Castro stated, "The mechanisms that ensure the correct selection, permanence and promotion of cadre must be improved constantly on the basis of thorough, critical, objective and systematic evaluations and with appropriate attention to development and training. Women's representation in keeping with their participation and their important contribution to the building of socialism in our country must be ensured, along with the existence of a growing reserve of promising young people born and tempered in the forge of the Revolution."

In 1986, women accounted for 21.5 percent of party membership. (The number of women in the CC had increased to 18.8 percent of the combined CC membership.) Ethnicity has become an important issue in the party, perhaps related to the growing influence, education, and expectations of the black population. A Communist Party document stated that "in order for the Party's leadership to duly reflect the ethnic composition of our people, it must include those compatriots of proven revolutionary merit and talents who in the past had been discriminated against because of their skin color."

Castro has noted that the "rectification of historical injustices" such as racial discrimination "cannot be left to spontaneity." By 1986, only 28.4 percent of the CC membership was black or mulatto. But the affirmative action policies adopted by the revolutionary leadership suggested that the failures in this area were acknowledged and steps were to be taken to address them.

The Communist Party internal organization was also confronted by the changes begun in 1985 in the Soviet Union, and then taken up by Eastern Europe in the late 1980s, as well as by Communist parties throughout the rest of the world. Thus, in mid-February 1990, the Communist Party leadership announced new plans to transform itself. The promised changes, however, did not imply the abolition of the one-party state. A party document stated, "What we are talking about is the perfecting of a single, Leninist party based on the principles of democratic centralism." (This happened precisely as the Soviets abandoned a constitutional monopoly on power.)

In 1990, the ten-member Secretariat was reduced to six persons. No explanations were given. As a consequence of the changes, the labor movement no longer had a representative (the peasant/farmer sector had no direct voice either). The representative of the labor movement (former head of the Cuban Confederation of Labor) was also dropped from the Political Bureau at that time.

In summary, while the permanent full-time membership of the Political Bureau remained fairly constant throughout the 1980s, the alternate membership experienced drastic change. However, the alternates have little power as long as they remain in that position. In a sense, the increasing number of alternates suggests that rising stars within the revolutionary ranks have been promised power and authority, but they have not been given enough of it to shape decisions within the Political Bureau and the Secretariat. True, the alternates have power vis-à-vis the society at large. They participate in controlling key social, economic, and governmental institutions; but since the core of power resides within the party, they merely implement the significant decisions made elsewhere.

At the 1991 Communist Party Congress, the Congress announced that religious persons could become members of the Communist Party and outlined the major policy changes that would follow—among them, opening major areas of the economy to foreign investments, developing a mixed economy under the guidance of the state, allowing a greater role to private enterprise, and establishing party cells at the neighborhood level (until that time, party cells were found only at the workplace). At the Fourth PCC Congress in 1992, the Secretariat was abolished. The position of candidates to the Political Bureau was also abolished, but the membership of the bureau itself was increased to twenty-five.

The Communist Party was supposed to have another congress in 1996, but it was postponed until the following year. The 1997 Fifth Congress of the Communist Party allowed the membership to reassess the results of the economic policies adopted since the collapse of the Soviet bloc (post-1991), when the country decriminalized the use of the dollar, fostered foreign investments, stressed the importance of tourism, legalized family remittances to the island, as well as made further openings to small private entrepreneurship in some areas of the urban economy, privatized most state farms, and the made widespread use of market relations among state enterprises. During the difficult and critical years from 1991 to 1996, some Party members dropped out or "lost their perspective." In August 1994, urban unrest led to serious concerns about the future political stability of the country. A 1996 party document noted that during the early years of the "special period" the PCC had to deal with all the objective material shortages as well as with "selfishness, a mercantile outlook, the desire of some to just make money, consumerism and the loss of revolutionary ethical norms." During that same period the pressure from the U.S. government increased, as manifested in the Torricelli Act (1992) and the Helms-Burton Bill (1996)(see chapter 14).

From 1994 to 1997, the PCC leadership—led by Raúl Castro—traveled around the country to revitalize its methods and membership. The national leaders demanded a more critical attitude on the part of the lower political levels of the party, stressing that local political and economic resources should be stressed to solve pressing problems. The key message was, "it can be done" if initiative is taken by the party ranks without expecting assistance from above. By 1994, despite the social problems, the Cuban economy began to improve. The next two years economic growth became significant and the political leadership was in a stronger position to have its Communist Party Congress.

Prior to the Fifth Party Congress of October 1997, the mass organizations held their own respective congresses, where the themes were political unity and grassroots initiatives. In the face of such difficulties, the ranks of the membership were opened to a greater number of workers. The Fifth Congress recognized the need to extend to all state enterprises the *nuevo sistema empresarial*, a managerial experiment initiated within the armed forces that provided incentives to workers, including the options of a portion of salaries in dollars or access to dollar-based goods. One unusual note at the Fifth Congress was that Fidel Castro did not speak; this led many analysts to assume that he was ill. However, the intent of having Raúl Castro play such a central role was to make the point that the older brother was, indeed, replaceable. In the 1980s, on a yearly average, about 27,000 persons joined the PCC. From 1992 to 1996, about 233,000 workers joined, an average of 46,000 annually. That meant that the political organization had about 30 percent new members during the most difficult times of the revolutionary period.

By May 2003, the PCC had 856,262 members organized in 62,800 grassroots cells, which are organized at workplaces, schools, military units, and by place of residence—the latter a uniquely Cuban feature. Since 1992 there has been significant leadership change at the municipal, provincial, and even national levels of the Communist Party; even some of the "historical" figures have been replaced, although control remains in the hands of much older members. Nonetheless, a growing number of cabinet members and state legislative and administrative leaders are now under the age of fifty. The majority of the new party leaders are professionals with technical training. The youth of the PCC at the provincial and municipal levels is even more extraordinary; the typical party leader is about thirty-four years of age.

At the Fifth Congress, the Central Committee membership was reduced from 225 to 150 members while the Political Bureau declined from 26 to 24.

This was a mechanism to reduce the influence of the so-called *históricos*, or the "old guard," within the revolutionary ranks. The Political Bureau had taken over functions previously undertaken by the Secretariat, such as dealing with the party's internal matters. A PCC Congress was due in 2003, but by the next year, it had not yet been held.

THE NATIONAL ASSEMBLY

In 1977, a National Assembly (NA) with formal legislative powers was established. The NA is a representative institution whose members are elected for five-year periods. Election is indirect, delegates being chosen by provincial assemblies. (Provincial elections are popular and direct.) The NA has 481 delegates and meets twice a year, usually for less than a week. It can generate legislation as well as approve it, but laws must be consonant with the general guidelines of the Communist Party. How much real power the NA possesses is debatable. Sessions are so short that there is little time to study, analyze, and debate. Recently, some delegates have tried to represent their respective local constituencies, but the NA is not receptive to that idea. In general, the NA serves to legitimize decisions made elsewhere.

The real work of the NA is done by standing work committees and the Council of State (CS). Committee members are appointed. Chosen for their specialized knowledge rather than for their political credentials, they need not be delegates to any legislative body. The NA has fifteen committees, fourteen commissions, and nine departments. It should be noted that the persons elected to the assemblies, whether on the national, provincial, or municipal level, do not run on a particular political platform. They have no individual set of policy proposals; instead, they are chosen for their personal characteristics. It is a given that a candidate's political platform will be that of the Communist Party.

The National Assembly has come under criticism by the general population, its members, and members of the Communist Party. The population, at meetings with their elected representatives, have expressed dismay at the institution's lack of power and its incapacity to deal with substantive issues. The members of the municipal and provincial assemblies, on the other hand, have begun to lobby their own constituencies as well as the National Assembly, to acquire a greater role in making policy decisions, particularly in the area of economic and social policy. Finally, National Assembly members have complained that they ought to be able to work for a longer period of time, taking for themselves the powers enjoyed by the executive committees. They also have demanded a say in determining budgetary priorities, the size of the budget, and real control over matters of foreign policy.

At the Communist Party Congress in 1991, these matters were addressed, and in 1992 the Cuban constitution was drastically changed to provide more power and influence to the National Assembly. The 1993 elections of the National Assembly produced a major overhaul of the elected members; new people entered the scene, most of them in their thirties. Direct elections were established at each of the three legislative levels: municipal, provincial, and national.

When the NA is not meeting, its functions and prerogatives are assumed by its executive committee, the Council of State, which is selected by the NA from its own ranks. The CS carries out the decisions of the NA as well as tasks outlined in the 1976 constitution. The CS, in 1982, had forty members. Its most important power is that of issuing laws when the NA is not functioning (in a sense, the CS is the country's real legislature). The CS also interprets the law, exercises legislative initiative, declares war or makes peace, removes or appoints members of the Council of Ministers, gives instructions of a general nature to the office of the attorney general and to the judiciary, supervises the diplomatic corps, vetoes ministerial decisions as well as those made at any other level, and exercises any other power that the NA may give it.

The president of the CS is expected to control and supervise the activities of all government ministries and administrative agencies. He could take over any ministry or government post and propose to the NA the members of the Council of Ministers. He is also commander in chief of the armed forces. The president, first vice president, and five vice presidents of the CS are all in the Political Bureau. The president and the first vice president also head the Secretariat. The other thirty-three members of the CS have been either in the PB, the CC, or, until recently, the Secretariat.

The National Assembly has had three elections since 1992—in 1993, 1998, 2003. The most recent legislature has 390 (64.04 percent) males and 219 females (35.96 percent). The average age was forty-seven years; 67 percent of the deputies were white and 378 of them (62 percent) new to the office.

THE COUNCIL OF MINISTERS

The government proper is the Council of Ministers (CM), whose members are appointed by the president of the Council of State and ratified by the NA. The CM has one president, one first vice president, twelve vice presidents, thirty ministers, forty-eight commission members, eight advisers, one deputy secretary, and one minister secretary. The CM administers the state apparatus, executes the laws, issues decrees in accordance with existing laws, develops and administers the national budget, carries out foreign policy, and organizes and directs social, economic, cultural, scientific, and military matters. The CM's Executive Committee (comprising the president, first vice president, and the twelve vice presidents) is the real power in government. In 1982, of the fourteen persons on the executive committee, nine were in the PB, two were in the Secretariat, five were full members of the CS, and six others were alternates.

Before 1976, the same individuals performed numerous functions although they had one role: They were revolutionaries with power. Revolutionary leaders assumed both political and administrative functions. Political leadership and administration are now separate. Charismatic authority is being transformed into a legal-rational system of authority, but during that transition, which may take years, the rules and regulations of the new political structure are elaborated, defined, and given content as well as life by the charismatic authority.

Fidel and Raúl Castro have a tremendous amount of power and control over the key institutions of Cuban society. But this is to be expected. A charismatic system of authority transfers legitimacy to a legal-rational type of authority by placing the representatives of the previous system in key positions. As time goes on and the charismatic leaders play by the new rules, the institutions themselves gain legitimacy. Of course, it remains to be seen whether such a process will continue to unfold. In 1982, Fidel Castro held the following posts: first secretary of the Political Bureau and the Secretariat; member of the Central Committee; deputy to the National Assembly; president of the Council of State, the Council of Ministers, and the Executive Committee of the Council of Ministers; and commander in chief of the armed forces. Raúl Castro was the second secretary of the Political Bureau and the Secretariat; member of the Central Committee; deputy to the National Assembly; first vice president of the Council of State, the Council of Ministers, and the Executive Committee of the Council of Ministers; and minister of the armed forces. Thus, the answer to the perennial question, What will happen when Fidel Castro dies?, has to be—on the basis of the institutionalization of authority and the resources that Raúl Castro commands—that Raúl would succeed his brother.

The succession question, a problem confronted by any political system based on charismatic authority, has become more acute as the revolution and its leaders have gotten older. To the concerns with a gerontocracy should be added the international situation as of late. The Communist movement is in disarray. In the Soviet Union as well as Eastern Europe the one-party state monopoly has disappeared; electoral politics are now accepted as a matter of political necessity, and Communists everywhere no longer claim to have all the answers. Elections in Nicaragua, the dissolution of Communist parties in Eastern Europe, the revamping of NATO, and the rediscovery of Western political "democracy" have imposed tremendous pressure on the Cuban political system.

The European Parliament, as well as traditional leftist friends of the Cuban Revolution, are demanding the establishment of a more open political system in the island. To these pressures should be added the very success of the revolution: It has created a more sophisticated political culture, a more educated population, and a more generalized belief that the people can rule themselves. The period of charismatic rule, in other words, confronts its major crisis. It has one option: to transfer authority from the charismatic leader to representative institutions that enjoy legitimacy.

How this will be accomplished has not yet been resolved. Nor is there a consensus within Cuba that this should be done. Many people still identify solely with Fidel Castro, the charismatic leader ("el original," the man who conceived, organized, made, consolidated, and maintained the revolution for over thirty-eight years). In fact, those who wish to preserve the charismatic type of political regime note that "in the face of the crisis of socialism and the aggressive euphoria of North American imperialism" it is impossible to play with

Western political models. Their reasoning suggests that the United States is now ready to attack Cuba, as the revolution becomes one of the few surviving socialist/revolutionary regimes in the world. In their view the only possibility for survival is to be in a permanent state of readiness, which only the mass mobilization qualities of charismatic authority can assure. Perhaps this reasoning would be easily dismissed if the revolutionaries thought that the United States had no intention of attacking the revolution, but U.S. policymakers, in a sense, have contributed to the fear of attack. (See "U.S.–Cuban Relations" on page 370.)

From 1989 to 1992, the Cuban revolutionaries returned to the methods of earlier years. Mass mobilization and calls to nationalism became a daily occurrence. The revolutionary leadership asserted that Cuba's independence and the very future of socialism depended on the survival and durability of the revolution. Thus, political reforms were defined as concessions that could lead to revolutionary defeat. According to Fidel Castro, in a number of speeches given in late 1989 and early 1990, Cuba's independence, national sovereignty, and the defense of "socialism" were inexorably linked. The battle cry "Fatherland or Death" of earlier years was transformed into "Socialism or Death."

After the 1991 Communist Party Congress and the 1992 constitutional reform, the political picture changed again. The nationalist theme was replaced by stress on economic efficiency and reorganization. One heard less talk of socialism as seminars on management, quality circles, and profitability became the order of the day. The regime had begun building a state capitalist economy without private capitalists.

Calls to emulate the experience of Eastern Europe are dismissed by Cuban revolutionaries as another form of "intellectual and political colonialism." Cuba's realities, they say, are different from those of Europe. Cuba, and the rest of Latin America, must find their own answers on the basis of their own material and cultural conditions. Moreover, the recent return to power by electoral means of socialists and even Communists in Eastern Europe had given cause for hope to those in power in Havana. The dismal economic problems in Russia and elsewhere in Eastern Europe further strengthen the point held by the Cuban revolutionaries that the state has to play a central role in economic policy. Moreover, the recent tilt to the left in the political landscape in Latin America (Lula in Brazil, Kirchner in Argentina, Chávez in Venezuela among them) means that Havana now has new allies in this hemisphere. The extremely rightwing and interventionist foreign and military policies of the George W. Bush administration have made new friends for Cuba throughout the world as well.

REDISTRIBUTION AND ECONOMIC EXPERIMENTATION

Cuba is a poor and underdeveloped country. When the Cuban revolutionaries attained power, the country confronted serious economic problems. Foremost among these was dependence on one crop—sugar—and one buyer—the United States. How much sugar the United States bought was determined by the U.S. Congress and the Agriculture Department. The sugar harvest lasted, at best, four months; thus, Cuba also faced serious unemployment and under-employment.

Prior to the revolution, the unemployment rate averaged 16.4 percent of the available workforce. However, when the sugar harvest ended, it could climb to 20–21 percent. In 1957, only 37.2 percent of the labor force worked the entire year. Social inequality was also a problem. According to a Labor Ministry report issued in 1957, 62.2 percent of the employed received an average monthly salary of less than 75 pesos (peso value was then equal to the dollar). Only 38 percent of the male workers earned more than $75 per month. In 1956, 34 percent of the total population of Cuba received 10 percent of the national income, and only 7.2 percent of the employees earned more than $1,000 a year. A family of six, on the average, had a yearly income of $548.75 and could spend about 17 cents per person for food daily. In the first year of the revolution, 73 percent of all families had an average income of $715 per year. Poverty was widespread, particularly in the rural areas.

Land was unequally distributed. A small portion of the landowners owned most of it. In 1959, 8.5 percent of all farms comprised 71.6 percent of the land area in farms; on the other hand, 80 percent of all farms comprised 13.8 percent of the farmland. At the time, 94.6 percent of the land was privately owned; the state controlled just 5.4 percent. Only 32.2 percent of the landowners worked their own land; 25.5 percent of the farmland was administered on behalf of the landowners, and 42.3 percent was rented out or share-cropped. Twenty-five percent of the best agricultural land was owned by U.S. companies, while 63.7 percent of the agricultural workforce had no land of its own. Most of those who owned their land were usually engaged in production for family use since their parcels were very small. Altogether, U.S. corporate interests controlled 2 million acres (810,000 hectares) of land in the island, out of a total surface of 23 million acres (9.3 million hectares)—that is, 8.7 percent of the national territory. In Camagüey Province, six companies controlled 20.7 percent of the land.

U.S. interests could be found elsewhere as well. Total U.S. investments had reached a little over $1 billion when the revolutionaries took power; this was the equivalent of 40 percent of the GNP. U.S. capital dominated 90 percent of the utilities, 50 percent of the railways, 40 percent of the production of raw sugar, 25 percent of all bank deposits. U.S. interests controlled more than 80 percent of mining, oil production, hotels, pharmaceuticals, detergents, fertilizers, auto dealerships, tires, imports, and exports. Of 161 sugar mills, U.S. companies owned thirty-six. U.S. capital was shifting away from traditional investments (sugar, utilities, mining) and moving toward new areas (loans, imports, exports, light industry). The reported rate of return on U.S. investments was 9 percent, but Cuban revolutionary authorities have estimated that the real rate was about 23 percent. From 1952 to 1958, U.S. companies repatriated an average of $50 million yearly (new investment during the period was $40 million yearly).

In 1958, the United States supplied 72 percent of Cuban imports and bought 69 percent of Cuban exports. Cuba's balance of trade from 1948 to

1958 was positive with most of the world, except the United States. It has been estimated that the rate of economic growth from 1945 to 1958 averaged 4.3 percent per year while the per capita income growth was 1.8 percent.

When the revolutionaries seized power, they found an economy that relied on sugar production, primarily controlled in its numerous facets by U.S. capital, as well as an economy that was unable to generate sufficient jobs in the primary or secondary sector to absorb the surplus labor. The Cuban economy was essentially capitalist in nature, with a large proletarian labor force in the countryside (over 64 percent of the rural laborers were wage earners).

In the first two years of the revolution two major trends developed. On the one hand, a progressive redistribution of income took place.

- February 2, 1959: All debts owed to the Cuban state suspended
- March 10, 1959: House rents lowered 50 percent
- May 17, 1959: Agrarian Reform Law began redistribution of land
- December 23, 1959: Social security made available to all workers
- October 14, 1960: Urban Reform Law established procedure by which renter will use rent payments as amortization in order to purchase home
- June 7, 1961: Free universal education established
- August 1, 1961: Transportation costs lowered
- September 21, 1961: Child care centers subsidized by the state
- March 12, 1962: Rationing introduced, price of all food items frozen (remained frozen until the early 1980s)

The second trend was a radical change in prevailing property relations. By the end of 1960, the critical areas of the Cuban economy had been taken over by the state: All of banking, export-import operations, energy, and utilities were owned by the state. More than three-quarters of industry, construction, and transportation was also in the hands of the government. Only the bulk of agriculture was in the hands of the private sector, and that was primarily the result of the redistribution of land.

During the period 1959–1960, there was no talk of socialism on the part of the authorities. Economic thinking revolved around the ideas of rapid industrialization, import substitution, and reducing the role of sugar while diversifying agriculture. There were no real controls of an economic nature. The capitalist market was not replaced; it disappeared, and nothing took its place. No one seemed to pay attention to capital accumulation. The central idea was simply to establish greater equality by increasing the income and resources of the lower classes. This was the distributionist phase of the revolution. As the state moved into the private economy, it found that it lacked the personnel to run the new enterprises; often those who were considered loyal were put in command. They had to learn their jobs while performing them. Consumption improved altogether, but it led to shortages because no effort was made to increase stocks.

In 1961, after the revolutionaries discovered that they had socialism, they began looking for a model to emulate. The Czechoslovakian model was copied, and industrialization was stressed; sugar was set aside. From 1961 to 1963, some problems developed with the emerging rural middle class. Since the revolutionary regime had little use for sugar and industry seemed more appealing, a second agrarian reform was issued that abolished the remaining medium-sized landholdings. During this period, the state further socialized the means of production so that it controlled 70 percent of the agricultural sector and more than 95 percent of industry, transportation, and construction. The private sector could sell only to the state. The Cuban economy had the highest index of state control in the world. A generalized process of centralization of economic decisionmaking took root, led by Ché Guevara from the Ministry of Industries.

It should be noted that this is the period when Cuba and the United States had reached the equivalent of a state of war (in 1961, the Bay of Pigs; in 1962, the October missile crisis). Within Cuba, the revolutionaries continued their distributionist policies. Health care, for example, became free in this period. Unemployment disappeared—primarily because the productivity of labor declined and more people were hired to do a job that in the past had been performed by one person. Also, many of the previously unemployed were absorbed by the service sector. From 1961 to 1962, sugar output dropped from 6.8 million tons to 3.8 million. Yet, few sectors were growing or generating the necessary foreign exchange. This led to a rectification of the economic policy.

In 1963, the revolutionary authorities abandoned their stress on industrialization; sugar was to be the pivot of Cuba's economic development. The new economic strategy was to be based on modernizing Cuban agriculture, introducing more up-to-date forces of production, and improving the skills of the workers. The effort would be centered on the state farms. At the time, two entirely different economic models for constructing the future socialist society were being discussed.

Meanwhile, the United States had imposed an economic blockade on the island in 1962, and except for Mexico, no country in the hemisphere traded with the Cubans. Moreover, Cuba's terms of trade deteriorated from 1964 to 1966 due primarily to the drop in the price of sugar (in 1963, the price was 8.3 cents per pound; by 1966, it had dropped to 1.8 cents). So the cost of imports increased greatly.

In 1966, Cuba's most original phase began. It lasted until 1970. The goal was to produce ever-larger amounts of sugar, regardless of the world market situation. Moreover, since the country did not have the material resources to reward effort, moral (that is, political) incentives were to be used to motivate the workers. The highly centralized economic plans of the previous period were replaced by sectoral, independent, decentralized plans. The plans (and enterprises) received money allocated through a central budget. Enterprises did not engage in mercantile relations with one another, and they did not have to show a profit. Cost accounting was disregarded altogether. Efficiency depended merely on meeting output goals, regardless of cost. During the period, a concentrated effort was made to avoid bureaucratic rigidity and to discourage criticism of the approach. Revolutionary consciousness and commitment, it was believed, would do the trick.

At the same time, the state took over complete control of industry, all of construction, 98 percent of transportation, and every single retail business. The labor force involved in harvesting sugar was militarized in 1969. Sugar output went through cycles. From 1966 to 1967, it went up from 4.5 million tons to 6.2 million; then it dropped to 5.1 million tons in 1968 and to 4.4 million in 1969. The 1970 harvest was the largest in the history of the country, but it had a tremendous negative impact on the larger economy, since most of the national resources were concentrated on meeting the goal of producing 10 million tons of sugar.

Economic efficiency dropped abruptly during this period. Economic growth averaged just 0.4 percent. The revolutionary authorities had ended the connection between output and salaries; that is, workers got paid regardless of production. Moreover, during this period, the state distributed, free, water, public phone service, and child care, among other things. Gratuities were on the increase, and labor productivity declined. An excess of money in circulation ensued; purchasing power exceeded goods available, contributing to labor absenteeism. During the period, the country invested up to 30 percent of its material product on economic growth, which forced it to rely more than ever on imports. The economy did not fare as poorly as one might have expected because the price of sugar consistently climbed during these years (in 1966, the price was 1.8 cents per pound; 1967, 1.9; 1968, 1.9; 1969, 3.2; 1970, 3.68).

In 1970, the revolutionary authorities reconsidered their strategy and revised it, shifting from the budgetary system of finance to what is called *cálculo económico,* or self-finance system. The new system stressed centralized economic planning, cost accounting and enterprise profitability, material rewards, mercantile relations among enterprises, and contracts between enterprises and labor unions. Productivity and efficiency came to be measured on the basis of the rate of return (connected to the cost of production). Managerial expertise on the administrative level began to take precedence over revolutionary zeal. The role of sugar was de-emphasized somewhat, as more attention was paid to the diversification of agriculture and the development of mineral resources. The *cálculo económico* had become nationwide in its application by 1977. Thus, 1971 to 1976 were years of transition. It should be noted that the shift away from the budgetary system coincided with the move toward institutionalization. This was not coincidental. Cuba's economic and political organizations are highly interrelated. Charismatic authority went hand in hand with moral incentives and mass mobilization to achieve economic goals; rational-legal authority now permeates the political as well as the economic spheres.

The new economic and political organization seemed to pay off very well. The gross material product (GMP)—that is, the gross value of production from agriculture, industry, and construction—showed some remarkable developments; for example, the GMP growth rates for the 1970s were as follows.

1971:   4.2%
1972:   9.7%
1973: 13.1%
1974:   7.8%
1975: 12.3%
1976:   3.5%
1977:   3.1%
1978:   8.2%
1979:   2.4%

The improvement and subsequent deterioration of the economy in the 1970s, however, were not due to internal conditions. Rather, the price of sugar in the world market affects the general performance of the Cuban economy. Sugar prices rose from 4.5 cents per pound in 1970 to 29.6 cents in 1974 and 20.3 cents in 1975 before they began to drop, reaching 7.4 cents in 1982. The cycle was reflected in the Cuban economy because, more than twenty years after the revolution, the export of sugar remained crucial to the overall functioning of the economy. In many years, sugar accounted for 80 percent of foreign earnings.

It should be stressed, however, that the revolutionary government worked out an arrangement with the Soviet Union that allowed the island to escape, to some extent, the cycles of the capitalist economy as far as sugar is concerned. Since the 1960s, the Soviets paid a much higher price for Cuban sugar than the price in the open world market. Only on three occasions (1963, 1972, 1974) were world market prices higher than those paid by the Soviets. By 1979, when the world price had reached a low point of 9.6 cents, the Soviets were paying 44 cents. The treatment that the revolutionary government received from the Soviet Union has been positive and extraordinary. In 1972, the Soviet Union agreed to postpone until 1986 the payment of Cuba's debt. The debt covered a period of twenty-five years during which Cuba paid no interest.

Approximately 20 percent of Cuba's trade in the early 1980s was with the capitalist market economies. The terms of trade were such, however, that while the price of sugar declined, the prices of the products Cuba had to buy to process the sugar cane and produce sugar went up. (A metric ton of urea in 1972 sold for $76, but by 1980 the price was $303. The same situation occurred with ammonia nitrate: Its price changed from $206 to $506.) In constant 1970 prices, a pound of sugar in 1982 sold for 2.8 cents. In order to import the same amount of goods, then, Cuba had to export much more.

Cuba's economic performance in the first five years of the 1980s was significantly better than that of the rest of Latin America (see Table 18.1). But the Cuban situation started to change in 1986, the year that Fidel Castro announced the initiation of the "rectification" campaign in the economy. The campaign denounced and took steps against private enterprise (the free peasants' market created in 1980, the appearance of private urban businesses, and the reliance on profitability as an indicator for the allocation of resources). The rectification campaign, in other words, put political decisions rather than "economic logic" in command. The overall performance of the economy suffered as a result.

Moreover, events in Eastern Europe and the Soviet Union damaged external trade. The Eastern European countries shifted toward convertible currency transactions, and the democratization of the Soviet political system led to a greater demand for consumer goods just as the situation produced tremendous uncertainty in the supply of goods from abroad. Cuban economic planning and performance hence suffered. The revolutionary government, with little foreign exchange in hand, adopted a policy of more import substitution. The strategy was accompanied by greater stress on export diversification.

In early 1990, Fidel Castro told the Cuban people that very difficult years could be expected and that rationing might be extended to new products. At the same time, the Cuban authorities contacted Mexican, Brazilian, and Japanese investors and made new offers to transnational corporations in the hope that the shortage of capital could be overcome. Cuban foreign reserves in 1988 and 1989 were less than $100 million.

In 1991–1992, Cuba's traditional economic allies disappeared, and so did all aid, credit, suppliers, and buyers. The Cuban economy suffered an almost overwhelming blow. From 1992 to 1993, imports collapsed, as did exports. Table 18.1 shows the pattern in imports from 1989, just prior to the collapse of the Soviet bloc, and its impact on Cuba, then the island's improvement—without any real assistance.

TABLE 18.1   Imports

Year	Growth Rate	Total (millions USD)
1989	3.40%	8,608
1990	-5.70%	8,017
1991	-37.00%	4,702
1992	-45.30%	2,737
1993	-5.40%	2,339
1994	19.20%	2,849
1995	11.50%	3,565
1996	24.30%	4,125
1997	11.00%	4,628
1998	8.00%	4,800

The absence of supplies and raw materials meant that economic output declined between 30 percent and 35 percent in just two years. By 1994, the economy touched bottom. The following year it grew by almost 3 percent, and in 1996 it achieved a growth of 7.6 percent.

TABLE 18.2   Gross Internal Investments, Growth Rate

Year	Growth Rate
1989	10.1%
1990	-2.9%
1991	-45.9%
1992	-58.3%
1993	-39.7%
1994	1.9%
1995	35.2%
1996	22.8%
1997	13.7%
1998	7.3%

Bouncing back, however, has not meant that the overall standard of living of the population has improved in a major way. In the late 1990s, Cuba still produced at a level below that of 1985. Yet the positive turn in the economy has been quite extraordinary. Foreign investments, tourism, and nickel exports are the three major contributors to the recovery. Not long ago most foreign analysts considered Cuba's economic prospects rather dim. The trend now appears to be moving in the opposite direction.

TABLE 18.3   Gross National Product

Year	Growth Rate	Per Inhabitant
1989	1.5%	1.0
1990	-2.9%	-3.9
1991	-9.5%	-10.4
1992	-9.9	-10.6
1993	-13.6	-14.2
1994	0.6	0.2
1995	2.5	2.2
1996	7.6	7.2
1997	2.5	2.1
1998	1.3	0.9

Despite Cuba's limited economic resources, the revolutionary government has been able to distribute social services in a manner that has produced profound positive results. The population of Cuba is about 11 million. The country is highly urban. In 1958, 58.7 percent of the people lived in cities; by 1983 the figure was 64.5 percent. The population in 2002 was 76 percent urban. From 1990 to the present the urban population has grown by 0.7 percent per year (the growth rate was 2.1 percent from 1970–1991). The mortality rate is 7.1 per 1,000 inhabitants, and life expectancy increased from 58 years in 1959

TABLE 18.4   Population Growth Rate

Year	Population Total (millions)	Growth Rate
1989	10.5	0.5
1990	10.6	1.1
1991	10.7	1
1992	10.8	0.8
1993	10.9	0.7
1994	10.9	0.4
1995	10.9	0.3
1996	11	0.4
1997	11	0.4
1998	11	0.5

to 74.8 years in 2001. The infant mortality rate, a major index of how much poverty and inequality a society has, has been radically changed—from a high of 33 it dropped to 6.5 in 2002. The age distribution of the population has changed as well. Before the revolution, 36.2 percent of the population was younger than fifteen; in 2000 the figure was 21.3 percent. At the same time, the percentage of people over sixty increased from 4.2 percent in 1958 to 14.5 percent in 2000. By 2002, 1.4 million Cubans lived off pensions. While the population is getting older and living longer, the birth rate has declined. In 1955 the population growth rate (per thousand) was 16, but in the year 2000 the rate stood at 2.3. As the population gets older there is further decline in the population growth rate. Opportunities offered to women, it has been shown, further contribute to a drop in the natality of the female population. The dependency ratio continues to increase (it stood at 55.0 in the year 2000). The city of Havana contains 17 percent of the population over the age of 60. The Cuban family tends to be small. In 1995 the typical household had 3.4 members, with little variation between urban and rural areas. About 54 percent of the families are nuclear, that is, two generations living under the same roof; however, 42 percent have three generations under the same roof or in close proximity.

Illiteracy has been reduced to less than 4 percent, and almost the entire population has received a primary education. At present, 96–97 percent of all the children of primary school age go to school. More than a million people have received a secondary education since 1959. One out of every 2.83 Cubans studies today. Full employment was achieved, although in the last few years unemployment has begun to grow (it is estimated that it was 2–4 percent of the male labor force in 1982). The social benefits that the population receives in the form of old-age pensions, workers' compensation, and maternity, illness, and social security allowances place Cuba at the forefront of all Latin American countries. It is by this means that the popularity and legitimacy of the revolution have been maintained. The distributionist policies of Cuba's revolutionary government have been far more successful than its economic policies—although one needs to acknowledge the numerous external political constraints imposed on the country.

Since 1993, however, the economic policies that have been introduced for the sake of survival have increased the degree of social inequality in the society. In a real sense, despite government policies to counter the trend, social stratification and inequality have gained ground. This phenomenon has been exacerbated by the remittances sent by Cubans living abroad, the increasing role of the market as one mechanism to distribute goods, and the emergence of tourism. In a sense Cuba has become a much more complex socioeconomic system. Poverty has become a real problem as well. Since the mid-1990s the Cuban government began to address the issue of a "population at risk." This was a serious matter in the eastern part of the island (Oriente) where by 1996 about 30 percent of the people were not earning enough to meet their basic needs. The estimated figure for the urban areas was 20 percent of the population. Yet, according to the Economic Commission for Latin America, it should be noted that Cuba remains the society with the greatest degree of social equality in all of Latin America.[1] In the period 1996–1998, Cuba's GINI Coefficient was 0.38 in urban areas.[2]

It remains to be seen whether the tremendous investment in human capital will pay off in the foreseeable future. The next few years, however, will be difficult ones for Cuba.

U.S.–Cuban Relations

From 1959 to 1961, relations between the United States and Cuba progressively deteriorated. From 1961 to 1965, the two countries were in a state of semi-war. After 1965, the situation relaxed somewhat, but the two had no contact with one another. This situation continued until the last years of the Nixon administration, when some unofficial talks began. Finally, when Jimmy Carter was elected president of the United States, relations began to thaw. Diplomatic relations were renewed on the section level (as opposed to the embassy level), but no steps were taken toward restoring trade relations. The U.S. economic embargo was relaxed somewhat, as well as travel restrictions between the two countries. When Ronald Reagan arrived at the White House, however, every major social upheaval in Latin America was interpreted as the work of Cuban subversion. Consequently, the United States returned to policies reminiscent of the Eisenhower administration. There were even claims from the Cubans that the Reagan administration attempted to assassinate the leaders of the revolution.

After eight years of the Reagan administration, the Cuban government assumed that President George Bush would improve bilateral relations. But relations, in fact, deteriorated. The dramatic changes in world communism led the White House to conclude that Cuba would be one more "domino" and that there was no need to take any initiatives that would change the island's isolation. Rather, the White House began to broadcast television programs to the island and tightened the economic embargo, while attempting to link improvement in the relations between the United States and Eastern Europe with the severance of their ties with the revolution.

In 1992, an election year, both Democratic and Republican parties ended up supporting the Torricelli Bill, which imposed stricter U.S. government policies on Cuba and, moreover, shifted policymaking away from the executive branch and placed that power in the hands of the U.S. Congress. Presidential candidate Bill Clinton campaigned in support of a harder line against the Cuban government. Once Clinton was elected president, the government in Havana adopted a wait-and-see policy but soon discovered that the new administration addressed Cuban policy on the basis of domestic political needs. The Clinton administration took a fairly aggressive approach of supporting human rights activists and political opponents, and the Cuban government reacted by imposing even harsher restrictions on anyone considered a political enemy. During the summer of 1994, as the standard of living deteriorated and political repression augmented in Cuba, the number of boat people leaving the island climbed. As the U.S. government continued to welcome the so-called *balseros,* the Cuban government opted to allow anyone who so wished to leave the island by sea in order to reach the United States. The initiative forced the White House to begin negotiations with Havana. The end result was a break with past migration policy on Cuba: The United States no longer would allow any Cuban to enter the country unless proper procedures were followed, including the granting of a visa (although Cubans who somehow manage to reach U.S. soil can claim refugee status, and remain).

Throughout 1995 there were hints and indications that perhaps relations between the two longtime adversaries would improve. Tension between the White House and the conservative exile organizations was manifested on many occasions. The conservative victory in congressional elections in 1994 meant that new forces pushed for a tougher stance on Cuba in U.S. politics. Exile organizations believed that the time was right to manufacture a crisis. In the fall of 1995 and early 1996, conservative exiles initiated a series of ventures against the Cuban government, the best known led by Brothers to the Rescue, a Miami group that began to fly over Cuban territory to drop political leaflets. In early 1995, two of the planes were shot down by the Cuban air force. This incited the Congress to adopt the Helms-Burton Bill, which President Clinton rapidly signed. The legislation signified a return to the worst days of U.S. interference in the domestic affairs of Cuba, at the same time creating the mechanism to attempt to impose a policy of economic isolation by third countries on Cuba. Thus, the policy of extraterritoriality was made into law and applied against Cuba and other countries as well.

With the George W. Bush administration, the most right-wing Cuban exiles got into strategic positions in the making of policy toward Latin America in general and Cuba in particular. The relations between the two countries have deteriorated in a number of areas, with the White House even announcing a set of policies that further limits the travels of Americans and Cuban-Americans to Cuba. The numerous people-to-people and cultural as well as educational contacts established during the Clinton administration have, for all practical purposes, come to an end. Family remittances by Cuban-Americans have been reduced since the Bush Treasury Department restricted the definition of what constitutes a Cuban family. Moreover, the administration has announced its commitment to produce "regime change" by providing more financial and other resources to the political opposition on the island (as long as it answers to the right-wing exiles). In early May 2004, the U.S. government released a document of more than 500 pages indicating what it intends to do once the revolution has been overthrown. It outlined how Cuba's economy, politics, society, and culture should be organized, all under the direct supervision of the executive branch. The announced policy went beyond the Platt Amendment itself.

But there is not much future for an internal political opposition. The more moderate and liberal opponents on the island will be more isolated now than ever, since the United States does not recognize them; they might try to seek assistance from social democrats in western Europe, but that does not seem a very promising prospect (the European Union has toyed with developing an alternative approach to that of the United States, but Washington, D.C. has torpedoed the initiative). The opposition on the island is disorganized and thoroughly penetrated by the Cuban police.

There are, of course, pressures from within the United States. Both the House and the Senate have gone on record favoring closer and normal relations with Cuba. Their position corresponds to what a growing sector of the business community wants. Moderate Cuban Americans also support such a change. Moreover, the demographics of the Cubans who live in the United States has changed; a greater number left the island in the 1990s, and they did so, primarily for economic reasons. Eventually those trends will assert themselves. In a sense, Cuban society has become more complex and the same can be said of Cubans abroad.

Cuba has a policy of opening to anyone who is willing to engage in respectful communication, as long as Cuba's right of self-determination is accepted. Havana has improved its relations with a large portion of the Cuban-American community, even getting rid of the condition by which an exile or emigre had to request a visa to enter the island. Normalization among Cubans on both sides of the Straits of Florida is preceding such action by the politicians in Washington, D.C.

The policy of confrontation, of course, reinforces the "besieged fortress" mentality in Havana. Thus the revolutionary authorities reply by establishing worldwide ties of all types with every country that is willing to engage them. Tourism itself has become a sort of self-defense, since the more one gets to know Cuba and its revolution, the less one will consider using military means against it. At present, however, there is little prospect of improvement in the relations between the United States and Cuba (see also chapter 14).

Regardless of what anyone may think, the Cuban Revolution is there to stay. It has radically affected every facet of Cuban life as well as of the country's international relations. What will happen as the population becomes better educated and the political system further institutionalized, no one knows. It is clear, nonetheless, that internal developments—as is the case with other social revolutions—will be affected by the international context.

NOTES

1. CEPAL, Equidad, Desarrollo y Ciudadanía, Santiago de Chile, 2001.

2. CEPAL, Politica Social y Reformas Estructurales: Cuba A Principios del Siglo XXI, Mexico, 2004

SUGGESTED READINGS

Periodical Literature

Following are a number of very useful periodical sources that can help the student of Cuba to keep up with events.

Bohemia. This major Havana weekly covers social, economic, cultural, and political events.

Cuba internacional. A glossy monthly portraying achievements of the Revolution.

Cuba Resource Center Newsletter. The main English-language publication presenting a friendly view of revolutionary Cuba. Published in New York City.

Cuban Studies. The best scholarly journal published on Cuba. Published in Pittsburgh, it concentrates on the post–1959 period. Each issue contains the best bibliography available on publications dealing with Cuba.

Foreign Broadcast Information Service. Daily translations of Cuban radio and television broadcasts monitored by U.S. intelligence agencies. Available on microfiche.

Temas. This is the leading cultural and social sciences journal in Cuba, required reading for anyone who wishes to know about the country.

Translations on Latin America. Translations of the documents and articles that are considered most important by the U.S. intelligence community. Deals with all of Latin America and has a section on Cuba. Published at least twice a week.

Numerous Internet resources offer information on Cuba:. The best resource is: http://sitioscubanos.cuba.cu/.

Books

Chomsky, Aviva, Barry Carr, Pamela Maria Smorkaloff, eds. *The Cuba Reader: History, Culture, Politics.* Durham, N.C.: Duke University Press, 2004.

Domínguez, Jorge I. *Cuba: Order and Revolution.* Cambridge: Harvard University Press, 1978.

Hernandez, Rafael. *Looking at Cuba: Essays on Culture and Civil Society.* Gainesville: University Press of Florida, 2003.

Jatar-Hausmann, Ana Julia, *The Cuban Way: Capitalism, Communism and Confrontation.* West Hartford, Conn.: Kumarian Press, 1999

MacEwan, Arthur. *Revolution and Economic Development in Cuba.* New York: St. Martin's Press, 1981.

Mesa-Lago, Carmelo. *The Economy of Socialist Cuba: A Two-Decade Appraisal.* Albuquerque: University of New Mexico Press, 1981.

Rosset, Peter, and Medea Benjamin. *The Greening of the Revolution: Cuba's Experiment with Organic Agriculture.* Gainesville: Ocean Press, 1995.

Sarduy, Pedro Pérez, et al. *Afro-Cuban Voices: On Race and Identity in Contemporary Cuba,* Gainesville: University Press of Florida, 2000.

Scarpaci, Joseph L., Roberto Segre, Mario Coyula, Andres Duany. *Havana: Two Faces of the Antillean Metropolis.* Durham, N.C.: University of North Carolina Press, 2002.

Pérez-Stable, Marifeli. *The Cuban Revolution: Origins, Course, and Legacy.* New York: Oxford University Press, 1998.

United Nations, Economic Commission for Latin America. *Cuba: Estilo de desarrollo y políticas sociales.* Mexico City, 1980.

Chapter 19

The Caribbean: The Structure of Modern-Conservative Societies

ANTHONY P. MAINGOT

In a geopolitical sense, it is best to define the Caribbean in terms of all the countries that border on that sea. This includes the islands as well as the countries of the mainland with eastern coasts that form the western perimeter of the Caribbean. Together, they make up a "basin" of which the sea is the crucial geopolitical feature.

Geographical definitions, however, are ultimately arbitrary. Their validity depends on the purpose or ends pursued, that is, on their utility. So El Salvador, which has no border on the Caribbean Sea, is regarded by some as a Caribbean Basin country, whereas Mexico, Colombia, and most Central American countries are two-ocean countries yet look more toward the Caribbean than toward the Pacific. A simple explanation lies in the fact that colonization and subsequent trade and cultural contacts developed as part of the Atlantic expansion, first of Spain and later the rest of Europe.

For the purpose of this chapter, "the Caribbean" is considered to be the islands plus those mainland territories that, until recently, were part of the British, Dutch, and French colonial empires. Clearly, it is difficult to generalize on any level about countries as varied as these. Haiti has almost six times more land and five times the population of Trinidad and Tobago but only one-fifth the gross domestic product (GDP). Haitians speak Creole, and a liberal estimate is that 50 percent of them are illiterate; Trinidadians speak English, and 96 percent are literate (see Table 19.1). The former has been governed by dictators throughout most of its 180 years of independence; the latter had a functioning parliamentary system even before it became independent in 1962.

As with any other geographical region or expression ("Africa," "Latin America," "Asia"), each unit in the region deserves to be studied individually. And yet, there is also value in an understanding of the broader continuities and similarities that make any region a culture area. Keep in mind, as Melville Herskovits

TABLE 19.1   The Insular Caribbean: Basic Statistics

	Population (1000)	Area (KM²)	GDP (1998) per capita	Language
Independent States (1)				
Cuba	11,000	114,500	—	Spanish
Dominican Republic	7,600	49,000	1,799	Spanish
Haiti	7,000	28,000	208	French/C
Jamaica	2,500	11,000	1,559	English
Trinidad & Tobago	1,290	5,000	4,618	English
Bahamas	272	13,900	12,944	English
Barbados	261	430	7,894	English
St. Lucia	153	620	3,907	English/C
St. Vincent/Grenadines	127	390	2,635	English
Grenada	108	340	3,347	English
Antigua/Barbuda	92	440	8,559	English
Dominica	96	750	3,310	English
St. Kitts/Nevis	48	270	6,716	English
On Mainland				
Guyana	760	215,000	825	English
Suriname	457	163,000	710	Dutch/C
Belize	211	23,000	2,725	English
Dependent Territories (2)				
Guadeloupe (F)	413	1,710	12,287	French/C
Martinique (F)	371	1,100	14,524	French/C
French Guiana (F)	135	90,000	13,044	French/C
Netherland Antilles (Neth.)	197	800	11,698	Dutch/C
Aruba (Neth.)	77	90	16,186	Dutch/C
Cayman Island (UK)	33	264	23,966	English
British Virgin Islands (UK)	17	150	14,010	English
Turks & Caicos (UK)	14	417	7,061	English
Montserrat (UK)	11	102	3,846	English
Anguilla (UK)	10	90	6,937	English
Puerto Rico (USA)	3,700	8,900	9,815	Spanish
U.S. Virgin Islands (USA)	104	347	12,038	English

Sources: (C= Local creole language)
(1) Norman Girvan, "Societies at Risk? The Caribbean and Global Change," Paris: UNESCO Discussion Paper No.17 (Aug. 1997), Table No.1. (2) Victor Bulmer-Thomas, "The Wider Caribbean in the 20th C.," Integration and Trade Vol. 15 (2001), Table 10.

reminds us, that the concept of culture area does not denote a self-conscious grouping. Rather than focusing on the details, it points to the broad lines of similarities and differences between cultures. In the Caribbean, these continuities and similarities result from a blending of modern and conservative features in the composition of major institutions as well as in social and behavioral dynamics. It is useful to call Caribbean societies modern-conservative systems.

THE CONCEPT OF MODERN-CONSERVATIVE SOCIETIES

Like all concepts or heuristic devices in the social sciences, the concept of modern-conservative societies is used to explain complex social structures and social processes. This is especially important in a region as varied as the Caribbean. The point is that the concept appears to describe Caribbean social structure well, and we conclude therefore that it will also help explain the political manifestations of that social structure.

It is important to note that we are not talking about traditional societies: those relatively static, passive, and acquiescent societies generally resistant to change. They approximate rather what Michael Oakeshott calls societies underpinned by "skeptical conservatism," a peculiar mixture of political conservatism and radical individualism and skepticism. The modern-conservative society is not only capable of social change, it is often prone to dramatic calls or movements for change. Several cases from the English-speaking Caribbean illustrate the latent explosive character of the modern-conservative society.

In 1970, the island state of Trinidad and Tobago was suffering from both a decline in oil production and low world prices for oil. OPEC had not yet managed to control the market; it would do this in 1972. The island economy had been radically changed by oil. The production of sugar, cacao, and other agricultural commodities was now subsidized; the state became the largest employer. By 1970, there was 22 percent open unemployment and 23 percent hidden unemployment, while the unemployment among moderately educated youth (more than eight years of schooling) was 40 percent higher than the average. Additionally, since 80 percent of the women indicated no desire to work outside the home, the problem was squarely centered on the young males. These youth were integrated into the modern sector: urban, educated, organized, and in close contact with the outside world.

With the Black Power movement in full bloom in the United States and Canada, two events outside Trinidad lit the spark of Trinidad's own Black Power uprising. One occurred in Jamaica, where authorities prohibited a Guyanese university lecturer, Walter Rodney, from reentering Jamaica from Canada. The so-called Rodney affair stirred the university students in Trinidad, as did the "riot" of a dozen Trinidadian students in Canada claiming racial discrimination. Racial grievances, unemployment, unrest among the professional military men, and accusations of graft and corruption against certain government ministers all came to a head in a massive movement against "the system." And yet, the motor, the driving force, was not class conflict but a deep sense of righteous indignation.

The target of the movement, Prime Minister Eric Williams, was repeatedly invited to join the moral crusade for black identity and ownership. Clearly, he had lost his moral authority but not his political legitimacy.

In 1970 in Trinidad, righteous indignation took on psychological and cultural dimensions: a return to history, to a purer and more integral past as a means of collective and individual cleansing and redemption. African names and apparel were adopted and modern European ways rejected to such an extent that the movement's leadership soon began to alienate large sectors of the Indian and colored populations as well as the black middle class. A reorganized police force put an end to the armed phase of the movement, and when ten years later the same leaders competed in a free election, they were soundly defeated. Had the problems of the society been solved by the massive influx of oil revenues since 1973? Not at all. Fully 83 percent of those who in 1981 felt that life was getting worse on the island attributed that deterioration to corruption.

Although the incumbent party won a sizable electoral victory in 1981, race again showed its strength: The victorious People's National Movement (PNM) won the safe "black" seats; the opposition United Labour Force (ULF), the safe "Indian" seats. As in 1970, a deterioration in the economy could again spark unrest, but it will have to play on certain moral chords and generate a sense of indignation among both leaders and followers, with totally unpredictable outcomes.

The case of St. Lucia in early 1982 illustrates this aspect of political behavior in modern-conservative societies. On January 16, 1982, the prime minister of St. Lucia resigned after widespread public protests. This forced the dismissal of Parliament and mandated the calling of elections within a few months. The caretaker government was led by a member of a radical party, the smallest of St. Lucia's three main parties. It was not this party, however, that had led the antigovernment movement, nor were the issues in the movement ideological ones in the political sense. That movement was headed by the chamber of commerce and other middle sectors, protesting what they regarded as official corruption and abuse of government authority.

The upheaval in St. Lucia was very similar to that which had occurred in Grenada three years earlier: Incompetence, corruption, and abuse of authority had engendered a massive sense of indignation among a multiplicity of sectors. In Grenada, the opposition movement was called the Committee of 21, indicating the number of groups involved in the opposition to Prime Minister Eric Gairy. The difference between Grenada in 1979 and St. Lucia in 1982 was that a small, radical clique managed to wrest power by force of arms in the former, while constitutional government was restored the middle classes in the latter. Although all groups participated in the 1982 elections in St. Lucia, the moderates won every seat in the House of Assembly. Similar defeats of radical parties had already occurred in Dominica, St. Vincent, St. Kitts, Jamaica, Barbados, and Trinidad. Elections in the Dominican Republic in mid-1982 also indicated a tendency toward the center in political-ideological terms; it appeared to be a Caribbean-wide phenomenon.

A decade later, similar moderate responses were evident in Trinidadians' response to an armed insurrectionary attempt. In 1991, a black Muslim group, the Jamaat al Muslimeen, played on the deep sense of malaise among the urban masses. After assaulting police headquarters, taking the prime minister and most of his cabinet hostage, and taking control of the television station, the rebels called on the populace to rebel. They did no such thing, and the terrorists had to surrender to the still-standing authorities. Although 60 percent of a national poll expressed sympathy with the Muslimeen's grievances, fully 75 percent rejected the use of force to achieve redress of these.

These illustrations allow us to identify some of the characteristics of the modern-conservative society. It should at the outset be understood that to speak of "structures" does not imply anything static: It merely means that certain underlying factors or interrelationships are more durable, more tenacious and retentive than many of the immediate and observable manifestations of those relationships suggest. Such ideas or concepts as history, life, being, and essence are central to this conservative view of life and are logical products of ex-colonial, multiethnic, and deeply religious societies, as we shall see. As Karl Mannheim has noted, these patterns of thought, far from becoming superfluous through modernization, tend to survive and adapt themselves to each new stage of social development.[1] Because it has a real social basis, conservative thought is functional and useful as a guide to action.

The modern conservative society, then, tends to mobilize politically around issues that strike chords of a conservative type, issues that engender a collective sense of moral indignation. Mobilization occurs, however, through modern mechanisms and institutional arrangements. The most conservative of values, if widely shared and if the spokespeople have access to modern institutions and mechanisms, can have impacts that have revolutionary manifestations though something less than revolutionary goals—if "revolutionary" implies a complete overthrow of the existing sociopolitical structure, not merely the regime.

The myth of the modern, revolutionary nature of Caribbean societies stems from a misunderstanding of the nature of many of the movements that brought revolutionary elites to power. Even in modern-conservative societies (as Lenin theorized and demonstrated), a determined elite can bring about a designed outcome. This is so because after the initial mobilization, the movement tends to enter into a qualitatively new phase. This phase has dynamics of its own, dynamics that tend to represent a combination of the unpredictability and complexity of all mass actions and the more predictable—or at least understandable—actions of revolutionary cadres and elites. The latter can turn the movement in a revolutionary direction even in modern-conservative societies; they are less capable, however, of initially generating a revolutionary mobilization in such societies.

This explains why the Suriname Revolution (1980) and the Grenadian Revolution (1979), like the Nicaraguan Revolution, had to coexist with strong private sectors, established churches, and other aroused but hardly revolutionary sectors. These regimes were confronted with the complexity of the modern-conservative society, which explains as much about the failure of revolution as does the implacable opposition of Washington (which certainly played its part).

Understanding the nature of political change in these societies, then, requires an analysis not only of the immediate political happenings in the area—the political landscape—but also of what might be called the structural or enduring aspects of Caribbean political dynamics: the political substructure. What is required, thus, is a political economy approach to the area in which demographics and economics are central, though not exclusive, topics of analysis.

The central questions, however, remain. Who reacts, why, and over what? What do the answers tell us about the ongoing and therefore relatively predictable aspects of Caribbean political culture and dynamics? Some answers might be forthcoming from an analysis of the ideology and behavior of a few of the major political leaders in recent Caribbean history.

POLITICAL-IDEOLOGICAL LEADERSHIP

The career of Trinidad's prime minister Eric Williams, who governed from 1956 until his death in 1981, illustrates the complexity of style and orientation of the region's leadership. Much has changed in the Caribbean since 1956, when Williams first came to power as a celebrated scholar-administrator. His Ph.D. thesis at Oxford, "Capitalism and Slavery," had become the standard radical interpretation of European industrialization (made possible by the triangular slave trade) and emancipation (made necessary by the very success of that industrialization). He was living proof that a man of color was indeed capable of great achievements in a mother country's highest centers of learning.

This success and his later "telling off" of the English, Americans, French, and Dutch in the Caribbean Commission—an agency set up by the colonial powers to assist in Caribbean development—were proof sufficient to make him the man to lead the island's decolonization movement. "Massa day done" became Williams's battle cry, a welcome prospect to the black and colored middle and working classes who followed his charismatic leadership. The psychic scars of colonialism had found their soothing balm. But where to turn for models?

Asia and Africa were also going through the pains and pleasures of decolonization, and those continents—more than neighboring Latin America—provided some, but not all, of the models. It was in the paths of Nehru, Nkrumah, Sukarno, and Kenyatta that Williams saw represented the post–World War II, nonwhite decolonization process. Like those leaders, Williams understood very early that decolonization had both racial and political connotations. The very concept of empire had been based on ideas of racial superiority and inferiority. These men had to give living rebuttals to the imperial myths that people of color could not govern themselves and that non-Western societies could never be viable nations. Not only did they have to prove their people's capacity by leading the political struggle, they also had to prove their personal worth through exceptional achievement. In colonial situations, the burden of proof is always with the colonized.

It is no surprise, therefore, that more often than not these decolonizers began to perceive themselves as the very—if not the sole—embodiment of their countries. This perhaps was the genesis of their eventual sense of indispensability. Williams acted for twenty-five years on that belief. Repeated victories at the polls did little to dispel the illusion.

But Trinidad, like the rest of the English-speaking West Indies, was in the Western Hemisphere, where the majority of the independent countries were Spanish-speaking and most were far from being democratic models. Surrounded by dictators who enjoyed warm relations with Washington and London, Williams understood that the decolonization of the English-speaking Caribbean was to be a lonely process in the Latin American setting. The parliamentary system adopted by the West Indies differed from the executive system of Latin America, and Williams always felt that the former suited the West Indies better.

This belief was shared by an array of truly exceptional West Indian leaders: Alexander Bustamante and Norman Manley in Jamaica, Grantly Adams and Errol Barrow in Barbados, and Cheddi Jagan in Guyana (a true constitutionalist despite his Marxist rhetoric). By the mid-1960s, these leaders had laid the foundations of West Indian constitutional democracy, thereby giving the lie to colonial racists and modern ideologists who argued that only authoritarian one-party states fit the Caribbean reality.

Williams governed long enough to deal with two elected Manleys (father and son) and two elected Adamses (father and son); to see the OPEC-created explosion in revenues from gas and oil; to see the collapse of the West Indian Federation and the rise of the Caribbean Common Market; and to see the decline of Britain and the rise of Cuba and Venezuela as regional powers. He lived long enough to see the rise and fall of Michael Manley's "democratic socialism" in Jamaica (1972–1980), and he appeared ready to deal with Jamaica's new leader, Edward Seaga, who emphasized the role of the private sector.

By the time of Williams's death in 1981, the Caribbean had witnessed many a social and economic experiment and was quite a different area. Although there were some governments "for life" (Cuba, Haiti, and probably also Guyana), there were democratic governments in virtually all the other Caribbean island states, making the Caribbean the largest area governed by democratically elected regimes in the hemisphere. The parliamentary system was working in the West Indies.

The first generation of post-independence leaders in the English-speaking Caribbean had sown well and, in so doing, left its marks on the immediate post-colonial era. By the mid-1980s, there were indications that the passing of that era meant not only generational change but also the passing of the charismatic, "indispensable" leader as a part of the political culture. This change was demonstrated by a trend in the region's politics, the emergence in the 1980s of the less-than-charismatic "manager" political type. Edward Seaga of Jamaica, Mary Eugenia Charles of Dominica, Tom Adams of Barbados, George Chambers in Trinidad, and Antonio Guzmán and Salvador Jorge Blanco in the Dominican Republic all fit this mold.

What explains this shift in leadership? Certainly there is some truth to the view that the trend is partly reactive: a response to the dismal administrative performance of some of the area's most celebrated charismatic leaders of the 1960s and 1970s—Fidel Castro of Cuba, Michael Manley of Jamaica, and Forbes Burnham of Guyana, for example. But a fuller explanation would bring us closer to the issue of complexity that was posited earlier, that dual process involving enduring, underlying relationships, values, and interests (substrata) and the changing political landscape. The careers of Caribbean leaders of Marxist or non-Marxist socialist persuasion, that is, the secular modernizers, are illustrative.

One such case is Aimé Césaire, mayor of Fort-de-France, Martinique, and Communist *deputé* to the National Assembly in Paris for over thirty-five years. When Césaire resigned from the French Communist Party in 1956, it was a sensational event. "Thinking of Martinique," he wrote, "I see that communism has managed to encyst us, isolate us in the Caribbean Basin." To Césaire, there was an alternative path: "Black Africa, the dam of our civilization and source of our culture." Only through race, culture, and the richness of ethnic particulars, he continued, could Caribbean people avoid the alienation wrought by what he called the "fleshless universalism" of European communism.[2]

This return to history, to culture, and ultimately to race has been a fairly consistent response to many Caribbean socialist modernizers—who never stop referring to themselves as socialists—faced with the difficulties of attempting secular revolutionary change in large, nonrevolutionary, and conservative societies. The counterpoint between a rational secular universalism and a particularism of "being" has resulted in some original and dynamic West Indian ideological modifications to Marxism and non-Marxist socialist thought. In Césaire's case, it led to his fundamental contributions to negritude, a literary-political movement highlighting African contributions to contemporary society, as well as to an accommodation with continued French-Caribbean integration (though not assimilation) into the French system. None of this is new.

Trinidad's first major socialist activist in the 1920s, Andrew Cipriani, yearly paid his homage to Fabian thought and the British Labour Party, but after decades of militancy he withdrew in the face of two challenges to his basic conservative view of the world: the divorce bill, which he saw as a threat to the family, and the use of violence in strike action. Those who used violence (such as Uriah Butler, the "spontaneous" leader in Trinidad's 1937 labor movement and uprising) themselves ended up turning to religion (quoting biblical passages) and to English history (studying the rule of Henry VIII). The pull of the conservative values and norms of the masses on the leadership has been powerful. Even Eric Williams, whose early historical writings were gems of Marxist thought and careful documentation, would eventually abandon what one admirer called "the infinite, barren track of documents, dates and texts" to write "gossip . . . which experience had established as the truth."

A review of Trinidadian C. L. R. James's five decades of thought on Trotskyite socialism and revolution indicates that he never resolved the universalism-particularism counterpoint. In his *Black Jacobins* (1938), perhaps the most influential West Indian work of the twentieth century, James vacillates and hedges but ends up on the side of the Dessalinean Black Revolution as distinct from the universalist experiment of Toussaint.

It is not at all evident that there can be in practice a working and productive relationship between racial or ethnic populism and a program based on premises of secular modernism, whether socialist or not. Even in theory, the reconciliation appears improbable. A case in point is the work of the Martinican Frantz Fanon. Like Césaire—whom he knew and greatly admired—Fanon wished to be liberated from the "fleshless shacks" of European thought; thus he searched for a key to what he called the "psycho-affective equilibrium" of the angry Third World intellectual. This search is central to an understanding of the dynamics of modern-conservative societies. Fanon felt compelled to describe and explain what he perceived as the relentless determination of revolutionary elites to return to history: to "renew contact once more with the oldest and most pre-colonial springs of life of their people." Fanon understood the enduring consequences of the racial hurts and angst inflicted during colonialism. "This state belief in national culture," he wrote, "is in fact an ardent despairing turning toward anything that will afford him anchorage."[3] Even such a lifelong and dedicated Marxist as Guyana's Cheddi Jagan finds a practical and perhaps even psychological need to blend his Marxism with an ongoing devotion to Hinduism. Clearly, then, race and desire for a return to history have been powerful forces blocking a universalist and secular approach to politics.

The rational and secular view of the world that is necessary for modern (especially socialist) revolution is not easily sustained in these societies. In the cases of Césaire, Williams, Norman Manley, Forbes Burnham, and others, Marxist or socialist thought was mediated by pressures from the multiethnic, religious, and conservative societies they led—and which eventually forced them to succumb to the particularistic note in the particularism-universalism counterpoint. It is a fundamental characteristic of a conservative society that views of the world and of social change resist any notions of dealing with problems in any way other than in terms of their historically perceived uniqueness. This characteristic has been, more often than not, part of the Caribbean experience.[4]

The experience explains how Dr. François Duvalier ("Papa Doc") could come into power in Haiti in 1957 advocating a radical Black Power revolution but revert to a very traditional form of political barbarism. He played the most retrograde chords of a deeply conservative society to entrench himself—and then his son, Jean Claude—in power.

CARIBBEAN POLITICAL ECONOMY

In part because development in the Caribbean involves modern societies with relatively skilled labor and a high degree of unionization, and thus high wages, the development process in the region has tended to be industrial and capital intensive. The overflow of available labor (because of reduced migration) has tended to be absorbed by the public sector. The financial and economic retrenchments made necessary by the energy crisis (and consequent balance-of-payments difficulties) have forced a slowing down of this public employment. The result is not merely unemployment but rather a process that is creating a whole generation of "never employed." The vast majority of this group has attained at least some high school education and has some skills and aspirations. Alas, they tend not to be the skills that are in demand nor the aspirations that would encourage needed activities such as agricultural enterprises. Only the latter, with its labor intensity, could in fact absorb the large numbers of people who annually enter the labor market.

Such an agricultural orientation and direction is to be found nowhere in the Caribbean except Haiti, which is still 50 percent rural. The decline of the agricultural sector is a fundamental fact of Caribbean political economy. The movement is toward the urban areas and, critically, migration abroad. In the English-speaking Caribbean, migration accounted for a 46,000-person decrease in the labor force during the 1960s. Because of a slowdown in migration, this labor force is calculated to have increased by about 400,000 during the 1970s, two-thirds of the increase being among young adults.

On every one of the Caribbean islands, youthful adults make up an ever-increasing percentage of the total population, and everywhere they share the restlessness of youth the world over. But the "complexity" approach cautions that it would be a terrible mistake to associate a priori all this modern political ferment and activity with a state of social revolution. Such an association might preempt a close look at the substratum—the political economy—of Caribbean society. Although the configurations and expressions of this conservatism vary, several aspects of Caribbean society show great similarities from one country to another.

Throughout the area, there is a deep and dynamic religiosity, even though the intensity and pervasiveness of religion—as doctrine and as institutions—do vary and are in a rapid process of change. It is startling, for instance, to discover that in Jamaica traditional religions such as Anglicanism and Roman Catholicism are now professed by only 5.5 percent and 4.1 percent respectively, while new U.S.-based faiths, such as the Church of God, claim 21.2 percent of the faithful.[5] The traditional picture of the dominant church in the central plaza, being attended by women and children once a week, is giving way to the storefront churches attended by the whole family. This is true of the whole Caribbean, Hispanic and non-Hispanic alike. Cuba and Puerto Rico were perhaps the least structurally conservative of the Caribbean societies, in large measure because of the considerable influence of secular North American values and interests.

Another situation is that of the English-speaking West Indies, where one finds multiple denominations and neighborhoods, urban and rural. This case illustrates a living presence of religion greater than a ceremonial one and is typical also of countries such as Haiti, where Christianity combined with West African religions to create a syncretism called voodoo (also called *Santería* in Cuba and *Shango* in Trinidad). This religiosity impinges on other spheres of life.

One attitudinal spinoff from the doctrines of the major religions in the area is the belief in private property, especially land. There is an intense love and respect for the land and a desire to own a piece of it. The popular Haitian saying *Se vagabon qui loue kay* (Only vagabonds rent their homes) expresses the desire for ownership, for full possession. On Nevis, 80 percent of the homeowners own their house lot; on St. Vincent, the figure is 75 percent. Although the figure is only 46.8 percent on Barbados, travel around that island reveals that even the smallest house has a name; the name represents the emotional dimension of property ownership. The little picket fence around the house is the physical expression of the emotional dimension. That picket fence (or cactus fence in the Netherlands Antilles) also expresses another characteristic of Caribbean peoples. In the midst of their gregariousness, they like their privacy, an expression of their intrinsic independence. This characteristic, usually identified as a rural phenomenon, is pervasive even in urban areas. This explains the living presence in West Indian language of old English sayings such as "A man's home is his castle" or, as used with an additional meaning in Creole, "Two man rat can't live in same hole."

This latter saying expresses the idea that in any house only one of the partners can wear the pants. It is taken for granted that the male partner does. And yet, these societies are fundamentally matriarchal and matrilocal: Because of the very high illegitimacy rate among the working class, it is the mother who raises the child, and the child lives where the mother (as well as the maternal grandmother) lives. As the 1981 study by Gary and Rosemary Brana-Shute demonstrates, there is a deep underlying conservatism in the socialization processes and aspirations of even the hard-core—and angry—unemployed youth in the area.

And yet, as Caribbean history has repeatedly shown, these generally moderate and family-oriented societies, and especially the youths, are capable of sudden, quite unpredictable political and social outbursts. This was very evident in Curaçao, in the Netherlands Antilles, in 1969 when a minor industrial strike exploded into a class and race attack on the system. Half of the buildings in the main commercial sector of the island were burned to the ground.

The basically conservative substrata of Caribbean societies also sustain very modern and highly mobilized societies and their corresponding agencies. Note the following dimensions and configurations of that modernity—with certain exceptions, such as Haiti, the populations are literate and schooled. On island after island, from 90 to 100 percent of the children of primary school age are in school, and literacy rates everywhere are above 85 percent. Although there is some evidence that conservative attitudes are positively correlated with greater degrees of education,[6] the fact is that a population that participates in the articulation of grievances and wishes and that can utilize the modern techniques of communication is one that has an increased capability for mobilization. Throughout the Caribbean, people are politically mobilized. There are everywhere political parties and interest groups with capacities for extensive articulation of interests and aggregation of these into policy options. No government today, of the left, middle, or right, can ignore the demands of the groups. Literacy and education also make the labor union system more effective in the West Indies, since 30 to 50 percent of the workforce is unionized, and historic ties with political parties give unions additional leverage in the bargaining processes.

Another of the modern agencies that a literate and schooled population makes possible is the state bureaucracy, which, according to Max Weber, is the most "rational" of all forms of organization. Such state bureaucracies are found throughout the Caribbean in the form of a relatively skilled public or civil service. In Trinidad, there are three and a half times more people with diplomas or degrees in the public service than in the private sector, and in Jamaica the institutionalization and legitimacy of the public service are evident in its capacity to survive dramatic shifts in political party fortunes. The top echelons of these bureaucracies are now being educated in the area. The University of the West Indies (UWI), with campuses in Jamaica, Trinidad, and Barbados, now makes university education accessible to a much broader sector, as do the universities in Guyana, Martinique, Surinam, Curaçao, and elsewhere. Whereas in 1957 there were 2,632 West Indians studying at universities abroad compared to only 566 at UWI, by 1982 the number abroad had doubled, but the number of students at UWI had increased twelve fold.

Caribbean modernity is reflected also in other areas. That Caribbean working people have largely developed both the habits and the skills required of labor in modern societies has made them very desirable as immigrant workers. This explains the long tradition of migration, and return, of Caribbean workers; they are and always have been a mobile population. Whether building the Panama Canal and Central America's railroads and ports or running the London public transportation system, Caribbean workers have had the attitudes and skills of urban workers. They return with new skills, but also with the hope of buying that house or piece of land for which they have saved. In Haiti, the "Bahamas" house was built with remittances from Haitians working in the Bahamas, whereas the newer "Miami" house points to the new destination of Haitian migrants and the source of their remittances.

While abroad, Caribbean workers are able to communicate with their compatriots. Mailboxes stand along every road; there is widespread use of radio and newspapers and direct-dialing telephones from the United States to many islands, and in the French West Indies, Netherlands Antilles, Jamaica, Trinidad, and Barbados, the widespread use of television. Modern communications assist both in modernizing the Caribbean and in preserving ethnic attachments. Literacy in one or more of the major languages of the world (English, Spanish, and French) gives Caribbeans access to the main currents of ideas and technology, while their native variations on those languages (Creole in Haiti, *papiamento* in Curaçao, *sranang*—also known as *Taki-Taki*—in Suriname) strengthen the sense of *Volk*, or nation, of *Gemeinschaft*, or community.

If one adds the fact that any particular sector of the islands is within, at most, a two-hour bus ride of some urban center, one understands something of the modernity of the society as well as its continued proximity to rural village life. Ties to the land and to tradition are not broken by a move to the city; rather, those links provide something of the underpinnings of the conservative values and orientations of the urban residents even as the diversification of memberships and involvements (churches, sport clubs, unions, political parties, service clubs) contributes to and expresses the society's modern dimensions. The glue that holds all together is the Caribbean family, both the nuclear and the extended family with its *compadres* (godfathers), *comadres* (godmothers), "cousins," and "aunties."

These, then, are some of the native aspects of these modern-conservative societies. Yet, an analysis of the substrata also has to take into account the external factors affecting change. Although on balance internal factors tend to carry more weight in any causal analysis of social change, the small size of the Caribbean states makes external factors somewhat more important than they would be for most states.

There can be no question that smallness makes them vulnerable to a host of problems. One of these is national insecurity, as was illustrated by the extraordinary 1981 attempted invasion and subversion of the government of Dominica by U.S. mercenaries in league with local politicians. Furthermore, securing a degree of national representation abroad is costly. But such representation is important not only to facilitate contact with foreign nations through traditional diplomatic ties, but also to attract attention from the increasing number of international and multilateral banking or lending agencies.[7]

Also contributing to the vulnerability are the cleavages created by the race and ethnic divisions that characterize the politics of nations such as Trinidad and Tobago, Guyana, and Suriname. In each of these countries, Indians (originally from British India) compose half or more of the population. Predominantly Hindu in religion (some 20 percent are Muslim), these sectors are in themselves prototypical modern-conservative groups. Reconciling Hinduism with secular ideologies such as Marxism is a difficult task in itself; to do so in a context in which major elements of that Indian population are capitalists, landowners, and merchants (as in the case of Guyana and Suriname) is an even more complex proposition. Whether the cleavage is black versus white, Indian versus black, or black versus mulatto, race and race conflict contribute to social division and to the vulnerability of Caribbean societies.

Understanding and awareness of the vulnerabilities resulting from smallness have led to many attempts at regional or subregional integration. Dreams of a united Caribbean are not new. They were expressed in José Martí's theme that Cuba and Puerto Rico were wings of the same dove; in Haitian president Jean Pierre Boyer's dream of liberating all the slaves, first of neighboring Santo Domingo (which his armies occupied from 1822 to 1844), then of other islands; and in the West Indies Federation, which lasted from 1958 to 1961. The repeated failures of such attempts, however, created skepticism about the viability and indeed the desirability of such union.

Despite constant talk about "integration," such as the mid-1990s creation of the thirty-five-member Association of Caribbean States, the mini–nation-state is now a reality of the Caribbean scene, and we probably have not seen the last of the newly independent entities. By the 1990s, the area was limiting itself to attempts at economic integration through such instruments as the Caribbean Common Market (CARICOM) and the Caribbean Development Bank. Even the

Organization of Eastern Caribbean States[8] emphasizes the economic aspects of association, leaving politics, including foreign policy, to each individual member.

Unfortunately, while insularity gathers strength on each island, globalization, impelled by international politics and transnational forces (including multinational corporations), presses for a reduction in state sovereignty. And today, as in the past, size and isolation make these territories targets for international expansion. During the Cold War (the 1960s through the 1980s), escalating ideological competition among international forces made the Caribbean a cockpit, the modern-day equivalent of the European battlegrounds of the seventeenth and eighteenth centuries. Marxism-Leninism, the Socialist International, the Christian Democrats, and international labor organizations as well as new regional actors such as Cuba, Venezuela, and Mexico all joined the battle for the minds of Caribbean peoples. The United States has long been engaged in the competition. To these may be added many proselytizing religious and semireligious groups, from Islam to the Seventh-Day Adventists and Mormons, to the Rastafarian movement (now of Pan-Caribbean character). Since the foreign offices and intelligence services of the major states never left the area, the ideational scene in the Caribbean was a bewildering panorama of competing radio broadcasts; roaming sports, cultural, and scientific missions; state visits; and sojourning consultants from international aid agencies—and these activities were only the overt ones. By the 1990s, with the end of the Cold War, the "taming" of Cuban internationalism, and the shocks of the denouements of the Grenadian and Surinamese revolutions, all that changed. The new Caribbean geopolitics has more to do with economics: In the search for markets and foreign investment capital, import-substitution economies have been opened up (that is, "liberalized") and forced to become export-driven. The private sectors, not the state, have been given the responsibility for economic development. It is all too recent to say whether this will prove to be a more productive strategy of development. It certainly is global in application and strongly pushed by the single power whose influence now stands unchallenged in the region, the United States.

The structural elements revealed in this bare-bones sketch of the internal nature and dynamics of Caribbean societies dispute the generalized idea that these societies were invariably or structurally revolutionary in nature. To be sure, these societies were never static; they often reacted violently when the sense of moral indignation and the collective democratic sensibilities were challenged. These were the responses of modern-conservative societies.

By the late 1990s, a new and arguably greater threat faced these vulnerable states: the threat of organized international crime, pushing every form of illegal activity from drugs to guns to money laundering to financial scams of every conceivable type. Accompanying these structural changes are new sources of threat: the fear that the greatest menace to these small states comes from the internationalization of crime, corruption, and violence. International criminal cartels are quite capable of corrupting whole states, subverting their electoral, legal, and police systems. Formal sovereignty does not mean much under such circumstances. The question is whether the moral conservatism that was so instrumental in withstanding the totalitarian temptation will also serve as a bulwark against the onslaught of organized crime. This question is the central challenge at the end of the twentieth century.

Conclusion

The first thing to keep in mind in analyzing the "new" Caribbean is the degree of social change, both in speed and in kind. Such rapid social change never occurs without consequences and this region is no exception. Two distinct processes can be identified. First, these recently decolonized societies are increasing their contacts with their former metropolitan masters. There are the benefits to be derived from links in the European Union, including assistance in many social and economic areas. The association clearly brings some relief from the sense of economic vulnerability in the context of globalization and, perhaps more immediately, from the challenges represented by the demand for economic "openness" and liberalization coming from the North American Free Trade Area (NAFTA). An increased European military presence also means a greater sense of security in the increasingly important area of law and order operations.

The second set of processes derive from the fact that race and ethnicity continue to be bridges that contribute to better understanding and relations with the United States. And yet, since nothing ever stands still, the erstwhile special relationship with the predominantly Afro-Caribbean islands is in relative decline as the U.S. racial and ethnic composition changes. Specifically, the rise in the United States of Hispanic political mobilization and the comparative decline of black political power has meant the relative decline of Afro-Caribbean influence. It is vital that several politically important U.S. cities such as Los Angeles and Miami, the former a gateway to Mexico and the latter a veritable gateway to the Caribbean, are essentially Latin cities. The growing Puerto Rican and Dominican populations in New York have come out of the shadow of the much older West Indian enclaves to assert an influence of their own. Competition for the attention of Washington has been, and continues to be, a fundamental task of the foreign policies of Caribbean states. It is evident that the task is becoming more difficult.

Both these processes challenge the region's sense of national identity and perception of sovereignty and highlight the vulnerability of small states in a globalized world. Yet, there is no reason to despair. The stalwart people of these islands have faced many threats and challenges before. As they say in the islands, "We have seen the best of times and the worst of times." Certainly true as an uplifting message. Hard facts, however, indicate that the new challenges are of such a transnational nature that they will surely test their mettle as never before. Be that as it may, the interpretation of Caribbean societies presented here does provide some grounds for cautious optimism. The wide acceptance of democratic forms is but one expression of political cultures that are at once very conservative about basic social and political issues and yet modern and adaptable in their capacity to adjust and even innovate. Such predispositions to incorporate the new without discarding what has worked historically will surely come in handy in the new era. Thus, it is useful to characterize Caribbean societies as modern-conservative societies, an ideal-type construct that helps us understand what otherwise might appear to be contradictory or even unintelligible in the behavior of this multilingual, multiracial, and multistate area.

NOTES

1. Karl Mannheim, "Conservative Thought," in Paul Keckskemeti, ed., *Essays on Sociology and Social Psychology* (New York: Oxford University Press, 1953), pp. 77–164.

2. Aimé Césaire, "Lettre à Maurice Thorez," *Présence Africaine* (Paris) (1956), p. 15.

3. Frantz Fanon, *The Wretched of the Earth* (New York: Grove Press, 1968), p. 217.

4. One interesting exception is the New Jewel Movement, which came to power in Grenada in 1979, attempting to portray that experience as an extension of a Caribbean decolonization process begun in Cuba. It was deposed through U.S. military intervention in 1983.

5. Martin Mordecai and Pamela Mordecai, *Culture and Customs of Jamaica* (Westport, Conn.: Greenwood Press, 2001), p. 41.

6. See Selwyn Ryan, Eddie Greene, and Jack Harewood, *The Confused Electorate* (St. Augustine, Trinidad: ISER, 1979); and Anthony P. Maingot, "The Difficult Path to Socialism in the English-Speaking Caribbean," in Richard R. Fagen, ed., *Capitalism and the State in U.S.–Latin American Relations* (Stanford: Stanford University Press, 1979).

7. This is not only a question of asymmetry of power but also a question of commanding respect and dignity.

8. Antigua/Barbuda, St. Vincent/Grenadines, Dominica, St. Lucia, and Grenada.

SUGGESTED READINGS

A good general treatment of the Caribbean as a whole is Franklin W. Knight, *The Caribbean: The Genesis of a Fragmented Nationalism,* 2nd ed. (New York: Oxford University Press, 1980). Knight also edited, with Margaret E. Crahan, *Africa and the Caribbean: The Legacies of a Link* (Baltimore: Johns Hopkins University Press, 1979). On the English-speaking Caribbean, several of Gordon K. Lewis's books are being republished. *The Growth of the Modern West Indies* (1968), is being republished in 2004 by Ian Randle Publishers of Jamaica with a new introduction by Franklin W. Knight. Lewis's *Puerto Rico, Freedom and Power in the Caribbean* (1963) is also reappearing under the Ian Randle imprint with a new introduction by Anthony P. Maingot who also wrote the new introduction to Lewis's classic, *Main Currents of Caribbean Thought* (1983), republished by the University of Nebraska Press in 2004. David Lowenthal's *West Indian Societies* (New York: Oxford University Press, 1972) is especially strong on race relations and the analysis of the "plural society." On the development of socialist politics and the region's conservative responses, see Anthony P. Maingot, *The United States and the Caribbean* (Boulder, Colo.: Westview Press, 1994).

Contemporary affairs are best followed through the newsletter from London *Caribbean Insight* and the magazine *Hemisphere* (Florida International University).

PART VIII

THE ANDES

Chapter 20

COLOMBIA'S SPLIT-LEVEL REALITIES

JAN KNIPPERS BLACK

For most of the past century, Colombia has been formally identified as a democracy. In fact, it has often been referred to as South America's oldest democracy; by some standards it has been an extraordinarily stable one, underpinned by a growing and modernizing economy. And for those who enjoyed *abolengo*—notable names—and lived in gated and guarded neighborhoods, the landed gentry and captains of industry whose family histories were threaded through the highest offices of Church and State, this formal identity may have seemed real enough. Even for the less well endowed middle-class families who have lived within a hundred mile radius of the capital, Bogotá, or of one of the other major cities, the social strife that has ravaged the countryside almost continuously may have intruded only episodically.

Those episodes of intrusion have called forth a variety of explanations or rationales and a continuous process of labeling and re-labeling, from the wars of conquest and of independence to partisan wars, to banditry and ideological wars overlain by the Cold War, and more recently to the ongoing drug war and the war on terrorism. All such wars are power struggles, of course, from local to global arenas, and all are to some degree about resources, particularly land.

Changes over the years in slogans and flags and in the resources at issue have served to obscure what is unchanging in this equation of anarchy: the hand played by Mother Nature herself—the divisions imposed by the steep and rugged ridges and isolated valleys of a three-pronged mountain range. In Colombia, as in Afghanistan and Appalachia, Papua New Guinea and the Caucasus, the ultimate saboteur of national or regional unity and the effective sovereignty of a central government is topography. But there is no glory, no partisan advantage, no budgetary windfall, and no victory to claim in fighting a mountain range.

The anarchy and generalized insecurity that constitute the ground floor of the Colombian reality—at least in rural areas and in the urban shantytowns where peasants driven off their land seek shelter—may be almost as old as the mountains that sustain it. But a couple of circumstances have caused it to intrude on the national consciousness more persistently and insistently in the past two decades. In the first place, while the spread of cash cropping and agroexport in general implies concentration of land ownership—turf wars—and thus a certain degree of violence, the cultivation and trafficking of cocaine is particularly conducive to violence. Addiction and criminalization ensure an inelastic market and high market value. The monetary stakes attract thieves from all classes and sectors, and criminalization enhances the budget, power, and autonomy of security forces, especially as they draw increasing support from the United States.

Finally, over more than a century, the Colombian government, like many governments elsewhere, has generally been willing to settle for the illusion of centralized control over the claimed territory. But the hemisphere's hegemon has become increasingly ambitious or increasingly delusional about what it is able or should be able to control and thus threatens to turn a condominium of split-level realities into a conflated reality of free-fire-zoned wasteland, spreading across national borders.

A Penthouse Perspective on Colombian Reality

The Origins of Oligarchy

Virtually all analysts of the Colombian political system use modifiers when speaking of the country's democracy. John D. Martz Jr. characterized the system as a "qualified" democracy. Others have spoken of limited or elitist democracy. Robert E. Scott went so far as to label its leadership a "ruling caste." While the frontier area between the upper and middle classes lacks the structure that might be provided, for example, by titles of nobility, and while there are varying interpretations by students of Colombian society of degrees of upward and downward mobility, there is considerable objective and subjective evidence that a self-perpetuating minority controls the key power resources of the society.

Robert H. Dix, whose study of the Colombian elite was among the first to involve survey and interview techniques, found that most of those who numbered among the upper class had their roots in the hacienda. Prestigious family names (*abolengo*) have been historically associated with land ownership, although they have served to some extent as autonomous sources of elite status. Light complexion, higher education in the arts or traditional professions, and cosmopolitanism are generally concomitants of *abolengo*. Wealth acquired from industrial or commercial pursuits or professional expertise may confer elite status, but by no means assure it. Some interlocking of landowning and industrial families has occurred through marriage, however, and many landowning families have invested in industrial and commercial enterprises, while some industrial entrepreneurs have invested in land. Members of both Liberal and Conservative party hierarchies, for example, have been officers of the powerful National Federation of Coffee Growers.

The two-party system, which in the early development of most Latin American countries involved only the upper classes, and which in most cases gave way in the twentieth century to a multiparty system, so pervaded the society in Colombia that as late as 1969 a leader of the National Popular Alliance (ANAPO), the only political movement that posed a credible threat to the dominance of the two traditional parties, described ANAPO as a bipartisan movement rather than as a third party. Such a pervasive two-party system has reflected and re-enforced, rather than mitigated, a system of rigid socioeconomic stratification and a traditional political culture that favored the maintenance of control by a relatively closed societal elite over the expansion of political participation.

Partisanship Takes Root

Although partisanship began to develop in Colombia in the 1830s, the Liberal and Conservative parties did not appear as such until 1848 when they took positions, respectively, against and for the government of Tomás Cipriano de Mosquera. Since that time the two parties, through armed conflict, electoral competition, or collaboration, have maintained control of the country's political system. In the nineteenth century that competition was manifested more often in armed conflict than in elections.

The Constitution drawn up by the Conservatives in 1886 established a unitary system and provided for separation of church and state, although a concordat with the Holy See established a close working relationship between the government and the Catholic hierarchy. Coffee production and export provided a financial base for centralizing state power and promoting investment also in industry. Coffee accounted for 70 percent of the country's export earnings by the 1930s. The Conservative Party ruled, largely in authoritarian fashion, from 1886 to 1930, successfully thwarting two attempts by the Liberals to gain control by force. The essentially partisan so-called Thousand Day War (1899–1902) devastated the country and left some 100,000 dead.

The constitution of 1886 was to last more than a century, until it was superseded in 1991. It was amended, however, by the Liberals to give the government power to deal with economic affairs which, when Enrique Olaya Herrera came to power in 1930, were in turmoil. The country was ruled by four Liberal presidents between 1930 and 1946. The first term of Alfonso López Pumarejo, (1934–1938), saw numerous reform measures enacted. As a result, the more centrist elements of the Liberal Party withdrew their support from López, who was then succeeded by Eduardo Santos, leader of the centrist faction. López was reelected in 1942 but resigned in 1945, his term being completed by Alberto Lleras Camargo.

Conservative Mariano Ospina Pérez was elected president in 1946 on a platform of quasi-bipartisanship, but partisan rivalry soon became more bitter than ever. It erupted into civil war after the *Bogotazo*—the uprising in Bogotá in 1948 that followed the assassination of Jorge Eliécer Gaitán. Gaitán, a Liberal, had become a national figure as a dynamic spokesman of peasant and working class interests. Laureano Gómez assumed the presidency in an uncontested election in 1948 and completed the trend toward authoritarianism that had been initiated by his predecessor, including the use of the armed forces and police to fight Liberals. Some 200,000 people were killed, mostly between 1949 and 1953, in an awful bloodletting that came to be known as *La Violencia*.

In 1953, Lieutenant General Gustavo Rojas Pinilla, after uncovering a plot, apparently inspired by Gómez, for his assassination, engineered a coup d'etat and assumed control of the government. Although this move was initially greeted with broad popular support, the military government became increasingly arbitrary and repressive. Following a display of public discontent in 1957, the armed forces, backed by political party leaders, removed Rojas Pinilla from office.

City-States, the Vertical Two-Party System, and Social Structure

By the mid-twentieth century the major issues that distinguished Liberals and Conservatives in the nineteenth century, those of a unitary versus a federal governmental system and the extent of the special prerogatives of the Church, were no longer seriously contended. Even so, almost all Colombians consider themselves either Liberals or Conservatives. This affiliation is a part of one's family heritage and, especially among the rural middle and lower classes, strongly influences marriage, business ties, and social contacts, although the majority of the adult population does not vote and actual participation in party affairs is extremely limited. The parties are similar in composition and organization, incorporating persons of all social classes, but deriving their leadership from the oligarchy. While on paper the parties have much of the framework of modern parties, in the functioning of their internal machinery, in methods of financing, in the role of the press, and in the approach to mass organization they reveal the patron-client orientation of their societal environment. In the rural areas, for example, landowners are expected to "deliver" the votes of the peasants in their domains.

The isolation of the various population centers, resulting from settlement patterns and topographic extremes, has fostered a type of political rivalry reminiscent of a system of city states or fiefdoms. Almost the entire population of many towns and villages consider themselves either Liberals or Conservatives. Thus the structures of the two parties merely reflect the pyramidal structure of the larger society, and the pervasiveness of the traditional parties has left little room for the emergence of modern parties organized along horizontal lines of common socioeconomic interests. Furthermore, armed clashes in the nineteenth century, resulting from political and economic rivalry in which peasants were called upon to defend their landlords, consolidated the political uniformity of some regions and communities to such an extent that to change one's party affiliation was to be considered a traitor.

Despite the general blurring of ideological differences between Conservatives and Liberals, positions traceable to the inception of the two parties—order, hierarchy, and strong central control by Church and state versus secularization of society, decentralization of government, and laissez-faire economic policy—regain significance from time to time. And new differences have emerged on occasion as one party or the other sought to expand its base. The Liberal Party was responsible for a considerable body of welfare legislation, for example, enacted in the twentieth century. Political expediency, however, has generally been more apparent than ideological considerations in the voting patterns of both parties and their factions, and the leadership of both parties remains firmly in the hands of the elites. While the leaders have been able to compromise on occasion when upper-class interests appeared to be threatened, members of the lower classes, with less comprehension of the ideological and practical issues dividing the parties, have been less able to overcome traditional party enmity in order to identify and articulate their common interests.

Until the mid-twentieth century only the elite evidenced a politically significant degree of class consciousness. A potential source of conflict that might have diluted the power of the upper class was avoided as the large landowners recognized that through accommodating the new industrialists they could prevent a major challenge to traditional political patterns. A middle class had begun by the 1930s to develop sufficient numerical strength to challenge the dominance of the elites, but individuals of this group recognized few common interests or values distinct from those of the elites. Thus, the ruling families were generally able to co-opt into the service of the existing two-party system those individuals who exhibited potential for leadership of a middle-class movement.

The failure of the lower class to develop class consciousness and structures for articulating and aggregating class interests may be attributed in part to the paternalistic attitude of the elites, the vertical organization of virtually all social institutions, the lack of leaders, with the notable exception of Jorge Eliécer Gaitán, from the middle class, and the paucity of large concentrations of the disadvantaged in a given social environment. Where wage-earning rural laborers have been concentrated in plantation "factories," such as in the sugar industry in the Cauca Valley, unionization and political radicalization have been common, but throughout most rural areas *minifundio* owners, squatters, tenants, and sharecroppers, who have little contact among themselves, predominate. The fact that industrial labor forces have been dispersed among several urban centers rather than concentrated in a few very large cities has inhibited the development of the labor movement. In fact, each of the two major labor confederations developed under the tutelage of one of the two major parties and, until the 1970s, suspicion and rivalry prevented effective aggregation of interests even on the most basic issues affecting labor.

Among elites, on the other hand, interest articulation often circumvents the party structures entirely. Informal ties based on kinship, friendship, or interlocking business interests allow individuals to take their appeals directly to the executive branch regardless of which party is in power. Periodic consultations between the president and representatives of the country's major pressure groups, such as the National Coffee Growers' Federation and the National Association of Industrialists, designed to reach mutual accommodation on matters of economic and social policy, have become virtually institutionalized.

A Brush with Ground-Floor Reality: La Violencia

Ironically, the protracted civil war known as *la violencia*, or the violence, initially fought on behalf of clashing loyalties in the traditional regional partisan pattern, uprooted masses of people and planted the seeds of class consciousness. By the late 1950s, evidence of change in the political culture, fostered largely by the *violencia* and by urbanization, raised the specter of a modification in the two-party system and a challenge to elite control.

The partisan war—or sometimes class war disguised as partisan—largely dissipated during the period of military rule, but revived to a degree in the late 1950s and early 1960s, as some who had led Liberal party guerrilla operations established foci, or occupied enclaves, in rural areas and supported themselves through banditry. Some also declared independence for their carved-out domains and learned the language of Marxism. These included the Revolutionary Armed Forces of Colombia (FARC) and the Army of National Liberation (ELN).

Widespread mistrust in the institutions of authority was to some extent both cause and effect of the *violencia*. Gaitán's denunciation of the elites, or *oligarquía*, and the sacking of buildings identified with the government or the Church after his assassination were indicative of the depth of alienation. The direct involvement of the police and the armed forces in the partisan conflict that followed further contributed to the undermining of authority and of the power structure on which it was based. The skepticism toward governmental institutions and the mistrust of the oligarchy that grew out of the *violencia* corresponded with the development among spokesmen of the lower class of a greater awareness of their potential political strength and of a conviction of their right to be heard on policies affecting them. What began as a partisan conflict evolved into a diffuse manifestation of an incipient class struggle.

Urbanization, spurred by rapid industrialization since the 1930s and accelerated in the 1950s by the *violencia*, has had a measurable impact on political attitudes. Rivalries based on kinship and community ties have been less relevant in the more anonymous context of urban life, and changing of hereditary affiliations in the city, while requiring some corresponding changes in personal relationships, has not assured social ostracism.

Furthermore, urban dwellers have been exposed more intensively to the communications media and to organizations, such as unions, where class interests are articulated. More or less spontaneous protest demonstrations have taken place with increasing frequency in response to the implementation of unpopular measures, such as increases in the costs of public services. Urbanization has been seen as a major factor in the general mid-century shift from a Conservative to a Liberal nationwide majority of voters. In the elections of March 1962 every city with a vote amounting to 25,000 or more returned a Liberal majority.[1]

Elite Consensus and Stabilization: The National Front

The temporary coalescence of Liberal and Conservative party leadership to effect a political truce or a gradual transfer of power that had taken place on various occasions prior to 1958 was short-lived and gave way to the hegemony of one party and the virtual exclusion of the other from representation in government. In the late 1950s, however, the undercurrent of class consciousness that had revealed itself in the latter stages of the *violencia*, the assumption of power by the military (1953–1957) for the first time in the twentieth century, and the complex demands on government of a rapidly developing economy apparently served notice on the elites of both parties that only through genuine sustained cooperation could they avoid losing control of the direction and pace of change. Thus a bipartisan agreement drawn up before the overthrow of Rojas Pinilla established a coalition system to be known as the National Front.

The arrangement embodied in the Sitges Agreement in 1957 and incorporated by plebiscite into the constitution institutionalized duopolistic control of the Liberal and Conservative parties over the machinery of government that was to remain in effect until 1974.The three basic pillars of this arrangement, parity in all elective and appointive offices, alternation of the presidency, and the requirement of a two-thirds vote on all legislation, contributed further to a system favoring accommodation over resolute action. Such accommodation did indeed pave the way for substantial economic growth, as a number of new products were added to the agroexport list.

In pitting faction against faction *within* each party, however, the arrangement magnified the already strong tendencies toward factionalism and personalism and often obscured from the public the issues of national policy involved in elections and in the legislative process. The low priority allocated to legislation by the legislators themselves was indicated by the high rate of absenteeism and the frequency with which congressmen yielded their seats to alternates.[2]

A system of proportional representation among the factions of the two major parties and the tolerance of the coalition government for the participation of non-establishment groups willing to run candidates under the traditional party labels operated as an escape valve for mounting opposition to the bipartisan arrangement and provided an indicator of the extent of that opposition. As dissident factions of the major parties and incipient third-party movements generally based their platforms on opposition to the system, elections between 1958 and 1974 were viewed, in effect, as plebiscites on the continuation of the National Front arrangement.

Between 1958 and 1969, the combined votes cast for opponents of the National Front rarely exceeded one-third of the total vote. However, the alienation and apathy evidenced by abstention rates of some two-thirds of the eligible voters in the elections of 1964, 1966, and 1968 weakened the credibility of the government's claim to a popular base. Voter turnout decreased from a high of about 70 percent in the 1957 plebiscite to approximately 30 percent in the 1968 congressional elections.

The abrupt dissolution of the National Front in 1974 called for in the original agreement had been viewed by elites with anxiety as an invitation to recourse to violence. A major constitutional revision adopted in 1968, however, alleviated many adverse aspects of the bipartisan arrangement, paved the way for a gradual transition over an eight-year period, and raised hopes that the return to a more competitive system could be achieved peacefully.[3]

Another major subject of speculation and concern was whether the transition would result in a reversion to two-party dominance or the emergence, for the first time in the country's history, of an authentic multiparty system. The major parties appeared geared up for the former eventuality. The Liberal Party was strengthened in 1967 by a merger, the first since the late 1930s, of its two largest factions, and the major Conservative factions were vociferous about the need for unity. It was assumed, however, that in the event that the Conservatives failed to unite and the Liberal merger came unglued, the right wing of the Liberals and the left wing of the Conservatives might unite to form a center party. As it turned out, partisan elites were to be blindsided by new power contenders who shunned electoral arenas or hijacked electoral processes.

REALITY FROM THE BOTTOM UP: CHRONIC WARFARE, DISPLACEMENT, AND DESPERATION

Frustrated Reform and Ill-Gotten Gain

Formally, the National Front arrangement was laid to rest on schedule in 1974 with the inauguration of President Alfonso López Michelsen of the Liberal Party. Nevertheless, in accordance with the constitutional amendment of 1968, the pattern of partisan parity in executive and legislative positions was followed by López and by his Liberal Party successor Julio César Turbay Ayala. Some aspects of the pattern were also revisited in the 1990s.

Over the course of the extended National Front period, the issues and interests that had previously divided Conservatives and Liberals and, in fact, had driven them twice to civil war—Church versus state, urban versus rural, agriculture and commerce versus industry—had almost become moot, and on both sides of the partisan divide, competition had moved inside the parties. The public in general was not expected to weigh in on this kind of competition and, in fact, it did not. Voter turnout, less than half of those eligible during the official period of the National Front, did not rebound thereafter.

Until the advent of the National Front, minor parties offered little challenge to the two-party system. Most of them were short-lived and were personalistic or Marxist-oriented or both. Few had sufficient membership to operate in all parts of the country. The Communist Party was the oldest and most durable of the minor parties, having functioned continuously since the 1920s, but it rarely received more than 1 percent of the vote and it was often sharply divided between pro-Moscow and pro-Beijing factions.

The National Popular Alliance (ANAPO), was initially a personalist party organized in the 1960s under the leadership of former dictator Gustavo Rojas Pinilla. It made steady gains, electing candidates on primarily Conservative, but also Liberal lists; and despite the "strange bedfellow" nature of its membership, the vagueness of its platform, and the confusion as to whether it was a party or a "bipartisan movement," it aroused considerable uneasiness among the elite. Such uneasiness proved well-founded in 1970 when ANAPO came very close, at least, to winning the presidential election. In fact, it was widely believed to have won that election and to have been deprived of its victory by electoral fraud.

Frustration with a seemingly impregnable system gave rise in the late 1970s to a new underground organization drawing participants especially from ANAPO and from the FARC. Formally calling itself the April 19th Movement after the date of the alleged electoral fraud, it came to be known simply as M–19. Unlike earlier guerrilla movements, it was from the start urban-based. Meanwhile other organizations representing lower-class interests began to break with their Liberal Party roots—as in the case of a peasant organization nurtured initially by the government of Carlos Lleras Restrepo (1966–1970)— or to rise independent of partisan support, like the union movement that culminated in 1986 in the formation of the United Workers Central (CUT).

Meanwhile rural violence, exacerbated by the spread of a new cash crop— cocaine—drove peasants from their land and into unsecured and unserviced shantytowns on the fringes of the cities. Thus the violence and vulnerability that had long plagued many rural areas moved into town and became a fact of city life as well.

Already, in the 1970s, Colombia's homicide rate was among the world's highest, and it continued to climb sharply. By the late 1980s, 20,000 people were being murdered each year, a roster that included party and union leaders, mayors and city councilors, journalists and newspaper editors, judges and prosecutors, a minister of justice, an attorney general, and, in 1989 and 1990, three presidential candidates.[4] Responsibility for the atrocities lay in part with the FARC and, to a lesser degree, with the ELN. Human rights monitors have found them to be responsible for most of the kidnappings, early on a fundraising strategy and more recently leverage for prisoner exchange as well. Monitors found, however, that the great majority of the murders were carried out by official security forces or the rapidly growing paramilitary death squads. Massacres, as such, have generally been the work of paramilitaries. Americas Watch, the Western Hemisphere branch of Human Rights Watch, reported in December 1992 that 40 percent of Colombia's political assassinations were attributable to government agents, 30 percent to paramilitary groups, 27.5 percent to the guerrillas, and 2.5 percent to the drug mafia.[5]

Paramilitaries supported financially by landowning drug barons and strategically, at least, by the military were operating with impunity in urban as well as rural areas. Massacres of whole villages were sometimes carried out with the open collusion of the army, which, incidentally, was also growing—from 80,000 members in 1978 to 135,000 in 1988—and operating with increasing autonomy from civilian authorities. On one occasion, in 1985, when M–19 guerrillas had occupied the Palace of Justice, the army stormed the palace, killing ninety-five people, including many staff members and casual visitors as well as twelve of the twenty-five Supreme Court justices.[6] Portions of the palace were torched, including those where narcotrafficking case files were being processed.

The storming of the Palace of Justice appeared to be an affront to President Belisario Betancur (1982–1986), of the left wing of the Conservative Party, who had made a serious effort to de-escalate insurrection and to rein in the repression practiced by security forces. Human rights concerns received official attention under his government, and the activities of right-wing death squads were investigated. Amnesty was offered to guerrillas who would lay down their arms. Many accepted the offer, and former affiliates of FARC went on to form a legitimate political party, the Patriotic Union (UP). The UP had considerable success initially in fielding and electing candidates, especially to local offices, but its leadership ranks were decimated between the mid-1980s and the early 1990s by more than 2,000 assassinations. Drug mafias shared responsibility for these murders with police, military, and paramilitary forces.

Violence continued to escalate under the presidency of Liberal Virgilio Barco, who succeeded Betancur in 1986 and who also attempted, to little avail, to reform the political system so as to make it more inclusive. The assassination in 1989 of the Liberal Party's popular presidential candidate, Luis Carlos Galán, by drug lords precipitated an all-out campaign against the leaders of the major Medellin- and Cali-based narcotrafficking organizations. That campaign had the effect of splintering and dispersing mafia operations. That plus the balloon effect of earlier U.S.-sponsored drug wars in pushing major operations out of Peru and Bolivia and into Colombia greatly expanded the territory under coca cultivation and the geographic distribution of cocaine-processing laboratories. Meanwhile, laundered drug money was burrowing more deeply into legitimate business and mainstream politics and competing more forcefully with government for the loyalty of security forces.

The Making of a Humanitarian Catastrophe

Peasants driven from the countryside by the *violencia* between the late 1940s and the mid 1960s doubled the urban population. Those driven out from the mid-1960s to the mid-1980s by the commercialization of agriculture doubled it again. The urban population reached about 20 million, 70 percent of the overall population, in the mid 1980s. Urban life, particularly in the largest cities—Bogotá, Cali, and Medellín—benefited in the 1960s and 1970s from a flourishing of diversified domestic industry. By the 1980s, however, deregulation and foreign competition, inflation, and debt had taken their toll. Government intervention in the late 1980s stopped the slide, but local industry did not recover to 1970s levels.

Narcodollars helped to finance the external trade balance, saving Colombia from the depths of recession experienced elsewhere in Latin America during that decade, but the off-budget windfall fueled inflation and, of course, corruption. Moreover, new economic growth was not matched by growth in jobs, much less in wages. Most employment was in the so-called informal sector, unprotected by labor organization or legislation.

The elections of 1990 saw the withdrawal of the Patriotic Union, following the assassination of its leader and presidential candidate, Bernardo Jaramillo;

the emergence of another party on the left—the Democratic Alliance, a vehicle primarily for former members of M–19—with 12.5 percent of the vote; a schism within the Conservative Party; and a victory for the centrist Liberal Party candidate Cesar Gaviria Trujillo. Only slightly more than a fourth of the eligible electorate turned out to vote. Twice as many as had voted for Gaviria, however, voted in favor of a Constituent Assembly to draw up a new constitution. That constitution, optimistically opening up more avenues for popular political participation, was adopted in 1991.[7]

Assuming office in 1990, Gaviria embraced neoliberal economic policies, stressing trade liberalization, privatization, competitiveness, elimination of price subsidies, and sharp reductions in public expenditures. Foreign investment rose sharply, but wage levels dropped, prices and unemployment figures rose, and public services declined. As popular opposition mounted, Gaviria's successor, Ernesto Samper (1994–1998), proposed social pacts with labor; but he returned to implementation of neoliberal measures as the U.S. Congress, citing allegations that narcodollars had corrupted Samper's election campaign, found the Colombian government insufficiently committed to derailing the drug trade. Colombia was thus "decertified" in 1996 as a drug war collaborator, triggering disruptions in trade with and aid from the United States. Disruptions in legitimate trade and slippage in the legitimate economy underscored the importance of the country's most lucrative cash crop.

Andrés Pastrana, of the Conservative Party (son of an earlier president), came to the presidency in 1998 with an ambitious plan. Along with strengthening security forces, *Plan Colombia* envisioned the strengthening of investigatory, judicial, and other capabilities of the civilian government as well as the promotion of rural development. Most of all, the plan originated as a peace initiative. Under that plan, Pastrana recognized a zone (under the de facto control of FARC) about the size of Switzerland, in the southern part of the country, as an autonomous—or demilitarized—zone, in which negotiations for a peaceful settlement might take place. Latin American and European countries offered their good offices, and for a time optimism prevailed.

Negotiations between the Pastrana government and the FARC leadership got under way at the beginning of 1999 and continued off and on for three years without producing so much as a ceasefire agreement. Prospects for negotiation were stymied on the one hand, particularly after 2000, by the insistence of the U.S. government—the major funding source for operations of the semi-autonomous Colombian security forces—on the militarization of *Plan Colombia*. On the other hand, prospects were hampered by the FARC's distrust of the government. Such distrust was born in part of the betrayal of FARC political and diplomatic leaders who had set themselves up for assassination by accepting amnesty and integrating the legitimate political system. That betrayal set in relief the underlying weakness of the traditional civilian partisan elite—especially its inability to control security forces—weakness heavily underscored by the fate of the Patriotic Union Party.

At the beginning of 2002, the combination of a Colombian government ultimatum and the intercession of United Nations envoy James LeMoyne, accompanied by Church officials and representatives of ten countries, finally produced a new plan for the peace process and a timetable for a ceasefire. Sadly, this seeming breakthrough was to be short-lived. In the weeks that followed, FARC provocations continued, culminating in the hijacking of a domestic airliner and the kidnapping of a senator who was on board. Thereupon, President Pastrana declared the peace process dead; on February 20, aerial bombardment signaled the beginning of a military campaign to retake the recently demilitarized zone.[8]

If Pastrana's election in 1998 had been seen as a mandate to pursue peace, the election in 2002 of Alvaro Uribe Vélez, a dissident Liberal, was seen as a mandate for security, or closure by reconquest. President Uribe, who assumed office in August 2002, had a reputation as a hardliner, and he promised to do all-out battle against the FARC. After two years of staunch refusal to negotiate, Uribe surprised the country on August 18, 2004, by offering the FARC conditions for a prisoner exchange. The conditions, however, were such that both the FARC and relatives of some of its hostages dismissed the offer as not serious. Since polls indicated that most Colombians support a prisoner exchange, some commentators linked the government's apparent about-face on the issue to the pending Congressional approval of a constitutional change that would open the way for Uribe to serve a second term.[9]

THE DEMOGRAPHICS OF DESPERATION

In May 2004, Jan Egeland, UN undersecretary for humanitarian affairs, called a press conference in New York to draw attention to the situation in Colombia, which he called "by far the biggest humanitarian catastrophe in the Western Hemisphere." Intractable warfare over political and military advantage, old and new grudges, the bounty of the illicit drug trade, and increasingly over control of territory had generated two million refugees. Colombia had become, after the Congo and Sudan, the country with the third greatest number of displaced persons in its midst.[10]

The two major guerrilla groups, the FARC and the ELN, were engaged in armed combat with official military forces and right-wing paramilitary groups. The contemporary cash crop of choice sustains combatants on all sides; left-wing guerrillas and right-wing paramilitaries alike finance themselves directly through drug-trafficking as well as through collecting protection "taxes" from coca growers. Taxation notwithstanding, small-scale growers, who produce most of the national crop, can earn far more on cocaine than on any other traditional or non-traditional crop.

Revolutionaries: The FARC and the ELN

Taxes paid in exchange for security are more important to the guerrillas and the territories they control than to the paramilitaries, who gain much of their

territory by killing off or driving off the previous inhabitants and taking possession of the land. Though the FARC has become more involved in trafficking
in recent years, most of its cocaine windfall, estimated at $500 million a year,
derives from the 10 percent tax it collects from growers. With that treasury, the
FARC has been able to field an army of more than 20,000—swelled at times by
peasants driven off their land by the paramilitaries—and to control, or at least
to move freely in, 40 to 60 percent of the national territory.[11] The ELN is much
smaller, having about 4,000 troops, and has been less intransigent with respect
to negotiation for peaceful settlement. It has been noted particularly for continual sabotage of operations and pipelines of the petroleum multinationals.

Now the hemisphere's oldest and most powerful revolutionary body, the
FARC originated as a Maoist-inspired peasant co-op under the leadership of
Liberal Party combatants "retired" after the *violencia* subsided. The isolated
community in southern Tolima department known as the Independent Republic of Marquetalia was transformed into a guerrilla organization after a
U.S.-supported attack on the community in May 1964. Survivors reported
that the raid pitted 16,000 military personnel against 1,000 villagers, of whom
only forty-eight were armed.[12]

A peasant-based and peasant-led movement from the start, the FARC is
clearly serious about social change. The movement, however, hardly lends itself
to the self-sacrificial, romantic revolutionary image of the Zapatistas, for example, of Mexico's southern province of Chiapas. As has so often been the case
in Colombia and elsewhere, a war without foreseeable end has generated its
own sustainable economy; and the FARC would be highly unlikely to place it
on a bargaining table, even if it could place full faith and credit in the government's bargaining position.

A factor contributing further to the intractability of this war is the nature
and experience of the FARC leadership. In 2004, it remained in the hands of
its septuagenarian founder, Manuel Marulanda—better known as *Tirofijo*, or
Sure-shot—who had been a warrior for half a century, since the onset of *La Violencia*. Like *Tirofijo* himself, his lieutenants are schooled and skilled in war-
making and have no apparent vocation for peacekeeping or civil governance.
Not coincidentally, those of the FARC leadership who had such vocation were
targeted for assassination by official and unofficial security forces whose skills
and interests, like those of the surviving FARC leadership, lay in sustaining
conflict, not in promoting peace.

Counterrevolutionaries: The Paramilitaries and the AUC

It is hardly surprising that where threadbare peasants organize to defend their
interests, armed bodies acting on behalf of estate or plantation owners will also
appear. Nor is it surprising that when the cash crop cultivated on many such
estates comes to be cocaine, those armed bodies will become increasingly robust. Compensation for such security services usually comes largely in the
form of impunity—the right to rape and pillage. The longer such forces enjoy
impunity and the greater the available loot, the more likely it is that they will

soon cease simply to serve private or public powers and rather become wielders of those powers.

The trajectory of Colombia's paramilitaries is not so different from those of vigilante groups or death squads elsewhere—Central America, for example—where rigid class structure and increasing inequity were challenged from below. That trajectory has led from private and locally contained activity to co-optation, disguised or open, by official military and intelligence operatives, and finally to major or commanding roles in government itself.

Paramilitaries, in order to coordinate their operations at the national level, in 1997 formed a loose confederation, the United Self-Defense Forces of Colombia (AUC); it tripled in size from 1998 to 2002, when its members numbered about 15,000. As generalized insecurity has moved into town, along with displaced peasants and dismissed workers, support for the paramilitaries has spread also within the urban middle class. This expanded base was manifested in the congressional and presidential elections of 2002; for reasons, reportedly, of affinity on the one hand and intimidation on the other, the AUC gained control of about 35 percent of the congressional seats as well as several governorships.

President Uribe's support base included both Liberals and Conservatives, but it was swelled particularly by nontraditional participants like the paramilitaries. Uribe, a former governor of the drug mafia-infested department of Antioquia, had been linked to the paramilitaries, reportedly, in myriad ways and to their collaborators in official military positions, and he was clearly their undeclared candidate. Though only 38 percent of the eligible voters turned out, Uribe's margin of 53 percent in a field of four was impressive. The official Liberal candidate, Horacio Serpa, came in second, at 31.7 percent. The United States had also weighed in, signaling its support for Uribe both privately and publicly. U.S. Ambassador Anne Patterson had met privately with Uribe at his home in Antioquia in late 2001, and she was quick to publicly congratulate him on his victory, well before Serpa had conceded.[13]

Deepening U.S. Involvement

Whether Colombia's power struggle is to be played out with bullets or ballots, the role of the United States has become ever more central to it. In the aftermath of the September 11, 2001, terrorist attacks on New York City and Washington, D.C., the Bush administration had begun to speak of its left-wing antagonists around Latin America, including Colombia, as terrorists. An emergency supplemental appropriations bill to expand counter-terror capabilities worldwide, rushed through the U.S. Congress in March 2000, included money for Colombia and language that allowed expansion of the mission there from fighting drugs to fighting terrorists as well. The Democratic Party opposition, unable to prevent passage of the legislation, managed nevertheless to designate the AUC, along with the FARC and the ELN, as terrorist organizations. It is unclear, however, whether the laundering, or "decommissioning," of the

AUC consequently pledged by Uribe will turn out to be a cold shower or a warm bath.

In the name of *Plan Colombia*, the U.S. Government by 2004 had spent some three billion dollars, more than 75 percent of it on military assistance. Until the U.S. invasion of Iraq, Colombia was the third-largest recipient of U.S. assistance, after only Israel and Egypt. About 400 military personnel were serving in Colombia, along with another 400 of the so-called civilian contractors, and the administration had proposed a near doubling of those numbers. The United States had used hundreds of thousands of gallons of highly toxic herbicides in aerial spraying of coca fields—and also, incidentally, of food crops and villages. Such spraying is most likely in the long term to increase the acreage planted in coca; the coca plant is more resilient than most and will grow in soil too damaged for replanting in food crops. In the short term, peasants whose food crops have been eradicated will be driven onto less fertile land that is fit for little else than the extraordinarily robust coca. There is no indication, in any case, that the almost forty-billion-dollar-a-year cocaine traffic into the United States—some 80 percent of it from Colombia—has abated.[14]

No Winners, Only Losers and Unsung Heroes

As of mid 2004, while paramilitaries had been literally gaining ground under the Uribe government, it was not clear who might emerge in the longer term as winners of the seemingly endless Colombian free-for-all. But there was no doubt at all about the losers. Civilians who were not targeted by the guerrillas were thereby under suspicion of being guerrilla sympathizers and thus were targeted by the paramilitaries. Some were targeted by both, and others were simply crushed in passing when their ancestral homes got in the way of bullets and bombs and herbicides, or, as in the case of some indigenous groups, in the way of the ambitions of multinational petroleum interests.

Eighty percent of the population was found to be living in poverty in 2004, with 46 percent falling into the category of "extreme" poverty; and the income gap continued to grow. Ninety percent of the land is owned by 10 percent of the population, and the trend is toward ever greater concentration rather than redistribution. It is hardly surprising that land seized by terror from the poor finds its way into the grasp of the already wealthy. Paramilitaries began in 2001 to sell of great chunks of land under their control to drug traffickers willing to pay fees based on cocaine production.[15]

Health care was generally unavailable for those in the herbicide spray zones who suffered from rashes, respiratory problems, and temporary blindness. Education was not readily available either. Though 75 percent of the population is now urban, one-third of the children of primary school age have never attended school. In the mushrooming shantytowns, children without schools or jobs were being impressed into one or another category of armed band or lured into prostitution.

Meanwhile, there was no escape from nagging insecurity. Wealthy businessmen could build the walls higher around their properties and hire more security guards, but even they could not avoid becoming prisoners in their own homes. Some Colombians hunker down and assume a low profile. But those who by profession or avocation have chosen to deal in truth and justice put themselves regularly at risk, and the poor, of course, are always vulnerable.

All wars have their heroes, but heroes of the most inglorious of wars, especially wars of the rich against the poor—of conquest and endless reconquest—are certain to be unsung. Among the unsung heroes and heroines of Colombia's chronic conflict are the citizens of rural communities—particularly in the province of Cauca—continuously threatened by marauding bands, who have organized and declared themselves to be "peace communities." At great personal and collective risk, they stand firm in unarmed resistance to guerrillas or, more often, paramilitaries who would drive them off their land and out of their villages. The best known and presumed oldest of these is San José de Apartado, which has maintained its integrity against all odds over some three decades of resistance. Victories are partial and always reversible, but the network of communities is spreading rapidly, capturing imagination and drawing support from many religious and nongovernmental organizations in Europe and the United States.

Even so, if there is to be a breakthrough to sustainable peace and human security at ground level—as opposed to the penthouse suites where "peace process" can so easily become the new designation of an ongoing war—its outline is yet to emerge. For now, the famous lament of the Liberator of South America, Simón Bolívar, remains sadly applicable to Colombia: "America is ungovernable; those who have fought the revolution have plowed the sea."

NOTES

1. Robert H. Dix, *Colombia: The Political Dimensions of Change* (New Haven: Yale University Press, 1967), p. 242

2. James L. Payne, *Patterns of Conflict in Colombia* (New Haven: Yale University Press, 1968), pp. 238–267.

3. U.S. Congress, 91st, 1st Session, Senate, Committee on Foreign Relations, *Colombia: A Case History of U.S. Aid* (Washington, D.C.: Government Printing Office, February 1, 1969), pp. 57–59.

4. Jenny Pearce, Colombia entry in Peter Calvert, ed., *Political and Economic Encyclopedia of South America and the Caribbean* (London: Longman Group, 1991), pp. 123–133.

5. Charles Bergquist, Ricardo Peñaranda, and Gonzalo Sánchez G., *Violence in Colombia, 1990–2000: Waging War and Negotiating Peace* (Wilmington, Del.: Scholarly Resources, 2004), p. xiv.

6. Pearce, *loc. cit.;* see also Marc Cooper, "Plan Colombia: Wrong Issue, Wrong Enemy, Wrong Country," *The Nation,* March 19, 2001, pp. 11–18.

7. A sampling of the reforms embodied in that new constitution is found in Charles Bergquist, et al., p. 213.

8. William Monning and Jeffrey Fields, "A Multilateral Negotiation/Mediation Simulation: The Civil Conflict in Colombia," Monterey Institute of International Studies (unpublished), 2004.

9. Latin America Database, NotiSur–South American Political and Economic Affairs, ISSN 1060–4189, Volume 14, Number 33, September 3, 2004.

10. Peter Canby, "Latin America's Longest War," *The Nation,* August 16/23, 2004, pp. 31–38.

11. Monning and Fields, *loc. cit.*

12. Monning and Fields, *loc. cit.*

13. Washington Office on Latin America, *Colombia Monitor,* Washington, D.C., July 2002.

14. Canby, *loc. cit.*

15. Robin Kirk, *More Terrible Than Death: Violence, Drugs, and America's War in Colombia* (New York: Public Affairs, 2004).

SUGGESTED READINGS

Bergquist, Charles, Ricardo Peñaranda, and Gonzalo Sánchez G., eds. *Violence in Colombia, 1990–2000: Waging War and Negotiating Peace.* Wilmington, Del.: Scholarly Resources, 2001.

Dix, Robert H. *Colombia: The Political Dimensions of Change.* New Haven: Yale University Press, 1967.

___. *The Politics of Colombia.* New York: Praeger, 1987.

Dudley, Steven. *Walking Ghosts: Murder and Guerrilla Politics in Colombia.* London: Routledge Press, 2004.

Fluharty, Vernon J. *The Dance of the Millions: Military Rule and Social Revolution in Colombia, 1930–1956.* Pittsburgh: University of Pittsburgh Press, 1957.

Galbraith, W. O., *Colombia: A General Survey,* 2nd ed. London: Oxford University Press, 1966.

Hartlyn, Jonathan. *The Politics of Coalition Rule in Colombia.* Cambridge: Cambridge University Press, 1988.

Holt, Pat M. *Colombia Today and Tomorrow.* New York: Praeger, 1964.

Hunter, John A. *Emerging Colombia.* Washington, D.C.: Public Affairs, 1962.

Kirk, Robin. *More Terrible Than Death: Massacres, Drugs, and America's War in Colombia.* Washington, D.C.: Public Affairs, 2004.

Kline, Harvey F. *Colombia—Democracy Under Assault.* Boulder, Colo.: Westview Press, 1995.

Livingstone, Grace. *Inside Colombia, Drugs, Democracy, and War.* New Brunswick, N.J.: Rutgers University Press, 2004.

Martz, John D. Jr. "Colombia: Qualified Democracy." Chapter XI in Martin C. Needler, ed., *Political Systems of Latin America.* Princeton, N.J.: Van Nostrand, 1964.

___. *The Politics of Clientelism in Colombia: Democracy and the State.* New Brunswick:, N.J.: Transaction Press, 1996.

Molano, Alfred. *Loyal Soldiers in the Cocaine Kingdom: Tales of Drugs, Mules, and Gunmen* (translation by James Graham). New York: Colombia University Press, 2004.

Payne, James L. *Patterns of Conflict in Colombia.* New Haven, Conn.: Yale University Press, 1968.

Smith, T. Lynn. *Colombia: Social Structure and the Process of Development.* Gainesville: University of Florida Press, 1967.

Taussig, Michael. *Law in a Lawless Land: Diary of a Limpieza in Colombia.* New York: The New Press, 2004.

Chapter 21

VENEZUELA: A "MODEL" DEMOCRACY IN CRISIS

STEVE ELLNER

VENEZUELA WAS AN UNLIKELY nation for the type of social and political turbulence that set in during the 1990s and peaked following the election of Hugo Chávez in 1998. For years political scientists had labeled Venezuela a "showcase" or "model" democracy, in large part because of its mass-based political parties, which provided organized labor and other institutions with input into decisionmaking, thus assuring political stability. Leaders of the struggle against the dictatorship of Juan Vicente Gómez (1908–1935) founded Venezuela's largest party, Democratic Action (AD), and subsequently came to power during a short-lived democracy of 1945 to 1948. AD and the nation's second largest party, the social Christian COPEI, alternated in power several times during the modern period of democracy beginning in 1958, at a time when military coups interrupted democratic rule in the rest of Latin America. Cold War imperatives contributed to the international renown of AD and COPEI leaders, who played a leading role in Washington's efforts to banish Cuba from the community of Latin American nations shortly after Fidel Castro's rise to power.

A week of mass disturbances in February 1989 known as the "*Caracazo*" signaled the end of AD and COPEI hegemony and coincided with other abrupt and difficult changes. Controversial formulas, including the privatization of the telecommunications and steel industries and the national airlines, replaced the strategy of state intervention in the economy (known as "sowing the oil"), which had enjoyed a near consensus among major political actors after 1958. In addition, erratic international oil prices since the mid-1980s contrasted with the previous half century and underlined Venezuela's dependence on the export of that commodity, leading Venezuelans to question the notion that they were a privileged third-world nation.

A second rupture occurred with Chávez's presidential election. The Constitution of 1999, drafted by Chávez supporters, established the model of direct popular participation known as "participatory democracy," in the process undermining the all-encompassing influence and privileges of political parties. In addition, Chávez's foreign policy, designed to promote a multipolar world, distanced Venezuela from the U.S. orbit more than at any moment until then. In other respects, however, Chávez's appeal to the marginalized poor who worked outside the formal economy was not completely new for Venezuela and Latin America. To a certain extent it represented a throwback to the 1930s and 1940s when radical Latin American leaders known as populists (such as Juan Domingo Perón in Argentina) promoted the incorporation of excluded sectors into their nation's social and political life.

VENEZUELA PRIOR TO THE OUTSET OF THE MODERN DEMOCRATIC PERIOD IN 1958

Colonial Venezuela's backwater setting and delayed institutional growth molded future developments, including the resistance to Spanish rule in the early nineteenth century. Thus, due to Venezuela's backwardness and lack of prosperity, few Spanish women arrived to marry into the native elite; as a result the colony was characterized by high rates of miscegenation both in rural areas and towns. Soon virtually all colonists were of mixed blood. Furthermore, the weak presence of Spanish authorities gave rise to widespread contraband, which in turn cemented ties with Spain's traditional adversary England and eventually generated interest in free trade. At the same time the colony's isolation facilitated contact with republican ideas, which also stimulated the wars for independence. Spain's neglect of Venezuela in the sixteenth and seventeenth centuries helped convert town councils (known as *cabildos*), controlled by the local elite but responsive to all citizens, into centers of decisionmaking. The attempts by the eighteenth century Spanish Bourbon kings to centralize power enhanced Caracas's position at the expense of the *cabildos* and created discontent. The relative weakness of Spanish authority in the colony goes a long way in explaining why an army led by Venezuela's Simón Bolívar not only liberated his nation from Spanish rule, but went on to win independence in Colombia, Ecuador, Peru, and Bolivia.

Traditional historiography portrayed the period between the death of Bolívar in 1830 and that of Gómez in 1935 as a lost century devoid of meaningful change, and characterized by ongoing clashes among *caudillos* (strongmen) lacking in scruples and programs. Such a simplistic thesis, which is still accepted by many, if not most, Venezuelans, belies the popular and democratic banners of the struggles and certain changes that occurred during those hundred years. A dynamic view of history would recognize the long-term importance of mobilizations around radical social and political slogans, and their influence on popular consciousness, even though most of those demands were neither well defined nor achieved at the time.

As a result of the "Federal War" between 1859 and 1863, the Liberal Party, which appealed to non-privileged sectors, gained power from the Conservatives, who had previously dominated politics. When the Liberal leaders landed at the port city of Coro marking the beginning of the war, they called for the abolition of both the death penalty and imprisonment for debt, as well as proclaiming religious liberty, direct elections, and equality before law. Their arrival at Coro sparked uprisings in several places, including the San Carlos prison in Maracaibo. The Liberal rallying cry "Federation" lacked a precise definition, but for the lower classes it signified a call for liberty, equality, and distribution of land. To raise money for the war effort, the most radical Liberal, General Ezequiel Zamora, decreed a 5 percent tax on the possessions of wealthy Venezuelans. Zamora, however, was killed in battle, possibly on orders from fellow Liberals.

Eventually, the rival Liberal leader Antonio Guzmán Blanco gained control and ruled Venezuela between 1870 and 1888. Guzmán Blanco was notoriously corrupt and he completely abandoned the Liberals' democratic commitments. Nevertheless, in his first year in power he decreed obligatory primary education. Subsequently the number of public schools increased nearly tenfold. At the same time, he curtailed the prerogatives of the Catholic Church, a bulwark of the oligarchy, by establishing a civil registry and conferring on the state a monopoly on legally recognized marriages. Guzmán Blanco also established a mechanism known as the *situado* for the distribution of fixed percentages of the federal budget to the states. The *situado* placated the regional *caudillos* by compensating for the central government's jurisdiction over customs and mineral wealth and the elimination of internal tariffs. Venezuelan historian Germán Carrera Damas has argued that the Liberals in power embraced a "national project" consisting of incipient state centralization and policies that favored the "advanced" enterprising sectors of the elite over the traditional oligarchy.

The next important political change occurred in 1899 when a makeshift army from the state of Táchira led by Cipriano Castro (who governed from 1899 to 1908) and Juan Vicente Gómez (1908–1935) took control of Caracas. Their war cry, "New Men, New Ideals, New Methods," proved deceptive as Castro ruled as a dictator and Gómez as a ruthless one. Nevertheless, Castro, who even before the invasion had embraced a nationalist rhetoric in opposition to British territorial encroachment, displayed courage in facing up to powerful national and foreign interests that were themselves linked. In 1902–1903, he put down an uprising known as the *"Revolución Libertadora,"* financed by U.S. investors who were irked by Castro's insistence on compliance with the terms of a contract involving the exploitation of asphalt. During the conflict the rebels hailed the blockade of British, Italian, and German ships that were sent to force the Venezuelan government to meet its debt obligations. Castro reacted by appealing to national unity and even released from jail a leading political adversary, José Manuel Hernández, who called on the nation to put aside differences to face the foreign invaders. Although Castro soon called on the United States to help settle the dispute, Washington ended up aiding his ex-comrade-in-arms Gómez in staging a successful coup in 1908.

In promoting centralism and building national institutions, Castro and Gómez continued where Guzmán Blanco left off. Most important, Castro created a standing national army while Gómez promoted its professionalization and centralized its command. As a result, the Venezuelan government was able to rein in regional *caudillos* and avoid a repetition of the *Revolución Libertadora* uprising.

Oil revenue under Gómez facilitated state building and specifically the formation of a well-equipped standing army. In the early 1920s, Venezuela began to export significant quantities of oil and by the end of the decade had become the largest international supplier. Venezuela's status as a single product exporter was maintained as the production of coffee and cacao, the nation's main cash crop during the previous century, declined precipitously in the 1920s. The state bureaucracy and programs fed by oil revenue produced opportunities for a burgeoning middle class and working class, which went on to form the social base of democratic political movements that challenged the Gómez dictatorship.

The year 1936 began the modern period of Venezuelan history. Even though President Eleazar López Contreras (1936–1941) and Isaías Medina Angarita (1941–1945) were former Gómez military officers and were called "*gomecistas*" by their adversaries, they promoted gradual democratization, including legalization of political parties and labor unions, freedom of expression, and electoral reforms. Equally important, both presidents contributed to the institution building and centralism that began with Guzmán Blanco. Thus, for instance, López passed the social security law in 1940 while Medina implemented it by creating the Venezuelan Social Security Institute (IVSS) in 1944.

The October 1945 coup that initiated the *trienio* period of AD rule between 1945 and 1948 deepened the steps toward reform, modernization, and democracy of the previous ten years. An example of gradual change was the *trienio* government's policy of "50–50," in which for every dollar of oil company profits, the state received at least one dollar in revenue. Although AD called the policy revolutionary, President Medina had established the "50–50" arrangement as a guiding principle in his Law of Hydrocarbons of 1943 (but in practice the calculation of taxes on oil profits during the next two years fell short of that goal). In some aspects, the *trienio* represented a qualitative change in favor of democracy and modernization. Most important, politics was characterized by popular mobilization and participation, including the proliferation of labor organizations, in contrast to the more elitist, restrictive political system operating until then. Another novelty was the government's strategy of assigning a significant portion of the national budget to the Venezuelan Development Corporation (CVF) in order to grant credit and subsidies to national enterprises.

The military rule under General Marcos Pérez Jiménez between 1948 and 1958 also combined elements of rupture with the past and continuity. By outlawing AD, the Communist Party, and hundreds of labor unions, and holding a notoriously rigged election (for a constituent assembly) in 1952 and plebiscite in 1957, the dictatorship interrupted democratic process dating back to 1936. It also halted the *trienio* government's policy of subsidizing national enterprises to promote economic development. Nevertheless, in carrying out ambitious development plans in the industrial Guayana region, including the creation of the state-owned steel company SIDOR, the government rejected laissez-faire (or state nonintervention) economics, thus adhering to general policy dating back to 1936.

The Modern Democratic Period: The Stable Years, 1958–1988

Following the overthrow of Pérez Jiménez by a broad alliance of political parties, dissident officers, and representatives of the Catholic Church hierarchy, Venezuelan politics evolved into a two-party system based on AD and COPEI. For the first three presidential elections, AD's Rómulo Betancourt (in 1958), AD's Raúl Leoni (in 1963), and COPEI's Rafael Caldera (in 1968) ran in an open field of candidates and were elected with less than 50 percent of the vote. In 1961, the diverse parties converged in drafting the nation's constitution, which would remain in effect for nearly forty years.

The emergence of the pro-establishment AD and COPEI as the dominant parties was due in part to the fatal decision of the Venezuelan left, inspired by the Cuban revolution, to participate in guerrilla warfare. The political tensions that led to the left's decisions to take up arms were partly the product of economic difficulties stemming from the international competition posed by emerging Middle-East oil producers. During Leoni's presidency, the pro-guerrilla Communist Party put forward the slogan "Democratic Peace" in order to negotiate its way back into legal life. Upon taking office, President Caldera granted amnesty to the Communists and subsequently to the insurgent Movement of the Revolutionary Left (MIR).

The guerrilla defeat was testimony to the attractiveness of the model of vigorous state intervention in the economy embraced by AD and COPEI as an alternative to the socialist system of exclusive state ownership defended by the left. Thus AD and COPEI governments actively promoted economic development and attempted to fulfill social objectives. While Venezuela was basically capitalist, the constitution of 1961 reserved "basic industry" for the state, although it failed to formulate a precise definition of the term. Along these lines, the Betancourt administration expanded the plans for Guayana formulated under the Pérez Jiménez dictatorship by creating the Venezuelan Corporation of Guayana (CVG) to run the steel and hydroelectric power industries of the region. In addition, Betancourt created the Venezuelan Petroleum Corporation (CVP), although he never made clear whether it was designed to compete with private oil companies or to serve as a mechanism to gauge their profits for tax purposes. Throughout the period, the nation's main labor confederation, the AD-controlled Confederation of Venezuelan Workers (CTV), put forward specific proposals to enhance the central government's role in the economy, and in doing so championed the interventionist model even more than did the governing parties.

President Carlos Andrés Pérez's election in 1974 initiated a new period in which the combined presidential vote of AD and COPEI approximated 90 percent of the voting population. Pérez's full-fledged application of the interventionist model in the form of ambitious social and economic programs was made possible by a windfall in oil revenue beginning in his first year in office. Pérez's most far-reaching actions on the economic front were his nationalization of the iron and oil industries (in 1975 and 1976), his increase in state ownership of the aluminum industry, and the vast sums of money invested in the expansion of the state steel company SIDOR. Shortly after he left office, Pérez claimed that the state takeover of private companies under his administration formed part of a strategy of "evolutionary socialism."

Sharp increases of international oil prices provided President Pérez and his successor, COPEI's Luis Herrera Campins (1979–1984), with a golden opportunity to promote national development. The economic contraction and deteriorating social conditions throughout the 1980s served as a reminder that the development strategy of previous decades had failed to produce the expected results. Neoliberal thinking (which minimizes the role of the state) attributed the stagnation to the inherent shortcomings of the interventionist strategy,

Other explanations for the economic shortcomings of the democratic period focus on specific practices that at any given moment could have been avoided. In the first place, the interventionist policies of the Venezuelan government were biased in favor of social as opposed to developmental objectives (a tendency that has led some political scientists to call Pérez and other presidents of the "period populists"). Thus, for example, the need to create job opportunities overshadowed the goal of increasing productivity and was often translated into the generation of artificial employment. In the second place, in spite of Venezuela's image as a showcase democracy, the widespread corruption and patronage practiced by the dominant parties were responsible for the state's low levels of productivity, particularly in telecommunications, steel, aluminum, and airlines companies that were subsequently slated for private takeover. Indeed, there is evidence that the deteriorating conditions in state-run industries in the 1980s were partially induced to pave the way for privatization. In the third place, the post-1958 governments generally failed to prioritize the goal of severing dependence on foreign capital and the promotion of technology and sophisticated products such as capital goods. Finally, even though the nation was awash in hard currency as a result of oil price hikes, the Pérez and Herrera Campins administrations greatly increased the foreign debt, thus shackling the state budget for many years to come. Political scientist Terry Lynn Karl points out that the magnitude of such indebtedness on the part of a nation in time of prosperity had parallels only with Spain in the sixteenth century.

The Deepening of the Political Crisis, 1989–2003

The critics of Venezuelan democracy have pointed to two distinct dates signaling the changes that inflicted the most damage on the nation and its political system. President Chávez and his supporters claim that the democratic system was flawed from the outset in 1958 due to the central role assigned to political parties and the key decisions that were reached by a political elite removed from the general population. Such a view ignores the popular will in favor of the electoral democracy replacing the Pérez Jiménez dictatorship. In addition, the politics of state intervention in the economy that was a hallmark of the post-1958 regime, for all its shortcomings, promoted economic development and diversification.

A second view pinpoints 1989 as the date when an abrupt change of economic policies implemented under the second presidency of President Carlos Andrés Pérez (1989–1993), coupled with an extended period of relatively low oil prices, aggravated social inequalities and sparked social unrest. Over the next ten years, the number of marginalized poor lacking steady work in the formal economy grew steadily, reaching nearly 60 percent of the population. As a result, leading actors, including politicians such as Pérez and political parties such as AD, lost credibility. Pérez's "shock treatment," consisting of the sudden application of neoliberal reforms, included deregulation of exchange rates (which had been frozen for priority imports), as well as of retail prices and interest rates. Like Pérez in 1988, Rafael Caldera in 1993 won the presidential elections on a platform that defended the interventionist model, only to implement neoliberal formulas in his third year in office on terms negotiated with the International Monetary Fund (IMF). In his last two years in office, Caldera signed legislation modifying the system of worker severance payments and privatizing social security along the lines that President Pérez had proposed in 1989, but then dropped due to lack of sufficient support. Both measures were widely perceived as tinkering with longstanding worker benefits that protected them in moments of difficulty. The CTV (along with business and state representatives) formed part of a presidentially created tripartite commission that drafted the legislation, and in doing so abandoned its traditional insistence on leaving both systems intact.

The reaction against Pérez's neoliberal reforms was immediate and at times violent. A week of nationwide disturbances known as the *Caracazo* broke out on February 27, 1989, just minutes after transportation price hikes went into effect. A wave of organized protests and spontaneous street actions encompassed Pérez's four years in office. On February 4, 1992, an abortive coup was staged by middle-level army officers led by Hugo Chávez and ten months later a second and bloodier one was led by senior officers including those of the navy and the air force. The following year Pérez was impeached, ostensibly as a result of accusations of misuse of public funds, but undoubtedly his removal was related to the widespread discontent generated by his economic policies.

Subsequently the series of protests subsided, in large part because of President Caldera's more sagacious approach. Not only did Caldera follow a policy of protracted implementation of neoliberal formulas, but he created the tripartite commission and forged a tacit alliance with AD that brought key actors into the decisionmaking process.

The presidential election of 1998 put in clear evidence the popular repudiation of the political establishment. Chávez with 56 percent of the vote and Henrique Salas Romer with 40 percent both blamed the major parties, and the coterie that ran them, for the nation's woes. In his antiparty rhetoric, Chávez an ex-rebel who had tried to overthrow an AD government, outdid Salas Romer, who formerly belonged to COPEI and who received eleventh-hour endorsement from AD and COPEI. Chávez's popularity rose during the two-year presidential campaign at the same time that he subordinated or modified radical positions such as nonpayment of the foreign debt and emphasized political objectives. His main campaign banner was the convocation of a constitutional assembly in order to replace "representative democracy," which was underpinned by political parties, with "participatory democracy" consisting of direct popular input.

In elections held in July 1999, Chávez's party, the Fifth Republic Movement (MRV), gained absolute control of the National Constitutional Assembly. A national referendum in December of the same year approved the document by 71 percent of the votes. The framers of the new constitution rejected the model embodied by those who drafted the previous constitution of 1961 that privileged political parties. Instead the new constitution established mechanisms for the direct participation of civil society and citizens as a whole in decisionmaking. Thus, for instance, while a majority of the members of the national electoral commission were previously party members, the 1999 constitution stipulated that all of them had to be unaffiliated with parties and assigned organizations of civil society a role in selecting them. The 1999 constitution also allowed for recall elections of elected officials and referendums on policies and legislation.

In his bid for the presidency in 1998, Chávez received campaign contributions from various powerful economic groups as well as political moderates such as the Movement toward Socialism (MAS) party. Chávez, however, did not hide his intentions of going beyond an initial political stage to a more radical one highlighted by socioeconomic changes at a future date, although it is possible that the moderates and capitalists who backed him underestimated his resolve. In 2001, Chávez radicalized his discourse and passed forty-nine controversial laws in one fell swoop. This legislation included an agrarian reform that forced owners of unproductive land to accept a state plan for cultivation or face expropriation; the Organic Law of Hydrocarbons, which assigned the state majority control of mixed oil ventures; and another law that undid the privatization of the social security system enacted under Caldera. According to an executive decree on February 4, 2002, committees established in slums that undertook surveys could distribute deeds to long-time residents who had illegally settled the land.

The opposition, consisting of AD, COPEI, MAS, the CTV, the business organization FEDECAMARAS, and the communications media in general, accused Chávez of moving in an authoritarian direction. The opposition pointed out that the new constitution strengthened the executive at the expense of the congress, which, for example, lost the right to veto proposed promotions of military officers to higher ranks. Opposition leaders added that President Chávez's domination of the various branches of government violated the system of checks and balances. Thus Chávez's MVR party maintained majority control of congress. Nevertheless, the supreme court, the national electoral council, and the attorney general's office, which originally were viewed as having been subordinated to the executive, reached decisions that at times favored Chávez and other times the opposition.

The opposition-sponsored indefinite general strike in April 2002 led to a coup that in turn set off mass mobilizations of slum dwellers in defense of Chávez, paving the way for his return within forty-eight hours. During those two days, FEDECAMARAS president Pedro Carmona assumed the presidency and proceeded to abolish congress and other elected institutions. A second effort to oust Chávez occurred in December of the same year, with a ten-week general strike. Given FEDECAMARAS's leading role in the strike it was difficult to determine whether the shutdown was supported by the workers or was (as the *Chavistas* claimed) a management decreed lockout.

By the beginning of 2004, one of the main challenges facing the opposition was the definition of programs and ideology. Over the previous two years, opposition leaders had sacrificed programmatic clarity for the sake of maintaining unity in the effort to oust Chávez, which eclipsed all other objectives and activities. After five years in power, Chávez also lacked a fully developed strategy of economic development and severance of foreign dependence. In spite of his economic nationalism, Chávez failed to establish mechanisms to oblige foreign investors to favor local capital and the local work force. Furthermore, as a result of his rhetoric in favor of the poor, developmental objectives were subordinated to social ones. Thus, for instance, the government allotted vast sums of money to small makeshift (or "macro") companies as well as cooperatives in an effort to alleviate unemployment and poverty, even though those firms were not particularly effective in promoting economic growth.

Conflict in the Nationalized Oil Industry

The nationalization of the oil industry under the first administration of Carlos Andrés Pérez in 1976 achieved a surprising national consensus, at the same time that it appealed to national pride. Nevertheless, the terms of nationalization soon generated controversy. Shortly after nationalization, a noncommercial magazine published secrete technological and commercialization contracts signed between the state oil company (PDVSA) and Exxon, Shell, and Gulf, which had dominated the Venezuelan petroleum industry over the previous half a century. PDVSA executives, who represented one line of thinking, defended the contracts as necessary to ensure the smooth transition to state control. At the same time they rejected public debate on grounds that the issues involved were technical matters that nonspecialists could not easily grasp. They also feared that excessive government interference would undermine long-term planning based on technical criteria.

A second current included politicians of different political stripes who insisted that major decisions in the industry be opened to public discussion and that the Ministry of Energy and Mines, not PDVSA, formulate oil policy. In addition, the PDVSA critics argued that the Venezuelan oil company should diversify its relations beyond the three multinational corporations that had traditionally controlled the industry. Some of those belonging to the second current viewed the PDVSA as a "state within the state" and its executives as representing an elite tied to the former big three multinationals and removed from the interests of the nation.

Following nationalization, PDVSA executives attempted to achieve autonomy in decisionmaking, particularly with regard to investments. In the early 1980s PDVSA embarked on the program of internationalization whereby it bought into companies and refineries in Europe and the United States, including Citgo. The transfer of PDVSA resources abroad deprived the Venezuelan government of the opportunity to use the state oil company's liquid assets to meet budgetary obligations, as it had occasionally done in the past.

The policy known as the "Oil Opening" initiated in the 1990s further insulated the oil industry from government interference and popular pressure. The new approach allowed private capital to become majority shareholders in joint ventures with PDVSA. Much, but not all, of the Oil Opening took in nonconventional, heavy oil and oil wells with reduced productive capacity, which required considerable capital and advanced technology. Nearly all the companies that associated with PDVSA under the terms of the Oil Opening were multinationals. Critics of oil policy feared that the Oil Opening formed part of a PDVSA strategy to bring about the total privatization of the oil industry, thus undoing the nationalization of 1976. They also argued that the sharp increase in Venezuela's productive capacity as a result of the Oil Opening weakened OPEC in that it disregarded the organization's policy of limiting supply in order to increase prices. Indeed, some PDVSA executives considered OPEC's system of production quotas contrary to Venezuelan interests in exploiting its immense reserves, and favored Venezuela's virtual withdrawal from the organization.

Chávez reversed Venezuela's oil policy of previous years and played an active role in strengthening OPEC. In the first place, he strictly abided by the production quotas OPEC assigned Venezuela, unlike the case during the previous administration of Caldera. The Chávez government also sponsored an OPEC summit in 2000, where it gained approval for a plan to maintain oil prices between $22 and $28 per barrel. Furthermore, Chávez halted the trend toward privatization by passing the Organic Law of Hydrocarbons, which ensured state control of all joint ventures. The same law modified the tax structure to minimize PDVSA's evasion of its financial obligations to the state.

PDVSA's top-level employees played a leading role in the two attempts to oust Chávez from power in 2002. They helped pave the way for the April coup by calling a strike to protest Chávez's alleged political appointments in the oil industry in violation of the merit system. The oil industry was also central in determining the outcome of the ten-week general strike against Chávez beginning in December 2002. The success of the government in restoring production to pre-strike levels without the thousands of professional employees who supported the strike lent credibility to its claim that PDVSA had over the years created a costly and unnecessary bureaucracy. In the aftermath of the shutdown, Chávez fired 18,000 oil employees on grounds that they had participated in the "insurrectional" general strike that had involved sabotage. With new executives in charge of PDVSA, the government proclaimed the total transformation of the company, including its sponsorship of social programs for surrounding communities. Such activity, however, ran the risk of detracting from PDVSA's fulfillment of its principal function, namely producing oil.

U.S.–Venezuelan Relations Under Chávez

The radicalization of Chávez's government during his first five years in office went hand in hand with the deterioration of relations with Washington. During the presidential campaign of 1998, Chávez avoided harsh words against the United States, even though the Clinton administration denied his request for a visa for the purpose of addressing the international business community in New York. John Maisto, the U.S. ambassador in Caracas under Clinton, set the tone for the strained tolerance that characterized the relations during Chávez's first two years in office. Maisto argued that in spite of Chávez's leftist discourse, the United States should avoid open confrontation with his government. The ambassador pointed out that not only was Chávez elected by a large majority of votes, but Venezuela continued to supply oil and make payments on its foreign debt. Nevertheless, tension did rise, as was put in evidence by occasional antagonistic remarks by State Department spokesmen. The most important source of friction at the outset of the administration was Chávez's refusal to allow U.S. surveillance planes to pursue drug smugglers out of neighboring Colombia in Venezuelan air space.

Diverse positions assumed by Chávez would have been to the dislike of either Democratic or Republican administrations. Most important, Chávez played a leadership role in OPEC, a role facilitated by the fact that Venezuela is the only non-Muslim member of the organization and thus exempt from internal feuds with religious implications. Chávez's efforts to promote OPEC unity led him to travel to each member nation in order to personally invite heads of states to OPEC's second summit meeting in Caracas in September 2000. On that occasion, Washington rebuked Chávez for meeting with Iraq's Saddam Hussein and Libya's Muammar Qaddafi. In the second place, Chávez's rhetoric in favor of a "multi-polar" world, in which various centers of power such as the European Union, the Latin American bloc of nations and OPEC coexisted, implicitly (and eventually explicitly) questioned the legitimacy of U.S. hegemony. Other stands and actions that annoyed Washington included Chávez's close ties with Cuba, as reflected by the sale of oil at discounts and the presence of a large mission of Cuban doctors in Venezuela; his vocal opposition to President Bush's target of 2005 for the initiation of the hemispheric economic union known as the Free Trade Area of the Americas (FTAA); Venezuelan criticism of the Plan Colombia to combat the drug trade and guerrilla movement in that nation; and Chávez's decision to order a U.S. military delegation to vacate the Venezuelan Army's Caracas headquarters on grounds that such an arrangement was no longer necessary in the aftermath of the Cold War.

Relations with the United States worsened after the September 11, 2001, attacks when the Bush administration explicitly ruled out a middle ground between Washington's allies and enemies. Although Chávez condemned the attacks, he also criticized the U.S. bombing of Afghanistan. Shortly thereafter, Secretary of State Colin Powell accused Chávez of failing to be fully supportive in the war against terrorism. The National Endowment of Democracy (NED) funneled money through conduits to organizations of the opposition, including political parties, NGOs, and the staunchly anti-government Confederation of Workers of Venezuela. The NGO Venezuelan Solidarity Network claimed that the NED had allocated $800,000 to Venezuelan organizations in 2002 and 2003. The NED itself placed on its web page the names of over a dozen Venezuelan recipients of the foundation's grants, some of which were in the anti-Chávez camp.

The White House at first attributed the April 11, 2002, coup to Chávez's own errors. On April 12, the Bush administration's Otto Reich, who had met with opposition leaders including coup head Pedro Carmona numerous times in the months prior to April 11, summoned Latin American ambassadors to his office. Reich assured them that the coup would not endanger democracy throughout the region. Nevertheless, as soon as the OAS condemned the coup and internal resistance to it began to mount, the United States adopted a more neutral stand. In the aftermath of the coup, relations assumed a lower profile until the general strike in December of that year, which set off an escalation of hostile rhetoric between the two nations. President Chávez for the first time used the term "imperialism" and denounced Washington for its close ties to the opposition. Washington, for its part, made a distinction between the nationalistic governments in Argentina and Brazil and the more leftist Venezuelan government, at the same time that it questioned Chávez's democratic credentials.

CONCLUSION

The founding and preservation of democracy in Venezuela after 1958 represented a major achievement for the nation, but the system also had serious defects and limitations. Modern democratic rule contrasted favorably with the previous century and a half of *caudillos* and military dictatorships following independence. Venezuelan democracy also stood in contrast to the rest of Latin America, which was subject to military governments in the 1960s through the 1980s. Furthermore, Venezuelan democracy after 1958 established a model of active state intervention in the economy, which promoted industrial diversification for the internal market, thus substituting many consumer products that were previously imported. On the downside, corruption, the use of the patronage system, and electoral manipulation at all levels became a standard feature of life. In addition, the governments of the period took but timid steps to break dependence on foreign technology and capital.

The difficulties that Venezuela faced in the 1990s highlighted the nation's similarities with the rest of the continent. Venezuela's two dominant political parties lost considerable prestige and a multiparty system replaced the prevailing two-party system. In addition, two military coup attempts were staged against the backdrop of intense social unrest. Finally, government economic policy failed to put a halt to the stagnation that characterized the nation's economy since the early 1980s. These developments forced many Venezuelans including political analysts to reconsider their view that Venezuela was a "privileged" third world country and a showcase for democracy due to its social and political stability. Most important, Venezuela's dependence on petroleum pegged the performance of the nation's economy to the fluctuations in world oil prices, thus accounting for the economic instability that translated itself into political instability.

SUGGESTED READINGS

Buxton, Julia. *The Failure of Political Reform in Venezuela.* Aldershot, England: Ashgate, 2001.

Coppedge Michael: *Strong Parties and Lame Ducks: Presidential Patriarchy and Factionalism in Venezuela.* Stanford, Calif.: Stanford University Press, 1994.

Coronil, Fernando. *The Magical State: Nature, Money, and Modernity in Venezuela.* Chicago: University of Chicago Press, 1997.

Crisp, Brian. *Democratic Institutional Design: The Powers and Incentives of Venezuelan Politicians and Interest Groups.* Stanford, Calif.: Stanford University Press. 2000

Ellner, Steve. *Organized Labor in Venezuela: Behavior and Concerns in a Democratic Setting.* Wilmington, Del.: Scholarly Resources, 1993.

Ellner, Steve, and Daniel Hellinger, eds. *Venezuelan Politics in the Chávez Era: Class, Polarization and Conflict.* Boulder, Colo.: Lynne Rienner Publishers: 2003.

Ewell, Judith. *Venezuela: A Century of Change.* Stanford: Stanford University Press, 1984.

_____. *Venezuela and The United States: From Monroe's Hemisphere to Petroleum's Empire.* Athens, Ga.: University of Georgia Press, 1996.

Friedman, Elisabeth J. *Unfinished Transitions: Women and the Gendered Development of Democracy in Venezuela, 1936–1996.* University Park, Pa.: Pennsylvania State University Press, 2000.

Karl, Terry Lynn. *The Paradox of Plenty: Oil Booms and Petro-States.* Berkeley: University of California Press, 1977.

Lombardi, John. *Venezuela: The Search for Order, the Dream of Progress.* New York: Oxford University Press, 1982.

McCoy, Jennifer, Andrés Serbin, William C. Smith, and Andrés Stambouli, eds. *Venezuelan Democracy Under Stress.* New Brunswick, N.J.: Transaction Publishers, 1995.

Wright, Winthrop R. *Café Con Leche: Race, Class, and National Image in Venezuela.* Austin: University of Texas Press, 1990.

Yarrington, Doug. *A Coffee Frontier: Land, Society, and Politics in Duaca, Venezuela, 1830–1936.* Pittsburgh: University of Pittsburgh Press, 1997.

Chapter 22

ECUADOR: POLITICAL TURMOIL, SOCIAL MOBILIZATION, AND FRUSTRATED REFORM

PABLO ANDRADE A.
LIISA L. NORTH

AT THE TURN OF the twenty-first century, and despite the emergence of active grassroots-based social movements, the hopes of democracy, economic prosperity, and social progress that attended Ecuador's 1979 transition from military to civilian rule had been shattered. In 2002, per capita GNP stood at 1980 levels while poverty affected more than 70 percent of the population. Poverty, moreover, was accompanied by increasing inequality, and it was most acute in rural areas, among indigenous peoples, and among women. The educational advances of the 1970s and 1980s, critical for the future development of the country, came to a halt in the 1990s as governments spent more and more on debt service and less and less on social programs. Indeed, debt service costs climbed from 5.2 percent to 12.5 percent of GNP between 1991 and 2000, absorbing more or less 40 percent of the public budget during the first years of the new century. Poverty, inequality, and lack of employment opportunities abetted criminal activity, reflected in rising homicide rates, and it also promoted migration out of the country, estimated to have reached one million people or 8 percent of the population during the 1990s. It was the remittances of the migrants rather than incomes earned at home that provided for the needs of increasing numbers of Ecuadorians.[1]

The dismal social and economic conditions were cause and consequence of political turmoil. The first four presidents of the post-transition period did finish their constitutionally mandated terms in office, but the party system that appeared to be consolidating during the early 1980s was in shambles by the mid-1990s. Between 1996 and 2003, five presidents rotated though the executive office. A combination of elite opposition and massive popular protest brought down the populist coalition of Abdalá Bucaram in February 1997, after only six months in office; the centrist government headed by Jamil Mahuad Witt lasted only eighteen months, toppled by an indigenous-military rebellion in early 2000. His term in office was completed by his Vice-President, Gustavo Noboa. Colonel Lucio Gutiérrez, one of the protagonists of the early 2000 rebellion, was elected in 2000.

While the political party system fragmented, social movements gained importance, the indigenous movement most prominently among them. Led by the *Confederación de Nacionalidades Indígenas de Ecuador* (Confederation of Indigenous Nationalities of Ecuador-CONAIE), the indigenous peoples of the highland and Amazonian regions united in nearly nationwide but peaceful *levantaminetos*, or uprisings, against government social and economic policies in 1990, 1994, 1997, 2000, and then again in 2001. Access to land featured prominently among the demands of the first two of these uprisings, along with protest against the privatization of water sources and the dissolution of communal lands that were proposed in agrarian modernization laws presented in 1994 by the rightist government of Sixto Durán-Ballén. However, neither the indigenous nor other social movements—the new women's and environmental activism or the old labor unions that had burst on the political scene in the early 1920s—were able to secure policies that might have counteracted the negative social trends.

How can Ecuador's dismal socioeconomic performance and political instability be explained? A good part of the explanation derives from the past: that is, from the historical evolution of the country's highly dependent primary export-oriented economy, its profound social class and ethnic divisions, and weak and exclusionary political institutions that led to repeated military interventions. However, the sorry mess in which the country finds itself today also emerges from neoliberal structural adjustment policies (SAPs) that Ecuador, under external duress, has pursued since the early 1980s. Below, after briefly reviewing this historical legacy, we turn to Ecuador's incomplete democratization since 1979, drawing attention to the fragmentation of the political party system, the rise of a vibrant indigenous movement, and the adoption of a new constitution that, among other things, recognized Ecuador as a pluri-national republic. The final sections of the chapter look at the ways in which the country's problems are being exacerbated by new forms of dependency generated by neoliberal policies and by the U.S. "wars" on drugs and terrorism.

THE HISTORICAL LEGACY

The prevailing patterns of Ecuador's twentieth century development, which excluded the majority of the population from political participation and the benefits of economic growth, can be traced to the colonial period. However, it was during the first two great waves of modern export growth—the cacao (roughly 1860–1920) and banana (1948–1972) eras—that the basic contours of contemporary patterns of exclusionary economic development and social inequality hardened into place. The efforts of reformist military governments to generate a more inclusionary model of economic growth and social transformation, first in the late 1930s, then in the mid-1960s, and once more at the beginning of the decade-long "petroleum boom" (1972–1982), remained truncated.

The Constitution of an Exclusionary Primary Export Economy

During the course of Ecuador's first modern export era, a powerful oligarchy of cacao producers, who also controlled banking and the export-import trade, was formed in the coastal city of Guayaquil. Employing cheap semi-servile (or semi-waged) labor on their great estates, this "handful" of landlord-financial-commercial families concentrated political power and the profits of export growth in their hands. Idealizing their European roots and inclined toward ostentatious consumption, both inside and outside the country, it has been estimated that, at the beginning of the twentieth century, these elite families transferred a 20 percent of cacao export profits to relatives who lived abroad, especially in Paris (Guerrero, 1980).

The second great export era of banana production expanded the network of intermarrying oligarchic families in Guayaquil and was associated with important investment in infrastructure (roads and ports), the acceleration of migration from highland to coastal regions, steady urbanization, the beginnings of import-substitution industrialization, the growth of the middle class, and the foundation of state economic and social planning institutions. The banana boom thus distributed its profits more broadly than cacao had done, but the basic patterns of social inequality remained intact and the political system highly exclusionary. Indeed, in the highlands, indigenous peoples, who formed the majority of the rural population, remained disenfranchised and subject to servile labor relations: the triad of the prefect, the priest, and the landlord continued to control the lives of rural peoples.

Analysts of the composition of Ecuador's elites in the 1960s and 1970s refer to ten Guayaquil-based "business empires" that were linked through family ties and controlled most commercial, financial, industrial, communications, and agricultural enterprises of the coast.[2] A parallel, although somewhat less concentrated set of Quito-based elite families, reigned over the highlands. The political power of these two sets of oligarchies was sufficient to block any thorough-going social and economic reform aimed toward redistribution of assets (most importantly land), incomes, and public services.

The divergent economic interests of the coastal and highland elites (and a third elite cluster in the city of Cuenca in the southern highlands) led to regional tensions and conflicts: The coastal elites were outward-oriented while the highland elites were more dependent on production for internal markets. Also, to the extent that the productive apparatus and social relations of production varied from region to region, regional political cultures emerged. These regional divisions/cultures cut across subordinate as well as dominant classes. But whereas regional elites, when faced with threats from below, united to defend their common interests, subordinate classes—divided by ethnicity, class, and region—found political unity difficult to achieve.

Civilian Authoritarians and Military Reformers

As the civilian elites equated their narrow private interests with national interests, it was military governments that pursued social reforms, in response to pressures from below, and turned the state into a sponsor of economic development. Indeed, military governments recognized indigenous communities in the Ley de Comunas of 1937; carried out the first agrarian reform that abolished the highland *huasipungo* in 1964 (a response not only to peasant demand but also to the Cuban Revolution and U.S. foreign policy, as expressed in the Alliance for Progress); carried out a second agrarian reform in 1973; and promoted industrial diversification and economic planning and invested in physical and social infrastructure—education in particular—during the remainder of the decade.

It was the last of those military governments (1972–1979) that coincided with the petroleum boom (1972–1982), which provided unparalleled resources to the state to pursue reformist and developmental policies. However, the reformist initiatives of the government headed by General Rodríguez Lara (1972–1976) were blocked by the country's dominant elites, who engineered his overthrow and replacement by a military triumvirate (1976–1979). In effect, elites managed to access petroleum boom income to diversify their portfolios into industrial activities in collaboration with foreign capital. Redistributive reforms remained truncated, although the boom's resources were spread widely enough to generate the rapid growth of an urban middle class. The institutional and social transformations of the decade also set the context for the social mobilizations of the past quarter century, to which we turn below.

THE DEMOCRATIC TRANSITION AND SOCIAL MOBILIZATION

In the course of the export booms and their attendant social transformations, Ecuador did not develop a strong party system, and the weak, clientilistic, and fragmented system that did exist was regionally based. Moreover, political organization was throttled under the military regime in the 1970s. The transition to civilian rule thus did not begin in favorable circumstances. Nevertheless, an incipient party system appeared to be forming, with major parties spanning the ideological spectrum from left to right. However, populism and political instability reemerged in the mid-1990s, along with new social movements.

The Political Party Spectrum of the Transition to Democracy

The transition to civilian rule in 1979 added a new ingredient to democracy in Ecuador. It was the electoral participation of illiterates (granted by the constitution of 1978), which in fact meant the political enfranchisement of the rural poor who, in the highlands, were largely indigenous peasants. This liberating political reform took place in a countryside where the agrarian reform initiatives of 1964 and 1973, although they had not distributed much land, had transformed the traditional structures of political power that were based on the domination of large estate owners. However, neither the traditional regionally based right-wing parties that had been linked to the landlord classes of the coast and the highlands nor the left that had spurred the creation of a strong peasant movement managed to establish strong and stable linkages with the new rural voters.[3] Nor did the center and center-left parties (the Christian Democrats and Democratic Left respectively) fare any better. Thus, until 1996, when indigenous organizations and social movements coalesced to form the Pachakutik United Pluricultural Movement (MUPP), the indigenous and peasant populations, for all practical purposes, did not enjoy political representation in either the national congress or in provincial and municipal governments.

In fact, the rapid urbanization and growth of peri-urban settlements that began in the 1950s turned the attention of all parties largely toward conquering the votes of the recently arrived migrants from the rural areas: The population residing in towns and cities climbed steadily from 28.6 percent in 1950 to 55.4 percent in 1990. Following patterns of behavior with origins tracing back to the country's first twentieth century period of democracy (1946–1963), political parties specialized in creating clientelistic networks to capture the votes of urban middle classes and the more or less recently arrived migrants who made up the urban popular sectors. On the one hand, political clientelism involved the direct exchange of goods and services provided by national and municipal governments for the votes of the popular sectors. On the other hand, the transformation of clientelistic networks into electoral machines depended on attracting and promoting the leaders of popular sector neighborhood organizations and, in the case of the middle classes, the leaders of their professional and business associations. These leaders were then transformed into the political figures that occupied positions in congress, the executive branches, and local governments (Menéndez Carrión 1986; Conaghan, 1995).

The alliances among these political leaders and the various parties remained fluid, however, and the parties did not succeed in transforming their capacity to win votes into a capacity to create stable groups of cadres. Perhaps even more importantly, the first four presidents of the contemporary democratic period—in order to implement neoliberal structural adjustment policies (SAPs) demanded by the International Monetary Fund (IMF), the World Bank, and the U.S. Treasury—abandoned their electoral machines and governed with ad hoc technocratic teams (Conaghan and Malloy, 1994). They thus dug a trench between their governments and the political parties that were supposed to provide support for their policies. The highly unpopular SAPs, pursued by all governments since the onset of the debt crisis in 1982, undercut both popular and elite support for the representatives the parties elected. And all this was reflected in the turbulent relations between governments and their own representatives in congress and in local governments, contributing to the further fragmentation of both parliamentary alliances and the political parties themselves.

TABLE 22.1   Ecuadorian Heads of State and Their Political Affiliations

1972–79	Military Rule	Reformist (1972–76); Conservative Right (1976–79)
1979–81	Jaime Roldós	Populist, Concentration of Popular Forces
1981–84	Osvaldo Hurtado	Centrist, Christian Democratic Party
1984–88	León Febres Cordero	Rightist, Social Christian Party
1988–92	Rodrigo Borja	Centre Left, Democratic Left Party
1992–96	Sixto Durán-Ballén	Rightist, Conservative Party
1996–97	Abdalá Bucaram	Populist, Ecuadorian Roldosist Party
1997–98	Fabián Alarcón	(Interim) Center Right, Liberal
1998–2000	Jamil Mahuad	Center Right, Christian Democratic Party
2000–02	Gustavo Noboa	Center Right, Christian Democratic Party
2002–	Lucio Gutiérrez	Populist, party alliance including Pachakutic

In this political milieu, the parties that eventually became most successful in attracting votes were not necessarily the same ones that best expressed the interests of the dominant groups—that is, the networks of Quito- and Guayaquil-based bankers, industrialists, large merchants, and landowners. Thus the quintessential bête noir of Ecuadorian politics, the erratic and flamboyantly populist leader of the Ecuadorian Roldosista Party, Abdalá Bucaram, was elected president in 1996 and the leader of the turn-of-the-century military indigenous revolt, Colonel Lucio Gutiérrez, in 2002.

The Emergence of New Social Movements

The period stretching from 1990 to 2000 is one of the most dramatic in recent Ecuadorian history, including the massive popular mobilizations surrounding the depositions of Presidents Bucaram in 1997 and Jamil Mahuad in 2000 and the rise of Ecuador's indigenous social and political movements. Indeed, during the 1990s, the indigenous movement converted itself into a leading and legitimate force in Ecuadorian politics, both through its principal organization, the Confederation of Indigenous Nationalities of Ecuador (CONAIE), and the entrance of the associated MUPP into electoral competition.

The historical origins of Ecuador's indigenous movement can be traced to the peasant movements of the 1930s (Becker 2000; Striffler 2002). Its recent origins, as noted above, can be located in the transformation of the social relations of rural power that originated from the agrarian reforms of the 1960s and 1970s and the modernization of agriculture, which liberated the mostly indigenous highland peasant populations from the ties of political domination that had prevailed in the countryside since the second half of the nineteenth century and before (Zamosc 1994; Clark 1998). This liberation was accompanied by the presence of two religious transformations that favored the reconstruction of the indigenous community: the adoption of liberation theology by the Catholic Church and the growth of evangelism.

Inspired by liberation theology, the Catholic Church abandoned its traditional orientation in favor of the country's landlord elites and moved toward a political alliance with, and support for, the indigenous peasantry. The new orientation sought to address the conditions of extreme poverty among indigenous and peasant populations through the transfer of land, the organization of agricultural cooperatives, and literacy training in native languages. The best known of these experiences took place in the province of Chimborazo. There, one of the leading Catholic bishops of the liberation theology movement in Latin America established Quichua-language community radio stations, literacy programs, and leadership schools for indigenous people. Another Church-sponsored development program, which was praised as an economic success by the Interamerican Development Bank (IDB) in the 1990s, was established in the highlands of the neighboring province of Bolívar (North 2003). The programs inaugurated by the Catholic Church propelled not only linguistic identity reconstruction among indigenous peoples but also the creation, in the political vacuum left by the retreat of the old landlord structure, of a new center of power. That center was the indigenous community, and it became the foundation on which the indigenous movement established itself and grew in the 1980s and 1990s (Korovkin 2001). Meanwhile, the leadership education initiatives undertaken by the Church in the early 1980s formed the people who became the political leaders of CONAIE and Pachakutic.

A similar although less well-known role was played by evangelical missions in the highlands (Muratorio 1980). Contrary to the stereotyped image of U.S.-based evangelical missions as "agents of imperialism" that encourage political passivity among peasants, the Protestant churches in the two most indigenous provinces of highland Ecuador—Chimborazo and Cotopaxi—played a broadly emancipating role by favoring peasant organization and literacy in Quichua. These processes that evolved over the last quarter of the twentieth century culminated in the creation of the Ecuadorian Federation of Indigenous Evangelicals (FEINE), one of the most politically active indigenous organizations of recent times.

The new indigenous leaderships began their political activism as intermediaries between the indigenous communities, the national state, and international development aid agencies. The connections with development agencies made it possible for some of the most well-known figures of the late 1990s, both CONAIE and Pachakutik founders, to establish early links to the international indigenous rights movement (Maiguashca 1992). Thus, in contrast to the fragmentation of the middle- and upper-class-led urban political parties and the decline of the labor movement, an indigenous leadership emerged in the early 1980s that, step by step, became more self-confident and capable of controlling the representation of the peasant and indigenous sectors of the highland and Amazonian regions (Guerrero 1994). The process culminated in the establishment of CONAIE, which burst dramatically on the political scene with the national "Indigenous Uprising" of 1990.

During the 1990s, the demand for cultural rights and an anti-neoliberal political-economic platform gained importance within the indigenous movement in comparison to the traditional peasant movement's demand for land.

The rights demanded by the indigenous peoples were strongly focused around an insistence on running their own affairs—taking charge of their own development and exercising the right to govern themselves according to their own laws and customs. These were rights that they claimed on the basis of international accords and treaties signed by Ecuador. The solidarity that these demands awakened among intellectuals and public and private union activists culminated, in 1996, in the establishment of a coalition between CONAIE and various popular organizations that formed part of the Coordinator of Social Movements (CMS). This was the coalition that ultimately founded the MUPP, which participated successfully in the national elections of 1996, placing third in the presidential race and winning ten out of the hundred seats in Ecuador's unicameral Congress. Then, in 2000, running alone or in alliances, the MUPP won the elections in five out of the country's twenty-two provinces and in twenty-nine out of 215 municipalities (with the exception of one coastal municipality, all of those victories were registered in the highland and Amazonian regions).

On this political institutional base and their capacity for mobilization, the indigenous organizations assumed a leadership role in the demonstrations that culminated in the downfall of President Bucaram in February 1997. Subsequently, in a climate of political crisis, distrust in the traditional political parties, and the weakness of interim President Fabián Alarcón (1997–1998), the indigenous movement, political parties from just about the entire ideological spectrum, and the media launched a campaign for a broader political transformation: that is, the rewriting of the country's constitution and a reform of the electoral system.

The Adoption of Yet Another Constitution

In the midst of intense social mobilization and political uncertainty, Ecuadorian voters in 1997 approved a plebiscite for the convocation of a National Assembly that would reform the constitution of 1978. Voters, political parties, and social movements hoped that constitutional reforms would create new political conditions for reforming the state, broadening popular participation in decisionmaking, checking the populist tendencies of the political system, and removing institutional barriers to the political inclusion of indigenous peoples.

The confused and difficult process of reform began with the election of representatives to a constitutional assembly. Contrary to the expectations of indigenous and other popular sector organizations, social movements won only minority representation in comparison to the established political parties. Later, these movements did not even succeed in establishing a stable coalition with their "natural allies," the parties of the left and the center left that were represented in the assembly. On the other hand, neither did the established political parties on any one part of the political spectrum, and least of all the parties of the right and center right, obtain a clear majority of seats that would have allowed them to impose their agendas on the assembly.

Thus, even though the reforms approved during 1997–1998 by the assembly were significant enough to speak of a new constitution, that document basically reflected a deadlock between political forces. It did not provide future governments, for example, with the institutional basis that the parties of the right sought for amending the state's active role in the economy. In fact, the constitution of 1998 ratified a political vision of the state that assigned it a key role in the management of the country's economic life through the regulation of the private sector as well as the ownership of key activities such as the production and provision of energy and communications infrastructure. Neither did the national assembly modify the obligations of the state with regard to the provision of social goods and services such as education, health, and social security.

In strictly political terms, the new constitution did create mechanisms that were expected to deepen democratization and improve governability. Among them, three fundamental changes vis-à-vis the constitution of 1978 stand out: the expansion of electoral representation; administrative decentralization; and the inclusion of mechanisms of "affirmative action" (*discriminación positiva*). While the constitution of 1978 permitted only candidates who were endorsed by political parties to contest elections, the new constitution allowed candidates to be sponsored by social movements and other organizations. This change was designed to complement a new constitutional provision regarding the transfer of responsibilities and capacities from the central state to provinces (headed by prefects), municipalities, and parish councils. This was a significant reform with respect to the previous constitution, which favored the centralization of functions and responsibilities, in addition to decisionmaking, in the national government. Finally, the 1998 constitution created a new juridical framework for increasing women's representation in government. Election laws were modified to force parties and other candidate-sponsoring organizations to include 35 percent women on the lists they presented for popular election. The impact of the 35 percent rule, in contrast to what has happened to extended political participation in general and to decentralization, could be seen in national politics. In 2002, women occupied 20 percent of cabinet posts and their political representation in congress increased from 12 percent in the 1980s to 15 percent at the beginning of the new century (UNDP 2002).

These constitutional innovations, however, were not the ones that attracted the greatest amount of political and academic attention in comparison to the issues of citizenship and self-government rights for indigenous peoples. These latter refer to two questions. First of all, the 1998 constitution ordains that the political category of "citizen" must include all Ecuadorians, without discriminating against any group. This, of course, was already consecrated in the 1978 constitution and further clarified in a constitutional reform in 1990, but it was reiterated once more in conjunction with the assembly's negative response to the demand of indigenous organizations for the recognition of Ecuador as a "pluri-national" entity (Andolina 1998). Second, and in place of the pluri-national state sought by indigenous organizations, the 1998 constitution prescribes the juridical recognition of the "collective rights" of indigenous peoples; specifically, it enshrines their rights to preserve their culture and pursue forms of self-government that recognize the role of "traditional authorities" and the legitimacy of customary law. The dominant political and academic interpretation of these constitutional reforms is that they have empowered Ecuador's indigenous peoples, providing them with the legal instruments to defend their cultural identity (Trujillo 2000).

It is too early to come to any conclusive evaluation of the benefits that these constitutional reforms might signify for the country's indigenous peoples. Certainly, Ecuador's indigenous movement, as noted above, has won broad parliamentary representation and controls various municipal governments, although effective empowerment through decentralization and local democratization remains immensely problematic (Cameron 2003). In addition, at least one government agency, the National Council of the Indigenous and Black Peoples of Ecuador (CODENPE)—staffed by indigenous and black community leaders and technocrats—is now explicitly mandated to advance indigenous interests. However, this agency was created before the constitutional reforms were enacted, and the advances in indigenous political representation can be attributed to the organizational capacity and actions of CONAIE, as well as the changes introduced by the 1998 Law of Political Parties and Elections, which favored the political representation of small parties and political movements over large electoral machines (Collins 2002; Crisp 2002).

The evaluation of the impact of the new constitution on resolving problems of governability and muscular populist parties, by contrast, is relatively straightforward. In effect, the 1998 constitution includes clauses intended to make the life of future presidents easier within Ecuador's fractious multi-party system. Among other things, it forces the larger parties to forge congressional coalitions—generally considered factors of stability; it eliminates the power of congress to censure and remove ministers; and it concedes broad legislative initiative to the president of the republic. These elements were tested during the first government elected under the new constitution: the Christian Democratic administration of Jamil Mahuad. The new constitutional dispositions clearly facilitated the adoption of radical economic decisions by the president (among them, the temporary elimination of income taxes and the adoption of the U.S. dollar as the official currency), and they provided the president with greater freedom in foreign policy negotiations with the United States. Nevertheless, those clauses did not assist the president in building a congressional coalition that could defend his government, which was overthrown in the "military-indigenous rebellion" of January 2000. Neither did they advance transparency or reduce corruption, which were among the other hopes of constitutional reformers. Nor was populism in any way controlled or diminished. In fact, both candidates in the second runoff round of the 2002 presidential elections came from populist parties (Quintero 2002; Andrade 2003).

Finally, the anticipated socially progressive impact of the political incorporation of indigenous peoples remained to materialize. The indigenous-populist governing coalition that emerged from the 2002 elections—with the ex-army colonel and former leader of the military-indigenous rebellion of 2000, Lucio Gutiérrez, occupying the presidency—quickly demonstrated its fragility and weakness. It proved itself incapable of reversing the neoliberal economic policies that had been institutionalized in earlier years or of moderating their destructive impacts on social conditions. It also demonstrated the near impossibility of standing up to the United States on issues that it considered central to its national security, such as U.S. militaristic policies in response to the expansion of drug trafficking and Colombia's civil war.

Exacerbated Dependency

Ecuador is a small and dependent country with hardly any capacity to buck international trends and pressures. Its dependency is economic (on foreign investment and fickle export markets) and ideological (an incapacity to formulate policies distinct from those imposed from the outside). If change has taken place over the past twenty years, it has essentially taken the direction of intensifying these historical trends.

Since the mid-1980s, with the adoption of neoliberal SAPs imposed by the IMF, the World Bank, and the U.S. Treasury, the relations between the state and the economy in Ecuador have been reconfigured. The most notable results of those policies have been: a renewed reliance on primary export commodities (petroleum and bananas as in the past, with cut flowers and maritime products added to the mix recently); dependence on foreign private capital in export production, commercialization, and finance; the weakening of labor standards, along with a weakening of the labor movement to attract domestic and foreign investment; the invasion of domestic markets by cheap imports, especially after the adoption of the U.S. dollar as the official currency; the general abandonment of redistributive reforms, with a resulting growth in inequality and poverty; and weak and erratic, when not negative (as during 1997–2000), growth. The social violence generated by these policies and their consequences has led to the rapid growth of private security forces, in the urban as well as the rural areas, that cooperate with public forces to control the increased number of crimes against property and new waves of protest in the countryside. All this has meant contraction of the domestic market—indeed, the abandonment of the policies that favored the domestic market growth and diversification that were pursued, albeit in erratic ways, by governments in the 1960s and 1970s.

The negative impacts of neoliberal adjustment policies were aggravated during the financial crisis of 1997–2000 when almost 60 percent of the financial system went bankrupt, generating losses estimated at around $7 billion. The financial crisis also further intensified the vulnerability of Ecuador's governments to external pressures regarding the adoption of policies favorable to domestic and international financial sectors, at the same time that it made governments more susceptible to the demands of domestic export and financial groups for measures that would protect their interests.

Thus, to overcome the financial crisis of May 1998 and maintain elite support, President Mahuad's government converted the debts that had been contracted by the insolvent private banks into public debts. This decision, together with the temporary suspension of income taxes and the adoption of a tax on bank transactions, worsened the difficult fiscal situation of the state, contributing to the devaluation of the national currency (the *sucre*), an increase in the number of business bankruptcies, and the risk of hyperinflation. To make matters worse, prices of petroleum, the principal export, plunged during 1998–1999, descending to less than ten dollars per barrel from an average of sixteen dollars in 1997. Finally, in December 2000, confronted with this economic and political instability, President Mahuad decreed the adoption of the U.S. dollar as the official currency of the country in an effort to buy the political support of the great commercial and banking groups of the city of Guayaquil.

Dollarization, however, did not save Mahuad's government or the country's economy. Although per capita income recovered in comparison to 1999, in 2003 it was still about 4 percent below what it had been in 1998. On the other hand, even though dollarization slowed down inflation, it did so by restricting economic growth: It increased the costs of production in Ecuador in comparison to its neighbors whose currencies continued to devalue, and it consequently punished exports and favored imports, including even food imports (World Bank 2003). According to the Guayaquil Chamber of Commerce, nearly half of the country's export companies went bankrupt between 2000 and 2003.

The expectations of the governments of Mahuad, his successor Gustavo Noboa, and his successor, Lucio Gutiérrez, for attracting foreign direct investment, through the supposedly favorable conditions that were to be created by dollarization, did not materialize. The construction of the Heavy Crude Pipeline (OCP/Oleoducto de Crudo Pesado) in 2001–2002 had a certain beneficial impact on macroeconomic indicators, but it was the only important example of foreign direct investment and raised conflictive issues regarding environmental contamination and the rights of the indigenous peoples of the Amazon region where the petroleum fields are located (Korovkin 2003). However, a new and unexpected financial bounty arrived that is simultaneously assisting economic growth and increasing the country's vulnerability to external decisions: It comes from the massive emigration of Ecuadorians and the remittances that they are sending to their families back home.

The seriousness of the problems identified above and the potentially dangerous impacts of the country's new economic vulnerabilities might be best appreciated from a historical perspective. First of all, Ecuador's economic growth during the last twenty years of the twentieth century was slower than at any other point in its history (Thorp 2000, World Bank 2003). Second, similar to other highly dependent primary export economies in Latin America, the country's economy has been characterized by cycles of boom and bust, especially when exports have been the fundamental motor of growth, as was the case between 1900 and 1945 and then again after 1981. By contrast, only during the period from 1945 to 1981, when the state partly regulated the economy and converted itself into a complementary motor to exports, did Ecuador experience relatively sustained growth. But one of the central characteristics of the current historical moment is that the state is no longer capable of performing that role (CEPAL 2002). Third, the exceptionally weak growth of the last few years, especially 1997–2002, demonstrates that, in contrast to the export booms of the beginning and middle of the twentieth century (cacao and bananas) and of the 1970s (petroleum), the capacity of the Ecuadorian economy to come up with a major new export commodity appears highly unlikely. Therefore, it is possible to argue that Ecuador, instead of having improved its insertion in the international economy, at the beginning of the twenty-first century is more vulnerable than ever before and probably also more irrelevant in the global scheme of things than it was at the beginning of the twentieth century.

Foreign Policy

It is possible to identify three periods in Ecuador's historic relations with the United States during the twentieth century. A first formative period extended from 1900 to 1942, characterized by the predominance of trade issues as the United States became the principal market for Ecuador's exports and the principal source of its industrial imports. This relationship was strengthened by the opening of the Panama Canal and reached its high points during the Kemmerer Mission's reorganization of the Ecuadorian economy during the second half of the 1920s; the U.S. mediation of the 1942 war with Peru and the negotiation of the Treaty of Rio de Janeiro; and Ecuadorian cooperation with the United States during World War II, as reflected in the establishment of a U.S. air base in the Galapagos Islands.

The second period, from the end of World War II to the present, has been characterized by Ecuador's search for a "special relationship" with the United States. That relationship acquired its definitive form during the 1950s, in the context of U.S. international development aid policies (Montúfar 2002). During the 1950s and 1960s, Ecuador's attempts to establish close ties to the United States were facilitated by the presence of modernizing governments, both civilian led (1948–1963) and military led (1963–1966).[4] The consolidation of USAID programs in Ecuador was the principal achievement of this period. Nevertheless, even though the military government of 1963–1966 clearly aligned itself with Washington's anti-Communist policies, U.S. technical and financial military assistance remained at low levels in comparison to other Latin American countries, in part due to the absence of a powerful left in Ecuador, either in the form of political parties, or union federations, or guerrilla groups.

The patterns of relationships established in the 1950s and 1960s endured through the 1970s, with only slight variations during the radical phase of the military government headed by General Rodríguez Lara (1972–1976), which, in addition to redistributive reforms, tried to pursue moderately nationalist policies. Although that government attempted to maintain a multilateral Third World orientation (for example, by working to consolidate the Andean Pact, joining the movement of nonaligned nations, and becoming an OPEC member), economic relations with the United States became more important than ever before. Two factors accounted for this. On the one hand, to exploit and export petroleum, the Ecuadorian state established an alliance with an American multinational corporation, Texaco, and that relationship endured until 1986. On the other hand, the economic development strategies of the military governments favored alliances between Ecuador's private sector (the most important national business groups of the oligarchy described earlier) and U.S. multinational corporations and financial institutions.

The third distinct period in Ecuador–U.S. relations began in the early 1980s, that is, with the transition to democracy. Three themes have characterized those years. The first involves the adoption of neoliberal economic policies that have been accompanied by cooperation with the United States regarding hemispheric trade liberalization. Second comes the concern for the maintenance of democratic stability in Ecuador and the hemisphere, as promoted by Washington and the multilateral organizations—the OAS, the United Nations, and the Andean Community of Nations most importantly. It bears noting that, given the instability that has characterized the country's politics since 1996, Ecuador itself has been the object of democracy promotion diplomatic intervention on the part of Washington. Finally, since 1998, the "war against drugs" has become more and more important in relations with the United States.

As indicated earlier, the permanent articulating element in Ecuador–U.S. relations has been the search, on the part of Ecuadorian governments, for a "special relationship." This policy continuity can be explained in part as the result of the structural conditions of the Ecuadorian economy (the dependence on the United States as the country's principal trade partner, which deepened with the adoption of the U.S. dollar) and partly as the result of the cognitive preferences of Ecuador's policy makers. Throughout the 1980s and 1990s, Ecuador's diplomatic stance bespoke a clear alignment with Washington's desires regarding those economic and diplomatic issues that the latter considered important (Hey 1993, 560). Ecuador's foreign policies manifested greater autonomy only on issues of little importance to the United States that Ecuador's presidents identified as susceptible to yielding "domestic political gains"; perhaps the most notable example of this was provided by the visit to Cuba by President Febres Cordero, a confessed neoliberal and admirer of Ronald Reagan. Nevertheless, it bears emphasizing that Ecuador has become more subservient to U.S. policy since the presidency of Mahuad who, together with his successor Noboa, accepted Washington's diagnosis of the problems of the Andean region in general and the rise of drug trafficking and the escalation of Colombia's civil war in particular. That diagnosis proposes:

- The strengthening of democratic institutions,
- The promotion of sustainable development through trade liberalization as the best way to combat the drug trade in Colombia (and to prevent it from emerging in Ecuador), and
- The need for greater assistance in drug-traffic control programs to the Andean armed forces as part of the broader anti-drug and "anti-terrorist" strategy of Plan Colombia.

The adoption of Washington's diagnosis and the Ecuadorian government's own interests in drug control have favored practical (but not always rhetorical) support for the U.S. war on drugs (Bonilla 2000). That support has manifested itself in the creation of a Forward Observation Base (FOB) at the air force base in Manta on the north coast of Ecuador, less than one-hour flying time from Colombia. It has also involved increased cooperation between Ecuador's armed forces and police with U.S. government agencies. In fact, in 1999, Ecuador adopted an anti-drug strategy including a combination of police and military actions against drug trafficking (such as interdiction of drugs and the import of precursor chemicals, steps to eliminate money laundering, and eradication operations), which, for the most part, have been zealously executed in collaboration with the United States. In 1999, the National Police created a National Anti-Narcotics Division (DNA) that has had a specific budget designation since 2002 and incorporated 942 personnel in 2003. In the year 2000, mixed police-army task forces were created and operated in the three provinces that border on Colombia.

In sum, the new channel for achieving a special relationship with the United States—that is, Ecuador's alignment in the drug wars and, after September 11, in the war on terrorism—was creating a step-by-step institutionalization of the ties between Ecuadorian security forces and U.S. agencies. Similarly, these policies appeared to be contributing to the primacy of the theme of security—over and above democracy and economic development—in the bilateral Ecuador-U.S. agenda. This not only reflected the central preoccupation of the Bush administration but also Ecuador's very limited capacity to chart an autonomous foreign policy.

CONCLUSION

During the last two decades in Ecuador, new social divisions and forms of inequality have compounded the country's historic lack of social integration arising from the differential integration of its regions into international markets, the absence of a shared national political culture, and in general, great social and ethnic distances. The efforts of the reformist and developmentalist governments of the 1960s and 1970s to overcome these divisions appeared to have been reversed. It could be argued that in certain basic respects Ecuador has reverted to the late nineteenth century within an international context that is even more unfavorable to sustainable development than that

Table 22.2   Ecuador in Context

Late 19th Century	Late 20th Century
Reliance on primary exports with strong, albeit boom-bust, growth under increasing U.S. dominance.	Reliance on primary exports with weak and erratic growth under IFI/U.S. dominance.
Reliance on foreign private capital for export production, commerce, and finance.	Reliance on foreign private capital for export commerce and finance.
Expropriation of church and indigenous community lands to favor "export oligarchies," with increases in inequality and the maintenance of forced labor regimes.	Reduction of labor standards, weakening of unions, and abandonment of redistributive reforms to favor foreign and local investors, with resulting increases in inequality and poverty.
Organization of professional military and police forces, alongside the private security forces of estate owners, to control rural rebelliousness and banditry.	Booming growth of private security forces in both urban and rural areas, often in cooperation with state forces, to control increasing waves of crime against property and new waves of protest or rebellion in the countryside in the context of increased U.S. police and military assistance.
Political opening toward urban middle and working classes, but with continued concentration of economic policy making power in the hands of "export oligarchies" and allied foreign interests.	Political opening toward some social sectors, women and indigenous people in particular, but with increasing concentration of economic policy making power among local and foreign financial elites, including the IFIs.

of a hundred years ago, given the pressures emanating from both the international financial institutions and the United States with regard to economic and political-military policies.

Notes

1. The statistics on poverty, inequality, and migration are drawn from Larrea and Sánchez, 2002: 17, 19–25, and 25; Acosta, López Olivares, and Villamar, 2003: 18, 46; and Portes and Hoffman, 2003: 67–70.

2. On the constitution of the elites, see Navarro, 1976; Fierro, 1991, Conaghan, 1988; Handelman, 2002.

3. On the political right, these parties were the Conservatives in the highlands and the Liberals on the coast since the nineteenth century and the Social Christians on the coast more recently; on the left, they were the Communist and Socialist parties since the 1930s and the Maoist Popular Democratic Movement since the 1970s.

4. There were also moments of tension during this period: in 1961 when president Carlos Julio Arosemena sought to differentiate Ecuador's policy toward Cuba from that of the United States; and later during the so called "Tuna War," when Colombia, Peru, Chile, and Ecuador defended their legal rights over maritime waters against U.S. demands for fishing rights.

SUGGESTED READINGS

Acosta, Alberto, Susana López Olivares, and David Villamar. *Análisis de coyuntura económica 2002*. Quito: Instituto Latinoamericano de Investigaciones Sociales and Fundación Friedrich Ebert, 2003.

Andolina, Roberto. "CONAIE (and others) in the Ambiguous Spaces of Democracy," paper delivered at the meeting of the Latin American Studies Association (LASA), Chicago, 1998.

Andrade, Pablo. "Fuerzas sociales y políticas en la Constitución ecuatoriana de 1988," paper delivered at the I Encuentro de Ecuatorianistas, Latin American Studies Association (LASA), Quito, 2002.

Becker, Marc. "Ecuador." In *The South American Handbook*, edited by Patrick Heenan and Monique Lamontagne. London and Chicago: Fitzroy Dearborn Publishers, 2002.

Bonilla, Adrián. "Alcances de la autonomía y hegemonía en la política exterior ecuatoriana." In *Orfeo en el infierno. Una agenda de política exterior ecuatoriana*. Edited by Adrián Bonilla. Quito: FLACSO-CAF-Academia Diplomática, 2002.

Cameron, John D. "Municipal Democratization and Rural Development in Highland Ecuador." In *Rural Progress, Rural Decay: Neoliberal Adjustment Policies and Local Initiatives*, edited by Liisa L. North and John D. Cameron. Bloomfield, Conn.: Kumarian Press, 2003.

Clark, Kim. "Racial Ideologies and the Quest for National Development: Debating the Agrarian Problem in Ecuador (1930–1950)," *Journal of Latin American Studies*, (1998) 30.

Conaghan, Catherine M. *Restructuring Domination: Industrialists and the State in Ecuador*. Pittsburgh: University of Pittsburgh Press, 1988.

_____. "Politicians Against Parties, Discord and Disconnection in Ecuador's Party System." In *Building Democratic Institutions in Latin America*, edited by Scott Mainwaring and Timothy Scully. Stanford, Calif.: Stanford University Press, 1995.

Conaghan, Catherine M., and James M. Malloy. *Unsettling Statecraft. Democracy and Neoliberalism in the Central Andes*. Pittsburgh and London: University of Pittsburgh Press, 1994.

Collins, Jennifer. "A Sense of Possibility. Ecuador's Indigenous Movement Takes Center Stage." *NACLA Report on the Americas*. Vol. XXXII, No. 5, 2002.

Fierro, Luis. 1991. *Los Grupos Financieros en el Ecuador*. Quito: CEDEP.

Guerrero, Andrés. Los Oligarcas del Cacao. Quito: Editorial El Conejo, 1980.

Handelman, Howard. "The Origins of the Ecuadorian Bourgeoisie: Its Implications for Democracy, Challenges and Limits to Latin American's Democratic Revolution." *Canadian Journal of Latin American and Caribbean Studies*. Vol. 27, No. 53, 2002.

Korovkin, Tanya. "In Search of Dialogue? Oil Companies and Indigenous Peoples of the Ecuadorian Amazon." *Canadian Journal of Development Studies*. Vol. XXIII, No. 4, 2002.

_____. "Cut-Flower Exports, Female Labor, and Community Participation in Highland Ecuador." *Latin American Perspectives*. Issue 131, Vol. 30, No. 4 (July 2003).

Larrea, Carlos, and Liisa North. "Ecuador: adjustment policy impacts on truncated development and democratisation." *Third World Quarterly*. Vol. 18, No. 5, 1997.

Larrea, Carlos, and Jeannette Sánchez. *Pobreza, Empleo y Equidad en el Ecuador: perspectivas para el desarrollo humano sostenible*. Quito: Programa de las Naciones Unidas para el Desarrollo (PNUD), 2002.

Maiguashca, Bice. "The Role of Ideas in a Changing World Order: The International Indigenous Movement," *Occasional Papers in Latin American and Caribbean Studies*, No. 4. Toronto: CERLAC/York University, 1992.

Menéndez-Carrión, Amparo. *La Conquista del Voto: de Velasco a Roldós*. Quito: FLACSO-Corporación Editora Nacional, 1986.

Montúfar, César. *Hacia una teoría de la asistencia internacional para el desarrollo: un análisis desde su retórica*. Quito: Corporación Editoria Nacional-Centro Andino de Estudios Inetnacionales, Universidad Andina Simón Bolívar, 2003.

Muratorio, Blanca. "Protestantism and Capitalism Revisited, in the Rural Highlands of Ecuador." *Journal of Peasant Studies*, Vol. 8, No. 1, 1980.

Navarro, Guillermo. *La concentración de capitales en el Ecuador*. Quito: Ediciones Solitierra, 1976.

North, Liisa L. "Externally Induced Rural Diversification: The communitarian experience of Salinas." In *Rural Progress, Rural Decay: Neoliberal Adjustment Policies and Local Initiatives*, edited by Liisa L. North and John D. Cameron. Bloomfield, Conn.: Kumarian Press, 2003.

Portes, Alejandro, and Kelly Hoffman. "Latin American Class Structures: Their Composition and Change during the Neoliberal Era." *Latin American Research Review*, Vol. 38, No. 1, 2003.

Quintero, Rafael. *Entre el Hastío y la Participación Ciudadana*. Quito: ILDIS-Abya Yala, 2002.

Striffler, Steve. *In the Shadows of Sate and Capital. The United Fruit Company, Popular Struggle, and Agrarian Restructuring in Ecuador, 1900–1995*. Durham, N.C., and London: Duke University Press, 2002.

Zamosc, León. "Agrarian Protest and the Indian Movement in the Ecuadorian Highlands." *Latin American Perspectives* 29, No. 3, 1994.

Chapter 23

PERU: ECONOMIC VULNERABILITY AND PRECARIOUS DEMOCRACY

CYNTHIA MCCLINTOCK

ALTHOUGH DEMOCRACY HAS REGULARLY been undertaken in Peru, to date it has not been sustained for a long period of time. As Jan Knippers Black highlights in the introduction to this volume with respect to the bleak democratic record in the region generally, there is plenty of blame to go around. Historical and cultural legacies were adverse; Peru's development performance was poor; and, overall, the U.S. government has not played a positive role in the advancement of democracy.

WORLDS APART: THE OLIGARCHY AND THE INDIGENOUS

The challenge to national integration was very severe in Peru. As the home of one of the Western Hemisphere's largest and most sophisticated indigenous civilizations and subsequently one of Spain's two viceroyalties, the Spanish conquest and colonial rule were especially traumatic. By the late nineteenth century, an agroexport elite emerged; its wealth and power were so great that it was simply called "the oligarchy." Two ethnic, class, and geographic poles endured into the 1960s: at one pole were the oligarchy and perhaps another 10 percent of the population who were Caucasian, Catholic, Spanish-speaking, wealthy, and based in Lima; at the other pole were some 40 percent of the population, called "Indians," who were dark-skinned, at most nominally Catholic, Quechua-speaking, impoverished, and based in the Andean mountains. As Peru's renowned novelist Mario Vargas Llosa put it, the country was "an artificial gathering of men from different languages, customs, and traditions whose only common denominator was having been condemned by history to live together without knowing or loving one another."[1] In Peru, mistrust of fellow citizens is more intense than in most Latin American nations, and in part as a result, political leaders have not been adept at negotiation and compromise—abilities that are essential for the development of political parties and democratic institutions.[2]

Gradually—and in particular after 1968—the number of Peruvians at points on the continuum between the two poles increased. The wealth and power of the oligarchy were eclipsed and the income distribution became less skewed. By the early 1990s, more than two-thirds of Peruvians were living in cities; roughly 70 percent of the relevant age group was enrolled in secondary school and 40 percent enrolled in universities. Still, at least in part due to Peru's unsatisfactory economic-growth patterns, the country's middle classes are precarious and more than half the population lives on less than two dollars a day.[3]

Peru's living standards and economic growth rates have been below regional averages. Per capita income in Peru for 2002 (calculated in purchasing power parity dollars) was $4,800, versus an average of $6,750 for Latin America and the Caribbean.[4] Between 1900 and 1987 Peru's real GDP growth averaged approximately 3.6 percent, versus 3.8 percent for the region.[5] For the three decades between 1960 and 1990, Peru's GDP growth per capita was roughly two percentage points below the regional average—although during the 1990s growth was slightly above the average.[6] Currently and for most of its history, Peru has followed what were formerly called "liberal" and now "neoliberal" or "free market" economic policies; economic growth has been based primarily on raw-material exports. Peru's economy has been vulnerable to cycles of boom and bust and serious poverty and inequality have continued. For example, in 2000, 25 percent of Peruvian children under five years of age suffered from chronic malnutrition—more than twice the percentage in Brazil, Argentina, or Chile; in Peru's poorest mountainous areas, the figure was above 50 percent, similar to such countries as Afghanistan and Ethiopia.[7]

As dependency theorists would predict (see chapter 1), the U.S. government has tended to prioritize immediate U.S. economic objectives in Peru—not democracy. The U.S. government considered various democratic regimes insufficiently favorable to free-market economic policies, and accordingly provided scant support; also, the U.S. government cooperated closely with several authoritarian regimes that were favorable to U.S. economic interests (most recently, the Alberto Fujimori regime).

Perhaps most striking about Peruvian politics is that—despite unfavorable social, economic, and international conditions—democratic ideals have been important since the nineteenth century and have become stronger over time. Although many of Peru's elected, civilian governments have been the victims of military coups, its authoritarian governments have been the victims of popular demand for elections and democracy. Since 1919, no Peruvian political regime—neither democratic nor authoritarian—has endured more than twelve years. While the twentieth century's four authoritarian governments (Augusto Leguía, 1919–1930; Manuel Odría, 1948–1956; Juan Velasco Alvarado/Francisco Morales Bermúdez, 1968–1980; and Alberto Fujimori, 1992–2000) gained popular support for a period, none achieved institutionalization or long-standing legitimacy. Repeatedly, as the economic performance of authoritarian governments deteriorated, they wore out their welcome and Peruvians' democratic aspirations triumphed.

THE CONQUEST AND THE COLONIAL ERA

The Spanish conquest of the Inca Empire was devastating for Peru's indigenous peoples. The Inca Empire extended from present-day Chile to Ecuador and embraced more than 7 million people; with vast irrigation networks and excellent food storage and distribution facilities, it was prosperous. Yet, in 1532, fewer than 200 Spaniards led by Francisco Pizarro brutally overwhelmed an Incan army that might have numbered as many as 80,000 warriors. Despite their small number, the Spaniards won because of their horses, gunpowder, swords, and a successful ambush strategy—and also because of Incan internal conflicts. After capturing the Incan emperor, Atahualpa, the Spaniards betrayed him; they promised him freedom in exchange for a huge ransom, but—after his payment—murdered him. About forty years later, Túpac Amaru, the last Incan ruler, was seized and asked to convert to Christianity; he did—but was nonetheless beheaded.

Peru became one of Spain's two viceroyalties in the hemisphere. Peru's gold, silver, and mercury mines were extremely rich. The Spanish forced the indigenous peoples to work in these mines under brutal conditions. By 1600, these labor conditions and new European diseases decimated the indigenous population. The Spanish also seized much of the best agricultural land in Andean mountain valleys. Angry, the native peoples rebelled sporadically, often proclaiming their goal to be the restoration of Incan rule. In 1780, a descendant of the Inca royal family, Túpac Amaru II, led the largest rebellion against the Spanish during the colonial era. Lasting almost two years, the rebellion gained substantial peasant support, but was crushed by the Crown's killing of thousands.

As the movement for independence grew in Latin America in the early nineteenth century, Lima became the center of the Spanish counterattack. Peru's *criollos* (descendants of the Spanish born in the colonies) were wary of independence. Lima was Spain's administrative center in South America; *criollos* received relatively greater political and economic advantage from the Crown. *Criollos* also worried that, upon independence, they would not be able to control the relatively large indigenous population. Accordingly, predominantly foreign forces, led by the Argentine José de San Martín and the Venezuelan Simón Bolívar, brought independence to Peru in 1824.

INDEPENDENCE TO 1930

The hundred-odd years between Peru's independence and 1930 were marked by the emergence and consolidation of what was widely called "the oligarchy"—forty-odd families who controlled large landholdings that produced Peru's key exports, in particular sugar and cotton. These elites favored liberal (in the traditional sense of the word), civilian, constitutional regimes, and worked to establish them. However, in most Peruvians' views, these regimes, favoring export-led growth, did not try hard enough to achieve modicums of social justice and social integration, and they were unable to sustain their legitimacy.

The first twenty years of Peru's independence were turbulent. From different regional bases, the military leaders of the struggle (*caudillos*) competed for power and fought over national boundaries. Amid political turmoil, the economy also declined.

The turbulence abated during Peru's first export-led economic growth spurt: the guano boom (1840–1879). It was discovered that guano (bird droppings) was an excellent fertilizer, and that large quantities were available on small islands off Peru's shores. Guano became a bonanza for Peru. During the 1850s and 1860s, the value of guano exports was more than $15 million annually; owning a monopoly on the guano, the state chose the recipients of licenses for its export and reaped about 70 percent of the profits. The profits funded the dramatic enlargement of civilian and military bureaucracies, the construction of railroads, and the development of sugar and cotton estates on Peru's coast.

The new agroexport elites favored free trade and economic liberalism as well as civilian government; they believed that Peru's military leaders were squandering the guano revenues. Under the leadership of Manuel Pardo, they formed Peru's first civilian-based political party, the Civilista Party. In 1872, after a hard-fought election, Pardo became Peru's first civilian president.

This liberal initiative under the Civilistas was not sustained. Economic crisis was virtually immediate. In 1873, amid a global depression, export prices fell; at the same time, guano reserves were almost exhausted. Problems of corruption and fiscal mismanagement became more apparent. Then, in 1879, the War of the Pacific broke out. Nitrates (also a valuable fertilizer) had been discovered in the Atacama Desert; claims to hundreds of miles of the territory were disputed by Peru, Bolivia, and Chile. Peru suffered a devastating loss. In January 1881, Lima was occupied by the Chilean military; in the highlands, armed peasant groups attacked both the Chileans and large landowners. Finally, in 1883, Peru ceded a southern nitrate-rich province to Chile (among other concessions) and peace was achieved.

In the aftermath of war, Peru was socially and politically demoralized and economically ravaged. The leader of the reconstruction effort was General Andrés Cáceres, who had led Peruvian peasants against Chileans in the highlands and who, in 1885, won the first presidential elections after the war. One of the most serious challenges was the restoration of Peru's international creditworthiness; the Cáceres government negotiated the Grace Contract, which gave the British the right to operate Peru's railroad system for sixty-six years plus other concessions in return for the cancellation of Peru's foreign debt. Peru returned to the good graces of international investors, but the cost was widely considered steep.

In 1895, Cáceres's political and military hold over Peru was broken. The Partido Demócrata (Democratic Party) and the Civilistas allied to oust Cáceres and establish what became known as the "Aristocratic Republic." Although suffrage was severely restricted, electoral manipulation was common, and political exclusion was practiced, the constitutional order was by-and-large maintained from 1895 to 1919, Peru's longest constitutional era to date. For most of the era, the Civilistas were the dominant political party.

The Aristocratic Republic was bolstered by robust export-led growth. Between 1898 and 1918, the value of total exports—primarily sugar, cotton, copper, and oil—multiplied eight times. As these exports expanded, Peru's oligarchy was consolidated. Amid economic growth, the demand for labor increased sharply, and a working class emerged. Educational opportunities expanded.

However, export-led growth also provoked social and economic problems. In general, working conditions were dismal. Large haciendas expanded at the expense of smaller farmers and peasants. Copper mines such as the immense U.S.-owned Cerro de Pasco Corporation used production processes that devastated the ecology of peasant communities for miles around.

At the end of World War I, commodity prices fell and export production was devastated. In Peru, serious strikes erupted. In 1919, presidential elections were won by Augusto Leguía, a former Civilista president who had broken with the party, had been exiled for several years, and had campaigned as a populist reformer. In what might now be called Peru's first *autogolpe* (coup by the president himself), Leguía secured military support for an end to the constitution of the Aristocratic Republic.

Leguía governed Peru between 1919 and 1930, an eleven-year period called the *oncenio*—the longest government to date in Peru's history. Fervently pro-American, Leguía enjoyed close ties with the United States. U.S. capital flowed into Peru. The Leguía government also borrowed millions from U.S. banks, at first using the funds for ambitious road, school, and irrigation projects. As a result of these projects and some reforms (establishment of the eight-hour day, a minimum wage, and legal standing for peasant communities), Leguía enjoyed popular support for a period. However, as his government wore on, it became more corrupt and repressive. In 1929, the global depression hit, and most Latin American governments collapsed. Leguía was overthrown by a mestizo army commander, Luis Sánchez Cerro.

1930–1968: Oligarchical Power under Stress

From 1930 to 1968, Peru's oligarchy and its favored economic model confronted serious challenges, in particular from a new political party, the American Popular Revolutionary Alliance (APRA). The prevailing perception was that Peru was behind other Latin American nations in the effort to attain social justice and national integration and that dramatic social and economic "reforms"—redistributive reforms—were necessary. However, virtually throughout this period, Peru's oligarchy and military on the one hand and APRA on the other remained intransigent opponents, and reform initiatives failed. Whereas many Latin American nations adopted import-substitution industrialization policies, Peru retained an open, export-led model without a significant redistributive component.

Indeed, by most measures Peru was behind other Latin American nations. Peru's income distribution was one of the most unequal in the region; in 1961 the wealthiest 1 percent of the economically active population received a staggering 30 percent of the national income.[8] Also, the Gini index of land distribution was the most skewed among fifty-four nations for which data were reported; a mere 280 families—less than 0.1 percent of all farm families—owned approximately 30 percent of the land and more than 50 percent of the best land. [9] Moreover, in part because of the inaccessibility of Peru's mountainous regions and in part because of successive governments' lack of concern, the disparity in living standards between these regions and urban centers was unusually severe. On numerous measures of political participation too, Peru was behind its neighbors.

Founded in 1924 by Haya de la Torre and first based on Peru's sugar-growing north coast, APRA is Peru's only political party widely considered to be institutionalized. Haya de la Torre was not only a charismatic speaker and a brilliant intellectual, but also the architect of a cohesive, disciplined political organization. While various leftist leaders of the 1920s, in particular José Carlos Mariátegui, embraced Marxism, Haya did not. He did, however, denounce U.S. imperialism and advocate dramatic economic and political reforms. Proclaiming that "Only APRA will save Peru," he also called for moral renewal.

In bitterly fought elections in 1931, Haya was defeated by Sánchez Cerro, the military commander who had toppled Leguía. Although Sánchez Cerro enjoyed the support of the oligarchy, his modest, provincial background and mestizo appearance appealed to popular groups as well. Sánchez Cerro denounced APRA as anti-Catholic, antimilitary, and closet communist. Without evidence, APRA repudiated the 1931 electoral result as fraudulent and quickly became obstructionist in the legislature. In retaliation, Sánchez Cerro deported APRA's entire congressional representation. In 1932, APRA members rebelled in Trujillo, executing sixty-odd members of the army. In reprisal, the military killed 1,000 to 2,000 Apristas. In 1933, Sánchez Cerro was assassinated by an Aprista. Under Sánchez Cerro's successor, General Oscar Benavides, repression of APRA intensified, and Aprista militants continued to resort to violence. APRA also sought to infiltrate the military and to plot against the government with its allies in the military—tactics that deeply antagonized officers.

Between 1931 and 1968, elections were held, but APRA was proscribed to one degree or another. The only civilian president to complete his term during this period was Manuel Prado (1939–1945). During World War II, the United States and the Prado government were strong partners; rejecting fascism, APRA collaborated with Prado.

At the end of the war, hopes for democracy and reform were high in Peru. In the 1945 elections, the distinguished legal scholar, José Luis Bustamante, triumphed; he was the leader of a new political alliance that incorporated the APRA party. The Bustamante government quickly implemented import substitution industrialization policies; the government raised tariffs, introduced import and exchange controls, and increased workers' wages and benefits. However, while these policies were insufficient for APRA, they outraged Peru's oligarchy. Politically inexperienced, Bustamante was unable to negotiate effectively with either APRA or the oligarchy. After Apristas assassinated the editor of an oligarchical family's newspaper, Bustamente sought to marginalize the party, but his attempt was considered irresolute. Also, the Bustamante government was unable to secure economic or diplomatic support from the U.S. government; the Truman administration did not sustain the pro-democratic policies of Franklin D. Roosevelt.

Amid political polarization and economic deterioration, Bustamante was ousted in a 1948 military coup led by General Manuel Odría. The Odría government immediately banned APRA and reestablished orthodox liberal economic policies. The government also forged a highly cooperative relationship with the United States. With the onset of the Korean War, Peru's metal sector boomed, and the economy grew. However, like Peru's other authoritarian leaders, Odría sought a personalist, populist relationship with Peru's poor and did not build a strong political party. When the Korean War and the concomitant export boom ended in 1953, dismay mounted. Odría appeared not only authoritarian but also incompetent and decadent.

The 1956 election was won by former president Manuel Prado. Remarkably, Prado came within days of completing his term once again. As in his first administration, no economic or social policies were launched. However, Prado again ameliorated social and political tensions by reaching out further to APRA than most oligarchs wanted.

In the wake of the Cuban revolution and the Kennedy administration's launching of the Alliance for Progress, reformist tides were sweeping Latin America. Many Peruvians saw the moment as their country's last, best chance for reform by a democratic government, and hoped that this moment would be seized by Fernando Belaúnde, leader of the new party Acción Popular (Popular Action). Indeed, after elections in 1962 were inconclusive, the military staged a coup and organized new elections in 1963, which were won by Belaúnde.

Although public expenditure for education and for infrastructure increased dramatically, Peruvians' hopes were not realized. Constrained in part by his own aristocratic proclivities and in part by APRA obstructionism, Belaúnde did not deliver the promised reforms. Agrarian reform was minimal. Belaúnde failed to resolve quickly a dispute with the International Petroleum Company (IPC), a U.S. company that had provoked intense nationalistic sentiments among Peruvians. Although Peruvians considered Belaúnde too accommodating toward IPC, the Johnson administration considered him too harsh; the United States did not provide Belaúnde the support that—as a democratic reformer—he had expected during the Alliance for Progress.

THE 1968–1980 MILITARY GOVERNMENT

In 1968, reflecting Peruvians' perception that the last chance for reform by a democratic government had been lost, General Juan Velasco Alvarado led a military coup. Proclaiming a "Revolutionary Government of the Armed Forces" that would build a "fully participatory social democracy," the Velasco government finally curtailed the power of Peru's oligarchy. Subsequently,

Peru's elites were more likely to have earned their position through work, and less likely to have inherited it. Peru's income distribution improved; the middle classes expanded. At the same time, however, the military government's reforms did little to alleviate the lot of Peru's poorest—subsistence highlands peasants.

The Velasco government's social and economic reforms were dramatic. Not only did the government implement one of the most sweeping agrarian reforms in Latin America, but it expropriated a broad spectrum of other enterprises—from fishing, mining, and banking companies to daily newspapers—most of which had been owned by oligarchic families. The state came to own more than 20 percent of the economy, and peasants' and workers' cooperatives owned another 10 percent. Tariffs were raised, and with the closed economy manufacturing production grew rapidly.

Although the Velasco government claimed that it sought social justice for the poorest Peruvians, it did not provide large material benefits for them. Public expenditure was not shifted toward highland agriculture. The government did, however, continue to expand educational opportunities, and it recognized Quechua as the second national language of Peru.

The Velasco government distanced Peru from the United States. It immediately expropriated IPC, and subsequently numerous other U.S. companies. Most previous collaborative activities with the U.S. military were ended and major arms purchases were made from the Soviet Union. The Velasco government championed the interests of developing countries against "the North." However, the Velasco government's political agenda was ambiguous and often contradictory. Although the government was not repressive by Latin American standards, it severely restricted opposition political parties. Expropriated, the major daily newspapers gradually became mouthpieces for the regime. The government created a political agency, the National System for the Support of Social Mobilization (SINAMOS, an acronym that meant "Without Masters"), but its role was muddled. Still, amid complex reactions to the military government's political agenda, worker and peasant organizations—to a considerable degree under the banner of the Marxist left—expanded dramatically. Political attitudes became more democratic, more participatory, and also more radical and confrontational.

In 1975, Velasco was ousted in a palace coup by General Francisco Morales Bermúdez. Velasco had fallen ill, factionalism within the military had intensified, and Peru's economy had weakened. As the International Monetary Fund (IMF) demanded austerity, popular protest mounted. In 1977, less than two weeks after a massive general strike, Morales Bermúdez announced a transition to democracy.

THE 1980–1992 ELECTORAL DEMOCRACY[10]

In 1980, given the return to democracy in much of the region, Peruvians' hopes were high that, this time, the country's democracy would endure. For the first time, an oligarchy was not looking out first and foremost for its own interest, and APRA was no longer politically excluded. However, Peruvians' hopes were dashed by what was called the debt crisis and the concomitant rise of the Shining Path guerrillas.

Peru's political spectrum was dramatically changed. For various reasons, including the military government's failure to help the most disadvantaged Peruvians, the Marxist left grew. In 1978, in elections for a constituent assembly, leftist parties won 29 percent of the vote and became Peru's second largest electoral force (they remained so throughout the 1980s). With 35 percent of the vote, APRA was the largest party in the assembly, and Haya de la Torre became its president—to no one's dismay. Only a few months before his death, Haya triumphed, building considerable consensus behind a new constitution that for the first time enfranchised illiterates.

In 1980, Acción Popular's Belaúnde was reelected president. Unfortunately, turning seventy years old, Belaúnde seemed unable to focus on the country's increasingly formidable problems. One severe challenge was the debt crisis; like most countries in the region, Peru faced an increase in external interest rates, a decrease in international prices for its main exports, and payments on its foreign debt that exceeded 35 percent of its export earnings. Belaúnde began negotiations with the IMF, but these broke down in 1984 and, quietly, the government stopped servicing the debt.

A second daunting (and related) problem was the expanding Shining Path (*Sendero Luminoso*). Mounting the most serious guerrilla challenge in Peru's history, the Shining Path was savage, sectarian, and virulently Maoist; among its victims were political leaders from other Marxist groups, development engineers, church people, and peasants who withheld their support from the movement. Based in the remote, impoverished Andean province of Ayacucho, the Shining Path appealed in particular to provincial teachers and young people whose professional aspirations had been frustrated. The Belaúnde government's response to the movement was ineffective. For almost two years, the government contended that the rebellion was insignificant and did nothing; then, it endorsed repressive military action, failing to urge respect for human rights.

In 1985, Alán García, a young, energetic, charismatic APRA leader, won the elections in a landslide. On the debt crisis, García staked out a position to the left of most of his Latin American counterparts. In his inaugural address, blaming the crisis on imperialism and the United States, García said that Peru would pay no more than 10 percent of its export earnings to service its debt. García's position pleased Peruvians (almost 80 percent of whom had voted either for García or for the leftist parties' candidate), but deeply alienated the international financial community and the Reagan administration. García introduced expansionary fiscal policies, which appeared to work—until the end of 1987, when Peru's international reserves ran out. The ultimate result was economic debacle.

At the same time, the Shining Path expanded, seemingly inexorably. García understood Sendero as a serious problem that was the result of the destitution of Ayacucho and rejected an exclusively military approach to the problem; he sought to provide economic aid to the area and to raise the military's respect for human rights. However, for various reasons, these efforts failed. By 1989, the Shining Path guerrillas numbered approximately 10,000 combatants, had the support of roughly 15 percent of Peru's citizens, and controlled about 28 percent of the country's municipalities.[11]

As the 1990 elections loomed, APRA was seriously discredited, and Peruvians appeared ready for a candidate from the political right or center. The odds-on presidential favorite was Mario Vargas Llosa, the renowned novelist. However, during the campaign Vargas Llosa appeared aloof and arrogant, and his emphasis on the need for drastic free-market policies—a "shock"—frightened Peruvians. Ultimately, Alberto Fujimori, a former mathematics professor and university head, was the surprise second-place finisher in the first round and the easy winner of the second round. The son of humble Japanese immigrants, Fujimori appeared, in the words of his slogan, *Un presidente como tú* (A president like you). Another campaign motto, "Work, Honesty, and Technology," reminded Peruvians of the qualities they respected in persons of Asian origin. Repudiating Vargas Llosa's "shock," Fujimori promised to restore prosperity through gradual changes. With no prior political experience, Fujimori was a political outsider; a vote for him was a vote against what many Peruvians considered a failed, corrupt political class.

It was immediately clear that Fujimori was a bold leader who liked power; within months, he was satirized in Peru's media as a would-be Japanese emperor. Although his party held only about a quarter of the seats in the legislature, he enjoyed the traditional president's honeymoon and support from Vargas Llosa's political coalition and was able to win legislative approval for most of his initiatives. Quickly reversing his campaign promise of gradualism, Fujimori implemented a drastic shock policy. Peru returned to free-market economic policies: State expenditure was slashed, foreign investment laws eased, tariffs reduced, and privatization initiated. Similarly, with the support of Vladimiro Montesinos (a former army captain and lawyer for drug traffickers), Fujimori gained control over appointments and promotions in the military. The government repeatedly expressed disdain for human rights and a government-authorized death squad emerged.

As 1991 ended, however, Fujimori faced some resistance from Peru's legislature. Disagreement about new counterinsurgency measures and about the 1992 budget was intense. Exonerated by Peru's Supreme Court from charges of illicit enrichment and reelected secretary general of APRA, Alán García hoped to galvanize the political opposition to Fujimori. In part as a result, on April 5, 1992, Fujimori launched an *autogolpe*: He suspended the 1979 constitution, arrested several opposition leaders, padlocked the congress, and moved to dismantle the judiciary. To the dismay of Peru's intellectuals and traditional political leaders, the *autogolpe* was supported, according to opinion polls, by almost 80 percent of Peruvians. These Peruvians agreed with Fujimori that most of Peru's politicians, legislators, and judges were corrupt and hoped that, via the *autogolpe*, Fujimori would be able to take the measures necessary to resolve Peru's economic and security crises.

THE FUJIMORI GOVERNMENT AFTER THE 1992 AUTOGOLPE

After the *autogolpe*, the Fujimori government became what scholars have called an "electoral authoritarian" regime. In such a regime, elections are held and democratic institutions persist, but at the same time any real threat to presidential power is blocked by whatever means necessary. From 1992 until September 2000, Fujimori and Montesinos, de facto head of the National Intelligence Service (SIN) and Fujimori's Rasputin or Siamese twin, rode roughshod over Peru's democratic institutions.

The first six months after the *autogolpe* were rocky. Although most Peruvians supported the *autogolpe*, in the early 1990s the Organization of American States (OAS) and the U.S. government were seeking to establish hemispheric democratic norms, and they opposed the *autogolpe*. Negotiations between the Fujimori government and international actors continued for several months. Ultimately, in November 1992, the Fujimori government held elections for a new legislature that would also write a new constitution; although the government's electoral machinations were manifold, the international community decided that it would tolerate the new regime. Similarly, despite numerous flaws in the referendum on Peru's new constitution in October 1993, the international community was accommodating.

The tolerant attitude of the international community was shaped in part by the Fujimori government's successes. In September 1992, a small, elite squad within Peru's antiterrorist police captured the leader of the Shining Path, Abimael Guzmán. Within the next few weeks, using information found in Guzmán's hideout, police arrested more than 1,000 suspected guerrillas. During the next few years, the Shining Path was decimated. Also, the economy recovered. Peru's foreign debt was renegotiated and Peru returned to the good graces of the international financial community. As in many Latin American nations during the early to mid-1990s, hyperinflation ended, foreign direct investment increased dramatically, and imports and exports boomed. During 1993–1994, economic growth was robust.

Elections were held as scheduled in 1995, and Fujimori won a landslide victory. His popularity was due to his counterinsurgency and economic successes and also to an increasingly populist strategy; funds from the privatization program were spent in part on social programs and infrastructure for poor communities. Dressed in a poncho and Andean-style hat, Fujimori helicoptered frequently to mountainous communities to inaugurate new schools and roads.

However, opinion polls suggested that, while most Peruvians endorsed a second term for Fujimori, they also wanted Peru's congress to be able to check his power. Prior to the 1995 elections, pollsters predicted that opposition political parties would win about two-thirds of the legislative vote. In the event, however, according to the official tally, the government's electoral coalition won 51 percent of the vote. Pointing to the unprecedented 40 percent of ballots declared invalid as well as wrongdoings with voting-table tally sheets, most Peruvian opposition leaders and many other experts believe that the 1995 congressional result was manipulated. For the government's subsequent authoritarian programs, this majority proved essential.

Not long after the 1995 elections, support for the Fujimori government eroded. As in much of Latin America, the economy slowed. Also, the government's authoritarian proclivities were increasingly obvious. Although the 1993 constitution limited a president to two consecutive terms, in 1996 Fujimori's congressional majority passed a law affirming his eligibility for a third consecutive term. The government derailed efforts by the National Elections Board, the Constitutional Tribunal, and a coalition of opposition leaders to deny, in one way or another, Fujimori's eligibility.

As the 2000 elections neared, Fujimori and Montesinos steeply tilted the electoral playing field. Television news was blatantly biased; it was subsequently proven that Montesinos paid millions of dollars in bribes to media magnates. Opposition candidates were slandered and their campaigns obstructed. The government lavished large sums on food programs so that it could condition the continuation of these programs on residents' votes. It sought to assure that election officials were, at a minimum, spineless. It appeared that Fujimori might actually win the electoral exercise.

However, most Peruvians were fed up, and one of the opposition candidates, Alejandro Toledo, began to rise in the polls. Born in the mountains of Peru, the dark-skinned Toledo boasted an impressive resumé that included a Ph.D. from Stanford University and employment with the World Bank. The founder of his political party (Perú Posible), Toledo was effective on the stump, emphasizing his commitment to job creation. In the first round of the elections, Toledo finished with more than 40 percent of the vote, and a runoff was scheduled for May 28. However, in mid-May, Peru's electoral authorities announced the introduction of a new computer program, and international election monitors worried that the government was plotting fraud. When the government refused to postpone the runoff to give the OAS monitors time to verify the new program, they declined to monitor the exercise and declared Peru's electoral process "far from one that could be considered free and fair." For his part, Toledo boycotted the runoff. On May 28, Fujimori claimed that he had won the presidency with 51 percent of the vote.

While the rigged election angered international monitors, it did not appear to dismay the U.S. government. From the mid-1990s through 2000, the Clinton administration and the Fujimori government were cooperating effectively on key components of the bilateral agenda. As indicated above, the Fujimori government implemented one of Latin America's most dramatic shifts toward the free market. Also, after Ecuador provoked a border war with Peru in 1995, a settlement was negotiated among international actors, Fujimori, and the Ecuadorian president. The Central Intelligence Agency and Montesinos enjoyed a close relationship and cooperated for such initiatives as the 1997 raid that rescued almost all the hostages who had been seized by rebels at the Japanese ambassador's residence. While for many years Peru had been the source of much of the cocaine in the United States, in the 1990s coca cultivation declined dramatically in Peru, and the U.S. government touted the decline as an important victory in the war on drugs. Accordingly, many U.S. officials were willing to disregard the rigged election. Rather than call for new elections or threaten to suspend aid, the U.S. ambassador maintained a very cordial relationship with Fujimori.

Almost immediately, however, the regime collapsed. In August, the U.S. Department of State became upset by revelations that Montesinos had masterminded the smuggling of arms to guerrillas in Colombia. In September, a video that showed Montesinos bribing an opposition congressman was leaked to Peru's media. The video was the smoking gun that definitively proved the regime's corruption; Peruvians exploded in disgust. Montesinos fled the country and, from Tokyo in November, Fujimori faxed his resignation.

THE 2000–2004 RETURN TO DEMOCRACY

Peru's return to democracy has been troubled. Currently, the Toledo government (2001-) is approved by only some 8 to 15 percent of Peruvians in opinion polls. Some of the reasons are economic dilemmas and political-party configurations beyond Toledo's control, but the president's leadership has been disappointing. Moreover, the Toledo government has been burdened by difficult legacies from the Fujimori government. These problems have been of such severity that Toledo's capacity to complete his term has been in doubt.

Toledo's government is teetering despite a procedurally smooth transition back to democracy. After Fujimori's departure, the head of Peru's congress, Valentín Paniagua, became the president of a transition government. Paniagua, an experienced constitutional lawyer and long-standing Acción Popular leader, formed an effective government and presided over impeccable presidential elections in 2001. In the first round, Toledo won a plurality; APRA's Alán García finished second, edging past Unidad Nacional's Lourdes Flores, a candidate of the center-right. In the runoff, Toledo narrowly defeated García.

The government is also teetering despite an economic growth rate of roughly 4 percent annually between 2002 and 2004, one of the best rates in Latin America. As in Peru prior to 1968, growth has been based primarily on raw-material exports, currently, in particular, gold, copper, and zinc mined largely by international enterprises. However, as in the past, open, export-led economic policies have not yielded the increases in jobs and wages that Peruvians want.

The Toledo government has suffered from the nature of Peru's political parties and from the partisan composition of the current congress. Toledo's party, Perú Posible, is a hodgepodge mix of amateurish political leaders; for this reason, Toledo has not brought many of them into his cabinets, opting instead for respected independents. However, numerous Perú Posible members are intent on well-paid jobs and do not hesitate to fight each other for them—sometimes honestly but sometimes dishonestly charging corruption or other wrongdoing. Also, within the congress, Perú Posible does not enjoy a majority; neither of the major opposition parties, the center-left APRA nor the center-right Unidad Nacional, has been particularly constructive.

Toledo's leadership has been flawed. For more than a year, he refused to acknowledge paternity of his daughter, Zarai, who had been born out of wedlock. Whereas Fujimori was regularly photographed inaugurating public works, Toledo is regularly photographed at exclusive beach resorts. He does not seem to understand that poor Peruvians resent his expensive life style. (At the same time, wealthy, Caucasian Peruvians resent the expensive lifestyle of a man they consider a *cholo*—an Indian who has adopted Western ways.)

Arguably, however, the Toledo government is precarious first and foremost because Montesinos and his allies—widely referred to as the "Montesinos Mafia"—are trying to undermine it. Peru's democracy was not restored through a pact between the corrupt authoritarian regime and the democratic opposition; whereas in many Latin American countries, officials from the authoritarian regime were granted political amnesties, but they were not in Peru. At least 1,400 officials and allies of the Fujimori government—including Montesinos himself—are facing charges of corruption and other crimes. It appears in late 2004 that these defendants are hoping that, if the Toledo government falls, they will be able to negotiate leniency with the new government. Even in custody, Montesinos has hyped scandals and manipulated the news media.

Peru's Prospects

As of the writing of this chapter in late 2004, it is a difficult moment for democracy in Latin America in general and Peru in particular. Although most Latin Americans and most Peruvians reject extremist ideologies and favor democratic ideals, they are chafing at the disappointing performances of their democratic government.

Notes

1. Mario Vargas Llosa, "Questions of Conquest: What Columbus wrought, and what he did not," *Harper's*, December 1990, p. 52.

2. On levels of mistrust in Peru and elsewhere in Latin America, see the polls by *Latinobarómetro*.

3. World Bank, *World Development Report 2003: Sustainable Development in a Dynamic World* (Washington, D.C.: The World Bank and Oxford University Press, 2003), p. 236. Survey year was 1996.

4. World Bank, *World Development Report 2004: Making Services Work for People* (Washington, D.C.: The World Bank and Oxford University Press, 2003), p. 253.

5. Shane Hunt, "Peru: The Current Economic Situation in Long-Term Perspective." In *The Peruvian Economy and Structural Adjustment*, ed. Efraín Gonzales de Olarte (University of Miami, Miami, Fla.: North-South Center Press, 1996), p. 15.

6. For the 1980s and 1990s, the Economic Commission for Latin America and the Caribbean, *Preliminary Overview of the Economies of Latin America and the Caribbean 2000* (Santiago, Chile: United Nations, 2000), p. 85; for the 1960s and 1970s, Inter-American Development Bank, *Economic and Social Progress in Latin America* (Washington, D.C.: the Inter-American Development Bank, various years), 1985 report, p. 152, and 1997 report, p. 221.

7. "Drama de Hierro," *Caretas*, No. 1812 (February 25, 2004), p. 23.

8. Richard Webb, *Government Policy and the Distribution of Income in Peru, 1963–1973* (Cambridge, Mass.: Harvard University Press, 1977), pp. 6–7.

9. Charles L. Taylor and Michael C. Hudson, *World Handbook of Political and Social Indicators*, 2nd ed. (New Haven, Conn.: Yale University Press, 1972), p. 267, and Daniel Martínez and Armando Tealdo, *El Agro Peruano, 1970–1980* (Lima: CEDEP, 1982), pp. 15–16.

10. "Electoral democracy" is a conceptualization for political regimes that hold genuinely competitive and fair elections, but whose democratic features do not extend much beyond this procedural criterion; see Larry Diamond, "Is the Third Wave Over?" *Journal of Democracy* 7 (July 1996): pp. 21–25.

11. Cynthia McClintock, *Revolutionary Movements in Latin America: El Salvador's FMLN and Peru's Shining Path* (Washington, D.C.: U.S. Institute of Peace Press, 1998), p. 73.

Suggested Reading

An outstanding history of Peru that begins with pre-Incan civilization and continues through the Fujimori government is Peter Flindell Klarén, *Peru: Society and Nationhood in the Andes* (New York: Oxford University Press, 2000). A classic history emphasizing Peru's social and economic dualities is Julio Cótler, *Clases, estado, y nación en el Perú* (Lima: Instituto de Estudios Peruanos, 1978). A brilliant study of Peru's oligarchy is Dennis Gilbert, *The Oligarchy and the Old Regime in Peru*, Latin American Dissertation Series (Ithaca, N.Y.: Cornell University Press, 1977). An excellent analysis of subalterns' perspectives is Florencia E. Mallon, *The Defense of Community in Peru's Central Highlands: Peasant Struggle and Capitalist Transition, 1860–1940* (Princeton, N.J.: Princeton University Press, 1983).

The 1968–1980 military government is the subject of many superb studies. Among these are Abraham F. Lowenthal, ed., *The Peruvian Experiment* (Princeton, N.J.: Princeton University Press, 1983); Cynthia McClintock, *Peasant Cooperatives and Political Change in Peru* (Princeton, N.J.: Princeton University Press, 1981); Henry Pease García, *El ocaso del poder oligárquico* (Lima: DESCO, 1977); and David G. Becker, *The New Bourgeoisie and the Limits of Dependency: Mining, Class, and Power in "Revolutionary" Peru* (Princeton, N.J.: Princeton University Press, 1983).

Excellent works on politics after 1980 include Maxwell A. Cameron and Philip Mauceri, *The Peruvian Labyrinth: Polity, Society, and Economy* (University Park, Pa.: Pennsylvania State University Press, 1997). The Shining Path guerrillas are examined in David Scott Palmer, *Shining Path of Peru* (New York: St. Martin's Press, 1994) and Cynthia McClintock, *Revolu-*

tionary Movements in Latin America: El Salvador's FMLN and Peru's Shining Path (Washington, D.C.: U.S. Institute of Peace Press, 1998). Outstanding analyses of the Fujimori government include Carlos Iván Degregori, *La Década de la Antipolítica* (Lima: Instituto de Estudios Peruanos, 2000) and Catherine M. Conaghan, "Making and Unmaking Authoritarian Peru: Reelection, Resistance, and Regime Transition," The North-South Agenda Papers No. 47, the North-South Center (June 2001).

There are also excellent studies of related themes. A cogent analysis of Peru's economy is Rosemary Thorp and Geoffrey Bertram, *Peru 1890–1977: Growth and Policy in an Open Economy* (New York: Columbia University Press, 1978). U.S. policy toward Peru, including the "war on drugs," is examined in Cynthia McClintock and Fabián Vallas, *The United States and Peru: Cooperation—at a Cost* (New York: Routledge, 2003).

Chapter 24

BOLIVIA: A RESUSCITATED
INDIGENOUS MOVEMENT

JOSÉ Z. GARCÍA

AFTER WEEKS OF VIOLENT street demonstrations protesting his policies in many parts of the country, Gonzalo Sanchez de Lozada ("Goni") resigned as president of Bolivia on October 17, 2003, and flew to Miami. Sánchez, who speaks Spanish with a U.S. accent—he was raised in the United States—was elected president as leader of the *Movimiento Nacionalista Revolucionario* (MNR), the dominant political force of the past half century. In better days the MNR had spearheaded the Bolivian revolution of 1952, a social and political movement that empowered the indigenous population in tangible ways and nationalized many of the country's industries. In recent years, however, the MNR had been at the vanguard of a drive on behalf of neoliberal reform to undo much of the policy framework the party had helped create. Some of the same forces that had backed the MNR in the 1950s were now behind efforts to get Sánchez to resign.

The departure of Sánchez, however, was not related solely to the changing status of the MNR. In recent years changing global conditions and international pressures have led to extreme hardships for large portions of the Bolivian population. The failure of the political system, including the MNR, to respond adequately to increasingly militant demands for relief plunged the country into a political crisis that pits haves and have-nots against each other more starkly than at any time since the early 1950s. Bolivia is an extreme case in which the pressures of external actors allied with sectors of the local elite have attenuated an already weakened, impoverished state, limiting its ability to deal with fundamental issues on the political agenda. The growing determination of civil society to force government to address these issues has been marked by an alliance of new and old organizations of political opposition engaged in violent confrontations with the national government, leading to a crisis of legitimacy. That crisis resulted in Sánchez's resignation and as of fall 2004 showed no signs of abating.

HISTORICAL BACKGROUND

Colonial authorities distinguished between what they called Upper Peru, or
Charcas—roughly the area now comprising Bolivia—and Lower Peru, site of
contemporary Peru. Charcas was subordinated to Lower Peru throughout most
of the colonial period, although geographic isolation in practice permitted a
good deal of local autonomy. In 1545, a phenomenal silver deposit was discovered at Potosí, the exploitation of which made Chuquisaca (today Sucre)
and Potosí among the richest cities in the world. While these cities nurtured an
outstanding tradition of religious painting and developed two superb universities during the sixteenth and seventeenth centuries, the wealth that made these
possible derived from the forced labor of indigenous populations at the hands
of a foreign-born white elite. Gradually silver production declined, due to rising costs of imports (especially mercury) essential to mining operations, periodic weaknesses in the international silver market, and exhaustion of silver
supplies. The area now encompassing Bolivia has been extremely poor by Latin
American standards for well over two hundred years.

During the drive for independence Upper Peru was torn between royal authorities representing Río de la Plata (Argentina) and Lower Peru, defending
the crown, and rebels fighting for independence. Power was seized by a native-
born conservative, Pedro Antonio de Olañeta, who refused to acknowledge the
legitimacy either of the Spanish authorities after the Liberal Revolution in
Spain in 1820 or a rebel army under Venezuelan Simón Bolívar. Antonio Jose
de Sucre, an officer under Bolívar, defeated Olañeta's army in 1825. Bolivia became independent and Simón Bolívar became its first president—hence the
name Bolivia—for five months before leaving Sucre in charge. Independence,
however, brought on a period of instability caused in part by disagreement over
the relationship between Peru and Bolivia. President Andres de Santa Cruz,
who had been president of Peru in 1826, tried to resolve the issue by creating
a federation between the two countries, but this elicited opposition from Argentina and Chile, and the federation broke up after Chilean forces defeated
Santa Cruz in 1839.

Traditional trade routes were severed by the independence movement in the
early part of the nineteenth century, causing the mining industry nearly to collapse. Power shifted away from mining elites, dominant in political life for centuries, toward a landed aristocracy. As land became more valuable, the
government confiscated Church-owned lands, selling or renting these on behalf of the state. Then the government began to confiscate communal lands—
some cultivated by Indian communities since before the conquest—forcing
Indian residents to purchase individual plots and destroying part of the foundation of Indian society. Mariano Melgarejo, a *caudillo* who ruled from 1864
to 1871, abrogated land titles of more than 100,000 peasants, about 10 percent of the population of Bolivia. Grievances resulting from these policies
would reawaken during the Revolution of 1952.

Within a few decades after independence, Bolivia had lost one-half of its territory to its more powerful neighbors: Brazil, Argentina, Chile, Peru, and, later, Paraguay. Territory was ceded to Brazil in 1867 by Melgarejo for questionable commercial advantages. A war with Brazil in 1903 resulted in further losses. In 1879, Chile occupied Bolivia's small coastal strip on the Pacific Ocean between Peru and Chile. With support from Peru, Bolivia declared war, but after several years of fighting a truce was declared in 1884 and Bolivia has been landlocked ever since. In 1904, Bolivia formally ceded the territory to Chile.

Bolivia's economy revived during the 1870s with the discovery of huge tin deposits near the old silver mines. Tin prices remained high on world markets for several decades thereafter, generating revenues that helped pay for the modernization of the country. Three railroad lines were built, connecting Bolivia with the rest of the world for the first time. Foreign investors were invited to participate. New highways integrated large areas of the country. A new era of prosperity set in.

With the economy finally able to generate surpluses, Bolivians began to debate alternative roles for government. Traditional silver mining interests and large landowners, geographically centered in Potosí and Sucre, formed the base of the Conservative Party, which advocated development of transportation networks and encroachment of large haciendas on traditionally Indian communities. These latter policies resulted in Indian uprisings and the migration of Indians to mining and urban areas, where they encountered ethnic discrimination. Tin-mining entrepreneurs were centered near La Paz, and formed the base of the Liberal Party. As revenues in the tin industry soared, the balance of power shifted from the Conservative to the Liberal party. Liberal governments moved the capital city from Sucre to La Paz, although they left the national judiciary in Sucre. A Republican Party was formed in 1914, representing the growing middle classes in urban areas. In the 1920s, socialist parties began to appear. In short, economic growth produced competing interests, upsetting the traditional balance of political power held by a tiny elite representing landowners and mine owners.

Although the tin-mining industry dominated much of the economy, its structure left the tin barons vulnerable to these new social forces. By the early 1920s, three families—Patiño, Hochschild, and Aramayo—had driven out smaller enterprises and owned the vast proportion of the tin industry. However, the complexities inherent in the organization of the tin industry required that the three families hire hundreds of middle-class overseers and create strong relationships with government officials and foreigners. When Simon Patiño—who owned more than half of the tin mines of Bolivia—and his family left Bolivia in the early 1920s to live in Europe, his estate was left in the hands of managers who did not always share his interests. One of Patiño's accountants, Victor Paz Estenssoro, would later nationalize the tin mines and lead one of the few social revolutions in Latin American history.

THE CHACO WAR

A dispute between Bolivia and Paraguay led to a protracted war between the two countries. The Chaco, a deserted area the size of Colorado, was believed to contain important oil deposits, and the boundary lines within the Chaco between Paraguay and Bolivia were contested. Bolivian President Daniel Salamanca, representing a conservative coalition of the Liberal and Republican parties, began building a powerful army during the Depression, paying for it by drastically cutting government services. During a border dispute in 1932 Salamanca ordered his troops to invade Paraguay, a move that would have disastrous consequences. The Paraguayan armed forces put up a spirited defense, inflicted many casualties, and eventually entered Bolivian territory in a rout of the Bolivian army. A peace treaty was signed in 1935, in which Bolivian territory in the Chaco was ceded to Paraguay.

Several groups in Bolivia were embittered by this experience. Military officers were outraged that a civilian president had instigated an unwinnable war with an unprepared military. For the next two decades, military officers ruled the country. Moreover, the war had mobilized 10 percent of the population of Bolivia, including Indian peasants and tin miners. The segregation of the army into castes—white officers, mestizo noncommissioned officers, and Indian front-line soldiers—led to obvious inequalities in casualty rates, raising ethnic consciousness among Indians. Finally, intellectuals, labor union activists, and disaffected urban groups, frustrated by their inability to help set the national agenda, saw in the defeat an opportunity to play a stronger role in the political life of the country. The loss of the Chaco War helped unify middle- and lower-class groups and served to discredit the traditional political parties responsible for the war.

From the end of the Chaco War in 1935 until 1939, young military officers deeply undermined the conservative political system that had ruled Bolivia since the 1880s. Standard Oil Company was nationalized without compensation, the first such confiscation in Latin American history. A constitutional convention in 1938 created an activist state for the first time, approving a far-reaching labor code favorable to the laboring classes. Large mining concerns were required to turn over their foreign exchange to the national bank, enabling the government to tax them more effectively. During this period various middle-sector groups, including the armed forces, strengthened the power of the state at the expense of conservative upper classes. But they were unable to consolidate reform or establish a ruling coalition.

THE RISE OF THE MNR AND
THE BOLIVIAN REVOLUTION OF 1952

With the weakening of the traditional parties after the Chaco War, several new political parties appeared. The most talented leadership came from the National Revolutionary Movement (MNR), led by Victor Paz Estenssoro. The

MNR openly advocated nationalizing the tin mines and granting stronger rights to workers. When conservative parties tried to regroup in the early 1940s behind the government of General Enrique Peñaranda, the MNR conspired with sympathetic officers in the armed forces, overthrew the government, and backed a military government headed by Major Gualberto Villarroel. Villarroel, however, was unable to control conservative opposition, demands from the left, and conspiracies against him from the armed forces and sectors of the MNR. In 1946, he was attacked by a mob of students, teachers, and workers who marched on the palace of government, killed him, and hanged his body from a lamppost. Again traditional conservative parties came to power. This time they exiled MNR leaders while struggling to manage an ailing economy hurt by deteriorating tin prices, high inflation, labor unrest, and stagnant agricultural production. Presidential elections were held in 1951. Paz Estenssoro received the highest number of votes, but the armed forces prevented the MNR from taking power. A year later the MNR received assistance from a faction within the armed forces. The MNR seized arsenals and distributed arms to supporters. Miners marched on La Paz, blocking loyalist troops from reaching the city. The army finally surrendered and Paz Estenssoro became president of Bolivia.

In power, Paz acted quickly. During the revolt Indians had overtaken many haciendas and distributed the land among themselves, and tin miners had occupied the tin mines. Now the MNR formalized the takeovers, and granted Indians full citizenship rights for the first time since the conquest. Peasants were allowed to keep their arms, and an agrarian reform law expropriated large, unproductive estates for distribution to peasants. Tin miners organized themselves into a powerful new labor federation (COB), and the armed forces were purged of officers associated with previous conservative governments. Finally, the MNR nationalized the tin mines of the three major families, creating a state-owned monopoly to administer the sale of all minerals.

At the head of a successful, extremely popular, social movement—composed of miners, peasants, government workers, and other urban middle-class groups—that had endowed the government with extraordinary power, Paz Estenssoro began preparing for long-term rule. A pact was forged among the top four leaders to rotate their candidacies for president under the MNR party for sixteen years until 1968. Paz would serve a term from 1952–1956. He would be followed by Hernan Siles Suazo (who ran for vice president with Paz in 1951) from 1956 to 1960. Siles would be followed by Walter Guevara Arce, another leader of the MNR, until 1964, when mineworker organizer Juan Lechin would become the candidate. Dissolution of the pact would drive a wedge within the MNR, permitting conservative forces to rise again.

Siles Suazo indeed followed Paz as the presidential candidate in 1956. He was elected and served out his term, consolidating the reform program of the MNR. But in 1960, Paz intervened to block the agreed-upon candidacy of Walter Guevara in favor of his own. Paz became president again, splitting the MNR. In office, Paz acted swiftly to strengthen the armed forces, badly weakened under President Siles and increasingly allied with conservatives. Then, as the 1964 presidential elections approached, Paz used his influence to amend the constitution to permit him to run for yet another term in office. In this effort he was assisted by elements of the U.S. government as well as the armed forces, both concerned that Juan Lechín, a Trotskyist, might come to power. In return for their support, however, the armed forces insisted that the vice presidential candidate would be a member of the military.

Paz was duly elected under these circumstances. But a few months later the armed forces overthrew him, allowing Vice President (General) René Barrientos to become president. Barrientos, a truly popular leader who tried to create a multi-class power base of his own, was killed three years later in a helicopter incident. A succession of military governments followed. The most unusual was the regime of General Juan José Torres, who allowed students and labor union activists to form a Popular Assembly, which elected Juan Lechín its president and began passing legislation. Another general, Hugo Banzer, was able to oust Torres from office in less than a year. Banzer forged a power base that included a highly conservative, newly emerging elite from Santa Cruz, in the east, as well as conservative sectors throughout the country.

Under pressure from the U.S. Carter administration to hold elections after years of dictatorship, Bolivia had some difficulty re-establishing constitutional rule. In elections scheduled for 1978, former President Siles Suazo ran in a contest that also included General Juan Pereda Asbun, favored by President Banzer. The tally eventually found that neither had received a majority of votes, throwing the election to the legislature. Siles apparently counted on enough votes, but before congress could meet Pereda staged a coup and assumed dictatorial powers. He was ousted a few months later by General David Padilla. New elections were scheduled in 1979.

The major candidates this time were former presidents Siles and Paz. Again, neither candidate received enough votes to win outright, throwing the election to the legislature, which then wrestled over the issue for days. It finally selected Walter Guevara Arce, who had been betrayed by Paz in 1960, and who was now president of the senate. Guevara had not been a candidate in the 1979 elections and the constitutionality of his selection is still disputed. His election, however, was widely viewed as an effort to correct an injustice committed two decades earlier. Guevara was overthrown a few months later by General Alberto Natusch Busch, known to be connected to international cocaine traffickers. Facing strong opposition, Natusch stepped down. The legislature was reconvened to select a new president. Lydia Gueiler, the first woman to serve as president of Bolivia, was chosen interim president until new elections could be held.

In 1980, Paz and Siles ran against each other again. Siles won a plurality of votes, but once again not enough. Before the legislature could convene to settle the issue General Luís García Meza toppled the government. Connected to drug trafficking, he was ousted after a year and later convicted of corruption and sentenced to jail. Finally, in 1982 the legislature reconvened, selecting Siles president. Of the four leaders of the MNR who in 1952 agreed to alternate their candidacies, three eventually became president; all were deposed at one time or another, and all remained active through the 1980s. The fourth, Juan Lechín, remained an outsider; but as undisputed leader of the labor movement, he was a force to be reckoned with until he retired in the late 1980s.

BOLIVIA SINCE 1982

Since the removal of the armed forces from power in 1982, constitutionally elected governments have struggled on the one hand to balance the conflicting demands of the nation's organized interest groups in a reasonably equitable manner—the normal task of government—while on the other hand struggling to satisfy the doctrinal demands for neoliberal reform from agents of the international system. The two projects, however, are not always compatible.

Bolivian governments in the past quarter century have opted to accept neoliberal reform as the price for badly needed international assistance. But the conditions attached to this assistance have deeply altered the domestic balance of power among the various actors—trade unions, peasant groups, teachers, business groups, and so on—that emerged from the revolution of 1952—often in favor of small, domestically well-connected groups of Bolivians with wealthy international partners. Since the electoral constituency for neoliberalism is relatively small, many politicians have adopted anti-neoliberal campaigns at election time. But after elections neoliberal policies have been the norm, and the honest-broker, conflict-resolving function of government has at times been deeply compromised, including instances of documented corruption affecting major national issues. That these patterns surfaced under the governing watch of the same party, the MNR, that spearheaded the revolution of 1952, is an irony that only heightens the sense of betrayal. The resulting crisis of legitimacy is severe, and at the time of writing no easy solution appears to be in sight.

President Siles Suazo tried governing in the traditional, post–1952 style, from 1982–1985. His government secured loans from the International Monetary Fund (IMF) to service heavy foreign debts incurred during the military regimes of the 1970s. Since the debt repayment schedule amounted to 70 percent of export earnings, Siles faced painful decisions about which government programs to cut to pay for the debt service. Relying on a well-established fiscal pattern in Bolivia under such circumstances, he tried to temporize by granting concessions to too many groups, setting off an inflationary spiral—nothing new in Bolivian history—escalating to well over 10,000 percent in early 1985. This angered IMF officials and provoked a political crisis that led to Siles's resignation later that year. Subsequent presidents were more careful to adhere to the discipline advocated by the IMF, but they did so at the cost of popular support.

In one of the great ironies of Bolivian history, Victor Paz Estenssoro took the first major steps toward undermining the social compact that he, more than any single figure, had galvanized during the Revolution of 1952. Immediately after his election as president (for the fourth time) in 1985 he introduced the neoliberal model to Bolivia: rapid privatization of government corporations, reduction in state subsidies, a diminished role for government in social investments, such as education, health care, and welfare. He resolved the immediate economic crisis with a mixture of economic austerity, severe repression of labor, and martial law. At one point, when debt service payments equaled 84 percent of the value of exports, his government virtually stopped spending on social programs. During his tenure in office expenditures on education dropped from nearly 20 percent of the national budget to less than 10 percent. Rates of illiteracy and infant mortality began to rise significantly as social spending dropped. These policies stabilized the economy but alienated the major beneficiaries of the 1952 revolution: peasant organizations, tin miners, labor unions, and the poor in general. Paz Estenssoro's enormous stature as founder of the MNR and leader of the 1952 revolution enabled him to enact these reforms without serious civil strife. Subsequent governments were not so fortunate.

Paz Estenssoro's nephew, Jaime Paz Zamora, was elected president in 1989, in part because he promised to reverse the direction of his uncle's policies. Once in office, however, his party, the formerly leftist Movimiento de Izquierda Revolucionaria (MIR), formed an alliance with General Banzer's Acción Democrática Nacionalista (ADN), a right-wing, pro-business party, agreeing to share cabinet positions to continue the neoliberal policies begun by Paz. By the end of his term in office the rising neoliberal order was being challenged in many sectors. Twenty-four political parties, twice the usual, contested for elected positions in 1993. Perhaps sensing the public's desire for new ideas, the MNR selected Victor Hugo Cardenas, an Aymara Indian and leader of the Tupac Katari Revolutionary Movement of Liberation (MRTKL), to run for the vice presidency in 1993. MRTKL was one of several new groups representing the grievances of indigenous people. As presidential candidate, however, the MNR selected Gonzalo Sánchez de Lozada, a strong advocate of neoliberal reform. Within weeks after being elected president, Sánchez announced his intentions to sell 49 percent of the government-owned oil company to private interests and to transfer the tin mining industry to the private sector. Foreign investors would also be given access to 49 percent ownership in state-owned airline, railroad, and electric power facilities, allowing foreign firms to assume managerial control over these firms. These measures passed through the legislature with little opposition. Severe employment cutbacks within these industries weakened the trade union movement, formerly the core of the MNR, and raised the unemployment rate. Pressures within the political system began to build.

COCA PLANTATIONS AND THE RISE OF MAS

In Bolivia 12,000 hectares of coca is planted legally in the Yungas region north of La Paz, to satisfy the local demand generated by indigenous groups who have consumed coca leaves for several centuries. However, as demand for cocaine escalated in the United States during the 1980s, illegal cultivation of coca rose dramatically in the Chapare region, where up to 35,000 hectares of coca were harvested for eventual conversion to cocaine. Illegal coca plantations in the 1990s provided a livelihood for over 70,000 peasant families, some of whom had migrated to the Chapare after the collapse of the tin industry in the 1980s. Up to 10 percent of the gross domestic income of Bolivia derived from coca production, and as many as 300,000 peasants—8 to 10 percent of the national workforce—depended on coca production in the Chapare. Facing extraordinary pressure from the U.S. embassy, which insisted on eradication of illegal coca plantations as a condition of further assistance, Bolivian governments agreed to initiate a program of crop substitution combined with coca crop destruction. From 1995 to 2001, Bolivian anti-narcotics operations, assisted by the U.S. government, destroyed about 70 percent of the country's illegal coca plantations—by far the most effective anti-drug effort in the Western Hemisphere. But as in the case of neoliberal reform, cooperation with the U.S. damaged relations between the Bolivian government and large sectors of the population.

In the early 1990s, coca producers began to organize themselves. The strongest organization was headed by a talented young coca producer, Evo Morales, who organized a confederation of six growers' associations representing over 35,000 producers. One of the most dramatic political developments in the past half-century has been the extraordinary rise of this organization, which has been skilled at forging alliances with other political groupings. Morales also organized the Movement Toward Socialism (MAS), a political party, and ran for congress. Morales led strikes and demonstrations. He has been jailed repeatedly. He was elected to Congress and then expelled from Congress. But MAS, allied with other groups opposing neoliberal policies, has dominated the national agenda, and in 2003 he came within 42,000 votes of being elected president of Bolivia, in spite of public warnings from the U.S. ambassador to Bolivia that his election would seriously jeopardize continued U.S. assistance.

In 1995, teachers, health workers, and public utilities employees organized dozens of work stoppages, demanding higher salaries, protesting privatization policies, and protesting the coca eradication program. A state of siege, lasting six months, was called by President Sánchez, suspending constitutional rights, imposing a nighttime curfew, and allowing the government to hold people without trial. These disturbances were followed in 1996 by protests against an agrarian reform bill approved by congress, apparently reneging on promises made to various agrarian constituent groups. Opposition to the bill included peasants, coca growers, labor unions, tenant farmers, and agribusiness leaders. In 1997, former dictator Hugo Banzer was elected president, promising to "humanize" the face of neoliberalism on behalf of a conservative party. Evo Morales was also elected to the national congress that year. Under pressure from the U.S. government, Banzer made coca eradication a centerpiece of his administration. Three thousand troops were sent into the Chapare to conduct military operations. They destroyed the livelihoods of thousands of peasants in a failed effort to reduce the availability of cocaine in U.S. markets three thousand miles away. Meanwhile, scandals have broken out periodically in which high-level government officials have been implicated in large-scale drug trafficking activities. In one such case a cargo plane loaded with four tons of cocaine was seized in Peru, apparently part of a drug enterprise run in Bolivia and protected by officials at all levels. Former Presidents Jaime Paz Zamora and Victor Paz Estenssoro were also accused of accepting large quantities of campaign contributions from Bolivian drug dealers. By 2003, the U.S. State Department was reporting that coca cultivation in Bolivia had increased 23 percent, despite destruction of 12,000 hectares in 2002.

PROTESTS OVER WATER PRIVATIZATION AND OTHER NEOLIBERAL PROJECTS

In the late 1990s, as a condition of granting debt relief and other funds for development, World Bank officials pressured Bolivian government officials to privatize the water utilities company of Cochabamba, Bolivia's third largest city, with a population of 600,000. In 1999, Bolivian officials, in secrecy and with no bidding process, leased the Cochabamba water utility company to Aguas de Tunari, a subsidiary of Bechtel Corporation, a large multinational engineering company. The contract guaranteed Bechtel a profit of 16 percent each year for forty years. Once Bechtel took over the utility, in January 2000, it announced water rate hikes of up to 200 percent, raising the effective rate to about ten dollars per month per household, in a city where the minimum wage was only sixty dollars per month. Almost immediately large-scale demonstrations protested the rate hikes. The city was paralyzed from January to April. Violent confrontations with authorities led to the declaration of a state of siege, as government officials negotiated with organizers of the revolt. Finally the government announced that the contract had been rescinded and that Bechtel had left Bolivia. Water rates were rolled back to where they had been before the contract.

A few months later the country was paralyzed by demonstrations, strikes, and roadblocks—the worst social unrest in two decades—when students, teachers, peasant organizations, and coca growers began protesting low teachers' wages, government agrarian policies, and the military campaign to eradicate coca plants in the Chapare. The month-long protests ended in October when the government negotiated an end to the strikes, which caused widespread food shortages in several cities. After another wave of demonstrations in May 2001, the Bolivian labor confederation (COB) signed an agreement in which the government promised to adjust the minimum wage upwards and to reexamine its policies of privatization. General Banzer was diagnosed with lung cancer, and he stepped down from the presidency in August 2001.

In 2002, Gonzalzo Sánchez de Lozada, of the MNR, was elected president of Bolivia again, and formed a coalition government with the MIR, headed by former president Jaime Paz Zamora. But by this time the Movimiento Al Socialismo (MAS) headed by coca organizer Evo Morales, was the second largest political organization in the country. Morales immediately acted to articulate an agenda for negotiation, including questions surrounding Bolivia's participation in the Free Trade Area of the Americas, proposed exports of Bolivian natural gas, continued eradication of coca fields, and priorities in the national budget.

In January 2003, more than twenty persons died in clashes between the government and the coca growers, now joined by Bolivia's largest labor confederation, headed by Aymara leader Felipe Quispe, a member of congress. In February more than thirty persons died in protests after police went on strike for higher wages. Police were supported by many groups, including the Confederation of Private Business, angered by a government plan to impose an income tax for the first time, in response to IMF insistence on cutting the government budget as a condition of a new loan. Demonstrators set fire to government buildings, including the office of the vice president and the offices of three political parties. In June opposition legislators went on a hunger strike to force the government to debate key bills dealing with land rights and agricultural subsidies, and miners blocked major highways demanding government support to reactivate the mining industry. In July, landless peasants began seizing haciendas in various parts of the country and demanding they be given land to cultivate; soldiers and police responded by evicting peasants from occupied estates.

President Sanchez was further undermined after strong protests broke out in September against plans to export natural gas to Chile. Bolivia has the largest natural gas reserve in Latin America and the government reached an agreement with a transnational consortium, Pacific LNG, to invest the equivalent of US$6 billion in a pipeline to the Pacific coast for export to Mexico and the United States. Opposition groups demanded that 250,000 Bolivian homes be supplied with gas before permitting any exports, and strongly objected when Pacific LNG insisted on building the pipeline to Chile, instead of Peru. Many Bolivians still resent Chile for taking away Bolivia's access to the sea in 1884. Evo Morales and his followers in MAS organized a Coordinating Committee to Defend Gas, which incorporated dozens of peasant and worker unions, and insisted that the government should receive 50 percent of gas royalties rather than the 18 percent paid by foreign companies. After clashes in October had killed another thirty persons, Sánchez resigned. His successor, Vice President Mesa, tried to defuse the violence by decreeing a referendum on the gas deal, and he proved far more popular than Sánchez.

Bolivia remains extremely poor, and competition for scarce resources is severe. While the revolution of 1952 greatly improved the political status of the Indian population, assimilation did not take place, and the country remains ethnically fragmented. A full 30 percent of the population speaks Quechua, another 25 percent speaks Aymara. Nor did government policy significantly improve the distribution of wealth toward Indian populations. Recently indigenous groups have reorganized themselves in large numbers, now holding more than one-third of the seats in congress—the strongest ratio in history. Efforts by recent governments to legitimize neoliberal policies have failed, in large part because they have been imposed from the top, pressured from abroad. Groups enfranchised for the first time after hard-fought victories and organizational struggles in the revolution of 1952 were simply asked three decades later to accept a sharply lower standard of living with only vague promises in return. Thus far the neoliberal project has only strengthened the transformation of ethnic and economic grievances into a well-organized movement with the capacity to make itself heard.

Suggested Readings

Gill, Leslie, *Teetering on the Rim.* New York: Columbia University Press, 2000.

Klein, Herbert S. *Bolivia: A Concise History.* Cambridge, U.K.: Cambridge University Press, 2003.

Grindle, Merrilee Serrill, and Pilar Domingo, eds. *Proclaiming Revolution: Bolivia in Comparative Perspective.* Cambridge, Mass., Harvard University Press, 2003.

Leons, Madeline Barbara, and Harry Sanabria, eds. *Coca, Cocaine, and the Bolivian Reality.* Albany, N.Y.: State University of New York Press, 1997.

Levy, Marcela Lopez., *Bolivia* (Oxfam Country Profiles). Oxford, U.K.: Oxfam Publications, 2001.

Olivera, Oscar, and Tom Lewis. *Cochabamba: Water Rebellion in Bolivia.* Cambridge, Mass., 2004.

Internet

Latin America Data Base, University of New Mexico: http://ladb.unm.edu.

Latin America Network Information Center, University of Texas at Austin: http://www.lanic.utexas.edu.

PART IX

BRAZIL AND
THE SOUTHERN CONE

BRAZIL: FROM MILITARY REGIME TO A WORKERS' PARTY GOVERNMENT

DAVID FLEISCHER

"I WAS DREAMING THE wrong dream!" With this phrase, on October 14, 2003, Rio de Janeiro Deputy Fernando Gabeira highlighted his disengagement from the Workers' Party (PT)[1]. Considered an icon of the Brazilian left, Gabeira had participated in the kidnapping of U.S. Ambassador Charles Elbrick in August 1969 that allowed the ransom of fifteen political prisoners, including José Dirceu, who became President Luiz Inácio Lula da Silva's all-powerful chief of staff in January 2003. Calling the new PT government "Fernando Henrique Cardoso's third term," Gabeira voiced the disappointment of many Brazilians with the conservative, neoliberal policies pursued by the new PT government elected in October 2002, after twenty-two years of political and electoral struggles against the last military government and its four successors.

What happened to Brazil in this forty-year period from 1964 to 2003? After twenty-one years of military rule, finally a civilian president was "elected" indirectly by an electoral college in January 1985. On the eve of his inauguration on March 15, president-elect Tancredo Neves was stricken with an intestinal disorder, hospitalized, operated on five times in Brasília and São Paulo, and finally died on April 21. His vice president, José Sarney, who had been until June 1984 the president of the Social Democratic Party (PDS), which supported the military government, became president for the five-year term until March 1990. In essence, this was the first "dream gone wrong"—Brazil's final transition from the military regime was in the hands of a former governor and senator who had been allied with the military government, and who governed under close tutelage by the military.

TWO BRAZILS—"BELINDIA"

Brazil has often been portrayed and characterized as a nation existing on two levels—the "two Brazils"—where an incredibly rich, developed, educated, and very small minority managed to dominate the poor majority, many living on a subsistence level, passive, semi-educated, unorganized, leaderless. This duality was first described by two French sociologists in the late 1950s—Roger Bastide's "contrasts" and Jacques Lambert's "archaic" and "modern" Brazil.[2] Economist Edmar Bacha characterized this dualism as a "Belindia" (Belgium versus India).[3] Two Brazils sharply cut into various dichotomies: rural and urban social and cultural environments, industrial and agrarian economies, coast and hinterland, plains and rain forests. The growing gap between the rich and the poor—less than 10 percent of the population currently own 50 percent of the national wealth—and conflicting demands for material modernization and social change that weak formal political institutions were unable to mediate led to an impasse in the early 1960s. The consequent demand for "order" against the "chaos" deriving from incipient social mobilization paved the way for the civilian-military coup of 1964.

Considerable change has occurred in Brazil's regional contrasts in recent years. In terms of the so-called "rich" families (monthly income over R$22.487,00–approximately US$7,500), in 2000, 1,162,164 such families were encountered. They constituted 2.4 percent of all families (58 percent of them in São Paulo), concentrating 33 percent of national income and wealth equivalent to 45.85 percent of Brazil's GDP. In 1980, the rich families were only 1.8 percent of the total.[4] The differences indicate that no longer is Brazil's wealth generated by production and labor, but by a financialization of the economy. In 2000, the average income of rich families was fourteen times the national average, compared to ten times in 1980. In this twenty-year period, the proportion of "rich" families in São Paulo increased by 102.9 percent, by 78.4 percent in Piauí, and 17.9 percent in Ceará; the proportion declined by 14.2 percent in Pará and by 28.8 percent in Bahia.

In terms of quality of life, Brazil scored 0.775 on the Human Development Index (HDI) elaborated by UNDP in 2004 and was ranked seventy-second out of 177 nations—sixty-second rank on education (0.88), one hundred eleventh rank on life expectancy (0.72), and sixty-third rank on income (0.73). In 1990, Brazil was in seventy-first rank (0.712) and in 1975 in eighty-first rank (0.643) on the HDI scale. In terms of income distribution, however, Brazil was ranked "the fourth worst" worldwide—only "better" than Namibia, Lesotho, and Sierra Leone. In Brazil, the 10 percent richest segment had 46.7 percent of national income while the 10 percent poorest had only 0.5 percent (a differential of eighty-five times). This was worse than in the 2003 HDI, where the differential for Brazil was 65.8, with the ninth worst income distribution. In Namibia, the difference was 128.8 times. Brazil's GINI index for income distribution was 0.591 and that of Namibia was 0.707. In contrast, Brazil is the fifth largest nation (slightly larger than the continental United States) and fifth in population with the fifteenth largest GDP, but is ranked sixty-third in terms of per capita income.

THE 1964 COUP AND THE
TWENTY-ONE-YEAR MILITARY REGIME

After Independence from Portugal in 1822, Brazil evolved into a constitutional monarchy with the son of the Portuguese king (Dom João VI), Dom Pedro I, as emperor. After a brief regency, Dom Pedro II ruled Brazil from 1840 until he was toppled in 1889 and a republic was installed—with two successive general—presidents until 1894, when a civilian president was elected. This *First Republic*, based on coffee exports and dominated politically by the two largest states (São Paulo and Minas Gerais), which alternated the presidency during much of this thirty-five-year period, continued until the 1930 revolution. After the period of centralized empire, the new political system was more decentralized, with considerable autonomy for the states.

The 1920s produced great social and economic turmoil with growth of the main urban centers, large volumes of immigrants (especially from Italy and Spain), incipient industrialization, two military rebellions, in 1922 and 1924, and a *long march* led by Army captain Luiz Carlos Prestes that crisscrossed the nation in an attempt to stir resistance to the regime. Finally, in the 1930 election, São Paulo broke the "alternation" agreement (with Minas Gerais) and proceeded to elect a second consecutive president from that state.

In October 1930, discontented with this situation and fearing that "we must make the revolution [from above] before the people do," the governors of Minas Gerais and Rio Grande do Sul organized a revolt that ended the decadent oligarchic system and installed Getúlio Vargas as "provisional" president. Except for a brief democratic interim (1934–1937), Vargas ruled as a dictator until the military removed him from power in November 1945, one month prior to general elections. This fifteen-year Vargas period was marked by modernization, political centralization, industrialization, and Brazilian participation in World War II in support of the Allies in the Italian campaign (1943–1945).

The 1946 constitution instituted a liberal, multiparty democracy with moderate autonomy for the states. Vargas returned to the presidency by direct election in 1950, but was again removed by the military in August 1954. Vargas then committed suicide, becoming a "martyr" and symbol for his Brazilian Labor Party (PTB) of the struggle of Brazilian workers against economic oppression.

In November 1955, the PSD governor of Minas Gerais, Juscelino Kubitschek, was elected by a simple majority, threatened by a military coup, and took office in January 1956 after a three-month state of siege. Most thought that he would not complete his five-year term. However, Kubitschek proceeded to mobilize Brazilians for "fifty years of progress in five," built the new interior capital city of Brasília, spurred industrial growth, expanded the country's highway and electric power infrastructure, and pushed Brazil into the twentieth century.

Kubitschek's successor, Jânio Quadros, took office in January 1961, stressing austerity. He condemned the "irresponsible spending" of his predecessor, visited Cuba, decorated Ernesto "Ché" Guevara, and instituted a new "independent foreign policy." Seven months later, constrained by a minority in Congress, Quadros abruptly resigned. Part of the military then attempted to impede Vice President João Goulart (PTB), considered a Vargas protégé, from acceding to the presidency. The military was divided, and with the threat of a civil war, congress devised a "solution" by installing a parliamentary regime; Goulart was allowed to become president, with reduced powers, in September 1961.

The first parliamentary cabinet, with Tancredo Neves (PSD) as prime minister, was quite successful until it had to "step down" four months before the October 1962 elections. Goulart then appointed a series of weak PMs and, in late 1962, congress authorized a national plebiscite in January 1963 that voted to end the short-lived parliamentary system and restore Goulart's presidential powers. The nation was undergoing considerable unrest caused by increased inflation, massive rural-urban migration, slowed economic growth, numerous farm invasions by landless peasants, and successive labor and student strikes that frequently outpaced Goulart's feeble attempts at achieving basic reforms—changes in land tenure, the banking system, the university, and the political system. Regarding political reforms, progressives (especially in southern, more developed Brazil) proposed a one-man, one-vote system for Brazil to reduce the political weight of the underdeveloped, smaller, and more conservative states in the northeast and north regions. They also called for the enfranchisement of illiterates, state military police, and noncommissioned Army officers.

While Brazil had undergone much political, social, and economic change since 1930, it was still not a modern nation by twentieth-century standards. Although women had been enfranchised in 1932, illiterates were still prohibited from voting. In the 1962 elections, only about 25 percent of Brazil's population was registered to vote and some 70 percent of the population still lived in rural areas.

The 1962 elections had produced some renovation in congress, and the PTB and PSD each controlled about 28 percent of the 409 seats in the lower house. In 1961 and 1962, Goulart's brother-in-law, Governor Leonel Brizola, expropriated the foreign-owned electric power and telephone companies in their home state of Rio Grande do Sul. Brizola was elected federal deputy from the new state of Guanabara with the then-largest vote total on record. The conservatives controlled a majority that blocked approval of Goulart's "Basic Reforms," which required a two-thirds constitutional quorum.[5] As a result, in early 1964, President Goulart initiated some reforms by decree. When he appeared to be stimulating the unionization of army sergeants and other noncommissioned officers articulated with the CGT labor union central, in late March, the armed forces led a coup that quickly ousted Goulart and instituted the twenty-one-year military regime.[6]

The Brazilian military regime can be divided into four distinct periods: 1) the pseudo-constitutional interval from April 1964 to December 1968—when Presidents Castelo Branco and Costa e Silva governed under the aegis of the 1946 and 1966 constitutions but with some exceptional changes; 2) the descent into dictatorship with the AI–5 (Fifth Institutional Act), signed on December 13, 1968, that abolished all constitutional guarantees for ten years, covering the second part of the Costa e Silva presidency and the Médici period;

3) the presidency of Ernesto Geisel (1974–1979), which promoted a certain controlled liberalization and reduced the powers of the military hard line; and 4) the last military president, João Figueiredo (1979–1985), who processed the final political opening without the exceptional powers of the AI–5.

Different from the military regimes of its South American neighbors (Argentina, Peru, Uruguay, and Chile), where the generals prohibited all political activities, with short exceptional periods the Brazilian Armed Forces maintained what President Geisel called "relative democracy." Regular elections were held for legislative office and local mayors (but with constant changes in the rules and indirect elections for president and state governors). Political parties continued to function (but with two total realignments forced by the military); and the national congress remained open (but with considerable reductions of its powers and prerogatives, and it was closed three times).

After President João Goulart was removed by the military coup in late March 1964, the military high command issued the First Institutional Act (AI–1), which "legitimated" the intervention and imposed certain limits on civil liberties. This AI–1 also allowed the military to cancel elected mandates, remove civilians and military from the public service, and decree the loss of political rights for ten years. Congress was convened on April 11 to ratify the choice of General Humberto Castelo Branco and Deputy José Maria Alkmin as president and vice president. Many political leaders were expurgated and lost their political rights, including former presidents João Goulart, Jânio Quadros, and Juscelino Kubitschek. By the end of the AI–2 in 1966, sixty-seven deputies and two senators were stripped of their mandates and five governors were removed, in addition to hundreds of labor union leaders, professors, intellectuals, civil servants, and military officers.

The Castelo Branco presidency was marked by tensions between the so-called hard- and soft-line factions in the military. The former pressured for major surgery on Brazil's political system requiring a long period of military rule, while the latter envisioned a short intervention, minor "plastic" surgery, and a quick return to a civilian president after the October 1965 presidential elections. However, the prospects for such a quick transition became quite difficult and eventually President Castelo decreed indirect elections for the next president and extended his own mandate until March 1967. However, he maintained the direct elections for governor in eleven states for October 1965 and promised that those elected would take office. Although conservative candidates performed well in these elections, two Kubitschek protégés were elected in the important states of Minas Gerais and Guanabara (city-state of Rio de Janeiro) and two days later JK returned from exile in Paris to savor this victory. The negative reaction of the hard-line military officers was intense and the mobilization of army officers in Rio de Janeiro threatened to depose President Castelo Branco. The minister of war, General Arthur Costa e Silva, stepped in to calm the situation, extracted concessions from the president, avoided a coup, and consolidated his political position to be Castelo's successor in 1967. Those elected were allowed to take office, but the president decreed the end of the post–1945 multiparty system and established criteria for a new two-party system to be enacted for the 1966 elections.

In 1966, two new political parties were organized, the National Renovating Alliance (ARENA, pro-government) and Brazilian Democratic Movement (MDB, opposition). The rules imposed by the military government required 120 deputies and twenty senators to form a new party. Initially, the MDB could muster only eighteen senators, but President Castelo Branco convinced two ARENA-leaning senators to temporarily join the opposition party. Deputies from three major parties during the 1945–1964 period joined ARENA and MDB in distinct patterns. Those from the largely anti-Goulart UDN joined ARENA (eighty-four out of ninety-four), whereas those from Goulart's PTB mainly joined the MDB (seventy-five out of one hundred nine). In a more even split, a majority from the conservative PSD joined ARENA (eighty out of one hundred twenty-four).[7] Castelo Branco had read the works of Maurice Duverger[8] and understood the connection between two-party systems and majority (district) election systems. The president instructed the TSE (National Election Court) to divide Brazil into 409 election districts for the 1966 elections, but later abandoned the idea after the ex-UDN politicians complained that this system would favor their arch rivals (ex-PSD deputies) in Brazil's vast interior regions.

By mid-1966, ARENA counted 260 deputies and MDB 148. On October 3, 1966, the state legislatures in the twelve states that had not held direct elections for governor in 1965 convened to select their respective "bionic" governors.[9] Direct elections were held for senator, state and federal deputies, mayors and city councils on November 15. In lieu of the restrictions imposed by the regime, ARENA fared quite well at the polls and elected 276 deputies (67.5 percent) versus 133 for the MDB. ARENA achieved forty-seven members (71.2 percent) of the upper house. Thus, the second military president, Arthur Costa e Silva, took office on March 15, 1967, with comfortable majorities in congress—and a new constitution. The latter had been hastily put together by the lame-duck Congress in December 1966 and January 1967 under heavy tutelage from the outgoing Castelo Branco government.[10]

The Economic Miracle and Repression

The 1967 constitution left the new president without the most oppressive powers available to the regime in the 1964–1966 period. However, repression of public assemblies, labor union strikes and articulations, and student demonstrations were frequent. Although the government support party (ARENA) enjoyed strong majorities, congress was now immune to summary removal of its members by the military government. As discontent increased, ARENA found it increasingly more difficult to approve government bills, especially in 1968.

Following a period of economic stagnation (1960–1964), the Castelo Branco government enacted public policies to curb inflation, reduce public deficits, and control labor's economic demands. That provoked a recession, with declines in the GDP and increased unemployment. In 1967, Costa e Silva's economic czar, Finance Minister Delfim Neto, enacted policies to stimulate consumer demand, new domestic and foreign investments, and incentives for Brazilian exports. These initiatives, together with a favorable international economic environment, produced what was called the economic miracle (1967–1973). During this phase, average annual GDP growth was 11.1 percent, led by the industrial sector at 13.1 percent. Imports grew faster than exports to feed this economic expansion, but the resulting trade deficits were offset by large inflows of capital resulting in balance of payments surpluses.[11] The military government expropriated all electric power and telephone concessions and quickly consolidated the latter into modern state enterprises—Eleitrobrás and Telebrás.[12]

Labor and student unrest and protests against the authoritarian system swept Brazil in 1968, with the "March of 100,000 [students]" in Rio de Janeiro and numerous strikes in São Paulo that were repressed by police. Similar student and labor protest movements erupted in Western Europe and the United States in the spring and summer of 1968. In August, police closed the state university in Belo Horizonte and invaded the University of Brasília, and censorship and repression increased dramatically. Urban guerrilla actions and bank robberies became very frequent and produced even more repression.

Just prior to Brazil's National Independence Day (September 7), an outspoken MDB deputy, Márcio Moreira Alves, delivered a fiery speech at the Chamber of Deputies on September 2. Alves exhorted Brazilians to "boycott militarism" and not attend the military parades on Independence Day. Furthermore, he urged young Brazilian women not to date military officers. The armed forces were outraged, claiming that their dignity had been offended. In reprisal, the Costa e Silva government demanded that the chamber suspend Deputy Moreira Alves' parliamentary immunity, so that he could be stripped of his mandate and prosecuted for this offense.

In early December, this political challenge to the military regime reached its climax. On December 11, the Chamber of Deputies Justice Committee (following the substitution of nine ARENA deputies) reported in favor of Alves's removal. However, the following day, the full chamber rejected the request by a 216-to-141 vote (with some 90 "Nay" votes from ARENA deputies). On December 13, the military government issued the AI–5, which closed Congress until October 1969 and instituted ten years of full dictatorial discretionary powers. In the following months, ninety-four deputies (twenty-eight from ARENA) and four MDB senators were expelled from Congress.

In 1969, the military government perpetrated new waves of purges, including many university professors, such as sociologist Fernando Henrique Cardoso from the University of São Paulo. Reportedly, Costa e Silva had constituted a group of scholars and jurists to prepare a new constitution that would embody many of the regime's "exceptional rules" but restore a "state of law" to Brazil. Before this task could be completed, the president suffered a crippling stroke on August 27 and the three military ministers formed a junta to impede civilian Vice President Pedro Aleixo from assuming the presidency. During this confusing interval, guerrillas kidnapped U.S. Ambassador Charles Burke Elbrick in Rio de Janeiro on September 4 and demanded the release of fifteen political prisoners. The ransomed prisoners were flown to Mexico two days later.[13]

Finally, the Army High Command selected General Emílio Garrastazú Médici to succeed Costa e Silva and on October 25 congress was reconvened to ratify this decision. The Médici government maintained harsh political repression while the economy boomed, and in 1970 it imposed considerable changes on the election system. The Chamber of Deputies was reduced from 409 to 310 members and state delegations became proportional to their respective electorates, rather than population. Proportionately, this measure increased the representation of the more developed states with large electorates (Minas Gerais and São Paulo), and reduced that of less developed states with smaller electorates. Pernambuco, for example, had its delegation reduced from twenty-four to fifteen deputies.[14]

The 1970 elections were held with harsh restrictions on the opposition MDB. Many candidates were not permitted to run; use of radio, TV and press advertising was censored; many politicians had been purged; freedom of expression and assembly were reduced; and a general economic euphoria helped promote ARENA candidates. Brazil's victory in the world soccer cup in mid-1970 enhanced government support even more. The result was a near landslide victory for ARENA and the MDB was reduced to only eighty-six deputies (27.7 percent) and seven senators (10.6 percent). In 1971, some discouraged members of the opposition proposed the dissolution of the MDB.[15] The mayors and city councils elected in 1970 were given two-year mandates. This change was adopted to set municipal elections two years out of phase from the elections for congress and state legislatures. Two such elections were held in 1972 and 1976.

1974: Economic Downtown and Political "Opening"

By 1973, the economic miracle had become somewhat frayed, and the first petroleum shock imposed by OPEC after the Yom Kippur Arab–Israel conflict impacted very heavily on Brazil because of its heavy dependence on imported oil. As a result, capital flows to Brazil declined and its balance of payments became negative. This situation caused the country to borrow heavily from international financial markets to maintain minimal economic growth. The economic legitimacy that had sustained the military regime since 1967 was eroding and needed a quick political fix.

Enter General Ernesto Geisel, a nationalist officer of German descent who began his career just prior to the 1930 revolution and participated in anti-Vargas military revolts in 1945 and 1954 and the movements against his successors in 1961 and 1964. He had been a close advisor to Presidents Jânio

Quadros and Castelo Branco and had directed Petrobrás after 1967. His older brother, Orlando, was the outgoing army minister under President Médici.

Aided by the chief of staff, General Golbery do Couto e Silva, the Geisel presidency pursued three policy objectives: 1) maintaining economic growth with a "deepening" of industrialization; 2) managing a "political opening" or liberalization, paving the way for a return to civilian rule; and 3) reducing the power and influence of the military by reasserting the command powers of the presidency.[16] Geisel still had the all-powerful AI–5 at his disposal to enforce his policy decisions.

In late 1973, Geisel had been challenged by an "anti-candidate"—Deputy Ulysses Guimarães (MDB-SP), who crisscrossed the country with his quixotic crusade and garnered 76 (15 percent) out of a total of 505 votes in the January 15, 1974, electoral college. Two months later, Geisel was sworn in as the fourth military president for a five-year term, through March 1979. Thus, he became the only military president to oversee two general elections—in 1974 and 1978.

The first petroleum shock, of late 1973, was impacting strongly on Brazil in early 1974. Although exports remained strong, Brazil's terms of trade were drastically reduced. Capital flows declined, forcing an increase in foreign borrowing and consequently exploding current-account deficits. GDP growth remained relatively strong—6.9 percent on average from 1974 to 1980—but the current-account deficit rose from US$1.7 billion in 1973 to US$12.8 billion in 1980, and the foreign debt soared to US$54 billion by 1980. The increase in foreign debt was sustained by an international financial market awash in petrodollars. This situation was further aggravated by the second oil shock and the interest rate shock in the late 1970s. Inflation also increased considerably—from 16.2 percent in 1973 to 110.2 percent in 1980—with salaries adjusted by monetary correction once a year, and biannually as of 1979. The economic miracle phase had ended, and the military regime was in need of an alternate source of legitimacy.

Geisel and Golbery sought to enhance legitimacy through a decompression, or political opening, with more or less unfettered elections in 1974. The MDB opposition party was allowed to select its candidates with little official coercion and the campaign suffered few restrictions. Embratel (Brazil's long-lines telecommunications state enterprise) had completed the system of microwave TV transmissions that unified coverage in all states and nationwide—after the initial hookup was put in place just in time to cover Brazil's victory in the 1970 World Soccer Cup. Thus, the free TV time made available to the parties by the TSE (election court) covered all states in the evening prime-time period. Unlike the 1970 campaign, in 1974 the MDB (and ARENA) candidates had live access to TV campaigning and in many states debates were organized between the candidates for senator.

In most states, the MDB did not foresee a favorable election outcome and its traditional leaders avoided the "sacrifice" of running for the senate. For example, in São Paulo, Deputies Franco Montoro and Ulysses Guimarães ran for reelection, while a young city council member, Orestes Quércia, became the party's senate candidate. In 1970, the opposition party had polled 28.6 percent of the national vote and elected only three senators, so MDB leaders were justifiably apprehensive.

However, Brazilian voters reacted quite differently in 1974 than in 1970. Although ARENA outpolled the MDB in votes for federal deputy (42.0 percent versus 36.6 percent, with 21.3 percent blank and null votes), the opposition achieved 50.1 percent of the vote for the twenty-two senate seats up for election—and more importantly, elected sixteen senators. From 19.5 percent of the total vote for federal deputy in 1970, the MDB amassed 36.6 percent in 1974 and advanced from eighty-seven (28.1 percent) to 165 (45.3 percent) deputies, thus impeding the government from amending the constitution (at that point a two-thirds quorum was required) in the 1975–1979 period.[17] The MDB also elected majorities to six state legislatures that in principle would allow the opposition party to indirectly elect the next governors in 1978.

Many of the new MDB senators were excellent orators, so that in 1975 the senate galleries were packed with spectators (including many deputies) to observe the eloquent and fiery debates between ARENA and MDB senators. In 1975, the fanatical hard line in the Armed Forces began an insidious campaign against Geisel and Golbery, accusing them of having "favored the left" in the 1974 elections. In October, Geisel countered with what appeared to be a "pendulum" strategy and struck hard against the clandestine Brazilian Communist Party (PCB) in São Paulo. That month, journalist Vladimir Herzog was found dead in his cell at the Sao Paulo police's infamous Division of Intelligence (DOI) detention/torture center. Massive student demonstrations ensued, with violent protest speeches in Congress. In January 1976, labor union leader Manoel Fiel Filho was found dead in the same São Paulo DOI. With the death of Herzog, Geisel had extracted a promise from the army generals that such an incident would not be repeated, or else. The Fiel Filho repetition caused the president to immediately sack the commander of the II Army in São Paulo, General Ednardo D'Avila Mello, and many hard-line officers were retired or transferred to remote garrisons. Many of Geisel's advisers counseled the sacking of the minister of the army.

In an effort to stem what was perceived as a possible MDB tidal wave approaching with the 1976 municipal elections, the Geisel government enacted restrictions on television propaganda that year and restricted campaign activities somewhat. This resulted in only some quite modest gains for the MDB. In 1977, Geisel adjourned congress for two weeks and decreed the "April Package" that imposed several important modifications in the rules for the 1978 elections, in which two senate seats were up for election in each state. The base for calculating the number of deputies per state was changed back to population (in 1970 and 1974, the base was the electorate), thus increasing the representation of states in the north and northeast where ARENA was stronger. One of the two senate seats became "bionic" (indirectly elected by an electoral college in each state). These same state electoral colleges (with ARENA majorities in all states but the state of Rio de Janeiro) would also elect the new state governors in 1978. The constitutional quorum was reduced from a two-thirds to an absolute majority, thus allowing ARENA to amend the constitution. These changes were expected to stem the opposition tide in 1978 and guarantee continued ARENA majorities in both houses of Congress. During his term, Geisel used the AI–5 powers to sack six MDB deputies and one ARENA senator. The latter had been accused of corruption.

Also in 1977, Army Minister Sylvio Frota began frequent visits to congress and initiated an active political dialogue with ARENA politicians, clearly demonstrating his presidential ambitions for the 1979–1985 period. When Frota's activities began to challenge and erode Geisel's authority, the president reacted decisively. On the Columbus Day holiday, Geisel summarily dismissed Frota from the cabinet. The general attempted a reaction by convoking a meeting of the army high command but to no avail. General Fernando Bethlem was swiftly sworn in as the new army minister and proceeded to impose order in the military sector. Geisel then had a free hand to conclude his term and install his hand-picked successor.[18]

Ernesto Geisel enacted a foreign policy—"responsible pragmatism"—that distanced Brazil from the United States. His predecessors (Castelo Branco, Costa e Silva, and Médici) had maintained closely articulated relations with the United States.[19] In 1975, Brazil signed a nuclear cooperation agreement with West Germany to build seven nuclear power plants to generate electric power in Brazil's southeast industrial region. However, some U.S. officials suspected that this agreement could permit Brazil to gain access to technology that would allow the nation to master the complete nuclear cycle and construct a nuclear weapon. At the same time, President Geisel was attempting to reduce violations of human rights and torture in Brazil. In early 1977, the new U.S. president, Jimmy Carter, began to pressure Brazil and West Germany to end their nuclear agreement. At the same time, the White House released a report prepared for Congress describing the very negative human rights situation in Brazil. Geisel reacted strongly, and in March 1977 renounced the military agreement that had been signed with the United States in the 1950s. The military aid involved was insignificant but Geisel's gesture had symbolic resonance. In June, Geisel received Carter's wife, Rosalynn Carter, "coolly" in Brasília after she had visited an American lay Roman Catholic volunteer who had been imprisoned and tortured in Recife. In 1978, President Carter made a state visit to Brazil. However, Germany and Brazil maintained their nuclear agreement. Geisel visited Japan, Germany, France, and the United Kingdom—but was the only military president of Brazil not to visit the United States. In 1975, Brazil became the first Western power to recognize the MPLA regime in newly independent Angola (the United States favored UNITA). On the other hand, Brazil followed the U.S. lead and established diplomatic relations with the People's Republic of China. In 1977, Brazil forced Uruguay to cancel the political asylum it had granted to Leonel Brizola in 1964, and immediately President Carter offered Brizola asylum in the United States.

Geisel completed his last year in office (1978) with two "successful" elections—that of his successor, Gen. João Batista Figueiredo, and of ARENA majorities in the congress that took office in February 1979. Neither victory was easy. In 1974, Geisel had named Figueiredo, then a two-star general, to head the SNI (National Information Service). He had served as chief of military household under President Médici (1969–1974) and together with Geisel on the senior staff of President Castelo Branco. To ready Figueiredo as candidate for the fifth and last military presidency, Geisel had to bend Army promotion rules and pass over several more senior generals to promote his *in pectore* candidate to the fourth star by early 1978. This accomplished, the docile ARENA majority in the electoral college duly elected Figueiredo to the presidency and the civilian governor of Minas Gerais, Aureliano Chaves, as vice president.

The April Package of alterations of the electoral system for 1978 helped produce the ARENA majorities, especially in the senate. These changes had little effect on the election of federal deputies, accruing perhaps four additional seats for ARENA. In the case of the senate, however, without these modifications (appointed—"bionic"—senators and the creation of three new seats from the new state of Mato Grosso do Sul), in the best of hypotheses, the MDB would have eked out a thirty-three to thirty-one senate majority. The "Package" delivered a forty-two to twenty-five majority to ARENA—in spite of a 46 percent versus 35 percent plurality vote favoring the MDB. The national vote for the chamber was evenly split, ARENA with 39.9 percent and MDB with 39.4 percent. However, the regional inequalities of state delegations produced a 231-to-189 majority for the military government support party. The MDB counted 45 percent of the deputies, quite similar to the 45.3 percent in 1974.[20]

General Figueiredo was sworn in to a six-year term in March 1979 but without the AI–5 exceptional powers that had been abolished by Geisel two months earlier. Golbery continued as chief of staff. The hard-line radicals who had been muffled by Geisel in 1977 again began to agitate military opinion and carried out several bombings of newspaper stands, the Brazilian Bar Association (OAB) headquarters in Rio de Janeiro, and the Riocentro convention center. In the latter attempt, an army captain was badly injured and a sergeant was killed. However, the new government made some significant positive changes in 1979: The social security system was modified; a two-way amnesty was voted by Congress; the end of the two-party system was approved by Congress in late 1979; direct elections for governor were set for 1982; new legislation benefited renters; a two-year extension of the mandates of mayors and city councils elected in 1976 was enacted; amnesty was granted to purged labor union leaders; and biannual salary readjustments were made. As a result, most exiles began to return to Brazil after September 1979—including Leonel Brizola.

The two-party system had been useful to the military government, but after the economic downturn and the results of the 1974 and 1978 elections this mechanism became a straight jacket. All discontent (even among business leaders) was channeled into support for the single opposition party (MDB).

Government strategists thought that, with the creation of a moderately plural party system having five or six parties, the government would have more room for maneuver in Congress, to negotiate its proposals and build party coalitions. ARENA was more or less transformed into the Social Democratic Party (PDS), but with a slight reduction from 231 to 225 deputies. The MDB became the PMDB, but was split in half (reduced from 189 to 94 deputies). A new center, swing party, Popular Party (PP), was organized with sixty-eight deputies that on occasion could ally with the PDS. Finally, the old PTB was resurrected with twenty-three deputies and the Workers' Party (PT) was organized with five deputies. However, in May 1980, the Electoral Court (TSE) allocated the PTB label to Ivette Vargas (niece of Getúlio Vargas), and Leonel Brizola was forced to split and form his own Democratic Labor Party (PDT).

The extra two years for local officials' mandates again synchronized local and general elections for November 1982. This change was necessitated because in 1980 the new political parties were still being organized, and it was thought that concurrent elections would benefit the new military government party—PDS. This move reversed the decision by the military government in 1969 that set municipal elections two years out of phase in 1972 and 1976.

In September 1981, President Figueiredo suffered a serious heart attack in Rio de Janeiro. His doctors recommended total rest with no political activity and, after he was stabilized, open-heart bypass surgery. Some of his advisers wanted a "Reagan solution" whereby the vice president would not assume the presidency and Figueiredo would govern from his hospital room. When the doctors countered that this alternative would quickly kill him, Chief of Staff Leitão de Abreu reminded the president's staff that the "Costa e Silva solution" had not worked in 1969 and that they must allow Vice President Aureliano Chavez to occupy the presidency—if not, some general would take over; "they" (the Figueiredo advisers) would be out; and even though Figueiredo might recover, he would not return to the presidency. Chaves was duly sworn in as acting president for two months. Figueiredo had successful bypass surgery in Cleveland and reassumed the presidency in mid-November—in time to sign the creation of the new state of Rondônia to further reinforce the PDS majority in the senate after the 1982 elections.

However, SNI research discovered that the PDS would have great difficulties in the November 1982 elections, in spite of the inclusion of municipal elections, because of coalition building already under way. Thus, in December 1981, the Figueiredo government again altered the election rules, as his four predecessors had done so many times. Voters were to use a tied, straight-ticket ballot (obliged to vote for candidates of the same party for all offices), coalitions were prohibited, and the parties had to run full tickets and not leave the top of the ticket (governor and/or senator) vacant. In October, Congress had already defeated an attempt to adopt "sub-lists" for senator and governor that could have helped unify the diverse PDS factions. As a result, leaders of the PP felt that these rule changes had severely limited their party's electoral chances. Thus, in early 1982, they abruptly abolished the party and merged with the PMDB.[21] In June 1982, Congress approved a government-sponsored amendment that altered the date and composition of the next electoral college, permitted a short period of party switching, and returned the quorum for constitutional amendment to a two-thirds majority. The latter change was in anticipation that the PDS would lose its absolute majority in the Chamber.

1984–1985: Political Transition and Transaction

This election strategy (a bottom-up "coattails" effect) functioned well with the "tied ballot" in the Northeast region where all nine states elected PDS governors and senators. However, in the other regions, where voters were freer from oligarchic tutelage, the coattails effect was top-down; the PMDB elected nine governors and the PDT elected Leonel Brizola governor of the state of Rio de Janeiro. As a result of the "tied" effect, the PMDB elected a large number of mayors in these states. The PDS maintained a 46-to-23 majority in the senate, but lost its absolute majority in the lower house, 235 out of 479 deputies (49.1 percent). Through an unstable coalition with the thirteen PTB deputies, the government eked out 51.8 percent majority.

As the nomination phase for the electoral college approached in mid-1984, the PDS suffered pre-election tensions with several pre-candidates, the most important being Vice President Aureliano Chaves, Interior Minister (retired Army colonel) Mário Andreazza, and former São Paulo Governor Paulo Salim Maluf. In April, an absolute majority of the Chamber of Deputies approved a constitutional amendment calling for direct presidential elections in November 1984, but was short by twenty-one votes of the necessary two-thirds majority. When President Figueiredo abruptly vetoed the idea of a PDS presidential primary (that Chaves probably would have won), a dissident PDS faction (the Liberal Front) declared its independence by supporting the PMDB candidate, Minas Gerais Governor Tancredo Neves, and supplying his running mate—former PDS national president, Senator José Sarney from Maranhão—forming the "Democratic Alliance" ticket. To become a candidate, Sarney was obliged to join the PMDB. Paulo Maluf eventually was nominated in the PDS national convention for the January 15, 1985, electoral college. The June 1982 amendment had changed this body's composition such that each state would now have six delegates (in addition to its deputies and senators) and the 1982 elections had produced a 359 out of 680 (52.3 percent) majority. With the "party loyalty" law, it was thought that Maluf would be easily elected; but that was not to be. The Tancredo–Sarney ticket campaigned vigorously and attracted many PDS governors, senators, deputies, and delegates, especially from states in the Northeast. The Army high command communicated an informal *nihil obstat* (no objection) vis-à-vis the "Democratic Alliance." Finally, in November 1984, the Supreme Court ruled that the party loyalty law did not apply to the electoral college, thus facilitating an avalanche in favor of the opposition candidates. The PMDB ticket was elected by a 480-to-180 margin over the PDS candidate.[22]

Tancredo assumed several commitments on his route to the presidency and in the constitution of his new government. First, he established pacts with Aureliano Chaves and Ulysses Guimarães in early 1984. With the latter (PMDB pact), it was agreed that if the direct elections amendment passed, Guimarães would be the ideal PMDB candidate; if not, Neves would be the better candidate in the indirect election. With Chaves (Minas Gerais pact), it was agreed that whichever politician achieved the nomination of his respective party, the other *mineiro* would close ranks within their state in support of the successful candidate. Neves also established hundreds of commitments with politicians from the PMDB and other parties regarding public policies, appointments and pork-barrel politics after his inauguration on March 15, 1985. Most of the latter were oral agreements made during one-on-one conversations. His cabinet, announced in late January, was an eclectic patchwork of leaders from nearly all parties and factions and included his nephew, Francisco Dornelles, as finance minister.

Unfortunately, Tancredo was never sworn in, having taken ill on March 14, the eve of his inauguration. He was quickly admitted to the central Brasília hospital with severe diverticulitis (intestinal blockage by adherences). The surgery resulted in an infection and blood poisoning (septicemia). He was operated on three additional times and transferred to a São Paulo hospital, but where he would die on April 21. But on March 14 the question remained—who should be sworn in as president? Some interpreted the constitution to read that the president of the Lower House, Deputy Ulysses Guimarães (PMDB), should become acting president for sixty days, and if Tancredo became incapacitated (or died) new elections should be convoked by the electoral college. Most thought that this solution would be unacceptable to the military. Supreme Court judges suggested that José Sarney be sworn in as vice president and temporarily occupy the presidency until Tancredo recovered. This alternative was accepted, but outgoing President Figueiredo refused to "pass the presidential sash" to Sarney and left the Alvorada palace by the back door.

Thus, José Sarney assumed the presidency for what was to be a six-year term. He came under considerable military tutelage—the two key generals who had articulated the *nihil obstat* in the army high command in late 1984, Leonidas Pires Gonçalves and Ivan de Sousa Mendes, had been named army minister and chief of the SNI, respectively, by Tancredo Neves. Sarney was also under tutelage by many PMDB leaders who never really accepted him in the party, much less as Tancredo's successor. Soon, Sarney was besieged by politicians asking him to honor the "commitments" that Neves had supposedly made with them. The Liberal Front faction that had split off from the PDS organized the Liberal Front Party (PFL) in early 1985 and quickly absorbed many party switchers. By mid-1985, the Democratic Alliance counted 199 PMDB and 100 PFL deputies. In mid-1986, the count was 222 and 127, respectively. On the other hand, this party migration in the Lower House reduced the former military support party (PDS) considerably—from 235 elected in 1983 to 135 in mid-1985, sixty-eight in mid-1986, and only thirty-five seated in the National Constituent Assembly (ANC) in February 1987.

In May 1985, Congress approved several measures to advance the process of re-democratization: direct elections for president were adopted; illiterates were allowed to vote; the party system was "unchained," allowing the formation of new parties, including the communist PCB and PCdoB; a National Constituent Assembly (ANC) was to be elected in 1986 and convened in 1987; and direct elections were set for November 15, 1985, in towns and cities that still had "bionic" mayors held over from the military regime. Inflation was becoming a serious problem and in August 1985, Sarney replaced Dornelles at finance with business leader Dilson Funaro. The new minister recruited a group of young economists to prepare a novel stabilization plan for 1986.

CONSTITUENT ASSEMBLY AND DIRECT ELECTIONS

The initial strategy of this task force was altered in February 1986, following Sarney's cabinet reshuffle, which was considered "conservative" by PMDB leaders. Sarney ordered economists to quickly devise a crash stabilization plan to reinforce his legitimacy, and thus the Cruzado Plan was born on February 28, 1986. This plan consisted of a wage-price freeze that corrected salaries from their last readjustment and greatly stimulated consumer buying power and demand. Sarney's popularity soared and the PMDB joined this new bandwagon. GDP growth was quite strong in the first two years of the Sarney period—8.3 percent in 1985 and 8.0 percent in 1986. The stabilization plan became a powerful election tool and enabled the PMDB to elect all but one governor in the November 1986 elections, giving the party an absolute majority—302 (257 deputies and 45 senators) out of a total of 559—54.0 percent in the 1987 National Constituent Assembly. Not since the PSD elected 54.1 percent of the 1946 ANC members had one party held an absolute majority in Congress.

The ANC labored diligently until September 1988 and produced a new, "from scratch" constitution. Final log rolling left some 300 points for posterior "regulation" that has hampered policy makers ever since. While the new *Carta Magna* was considered liberal in the areas of political and social rights, it was considered conservative or status quo in the section dealing with the economic order and it reinforced the role of the state in the economy, the role of state enterprises, and central planning. The ANC rejected a parliamentary system, reduced Sarney's mandate to five years, and introduced the *medida provisória* (provisional measure-MP), a modification of the decree-law concept that went into effect immediately. The progressive group that had produced the first draft of the new constitution was superseded by a new conservative "Big Center" (*Centrão*) majority and was able to reverse the content of some of the articles on the second round item-by-item votes.[23] To placate the supporters of the parliamentary system, the ANC determined that a plebiscite would be held five years (1993) after the promulgation of the new constitution to decide Brazil's system of government—presidential or parliamentary republic, or a constitutional monarchy. Unfortunately (some remembered retrospectively), the ANC had finished its work prior to the fall of the Berlin Wall (1989), German reunification (1990), and the subsequent demise of the socialist systems in Eastern Europe—followed by major changes in the world economic order.[24]

In anticipation of the November 1988 municipal elections, a progressive faction in the PMDB splintered in June 1988 to form the PSDB (Brazilian Social Democratic Party) along the lines of the Western European Social Democratic parties—with forty deputies and eight senators. By 1989, the party counted fifty deputies, and by 1990, sixty. However, after the 1990 elections, the PSDB was reduced to thirty-eight deputies and ten senators, with one governor—Tasso Jereissati (Ceará).[25] The PMDB also lost deputies to other parties in the 1988–1990 period, and was reduced from 257 elected in 1986 to 108 in 1990—similar to the fate of the PSD after the 1946 constituent assembly. In these elections, the PT more than doubled its representation from sixteen elected in 1986 to thirty-five in 1990.

Brazil's first direct elections for president after 1960 were scheduled for November 15, 1989, and twenty-two parties fielded candidates. The PMDB chose the president of the ANC, Deputy Ulysses Guimarães; the PFL ran former Vice President Aureliano Chaves; the PDT chose former governor Leonel Brizola, while the PT selected its charismatic metalworkers labor union leader, Luiz Inácio *Lula* da Silva.[26] However, a little-known governor from Alagoas, Fernando Collor de Mello, organized the PRN (Party of National Renovation) in early 1989 and with a very flashy media campaign took the lead as an "anti-party" candidate, in a style reminiscent of Jânio Quadros in 1960. Collor received 30.48 percent of the valid vote on the first round, followed by Lula with 17.19 percent and Brizola with 16.51 percent. The PT candidate had edged Brizola out of the second round by some 455,000 votes. The ANC had imposed the absolute-majority concept on Brazilian elections for executive office, so Collor and Lula disputed the second round runoff on December 17. Collor was victorious over Lula by 49.9 percent to 44.2 percent.[27]

The Collor Disaster and Impeachment

President Collor was sworn in on March 15, 1990, and immediately issued a series of MPs that imposed a heterodox stabilization plan whereby all financial liquidity (over a certain minimum) was confiscated, held by the government for eighteen months and then dribbled out to the owners in twelve monthly payments with a below par monetary correction. This desperate operation was an effort to stem Brazil's inflation, which was running at about 90 percent per month. GDP growth in the final part of the Sarney presidency had declined considerably: 2.9 percent in 1987, 0.0 percent in 1988, and 3.6 percent in 1989. The "Collor Plan" indeed stabilized prices quickly and inflation dropped below zero (deflation). The U.S. dollar exchange rate dropped from Cr$ 84,00 to Cr$ 40,00 in two days. However, this stabilization plan lacked the staying power of the Cruzado Plan in 1986, so that before the November 15, 1990, elections the initial effects had dissipated into economic stagnation. Collor attempted a disorganized modernization of Brazil by: consolidating and reducing the number of cabinet ministries, extinguishing twenty-four state enterprises, sacking many public servants, raising taxes on industrial and agricultural production, beginning a privatization program for state firms, deregulating markets, and liberalizing trade with successive reductions in import levies and quotas. These efforts were in harmony with the main lines of the so-called *Consensus of Washington*. However, Collor's popular approval rating declined from 71 percent in February 1990 to 34 percent by September, seven months later. Inflation had returned and in December 1990 reached 20 percent per month. The Collor Plan caused a strong recession in 1990, as GDP declined by 4.2 percent and then stagnated in 1991 and 1992.[28]

The November 1990 elections did not produce a majority in congress for Collor's support coalition. Collor's group counted 170 deputies (34 percent) as follows: PRN (40), PFL (82), PTB (38), PTR (4), and PSC (6). The opposition was led by the PMDB (108), PSDB (37), PDT (47) and PT (35). In 1990, Collor tried to induce the PSDB to join his coalition and offered several cabinet positions, including foreign minister (Senator Fernando Henrique Cardoso). The PSDB refused this overture, as did several other parties.

In early 1992, an avalanche of corruption accusations culminated in a long denunciation in a *Veja* magazine interview in late May with his younger brother, Pedro Collor, that revealed extensive bag-man bribe operations. A Congressional Investigating Committee (CPI) was installed in June. Finally, the lower house approved the suspension of President Collor's mandate in late September (on an open, televised roll-call vote), just four days before the municipal elections; the senate then deliberated his impeachment. Finally, on December 30, 1992, Fernando Collor was impeached (the first such case in a democratic presidential system) by another open roll-call vote in the senate and his political rights were suspended for eight years.[29]

THE ITAMAR FRANCO INTERIM

Collor's vice president, former PMDB Senator Itamar Franco (Minas Gerais), became interim president in late September and president de jure in late December 1992 to complete the remainder of Collor's term through December 1994. He assembled his first cabinet based on many of his former senate colleagues, including Senator Fernando Henrique Cardoso (São Paulo) who became foreign minister. The problem of how to reactivate the stagnating economy plagued Itamar during the first seven months of his government. After a sequence of four finance ministers, and strengthened by the April 21 national plebiscite that reaffirmed Brazil as a presidential republic, on May 21 Franco named F. H. Cardoso to the finance ministry. Cardoso proceeded to recruit a team of top economists who elaborated new policies to stimulate GDP growth (4.9 percent in 1993) and develop a strategy for a different type of stabilization plan.

Nearly one year after the Chamber of Deputies had voted Collor's impeachment, in October 1993 the so-called *Budgetgate* crisis erupted in Brasília. Testimony by the former chief of staff of the Joint Budget Committee in Congress revealed a complex conspiracy to rig the budget for construction projects. A CPI was installed and discovered that: 1) the committee leaders made sure that these items remained in the budget; 2) key executive branch staff arranged the inclusion of these items in the budget proposal and assured the intended result of each procurement bid; and 3) the cartel of these firms designated the "winner" and "loser" for each contract.

The CPI filed its report in January 1994 and recommended the sacking of several of the deputies and senators involved. The senate declined to take action against its members, but the chamber expelled eight deputies and absolved twelve. Another four opted to resign. New procedures for budget elaboration by Congress were suggested.[30]

The *Real Plan* Elects Cardoso

In March 1994, Finance Minister Cardoso and his economic team launched the new stabilization plan, based on the Reference Value Unit (URV), which became the price and wage reference unit. Every day the currency value of the URV was adjusted. Congress approved the Emergency Social Fund (FSE) that allowed the government to impound (and/or transfer) up to 20 percent of constitutional bloc grants in order to reduce the fiscal deficit. After four months of price-wage alignments by the URV, this unit was converted into the new Real currency unit on July 1, 1994, at the final rate of Cr$2.750,00 to each URV/Real. A total new currency (bills and coins) had been manufactured with the assistance of government mints in the United States and Europe. Brazil's GDP expanded by 5.9 percent in 1994, and annual inflation declined from 916.5 percent in 1994 to 22.4 percent in 1995.[31]

However, Cardoso was no longer finance minister when the Real Plan was launched, for in April he had stepped down to become a PSDB presidential candidate in the October 1994 elections. At that point, inflation was still rampant. For this reason, the PT candidate (Lula) was leading public opinion and had reached 42 percent in the *Datafolha* poll conducted in early May, versus only 16 percent for Cardoso. However, by mid-July (two weeks after the Real Plan was launched), popular preferences were 34 percent versus 25 percent. In early August, Cardoso was leading 36 percent to 29 percent, and by the end of September, Cardoso led by 47 percent to Lula's 23 percent. In the October 3 election, Cardoso achieved a first-round victory with 54.3 percent of the valid vote, and Lula trailed with 27 percent. The *Real Plan* had propelled Cardoso into the presidency.

The 1994 elections confirmed the PMDB as the largest party in Congress— 107 deputies and 22 senators, followed by the PFL (89 deputies and 19 senators). President Cardoso's party (PSDB) enhanced its chamber delegation vis-à-vis the 1990 elections, from thirty-eight to sixty-two deputies, but remained at ten senators. The PT increased from thirty-five to forty-nine deputies. Cardoso's election alliance (PSDB-PFL-PTB) counted 182 deputies (35.5 percent). To achieve an absolute majority, Cardoso's support coalition in the chamber needed to be expanded. Moving to the Left was numerically impossible, and so Cardoso moved his support locus to the right to include the PMDB (107), the PDS (53), and the PP (36), giving him a comfortable 378 (73.7 percent) majority.

Although the Real Plan had stabilized inflation and elected Cardoso in 1994, in spite of the FSE control of revenue transfers to state and municipal governments, the federal deficit continued to expand due to state enterprises and the social security system. For this reason, Cardoso's top priority in 1995 was reform of the economic order section in the 1988 constitution to permit further privatizations and restructuring of the economy. In rapid sequence, congress approved constitutional amendments to permit privatization of the telecommunications and electric sectors, gas distribution, and coastal and river shipping. The main jewels among Brazil's state enterprises were privatized—CSN-Steel (1994), CVRD-Mining (1997), and Telebrás (1998)—plus most of the state-government-owned electric generation and distribution systems and state-owned banks. The revenues from these privatizations helped reduce federal deficits somewhat in lieu of further reforms (fiscal/tax, social security and administration).[32]

However, Cardoso made some advances in administrative reform and attempted social security reforms. In 1998 and 1999, congress passed a social security reform package that would have reduced the deficit caused by benefits paid out to retired public servants—but the supreme court declared this unconstitutional. Several attempts by congress to approve tax/fiscal reform packages were derailed by Cardoso's finance minister, Pedro Malan. Finally, after much debate, congress approved the Fiscal Responsibility Law in April 2000, which imposed severe penalties (including jail terms) for governors and mayors who over-spent their budgeted revenues. In 1997 and 1998, Minister Malan negotiated debt consolidation packages with each Brazilian state government. The federal government assumed the public debts of each state to be paid off in thirty years at 6 percent a.a., with monthly installments of up to 13 percent of the state's revenues.

Former President Itamar Franco was conveniently removed from Brazilian politics when President Cardoso appointed him ambassador to Portugal and then to the OAS in Washington, D.C. However, in 1998, he returned to Brazil to run for president. In 1997, after considerable pressures and arm-twisting, congress approved the reelection amendment allowing presidents, governors, and mayors to be elected to a second consecutive term. Thus, Cardoso could stand for re-election in the October 1998 elections. At that time, Itamar Franco was a member of the PMDB, and in two national conventions (March and June 1998) the party decided not to field a presidential candidate, nor to support any other party's candidate that year. Itamar was offered the PMDB candidacy for governor of Minas Gerais as a consolation prize that he grudgingly accepted, and he was duly elected. However, in early January 1999, Itamar's comeuppance was devastating. In his first week in office, Governor Itamar Franco suspended payments of some his state's foreign loans, which produced a run on Brazil's currency and forced Cardoso to intervene in the Central Bank to free-float the real with a devaluation of some 60 percent. The new governor of Rio Grande do Sul, Olívio Dutra, (PT) followed Itamar's lead. Finance Minister Malan wrote letters to the World Bank and Interamerican Development Bank withdrawing federal cover of loan operations with these states and immediately both institutions suspended all loan disbursements. Dutra quickly capitulated, but Itamar stubbornly held out for a few months.[33]

Enhanced by the *Real Plan*, Cardoso's PSDB made big gains in the 1996 municipal elections. Having elected 317 mayors in 1992, the party's so-called *tucanos* nearly tripled this number to 917 in 1996. From this expanded municipal base, the PSDB was able to increase its chamber delegation from 62 to 99 deputies in the 1998 elections.[34] Cardoso's reelection was relatively tranquil in 1998, with 53 percent of the valid vote. This time, the PT and PDT formed a coalition, with Leonel Brizola as Lula's running mate, and they polled 31.7 percent of the valid vote. This team more or less repeated the sum of the vote totals each had received in 1994 (PT 27% plus PDT 3.2% = 30.2%). The former Ceará PSDB governor, Ciro Gomes, who became Itamar Franco's last finance minister in 1994, ran on the PPS-Popular Socialist Party (former PCB) ticket in 1997 and received 11 percent of the valid vote.

The PSDB elected seven governors and the PFL and PMDB three each. The opposition elected six governors—PT (three), PSB (two), and PDT (one). The PMDB increased its senate delegation to twenty-seven, the PSDB expanded to sixteen, and the PFL remained at nineteen, while the PT-PDT-PSB-PPS bloc to the left totaled fifteen. In the lower house, the PMDB declined to eighty-three, and the PFL (105) and PSDB (99) gained deputies. The left bloc elected 112, led by the PT with fifty-nine deputies. Of the twenty-seven governors, twenty-two ran for re-election, but only fifteen were victorious, and the elections in thirteen states went to a second round. For the first time, a 25 percent quota for women candidates for deputy was used. In spite of this "advantage," only twenty-nine women (5.7 percent) were elected to the chamber versus thirty-four (6.6 percent) in 1994 without the quotas.

Cardoso's legislative initiatives in his second term were less successful than in his first. In part this was due to a burgeoning list of scandals that threatened to affect some governors, senators and deputies. Finally, in 2000, for the first time in Brazilian history, a senator was sanctioned by his peers, and later in 2001 three others decided to resign rather than be sacked. All three of the latter were reelected in 2002 (one to the senate, and two as federal deputies). In late 2001, the election court removed the governor of Piauí for violations of election laws in 1998, but he was elected to the senate in 2002. Also, the impact of the Real Plan on the economy had declined as GDP growth slowed in 2001 and 2002, following the electric sector crisis and blackouts in May 2001.[35]

The left made further gains in the 2000 municipal elections. The PMDB (1,257), PFL (1,028), and PSDB (990) made modest gains over their performance in 1996. The PT elected 187 mayors, including that of Brazil's largest city of São Paulo. The left advanced in urban Brazil and captured forty-nine of the hundred largest cities (compared to Thirty-two in 1996), as well as twelve of the twenty-six state capitals (eight in 1996). To a certain extent, these results were cues for what would happen in the 2002 general elections.[36]

2002: LULA WINS THE PRESIDENCY

In late 2001 and early 2002, the PT's perennial candidate, Lula, was again leading in the polls, as he had in 1994—before the Real Plan was introduced. However, 2002 would not have another such stabilization plan and the 1994/1998 Cardoso coalition was disorganized. The PFL had left the Cardoso support bloc and his cabinet in 2001, and in March 2002, severed all links with the PSDB because of the implosion of the pre-candidacy of the PFL governor of Maranhão—Roseana Sarney, the daughter of former president José Sarney. Different from 1994 and 1998, the PFL decided not to run any presidential candidate or support any other candidate in coalition. The PSDB chose Senator José Serra (SP) and then began organizing a coalition with the PMDB. With great difficulty, PMDB leaders were able to force approval of this linkage in late June at the party's national convention and selected Deputy Rita Camata (ES) as Serra's running mate. However, many state sections of the PMDB rejected this alliance and threw their informal support to Lula.

The PT, on the other hand, understood that it needed a different strategy for the 2002 race, and proceeded to move to the center. First, Lula's party concluded a coalition with the more conservative PL (Liberal Party) that chose a self-made businessman, Senator José Alencar from Minas Gerais, as Lula's running mate. Second, the PT reached out to progressive business leaders for financial and political support. Third, the party drafted a "Letter to Brazilians" explaining its policy objectives for the 2003–2006 period in quite a realistic and moderate proposal—quite different from past PT platforms.

The PPS again ran Ciro Gomes, but this time in coalition with the PTB (which had supported Cardoso in 1994 and 1998) and the PDT (which had supported Lula in 1998). Finally, the PSB (Brazilian Socialist Party) governor of Rio de Janeiro, Anthony Garotinho, stepped down to become a presidential candidate, with considerable support from evangelical Protestants.

Coalition building in 2002 was more complicated than in 1994 and 1998, because, in February 2002, the TSE (Election Court) imposed the concept of "verticalization of coalitions" that obliged parties to maintain the same coalitions for governor that they had joined for president. That meant, for example, that the PSDB-PMDB presidential coalition would be replicated in all twenty-seven elections for state governor. Of the major parties, only the PFL and the PPB (which did not participate in any presidential election coalition) were free to join any state coalition they desired. Initially, it was thought that this TSE decision would favor the PSDB candidate, but the election results proved otherwise.

In the October 6 first round, Lula came close to an outright victory with 46.4 percent of the valid vote versus 23.2 percent for Serra, 17.9 percent for Garotinho, and 12 percent for Ciro Gomes (equal to his 1998 result). Three weeks later, Lula obtained a resounding victory in the runoff election—62.5 percent of the valid vote. Like Salvador Allende in Chile and François Mitterrand in France, Lula was finally elected on his fourth attempt.

The parties that had been allied with Cardoso fared well in the races for governor, but their base declined in Congress. The PSDB elected seven governors, the PMDB five, and the PFL four. On the left, the PT gained three governorships, the PSB four, the PDT one, and the PSB two. In the senate, the PMDB was reduced from twenty-seven to nineteen, the PFL was steady at nineteen, and the PSDB declined from sixteen to eleven, while the PT doubled its delegation from seven to fourteen. In the lower house, the Cardoso support group declined considerably, the PFL from one hundred five to eighty-four, the PMDB from eighty-three to seventy-five, and the PSDB from ninety-nine to seventy-one. Capitalizing on its gains in the 2000 municipal elections and on Lula's 2002 coattails, the PT delegation jumped from fifty-nine to ninety-one deputies to become the largest delegation—allowing Lula's party to elect the president of the lower house in February 2003. Many thought that these results forebode profound reforms and changes for economic and social policies in Brazil—but they were mistaken.[37]

2003–2004: "Dreaming the Wrong Dream"

Twenty-two years after it had been organized, the Workers' Party finally achieved national political power with Lula was president. The pent-up election anxieties and vocations for political power climaxed with the inauguration of Lula and Alencar on January 1, 2003. However, during the transition in November and December 2002, President-elect Lula initiated a series of "heresies" that surprised many PT militants. Most expected Lula to quickly abandon his 2002 campaign rhetoric and revert to the PT's original policy objectives— reverse the privatizations, adopt developmentalist economic policy, enhance state participation in the economy, and so forth.

The first "heresy" involved Lula's choice for Central Bank president, a key appointment aimed at restoring the confidence of the international financial community. The choice fell to the former Bank of Boston CEO, Henrique Meirelles, who had just been elected federal deputy by the PSDB in Goiás. He promptly resigned his seat and his membership in the PSDB, and Lula requested President Cardoso to send the nomination to the senate so that it could be approved before the Christmas recess.

The second disappointment for the PT militants was the appointment of former PT Mayor of Ribeirão Preto, SP, Antônio Palocci Filho, to be finance minister. A medical doctor by training, Palocci had been Lula's campaign manager in 2002. He quipped to the press, "You say Brazil's economy is in the Intensive Care Unit, so Lula chose a doctor to cure the patient." Although the PT has a number of militants who are trained economists, Palocci set Finance off limits and none were recruited for the economic team.

The third heresy that went against all past PT demands was the continuation of the fifteen-month emergency agreement that Cardoso and Malan had signed with the IMF in August 2002. For twenty years the PT had ranted against the IMF and its policies as highly detrimental to Brazil.

The fourth heresy was announced at the new government's first cabinet meeting in January 2003—a continuation of the Cardoso fiscal austerity modus operandi with a R$14 billion cut in the 2003 budget. Stricter fiscal targets were adopted (the primary surplus goal was upped from Cardoso's 3.75 percent to 4.35 percent of GDP) and the Central Bank monetary policy committee quickly increased the basic interest rate to 26.5 percent a.a.

The fifth heresy was announced in February—a major social security reform that aimed at reduction of the massive deficits in the public sector, where employees were allowed to retire at full salary. Traditionally, public servants had been staunch PT supporters and now they felt "their" PT had betrayed them. This reform was eventually approved by congress in December; it placed caps on public salaries and retirement benefits and imposed a new model on all new entrants to the public service as of 2004 (limited benefits and a parallel private pension fund arrangement).

The final 2003 "heresies" involved the construction of the Lula support base in congress in 2003. The coalition that had supported Lula on the second round run-off against Serra (PT, PL, PCdoB, PPS, PTB, PDT and PSB) had elected 218 deputies (42.5 percent) and 31 senators (38.3 percent) in October 2002. Thus, comfortable absolute majorities had to be constructed. Lula's chief of staff, Deputy José Dirceu (SP), and his operatives began this task, and before the newly elected deputies were sworn in on February 1, 2003, the Lula bloc could count 252 deputies (49.1 percent). These party migrants were attracted away from the PFL (eight), PSDB (seven), PMDB (five) and PPB (five). The PT did not accept any of these "joiners," who were channeled to the PTB (up fifteen), PL (up seven), PSB (up six), and PPS (up six). By the time Lula submitted the social security and tax reforms to Congress on April 30, the PMDB and the PPB had joined the Lula bloc, which swelled to 370 deputies (72.1 percent) and 53 senators (65.4 percent). The PPB is the party of the eternal anathema of the PT—Paulo Maluf. In four months, the Lula team had achieved nearly the same-sized congressional coalition that Cardoso had assembled in 1995. This and other comparisons led some critics to call the Lula government "Cardoso's third term." Newspaper cartoons depicted Lula and Cardoso fighting over the agenda.

Lula chose his cabinet ministers from the coalition allies with a predominance of the PT, concentrated in São Paulo and Rio Grande do Sul. Several defeated PT candidates (for governor and senator) were rewarded with cabinet appointments. Lula's first-round adversary, Ciro Gomes, became minister of national integration. In late January 2004, Lula processed his first cabinet reshuffle. The PMDB had supported all the reform and legislative packages in 2003 and finally received two cabinet posts. Three social promotion posts were consolidated into a new Social Development Ministry; other ministers were switched or removed. However, in mid-February the first of a series of scandals erupted and the Lula government was thrown into turmoil. The chief of congressional relations was accused of taking bribes from numbers racket operators and attempting to intermediate certain contract renewals. In the process of the scandal, the Lula bloc lost its majority in the senate, as five PT senators and three PL senators left the coalition. The government lost key votes—the new minimum wage, outlawing bingo games, and an amendment to allow the re-election of the presidents of the senate and chamber of deputies. In early May, the *New York Times* published an article questioning the impact of Lula's excessive "tippling".[38] The president reacted angrily and ordered the correspondent's visa revoked. Cooler heads prevailed subsequently and the order was rescinded. Later, at the end of June, the *New York Times Magazine* published a long cover story about Lula, his origins, political ascent, and presidency.[39]

Conclusions

Rhetorically, the *NYT Magazine* story asked whether Lula was "Latin America's Last Leftist Leader?" More likely, Brazil's PT president is neither the first nor last national leader from a left-socialist political party to assume power only to enact neoliberal policies and reforms that his more conservative predecessors were unable to accomplish. This was the case of French Socialist François Mitterrand (1981), Spanish Socialist Felipe Gonzalez (1983), and Polish labor leader Lech Walesa (1990). At the end of the terms of these three leaders, more conservative parties returned to power. Two South American presidents elected by parties characterized as leftist or progressive were having difficulties in mid-2004: Alejandro Toledo (Peru) and Lucio Gutiérrez (Ecuador). On the other hand, President Ricardo Lagos was faring better in Chile. Lula himself has several times declared "I am not, nor have I ever been, a socialist or a leftist." By comparison Professor Fernando Henrique Cardoso followed a similar sequence. He began his academic career at the University of São Paulo in the late 1950s as a Marxist, evolved into a progressive social democrat in the Senate after 1983, and finally enacted so-called neoliberal reforms as president (1995–2002).

The policies, programs, and reforms introduced by President Lula in 2003 and 2004 led PT deputy Fernando Gabeira (RJ) to abandon the party in October 2003 and declare "I was dreaming the wrong dream."[40] During the crucial rounds of voting on the social security reform in 2003, a small group of PT deputies agreed with Gabeira and either voted against parts of the reform, abstained, or were absent. In mid-December 2003, three PT deputies and one senator were expelled from the party by its national executive committee. In mid-2004, twelve senators from parties in the Lula coalition declared themselves "independent" of government directives.

Once in power, the PT quickly discovered the hard and difficult political and economic restraints on governing. Its leaders complained about the "negative inheritance" received from the Cardoso presidency. The ensuing austerity policies enacted by the PT in 2003 constricted the economy, unemployment increased, average wages declined, and Brazil's GDP shrunk by 0.2 percent. On the other hand, the former government parties (PFL and PSDB) had difficulties adjusting to their new role as opposition, especially vis-à-vis Lula's social security reform proposal, which was very similar to what Cardoso had proposed and seen rejected by the Supreme Court.

Since the end of the military regime in 1985, Brazilian representative democracy has suffered considerable trials and tribulations—Tancredo Neves died on the eve of his inauguration; the first popularly elected president since 1960 was constitutionally impeached in 1992; several major congressional investigations shook the foundations of Brazil's political and economic institutions. Eleven elections and one plebiscite have been held since 1985; illiterates have been enfranchised; the voting age was reduced to sixteen; and some 65 percent of Brazilians are now eligible to vote. In mid-2004, the nation appears united and economically and politically stable, but Lula's presidency was seeing declining approval ratings after eighteen months in office. The questions remain—Will the PT and its allies expand their local base in the October 2004 municipal elections enough to repeat the 2000–2002 algorithm in the next general elections in 2006? Will enough additional political momentum be thus accumulated to boost Lula's re-election and with him even stronger majorities in Congress, in order to complete the cycle of reforms in Brazil?[41]

NOTES

1. *Folha de São Paulo,* October 15, 2003, p. A5.

2. The concept of the "Two Brazils" was first used by Jacques Lambert, *Os Dois Brasis* (Rio de Janeiro: INEP/CBPE, 1959). The concept of "contrasts" was applied by Roger Bastide, *Brésil Terre des Contrastes.* (Paris: L'Harmattan, 1957). For an extensive discussion of the "basic dualism of Brazilian society," see Helio Jaguaribe, *Alternativas do Brasil* (Rio de Janeiro: José Olympia Editora, 1989), chapter 2.

3. Edmar Bacha and Herbert S. Klein, eds., *Social Change in Brazil, 1945–1985: The Incomplete Transition* (Albuquerque, N.M.: University of New Mexico Press, 1989). For a treatment of Brazil's regional socioeconomic differences and their impact on the unequal distribution of political power before 1964, see: Glaucio Soares, *A Democracia Interrompida* (Rio de Janeiro: Fundação Getúlio Vargas, 2001), chapter 11.

4. Márcio Pochmann org. *Atlas da Riqueza no Brasil* (São Paulo: Editora Cortez, 2004). In 2000, the average monthly income of Brazilian families was R$1.608,59 (US$563.00).

5. For an analysis of this deadlock in the early 1960s, see: Glaucio Soares. *A Democracia Interrompida*, op. cit., chapters 12, 13 and 14; and Barry Ames, *Political Survival: Politicians and Public Policy in Latin America* (Berkeley: University of California Press, 1987).

6. See Élio Gaspari, *A Ditadura Envergonhada* (São Paulo: Companhia Das Letras, 2002), part 1; and René A. Dreifuss. *1964: A Conquista do Estado: Ação Política, Poder e Golpe* (Petrópolis: Editora Vozes, 1981).

7. Robert Wesson and David Fleischer, *Brazil in Transition* (New York: Praeger Press, 1983), pp. 103–105.

8. Maurice Duverger, *Les Partis Politiques* (Paris: Armand Colin, 1951).

9. Because the TV series *Bionic Woman* was popular in Brazil, persons indirectly elected to office were nicknamed "bionics."

10. For an analysis of this period, see: Élio Gaspari, *A Ditatura Envergonhada* (São Paulo: Companhia Das Letras, 2002), pp. 129–266.

11. For a description of this economic expansion phase, see Werner Baer, *The Brazilian Economy: Growth and Development* (New York: Praeger, 1989).

12. Ironically, the progressive left had called for the expropriation of foreign-owned public utilities in the early 1960s.

13. This episode is described in: Fernando Gabeira, *O que é isso, companheiro?* (Rio de Janeiro: Codecri, 1980), and the movie *Four Days in September*, released by Miramax films in 1997.

14. For an analysis of the "never-ending" sequence of election law changes in Brazil, see David Fleischer, "Political Reforms: Cardoso's Missing Link," in Mauricio Font ed. *Reforming Brazil*. (Lantham, Md.: Lexington Books, 2004), pp. 121–139. For an analysis of the regional inequalities in the Chamber of Deputies produced by the election system prior to 1964, see Glaucio Soares, *A Democracia Interropida*, op. cit., chapter. 12.

15. For a description of the tribulations of the MDB in the early 1970s, see Maria D'Alva Kinzo, *Legal Opposition Politics under Authoritarian Rule in Brazil—The Case of the MDB, 1966–1979* (London: Macmillian, 1988).

16. Geisel's own taped recollections of his presidency are found in Maria Celina D'Araujo and Celso Castro, orgs., *Ernesto Geisel* (Rio de Janeiro: Fundação Getúlio Vargas, 1997), pp. 255–415. For a broader analysis of this period, see Élio Gaspari, *A Ditatura Encurralada* (São Paulo: Companhia Das Letras, 2004).

17. For details regarding this MDB "victory," see Maria D'Alva Kinzo, *Legal Opposition Politics*, op. cit., and Sebastião Nery. *As 16 Derrotas que Abalaram o Brasil* (Rio de Janeiro: Francisco Alves, 1975).

18. Élio Gaspari, *A Ditatura Encurralada, pp. 407–481.*

19. Jan Knippers Black, *United States Penetration of Brazil.* (Philadelphia: University of Pennsylvania Press, 1977).

20. Maria D'Alva Kinzo, *Legal Opposition Politics.*

21. Wesson and Fleischer, *Brazil in Transition*, pp. 110–116.

22. The 1985 Electoral College sequence is described in David Fleischer, "Manipulações casuísticas do sistema eleitoral durante o período militar, ou como usualmente o feitiço se voltava contra o feiticeiro," in Soares and D'Araujo, eds., *21 Anos de Regime Militar* (Rio de Janeiro: Fundação Getúlio Vargas, 1994), pp. 188–194.

23. Maria D'Alva Kinzo, "O Quadro Partidário na Constituinte," *Revista Brasileira de Ciência Política* [Brasília], 1(1):91–123, 1989.

24. For analyses of the ANC, see: Xavier Martinez-Lara, *Building Democracy in Brazil: The Politics of Constitutional Change, 1985–1995* (London: Macmillian, 1996); Celina Maria de Souza, *Constitutional Engineering in Brazil: The Politics of Federalism and Decentralization*

(London: Macmillian, 1997); and Luiz Werneck Vianna. *A Transição: Da Constituinte à Sucessão Presidencial,* (Rio de Janeiro: Ed. Revan, 1989).

25. For the chronicle of the *tucano* party, see Jales Ramos Marques and David Fleischer, *PSDB: De Facção a Partido.* (Brasília: Instituto Teotonio Vilela, 1998). For an analysis of the *tucanos'* performance in the state of Ceará, see Judith Tendler, *Good Government in the Tropics* (Baltimore: Johns Hopkins University Press, 1996).

26. Margaret E. Keck, *The Workers' Party and Democratization in Brazil* (New Haven, Conn.: Yale University Press,1992).

27. Emir Sader and Ken Silverstein, *Without Fear of Being Happy: Lula, the Workers' Party and the 1989 Elections in Brazil* (New York: Verso Books, 1991).

28. For a review of economic policy in this period, see Edmund Amann, "Economic Policy and Performance in Brazil since 1985," in Maria D'Alva Kinzo and James Dunkerley, eds., *Brazil Since 1985* (London: ILAS/University of London, 2003), pp. 107–137.

29. A detailed anlaysis of the Collor impeachment is found in Keith S. Rosenn and Richard Downes, eds., *Corruption and Political Reform in Brazil: The Impact of Collor's Impeachment* (Coral Gables, Fla.: University of Miami Press, 1999).

30. For an analysis of *Budgetgate,* see David Fleischer, "Beyond Collorgate: Prospects for Consolidating Democracy in Brazil through Political Reform," in Rosenn and Downes, eds., *Corruption and Political Reform in Brazil,* pp. 49–71.

31. For a review of the Real Plan and its consequences, see Edmund Amann, "Economic Policy and Performance in Brazil Since 1985," in Kinzo and Dunkerley, eds. *Brazil since 1985,* pp. 116–126.

32. Brazil's reform program is evaluated in Kurt Weyland, *Democracy without Equity: Failures of Reform in Brazil* (Pittsburgh: Pittsburgh University Press, 1996).

33. David Fleischer, "Political Reforms: Cardoso's 'Missing Link,'" in Mauricio Font et al., eds., *Reforming Brazil* (Lantham, Md.: Lexington Books, 2004), pp. 112–139.

34. For a review of the *tucanos'* performance in the 1996 and 1998 elections, see Marques and Fleischer, *De Facção a Partido,* pp. 109–123 and 133–155.

35. Analyses of the Cardoso presidency can found in "Brazil: The Challenge of Constitutional Reform," a special issue of the *Journal of Interamerican Studies and World Affairs* [Miami], Vol. 40, No. 4, (Winter 1998); Bolivar Lamounier and Ruben Figueiredo, eds., *A Era FHC: Um balanço* (São Paulo: Cultura Editores, 2002); and Mauricio Font et al., eds., *Reforming Brazil.* Studies of Cardoso, the intellectual and the politician, respectively, are found in Carlos Michiles, *Ciência e Política sobre a Perspectiva do Realismo Utópico* (Brasília: University of Brasília Press, 2003); and Mauricio Font. *Transforming Brazil.*

36. For an analysis of the 2000 municipal elections, see David Fleischer, "As Eleições Municipais no Brasil: uma análise comparativa (1982–2000)," *Opinião Pública* [Campinas], 8(1):80–105, 2002.

37. For a review of these expectations, see Sue Branford et al, *Lula and the Workers' Party in Brazil* (New York: The New Press, 2004).

38. Larry Rohter, "Brazilian leader's tippling becomes national concern," *New York Times,* May 9, 2004, p. 1 passim.

39. Barry Bearak, "Poor Man's Burden: The hard times and letdowns of Lula," *New York Times Magazine,* June 27, 2004, p. 30 passim.

40. Cited in the *Folha de São Paulo,* October 15, 2003.

41. Leslie Bethell, "Politics in Brazil: From Elections without Democracy to Democracy without Citizenship," in Kinzo and Dunkerley, eds., *Brazil since 1985,* pp. 21–41; and Maria Victória Benevides et al., eds., *Reforma Política e Cidadania* (São Paulo: Editora Perseu Abramo, 2003).

Suggested Readings

In English

Abers, Rebecca Neaera. *Inventing Local Democracy: Grassroots Politics in Brazil.* Boulder, Colo.: Lynne Rienner, 2000.

Amann, Edmund. "Economic Policy and Performance in Brazil since 1985," in Kinzo and Dunkerley, eds., *Brazil since 1985*, pp. 107–137.

Ames, Barry. *Political Survival: Politicians and Public Policy in Latin America.* Berkeley: University of California Press, 1987.

————. *The Deadlock of Democracy in Brazil.* Ann Arbor: University of Michigan Press, 2001.

Bacha, Edmar, and Herbert S. Klein, eds. *Social Change in Brazil, 1945–1985: The Incomplete Transition.* Albuquerque, N.M.: University of New Mexico Press, 1989.

Baer, Werner. *The Brazilian Economy: Growth and Development.* New York: Praeger, 1989.

Bearak, Barry. "Poor Man's Burden: the hard times and letdowns of Lula," *New York Times Magazine*, June 27, 2004, p. 30 passim.

Bethell, Leslie. "Politics in Brazil: From Elections without Democracy to Democracy without Citizenship," in Kinzo and Dunkerley, eds., *Brazil since 1985*, pp. 21–41.

Black, Jan Knippers. *United States Penetration of Brazil.* Philadelphia: University of Pennsylvania Press, 1977.

Branford, Sue, and Bernardo Kucinski. *Carnival of the Oppressed: Lula and the Brazilian Workers Party.* London: Latin American Bureau, 1995.

———— et al. *Lula and the Workers Party in Brazil.* New York: The New Press, 2004.

Branford, Sue, and Jan Rocha. *Cutting the Wire: the Story of the Landless Movement in Brazil.* London: Latin American Bureau, 2002.

Figueiredo, Angelina C., and Fernando Limongi. "Congress and Decision-Making in Democratic Brazil," in Kinzo and Dunkerley, eds., *Brazil since 1985*, pp. 62–83.

Fleischer, David. "Government and Politics," in Hudson, ed., *Brazil: A Country Study*, pp. 253–332.

————. "Beyond Collorgate: Prospects for Consolidating Democracy in Brazil through Political Reform," in Rosenn and Downes, eds., *Corruption and Political Reform in Brazil*, pp. 49–71.

————. "Political Reforms: Cardoso's 'Missing Link'," in Font, ed. *Reforming Brazil*, pp. 112–139.

Font, Maurício A. *Transforming Brazil: A Reform Era in Perspective.* Lantham, Md.: Rowman and Littlefield, 2003.

———— et. al., eds. *Reforming Brazil.* Lantham, Md.: Rowman and Littlefield, 2004.

Hudson, Rex A., ed. *Brazil: A Country Study.* Washington, D.C.: Library of Congress, 1997.

Hunter, Wendy. *Eroding Military Influence in Brazil: Politicians against Soldiers.* Chapel Hill: University of North Carolina Press, 1997.

Keck, Margaret E. *The Workers' Party and Democratization in Brazil.* New Haven, Conn.: Yale University Press, 1992.

Kingstone, Peter R., and Timothy J. Power, eds. *Democratic Brazil.* Pittsburgh: Pittsburgh University Press, 1999.

Kinzo, Maria D'Alva. *Legal Opposition Politics under Authoritarian Rule in Brazil: The Case of the MDB, 1966–79.* London: Macmillan, 1988.

————. "Parties and Elections: Brazil's Democratic Experience since 1985," in Kinzo and Dunkerley, eds. *Brazil since 1985*, pp. 42–61.

_____, and James Dunkerley, eds. *Brazil since 1985: Economy, Polity and Society*. London: ILAS/University of London, 2003.

Macaulay, Fiona. "Democratization and the Judiciary: Competing Reform Agendas," inKinzo and Dunkerely, eds. *Brazil since 1985*, pp. 84–104.

Mainwaring, Scott. *The Catholic Church and Politics in Brazil, 1916–1985*. Stanford, Calif.: Stanford University Press, 1986.

_____. *Rethinking Party Systems in the Third Wave of Democratization: The Case of Brazil*. Stanford: Stanford University Press, 1999.

Martinez-Lara, Xavier. *Building Democracy in Brazil: The Politics of Constitutional Change, 1985–1995*. London: Macmillan, 1996.

Mueller, Charles C., and Werner Baer. "The Economy," in Hudson, ed. *Brazil: A Country Study*, pp. 137–252.

O'Donnell, Guillermo. "Challenges to Democratization in Brazil: The Threat of a Slow Death." *World Policy Journal*, Spring 1988, pp. 281–300.

Porto, Mauro P. "Mass Media and Politics in Democratic Brazil," in Kinzo and Dunkerley, eds. *Brazil since 1985*, pp. 288–313.

Power, Timothy J. *The Political Right in Brazil: Elites, Institutions, and Democratization*. University Park, Pa.: Pennsylvania State University Press, 2000.

Rosenn, Keith S., and Richard Downes, eds. *Corruption and Political Reform in Brazil: The Impact of Collor's Impeachment*. Coral Gables, Fla.: University of Miami Press, 1999.

Sader, Emir, and Ken Silverstein. *Without Fear of Being Happy: Lula, the Workers' Party and the 1989 Election in Brazil*. New York: Verso Books, 1991.

Sallum Jr., Brasilio. "The Changing Role of the State: New Patterns of State-Society Relations in Brazil at the End of the Twentieth Century," in Kinzo and Dunkerley, eds., *Brazil since 1985*, pp. 179–199.

Sawyer, Donald R. "The Society and its Environment," in Hudson, ed., *Brazil: A Country Study*, pp. 90–156.

Skidmore, Thomas. *Politics in Brazil*. New York: Oxford University Press, 1966.

_____. *The Politics of Military Rule in Brazil, 1964–85*. New York: Oxford University Press, 1988.

Souza, Celina Maria de. *Constitutional Engineering in Brazil: The Politics of Federalism and Decentralization*. London: Macmillian, 1997.

Stepan, Alfred. *Rethinking Military Politics: Brazil and the Southern Cone*. Princeton, N.J.: Princeton University Press, 1988.

_____, ed. *Democratizing Brazil: Problems of Transition and Consolidation*. New York: Oxford University Press, 1989.

Tendler, Judith. *Good Government in the Tropics*. Baltimore: Johns Hopkins University Press, 1996.

Tolefson, Scott D. "National Security," in Hudson, ed., *Brazil: A Country Study*, pp. 333–412.

Wesson, Robert, and David Fleischer. *Brazil in Transition*. New York: Praeger, 1983.

Weyland, Kurt. *Democracy without Equity: Failures of Reform in Brazil*. Pittsburgh: Pittsburgh University Press, 1996.

In Portuguese

Bastide, Roger. *Brasil: Terra de Contrastes*. São Paulo: DIFEL, 1959.

Benevides, Maria Victória et al., eds. *Reforma Política e Cidadania*. São Paulo: Editora Fundação Perseu Abramo, 2003.

Bresser Pereira, Luiz. *Pactos Políticos: Do Populismo à Redemocratização*. São Paulo: Editora Brasiliense, 1985.

Carreirão, Yan de Souza. *Decisão do Voto nas Eleições Presidenciais Brasileiras.* Rio de Janeiro: Fundação Getúlio Vargas, 2002.

D'Araujo, Maria Celina, and Celso Castro orgs. *Ernesto Geisel.* Rio de Janeiro: Fundação Getúlio Vargas, 1997.

D'Alva Gil Kinzo, Maria. "O Quadro partidário e a Constituinte." *Revista Brasileira de Ciência Política* [Brasília]1, 1 (March 1989), pp. 91–124.

DaMatta, Roberto. *O Que Faz O Brasil, Brasil?* São Paulo: Rocco, 1986.

Dreifuss, René A. *1964: A Conquista do Estado: Acão Política, Poder e Golpe do Estado.* Petrópolis: Editora Vozes, 1981.

_____. *O Jogo da Direita* (Petrópolis: Editora Vozes, 1989).

Faoro, Raymundo. *Os Donos do Poder: Formação do Patronato Político Brasiliero.* Editora Globo, 1958.

Fleischer, David. "Manipulações casuísticas do sistema eleitoral durante o período militar, ou como usualmente o feitiço se voltava contra o feiticeiro," in Gláúcio Soares and Maria Celina D'Araujo, eds. *21 Anos de Regime Militar.* Rio de Janeiro: Fundação Getúlio Vargas, 1994.

_____. "As Eleições Municipais no Brasil: uma análise comparativa (1982–2000)," *Opinião Pública* [Campinas], 8(1):80–105, 2002.

Gabeira, Fernando. *O que é isso, companheiro?.* Rio de Janeiro: Codecri, 1980.

Gaspari, Élio. *A Ditatura Envergonhada.* São Paulo: Companhia Das Letras, 2002.

_____. *A Ditadura Escancarada.* São Paulo: Companhia Das Letras, 2002.

_____. *A Ditadura Derrotada.* São Paulo: Companhia Das Letras, 2003.

_____. *A Ditatura Envergonhada.* São Paulo: Companhia Das Letras, 2004.

Jaguaribe, Helio. *Alternativas do Brasil.* Rio de Janeiro: José Olympio Editora, 1989.

Kinzo, Maria D'Alva. "O Quadro Partidário e a Constituinte," *Revista Brasileira de Ciência Política* [Brasília], 1(1):91–123, 1989.

Lambert, Jacques. *Os Dois Brasis.* Rio de Janeiro: INEP/CBPE, 1959.

Lamounier, Bolivar, ed. *De Geisel a Collor: O Balanço da Transição.* São Paulo: Ed. Sumaré.

_____, and Rubens Figueiredo, eds. *A Era FHC: Um Balanço.* São Paulo: Cultura Editores, 2002

Marques, Jales Ramos, and David Fleischer. *PSDB: De Facção a Partido.* Brasília: Inst. Teotonio Vilela, 1998.

Michiles, Carlos. *Ciência e Política sob a Perspectiva do Realismo Utópico: Análise Habermasiana do Discurso Argumentativo de Fernando Henrique Cardoso.* Brasília: Ed. Universidade de Brasília, 2003.

Nery, Sebastião. *As 16 Derrotas que Abalaram o Brasil.* Rio de Janeiro: Francisco Alves, 1975.

Pochmann, Márcio org. *Atlas da Riqueza no Brasil.* São Paulo: Editora Cortez, 2004.

Soares, Glaucio A.D. *A Democracia Interropida.* Rio de Janeiro: Fundação Getúlio Vargas, 2001.

_____, and Maria Celina D'Araujo, eds. *21 Anos de Regime Militar: Balanços e Perspectivas.* Rio de Janeiro: Fundação Getúlio Vargas, 1994.

Vianna, Luiz Werneck. *A Transição: Da Constituinte à Sucessão Presidencial.* Rio de Janeiro: Ed. Revan, 1989.

Chapter 26

CHILE: THE DEVELOPMENT, BREAKDOWN, AND RECOVERY OF DEMOCRACY

J. SAMUEL VALENZUELA
ARTURO VALENZUELA

CHILE, A COUNTRY OF nearly 16 million people isolated by the formidable Andes mountains on a narrow and elongated strip of land running 2,650 miles into the far southern reaches of the earth, developed early on a distinctive political system that set it apart from its Latin American neighbors. Soon after independence from Spain, conservative leaders were able to establish a national government that successfully resisted armed challenges to its authority, thereby avoiding the instability that plagued most of Spanish America. Through successive reforms in a pattern reminiscent of British history, Chile toward the end of the nineteenth century had built a democratic regime, although suffrage in national elections was limited to literate males until 1949. The regularity of electoral contests led to the rise of strong parties that have dominated political life into the twenty-first century. Running the full range of the ideological spectrum from left to right, the Chilean party system has had more in common with those of Latin Europe than of Latin America.

This unusual history and party system permitted the election in 1970 of President Salvador Allende, whose leftist government tried to lead the nation to socialism within its constitutional and democratic framework. Allende's experiment attracted world attention and was observed with particular interest in Italy and in France, where the left was attempting to follow the same political path. The experiment ended on September 11, 1973, when General Augusto Pinochet staged a bloody military coup that destroyed Chile's democracy and inaugurated a sixteen-and-a-half-year eternity of harsh authoritarian government. Within the context of Chilean history, such military rule was highly exceptional. Prior to Pinochet's regime, Chile had only once before, for less than five months in 1924, been governed by a strictly military junta. The crisis years of 1891 and 1932 produced juntas with military and civilian figures that lasted only a few weeks. The great majority of Chilean presidents had been regularly replaced by their successors following constitutional procedures. The national Congress, an institution that played a crucial role in Chilean political history, was also closed by the Pinochet for the first time since independence.

With the inauguration of President Patricio Aylwin on March 11, 1990, in highly emotional ceremonies attended by delegates from sixty-seven countries, including sixteen heads of state, Chile recovered its more-than-centennial democratic tradition.

This chapter examines the origins, evolution, characteristics, and breakdown of Chile's democratic system. It also reviews the main features of the military regime that ruled during the 1970s and 1980s and evaluates Chilean politics after the re-establishment of democracy.

An Overview of Chilean Political History, 1818–1970

Phase 1: The Founding of an Oligarchical Proto-Democracy (1818–1850)

As elsewhere on the continent, the defeat of Spanish and Chilean royalist forces after the wars of independence (1810–1818) did not lead to an easy transition toward autonomous rule. The break with Spain did not alter the socioeconomic order. The predominantly rural population, located mainly between Valparaíso and Concepción, continued to live in poverty without sharing the fruits of a weak economy based on exports of animal products, grain, and copper. The break, however, clearly disrupted the political system. Gone was the omnipresent and complex colonial administration, as well as the legitimating power of the Crown, the final arbiter of all conflicts. The nation became engulfed in political anarchy as different family, regional, and ideological groups fought each other only to produce unsuccessful dictatorial governments and a series of paper constitutions.

Political anarchy ended in the early 1830s, but it is a mistake, often made in Chilean historiography, to look to those years for an explanation of the subsequent stability of government. Surely the defeat of what were viewed later in the nineteenth century as the liberal factions in the Battle of Lircay (1830), the skillful political and financial maneuvers of ministers Diego Portales and Manuel Rengifo in the administrations of President Joaquín Prieto (1831–1836; 1836–1841), and the adoption of a centralizing constitution in 1833 were important steps in establishing new authority structures. But there is a difference between *establishment* of such structures and their *consolidation*. Consolidation involves the acceptance of the viability and legitimacy of new institutions by the political elites. It is a lengthy process, subject to continuous challenges and reversals. It took many years and was aided by several factors.

The first was the victory of Chilean forces over those of the Peru–Bolivia Confederation. Though the confederation, led by General Andrés Santa Cruz, had sought to extend its dominion southward, the real spark that ignited the

Chilean war effort was the assassination of Portales in 1837. Portales's policies, repressive measures, and advocacy of the war had made him the target of great enmity in Chile. Ironically, because it was rumored that he had been assassinated by agents of Santa Cruz, his death stirred a wave of patriotic emotions that were channeled to military preparations. For the first time Chilean elites mounted a joint endeavor to fight a common enemy, since the war of independence had been as much a civil war as a struggle against colonialism. Plots against the government were forgotten, and victory led to internal amnesty and to a restitution of pensions and ranks for the defeated forces of the 1829–1830 civil war. It also led to the election of the first truly national hero, Manuel Bulnes, to the presidency in 1841. A Chilean defeat in the war would have magnified factional disputes and threatened the stability of fragile institutions. The clear-cut victory, with no parallel in Latin America, created common symbols and a new sense of unity, leading the inauguration of an elected government with unprecedented support.

The second factor was the decisive control of the military by civilian authorities. As leader of the victorious army, Bulnes did not experience much opposition from the military in his first years in office. However, under his leadership the government deliberately reduced support for the regular army, so that by the end of Bulnes's term there were fewer soldiers than at the beginning and the budget for the regular military was severely curtailed. In place of a regular army, the executive encouraged the development of a highly politicized National Guard. Led by loyal government supporters (leadership positions became patronage devices for the president), the part-time guard was composed mainly of lower-middle-class civilians such as artisans, shopkeepers, and small proprietors. It numbered ten to twenty-five times the size of the peacetime army. The outbreak of a revolt against the government in 1851 was partly the reflection of the discontent of regular army officers, based in Concepción, with military policy. Bulnes himself led National Guard forces to suppress the uprising aimed at preventing his elected successor from taking office, even though his cousin was the rival leader. A similar revolt in 1859 was put down by mobilizing loyal army and National Guard forces.

As illustrated by Bulnes's decisive 1851 action, the third factor in the consolidation of the regime was the deliberate support he gave to the fledgling institutional system during his two five-year terms in office (1841–1851). Indeed, Bulnes's role in the consolidation process was, contrary to assertions in Chilean historiography, much greater than that of Portales, whose actual ministerial tenure was short. A written constitution based on democratic precepts, with fixed terms of office and elected authorities governing impersonally through the rule of law, were revolutionary notions at the time. Bulnes was certainly in a position to ignore these principles and to draw on his prestige and military strength to impose personal rule, as did his counterparts in Argentina, Mexico, and Venezuela. Instead, under his leadership the formal rules of the Constitution of 1833, with its separation of powers between the executive, the Congress, and the courts, became a reality.

The most important single element contributing to this process was the president's refusal to rule autocratically. Following the example of his predecessor, he relied on a strong collegial body, the cabinet, to carry out the main tasks of government. But, unlike those of his predecessor, Bulnes's cabinets drew from different sectors of public opinion, and its members were periodically changed to reflect new pressures and interests.

Though the executive took the initiative, Congress had to approve all legislation. The legislature gradually became more assertive and a platform for dissenting views. As early as the 1840s, the Congress resorted to delaying approval of the budget law in order to extract government concessions. Rather than defying this challenge to his authority, Bulnes sought compromise with the legislature. The legitimacy of Congress was therefore not questioned, even if cabinet officials manipulated the electoral process in favor of the official list of congressional candidates. This set the rudiments of the political game for the rest of the century.

Throughout the nineteenth century all relevant factions gained representation in the cabinet or in the legislature, and diverse opposition groups had to learn to collaborate within the shared institutional base to further their interests. It is noteworthy that every nineteenth-century head of state, with the exception of Jorge Montt, who became president after the 1891 civil war, had extensive prior experience as an elected representative in Congress. And the five presidents who succeeded Bulnes until 1886 began government service as young men in his administration.

The fourth factor contributing to regime consolidation was economic prosperity. The break with the colonial trade limitations opened the country to the international market, and Chilean exports thrived. Mining, primarily of silver and copper, expanded with the opening of new mines, and the new markets of California (after the gold rush), Europe, and Australia led to a boom in agricultural sales, mainly of wheat. The state played an important role in encouraging economic development based on external markets: It obtained foreign credit, improved dock facilities, opened new ports, began railway lines, and established a merchant marine. From 1844 to 1864, Chilean exports increased five times, and foreign creditors were quick to take note as Chilean issues brought higher prices on the London market than those of any other Latin American country.

Underlying the success of the government in promoting economic growth, and indirectly the success of the consolidation process itself, was the broad elite consensus on the merits of an "outward-oriented" development policy. Landowners in the central valley, miners in the north, and merchants in Santiago and in port cities all benefited from and promoted an economy based on the export of primary goods in the production of which the country had a decisive advantage. Most manufactured products were imported. There was no protectionism for domestic industry and no effective political force to press for it. The potential internal market for Chilean industry was small, and many obstacles, including the long distances from Europe and the United States and the tariff barriers that protected their own industries, discouraged manufacturing for export. However, an incipient industrialization did begin around textiles and iron works in the 1850s and 1860s. It supplied the military and produced materials used in mining, construction, and railways. Chilean artisans also built most of the boats that made their way up and down the long coast.

In sum, by mid-century, Chile had laid the foundations for constitutional republican rule based on the separation of powers. Victory in an international war, the control of the military by the constitutionally established authorities, political leadership respectful of the formal rules, and economic growth had contributed to this result that set Chile on a unique course in Latin America. The Congress had, in particular, taken its place as a basic arena for political accommodation, compromise, overview of the executive, and opposition. And although the franchise was limited and subject to intervention, it became the only mechanism for selecting political officeholders.

Phase 2: State Expansion and Elite Reaction (1850–1890)

Sharp political differences developed among nineteenth-century elites. The differences stemmed from the reaction of local and national notables, particularly those close to the Church, to the expansion of the state. When state institutions began to expand into the local level, rationalize taxes and duties, invest in public-works projects, and reduce church influence over national life, they generated bitter opposition. Our perspective is different from that of many historians, who have interpreted nineteenth-century controversies as a struggle between a rural "aristocracy" linked to the Conservative Party with a firm grip on the state and a rising group of miners, bankers, merchants, and professionals seeking political control. That view presupposes that political differences were the product of a fundamental, economically based cleavage among the elite. In fact, as already suggested, there was broad consensus on the merits of free-trade policies and on the pursuit of a development model based on primary goods exports. Moreover, socioeconomic divisions among the dominant sectors were not so clear-cut: The wealthiest families often had cross-investments in all areas of the economy. It is also clear that the conservatives STET were far from controlling the government. Quite to the contrary, they were driven into opposition at an early date and remained so for most of the century.

Moreover, by mid-century the state was not simply a tool of economic elites but had a considerable degree of autonomy. An entirely new profession of urban-based government officials and politicians had appeared on the political scene. Like President Manuel Montt (1851–1856; 1856–1861) himself, they relied on the state for their positions and had a real stake in the expansion of governmental authority. By 1860, over twenty-five hundred persons worked for the state, not counting thousands of workers hired by municipalities and government-financed public-works projects or the many individuals associated with the National Guard and the armed forces.

State autonomy was in part a function of growing governmental institutionalization and of the ability of state officials to manipulate the verdict of the electorate. But it was also the product of a system of revenue collection tied to an export economy. Reliance on customs revenues in a time of export expansion meant an incremental and automatic infusion of larger sums of money into state coffers without imposing large-scale domestic taxation. From 1830 to 1860, government revenues from customs duties, representing about 60 percent of all revenue, increased seven times. State revenues enabled the construction of numerous public-works projects, including the second railroad system of Latin America and the first to be operated by a government. In the fifteen-year period 1845–1860, expenditures on education alone quadrupled.

Given the encroachment of the state on the localities, it is not surprising that control of the state and its expenditures became the most important political issue of the time. Were urban or rural areas to be favored by state resources? Which port facilities should be improved? Where were the railroad lines to be built? Should local officials remain subordinated to the national government's decisions and largess, or should they be autonomous from it? And most importantly, should the state or the Church control the expanding educational system, civil registry, cemeteries, and hospitals?

The Conservative Party became the foremost expression of elite discontent over the increasing encroachment of the central state over national life and, in particular, its challenge to the Church's monopoly over educational, cultural, and family life, the maintenance of which conservatives viewed as essential to the preservation of the traditional social order. The party was originally formed by a group that split away from the Montt government when Manuel Montt supported the authority of civil courts in a matter of Church governance. In opposition, the Conservatives soon made alliances of convenience with some ideological Liberals who, while supporting the concept of a secular state, wanted more decentralization of political authority and an expansion of electoral participation. An unsuccessful 1859 uprising reflected the seriousness of the political controversies as progressive Liberal and some Conservative groups attempted to prevent Manuel Montt's closest associate from succeeding him to the presidency. Though the government forces, known as the Nationals, controlled the rebellion, Montt's associate wisely withdrew his candidacy. The new National president, José Joaquín Pérez (1861–1866; 1866–1871), saw the political wisdom of granting amnesty to the rebels and, following the Bulnes precedents, of incorporating both Conservatives and Liberals into cabinets of national unity in what became known as the Liberal-Conservative Fusion.

A few measures were adopted during the Pérez administrations to curb the power of executive authority. The president was restricted to one term, armed personnel were barred from voting booths, and other electoral reforms were made. However, the basic character of the state remained unchanged. With Pérez's support, the Liberals outmaneuvered their Conservative allies and continued the basic policies of the preceding National governments. State power transformed the Liberals, not vice versa. State authority expanded further, state-sponsored projects increased, and the secularization of public institutions continued.

By the midpoint of the administration of Liberal president Federico Er-rázuriz (1871–1876), the Conservatives had had enough. They left the government determined to oppose the drift toward a secular society and the continued encroachment of the state over national life. Ironically, the Conservatives once again made an alliance of convenience with another opposition group, the anticlerical Radical Party, which upheld the Liberal principles its government colleagues had seemingly abandoned. This unlikely alliance held a majority in Congress. The Conservatives took advantage of this majority in 1874 to stipulate in a new electoral law that anyone who could read and write had the income required by the constitution to vote. As a result the electorate tripled from 50,000 to 150,000 by 1878. Given that many women registered to vote in 1876, a new law in 1884 approved by an anticlerical majority clarified that voting rights were limited to literate men.

The 1874 reforms were not sufficient to counteract the strong intervention of local agents of the executive in the electoral process, an intervention that became more blatant and violent as the government's control over the electorate diminished. Hence, in 1890 the Conservatives successfully pressed for the secret vote, including the establishment of secret chambers in all voting places and government issued enveloppes to hide the vote from onlookers. And in 1917 Conservatives presented the first bill, unsuccessfully, that sought to enfranchise women; as the bill's authors recalled at the time, a Conservative leader had first proposed this measure in 1865.

The Conservatives stood to gain from these reforms. Given the failure of armed conspiracies, their only hope of curbing state authority and of gaining control of government resources lay in the expansion of suffrage and in the reduction of government manipulation of the voting process. Like their counterparts in northern European countries, the Conservatives knew that their relatively larger support in small towns, in rural areas, and among women would boost their electoral fortunes. The key role played by the Conservatives in suffrage expansion (which, surprisingly, has been attributed to the Liberals and Radicals by most historians) meant that the principal party of traditional Chilean Catholics became committed to expressing its power capabilities *through the electoral system,* not through conspiracies within the armed forces or by gaining the allegiance of the central bureaucracy. It also meant that Church opposition to republican electoral democracy, typical of Latin Europe until the early twentieth century, did not develop in Chile. The use of the electoral system as a mechanism for national leadership selection was reinforced by these circumstances.

The stakes involved in the control of the executive increased dramatically with the Chilean victory in the War of the Pacific (1879–1883), again against Peru and Bolivia. In the 1860s and 1870s, customs duties as a percentage of government revenue had declined to as low as 40 percent. After the war, with the incorporation of Peruvian and Bolivian land with enormous nitrate wealth into Chilean territory, customs duties once again climbed to over 70 percent of government income, eventually eliminating the need for internal property

taxes. Though a majority of nitrate fields fell into the hands of foreign interests, the Chilean state was able to retain close to 50 percent of all profits
through taxation. From 1870 to 1890, government revenues climbed over 150
percent, leading to a new wave of public-works projects and other government
expenditures.

The struggle over the role of the state in society finally resulted in the civil
war of 1891, during the closing months of José Manuel Balmaceda's government (1886–1891). With burgeoning nitrate wealth, his administration embarked on the most ambitious effort yet to channel governmental resources
into massive public-works projects. Though some of his detractors objected to
his hostile attitude toward British nitrate interests, opposition to Balmaceda
crystallized over the perennial issue of the nineteenth century: control over
state resources and the fairness of the electoral system. The anti-Balmaceda
forces included a wide spectrum of political opinion ranging from dissident
Liberals to Conservatives and Radicals, not to mention the British nitrate entrepreneurs. The defeat of Balmaceda led to the application of the new electoral institutions devised in 1890 that ended government intervention in the
electoral process. From then on presidents were unable to manipulate elections
into producing pro-government majorities, or to select their successors and impose them on the nation.

Phase 3: The Party System, Urbanization, and the Rise of Unions (1890–1925)

After 1891 the center of gravity of the Chilean political system shifted dramatically from the center to the locality. Municipal autonomy and electoral reform finally gave local notables control over suffrage and, therefore, over
congressmen and senators. Acting as agents of their local sponsors, the legislators sharply reduced the role of the executive by subjecting cabinet appointments to congressional ratification. Politics in the so-called Parliamentary
Republic (1891–1925) became an elaborate logrolling game in which legislative factions jockeyed for influence. Budget laws were carved up to please local
supporters, and public employment became a primary source for congressional
and party patronage. Central government employees increased from 3,048 in
1880 to 13,119 in 1900 and 27,479 in 1919, and the monolithic character of
the state changed as its structures were permeated by different political elites.
The incredible ministerial instability of the period, with its constant coalition
shifts and complex electoral pacts, must be seen in this light.

A key organization of twentieth-century politics, the political party with extensive local bases, developed principally during the Parliamentary Republic.
An unanticipated consequence of the liberalization of suffrage was the transformation of elite factions and protoparties into large-scale party organizations
and networks. Buying of votes and the manipulation of the electorate became
a complex and demanding job, and much of the day-to-day party activities
shifted from the hands of notables to those of professional politicians and brokers of lesser status. A new political class began to take shape.

The Conservative Party gained influence with the electoral reforms. But the profound socioeconomic transformations set in motion by nitrate production as well as by industrialization and urbanization gave other political groups new electoral constituencies. Nitrate fields soon employed 10 to 15 percent of the active population and, by expanding the internal market, generated a host of other activities, including metallurgical works, textile production, and transportation. Rural areas and their commercial and agro-industrial networks also experienced changes, as agriculture sought to meet the demand for food in the arid north. The urban population increased dramatically from 26 percent of the total in 1875 to close to 45 percent by the early 1900s, and the Radicals as well as a new group of Social Democrats assured themselves an increased role in politics with their skillful organizational efforts in changing cities, towns, and nitrate areas.

Political parties with direct access to the legislative process developed simultaneously with the expansion of the state bureaucracy. The growth of the public sector in this period was thus shaped by organizations whose primary goal was electoral success and accountability, organizations that continued to exert a major influence over state institutions and the policy process until the military coup of 1973.

Parties were not the only important organizations with local bases to appear in this period. Labor unions mushroomed, as nitrate, dock, railway, and industrial workers and artisans sought to improve their lot. However, labor unions were restricted and repressed. Dominant government and business elites thought labor militancy threatened the viability of the whole system. Since nitrate revenues were the lifeline of the state and of the economy, any cut in export revenues because of strikes would have devastating repercussions. The army was repeatedly used to put down strikes, often with great brutality, as in the Iquique massacre of 1907 when hundreds of workers were killed. Repression of labor union activities created a radical union leadership, since radical workers were more likely to assume the great personal risks involved.

Ironically, the openness of the political system, a product of the intense conflict among established elites, meant that repression when workers made demands at the workplace was not accompanied systematically by political repression. Working-class leaders were allowed to publish newspapers, create cultural associations, lobby Congress, and create political parties. Despite their radical outlooks, they soon realized that their cause could best be advanced politically through alliances of convenience with traditional parties eager to maximize their fortunes. Thus in 1921, the founding father of the labor movement and of the Communist party, Luis Emilio Recabarren, and one of his comrades were elected to Congress through an electoral pact with the Radical Party. This repeated earlier successes in local elections in which pacts had been forged with either Radicals or Democrats. The repression of the working class therefore contributed to the formation of a Marxist labor union and party leadership, and the relatively open and representative character of the political system meant that such leaders were able to organize politically and make deals with other forces to advance their positions.

The freewheeling and free-spending Parliamentary Republic was affected by the decline in nitrate exports given the discovery of synthetic nitrate during World War I, and its complex logrolling process to reach legislative decisions was unable to come up with solutions to many of the social pressures spawned by a changing society. President Arturo Alessandri's (1920–1925) populist politics violated many of the norms of political accommodation and led to demands to do away with politics and to obtain order. A crisis point was reached when young army officers intervened in politics in September 1924 and sent the president into exile. Although the officers had reformist objectives and pressed the congress to approve wide ranging social legislation, including the legalization of unions and a social security system establishing sickness and old age pensions, their intervention marked the end of the Parliamentary Republic. President Alessandri returned to power in early 1925 and dictated a new constitution. However, the many rapid changes eventually opened the way for the accession to power of a "nonpolitical" figure, Colonel Carlos Ibáñez. During his government (1927–1931), Congress lost influence and the president resorted to heavy-handed tactics in an attempt to reduce the influence of parties and the strength of the Communist-controlled labor federations, which represented a majority of organized workers.

Ibáñez expanded the state bureaucracy, revised the budgetary system, and created a national police force. Interpreting the comprehensive labor laws approved in 1924 to suit his own end, Ibáñez established legal unionism only where his agents could find leaders who agreed to support his government. But the military president failed. Party politics were too entrenched to be easily purged or manipulated from above. His use of the 1924 labor laws only delayed their full and correct implementation until the late 1930s. With the catastrophic effects of the Great Depression (in which Chilean exports dropped to less than a fifth of their value by 1931), another political crisis erupted, forcing Ibáñez to resign. And after a short interval of unrest, Arturo Alessandri was reelected president by a large margin.

Phase 4: Political Polarization and Mass Participation (1925–1970)

The 1925 Constitution restored presidential prerogatives and introduced the separation of Church and state. And yet an even more important political change during the 1920s was arguably the rise of the left. The Communist party was officially founded when the Socialist Workers' party convention of December 1921 voted to adhere to the Third International. By the end of the decade, a Trotskyite splinter had been expelled from the party, and various Socialist groups had been created. After Ibáñez's resignation, all these organizations emerged from their underground work to produce a confusing array of political groups on the left. However, in April 1933, a core of highly popular leaders formed the Socialist party of Chile by bringing together some of the pre-existing Socialist and Trotskyite organizations. The new Socialist party quickly gained significant working-class bases by attracting the support of the country's legal unions, with which the Communists had refused to collaborate because of their origins. Thus by the early 1930s, two major parties claiming to represent the workers had emerged on the political landscape, leading to a complex relationship of competition and/or cooperation between them that continues to this day. And with the rise of the Marxist left, the party system became highly polarized, covering the full range of the ideological spectrum.

Following the Popular Front strategy adopted in late 1934 by the Third International, the Communist party agreed to a previous Socialist initiative designed to unite the labor movement and to coordinate political strategies. With an eye on the next presidential elections, the by-then-historical Radical Party decided to withdraw its support of the conservative second Alessandri administration (1932–1938) and to join the left's discussions. These resulted in the merger of the labor movement into a single federation in 1936 and in the creation of a Popular Front coalition that elected the Radical Pedro Aguirre Cerda to the presidency in December 1938. This electoral victory over the candidates of Liberals and Conservatives marked the success, for the first time, of an anticlerical center-to-Marxist left coalition, which would govern the country until 1947. The coalition government expanded state social services in areas such as health, education, and social security. It also encouraged the rise of legal unionism, including Communist-led unions, within the framework of the 1924 labor laws that shaped Chile's elaborate industrial-relations system. And the Aguirre Cerda government created a State Development Corporation (CORFO) to plan and direct industrial growth.

The creation of CORFO was symptomatic of a change of direction in the Chilean economy and economic policy. The depression had dealt the final blow to the crippled nitrate industry, and by the late 1930s copper had become Chile's principal export, representing roughly 55 percent of export earnings in the 1940s and 80 percent by 1970. With the drastic decline of the capacity to import in the early 1930s, policymakers became convinced that the nation should not rely on imported consumer goods to satisfy most of its needs. They sought to encourage industrial production by establishing new lines of credit, protectionism, direct and indirect subsidies, price controls, and state investments in key areas such as steel and energy, which required large capital outlays. As a result, by the late 1960s, Chile's industrial sector produced a broad range of consumer goods, if not always at internationally competitive levels of efficiency.

One of the Popular Front government's objectives in fostering industrialization was the creation of jobs in urban areas, which were urgently required because of the decline of the labor-intensive nitrate industry and of the influx of new migrants into the cities. By 1940, 53 percent of the population lived in urban areas, a figure that increased to 76 percent by 1970. The population in cities with more than twenty thousand people increased at an even faster rate. The new industrialization, however, in the long run did not generate employment at a faster rate than the increase in urban population. The secondary sector (including for present purposes mining, construction, transport, and particularly manufacturing) absorbed roughly the same proportion of the economically active population in 1970 as it had in 1940, even though its proportion of the gross domestic product increased from 38 percent in 1940 to 48 percent in 1970. It was the service sector that absorbed increasing shares of total employment while contributing a smaller share of the GDP, while the primary sector (agriculture, forestry, and fishing) declined on both counts.

The Popular Front coalition broke down in part because of bitter internecine squabbles among Socialists and between Socialists and Communists and in part because of the fear of both Socialists and Radicals (particularly after the 1947 municipal election) that the Communists were making too much electoral progress. The onset of the Cold War and U.S. pressures also played a role in the Radicals' decision not only to expel the Communists from the cabinet but also to declare the party illegal in 1948. The disarray of the left and the unpopularity of the Radicals after so many years of opportunistic bargaining with both the left and the right finally led the electorate back to military populism, Gen. Carlos Ibáñez, who once again promised progress at the margin of party politics. Ibáñez (1952–1958) was easily elected to the presidency by a surge movement ranging from the far right to the Socialist left.

Ibáñez's heterogeneous movement did not become a durable political force. As he began his term, the economy entered a recession and inflation increased sharply, finally reaching a high of 86 percent in 1955. Ibáñez abandoned the populist appeal of his campaign and early programs and attempted to apply an austerity economic program.

The disintegration of the Ibáñez movement might have allowed the Radicals to move once again to fill the center of Chilean politics. However, they were challenged in that role by the emerging Christian Democratic (DC) party, whose candidate, Eduardo Frei, outpolled the Radicals in the 1958 presidential contest. But the real surprise of that election was the showing of Salvador Allende, the candidate of the Communist and Socialist parties. With 28.9 percent of the vote in the sharply divided contest, he failed by a fraction (2.7 percent) to defeat the winner, Jorge Alessandri.

In office, Alessandri (1958–1964), a businessman supported by the right and occasionally by the peripatetic Radicals, applied a new set of austerity measures and obtained increased foreign aid to attempt economic stabilization. In the wake of the Cuban Revolution, the United States became determined to prevent a growth of leftist influence in the rest of the hemisphere. Chile, with its large Marxist parties, became a priority of the Kennedy and Johnson administrations' foreign-aid programs and covert intelligence operations.

During the 1964 presidential election, the Chilean center and right as well as the U.S. government sought to prevent what almost occurred in 1958—an Allende victory. As a result the right decided to support the centrist Frei candidacy, which promised a "Revolution in Liberty," and the CIA contributed $1.20 per Chilean voter to the anti-left propaganda effort, over twice as much as the 54 cents per U.S. voter that Lyndon Johnson and Barry Goldwater jointly spent in their own presidential campaigns that year. Frei was elected with an absolute majority of the votes. His government, that of his successor, and the breakdown of democracy will be discussed after reviewing the principal aspects and actors of the political game of twentieth-century Chilean politics.

POLITICAL GROUPS AND THE STATE: THE POLITICAL SYSTEM AT MID-CENTURY

By mid-century the Chilean state had evolved into a large and complex set of institutions. Even before the election of Salvador Allende to the presidency in 1970, total state expenditures represented about 24 percent of the GDP. The state also generated over 55 percent of gross investment and roughly 50 percent of all available credit. About 13 percent of the active population worked for the state, not counting the employees of the thirty-nine key corporations in which CORFO owned majority shares or the forty-one other enterprises where its participation was substantial. Government agencies were responsible for health care and social-security benefits, for the regulation of prices and wages, and for the settlement of labor disputes. Indeed, the dominant role of government in regulatory, distributive, and redistributive policies meant that private groups were constantly turning to state agencies and to the legislature, at times through elected local government officials, to gain favorable rulings and dispensations.

Over the years, myriad interest groups developed, closely paralleling the expansion of the state. They ranged from professional societies and business organizations to student unions, trade and pensioners' associations, youth and church groups, mothers' clubs, and neighborhood councils. Workers were represented by industrial, craft, and peasant unions (the latter legalized only in 1967), which were subjected to a series of state regulations and restrictions, although their leadership was democratically chosen by the rank and file. Civil servants were organized into a series of associations that, though acting as unions, were never officially recognized as such. Most groups sought to maximize their political clout before the state by organizing national associations with national headquarters. Large industrial, agricultural, and commercial interests were, for example, respectively organized into the Society for Industrial Advancement (SOFOFA), the National Agricultural Society (SNA), and the Central Chamber of Commerce. Professional societies were grouped in the Confederation of Professional Associations. Roughly 60 percent of all unionists were affiliated directly or indirectly with the Central Labor Federation (CUT). Some categories of specialized workers, small industrialists and retail merchants, truck owners, and so on also had national confederation offices.

Following the 1925 Constitution, the president—elected for a six-year term—was the source of major initiatives in the political process. Yet the president was far from an all-powerful figure. The most important checks on executive authority came from the competitive party system, which will be described in the next section. But presidential authority was also checked by the differentiation of governmental institutions and the marked autonomy of agencies even within the executive chain of command.

The legislature was no longer the focal point of the system, as it had been in the Parliamentary Republic. Nevertheless, the Chilean Congress remained the most powerful in Latin America, with the ability to modify and reject executive proposals. The Congress was the main arena for discussion and approval of budgetary matters as well as for the all-important issue of wage readjustments for public and even private employees.

In the final analysis, legislative politics was party politics, and presidents could cajole and bargain with allied as well as with adversary political groups for mutual advantage. By contrast the two other branches of government, the court system and the comptroller general (Contraloría), were well insulated from both presidential and legislative scrutiny. Judicial promotions were determined by seniority and merit, and though the president retained some power of appointment, his candidates had to come from lists prepared by the judges themselves. Equally independent was the comptroller general, who, like the Supreme Court judges, was appointed for life. His agency was charged with auditing public accounts and ruling on the legality of executive decrees. The comptroller's rulings on financial matters were final; on other matters, the president could, with the concurrence of his cabinet, overrule the comptroller. However, because of the prestige of the comptroller's office, this could be done only at the risk of considerable controversy, and until the Allende years presidents rarely overruled the comptroller.

Even within the executive branch presidential authority was circumscribed. Forty percent of public employees worked for over fifty semiautonomous agencies that, though nominally under government ministries, enjoyed significant managerial and even budgetary autonomy. As elsewhere, the web of private interests affected by a particular agency soon learned to develop more or less workable relationships of mutual benefit with it. Vested interests often made it difficult for a new administration to abolish old programs and bureaus, and innovations often required the creation of new agencies to administer the new projects, thus contributing to the progressive expansion of the state apparatus. Civil-service organizations and professional associations anxious to place their members in the expanding state sector further complicated the picture. Some state agencies became virtual fiefdoms of architects, civil engineers, lawyers, or doctors.

Though many agencies actually had formal interest-group representation on managing councils, such representation never became as important as the more informal and fluid constituency ties. Chilean politics never became corporative politics. Most private groups did obtain legal recognition. But that was a routine procedure and hardly meant that the government was officially sanctioning particular associations with exclusive rights to represent functional segments of society before the state. Indeed, most claims on the state were made by highly competitive groups, often representing interests drawn from the same horizontal or class lines.

If Chilean politics was not corporative, neither was it praetorian. Despite the vast and disarticulated state apparatus and the claims of a multiplicity of interests jockeying for advantage, Chilean politics did not involve the naked confrontation of political forces, each seeking to maximize its interests through direct action in the face of weak or transitory authority structures. The key to the Chilean system, which discouraged both corporatist and praetorian tendencies, was the continuing importance of political parties and a party system tied to the legislature, the principal arena for political give-and-take. From the turn of the century on, the norm in Chile was not the direct link between government agencies and interest associations or the unmediated clash of organized social forces. Rather, party structures, permeating all levels of society, served as crucial linkage mechanisms binding organizations, institutions, groups, and individuals to the political center. Local units of competing parties were active within each level of the bureaucracy, each labor union, each student federation. Parties often succeeded in capturing particular organizations or in setting up rival ones. Once an issue affecting the organization arose, party structures were instrumental in conveying the organization's demands to the nucleus of the policymaking process or in acting as brokers before the ubiquitous bureaucracy.

As the historical discussion noted, the Chilean party system was fragmented and very competitive. With the exception of the Christian Democrats in the mid-1960s, no single party received more than 30 percent of the votes in congressional or municipal elections from 1925 to 1973. The party system was also highly polarized. During the 1937–1973 period, the vote for the left (Socialists and Communists) averaged 21.5 percent (or 25.7 percent if one excludes the 1949, 1953, and 1957 elections in which the Communists were banned from participation), and the vote for the right averaged 30.1 percent. Since neither the right nor the left could obtain an effective majority on its own, center groups, especially the Radical Party, played a very important if little-appreciated role in the polarized system: By dealing with both extremes, they were essential elements in most legislative majorities or in winning presidential coalitions—all of which permitted the political system to muddle through despite the sharp ideological divergences. And yet the center movements could not succeed in establishing themselves as a majority force, although they occasionally eroded the strength of either the left or the right. For example, supported by voters on the right, the Christian Democrats scored a dramatic gain in the 1965 congressional election, obtaining 42.3 percent of the vote. But the Liberals and Conservatives, having merged to form the National Party in 1966, regained much of their historical strength by 1969, and their candidate outpolled the Christian Democratic nominee in the 1970 presidential election.

Given the fact that no single party or tendency could capture the presidency alone, coalitions were necessary. These were either formed before the election and resulted in winning an absolute majority, as was the case in 1964, or they had to be put together after the election in order to obtain the constitutionally mandated congressional approval of a candidate receiving only a plurality of the vote, as occurred in most cases. But, invariably, coalitions tended to disintegrate shortly after the election. The president could not succeed himself, and party leaders scrambled to disassociate themselves from the difficulties of incumbency in order to maximize electoral fortunes in succeeding contests. This meant that presidents had to compromise often with new supporters in the legislature, to salvage part of their programs and to govern.

Despite the polarization of the party system, politics did not revolve around only ideological and programmatic discussions. Obtaining benefits for groups and even favors for individuals, the essence of politics during the Parliamentary Republic, continued to be an important part of party activities. In fact, officials from all parties spent most of their time acting as political brokers—processing pensions for widows, helping Protestant ministers qualify for the white-collar social-security fund, interviewing the labor minister on behalf of a union leadership, seeking a job for a young schoolteacher, obtaining bridges and sewer systems for communities, and so forth. Legislators had particular access to state agencies because of congressional influence over purse strings, promotions, and programs affecting the bureaucracy.

An important political issue that led to extended bargaining in the legislature and to a flurry of demands and pressures from organized groups was the yearly discussion of the wage readjustment law. The law was intimately related to the budgetary approval process and gave the legislators (and therefore the parties) an input into the economic policy planning process. The state-controlled wage scales in the public sector were used as guidelines for the private sector, and therefore the readjustment laws, which also regulated social-security benefits, were of direct concern to the various party constituencies. In an economy averaging over 25 percent inflation with sharp yearly variations, a fundamental demand would be readjustments that would exceed, or at least match, the rate of inflation. Occasionally, amendments favoring specific groups or unions, but not all in the same category, would be approved as the legislators in the majority group sought to pay off political debts or favor their party comrades in positions of leadership. And yet the political ramifications of class cleavages in the society would become apparent as the left would, in the middle of dense and legalistic discussions over specifics, normally press for higher wages and benefits for working-class sectors, and the right would generally favor the restrictive readjustments tied to fiscal and economic austerity policies.

There were no giants in the Chilean political system. No single group could win a complete majority or totally impose its will on the others. In fact, since there was no ideological or programmatic consensus among the polarized political forces, the Chilean polity was in many respects a stalemated one, in which each decision led to extensive debates and long processes of political accommodation—or to lengthy protests by the dissatisfied groups. In such a setting, change could only be incremental, not revolutionary. Though upper-class sectors were favored by existing arrangements, the intricate stalemate reflected a situation in which each group derived benefits from participating in the system and thus had real stakes in its preservation. This buttressed the strong consensus over following all legal procedures, and affirmed the legitimacy of

Chilean democracy. But as the left gained positions through the commonly shared political process, the right and the sectors it represented began to question the validity of the process itself.

THE BREAKDOWN OF DEMOCRACY

Chile Under Eduardo Frei

The election of Eduardo Frei to the presidency in 1964 marked a significant shift in the center of Chilean politics. Unlike the Radical Party or the Ibáñez movement, the Christian Democrats (DC) claimed to be a new and cohesive ideological center, intent on breaking the political stalemate. They argued that their reformist strategy would lead to genuine economic and social progress and that it represented a viable third way between the right and the Marxist left. The Christian Democrats therefore ignored the fact that they had achieved the presidency with official endorsement from the rightist parties and that their unprecedented 1965 majority in the Chamber of Deputies was obtained with the support of traditionally right-wing portions of the electorate. They tried to govern as if they had become a majority party that would monopolize the presidency without coalition support for decades to come. The Radicals, rather than being cultivated as a potential ally in the political center, were maligned as pragmatic opportunists and were forced to relinquish some of their hold over the state bureaucracy. With the exercise of rigid party discipline in the Chamber of Deputies, which prevented the legislature from overruling presidential initiatives, the lower house became more and more a rubber stamp and the Senate a negative force.

The animosities created by the DC's disdain for coalition politics were compounded by the reforms it set in motion. These were ostensibly designed to raise the living standards and political participation of lower-class sectors as well as to modernize the social and economic systems. Two new groups, in particular, were mobilized as never before: the urban shantytown dwellers and the peasants. The first were encouraged to set up neighborhood councils and a variety of self-help organizations with cultural and community-development ends. The second rapidly became unionized once the peasant unionization law was approved in 1967 or were included in the peasant cooperatives that were set up in the lands expropriated under the government's new agrarian-reform program. Small landholding peasants were also encouraged to form cooperatives. As a result, roughly half the peasant labor force had become organized one way or another by 1970. Many new (particularly craft) unions were also formed among urban workers. Training programs were begun for both workers and peasants to increase their skills, and an educational reform increased the minimum number of mandatory schooling years.

The reforms, especially those in the countryside, engendered great opposition on the right, which traditionally had a strong political base among the landowners, who were threatened with expropriations and peasant unionization. The reforms also caused resentment and bitterness on the left. As the many young Christian Democrats in charge of the new programs spread throughout the country displaying new equipment, it became clear that the party was attempting to build a strong political base among popular sectors, precisely those sectors that Communists and Socialists considered their own natural base of support. This led to an intense effort by the left to compete with the Christian Democrats in the creation of the new popular organizations. As a result, sharp party conflicts were extended to broader sections of the population, creating sectarian divisions and feelings at the grassroots as never before. The threat to the left and the overall party competition for popular support were enhanced by the rise of an extreme left movement that also sought to organize its following.

The popular mobilization of the 1960s should therefore be seen as the result of party competition, with primarily political consequences. It cannot be said that the process got out of hand, either in terms of the capacity of party elites to control it or in terms of its having overburdened the nation's economy. In fact, during the Frei administration the general economic situation improved and state income increased, thereby generating greater economic capacity to increase the income of the newly mobilized popular sectors as well as a larger government capability to finance new programs. Though state income rose with better tax collection, the economic and fiscal improvements of the period were largely due to a rise in the price of copper during the Vietnam War and to foreign credit, mainly from U.S. government and private sources. The latter caused an increase in Chilean external debt to US$3 billion by the end of Frei's term and debt-service payments equivalent to roughly a third of export earnings.

Despite all its efforts, the Christian Democratic vote in the 1969 congressional elections was reduced to 29.8 percent. And given the events of the previous six years, it proved impossible to have anything but a three-way race in the 1970 presidential elections. The right would have nothing to do with the Christian Democrats and decided to rally behind the candidacy of former president Jorge Alessandri. The Radicals and other small centrist and leftist groups joined the Socialists and Communists in forming the Popular Unity (UP) coalition, which presented Salvador Allende as candidate. Allende obtained 36.2 percent of the vote, Alessandri came in a close second with 34.9 percent, and the Christian Democratic nominee trailed with 27.8 percent. It must be noted that the result was not the expression of heightened electoral radicalism. Allende, in fact, received a smaller percentage of the vote than in 1964, when he was supported by only Socialists and Communists, and fewer new voters than his conservative adversary. Moreover, although the Christian Democratic candidate ran on a leftist platform, it is clear from survey and electoral data that his voters would have gone to the right rather than the left.

Following constitutional procedure, the Congress had to elect the president from the two front runners, since none of the candidates received an absolute majority of the vote. In the most flagrant foreign intervention in Chilean history, U.S. president Richard Nixon ordered the CIA to do everything necessary to prevent Allende from coming to power, including economic sabotage and provoking a military coup. The Christian Democrats, unable to vote for their own candidate, held the key swing votes in the legislature, and President Frei and his colleagues were subjected to numerous internal and external pressures to get them to vote for Alessandri. When it appeared that they would honor tradition by selecting the front-runner, the CIA helped to organize an attempt to kidnap the chief of staff of the armed forces to provoke a military coup. General René Schneider was killed and the coup attempt backfired. It was the first assassination of a major Chilean leader since that of Portales in 1837.

The Allende Years

Allende's inauguration as president represented the first time that a coalition dominated by the Marxist parties took control of the executive. The coalition had campaigned on a program designed to initiate a transition to socialism while preserving Chile's traditional democratic freedoms and constitutional procedures, and the new administration moved swiftly to implement it. With the unanimous consent of the Chilean Congress, U.S. interests in the copper mines were nationalized. Resorting to executive powers, some of which were based on admittedly obscure though never repealed legal statutes, the government purchased or took over a broad range of industries as well as the private banking sector and, using Frei's agrarian-reform law, accelerated expropriations of farmland. Some industry and land takeovers were instigated by their workers or peasants, led in most cases by leftist or extreme leftist militants, who began sit-in strikes demanding the expropriations. This phenomenon was aided by the overall political climate created by the Allende inauguration, one that favored rather than repressed working-class actions.

The government also quickly set in motion a plan to raise wages, salaries, and benefits, particularly for the lowest-paid workers, and to increase the social services in poor communities. These measures were taken to stimulate the economy by increasing demand and as an attempt to strengthen the government's electoral support by satisfying the expectations of the left's working-class bases, for whom socialism principally meant a better standard of living. The policies were apparently successful, as the economic growth rate during 1971 was the best in decades, and the Popular Unity obtained roughly 50 percent of the vote in the 1971 municipal elections.

The initially favorable economic trends were, however, quickly reversed. Reflecting the poor's needs, the rising demand was disproportionately channeled to a greater consumption of basic consumer items such as food and clothing, areas of the economy that were least able to respond with rapid production increases. Inflationary pressures were therefore strengthened, particularly since government deficit spending increased, partly as a result of greater tax evasion. By the end of 1972, inflation had reached 164 percent and currency emissions accounted for over 40 percent of the fiscal budget. Moreover, the economy was clearly hurt by politically motivated cutbacks in credits and spare parts from the usual U.S. private or governmental sources. Foreign-exchange reserves dwindled rapidly as Chile imported more food and equipment with less recourse to credit and as it sought to meet payments, though partly rescheduled, on the foreign debt. The price of copper dropped to record lows, adding to the difficulties.

Early political success also proved short-lived. In 1972, the UP suffered reverses in key by-elections as well as in important institutional elections, such as those of the University of Chile or of labor federations. The courts, Contraloría, and Congress also increasingly objected to government initiatives. And most importantly, the early tacit support of the Christian Democrats turned into active opposition, leading to congressional censorship of ministers and to attempts to limit presidential authority.

The process that led to the brutal 1973 military coup that ended the Allende experiment is a highly complex, multidimensional, and dialectical one. It cannot be reduced to a simple set of causes that are easily construed with the benefits of hindsight. Surely the government made many unwise decisions or proved indecisive at important turning points; the sabotage and conspiracies of foreign and domestic interests seeking to preserve privilege at all costs helped to create an acute economic and political crisis; the actions of revolutionary groups both within and without the government coalition contributed to the exacerbation of an atmosphere of extreme confrontation that strengthened the disloyal and reactionary opposition; elements in the armed forces proved to be less than totally committed to the constitution and the democratic system; the capacity of the state to control and direct civil society disintegrated; and taking a longer view, the dependency of the economy on the United States for everything from financing to spare parts made the Allende experiment excessively vulnerable. All these are important factors, but they are not sufficient to explain the final result if viewed apart from a historical process in which contingent events played an important role. The breakdown of the regime was not preordained. It is a mistake to view the middle sectors as hopelessly reactionary, the workers as so radicalized that they would not stop short of total revolution, the army so antidemocratic that it was only waiting for its opportunity, the economy so dependent and the United States so single-handedly powerful and intransigent that the only possible denouement was full-fledged authoritarianism. There was room for choice, but with each unfolding event in the historical process that choice was markedly reduced.

If a single factor must be highlighted, the breakdown of Chilean democracy should be viewed as the result of the inability and unwillingness of moderate forces on both sides of the political dividing line to forge center agreements on programs and policies as well as on regime-saving compromises. The UP could not obtain a workable majority on its own, and the option of arming the workers as demanded by revolutionary groups was not a realistic alternative. The Chilean left was organized to compete in elections, not fight in battles; to change strategy would not have been easy, and any attempt to do so would have provoked an even earlier coup d'état. Without support from centrist forces, principally from the Christian Democrats who had made Allende's election possible in the first place, the UP government would remain a minority government without sufficient power to carry out programs, given the vast and unwieldy character of the Chilean institutional system.

The failure of center agreements resulted from political pressures originating in the extremes of both sides of the polarized party system. The government coalition was in fact sharply divided, the basic disagreements being those separating the Communists from the majority faction in the Socialist party. The latter wanted to press as fast as possible to institute the UP program and felt that support for the government would increase only insofar as it took decisive action to implement a socialist system. Compromise with the DC would, in the Socialists' view, only divert revolutionary objectives and confuse the working class. They therefore sought to undermine UP-DC collaboration and agreements. The Communists were much more willing to moderate the course of government policies in order to consolidate a narrower range of changes and to broaden the government's legislative base by resolving differences with the Christian Democrats. Both Socialists and Communists were pressured by the non-UP extreme left, which sought to accelerate changes through direct action outside constitutional procedures. Their influence in the UP coalition was magnified by the proximity of their positions with those of elements in the Socialist party majority; therefore, the extreme left was not marginalized at the fringe of the political process.

Allende shared the Communists' position but did not wish to cause a break with his own Socialist party. He therefore projected an ambivalent image and at times failed to take decisive action—for fear of alienating his party—without the certainty of receiving consistent support from the center forces in exchange. These political differences affected the daily operations of government agencies; employees, for example, often would not take orders from superiors belonging to other parties. The president and the ministers were so often involved in tending to these daily crises that they had little time to structure long-term policies, analyze the consequences of short-term ones, or develop a coherent strategy to deal with the moderate opposition.

The Christian Democrats were also torn by internal differences: The party was divided into left- and right-leaning factions of approximately equal strength. The 1971 party leadership came from the left-leaning group, and it sought to maintain a working relationship with the government, while the right-wing faction pressed for the adoption of a tougher opposition stand. However, the party leadership was at first rebuffed by an overly confident UP government exhibiting the same arrogance the DC had shown previously, a situation that only strengthened the position of the right-wing sector within the party. Ironically, constitutional reforms adopted in 1970 by the DC and the right had diminished the role of the legislature, thus reducing the executive's need to reach agreements with the opposition. The right-wing faction was also strengthened by the vehement attacks on prominent DC leaders in the leftist media and by the assassination of a former Frei cabinet minister. Though this killing was the action of a small leftist fringe, the DC blamed the government for tolerating a climate of violence that, it argued, led to such incidents.

As a centrist opposition force, the DC was also extremely vulnerable to pressures from the right of the party system. If the DC leadership could not show that its tacit support for the government had resulted in moderating UP policies, the party stood to lose the anti-UP vote to the right without gaining greater support from the left. Therefore, the DC was soon forced to work with the right in opposition. The turning point came in mid-1971 with the first special by-election to fill a vacant congressional seat in which, given the winner-take-all nature of the contest, a UP victory was certain if the opposition fielded separate candidates. Consequently, the DC approached the government suggesting an agreement that would have led to a joint UP-DC candidacy, an offer that Allende accepted but the Socialist party vetoed. In view of this rejection, the DC turned to the right, and the joint opposition candidate won decisively. As a result of this experience, a leftover splinter group decided to leave the Christian Democratic party, which further strengthened the right wing within it. The DC alliance with the right-wing National Party continued in future elections, adding to the polarization of forces.

In February 1972, the DC obtained congressional approval of legislation severely limiting the president's ability to intervene in the economy, thereby challenging the essence of the government's program and marking the beginning of a fundamental constitutional confrontation between the president and the Congress. Interpreting 1970 constitutional amendments differently from the president, the opposition argued that Congress required only a simple majority to override a presidential veto of the new legislation, while the UP maintained, in fact more correctly, that a two-thirds majority was needed. It then became clear to moderates on both sides that accommodation was essential. On two separate occasions government and DC representatives met in an attempt to reach a compromise that would have allowed the government to keep a substantial public sector of the economy while giving the private sector certain guarantees. But the talks collapsed. The Nationals suggested a DC sellout, while the Socialists and other leftist groups stepped up factory expropriations in order to present the DC with a fait accompli. They thus undermined the negotiating position of the moderate Radical splinter group entrusted by Allende with conducting the discussion, and as a result this group left the UP coalition to join the opposition. Again, this only polarized the political forces further, reducing the potential success of a center agreement.

By mid-1972, the critical situation of the economy and the growing aggressiveness of the opposition led the government to try once again to hold talks with the Christian Democrats. This time Allende was strongly committed to reaching a compromise, and the UP made substantial concessions leading to agreement on a broad range of issues. However, the more conservative faction within the Christian Democratic party maneuvered successfully to prevent the negotiators from finishing their work. By that point, most sectors within the DC felt that the government was clearly on the defensive and thought that by concluding an agreement with it, the party would surely lose support among the increasingly discontented middle sectors, thereby running the risk of being routed by the Nationals in the March 1973 congressional elections. Considerations of short-term party interest thus carried the day.

Toward the end of 1972, qualitative changes had begun to take place in Chilean politics. The parties had repeatedly called the mass rallies that characterized the Allende years not only to increase their bargaining stakes but also to prove their capacity to mobilize people. Nonetheless, the nature of this mobilization soon changed. Business and professional associations increasingly took matters into their own hands, and before long the DC and the Nationals were falling over each other not to direct but to pledge support for the independent action of a whole range of groups. These demonstrations culminated in the massive October 1972 strike and lockout by hundreds of truck owners, merchants, industrialists, and professionals. The government parties countered by mobilizing their own supporters, also engendering a significant organizational infrastructure that could operate at the margin of party leadership directives. These demonstrations and counterdemonstrations by a vast array of groups, the numbers of which continued to increase during the Allende years, were partly stimulated by a vitriolic mass media giving at least two totally different interpretations of every event, generating a dynamic in which falsehoods turned into hysterically believed truths, and perceived threats were taken as imminent. The climate of agitation was also increased by the CIA funds that flowed to opposition groups, strengthening them significantly as political actors independent of party control. For government leaders the decreased capacity of party elites to control group mobilization and confrontation was more serious than for the opposition. It meant that the government lost an important measure of authority over the society, that the state itself would be bypassed as the central arena for political confrontation, and that the legitimacy of the regular processes of bargaining was undermined. In this crisis atmosphere, Allende turned to a presumably neutral referee who would ensure institutional order until the March 1973 congressional elections could clear the political air. Military men were brought into the cabinet, and the chief of staff was made the minister of the interior.

The incorporation of the military into the government ended the strikes of October 1972 and freed the political forces to concentrate on the congressional elections, which party leaders saw as the decisive confrontation. But in serving as a buffer between contending forces, the military itself became the object of intense political pressures. The left within the UP criticized the military for slowing down government programs and initiatives, while the more strident elements on the right accused it of helping a government that would otherwise fall. Other sectors went out of their way to praise the military, a tacit recognition that they were the only force with real power. These pressures politicized an institution that had largely remained at the margin of political events. Though it was hardly perceived at the time, a cleavage began to appear within the military between officers supporting the government because they saw it as the constitutional government and those more receptive to the increasingly louder voices of opposition elements calling for the government's downfall.

The March 1973 elections symbolized the final polarization of Chilean politics as the government and the opposition faced each other as two electoral blocs. Not surprisingly, the elections did not help resolve the political crisis. The opposition failed to gain the two-thirds majority it needed to impeach Allende, and the government failed to obtain majority control in either house of Congress. Given the massive inflation and serious shortages of basic goods as well as the climate of political uncertainty, the government's showing was commendable since it managed to win seats at the expense of the opposition. And yet the final results were not dramatically different from those that the two blocs had obtained as separate parties in the previous congressional contest. The electorate did not provide the magic solution. Its task done, the military left the cabinet.

Soon after, a decisive event initiated the final stage in the breakdown of the regime. On June 29, 1973, a military garrison revolted. Though the uprising was quickly put down, President Allende and his advisers realized that it was only a matter of time before the pro-coup faction of the armed forces consolidated its strength. They again dismissed the far left's counsel to arm the workers, arguing that the creation of a parallel army would only accelerate the coup. Ironically, military officers were quicker to believe, or to make believe, not only that the workers could be a potent force but that sectors of the left had already structured a viable military force. But the well-publicized efforts of military commanders to find secret arms caches uncovered nothing of importance, although they attempted to convey the impression that they had.

To the consternation of the leadership of his own Socialist party, Allende once again called for talks with the Christian Democrats. And despite the vocal opposition of many of their followers, the Christian Democratic leaders, urged to do so by the cardinal, agreed to the new negotiations. However, an agreement at that point was unlikely. The hard-line faction of the Christian Democrats had replaced the more moderate leadership, and Allende was thus obliged to deal with the group most hostile to his government and policies. Moreover, the country was once again in the throes of massive lockouts, strikes, and civil disobedience campaigns led by business and professional associations (with considerable CIA funding), all demanding the president's resignation. By that time significant working-class groups, such as the copper miners, had also staged strikes to express their discontent with specific government policies, which only reinforced the confidence of the opposition. Any form of support for the government by the Christian Democrats would therefore have been seen as a sellout by the opposition. The political arena had been reduced to a few men attempting to negotiate a settlement. Even though these men no longer had the kind of control over social forces they once had, a dramatic announcement from the talks would still have placed the nation's largest parties and most respected leaders on the side of a peaceful solution and would have seriously undermined the subversive plans of military officers.

But agreement was not forthcoming. The Christian Democrats did not trust Allende's word that he really wanted a settlement, believing instead that he merely sought to buy time in order to force an armed confrontation. However, it is clear from the president's actions that he sought an agreement. He kept moderate leaders in his cabinets, even though they were severely attacked by the left within and outside the UP, and he virtually broke with his own party. Furthermore, Allende finally did agree to the Christian Democratic demand of bringing the military back into the government. In combating to the end the dubious prospect of "Marxist totalitarianism" and in constantly increasing bargaining demands, the DC leaders failed to realize how much stake they had in the political order they thought they were defending. By not moving forcefully to structure a political solution, they undermined the fragile position of the president and his advisers, who were seeking accommodation. Instead the DC supported a Chamber of Deputies declaration calling on the military to safeguard the constitution and declaring that the government had violated the constitution and disregarded key laws.

Two weeks later, prominently displaying the chamber's resolution as evidence of the legitimacy and broad-based support for their action, the top military leadership led the brutal revolt against the government. Air force jets bombed and strafed the presidential palace, in which Allende himself, after offering resistance, apparently committed suicide. Thousands of government supporters, or presumed government supporters, were arrested, mistreated, tortured, or killed in the months that followed.

Some prominent Christian Democrats condemned the coup in the initial moments. But others, including the leadership, welcomed it as inevitable and blamed the government for all that had transpired. Little did they realize what the "saving" action of the military would mean for the country's and their own future.

The Military in Government

The September 11, 1973, coup marked the most dramatic political change in Chilean history. A military junta headed by the commanders of each of the services and the national police took power and argued at first that they had overthrown the Allende government in order to protect democracy and restore constitutional government. But the new authorities soon defined the Chilean crisis as one of regime rather than of government. They placed the blame for the breakdown of Chile's institutions not only on the Popular Unity government but also on liberal democracy itself. Democracy had permitted divisive party competition and the rise of Marxist political leaders intent on defining the nation's politics in class terms. It had also generated demagogic politicians who contributed to economic mismanagement. Government was best left, in their view, in the hands of "technicians" who could formulate the "best" policy choices with administrative efficiency until the people had the necessary "maturity" to exercise better judgment.

The goal of the new junta thus became one of creating a "new" democracy and a "new" citizen, devoid of the "vices" of the past. The Congress was closed, local governments disbanded, and elections banned. Newspapers, radio stations, and magazines were shut down, and those allowed to publish were subjected to varying degrees of censorship. Officials and leaders of the Popular Unity government and parties were arrested, exiled, and, in some cases, killed. Within months of the coup, Christian Democratic leaders, unwilling to accept an indefinite military regime, saw their activities severely curbed as well.

The military authorities sharply restricted the activities of traditional political parties and ignored the strong pressure of right-wing supporters to create a massive progovernment party or "civic-military movement." For this reason it is inappropriate to label the Chilean regime as fascist. The military regime sought political demobilization.

Neither is it appropriate to view the regime as corporatist. Despite early pronouncements that the junta intended to consult organized groups, all of the country's major interest groups, including employer and professional associations and trade organizations (many of which had supported the coup with enthusiasm), saw their influence markedly diminished. The new authorities were simply not interested in bringing into the decisionmaking process any expression of societal interests. They were convinced that through disciplined administrative management and the advice of qualified experts they would be able to govern and modernize the country without the advice of "interested" or "partisan" groups. They thus sought to replace party politics and interest-group politics with techno-administrative solutions imposed by fiat. The governing style for the country as a whole paralleled the internal governing style of the military institution itself.

The Chilean military regime was extraordinary in the extent to which General Pinochet succeeded in concentrating power in himself. Since he commanded the largest and most important service, the army, his fellow officers named him the first president of the junta but early suggestions called for the rotation of this position among its four members. Both executive and legislative power rested in the junta. Within a year, Pinochet had acquired greater power than his colleagues. With the adoption of a "Stature of the Military Junta," a protoconstitutional document, together with declaring himself "Supreme Chief of the Nation," Pinochet assumed control of executive power, although it still formally remained in the junta, which had to approve all cabinet and ambassadorial nominations. Half a year later a new constitutional decree named him "President of the Republic of Chile," the traditional designation of Chilean presidents, in addition to preserving the prior titles of "President of the Governmental Junta" and "Supreme Chief of the Nation," and stated unambiguously that he exercised executive power. General Pinochet's position as "President of the Republic," and the junta's as the "legislative power," was reaffirmed in the so-called transitory articles of the constitution adopted in 1980. Pinochet also changed his military title in order to emphasize a position of preeminence over his colleagues in the other services, who then became his subordinates in rank. In 1979, he adopted the designation of "Generalissimo of the Armed Forces" and later that of "Captain General." He controlled as the ultimate authority all military promotions and retirements, carefully overseeing in particular those in his own service.

This concentration of power had no parallel in other military regimes in Latin America. Pinochet was not a retired military officer, like most of his Argentine counterparts, nor did he serve at the behest of the corps of generals, like Brazilian military presidents. Policy decisions never originated among high-ranking officers and were never reviewed by them. Pinochet stressed repeatedly that the armed forces were not to deliberate political matters. In this sense, their relation to the executive power was one of subordination just as it had been, in the past, to the Chilean presidents. Military officers occupied a majority of all positions in the government, but they reported to their superiors, be they military or civilian, within the government. General Pinochet led a military regime, but it was not, strictly speaking, of the military. It is best described as a dictatorship of the commander in chief. As such, it was a curious, personalized regime in which power derived from occupancy of the top office of a military bureaucracy.

This type of dictatorship was made possible by the highly professional, obedient, and hierarchical nature of the Chilean military. Paradoxically, these were qualities that stemmed from Chile's democratic past. The military was not involved in politics, and Chilean politicians did not expect it to be the source of political instability or coups. It is highly symptomatic that the coup against President Allende did not break the military line of command: The president had appointed General Pinochet to the top position in the army shortly before.

Policy Initiatives of the Military Government

The Pinochet government undertook more far-reaching changes than any of those that preceded it over the last fifty years. The repressive apparatus of the state increased enormously, as did the jurisdiction of military courts over offenses by civilians. But in other respects the size of the state and its role in national life were drastically reduced.

The government pursued an aggressive policy of privatization. All land held under the agrarian reform program was turned over to individual property holders. Only a handful of companies remained in the public sector (aside from the railways and utilities, the most important of these is the copper company, CODELCO, that controls the principal established mines). The rest of the companies were sold to national and foreign private investors, often at bargain prices. New mineral deposits have been developed by private, mostly foreign, capital as well. As part of debt-for-equity swaps to reduce an external debt that increased to $20 billion by 1986, many formerly Chilean firms have been denationalized.

The authorities put in place a radical program of privatizing state services in social security and health, which meant dismantling long-standing publicly funded institutions. The public housing development program was also turned over to the private sector. Labor legislation was extensively revamped, making it more difficult for workers to pressure employers through collective action. The size of the unionized workforce declined by about 60 percent compared to its highest membership point in the last two years of the Allende government. Wages and salaries declined in real terms by as much as 50 percent with respect to their levels in 1970, and did not recover fully—even during the years of strong growth—during the whole period of military government. The combination of the incomes and welfare policies led to a significant regression in the distribution of income.

The government also undertook educational reforms. Public, primary, and secondary schools were turned over to municipal administrations (led by mayors appointed by the government), and new legislation encouraged the formation of private schools and even universities.

The economy was opened up to external competition by drastic cuts in import duties, resulting in numerous bankruptcies as industries were unable to adjust to the shock. Except for a few years in the late 1970s and early 1980s in which the government's economic team greatly overvalued the national currency with catastrophic results, economic policies generally sought to stimulate growth through the development of new exports. These policies were successful and reduced the reliance on copper exports from about 85 percent of export earnings in the early 1970s to about 45 percent in the late 1980s.

Economic growth rates were very spotty during the sixteen years of military government. There were severe recessions in 1975 and in 1982 (in each of those years the economy declined by about 14 percent) and periods of significant growth (or recovery) with positive rates of between 5 and 9 percent in the late 1970s and late 1980s. Given this zigzag pattern of growth, the per capita income of Chile by the end of the 1980s was roughly equivalent to its 1970 level measured in constant dollars. And yet the military government prided itself on its economic management, given the fact that the economy registered strong growth in the last three years of authoritarian rule; moreover, inflation was low, the external debt shrunk by $3 billion, and unemployment dropped significantly. Chilean businessmen also developed a new confidence in their abilities and in the economic future of the country, which they associated with the free-market and open-economy policies of the regime. This sense of success was magnified by the disastrous economic performance of Latin America during the 1980s.

Economic and social policy initiatives were in the hands of a team of young economists who came to be known as the Chicago Boys due to the free-market and monetarist approaches they drew from the University of Chicago. They appealed to Pinochet because of their lack of identification with Chilean parties and their technical competence. Their belief that Chilean underdevelopment could be attributed to an overbloated state that restricted private initiative corresponded well with the effort to drastically restrict state institutions for political reasons, given the association of those institutions with party-sponsored clientelistic politics in the democratic past.

Opposition to the Military Regime

Many authoritarian rulers think that they can drastically reduce support for their oppositions through a combination of repression and political, social, and economic changes. This goal proves to be elusive in countries, like Chile, with strong party systems. Citizens by and large retain their political predilections, and these are passed on from one generation to the next supported by family and community ties creating a collective political memory. Party militants are also able to retain at least the rudiments of their organizations, and they often remain active as leaders in social groups and associations whose activities are allowed by the regime.

Chile was no exception to this rule. The parties retained their organizations despite the severe repression directed especially at those of the left. Many party militants remained in positions of leadership in the same social groups where they found an audience before, be it the labor movement, student federations, or community associations. Supporters of the military government rarely won the internal elections of these groups when they were held freely. The Catholic Church assumed a very important role in the overall opposition to the regime. It continually called for national reconciliation and for a return to liberal democracy and refused to lend any credence to the attempts by the authorities to use Catholic social doctrine—in its most conservative interpretation—as a formula to legitimize the regime. The Church also took decisive steps to challenge the regime for its many abuses of human rights and protected the lawyers and other professionals who actively documented such abuses and defended their victims in court. Moreover, the Church gave legal cover and other forms of support to many groups, such as social science researchers, journalists, unions, and popular community associations through which opposition views were expressed and organizing took place. It was through such Church-sponsored activities that the Christian Democrats and the left gradually came together in the first years of the military regime, leaving behind their bitter divisions from the Allende period.

Through a combination of social mobilization, calls for negotiations, and international pressures, the opposition continually tried to force the military to abdicate and accept a transition to democracy. Militants on the extreme left, some associated with the Communist party, also attempted to organize armed resistance to the regime. All actions undertaken by such groups, including a failed assassination attempt against Pinochet himself, were sharply criticized by the rest of the opposition, on grounds of both morality and expediency. The bulk of the opposition condemned all forms of violence, and such incidents— some of which were of very dubious origins—seemed to play into the hands of the regime by lending credence to its claims that the country, suffering terrorist threats, was not ready for democracy.

The opposition's attempts to mobilize people against the regime were at times enormously successful in the major cities. There was a series of massive "protests" for several years beginning in May of 1983. The movement, called by labor leaders initially, consisted of banging pots at a certain hour in the evening, boycotting classes, staging work slowdowns, and refraining from using public transportation and from shopping. The military regime eventually met such protests, which were initially held monthly, with massive displays of force and random, brutal repression by the army and police. The protests increasingly led to violence, which the government tried, with characteristic aplomb, to blame entirely on the opposition.

The moderate opposition eventually called the protest movement off in order to break the increasing cycle of violence. And yet, the movement served an important function. It demonstrated both to the government and to the opposition itself that after ten years of military rule, in which the government, controlling television and most of the rest of the mass media, relentlessly diffused a single interpretation of all events, the opposition could still generate a massive demonstration against the authorities. This emboldened the parties to seek new forms of exercising political leadership, and it convinced many civilian politicians on the right that the military government's long-term project was not entirely viable. Such politicians, whose concerns were dismissed highhandedly by Pinochet, began to organize a new political party of the right, taking some distance from the military regime. This eventually generated a division on the right of the Chilean party spectrum between those who identified closely with the military regime and those who did not.

While the moderate opposition continually expressed its willingness to negotiate with the military regime over forms of transition to democracy, Pinochet himself steadfastly refused to entertain any such discussions. The personalized Chilean military regime had a very narrow and tight inner circle of power, allowing no space for the development of moderate but influential segments of political leadership within the ruling circles. If such segments had existed, it is conceivable that the opposition could have found a willing partner in the regime to search for a suitable transition formula. But all dissenters from Pinochet's leadership who emerged within the regime were simply excluded from it, and the opposition's attempts to press the government and the armed forces to negotiate came to nothing.

Throughout the military regime, the opposition enjoyed many expressions of international solidarity. The international community repeatedly condemned the government's violations of human rights. When the AFL-CIO threatened to boycott the unloading of Chilean exports in the United States in 1978, the government prepared labor legislation that allowed a significant reactivation of Chile's unions. And arms sales to the Chilean military from major American and European manufacturers were significantly curtailed. Given the orthodoxy of its economic management and commitment to its debt obligations, the Chilean government was well received only in international financial circles.

THE TRANSITION TO DEMOCRATIC GOVERNMENT

The opposition was finally able to force the military government into a transition to democracy by using the procedures Pinochet himself had put into the

1980 Constitution. The origins of this document go back to the immediate post-coup period. The new military authorities were in a juridicially untenable position. They justified their seizure of power in part by noting that the Allende coalition had violated the 1925 Constitution, but they themselves were violating it daily through their de facto exercise of power and by not reverting—as many early supporters of the coup expected—to constitutional procedures in order to reconstitute the government. The junta therefore argued that the existing constitution was inadequate to "protect" democracy and announced that a new one would be written. A committee of civilians identified with the right and the extreme right was charged in 1974 with the task of preparing the draft of a new charter.

The committee ran into disagreements between its extremist and more moderate members. Eventually, as head of a "Council of State," former president Jorge Alessandri took a leading role in drafting the constitution, which he presented to General Pinochet in 1978 for his approval. The document adhered to a very large extent to Chilean constitutional traditions. It also called for a transition period of five years in which General Pinochet would continue to govern as president, but would share legislative responsibilities with a Congress whose members would initially be designated.

Pinochet changed the draft in significant ways, strengthening the power of non-elected and military officials and extending the presidential term of office to eight years. Moreover he added twenty-nine "transitory articles" that suspended the application of the bulk of the constitutional provisions until the beginning of a second presidential term after the enactment of the constitution. One of these articles named Pinochet to the presidency for a first term, which was to begin on March 11, 1981, and others assigned the legislative power to the junta. The transitory articles therefore permitted Pinochet to extend his personalistic regime for another eight years.

What was to prove decisive for the transition to democratic government were the stipulations Pinochet added to the transitory articles for the presidential succession at the end of the first term. At that point the commanders in chief of the armed services (including Pinochet himself) would select a new presidential candidate, whose name would be submitted to the voters in a plebiscite. If that individual won the plebiscite, congressional elections would be held within a year, and the constitution would be fully applied. If the candidate lost the plebiscite, within a year there would be open presidential as well as congressional elections. It is safe to assume that Pinochet had every intention of running for a second term, and he had no difficulty, when the time came, in obtaining the nomination from his colleagues. Pinochet felt confident of his ability to win plebiscites. He did so by a large margin in 1978, and he obtained what was announced as 65 percent approval in the plebiscite held on September 11, 1980, to ratify the 1980 Constitution and his own "first presidential term" along with it.

But both of these plebiscites were held in highly irregular manners, and the opposition had little difficulty in contesting their validity. This rejection of the plebiscites' legitimacy, especially of the one that presumably had approved the constitution and Pinochet's own "presidential term" along with it, struck a raw nerve in ruling circles. Hence, Pinochet and his supporters took pains continually to stress the "constitutionality" of the government. Moreover, adherence to the 1980 Constitution became the centerpiece of the government's political program. The authorities also turned the defense of the "institutionality" enshrined in the constitution into one of the principal missions of the armed forces.

By late 1986, the opposition had exhausted all its efforts to force the government into a transition through social mobilization and other forms of pressure, and it therefore began to look forward to the 1988 plebiscite as a possible mechanism to defeat the government. Recalling its criticisms of the prior plebiscites, the opposition stipulated a series of conditions that would have to be met for the new plebiscite to be considered a valid expression of the voters' will. These included the re-establishment of a proper electoral registry (the previous one had been burned by the military), a sufficient amount of time for the registration process to ensure that large numbers of citizens actually registered, television access for advocates of the "no" ("no" to another term for Pinochet), the necessary voting procedures to ensure secrecy, and assurances that opposition delegates would be able to observe the balloting and vote-counting processes. The American ambassador in Santiago, Harry Barnes, made it very clear to the members of the military junta that the United States agreed with all these conditions and that it would not consider the plebiscite valid unless they were all met. Given its sensitivity to charges of illegitimacy, and given a ruling of the Constitutional Court favoring these procedures, the military government agreed to all of them.

As the campaign preparations began, the opposition organized a broad coalition for the "no" that included all groups except the Communist party, whose leaders only very belatedly saw any value in the process. The opposition used the half-hour segment the authorities gave it on television very effectively, with a message focused on future happiness and reconciliation. It also organized poll watchers in every single locality of the country and an alternative vote-counting system that would give it the possibility of checking the veracity of official figures. Citizens were to vote "yes" or "no" to Pinochet's continuing in the presidency, and when the votes were counted on the night of October 5, 1988, 54.7 percent had voted "no," and 43 percent "yes." Over 90 percent of those eligible to register had done so, and over 90 percent of registered voters cast ballots.

Pinochet was shocked by this result. Yet there was little he could do to set it aside. The plebiscite was a procedure that he introduced into the transitory articles of the constitution himself, and he could not easily turn against the "institutionality" he had for years urged the armed forces and his civilian supporters to uphold. The opposition also gave the regime no excuses to suspend the plebiscite or the vote count. From beginning to end, it conducted an orderly campaign, refraining from staging demonstrations that might be construed as provocations. The night of the vote count some government officials did seek to tamper with the vote count. But while this effort was under way, the commander in chief of the air force freely admitted to a journalist that the figures released by the opposition were correct, thereby undermining any tinkering with the results.

The outcome of the plebiscite meant that within a year, open presidential and congressional elections were held. The opposition parties agreed to support a single presidential candidate, Christian Democrat Patricio Aylwin, and to present basically a single list of candidates for the Senate and the Lower House. The opposition demanded that the 1980 Constitution be revised, and in subsequent negotiations the government agreed to significant changes including the elimination of the prohibition of parties of the Marxist left and the dilution of the power that the military would have over civilian authorities. In turn, the opposition called for the public to accept the amended constitution in a plebiscite, held in July of 1989, thereby giving it popular legitimacy and signaling that it would accept it itself as the basic legal framework of the country.

The presidential and congressional elections were held on December 14, 1989. Aylwin won 55.2 percent of the validly cast vote, defeating two candidates of the right, and his democratic coalition obtained 56.5 percent of the vote for seats in the Lower House of Congress.

Rebuilding the Democratic Regime

President Aylwin's term in office was shortened to four years as part of the agreement with the military regime that altered the Constitution in mid-1989. The right and even the military thought that they could recapture the presidency after four years, because they assumed that the incoming opposition would prove to be incompetent in office. Pinochet even created a virtual shadow cabinet with thirty-five advisers in charge of covering developments in all areas of public policy. Supporters of the military regime assumed that labor conflicts over long-standing grievances would emerge; leftist insurgencies and terrorism would expand; demands for accounting of human rights violations would magnify tensions; the political alliance of Christian Democrats, Socialists, radicals, and others would soon break up; and the economy, already overheated as a result of the military government's overspending for electoral purposes, would deteriorate as investments dried up in a climate of uncertainty. Such perceptions were buttressed by the experience of democratization in neighboring countries, where it had been accompanied by adverse economic results.

However, these predictions proved to be grossly incorrect. After his term in office ended in 1994, President Aylwin turned the government over to Eduardo Frei Ruiz Tagle, another Christian Democrat and the son of the former President, who was elected in December 1993 by the same coalition that had won the plebiscite against Pinochet, this time to serve a new presidential term of six years. Frei in turn handed over power in the year 2000 to Socialist Ricardo Lagos, one of the architects of the alliance that defeated Pinochet in 1988. Lagos took office for a term extending until March of 2006. As President Lagos nears the end of his term, the governing alliance, known as the Concertation of Parties for Democracy, has become the most stable and successful governing coalition in Chilean history. The Concertation governments have built on the economic reforms of the military regime while strengthening the social safety net, cutting the number of poor households by half to about 20% of the total, doubling the national product, drastically reducing inflation to yearly rates of less than 3%, and consolidating democratic institutions.

Although the first year of the Aylwin government required an economic adjustment that reduced growth to 2 percent, since then the economy has boomed, despite a dip between 1998 and 2003, and Chile now has the highest per capita income (using a purchasing power parity exchange rate) in Latin America. The rate of savings and investment increased by the mid-1990s to about 27 percent of GNP, a level nearly equal to those of the high-performing Asian economies, and there has been a yearly fiscal budget surplus of 1–3 percent of GNP. Social spending on education, health, and housing has increased on average by 10 percent per year since 1990. The lowest pensions and the minimum wage have risen about 150 percent, and after a slow start, by 1996 real wages have reached their highest levels ever with each passing year. A highly successful housing policy has steadily replaced urban shantytowns, and about 75% of all Chilean households currently own the dwellings they live in. A new network of super highways and paved secondary roads leads in all directions. Despite an increase in labor conflict, including that of public-sector workers and teachers, the new levels of such conflict are very low by international standards and minimal when compared to those of the late 1960s and early 1970s in Chile. Foreign investors have flocked to place their money in Chile, international credit agencies have given Chilean paper investment grade, and the nation's business sector has begun to invest heavily in neighboring economies. The government has negotiated free-trade agreements with Mexico, Canada, the United States, the European Union, and South Korea, and has joined the Mercosur block of South American countries as an associate member. A new free trade agreement is currently being negotiated with China. Products from all over the world fill market shelves in Chile, and yet the country enjoys a positive balance of trade year after year. Access to education has improved to the point that nearly 65% of all adults in Chile have now completed secondary school. And access to health has led to national health indicators that now compare favorably to those of the most developed countries in the world. The main deficiency in this favorable overall socio-economic picture has been that income distribution retains the regressiveness it reached under the military regime.

One of the most difficult issues of the Chilean transition has been the legacy of human rights violations by the Pinochet regime. President Aylwin initiated a review of the 384 political prisoners who remained in jail when he took office, most of whom were rapidly released. The last handful of prisoners had their sentences changed to exile abroad. Aylwin also appointed a Truth and Reconciliation Committee with representatives of all segments of opinion that documented over 3,000 cases of disappearances and produced a general report providing the country with a common interpretation of the recent and very conflictual past. Only the military and the Supreme Court took objection to that interpretation. The families of the disappeared persons were compensated by the state, including lifelong pensions for parents, widows, or widowers, stipends or scholarships for children, and were given free medical attention. In addition, people who were fired for political reasons had their pension benefits restored, and those who were exiled were assisted in returning to the country. By 2004 there were about 255,000 beneficiaries of all these programs. In addition, the Frei government sponsored a dialog between human rights lawyers and the heads of the military services, leading the military to call human rights crimes "abominable acts." And the Lagos government appointed a committee to investigate cases of torture. It has reported that about 35,000 Chileans were tortured by the military regime's agents; all of them are to received a modest compensation. In reaction to this information, the head of the army appointed by President Lagos, General Emilio Cheyre, has recognized that the military did indeed have a systematic policy of torturing detainees. General Cheyre has pledged that the military will "never again" engage in violations of human rights.

The evidence that was gathered by the Truth and Reconciliation Commission was made public and could be used by the families for prosecuting the perpetrators of human rights violations. The government initiated a new interpretation of Pinochet's 1978 amnesty law stating that unless the body of a disappeared person was found the amnesty could not be applied; this opened the way for judicial inquiries into these human rights violations. New laws have also drastically reduced the jurisdiction of military courts over crimes by military personnel involving civilians. As a result of all these measures, many cases were reopened, and by mid-1996, while Pinochet still remained the head of the Army until 1998 following the stipulations in the transitory articles of the 1980 Constitution, there were about 250 such cases under active review by the courts. By 2003, around 120 military officers had been removed from military ranks after judicial determination of their participation in human rights violations. Moreover, by 2004 about fifty military and police officers and some civilians have served or are serving sentences for crimes committed during the dictatorship but not covered by the amnesty law. These include the former head of the military regime's intelligence service during the worst period of human rights violations, General Manuel Contreras, as well as his closest collaborators.

The human rights policies of the Aylwin government led to sometimes severe tensions with the military. Aylwin twice urged General Pinochet to resign. Led by Pinochet, officers demonstrated, producing serious incidents of military insubordination. However, these incidents led to no changes in government policies. No laws calling for an end to prosecutions, such as those approved in Argentina and Uruguay, were ever approved.

The demand for prosecution in Chile of General Pinochet for human rights crimes began the very day he retired from his position as head of the Army in January 1998. He took refuge in the immunity from prosecution afforded to him by the fact that he had the right, as a former "President of the Republic," to become a Senator for life. Consequently, Judge Juan Guzmán, who took charge of the cases presented against Pinochet, had to first remove this immunity. He was in the midst of the investigations that were necessary to do so when Pinochet was arrested in London under a warrant issued by a Spanish judge. The ensuing court procedures in London had implications for international human rights law worldwide. But after about a year in London Pinochet suffered a series of minor strokes that impaired his ability to recollect events, and he was therefore freed to return to Chile. At that point Judge Guzmán resumed his proceedings, and the Chilean courts accepted his verdict removing Pinochet's immunity from prosecution. However, Pinochet's medical condition prevented Judge Guzmán from prosecuting Pinochet in a criminal trial. The time he spent in London turned out to be precious time lost for this purpose.

The Chilean judicial system had already condemned several human rights violators to jail terms before Pinochet was arrested in London. And yet Pinochet's arrest had the effect of giving a psychological boost to judges who had always felt that they should make an effort to prosecute vigorously human rights cases. They had to work in a judicial environment dominated by the conservative and pro-military regime judges that had been promoted to the higher courts under Pinochet, and his arrest in London vindicated their views. Similarly, Pinochet's arrest forced people on the right to finally accept the notion that human rights violations were a serious matter, and not an invention of opponents of the military regime or an aberration produced by a "few bad apples" in the security services—a view that General Cheyre has now accepted. Finally, the discovery in 2004 that Pinochet also had accumulated up to 8 million dollars in secret foreign bank accounts further served to tarnish his image among his Chilean followers. Allegations of corruption have always been taken very seriously in Chile, and the country prides itself for having little of it.

Despite the changes to the 1980 Constitution in mid-1989, when the Aylwin government began the constitution still contained elements that were contrary to democratic constitutional theory. These were, in the main, corporatist mechanisms of representation and governance at the local government level; the capacity of a National Security Council (half of which was composed of the commanders of military services) to convene by initiative of a fraction of its members in order to ask the president or other high authorities for explanations on a broad range of matters; the presence in the Senate of ten senators who were not elected by popular vote but designated by various authorities, including four who had to be former heads of the armed services who were to be chosen by the National Security Council; and the lack of a presidential power to remove commanders of the armed services from their positions and to force career military or police officers into retirement. Chilean redemocratization could not be complete until these anomalous institutions were eliminated.

The local government institutions were the first to be changed. The discussions with the rightist parties over this matter began soon after Aylwin became president. Although the parties of the right have always tried to retain what they saw as the positive policy and institutional legacies of the authoritarian regime, they rejected the Pinochet model in this aspect. They preferred to measure their local support in open elections and to place, where they had the necessary votes, members of their parties in positions of local government leadership. The constitutional change simply reinstated the type of municipal government that existed prior to 1973. The first municipal elections were held in mid-1992; twenty-two years had passed since such elections had last been held.

The other aspects that were counter to democratic constitutionalism in the 1980 Constitution were much more difficult to change. The right defended the designated senators because, having been originally named at the end of the Pinochet government for eight year terms, all of them favored the right and allowed it to gain a majority of the Senate. The rightist parties also sought to prevent the president from having the power to remove armed services commanders, arguing that such power would dilute their role in the National Security Council. And they noted that this Council was necessary as a check on presidential power as part of the function of the armed forces as "guarantors" of Chile's political and institutional stability.

No argument sufficed to convince the right that these were inappropriate institutions in a democracy. However, as the years went by the Concertation governments could begin to appoint designated senators that would favor the Concertation coalition. Moreover, the stability of the country meant that the National Security Council's role as watch dog made no sense. Hence, after long discussions with the rightist parties, they finally agreed, in a vote in Congress in October 2004, to do away with all of the anomalous institutions mentioned above. The current designated senators will not be replaced, the National Security Council has been reduced to an advisory body to the president to be convened at his initiative, and the president has been given the power to retire the top commanders of the armed services. To do so the President only needs to inform the senate of his actions. Consequently, the transformation of the 1980 Constitution into one which follows the basic outlines of democratic precepts is now complete.

The results of municipal elections, the only ones held with a proportional representation system that is similar to that employed before 1973, show clearly that Chilean voters are still divided into right, center, and left tendencies in about the same proportions as they were before the military dictatorship. The Communist party has, at about 6%, a slightly smaller electorate than before, but in alliance with other groups it can obtain about 10% of the total as demonstrated by the 2004 elections. This does not mean that there are no important differences between the pre- and post-dictatorship party systems. The current system is divided into two grand coalitions, with the Christian Democrats in alliance with the center and leftist parties, including a now moderate Socialist party. In turn, the right is presently divided into two main parties, not one as was the case after 1967. One of these parties, the Unión Demócrata Independiente (UDI) is closer to the military regime's legacy than the other, Renovación Nacional (RN). The UDI also has close ties to the more conservative groups in the Catholic Church, including Opus Dei. The continued organization of the current party system into two large coalitions is not only the result of the alliances forged originally for the "yes" or "no" plebiscite that defeated Pinochet. It is also a function of the fact that congressional elections are held with a highly unusual electoral system devised by the outgoing military regime to favor the right. It calls on parties to present only two candidates per district, and it gives both seats to a list only if it has more than twice the votes of the second, runner up list. This system rewards parties that forge alliances, and tends to produce a parity of representation between the two top vote-getting alliances. While the Concertatión governments have sought to change this system, it is strongly supported by the parties of the right and it even has its defenders among the leaders of the Concertatión. The latter argue that the two large coalitions have helped moderate political competition and have made the country more "governable" than it was in the past. Indeed, legislators are forced by the electoral system to remain disciplined members of the two coalitions.

And yet, the pragmatism of political leaders and the effort to search for consensus on all kinds of issues, features that make current Chilean politics so different from the past, are largely the result of a process of political learning. There is a widely held consensus that the crisis of Chilean democracy was one that emerged from excesses committed by all sides. And there is a yearning to cultivate order, progress and prosperity within the framework of a reinvigorated democracy. A large part of the success of Chilean democratization stems from the depth of this frame of mind throughout Chilean society.

There is also considerable awareness that in the economic sphere Chile cannot rest on its achievements to date. Most of the investment in Chile has gone into mining, fishing, agriculture, and forest products including cellulose and paper. The bulk of Chilean exports are still primary commodities. For the country to reach its goal of advancing into the group of developed economies of the world it must increase the technological sophistication of its export menu. This requires further improvements in the country's competitiveness, which can only be achieved with even greater public investment in infrastructure and in human capital, particularly in education. Policymakers know the challenges that lie ahead and are committed to overcoming them. And Chileans of all walks of life are more optimistic now about the future than they have ever been.

Suggested Readings

Angell, Alan. *Politics and the Labour Movement in Chile.* London: Oxford University Press, 1972.

Arriagada, Genaro. *Pinochet: The Politics of Power.* Winchester, Mass.: Unwin Hyman, 1988.

Bauer, Robert J. *Chilean Rural Society from the Spanish Conquest to 1930.* London: Cambridge University Press, 1975.

Bethell, Leslie, ed. *Chile since Independence.* New York: Cambridge University Press, 1993.

Blakemore, Harold. *British Nitrates and Chilean Politics, 1886–1896: Balmaceda and North.* London: Athlone Press, 1974.

Boorstein, Edward. *Allende's Chile: An Inside View.* New York: International Publishers, 1977.

Collier, Simon, and William F. Sater. *A History of Chile, 1808–1994.* New York: Cambridge University Press, 1996.

Constable, Pamela, and Arturo Valenzuela. *A Nation of Enemies: Chile Under Pinochet.* New York: W. W. Norton, 1991.

Davis, Madeleine. *The Pinochet Case: Origins, Progress and Implications.* London: Institute of Latin American Studies, 2003.

DeShazo, Peter. *Urban Workers and Labor Unions in Chile, 1902–1927.* Madison, Wis.: University of Wisconsin Press, 1983.

De Vylder, Stefan. *Allende's Chile: The Political Economy of the Rise and Fall of the Unidad Popular.* Cambridge: Cambridge University Press, 1974.

Drake, Paul W. *Socialism and Populism in Chile, 1932–52.* Urbana, Ill.: University of Illinois, 1978.

Edwards, Sebastian, and Alexandra Cox Edwards. *Monetarism and Liberalization: The Chilean Experiment.* Boston: Ballinger Publishing Co., 1987.

Ensalaco, Mark. *Chile under Pinochet: Recovering the Truth.* Philadelphia: University of Pennsylvania Press, 2000.

Foxley, Alejandro. *Latin American Experiments in Neoconservative Economics.* Berkeley: University of California, 1983.

Galdames, Luis. *A History of Chile.* Translated and edited by Isaac J. Cox. Chapel Hill, N.C.: University of North Carolina Press, 1941.

Garretón, Manuel Antonio. *The Chilean Political Process.* Winchester, Mass.: Unwin Hyman, 1989.

Gil, Federico. *The Political System of Chile.* Boston: Houghton Mifflin, 1966.

Gil, Federico, Ricardo Lagos E., and H. A. Landsberger, eds. *Chile at the Turning Point: Lessons of the Socialist Years, 1970–73.* Philadelphia: Institute for the Study of Human Issues (ISHI), 1979.

Hutchinson, Elizabeth Quay. *Labors Appropriate to their Sex.* Durham, N.C.: Duke University Press, 2001.

Kaufman, Robert R. *The Politics of Land Reform in Chile 1950–1970: Public Policy, Political Institutions, and Social Change.* Cambridge: Harvard University Press, 1972.

Kornbluh, Peter, ed. *The Pinochet File: A Declassified Dossier on Atrocity and Accountability.* National Security Archive, The New Press, 2003.

Loveman, Brian. *Chile: The Legacy of Hispanic Capitalism.* New York: Oxford University Press, 1979.

Mamalakis, Markos J. *The Growth and Structure of the Chilean Economy: From Independence to Allende.* New Haven, Conn.: Yale University Press, 1976.

Petras, James, and Morris Morley. *The United States and Chile: Imperialism and the Overthrow of the Allende Government.* New York: Monthly Review Press, 1975.

Pike, Fredrick. *Chile and the United States.* Notre Dame, Ind.: University of Notre Dame Press, 1963.

Roxborough, Ian, Philip O'Brien, and Jackie Roddick. *Chile: The State and Revolution.* New York: Holmes & Meier Publishers, 1977.

Scully, Timothy R. *Rethinking the Center: Party Politics in Nineteenth and Twentieth Century Chile.* Stanford, Calif.: Stanford University Press, 1992.

Sigmund, Paul E. *The Overthrow of Allende and the Politics of Chile, 1964–76.* Pittsburgh: University of Pittsburgh, 1977.

_____. *The United States and Democracy in Chile.* Baltimore: Johns Hopkins University Press, 1993.

Smith, Brian H. *The Church and Politics in Chile: Challenges to Modern Catholicism.* Princeton, N.J.: Princeton University Press, 1982.

Spooner, Mary Helen. *Soldiers in a Narrow Land: The Pinochet Regime in Chile.* Berkeley: University of California Press, 1999.

Stallings, Barbara. *Class Conflict and Economic Development in Chile, 1958–1973.* Stanford, Calif.: Stanford University Press, 1978.

Valenzuela, Arturo. *Political Brokers in Chile: Local Politics in a Centralized Polity.* Durham, N.C.: Duke University Press, 1977.

_____. *The Breakdown of Democratic Regimes: Chile.* Baltimore: Johns Hopkins University Press, 1978.

Valenzuela, J. Samuel, and Arturo Valenzuela, eds. *Military Rule in Chile: Dictatorship and Oppositions.* Baltimore: Johns Hopkins University Press, 1986.

Winn, Peter. *Weavers of Revolution: The Yarur Workers and Chile's Road to Socialism.* New York: Oxford University Press, 1986.

Chapter 27

ARGENTINA:
DECLINE AND REVIVAL

PETER CALVERT

ARGENTINA, THE EIGHTH LARGEST country in the world, presents many paradoxes. With an area of some 2,767,000 square kilometers, it had a population of only 38 million in 2003. It is incredibly rich in agricultural land: The vast pampa, stretching westward between Buenos Aires and the Andes, makes Argentina one of the world's few grain-exporting nations and the only one in the Southern Hemisphere. Yet some three-fifths of the population live and work in the sophisticated urban environment of Greater Buenos Aires. Argentina is also self-sufficient in oil and natural gas and wealthy in mineral resources. Although comparable in size to Australia, it has failed to develop along the same lines; in 1930 it entered on a long period of decline. In 1930, in fact, Argentina was the seventh richest country in the world. By 1980, it was seventy-seventh, and its rulers, it seemed, were resigned to permanent membership of the Third World. A literate and sophisticated people had been subjected to an exceptionally brutal military dictatorship. "Argentina," people said, "is the land of the future, always has been and always will be."

The jury is still out on whether the country's economy can be stabilized in the near term, but democracy itself has survived a sequence of economic crises more successfully than anyone expected.

BUENOS AIRES VERSUS THE PROVINCES

In colonial times, Argentina lay on the furthest edges of the Spanish Empire. The first Spanish settlers in what is now Argentina came from Peru, and until 1776 the region remained backward and neglected. Founded in 1580 and a fine natural port, Buenos Aires long stagnated while all trade had to be channeled through Lima. Direct trade between Buenos Aires and Spain (notably in hides and in silver from what is now Bolivia) only later stimulated the growth of the town. In 1776, the Viceroyalty of the River Plate (Río de la Plata) was established. Buenos Aires began to grow rapidly. In 1807, the doomed attempt

541

of Sir Home Popham to seize the city for the British Empire taught its inhabitants that they could defend themselves. It went on to free itself from Spanish rule in 1810, its *Cabildo* (town council) governing on behalf of the Spanish king, Ferdinand VII, though he was at the time a captive of the French Emperor Napoleon Bonaparte. In 1816, when the Spanish moved to recapture Buenos Aires, the independence of what were then called the United Provinces of South America was declared at Tucumán.

Buenos Aires in 1810 was already bigger by far than the other main towns scattered along the River Plate and in the west and northwest, in the lee of the Andes. The colony was underpopulated for its size, although the vast and largely treeless plains, the hinterland of Buenos Aires known as the Pampas, still contained a substantial native American population. In the vast, flat, rural plain of the Province (as opposed to the City) of Buenos Aires roamed the Argentine cowboy, the *gaucho,* who opened up the interior and gave Argentina its national myth.

Argentina remained disunited for much of the nineteenth century, owing to the rivalry between Buenos Aires and the other provinces. The former favored a centralized structure, with Buenos Aires dominant, whereas the latter wanted a federal structure with provincial autonomy. Buenos Aires derived its revenues from the port, whereas the prices of provincial manufactures, such as textiles, were undercut by cheaper foreign imports. Buenos Aires did not share its wealth with the other provinces and, moreover, grew more European in its outlook and amenities; the provinces remained backward, dominated by autocratic, often savage leaders (*caudillos*). The struggle between federalists and centralists was overshadowed after 1835 by the dictatorship of Juan Manuel de Rosas, *caudillo* of Buenos Aires. He ignored the national problem, giving the provincial rulers complete freedom of action in return for their recognizing him as national leader. Paradoxically, this helped create the national unity he opposed. In 1852, he was deposed by a coalition of his political opponents and died in exile on his farm just outside Southampton, England, in 1877.

In 1853, a federal constitution was created for the new Argentine Republic. Buenos Aires seceded from the federation but in 1859 was defeated in a military confrontation with the other provinces. In 1861, its forces were victorious and it joined the union in order to dominate it. In 1880, three centuries after its founding, the city of Buenos Aires replaced Rosario as the federal capital. A new capital for the old Province of Buenos Aires was built at La Plata. The provincial *caudillos* made the transition to being more conventional politicians, though it was the great landowners, the *estancieros,* who dominated national life.

The next four decades were years of economic transformation as the combined impact of British investment, European immigration, the expansion of the railways, and the beef, grain, and wool of the Pampas made Argentina rich. These developments first benefited the cattle barons and big landowners who dominated politics, but two new classes emerged to challenge their hold on power: professionals such as bankers, brokers, and lawyers and an urban working class composed largely of recent immigrants. In any one decade from 1880 to 1950, there were proportionately three times as many immigrants to Argentina as to the United States.

MODERN PARTIES AND AN OLD-FASHIONED MILITARY

The first challenge came in the 1890s with the foundation of the Radical and Socialist Parties, but fraudulent elections kept the oligarchy of landowners, merchants, and bankers in power. In 1912, however, President Roque Sáenz Peña, though a conservative, insisted on the adoption of a law introducing secret ballots, to reduce electoral corruption. As a result, in 1916 Hipólito Yrigoyen, nephew of the founder of the Radical Party, the Unión Cívica Radical (UCR, Radical Civic Union), became Argentina's first popularly elected president. The economy was still growing strongly in 1922 and a manufacturing industry developed under Yrigoyen's Radical successor, Marcelo T. de Alvear. In 1928, Yrigoyen was elected to a second term, causing a split in the party in opposition to Yrigoyen's personalism. Before the effects of the 1929 depression were felt, Yrigoyen's reclusiveness and society's lack of perception with regard to the threat of a military takeover made it possible in 1930 for a small band of cadets, armed with wooden rifles and led by a retired general, José E. Uriburu to seize power.

From 1932 to 1943, a period known as the Infamous Decade, the oligarchy resumed power in the form of a loose coalition (the *Concordancia*) of Conservatives and antipersonalist Radicals, supported by the armed forces. It was their friends and supporters who benefited from the economic recovery and from Argentina's role in supplying the Allies with meat and grain during World War II. But the war divided Argentine society further. Some leaders were strongly pro-Allies, but a suspicious isolationism had become the norm, and important elements in the armed forces, admiring German military prowess, were openly pro-Axis. When in 1943 it seemed that the civilian politicians would install a pro-Allies president, the army intervened again.

The year 1943 was a turning point. Colonel Juan Domingo Perón, secretary of the army lodge that planned and executed the coup, became minister of war and secretary for labor and social welfare in the military government. He promoted labor reforms and encouraged unionization, becoming immensely popular with the masses, though not with the oligarchy. In 1946, in a free election, he won the presidency decisively. In 1949, he amended the constitution to permit his re-election in 1951; he held power until 1955.

Perón's populistic and personalist regime had many of the marks of a dictatorship. The media were controlled, dissent suppressed, a single ruling party established, the cult of personality encouraged. However, his rule was based on an alliance with the trade unions and mobilized the popular support of the urban underprivileged, the *descamisados* (shirtless ones). Large welfare programs not only brought Perón a devoted following but yielded real benefits to the poor, dramatized from the ministry of social welfare by Perón's charismatic wife, Eva Duarte de Perón ("Evita"), who came to be regarded virtually as a saint, and for many still is.

A staunch nationalist, Perón bought out the British-owned railways, greatly accelerated industrialization under strong government control, and increased the role of the state in the economy. In his foreign policy he sought a "third position," later to be termed nonalignment, and the leadership of South America. However, he neglected the agricultural sector, formerly the basis of Argentina's export trade. Rural migration increased, and serious economic imbalances developed. As inflation rose and agricultural output fell, the economy's growth slowed down. Evita Perón died in July 1952, depriving her husband of his strongest ally with the masses.

During his second term, from 1951, after surviving an attempted military coup, Perón tempered his policies. He resisted workers' wage demands, supported the farmers, and as of 1954 encouraged foreign capital in the petroleum industry. Such changes alienated many former supporters. Discontent grew with both the repressive nature of the regime and the large bureaucracy. Attacks by overzealous supporters on the Roman Catholic Church compounded Perón's problems. Finally, in September 1955, the armed forces intervened. Perón went into exile in Spain. However, his legacy and his political movement survived to form the fundamental divide in Argentine politics for the next four decades.

The Peronists, the Military, and the Guerrillas

The armed forces sought in vain to exclude both Perón and his supporters from national politics. The leader of the coup of 1955, General Eduardo Lonardi, was himself prepared to work with the Peronists but was soon deposed by the more intransigent General Pedro Aramburu. For three years (1955–1958), Aramburu attempted to suppress all vestiges of Peronism. Elections from which the Peronists were barred installed a left-wing Radical, Arturo Frondizi (1958–1962), under whom economic development accelerated. Promising fifty years of development in five years, he delivered forty years of inflation in four. Inflation became an endemic problem. When Frondizi, too, proposed to allow the Peronists (though not Perón himself) to stand for election, he too was deposed by the army.

New elections were held in 1963, and Arturo Illia, another Radical, was elected. However, in 1966 the military ousted him as well, claiming that he had been ineffective. The new military government headed by Juan Carlos Onganía (1966–1970) made it clear that it intended to stay in power as long as was "necessary" to revive the economy. Supported by authoritarian controls, his minister of economy and labor, Adalberto Krieger Vasena, produced a viable but austere recovery plan. But Krieger Vasena was forced to resign in May 1969 in the wake of a massive demonstration in the city of Córdoba (the *Cordobazo*). Further strikes and protests followed.

Meanwhile, under the influence of the Cuban Revolution and its aftermath, two main urban guerrilla movements emerged, a pro-Cuban organization called the Revolutionary Army of the People (ERP, Ejército Revolucionario del Pueblo), and a Peronist group known as the Montoneros. The Montoneros kidnapped and murdered former president Aramburu, thereby undermining Onganía, whose colleagues deposed him in June 1970. An unknown general, Roberto Levingston, was appointed to head the government but was replaced in March 1971 by General Alejandro Lanusse, the organizer of the 1970 coup, who took over the presidency himself.

Lanusse inherited an impossible situation. With guerrilla violence growing and with the economy suffering from such frequent political changes that long-term, consistent policies could not be implemented, he took the ultimate gamble of holding fresh elections in March 1973 and allowing the Peronists to take part for the first time in twenty years. Perón's candidacy was disallowed (he had now been in exile for eighteen years), but his proxy, Héctor Cámpora, was allowed to stand and was duly elected. Cámpora's presidency lasted only a few weeks. Having offered freedom to captured guerrillas, he resigned in order to force Perón's return. The military, internally divided, yielded to the demand for new elections. Perón's return to the country in June 1973 was marred by violence at Ezeiza Airport in which many died. In September, nevertheless, he was returned to the presidency, with his third wife, María Estela ("Isabelita") Martínez de Perón, as vice president.

However, the hopes of Perón's supporters were soon dashed. Perón, by then a sick man of seventy-eight, was unable to meet the many conflicting demands made on him during his short third term as president, though much was said and planned along the social democratic lines he had seen working well in Europe. He tried to distance himself from the leftist fringe that had infiltrated the movement during the last years of military proscription, only to find that political violence originating from both the left and the right increased. The two major insurgent movements, the Peronist Montoneros and the Marxist ERP, battled openly for power with kidnappings, bombings, and assassinations.

At Perón's death on July 1, 1974, his widow, Isabelita, became, by an irony of history, Latin America's (and indeed the world's) first woman executive president. The Peronist movement was not only divided, but its extreme wings were in fact at war, and as chaos spread rightist death squads appeared, controlled by Isabel Perón's chief confidant, the influential minister of social welfare, José López Rega (*El Brujo*, or "the Sorcerer"). The country slid into anarchy. Violence increased as inflation rose to 364 percent in 1976, and the government did little to stop it. In March 1976, the armed forces again seized power.

THE JUNTA AND THE DIRTY WAR

The governing junta of service chiefs chose the commander of the army, General Jorge Videla, as the new president. Under the chiefs' leadership, there began what the government termed euphemistically the "process of national reorganization." The period has since become better known abroad as the dirty war (*la guerra sucia*).

The process was a concerted attempt to eradicate terrorism by the use of terror. Tens of thousands of "suspects" were arrested, tortured, and murdered. People were arrested simply to fulfill the quotas imposed on provincial agencies. Early conservative estimates put the number of people killed, or who "disappeared," at over 10,000; more recent estimates range from 15,000 to 30,000. Such a wholesale purge inevitably included some genuine terrorists, and by 1978 the capacity for disruption by the Montoneros and the ERP had been drastically reduced by the death, exile, or imprisonment of their known leaders.

Meanwhile, massive borrowing and the overvaluation of the currency led to a rapid growth in consumer spending, giving the middle classes a false sense of prosperity. Videla, who had retired from the army and junta in August 1978, was succeeded as president in a quasi-constitutional fashion by General Roberto Viola in March 1981, just at the start of a new economic recession. Ill health and the opposition of military conservatives to his relatively conciliatory policies forced Viola out of office in November. A right-wing nationalist, General Leopoldo Fortunato Galtieri, took over in December as president and head of the junta.

THE FALKLANDS/MALVINAS WAR

At the beginning of 1982, there was a series of labor demonstrations and strikes, culminating on March 30 in a violent confrontation between demonstrators and government forces in Buenos Aires. Galtieri had however siezed power with a plan that, he believed, would guarantee his position. On April 2, Argentine forces seized the British-ruled Falkland Islands (Islas Malvinas) in the South Atlantic, title to which had been disputed by Argentina since British occupation in 1833. The tiny British garrison of eighty-seven was rapidly overwhelmed by 10,000 Argentine soldiers, and Argentine sovereignty was proclaimed. Initially the seizure of the islands was a resounding success for the government—the Peronists had always supported it. However, the final defeat of the Argentine forces by a small British naval task force on June 14 was a catastrophe and a national humiliation. The military government of Galtieri, inept politically and economically, had failed in combat, the professional field in which lay its claim to national preeminence. Galtieri was abruptly replaced and a retired general, Reynaldo Bignone, selected to head an interim government under which the military could retreat from power without having to pay the penalty for its misdeeds.

Bignone, having established a dialogue with the political parties, called elections for October 30, 1983, in an atmosphere of deep economic crisis and national confusion, fueled by growing civilian demands for the investigation of human rights abuses committed by the services. The UCR (Radicals) and the Partido Justicialista (Peronists), the two main parties, chose as their respective presidential candidates Raúl Alfonsín and Italo Luder. The former, a fifty-seven-year-old lawyer who had courageously opposed the war and had a record of defense of human rights, obtained a massive victory over Luder, who lacked charisma and whose party was deeply divided.

A Halting Redemocratization

Inaugurated as president in December 1983, Alfonsín faced massive problems. Of a foreign debt of $40 billion left by the military government, one-quarter at least had been wasted and another quarter was never traced. Meanwhile, hyperinflation and economic stagnation combined to frustrate the hopes that Alfonsín's victory had aroused—for fifteen consecutive years, Argentina had triple-digit inflation, a world record. The trade unions, still largely in Peronist hands, reacted to the new government's imposition of austerity measures by staging a one-day general strike in May 1985, while the military carefully watched the progress of trials of former leaders of the armed forces. During the first year of Alfonsín's presidency, after very protracted negotiations, he managed to renegotiate the foreign debt, maintain political stability, and reach some accord with the Peronists. Abroad, he finalized with Chile a long-standing dispute over possession of three islets in the Beagle Channel at the extreme south of Tierra del Fuego, which had almost brought the two countries to war in 1978.

Two issues dominated Alfonsín's government: relations with the military and the resuscitation of the economy. In theory committed to eradicating the military from Argentine politics and to establishing a working democratic system, Alfonsín soon had to temper his policies with reality. The problem was the popular demand for the trial of service personnel for gross abuses of human rights during the "dirty war." Ostensibly an asset to Alfonsín, public pressure on this issue was in fact a two-edged weapon. Alfonsín was sensitive to the dangers of isolation of the armed forces from civilian society and sought to maintain national unity. Few objected—even within the reconstituted services—to the court-martial in 1985 of the first three military juntas to rule Argentina after the 1976 coup, for offenses that included abduction, torture, and murder. (In December, four of the accused were acquitted, but sentences were passed on the remaining five, including sentences of life imprisonment for General Videla and Admiral Eduardo Massera.) Nor did many complain at the prosecution of the high command that had held office during the South Atlantic conflict.

However, as evidence of military atrocities increased, so, too, did the claims of the military that the dirty war was a just war and that a general amnesty should be enacted. Alfonsín attempted to resolve this conflict in December 1986, when Congress approved a law, known popularly as the "Punto Final" (Full Stop) Law, which established a sixty-day deadline for new indictments. The government had expected that only some seventy such cases might be presented. But by the deadline, over 250 indictments had been accepted. Moreover, for the first time, serving officers as well as retired ones were accused.

In April 1987, military rebellions broke out in Córdoba and later at the Campo de Mayo itself. There the rebels included veterans of the Falklands campaign in full service camouflage and painted faces (*carapintadas*). Although there were popular demonstrations in support of democracy, concessions were made to the military, despite the ensuing controversy. A new army chief of staff was appointed, and Alfonsín submitted to Congress legislative proposals that came to be known as the "Obediencia Debida" (Due Obedience) Law, absolving most junior military officers. Out of some 370 members of the armed forces due to be tried for human rights offenses, only between thirty and fifty were left to face charges. Even this number was too many for some sectors of the military, and there were minor insurrections in January and December 1988. Then in January 1989, the army claimed to have successfully defeated an attack by forty left-wing activists on a military base at La Tablada, 25 kilometers west of Buenos Aires. The alleged guerrillas, thirty-nine of whom were already dead, were said to have been members of a hitherto unknown organization, Movimiento Todos por la Patria ("All for the Country Movement," or MTP). Alfonsín publicly congratulated the military on its swift suppression of the uprising and reestablished the military's official right to act against "subversion" by creating a National Security Council. Opposition groups (including the Peronist presidential candidate, Carlos Saúl Menem) accused government and military bodies of having deliberately provoked the attack in an attempt to discredit all opposition factions. But it has since been confirmed to have been a real, if doomed, attempt to resuscitate the guerrilla conflict on the part of Enrique Gorriarán Merlo and a small group of former members of the ERP.

ECONOMIC CRISIS

What defeated Alfonsín was the Argentine economy. After pursuing gradualist policies to reactivate it in 1984–1985, the government turned in June 1985 to the fashionable doctrine of the "heterodox shock." The Austral Plan was named after the new currency that was to end inflation, by then running at an estimated annual rate of 1,129 percent. But the accompanying freeze on wages led to labor unrest, with the Peronist-dominated trade unions holding a series of one-day strikes. Hence, despite its initial promise, the plan was effectively abandoned while the midterm elections took place.

With the elections out of the way and inflation again soaring, in February 1987, a second Austral Plan (the "Australito") was announced. Old devices, such as devaluation; the pegging, or linking, of wage increases to price rises; and lower interest rates were tried again. Again the government's attempts at achieving economic stabilization were unsuccessful; the deficit on the public-sector account worsened, and inflation continued to spiral upward. These problems led to a deterioration in relations with foreign creditors and pushed the currency to the edge of collapse. In early 1989, the World Bank, which until that time had broadly supported Alfonsín, suspended all its financing in Argentina. Negotiations with international creditors were deferred indefinitely. Despite the efforts of two new finance ministers in as many months, no credible economic strategy emerged, and control over inflation was abandoned while the elections of May 1989 were held.

A New Kind of Peronist

With his economic policy in ruins, Alfonsín's sole remaining aim at the end of his presidency was to be succeeded by another democratically elected president. Despite the crisis the elections were both peaceful and orderly. The candidate of the UCR, Eduardo César Angeloz, proposed widespread privatization and economic austerity in order to combat the economic crisis but was saddled with the burden of Alfonsín's failure. Victory went to the Peronist candidate, Carlos Saúl Menem, the flamboyant former governor of the inland province of La Rioja. In his campaign, Menem captured the popular vote and a Peronist majority in the Senate with the promise of a production revolution based on wage increases and significant aid to industry. Yet long before he was due to take office, food riots, looting, and bombings in several Argentine cities forced Alfonsín to impose a state of siege and to hand over presidential power to Menem five months early, on July 8, to avoid a total breakdown of public authority.

When Menem succeeded Alfonsín, it was the first time since 1928 that an elected president had handed over the office to his successor without military pressure. Democracy, even in the midst of the greatest economic crisis of the century, was still immensely popular. It was immediately clear, moreover, that Menem's economic strategy, to turn Argentina into what he called a "popular market-capitalist country," was much closer to that of the Radicals than his campaign had suggested. The results, too, were much the same—the collapse of the currency and a second hyperinflationary wave. Menem's relaxed use of presidential authority, divisions in the cabinet, and reluctant support for policies so different to traditional Peronism increased the difficulty in reducing state expenditure and in selling state-owned enterprises. The government's troubles were further exacerbated by the public airing of the president's marital problems.

With regard to the military, Menem, who had spent the entire period of the military regime under house arrest, from the outset advocated conciliation, despite strong resistance from among his own supporters. After weeks of rumor, a series of pardons affecting 277 individuals, including guerrillas but, more important, members of the military junta responsible for the Falklands debacle, was issued in October 1989. At the end of 1990, however, military discontent reemerged. The government was taken by surprise when some supporters of Colonel Mohammed Ali Seneildín, leader of the December 1988 revolt, rebelled on December 3 and seized the military headquarters, with the loss of at least three lives. Any question of negotiation was speedily rejected; the headquarters were stormed and the leaders charged with insurrection.

They were sentenced to indefinite imprisonment and discharge from the service. The price was Menem's irreversible decision on December 29 to pardon General Jorge Videla and all others convicted for human rights crimes during the dirty war.

From then on, though, the relative strength of the armed forces continued to decline. In February 1990, Menem took the personal decision to resume diplomatic relations with the United Kingdom, keeping the issue of the sovereignty of the disputed islands, as he put it, "under an umbrella." In June 1991, the government announced that the armed forces would be reduced from 75,000 to 55,000 in number and the period of conscription reduced from one year to six months.

Meanwhile, in January 1991, a series of ministerial changes were to transform the country's economic prospects. The new minister of the economy, Domingo Cavallo, proceeded to implement his so-called Convertibility Plan. This had three main planks. The first was the so-called dollarization of the economy, whereby the Argentine economy was linked to the U.S. economy by the establishment of a fixed exchange rate of 10,000 australes (or one new peso) to the U.S. dollar. This brought inflation down into low single figures in a few weeks and brought some US$20 billion of "hot money" back into the country. The second was a program of privatization that would reverse forty years of Peronist policy and buy time to fulfill the third plank, a plan to improve government finances by collecting taxes that had been widely evaded. By the time of Menem's state visit to the United States in November, he was celebrated as Latin America's leading free-market reformer and U.S. ally. As a result, in March 1992 Menem secured a promise of debt reduction under the Brady Initiative. Argentina's accumulated debt was reduced from over $60 billion to some $48 billion.

At the same time, support for the ruling Peronist party strengthened. In the provincial elections, the Peronists won fifteen of the twenty-one governorships at stake, including that of the key Province of Buenos Aires, where Vice President Eduardo Duhalde won 47 percent of the votes cast. Although their opponents were in disarray, the Peronists were not free of problems, of which the two main ones were the persistent accusations of corruption leveled against them and their inability to agree on a successor to President Menem. Thus, in February 1993, a campaign was begun by the leadership of the Peronists for a constitutional amendment to permit Menem's reelection.

In legislative elections held on October 3, 1993, the Peronists won 42.3 percent of the votes cast, which resulted in their holding 123 seats of the 254-seat Chamber of Deputies, less than the two-thirds majority necessary in the lower house to approve a constitutional amendment. But anxious to avoid another humiliating defeat for his party in a national referendum on the question of constitutional reform, former president Alfonsín, who was re-elected as UCR leader in November 1993, entered into a dialogue with President Menem. The terms of their agreement were endorsed by a UCR national convention in early December. The main proposals detailed in the agreement were allowing a president to seek a consecutive term in office; the creation of the post of coordinating minister to fulfill a prime-ministerial function; an increase in the number of seats in the Senate and a reduction in the length of mandate of all senators; and changes of the procedure for judicial appointments. This last proposal was important in securing UCR support, as the Supreme Court was Peronist-dominated. No action was taken, however, to correct the problem that had helped bring down Alfonsín, the ability of the provinces to run up debts that then had to be met by the federal government. President Menem immediately declared his intention to seek re-election in 1995.

Constitutional Reform

Elections to a 305-seat constituent assembly, which was to draft and approve the proposed constitution, took place on April 10, 1994. The Peronists won 37.7 percent of the votes cast and the UCR only 19.9 percent—the party's worst election result since Argentina's return to democracy in 1983. The Frente Grande, a loose left-wing coalition formed in mid-1993 to oppose the proposed reforms, came in third, receiving an unexpected 12.5 percent of the ballot. However, on August 22 the assembly approved the new constitution, which came into force on the following day. Concessions included the reduction of the presidential mandate from six years to four; the creation of the post of chief of cabinet; a runoff election for presidential and vice-presidential candidates when neither obtained 45 percent of the votes cast, or 40 percent when the nearest candidate gained less than 30 percent of the ballot; the establishment of an autonomous government in the City of Buenos Aires with a directly elected mayor; the extension of congressional sessions to nine months; an increase in the number of senators from two to three from each province; the creation of a Council of Magistrates and other judicial reforms.

In any event, the presidential elections of 1995 were overshadowed by the impact on the economy of the Mexican economic crisis (the "tequila effect"). Unemployment, which rose between April and July from 12.5 percent to 18.6 percent of the economically active population, was the subject of a $1.5 billion initiative. Yet it was not the UCR candidate, Governor Horacio Massaccesi of Río Negro, who made the run-off, but a dissident Peronist, Senator José Octavio Bordón of Mendoza, whose Frente Grande, now the center-left Front for a Country in Solidarity (*Frepaso*) took support from both Radicals and dissident Peronists. So, President Menem won re-election decisively, gaining 49.8 percent of the votes cast in the only round of balloting. The president had carried every province, and his party, the Peronists, gained an overall majority of three seats in the 257-seat Chamber of Deputies

In the aftermath of his victory, President Menem confirmed his intention to retain Cavallo as economy minister. But later in the year tension grew between the two as Cavallo complained publicly of resistance to free-market reform among entrenched interests in government. Eventually, in 1996, Cavallo was dismissed. But his plan had been so successful that even after recession set in 1997, the government was reluctant to contemplate devaluation. At the same time falling revenues, and the inability to control expenditure by the provincial governments, created a widening fiscal gap, which could only be filled by increased borrowing. Meanwhile, though Menem was able to see out his second term, his efforts to prevent Governor Duhalde from succeeding him further split the Peronists, while Cavallo formed a new party, Action for the Republic, and attracted some support. Hence at the 1999 elections, the conservative UCR Mayor of Buenos Aires, Fernando De la Rúa Bruno, heading an Alliance between UCR and Frepaso, won the presidency decisively. The Peronists lost control of the Chamber of Deputies, but retained their majority in the Senate.

Unfortunately by the time that De la Rúa took office the country was already deep in recession. Unemployment was reaching record levels. In March 2001, therefore, he brought Cavallo back for a second spell as economy minister. The appointment stabilized the situation briefly. However the government was so weak that when Cavallo announced his plan to reduce the budget deficit in 2001 by $3 billion, it was to be achieved by tax increases rather than by spending cuts, which would have involved dismissing public sector workers, cutting their salaries, or reducing state retirement benefits. Confidence was further undermined by Cavallo's frenetic activity, constantly unveiling new measures and holding press conferences three times a day. After a deal with fourteen powerful provincial governors in July, the Senate was finally persuaded to pass the "zero deficit" law. With this as an excuse, the IMF in August reluctantly agreed to disburse $1.2 billion due in September and even lend a further $8 billion, despite clear signs that the situation was already out of control and in the face of strong reservations of Bush administration officials in the United States, who wanted to make an example of Argentina to other states.

THE 2001 CRISIS AND ITS AFTERMATH

At the mid-term elections on October 14, the voters showed their anger in the most unmistakable way, by giving the opposition Peronists a majority in both houses of Congress. From there they watched as Cavallo made a desperate effort to avoid default. In response to a massive run on the banks, the government on November 30 imposed limits both on cash withdrawals (the *corralito*) and on capital movements, effectively ending peso convertibility. Throwing gasoline on the flames, the IMF in response held back the $1.3 billion due to be paid in December. On the weekend of December 15–16, public order began to break down as desperate people started to loot supermarkets. Others banged empty pots (*cacerolazo*) and hammered on the shutters of the banks in frustration. Huge crowds collected in the Plaza de Mayo shouting for the government to go. Heavy-handed police intervention claimed twenty-five lives, injured hundreds, and led to thousands of arrests, which only made matters worse. Finally, on December 20, President de la Rúa asked the Peronists to join a government of national unity. They prudently refused. He resigned and was lifted off the roof of the Casa Rosada by helicopter, while Cavallo, in fear of his life, fled to Patagonia.

Over the next two weeks, five people served consecutively as interim president. When on January 1, 2002, the Peronist-dominated Congress chose Eduardo Duhalde to serve out De la Rúa's term, therefore, the country had already gone into default on its debt. Congress granted the new president emergency powers and the peso was devalued on January 7. But the peso's new value could not be sustained; the stock market reopened on January 17 to a sharp fall and violent demonstrations continued across the country against the shortage of cash brought about by the corralito. When on February 9 the government unveiled plans to cut the already spartan federal budget by $370 million, some 3,000 demonstrators again filled the Plaza de Mayo for a *cacerolazo*. In response the government restored convertibility and agreed to allow people at least to cash their pay checks in full.

Fresh rioting followed. Even so, at the beginning of April, Argentina was given the uncompromising message by the IMF that no further help would be available unless even more drastic cuts were forthcoming. On Monday, April 22, therefore, the banks were all closed again by government decree. The following day, after failing to win support for an emergency plan to exchange frozen bank deposits for government bonds, the economy minister resigned, together with most of the rest of the cabinet. At that point the peso had fallen to $3.50 to the U.S. dollar, having lost just under 69 percent of its value since the beginning of the year. Inflation had risen to 20 percent, millions had effectively lost their savings, public sector workers were rioting, and half the population was said to be living below the national poverty line. In consequence there had been a steep rise in robberies, kidnappings, and other crimes, which the underpaid police were either unable or unwilling to combat. Thieves who stole nearly 3,000 miles of copper wire between January and September seriously disrupted the telephone service, and utility workers were physically attacked when they tried to carry out repairs.

To his credit, President Duhalde remained calm and avoided inflammatory language, and throughout constitutional processes were maintained. By the time elections came round in March 2003 the economy had fallen so far that it was already beginning to pick up. With Duhalde himself ruled out, the Peronists chose Néstor Kirchner, the charismatic and financially successful governor of Santa Cruz, as their presidential candidate. Menem, who had been scheming for re-election, ungraciously withdrew. But Kirchner's victory gave Argentina a promising start in trying to rebuild on a more realistic basis.

FOREIGN RELATIONS

The improvement of relations between Argentina and the United States continued into the 1990s under U.S. President Bill Clinton's administration. In late August 1994, Argentine–British relations became more strained after the reiteration in the new constitution of Argentina's claim to sovereignty over the Falkland Islands. However, Argentine and British troops together patrolled the "green line" in Cyprus. By signing the Treaty of Tlatelolco, sending a naval force to the Persian (Arabian) Gulf in 1990, and supporting UN operations in Bosnia-Herzegovina and in Haiti, President Menem signaled his country's intention of playing a new and wider role in the "new world order" and of being an active participant in UN peacekeeping operations. Meanwhile, with the excuse of economic constraint, the military budget was cut; the army's strength reduced by a further 15 percent, to 23,000, in 1995; and conscription officially ended. With the issue of sovereignty still "under an umbrella," talks led to an agreement signed in New York on September 27, 1995, on joint exploitation of the Malvinas Basin, which enabled oil companies to bid for licenses in the disputed area without incurring penalties. Had the area been as rich as many believed, Argentina stood to gain handsomely from rising world prices, but in fact the basin turned out to be dry.

Menem decisively rejected the Radical Party's policy of seeking leadership of the Third World and took Argentina out of the Nonaligned Movement. Re-emerging as a candidate member of the First World, Argentina rejected its traditional posture of suspicious isolationism to come out as a strong ally of the United States and an example to the world of the success—fleeting as it turned out—of the free market.

Argentina's economic collapse at the outset of 2002 left a residue of popular distrust of neoliberal policy and of political leaders subject to guidance by public and private creditors, including the United States and the IMF. Public frustration and the widespread grassroots organization to which it gave rise thus provided a base for a major policy shift. With the inauguration of Nestor Kirchner in 2003, Argentina aligned itself with Brazil, by then governed by the Workers' Party, in seeking to strengthen MERCOSUR and with Latin America and other Third World countries in challenging First World blueprints for the World Trade Organization(WTO) and the Free Trade Agreement of the Americas (FTAA).

SUGGESTED READINGS

Alexander, Robert J. *Juan Domingo Perón: A History.* Boulder, Colo.: Westview Press, 1979.

Argentina, Republic of. Comisión Nacional sobre la Desaparición de Personas. *Nunca Mas: Informe de la Comisión Nacional sobre la Desaparición de Personas.* Buenos Aires: Editorial Universitaria de Buenos Aires, 1986.

Calvert, Susan, and Peter Calvert. *Argentina: Political Culture and Instability.* London: Macmillan, 1988.

Crawley, Eduardo. *A House Divided: Argentina 1880–1980.* London: C. Hurst & Co., 1984.

Di Tella, Guido. *Argentina Under Perón, 1973–76: The Nation's Experience with a Labour-based Government.* London: Macmillan, 1983.

Falcoff, Mark, and Ronald H. Dolkart, eds. *Prologue to Perón: Argentina in Depression and War 1930–1943.* Berkeley, Calif.: University of California Press, 1975.

Fraser, Nicholas, and Marysa Navarro. *Eva Perón.* London: André Deutsch, 1980.

Graham-Yooll, Andrew. *A State of Fear: Memories of Argentina's Nightmare.* London: Eland, 1986.

Imaz, José Luis de. *Los que mandan.* Buenos Aires: Editorial Universitaria de Buenos Aires, 1964.

Kirkpatrick, Jeane. *Leader and Vanguard in Mass Society: A Study of Peronist Argentina.* Cambridge: Massachusetts Institute of Technology, 1971.

Mallon, Richard D., and Juan V. Sourrouille. *Economic Policymaking in a Conflict Society: The Argentine Case.* Cambridge: Harvard University Press, 1975.

Martínez Estrada, Ezequiel (trans. by Alain Swietlicki). *X-Ray of the Pampa.* Austin: University of Texas Press, 1971.

Milenky, Edward S. *Argentina's Foreign Policies.* Boulder, Colo.: Westview Press, 1978.

O'Donnell, Guillermo. *Modernization and Bureaucratic-Authoritarianism: Studies in South American Politics.* Berkeley: University of California Press, 1973.

Page, Joseph A. *Perón: A Biography.* New York: Random House, 1983.

Platt, D. C. M., and Guido di Tella, eds. *Argentina, Australia and Canada: Studies in Comparative Development, 1870–1965.* London: Macmillan, 1985.

Potash, Robert A. *The Army and Politics in Argentina 1928–1945: Yrigoyen to Perón.* Stanford, Calif.: Stanford University Press, 1969.

_____. *The Army and Politics in Argentina 1945–1962: Perón to Frondizi.* London: Athlone Press, 1980.

Rock, David. *Argentina 1516–1982: From Spanish Colonization to the Falklands War.* Berkeley: University of California Press, 1985.

Schoultz, Lars. *The Populist Challenge: Argentine Electoral Behaviour in the Postwar Era.* Chapel Hill, N.C.: University of North Carolina Press, 1983.

Scobie, James R. *Argentina: A City and a Nation.* New York: Oxford University Press, 1971.

_____. *Buenos Aires: Plaza to Suburb, 1870–1910.* New York: Oxford University Press, 1974.

Snow, Peter G. *Political Forces in Argentina.* Boston: Allyn & Bacon, 1971.

Tamarin, David. *The Argentine Labor Movement, 1930–1945: A Study in the Origins of Peronism.* Albuquerque: University of New Mexico Press, 1985.

Timmerman, Jacobo (trans. by Tony Talbot). *Prisoner Without a Name, Cell Without a Number.* Harmondsworth, Middlesex: Penguin, 1982.

Turner, Frederick C., and José Enrique Miguens, eds. *Juan Perón and the Reshaping of Argentina.* Pittsburgh: University of Pittsburgh Press, 1983.

Wynia, Gary W. *Argentina in the Postwar Era: Politics and Economic Policy Making in a Divided Society.* Albuquerque: University of New Mexico Press, 1978.

Chapter 28

URUGUAY AND PARAGUAY:
AN ARDUOUS TRANSITION

DIEGO ABENTE BRUN

URUGUAY AND PARAGUAY, two of the smallest nations of South America, are often confused with one another because their names are so similar. However, their differences are probably among the greatest between any two countries in Latin America and can be traced back as far as the beginning of the Spanish conquest in 1536.

Both countries developed around a city; Asunción in the case of Paraguay, Montevideo in the case of Uruguay. The former, established in 1537, is the oldest city in the Río de la Plata Basin. It remained the center of the Spanish domain in the area until the end of the seventeenth century, when it lost its supremacy to the port city of Buenos Aires due to the administrative partition of the province of Paraguay. Yet it was not until 1680 that the Portuguese established the first settlement, the Colonia del Santísimo Sacramento, in what is now Uruguayan territory. Some forty-five years later, the Spaniards expelled the Portuguese and, in 1726, established the city of Montevideo.

Asunción was for several reasons a suitable center for the Spanish domain. It was located on a bay overlooked by the hills of Lambare and therefore easy to defend from nearby Indian populations. Furthermore, the Spaniards were able to work out a political alliance with the Indians living in that particular area, a factor that in time contributed to some of the unique features of the Paraguayan nation. As an aspect of the alliance, the Indians gave to the Spaniards some of their women, whose brothers, in turn, were because of that very link obliged to work certain days a week for the *cuñados* (brothers-in-law). This hastened the process of racial integration, or *mestizaje,* and made Paraguay one of the most homogeneous mestizo countries in Latin America. The practice also contributed to the preservation of the Indian language, Guaraní, because the mestizos learned the Indian tongue from their mothers and Spanish from their fathers. Although with heavy racial overtones, this bilingual situation persists to the present.

In the area surrounding Montevideo, by contrast, there were but a few Indians; they did not enter into close contact with the Spanish settlers, who were mostly cattle ranchers. As a result, the country was populated basically by *criollos* (Hispanic Creoles), and *mestizaje* was almost unknown. In addition, the waves of European, especially Italian and Spanish, immigrants in the second half of the nineteenth century and the first decades of the twentieth ultimately made of Uruguay a country racially European.

Paraguay, having acquired through the colonial years some sort of cultural, linguistic, and economic identity, proclaimed its independence from Spain in 1811, but at the same time rejected the domination of Buenos Aires, the city to which it had been administratively linked before the breakdown of the Spanish empire in the Americas. Soon after independence, José Gaspar Rodríguez de Francia was appointed dictator in 1814 in a truly Roman fashion— first for a two-year term and then for life. Ruling until his death in 1840, he succeeded in completely isolating the country and in defeating the pro–Buenos Aires tendencies. He tolerated no political activity at all and instituted an all-embracing repressive state.

Uruguay, meanwhile, was invaded and annexed by the Portuguese-Brazilian Empire in 1816 and became the Cisplatine Province until 1828. In 1830, it became an independent republic, probably the first buffer state in Latin America, created after long negotiations between Brazilians (Portuguese) and Argentineans with the important intermediation of the British envoy, Lord Ponsonby.

In Paraguay, Francia was succeeded by Carlos Antonio López, who followed some of Francia's policies but opened the door to greater commerce and allowed some very limited political liberalization. Nevertheless, he secured total power for himself and his family, particularly for his son Francisco Solano, who was made brigadier general of the Paraguayan army at the age of eighteen. In quasi-monarchic fashion, Francisco Solano López succeeded his father, who died in 1862. Solano López had been in Europe in 1852–1853 and was heavily influenced by the France of Napoleon III as well as by European geopolitical doctrines. Thus, in 1864, arguing that a partial invasion of Uruguayan territory by Brazilian troops constituted a threat to the equilibrium of the nations of the Rio de la Plata, he declared war on Brazil. Later he declared war against Argentina because of its refusal to let Paraguayan troops cross Argentine territory to engage the Brazilian army. Finally, Uruguay itself declared war on Paraguay, although its participation was minor. The war ended five years later with the almost total destruction of Paraguay and the death of Marshal López, who, true to his previous statements, heroically accepted death but not surrender.

URUGUAY

Democracy: Practice and Tradition of Coparticipation

Until 1973, Uruguay was considered one of the most stable democracies of Latin America, a model of freedom and progress. Although such enthusiastic claims were somewhat exaggerated, it is certainly true that until the late 1960s Uruguay had a relatively stable polity and ranked among the most democratic regimes in Latin America. Let us therefore examine how this situation came into being.[1]

Early in the nineteenth century, the Uruguayan *caudillos* (later the political elites) came to a conclusion that was to be of foremost importance in the future: that institutionalized compromises were necessary. Thus, since 1830, the history of Uruguay is one of compromises among *caudillos*—broken from time to time but replaced soon thereafter by other compromises reflecting the characteristics of the new situation and the relative forces of the contending parties. This process led to the institutionalization of a practice known as co-participation, a constant in Uruguayan history and the ideological and practical framework within which Uruguayan politics evolved until the late 1960s. Hence, regardless of which of the two traditional parties, the Blancos (whites, conservatives) or the Colorados (reds, liberals), was in power, there was always room, a coparticipative role, for the opposition.

The first half of the twentieth century was dominated by the figure of the Colorado populist leader José Batlle y Ordóñez. Batlle, president from 1903–1907 and 1911–1915, represented the most advanced and progressive wing of the Colorado Party, and his influence in Uruguayan politics had far-reaching consequences. Under his leadership, Uruguay underwent a rapid process of modernization financed, in part, by rising export revenues. However, it is in the fields of economic and social reforms that his influence was paramount and most lasting. Among other things, he nationalized foreign banks and the public service companies, enacted a law concerning pensions and retirements, established provisions for rest days and workmen's compensation for industrial accidents, and legalized the eight-hour working day. His policies also opened the door for the newly mobilized social and political forces of Montevideo, most of them immigrants or sons of immigrants, to enter the political arena. These new forces, representing the middle and working classes, in turn generated support for the party and faction that implemented such reforms. If one considers that by the turn of the century the population of the capital city of Montevideo already represented 30 percent of the population of the country and that 47 percent of that population was composed of immigrants, one can understand how deeply Batlle's policies changed the map of the country. In electoral terms, his reforms meant that the total number of voters jumped from 31,262 in 1910 to 299,017 in 1928.[2]

As a result of Batlle's influence, the situation in Uruguay changed drastically in the 1920s and 1930s. Two elements were of particular importance. First, the power and role of the state were greatly enhanced through state intervention in the economy. Public and semipublic corporations (*entes autónomos*) were created, necessitating a tremendous expansion of the state bureaucracy. By the 1930s, the budget of the state *entes* represented 62 percent of total national expenses, and the total number of public employees had reached 52,000—approximately 5 percent of the national population.[3] Second, through the reforms promulgated by Batlle, the middle and working classes of Montevideo gained a position as participants in the political system.

This gain was also facilitated by the expansion of the industrial sector. For example, the number of industrial establishments increased from 714 to 7,403 between 1901 and 1930.[4]

This new situation did not supersede coparticipation, the old and resilient political tradition; in fact, a new collegial system (*colegiado*) was introduced for the exercise of executive power. The first *colegiado* (1917–1933), a personal triumph for Batlle, consisted of a dual executive power. On the one hand, the president was in charge of foreign affairs and defense, political, and police matters, while on the other, the National Council of Administration, composed of six members representing the majority party and three the largest minority party, was in charge of all other administrative matters. The second *colegiado* (1952–1966) went further and eliminated the figure of the president. It vested all powers in the council, which, like previous ones, had one-third of its seats reserved for the first minority party.[5]

Two factors are of particular importance in explaining the long-lasting success of coparticipation. The first is the country's steady rate of economic growth in the first half of the twentieth century. That growth allowed the political system to respond quite successfully to increasing political and economic demands from different social sectors and to foot the bill for a semi-welfare state. The 1900–1930 period, considered the period of *crecimiento hacia afuera* ("outward-looking growth"), was characterized by an export boom based on meat, wool, and hides. The total value of exports increased from 29.4 million pesos in 1900 to 73.3 million pesos in 1915 and 100.9 million pesos in 1930. By the 1930s, that model of growth had been gradually replaced by a model of *crecimiento hacia adentro* ("inward-looking growth"), though exports, particularly wool, continued to provide the hard currency that ultimately financed the model. The internal dynamic of growth, however, was provided by an industrial process of import substitution. The number of industrial establishments increased from 6,750 in 1930 to 23,080 in 1952, and the number of jobs provided by them jumped from 54,000 to 141,000.[6] The proportion contributed by industrial production to the GDP grew from 12.5 percent in 1930 to 20.3 percent in 1950.[7] The fact is that, either through exports or through import substitution, the rate of growth increased steadily, thus providing the government with the necessary resources to accommodate social, economic, and political demands and maintain its political efficacy.

A second important factor in explaining Uruguay's democratic stability until the late 1960s is its peculiar legal-constitutional framework. That framework, by accepting the political reality of a highly fragmented political scene and a machine-type political party system, institutionalized a stable and mutually accepted formula for resolving political disputes. An important part of this framework of practical and legalized coparticipation was the electoral law, passed in 1910, whereby parties were able to withstand fractionalization without losing electoral strength. The law, known as the *ley de lemas* (law of party designations), established a system in which the voter, in national elections, chose, simultaneously, the party of his preference and, within that party, the candidate of his preference. In U.S. terms, that would be tantamount to having the primaries and the national elections held on the same day, the winner being the most popular candidate of the most popular party.

Breakdown of Democracy and Emergence of the Military Dictatorship

The decade of the 1950s signaled the beginning of the end of the economic bonanza and of the political model that this bonanza helped to sustain. The excessive dependence on exports, particularly on a few products, and the nature of an industrialization process that relied too heavily on protectionist measures and on foreign currencies generated by a depressed export sector brought about a series of crises of increasing gravity. Total exports dropped from US$254.3 million in 1950 to US$129.4 million in 1960. Recurrent balance-of-payments problems forced the continuing devaluation of the peso, from 1.90 to the dollar in 1950 to 11.30 to the dollar in 1960 to 250 to the dollar in 1971.[8] The average annual rate of growth declined from 4.8 percent in the 1945–1955 period to 0.9 percent in the 1955–1970 period while the per capita rate of growth for the last period was –0.3 percent.

The industrial sector lost the dynamism of the earlier period. The number of people employed by industries dropped from 200,642 in 1960 to 197,400 in 1968. The annual rate of growth of the industrial sector decreased from 6 percent for the 1945–1954 period to 1.6 percent for the 1960–1970 period.[9] The inflation rate, which had been 9.8 percent in 1955 and had never before surpassed the 15 percent mark, reached a record high of 125.4 percent in 1968.[10] There was also a dramatic decline in the real wages of workers and employees, especially after 1970. The index of real wages dropped from a base of 100 in 1957 to 76.5 in 1967[11] and from an index of base 100 in 1968 to 66.2 in 1979.[12] This last figure means that workers in 1979 earned an average of 33.8 percent less than in 1968.

This economic panorama of stagnation combined with high rates of inflation and continued balance-of-payments deficits provoked strong reactions from all economic sectors, but particularly from the landed upper classes. In the 1958 elections, the landowning elites threw their most active support to the conservative Blanco Party, which won its first national election in the twentieth century. In order to reverse what the landed elites considered a virtual confiscation of their export earnings through the mechanism of multiple exchange rates, the Blanco government in 1959 passed the Exchange Reform Law, which heavily favored the landowning class. The government was also forced to enter into a number of agreements with the International Monetary Fund (IMF) to regularize the constant balance-of-payments deficits. The crisis, however, continued to deepen. The *colegiado* system of government, implanted by the 1952 constitution, was blamed for many of the difficulties, and in 1966, concurrent with the national election, a new constitution that restored the presidential system was approved.

The elections were won by retired general Oscar Gestido of the Colorado Party, but he died less than a year after taking office and was replaced by his vice president, Jorge Pacheco Areco. By the time Pacheco replaced Gestido, the Tupamaro National Liberation Movement, an urban guerrilla group, had become very active. The Tupamaros, who aimed to overthrow the capitalist regime, were mainly young members of the petite bourgeoisie—intellectuals, students, and salaried members of the middle class. They established a highly efficient organization and were able to carry out some spectacular coups de main, including the kidnapping of the British ambassador, the Brazilian consul, and the U.S. police adviser, Dan Mitrione. Mitrione was later killed when the government refused to accept the Tupamaros' conditions for his release. Pacheco was thus forced to employ increasingly greater violence, and the general level of repression gradually rose.

Hence, the 1971 elections took place in a tense climate. The Uruguayan left coalesced in the Frente Amplio (Broad Front), composed of Christian Democrats, Socialists, Communists, and independent leftists. Its presidential candidate was retired general Liber Seregni, a prestigious and widely respected military man. The Broad Front, as expected, did well in Montevideo, where it captured 30 percent of the votes, but it fared poorly in the countryside. Colorado candidate Juan M. Bordaberry, with the support of his party's conservative *pachequista* faction, became the new president. Whereas Pacheco was from the upper classes of Montevideo, Bordaberry was closely associated with the even more conservative landowning classes.

The truce declared by the Tupamaros during the pre-electoral and electoral periods, designed to help the Broad Front, was soon over, and increasing repression and rising guerrilla activities began to escalate. The army, which had been called in September 1971 to lead the anti-subversive campaign, prepared a full-scale offensive. The killings of a frigate captain and an army colonel (the brother of General Gregorio Alvarez, who became president in 1981) enraged the military, and by September 1972 they had almost completely wiped out the Tupamaro Movement. Simultaneously, a whole array of right-wing terrorist, counterguerrilla movements—death-squad-type organizations—succeeded in generalizing an anti-leftist persecution. The army's success was based not only on its military superiority but also on the extensive and undiscriminating use of torture against anybody suspected of having any type of connection with the Tupamaros.

Once the process of overt military intervention in the political life of the country was set in motion, it became increasingly difficult, and ultimately impossible, for civilian political leaders to reverse it. Thus, although the anti-guerrilla campaign was almost completely successful by the end of 1972, the military gradually assumed a larger role in the decisionmaking process. With documents seized from the Tupamaros, the military launched a campaign against "corruption" and demanded a greater role in the management of state corporations and other state agencies. President Bordaberry caved in to virtually every demand, and by early 1973 he was a puppet of the military.

The first stage of the final crisis began in February 1973 when the army and the air force resisted Bordaberry's designation of a new defense minister. They further demanded the establishment of a National Security Council (COSENA), composed of officers and civilians, to deal with security and economic matters.

Parliament, in trying to stop the military from completely taking over the government, conducted a series of investigations into the extensive use of torture in army detention centers. On June 27, 1973, the generals retaliated by closing Parliament and replacing it with a Council of State, composed of forty-six members handpicked by the military. Political parties and activities were banned, the National University closed, workers' organizations outlawed, and the most terrible political persecution in Uruguayan history unleashed. From that time on, the only significant changes were in the degree and scope of repression. In 1976, Bordaberry was forced to resign and was replaced by a civilian chosen by the military, Aparicio Méndez, who was never more than a figurehead.

Early in the 1980s, the military started essaying some kind of political institutionalization of the dictatorship. Following the Brazilian model of changing presidents without changing the regime, the National Security Council elected a new president, General Gregorio Alvarez, in 1981. Soon after assuming power, Alvarez called a national referendum to approve a new constitution greatly restricting political activities—particularly those of the nontraditional parties—and perpetuating a growing role for the military. The plebiscite was a crushing defeat for the military as 54 percent of the voters, ignoring official intimidation, rejected the constitution. The process of controlled liberalization continued, however, and the military promised to hold free presidential and congressional elections in November 1984. Late in 1982, the Colorado and Blanco parties were allowed to organize internal elections, and the antigovernment factions scored a major victory, winning over 70 percent of the votes. In mid-1983, the government-opposition talks regarding the transition collapsed, due to the intransigence of the military in its attempt to secure control over the decisionmaking process even after the elections. The government responded by increasing the levels of political repression and press censorship, but the result was a series of mass rallies (the first public gatherings in Montevideo in years) demanding the immediate return to democracy.[13]

Finally, after a prolonged period of negotiations, the military retreated to the barracks in 1984 and Colorado candidate Julio María Sanguinetti was elected president. Sanguinetti led the first post-military government through rough waters, particularly because of the adamant refusal of the military to allow officers to stand trial for human rights violations and political crimes. Sanguinetti, however, managed to consolidate the restored democratic system. In the elections of November 1989, Luis A. Lacalle Herrera of the Blanco Party won the presidency.

Meanwhile, the economic situation improved in some respects in the late 1970s. Inflation was relatively controlled at the tremendous social cost of a drastic reduction in the living standards of wage earners, especially industrial workers. International prices for some traditional Uruguayan exports rose, with a consequent improvement of the balance of payments. The most significant change, however, was in the composition of Uruguayan exports. The nontraditional exports share of total exports increased from 25 percent in 1972–1973 to 64 percent in 1978, thanks to increasing tax rebates for these items. In the early 1980s, however, Uruguay plummeted into one of its worst recessions, with negative rates of growth of –1.3 percent in 1981, –10.0 percent in 1982, and –8.5 percent in 1983. Inflation, on the other hand, returned to a high of 57.5 percent in 1983, and remained hovering around 60 percent thereafter.

The sectors that benefited most from the policies of the military dictatorship were precisely those linked to the export of nontraditional goods, along with bankers. The landowning classes benefited too, especially to the extent that they provided the raw materials for most of the nontraditional export industries, such as tanning and leather goods. The sectors that suffered most were industrialists producing for domestic consumption, because of the contraction of the market, and salaried workers and employees, because real wages and salaries declined 35 percent in the 1972–1979 period. Labor unions were all but destroyed, and workers were left absolutely defenseless against the military dictatorship.

The U.S. Role

U.S. private investment in Uruguay has never been substantial. In 1960, it totaled only $47 million.[14] By 1980, total U.S. investment in Latin America was more than $38 billion, but Uruguay, Paraguay, and Bolivia shared less than 2 percent of that amount. Nor has U.S. economic aid been significant. U.S. loans and grants (excluding military programs) grew from $10.1 million in 1972 to $13 million in 1975 but declined sharply thereafter to $200,000 in 1978, reflecting the general deterioration of U.S.–Uruguayan relations in the 1977–1980 period. This deterioration was due to the Carter administration's human rights policy and the failure of the Uruguayan dictatorship to take positive steps toward stopping the systematic violation of human rights and civil liberties.

U.S. military aid, however, has been a different matter. The total extended to Uruguay during the 1950–1966 period was $33.2 million. The figure for 1969 was $1.6 million, increasing to $5.2 million in 1971. Thereafter, it decreased somewhat until 1973 and then jumped to a high of $8.2 million in 1975.[15] In 1977, Secretary of State Cyrus Vance announced that because of the pattern of gross violations of human rights by the Uruguayan government, the United States was suspending all military aid to that country. That policy was reversed by President Reagan in 1981.

It is clear that regardless of the specific amount of money appropriated for military aid to Uruguay each year, there was some sort of U.S. involvement during the heyday of the repression, that is, the 1970–1975 period. The role of U.S. police adviser Dan Mitrione, for example, killed by the Tupamaros on charges of training Uruguayan policemen in torture methods, has never been adequately explained.

From Democracy to Dictatorship: A Reassessment

The history of the rise and fall of democracy in Uruguay permits us to draw some interesting conclusions. The uninterrupted economic growth from 1900 to 1950 allowed the political process to become relatively autonomous from the pressures of the dominant classes. The extent to which these classes were able to function normally and make a satisfactory profit was related to their willingness to maintain a low profile in the political arena and to give a free rein to the politicians. The landowning elites, for example, may have considered that their earnings were being confiscated by exchange laws, but the continuing rise in the price of products they sold allowed them to prosper anyway. In fact, it was not until almost a decade after the crisis in the export sector began that they became directly involved in purely political matters.

The relative autonomy of the political process from economic pressure by the dominant classes was also favored by the development of a system of political machines that promoted the "welfarization" of the country. Hence, whereas the economically active population represented some 39 percent of the total population, the number of people on the government payroll plus the passive groups (that is, retirees and pensioners) represented, in 1969, almost 20 percent of the total population.[16] The state thus became a tremendous source of patronage for whose control parties developed increasingly larger political machines. The machines, in turn, restricted the ability of party leaders to implement sound policies because the parties were virtually mortgaged to the interests of the clientele that had helped them to gain power.

When the crisis emerged in the late 1950s, due to depression of the export sector and decline in the growth rate of the domestic industrial sector, it became increasingly difficult for any government to respond to the contradictory demands of various classes and economic sectors. The emergence of an armed challenge to the regime, the Tupamaros, aggravated the situation. Both the dominant classes—particularly the landowning elite—and the military felt that their interests were threatened. The process that followed the military defeat of the Tupamaros, however, suggested that the army had plans of its own—plans that presupposed the maintenance of a capitalist system but that were not necessarily inspired by the economic elite.

An external factor that may have heavily influenced the Uruguayan process is the involvement of more powerful neighboring states in internal power struggles. One should not forget that the three most powerful countries in the area—Brazil, Argentina, and Chile—were also suffering military dictatorships (except for the 1973–1976 Peronist parenthesis in Argentina) at the time of the militaristic drive in Uruguay. The influence of Brazil, especially, appears to have been quite strong. Likewise, when the winds of liberalization began to blow in Southern Cone countries, it became increasingly difficult for the military to continue refusing the domestic demand for democratization.

Uruguay in the 1990s: A Rebirth

As elsewhere in Latin America in the 1980s and 1990s, the retreat of the military has been halting and incomplete and the return of elections has not meant the return to full-blown class- or sector-interest competition or to constituency representation and accountability. Even so, the vitality of the born-again democratic system is impressive in light of the repression suffered in the 1970s and the constraints on resource allocation in the 1990s.

The general elections of 1984, heralding a return to civilian rule, were marred, to say the least, by prohibition of the candidacy of two very popular antimilitary leaders, Wilson Ferreira Aldunate of the Nationalist (Blanco) Party and General Liber Seregni of the Broad Front (Frente Amplio). Military intimidation forced the parliamentary adoption, at the end of 1986, of a measure granting amnesty to all military personnel accused of human rights violations.

Military restiveness on a lesser scale continued into the early 1990s, but it was popular opposition to the austerity measures upon which foreign credit was conditional that forced the major traditional parties into a National Accord. That accord carried over with respect to economic strategy from the tenure of the Colorado Party's Sanguinetti to the Blanco Party government of Luis Alberto Lacalle, elected in 1989, and to the subsequent government of Sanguinetti, returned to office in 1994.

The fact that the traditional parties had moved right and become almost indistinguishable opened political space to the left. Occupying the space on the political spectrum where factions of the Colorado Party were found in midcentury is the Ecuentro Progresista (EP, Progressive Alignment), led by former mayor of Montevideo Tabaré Vázquez.

In the 1994 elections, the traditional parties and the EP essentially divided the electorate into thirds. The EP portion, centered in Montevideo, coincided more or less with the constituency of the previously "subversive" Broad Front. Its tempered program calls for sparing from privatization those government services that are being frugally and efficiently run.

The economy, by all counts a disaster as transition to civilian rule got under way, has made something of a comeback. Recovery has followed a zigzag course but without the dramatic setbacks of the 1970s and early 1980s.

"Offshore-style" banking confidentiality and beachfront resort development, among other things, attracted major investments in the late 1980s and early 1990s. GDP growth registered an impressive 7.5 percent in 1992, dropping to 1.7 percent in 1993 and leveling off at about 4 percent in 1994. Foreign debt, inflation, and unemployment remained high in the mid-1990s, though they were generally edging downward, in part because of increasing agricultural exports and industrial production. The country confirmed its commitment to the Southern Cone Common Market (Mercosur) by implementing the custom union's common external tariff on most tradable goods at the beginning of 1995.

In the elections of late 1999, Jorge Battle, an old patriarch of the Colorado Party, became president only after a run-off election against Tabaré Vázquez, the candidate of the leftist Frente Amplio. The new electoral system was adopted a few years earlier to ensure the elections of presidents with strong mandates. In the first round the electorate was again divided in thirds, but this time the Frente Amplio ran a strong second place.

With a minority in Congress, President Battle invited the Blancos to a coalition government, which turned out to be of short duration. Argentina's economic meltdown had a devastating impact over the economy of Uruguay and soon emergency measures, including tax increases and a one-week banking holiday to prevent a massive withdrawal of deposits, were taken.

In the presidential elections of 2005, Tabaré Vázquez was finally successful. Uruguay thus became the third Latin American country in having an elected openly leftist government, after Allende in Chile and Lula in Brasil.

PARAGUAY

A Society in Conflict: 1870–1940

The War of the Triple Alliance (1864–1870) left Paraguay reduced to ruins, the economy in bankruptcy, the physical infrastructure destroyed, the population decimated, and the national territory reduced by some 60,000 square miles. In 1870, a liberal constitution was approved, but it was a dead letter. The two traditional parties, the Conservative, or Colorado (Red), and the Liberal, or Azul (Blue), were founded in 1887, but the former remained in power until 1904, not precisely through democratic means. Widespread corruption among government officials made things even worse. The enactment in 1883 and 1885 of the Laws of Sale of Public Land and *Yerbales* (maté plantations) brought about not only the beginnings of the great *latifundio* but also the eviction of poor peasants who had occupied those lands for generations. One Spanish-Argentine capitalist alone bought 14 million acres (5.7 million hectares) of land in the Chaco. In general, most of the 74.1 million acres (30 million hectares) of public lands were absorbed by private claimants.[17]

At the end of the nineteenth century, the situation could not have been worse. A few *estancieros* (ranchers) owned most of the land. A few foreign enterprises had a quasi-monopoly of tannin and yerba maté, two of the main export products. Poverty and backwardness were widespread. The violation of political and civil rights was routine, and the political elite was unresponsive. With public indignation aroused by this situation, the Liberal Party organized a successful revolt that quickly won widespread popular support. The 1904 Revolution, however, promised much but accomplished little. The main sources of wealth, including the newly developed *frigoríficos* (meat packing and processing plants), continued to be in foreign hands.[18]

By the 1920s, tensions with Bolivia regarding the territory of the Chaco quickly escalated to a point of no return, and in 1932 war broke out. The Paraguayan victory heightened social and economic mobilization, generating demands that existing institutions could not meet. On February 17, 1936, President Eusebio Ayala was overthrown and replaced by Colonel Rafael Franco, a Chaco War hero. Although the *febrerista* (after the month of the revolution) movement was quite heterogeneous, its ranks filled by Nazi-fascists, social democrats, and Marxists alike, it set in motion some of the major social and economic reforms in Paraguayan history.

In August 1937, a military uprising toppled the *febreristas*. The provisional government held elections in 1939, and the candidate of the Liberal Party, another Chaco War hero, General José F. Estigarribia, ran unopposed. In 1940, Estigarribia assumed dictatorial powers and replaced the 1870 constitution, but he died shortly thereafter in an airplane crash.

The Rise of Militarism

The army, which between 1936 and 1939 had been playing the role of arbiter, slowly moved toward assuming permanent and direct control of power. When Estigarribia died in 1940, his successor, General Higinio Morínigo, was selected by the military with little—if any—civilian influence. He assumed dictatorial powers and became the first strictly military dictator in Paraguayan history.

Morínigo found his military support in a Nazi-fascist lodge known as the Frente de Guerra (War Front) and, among civilians, in a group known as the *tiempistas* (after their newspaper *El Tiempo*), which had an ambiguous, conservative Christian-corporatist ideology. Fortunately for him, World War II helped to keep exports at high levels and to increase foreign exchange reserves. Besides, although Morínigo's sympathies for the Axis powers were never a secret, he astutely managed to sell his hemispheric loyalty to the United States, thus securing a U.S. offer of some $11 million in lend-lease military aid as well as $3 million in economic aid.[19]

Morínigo's economic policies were characterized by the increasing intervention of the state—a trend that started in the early 1930s leading to the creation of public corporations. Among them were COPAL (now APAL) in the field of alcohol production and sale, COPACAR in meat commercialization, and FLOMERES, the state merchant fleet. The cost of living increased dramatically from an index of 110 in 1940 (base: 1938 = 100) to 432 in 1948, an average annual increase of 41.5 percent.[20]

Morínigo's regime was far more repressive than had been any of its predecessors. His corporatist and authoritarian views were well expressed in the motto of his "revolution": Discipline, Hierarchy, Order. In 1942, he decreed the dissolution of the Liberal Party. With a Colorado-military coalition, Morínigo returned to harshly repressive policies, which prompted the rebellion of the Concepción military garrison in March 1947 and, with it, the outbreak

of a bloody five-month civil war. With the majority of the army and the officer corps against the dictator, the Colorados turned to the United States for
help. They needed it—the petition said—"to protect hemispheric security
from the bloody designs of Stalinist imperialism," but the U.S. State Department, after sending a CIA man to check on that claim, concluded that the rebellion was "far from being communist-dominated," and the request of the
Colorados was turned down.[21] Argentine president, Juan D. Perón, though,
viewed a similar petition sympathetically and secretly provided the weaponry
that permitted the Paraguayan government finally to defeat the rebels in the
outskirts of Asunción. Morínigo's victory was a Pyrrhic one, however, for the
Colorados grew stronger and, fearing that Morínigo would not turn over
power to their presidential candidate, Natalicio González, overthrew him in
February 1948.

The Era of Stroessner

The period that followed the 1947 government victory was marked by the
increasing "Coloradization" of the country. Civil service positions and access
to and promotion within the army were contingent upon having a proven
Colorado background. Meanwhile, the Korean War helped keep exports at
high levels from 1949 to 1953. Monetary reserves, which had dropped from
$11 million in 1946 to $3.1 million in 1949, jumped to $17.7 million at the
end of 1953. In spite of that, the internal economic situation deteriorated
rapidly. Inflation grew at an annual average rate of 67 percent in the
1947–1953 period and reached a record high of 157 percent in 1952. The
value of the local currency, the guaraní, decreased by more than 700 percent
in the 1946–1954 period.[22]

The worsening internal economic situation coupled with the intense con-
spiratorial activities of almost every *presidenciable* politician submerged the
country into one of the most unstable periods of its history. There was, indeed,
a brief but full-scale return to praetorianism, for the Colorados themselves were
bitterly divided by factional struggles, each faction seeking the support of some
key army officers to advance its particular goals. As a result, the public mood—
which in 1936 had favored change—in 1954 called for peace and order.

On May 4, 1954, taking advantage of that situation, forty-two-year-old
General Alfredo Stroessner staged a coup that overthrew the Colorado president, Federico Chávez. Three months later, replacing a provisional president,
Stroessner assumed power as the victorious candidate in a one-man presidential election. Although he was believed to be a transitional figure, Stroessner
quickly proved that all forecasts were wrong. He skillfully played military and
civilian sectors against each other, and in 1959, after almost a year of increasing labor and student unrest, he consolidated his position by closing the Colorado Parliament and expelling from the country almost one-half of its
members. By the beginning of the 1960s, he had become the unquestionable
leader; few *políticos* (politicians) or military men dared to challenge him.

The Socioeconomic Structure

Between 1954 and the early 1970s, the Paraguayan economy was characterized by very low rates of growth within the framework of a traditional social structure with widespread pre-capitalist forms of production in the countryside. Vast sectors of the peasantry were virtually excluded from the monetary economy and were devoted to subsistence crops on lands they did not own. By the end of the 1950s, for example, 1,549 landowners controlled some 85 percent of the land, and only 0.9 percent of the territory was dedicated to agriculture.[23] In addition, Paraguay did not undertake import substitution, like most other Latin American countries; the industrial sector, therefore, was quite underdeveloped. By 1963, for example, out of a population of some 1.9 million, only 35,000 were employed by industrial establishments. Nearly half of them, 17,482, worked in plants employing fewer than ten workers; there were only thirty-one industrial firms that employed more than 100 persons each.[24] Foreign investment, mostly British and Argentine, was concentrated in a few relatively dynamic sectors, particularly the meat-packing and processing industry, lumber, banking, and, more recently, cottonseed-oil manufacturing.

The economic situation in general was one of quasi-stagnation. The GDP increased between 1954 and 1969 at an annual rate of 3.7 percent, while the GDP per capita increased at an annual rate of only 1.3 percent.[25] The government, nevertheless, was successful in regard to two goals: controlling inflation and developing infrastructure. The former was achieved through an extremely tight monetary policy; the latter, through foreign loans and grants. The government also achieved some equilibrium in the balance of payments thanks to standby agreements signed with the IMF and to U.S. economic aid, especially the U.S. PL–480 program that allowed Paraguay to import wheat with credit granted on favorable terms.

Economic stagnation was accompanied by highly unequal income distribution. Although there are no reliable studies for that period, economist Henry D. Ceuppens estimated that 5 percent of the population had an income share of 50 percent of GNP; 15 percent, an income share of 20 percent of GNP; and 80 percent of the population shared the remaining 30 percent of GNP.[26]

The 1970s witnessed the most rapid and thorough process of modernization in recent Paraguayan history. Two basic factors account for the dynamics and characteristics of this process. First is the Itaipú hydroelectric dam, a project jointly undertaken by Paraguay and Brazil at a cost of $15 billion—almost five times the GNP of Paraguay in 1980. In full operation, the dam is the greatest in the world, producing 12.6 million kilowatts per hour.

The second factor was an agricultural boom associated with a shift to commercial export agriculture, particularly soybeans. The construction of the Itaipú dam and the agribusiness boom brought about a massive influx of foreign capital. As a result, foreign exchange reserves increased dramatically from $18 million in 1970 (the same level as 1953) to $781 million at the end of 1981. The process was also marked by a decline in the importance of

Anglo-Argentine investments in relation to Brazilian, U.S., European, and Japanese investments. Meanwhile, there emerged a powerful commercial agricultural sector, dominated by multinational companies, that dramatically transformed the countryside.

The rate of GNP growth increased from an average of 6.4 percent for the 1970–1975 period to an average of 10.2 percent for the 1976–1978 period. In 1979, the rate was 10.7 percent and in 1980, it reached a record high of 11.4 percent. In 1981, it dropped to a more modest 8.5 percent,[27] and 1982 and 1983 witnessed a deep recession and negative growth rates. The commercial deficit increased dangerously and reached a record high of $545 million. Moreover, the factor allowing substantial balance-of-payments surpluses in spite of increasing commercial deficits over the previous five years—the influx of foreign capital, mostly related to the Itaipú project—started to decline in 1981. The foreign debt, on the other hand, increased from $98 million (16.7 percent of the GNP) in 1970 to $2.2 billion (52 percent of the GNP) in 1988.[28]

The modernization process has had other negative consequences. Inflation reached a high of 28.1 percent in 1979; it decreased to 22.4 percent in 1980 and to 13 percent in 1981, but the real rate may have been much higher than these official figures. The government reacted with tough monetary restrictions, so tight that the country was thrown into one of its worst recessions. The real minimum wage fell by some 17 percent between 1964 and 1980. Although the GNP per capita in 1980 was $1,131, 62 percent of the urban population had an income of between $150 and $440.[29] In Asunción, the capital city, 13 percent of the population, or 68,000 people, live in eighty-nine *villas miserias* ("shantytowns") scattered around the city.[30]

The most important consequence of the rapid process of economic modernization, however, is the parallel process of social mobilization that is, in turn, greatly increasing social and economic demands on the political system.

The completion of the Itaipú project and the cutoff of the capital influx associated with it placed a considerable strain on the government. The approximately 12,000 Paraguayan workers employed in the project were gradually laid off in the early 1990s, and with continual delays in the start-up of the Paraguayan-Argentinean Yacyreta hydroelectric project, there was no new project big enough to absorb them.

THE POLITICAL PROCESS

By the early 1960s, Stroessner was able to consolidate a power structure based on three pillars: Stroessner himself, the army, and the Colorado Party. He was able to erect and sustain this structure first by demonstrating his ability to remain in power against all odds; second, by harshly repressing people opposed to him; and third, by co-opting the rest, particularly army officers and members of the Colorado Party. Corruption and contraband for the benefit of a small clique became widespread and were part of the arsenal of payoffs at the regime's disposal. Officially, it was considered *el precio de la paz* (the price of peace).

The dominant economic classes readily and happily "exchanged the right to rule for the right to make money," to borrow Barrington Moore's phrase. In actuality, they had never quite governed, and therefore the transaction was most favorable. Their pressure groups, chronically weak, were satisfied with the "peace" that few other rulers had been able to deliver over such an extended period of time. Important sectors of the population, discouraged by the high level of political repression from any type of political activity, also accepted the situation as an unchallengeable fait accompli.

During a first period (broadly 1954–1962), the regime relied heavily on massive repression and coercion. That approach gradually gave way to an authoritarian model that, without renouncing repression as an occasional necessity, placed increasing emphasis on limited co-optation. Co-optation in Paraguay, however, did not involve access to public offices. Because of the very rigid structure of power, it implied only the absence of politically motivated harassment or repression of individuals as long as they stay away from the political arena. However, the regime continued to unleash periodic waves of repression to remind the real and potential opposition, as well as its own followers, that should they opt for a change in the status quo, they would have to pay a very heavy price. The elements of psychological terror and latent threat therefore remained very effective.

The turning point in the transition from a naked dictatorship to an authoritarian regime was the legal recognition, in 1962, of a splinter Liberal group. In exchange for recognition, the group participated in the 1963 presidential "elections," thus providing a token opposition. Soon afterward, the participationist groups within the opposition prevailed over those proposing an insurrectionary strategy. In 1964, the Febrerista Party was legally recognized, and most of the exiled Liberal leaders were allowed to return. The municipal elections of 1965 witnessed the participation of a Lista Abierta (Open List) registered by the Febreristas but headed by a distinguished independent physician and supported by the mainstream of the Liberals. The "elections," as usual, were plagued by widespread official fraud, but they demonstrated that the majority of the Liberals did not support the Liberal minority splinter group recognized in 1962. That helped the leaders of the majority to win legal recognition as the Liberal Radical Party, the word "radical" being added to distinguish the group from the one legalized in 1962. In 1962 and again in 1967, as well as in the 1964 recognition of the Febrerista Party, U.S. pressure for liberalization played a significant role.

In 1967, with the participation of four opposition parties, a national convention was held to amend the 1940 constitution. In reality, the only important issue was the addition of an article allowing Stroessner to run for reelection two more times. He did so, in 1968 and 1973, winning easily in elections characterized by widespread fraud.

Participation, however, proved to be a one-way street: All the benefits accrued to the government. Legal opposition parties, though not openly repressed, had their activities restricted to such an extent that they gained very little political ground. An office-seeking elite within those parties remained satisfied to the extent that they had access to some thirty seats in the Senate and Chamber of Deputies, with the corresponding salaries and benefits. Soon, however, it became clear that there were too many politicians and too few sinecures. Politicians began to fight fiercely for the spoils that the regime put at their disposal. Such party infighting further debilitated the legal opposition, already perceived by the public as a highly ineffectual ornamental device.

It was in this context of the debilitation of the legal opposition that student and peasant movements rose to prominence in the late 1960s and early and middle 1970s. Both groups had become disenchanted with the legal opposition, not only because of its chronic inefficacy but also because it failed to provide a real ideological alternative to the right-wing regime. In a few years, they succeeded in organizing some of the largest mass movements in recent Paraguayan history. As a result, peasants and students were harshly repressed. The persecutions unleashed in the 1975–1980 period were of such magnitude that the mass movements were badly crippled.

Other sources of opposition to the regime were the Catholic Church and Church-related groups. Since the late 1960s, the Catholic hierarchy had steadfastly opposed and denounced abuses of the regime as a matter of public posture. The Church, however, did not perceive itself as being an opposition force and therefore did not have a clear political strategy.

Hence, the decade of the 1970s was characterized by the increasing strength of the government vis-à-vis the opposition. The general improvement in economic conditions and the Itaipú-related boom of the late 1970s further reduced the ability of the opposition to draw support from wide sectors of the population. In 1977, the government succeeded in further dividing the legal opposition by isolating those sectors that refused to go along with a 1977 constitutional amendment devised to allow Stroessner to run for re-election indefinitely. Splinter groups of the Liberal Party took advantage of the government search for potential "opposition" parties. At one moment, there were five Liberal parties, four of them bidding for recognition from the government to participate in the 1978 elections. Two of them were finally selected, thus assuring for themselves the highly contested parliamentary seats and for the government the continuation of the democratic façade.

Strengthened by its political and economic success, the regime continued to harass the non-participationist opposition. In the late 1970s, these sectors succeeded in articulating a joint opposition front, the Acuerdo Nacional (National Accord), uniting the Liberal Radical Authentic Party, the Febrerista Party, the Christian Democratic Party, and the Popular Colorado Movement (MOPOCO), a Colorado group expelled from the country by Stroessner in 1959. The Acuerdo was born under and encouraged by international, and particularly U.S., pressures against the Stroessner regime for its violation of human rights. It grew stronger as this pressure grew stronger during the Carter administration years. But as international pressure decreased, particularly after the election of Ronald Reagan in November 1980, the importance of the Acuerdo gradually diminished. Its activities, in any case, had been confined to public condemnation of the regime, but it did attain high visibility and have significant public impact.

For the government, nevertheless, there were problems. The international criticisms of its human rights violations were translated into actual sanctions when the U.S. government almost terminated its military assistance program and greatly reduced its economic aid. Moreover, the country was unable to obtain some loans from international institutions on the preferential terms it was accustomed to because of the U.S. refusal to vote favorably on those credits. Internally, the government faced some of its most severe domestic problems since the late 1950s. Within the Colorado Party, there were numerous confrontations among sectors competing for control of the party organization, particularly local branches or sections (*seccionales*) and student organizations. Furthermore, discontent among the youth whose potential role was being postponed while the ruling old guard refused to leave them room for upward mobility increased significantly. Moreover, growing politicization of student and labor sectors resulted in mounting pressures for liberalization. The transition to democracy in neighboring Argentina and Brazil further undermined the Stroessner regime.[31]

But the final blow to the thirty-five-year-old Stroessner dictatorship came as a result of the military ramifications of a major split in the ruling Colorado Party. In August 1987, an aging Stroessner moved virtually to expel from the party a sizable part of its leadership. That group became known as the traditionalists and was believed to be considering ending the automatic endorsement of the Stroessner candidacy for president. The attack on the traditionalists was led by a group of extreme right-wing zealots and diehard Stroessner loyalists known as militants.

Upon seizing control of the party, the militants moved to secure their positions in the state apparatus and the military. When Stroessner underwent major surgery in late August 1988, and his health became increasingly worrisome, the militants sped up their moves and sought to position Stroessner's eldest son, a just-promoted air force colonel, next in the line of military succession. To do so, a large number of generals and colonels had to be retired or reassigned, a move that began in early January 1989. But when, on February 2, Stroessner sought to retire General Andrés Rodríguez, his major military rival and First Army Corps commander, Rodríguez struck back and with widespread support from all units overthrew Stroessner on the morning of February 3, 1989, after ten hours of bloody battles.

General Rodríguez became provisional president and called for elections within ninety days as the first step in a process of transition to democracy. He ran as the candidate of the Colorado Party. Adopting a strong pro-democracy message, Rodríguez won the elections of May 1 by a landslide; he captured slightly more than 70 percent of the votes, against 20 percent for his closest competitor, PLRA leader Domingo Laíno. Opposition parties complained that they could not organize for elections in such a short period of time after three decades of repression. While the pre-electoral campaign allowed parties full political freedoms, and although General Rodríguez became a very popular candidate who would have won anyway, the elections were marred by many irregularities and systematic and widespread, although not massive, fraud.[32]

Upon assuming the presidency, General Rodríguez began to move decisively in the direction of greater liberalization and the incorporation of opposition or independent leaders into positions of leadership, including the Supreme Court and some ambassadorships. Nevertheless, much remained to be done before a true democratic system might emerge.

THE TRANSITION

In 1989, few believed that Paraguay could experience a transition to a democratic system along the lines followed by other countries in the region. Guided by deterministic and historic dogmas, many could not understand the present but as the endless repetition of the past. Yet, neither the historic legacy of Paraguay nor the specific nature of the Stroessner regime constituted insurmountable obstacles to a transition to democracy. The coup of February 3, 1989, began a process of transition from above and within that, once unleashed, gradually assumed a dynamic of its own and is now approaching a successful conclusion.

In the early stages of the process, General Rodríguez sought to gain the support of the international community by committing himself to democratize the country but without jeopardizing the old basis of political power of the Colorado Party: its privileged and incestuous relation with the armed forces, its unlimited and exclusive access to state patronage, and its thorough manipulation and control of the electoral process. Democratization thus in reality meant liberalization. To legitimize this, elections were called for May 1, at which time Rodríguez was elected president and a Colorado-controlled Congress was installed.

The process of liberalization, though, strengthened the opposition and allowed it gradually to gain bargaining power. Simultaneously, it fostered the fragmentation of the Colorado Party, as different factions vied for control of the party. As a consequence, political power became more dispersed and major political decisions began to require the give-and-take that characterizes coalition building. And inasmuch as power became less centralized and concentrated the chances for furthering the process of liberalization and acceleration, that of democratization improved.

It was in this context that a convention to write a new constitution to replace Stroessner's 1967 charter met in the first months of 1992. The new document neatly reflected the political reality. A presidential system with a very strong Congress was adopted as its framework. Important principles, such as decentralization and many programmatic statements about agrarian reform, social justice, and workers' rights, were also incorporated. But the most far-reaching clauses were those concerning the transfer of power.

To begin with, the constitution banned all forms of re-election and included, in its transitory part, an article tailor-made to impede a possible Rodríguez bid for re-election. This caused considerable tension, and generals loyal to him subtly threatened a coup. Rodríguez refused to swear allegiance to the new constitution, but the ceremony was held nonetheless before Congress and the document entered into effect on June 20, 1992.

Within less than a year, on May 9, 1993, the first relatively competitive elections were held. Three candidates—Juan Carlos Wasmosy for the Colorado Party, Domingo Laíno for the Authentic Radical Liberal Party, and Guillermo Caballero Vargas for the newly formed Encuentro Nacional—competed, and Wasmosy won with some 39 percent of the vote.

The elections brought into sharp relief both what had been achieved in terms of democratization and what remained to be done. On the one hand, the hotly contested primary elections within the Colorado Party threw a shadow of doubt over the legitimacy of Wasmosy's candidacy, as most observers believed his opponent, Luis María Argaña, won the election only to be deprived of it by means of the manipulation of the vote-counting process. On the other hand, the failure of both opposition candidates to join forces reflected the inability of political actors to develop effective mechanisms of coalition building. But perhaps more important, extensive political manipulation was exhibited throughout the electoral process. In fact the Colorado-run electoral board thoroughly controlled the process and excluded the opposition from any meaningful oversight of elaboration of registration rolls, distribution of polling places, and appointment of electoral officers, not to speak of the thorough utilization of the state apparatus and resources to support the campaign of the official candidate. Furthermore, there was open intervention of a sector of the military establishment, led by Major General Lino Oviedo, in support of Wasmosy's candidacy.

Considering all these problems part and parcel of the transition process, and taking into account that in spite of them the opposition parties, combined, had won a majority in Congress, both the Authentic Radical Liberal Party and the Encuentro Nacional formally recognized the results as valid and lent legitimacy to the Wasmosy government.

As expected, the first four years of Wasmosy's term were characterized by his constant inability to muster the support of his own party for his program. Much of the backing needed to weather the difficulties was provided by the opposition parties in the belief that it was fundamental for the success of the transition process that Wasmosy complete his term without interruption. In exchange, the opposition won some very important concessions, including the reorganization of the judiciary and the appointment of a more balanced nine-member Supreme Court. Of equally fundamental importance was the establishment of a three-member Supreme Electoral Tribunal, which promises a true reform of the electoral process.

A major military crisis erupted in April 1996 when Wasmosy dismissed the commander of the army, General Lino Oviedo, and he refused to step down. Oviedo had become a sort of power behind the throne, and there was the general perception that Wasmosy could not adopt major decisions without his agreement. Thanks to the prompt reaction of the Congress, the youth, political parties, the international community, and the institutionalist sector of the armed forces, Wasmosy stood firm, and within twenty-four hours Oviedo resigned. This outcome represented the removal of the last obstacle to the complete subordination of the military to the constitution and civilian control.

In this context, the first truly clean and competitive municipal elections were held in November 1996. The results demonstrated an almost even distribution of votes between the Colorado Party and opposition forces.

Wasmosy's legal mishandling of the aftermath of the 1996 military crisis, however, permitted Oviedo to run for president at the Colorado primary elections previous to the general elections of 1998. In a three-way race the former general won by a razor-thin margin but the Supreme Court finally ruled him ineligible and ratified a ten-year prison term. His vice-presidential candidate, Raúl Cubas, led the Colorado ticket with Argaña, who came second, as vice-presidential candidate.

The opposition united behind PLRA leader Domingo Laino as presidential candidate accompanied by Carlos Filizzola, of the Encuentro Nacional, as the vice-presidential nominee. The result was a total disaster for the opposition as the Colorado ticket won 54 percent of the votes against some 42 percent for the opposition.

Soon the political crisis re-emerged in full force as Cubas attempted to force the re-entry of Oviedo, bending legal and constitutional rules. The crisis led to the initiation of a process of impeachment of Cubas. As the procedures developed, Vice President Argaña was assassinated. Massive demonstrations against Cubas were violently dealt with and eight students were killed in the plaza of the Congress. The result was the resignation of Cubas, who fled to Brazil, while Oviedo escaped to Argentina.

Following constitutional procedures the president of the Congress, Luis González Macchi, assumed the presidency to complete the term. He invited opposition parties to be part of a government of national unity, but his lack of leadership and the constant infighting within his coalition lead to a government weak and marred by corruption and inefficiency.

The elections of 2003 presented yet a new scenario. The Colorado Party ran with the candidacy of Nicanor Duarte Frutos, a young former minister of education. The Liberal Party put up the candidacy of Julio C. Franco, who had been elected vice president after González Macchi assumed the presidency. A new political party, Patria Querida, emerged with force around the candidacy of Pedro Fadul, a businessman of the financial sector, and displaced the Encuentro Nacional, whose participation in the government of González Macchi made them lose credibility. And the oviedistas run with his own party, UNACE. Duarte Frutos won with 37 percent, followed by Franco with 23 percent and

Fadul with 21 percent. Unace won 13 percent of the votes and the Encuentro Nacional was relegated to a distant fourth with approximately 2 percent of the votes.

So far, Presidente Duarte has demostrated strong leadership skills and appointed a respected independent economist as minister of finance, which managed to revert the economic crisis and has made significant inroads in the fight against corruption. But the combination of complex political and economic problems, and the fact that the government lacks a majority in the Senate and has a fragile one in the Chamber of Deputies, makes it difficult to predict the result of his term. Should his presidency be a new failure—as the previous ones—the future of the democratic system will be endangered. Should he be able to tackle the main economic and social problem with a minimum of success, democracy would win another chance.

NOTES

1. For an elaboration on the theme of coparticipation as a framework to study Uruguayan politics see Martin Weinstein, *Uruguay: The Politics of Failure* (Westport, Conn.: Greenwood Press, 1975), whose general approach this section follows.

2. Juan E. Pivel Devoto, "Uruguay independiente," in Antonio Ballesteros, ed., *Historia de America y de los Pueblos Americanos*, vol. 21 (Barcelona: Salvat Editores, 1949), pp. 628–632, and Martin H. J. Fynch, *A Political Economy of Uruguay Since 1970* (New York: St. Martin's Press, 1981), pp. 11–13.

3. Weinstein, *Uruguay*, p. 69.

4. Luis Macadar, Nicolas Reig, and José E. Santías, "Una Economía Latinoamericana," in Luis Benvenuto et al., *Uruguay Hoy* (Buenos Aires: Siglo 21, 1971), pp. 50–52.

5. Victor Pastorino, *Itinerario del colegiado* (Montevideo: Agencia Periodística Interamericana, 1956).

6. Walter Luisiardo, *Reflexiones sobre aspectos de la historia económica del Uruguay: Período 1900–1979* (Montevideo: Comisión Coordinadora para el Desarrollo Económico, 1979), pp. 12–24.

7. Fynch, *Political Economy of Uruguay*, p. 171.

8. Luisiardo, *Reflexiones*, pp. 44–48, 69.

9. Fynch, *Political Economy of Uruguay*, pp. 220–223; Luisiardo, *Reflexiones*, p. 68.

10. James W. Wilkie and Peter Reich, *Statistical Abstract of Latin America* (Los Angeles: University of California Press, 1979), p. 332.

11. Weinstein, *Uruguay*, p. 119.

12. Luisiardo, *Reflexiones*, p. 95.

13. For an excellent analysis of this complex process, see Charles G. Gillespie's "Uruguay: Transition from Collegial-Technocratic Rule," in *Transitions from Authoritarian Rule*, edited by Guillermo O'Donnell, Philippe Schmitter, and Laurence Whitehead (Baltimore: Johns Hopkins University Press, 1986), II, pp. 173–195.

14. Fynch, *Political Economy of Uruguay*, pp. 183–184, 264.

15. Wilkie and Reich, *Statistical Abstract*, pp. 144, 518.

16. Macadar, Reig, and Santías, "Una Economía Latinoamericana," p. 102. The estimation goes as follows: 213,000 public employees + 346,000 pensioners = 559,000, which of a population of around 2.8 million is 19.96 percent.

17. Domingo Laíno, *Paraguay: De la Independencia a la Dependencia* (Asunción: Ediciones Cerro Corá, 1976), p. 171, and Harris G. Warren, *Paraguay and the Triple Alliance: The Post-*

War Decade 1869–1878 (Austin: Institute of Latin American Studies, University of Texas Press, 1978), p. 286.

18. U.S. Department of Commerce, *Commerce Yearbook* (Washington, D.C.: Government Printing Office, 1928–1932), and *Foreign Commerce Yearbook* (Washington, D.C.: Government Printing Office, 1932–1950).

19. Michael Grow, *The Good Neighbor Policy and Authoritarianism in Paraguay* (Lawrence, Kan.: Regents Press of Kansas, 1981), p. 115.

20. U.S. Department of Commerce, *Investment in Paraguay: Conditions and Outlook for United States Investors* (Washington, D.C.: Government Printing Office, 1954), pp. 15–17, 84.

21. Grow, *Good Neighbor Policy,* pp. 63, 118, 146–147, n 27.

22. U.S. Department of Commerce, *Investment in Paraguay,* pp. 84–85.

23. Carlos Pastore, *La Lucha por la tierra en el Paraguay* (Montevideo: Editorial Antequera, 1972), p. 422.

24. Censo Industrial 1963, cited in Henry D. Ceuppens, *Paraguay Año 2,000* (Asunción: Editorial Gráfica Zamphirópolos, 1971), p. 61.

25. Wilkie and Reich, *Statistical Abstract,* p. 262.

26. Ceuppens, *Paraguay Año 2,000,* pp. 37, 124–126.

27. Banco Interamericano de Desarrollo (BID), *Progreso económico social en America Latina: Informe 1980–1981* (Washington, D.C., 1981), pp. 358–360. *ABC Color,* "Suplemento económico," July 25, 1982, pp. 4–5.

28. Ricardo Rodríguez Silvero, "Paraguay: El Endeudamiento externo," *Revista Paraguaya de sociología* 17:50 (January–May 1980), p. 81. *Ultima Hora,* February 26, 1989, p. 12.

29. Fernando L. Masi, "Paraguay: Analysis of the Socio-Economic Evolution" (Manuscript prepared in Washington, D.C., at the American University, 1982), p. 21.

30. Study done by the *Comité de Iglesias,* cited in *ABC Color,* "Actualidad profesional," March 5, 1982, pp. 2–3.

31. An extended discussion of these issues can be found in Diego Abente, *Stronismo, Post-Stronismo and the Prospects for Democratization in Paraguay,* Working Paper No. 119, Kellogg Institute, University of Notre Dame, 1989, and "Constraints and Opportunities: External Factors, Authoritarianism, and the Prospects for Democratization in Paraguay," *Journal of Interamerican Studies and World Affairs* 30:1 (Spring 1988), pp. 73–104.

32. For a discussion of the elections, see the Report of the Latin American Studies Association International Commission to Observe the Paraguayan Elections, "The May 1, 1989, Elections in Paraguay: Toward a New Era of Democracy?" *LASA Forum XX,* 3 (Fall 1989), pp. 39–48.

Suggested Readings

Uruguay

Benvenuto, Luis, et al. *Uruguay Hoy.* Buenos Aires: Siglo 21, 1971. Uruguay as seen by the Uruguayans; interesting perspectives.

Fynch, Martin H. J. *A Political Economy of Uruguay Since 1970.* New York: St. Martin's Press, 1981. An excellent analysis of the Uruguayan economic process until the late 1970s; a must.

Handelman, Howard. *Military Authoritarianism and Political Change in Uruguay.* AUFS Report. Hanover, N.H.: American Universities Field Staff, 1978. A good short analysis of contemporary trends and events.

_____. *Economic Policy and Elite Pressures in Uruguay.* AUFS Report. Hanover, N.H.: American Universities Field Staff, 1979. A good short study on recent changes regarding the decisionmaking process.

Kaufman, Edy. *Uruguay in Transition*. New Brunswick, N.J.: Transaction Books, 1979. An interesting, up-to-date work on Uruguayan politics.

Pivel Devoto, Juan E. "Uruguay independiente." In Antonio Ballesteros, ed., *Historia de America y de los Pueblos Americanos*, Vol. 21: 405–638. Barcelona: Salvat Editores, 1949. One of the many good and short historical introductions to Uruguay.

Quijana, José M., and Guillermo Waksman. "Las Relaciones Uruguay–Estados Unidos en 1977–1979." In *Cuadernos semestrales* 6 (2? semestre, 1979), pp. 310–343. A good study on recent trends in U.S.–Uruguayan relations with a useful statistical appendix.

Verdisco, Aimee E. "Between Accountability and 'Reivindicación': Development and Intranational Differentiation in Uruguay." Ph.D. diss., State University of New York at Buffalo, 1996.

Weinstein, Martin. *Uruguay: The Politics of Failure*. Westport, Conn.: Greenwood Press, 1975. A comprehensive analysis of Uruguayan politics; especially good for the study of the 1900–1960s period.

Paraguay

Abente, Diego. *Stronismo, Post-Stronismo, and the Prospects for Democratization in Paraguay*. Working Paper No. 119, Kellogg Institute, University of Notre Dame, 1989.

Bouvier, Virginia M. *Decline of the Dictator: Paraguay at a Crossroads* (Washington, D.C.: WOLA, 1988).

Cardozo, Efraim. *Breve historia del Paraguay*. Buenos Aires: EUDEBA, 1965. A good and short introduction to Paraguayan history.

Grow, Michael. *The Good Neighbor Policy and Authoritarianism in Paraguay*. Lawrence, Kan.: Regents Press of Kansas, 1981. A very well-documented study of the 1939–1949 period.

Hicks, Frederick. "Interpersonal Relationships and Caudillismo in Paraguay." *Journal of Inter-American Studies and World Affairs* 13 (January 1971), pp. 89–111. A very interesting, although somewhat outdated, study of Paraguayan politics.

Lewis, Paul H. *The Politics of Exile: Paraguay's Febrerista Party*. Chapel Hill, N.C.: University of North Carolina Press, 1968. An in-depth study of the Febrerista Party.

———. *Paraguay Under Stroessner*. Chapel Hill: University of North Carolina Press, 1980.

Pastore, Carlos. *La Lucha por la tierra en el Paraguay*. Montevideo: Editorial Antequera, 1972. A very good social history of Paraguay with special emphasis on an analysis of the agrarian process.

Warren, Harris G. *Paraguay and the Triple Alliance: The Post-War Decade 1869–1878*. Austin: Institute of Latin American Studies, University of Texas Press, 1978. The best analysis of the first postwar decade.

Chapter 29

CONCLUSION:
A TROUBLED NEIGHBORHOOD

JAN KNIPPERS BLACK

GETTING TO KNOW THE NEIGHBORS

One of the complaints commonly voiced by Latin Americanists at the dawn of the new century is that the U.S. government is paying too little attention to Latin America. Central Americans on the receiving end of U.S. bombs and bullets in the 1980s and Colombian peasants being sprayed now in their fields of corn as well as of cocaine with U.S. biochemical toxins might counter that official U.S. attention is, at best, a mixed blessing.

The relative inattention of the late 1990s was owing in part to the shift from muddled Cold War concerns to more straightforward commercial ones, and thus a shift in watchdogs from military and intelligence operatives to international financial institutions. In fact, since September 11, 2001, the all-purpose rationale of anti-terrorism and the popular movements in protest of neoliberal policies are generating now more attention of the cloak-and-dagger kind. On the part of pundits, however, a general perception remains that this recently raucous part of the world has "matured." In fact much of what Anglo-Americans are inclined to see as change in Latin America actually represents change in our perceptions of Latin America, as well as in our perceptions of our own society.

Latin America is more familiar to us now. That is due only in part to the enormously increased volume of academic studies inspired by the birth of a multidisciplinary field. It is also due to increased travel and investment by U.S. citizens and to expanded U.S. public and private programs of exchange, propaganda, proselytizing, relief, and development. The perspectives of diplomats and others, whose writings provided our images in decades past, derived almost exclusively from contacts with the political and economic elites. But thousands of Peace Corps volunteers and other Americans coming of age since the 1960s have come to know Latin America's peasants and workers and marginalized would-be workers as real people—friends.

Can it be that Latin America's poor, stereotyped in the not-so-distant past as ignorant and passive, have only recently become clever, energetic, and enterprising? Or is it that we are only beginning to learn of the courage required to overcome official intimidation and of the ingenuity required to survive on the edge? Is it possible that Latin America's middle classes, traditionally hedonistic and lackadaisical, have only recently been energized? Or can it be that we have only recently realized that the professional who seems never to be in his office actually juggles three offices: his bureaucratic post, his chair at the university, and his private practice?

A student of mine once commented that "Brazilian women don't work; they have maids." No doubt there are still women throughout the Americas who are pampered and cloistered. But now that we know the maids as well as the mistresses, we know that the issue "to work or not to work" is even phonier for most Latin American women than for their Anglo-American counterparts. In fact, we have now seen that the greater the economic or political threat to survival, the more central will be the role of women in combating that threat. Women have long been the economic and organizational mainstays of the poorest urban shantytowns. More recently, the large-scale involvement of women in danger-fraught human rights networks and in revolutionary movements has been particularly striking. To declare that Latin Americans, for reasons of work roles or sex roles, intellect or temperament, are unequal to the task of their own development on their own terms is to declare our ignorance of them.

While Latin America has been overrun in the past half century with U.S. slogans, products, and advisers, there has also been movement in the other direction. Latin American scholars have set the tone for studies by U.S. academic specialists in Latin American affairs. Some of the best U.S. novelists have experimented with literary styles pioneered by Latin American novelists. Latin American graphic arts, music, and cinematography have gained in popularity with U.S. audiences. U.S. churches have been influenced by the liberation theology that swept first, like a firestorm, through Latin America's religious communities. Some of Latin America's "best and brightest," driven from their own countries by dictatorial regimes supported by the U.S. government, have settled in the United States and have deepened our own national debates about domestic and foreign policy.

Of course, Anglo-America and Latin America share the shame of past and present mistreatment of native American and Afro-American populations. Furthermore, much of what is now the United States shares with much of Latin America the heritage of Spanish conquest and settlement and 300 years of Spanish colonialism. Indian and Spanish cultures, never quite suppressed in the southwestern United States, are now being revitalized by the annual influx of Mexican and Central American workers, estimated to be in the millions, seeking employment that eludes them at home. Miami, of course, has been Cubanized, and the northeastern part of the United States has absorbed great numbers of Caribbeans. As these workers, refugees, and immigrants, documented or otherwise, move from state to state and city to city in search of work, no part of the United States is wholly immune from the process of Latinoization.

There were some 30 million Hispanics in the United States in 1996. It is estimated that before the year 2010 they will surpass blacks in numbers to become the largest ethnic minority in the United States. Although some people lament the trend, I lament only its causes. There is no denying that Latin Americans are enriching our culture and our national life as have past waves of immigrants.

Finally, we are getting to know Latin Americans as a consequence of our government's incessant meddling in their affairs. Despite the wonders of technology and imaginative methods for intimidating whistleblowers, government secrets have become ever harder to keep. The media sooner or later catches up with our boys in camouflage. Their exploits in the 1980s, along with the images of peasants fighting and dying and of leaders pleading, in flawless English, for arms or for reason, were brought into our homes nightly in living color.

A question raised urgently and often in the United States in the 1980s was "Will Central America become another Vietnam?" There are many arguments as to why it did not, but the most important may be that the Central Americans are our neighbors. The Vietnamese were to North Americans a most exotic people. While we opposed U.S. involvement in that distant war for a myriad of reasons, we were not prepared to understand the problems and aspirations of the people of Indochina. Latin Americans, by contrast, are now a familiar people. It may be the case in the early 2000s that U.S. intervention in Colombia remains at the level of "low-intensity conflict" in part because the U.S. public would balk at the idea of an assault there on the scale of what we have recently seen in Iraq.

America Is One

U.S. presidents always begin their speeches before the assembled dignitaries of Western Hemisphere summits with the assertion that America is one—one society and one market. Such assertion is followed by rhetorical fluff about individualism, democracy, godliness, private enterprise, and the security threat. But there is a growing unacknowledged reality to the oneness of America. Latin America is increasingly sharing not only the blessings of U.S.-style modernization but its demons as well. And many of the problems that have long plagued Latin America are more and more apparent and bedeviling in the United States itself. The clearest trend in the Americas is a trend toward convergence—if not of interests, at least of problems.

Latin America, now predominantly urban—in fact, the world's most urbanized region—boasts or frets of several of the world's largest cities. To Latin America, as to the United States, urbanization has brought both advantages and disadvantages. It has led to new, more effective forms of political organization and has facilitated the extension of services—electricity, running water, health care, public schools—to a greater proportion of the population. It has extended the reach of the communications media, enhancing their ability to disseminate information, misinformation, and disinformation. In Latin America, as in the United States, urbanization has weakened the constraints, but also the socialization and the security, that flowed from extended family systems. To Latin America, more recently than to the United States, it has also meant traffic congestion, pollution, and anonymous, impersonal street crime.

Latin American economies have long suffered from fluctuations in world prices for a limited number of minerals or agricultural products and from deterioration in the terms of trade for such primary products. Before World War II, agriculture contributed twice as much to regional gross product as manufacturing did. Although most Latin American countries are still highly dependent upon the export of one or two primary products, manufacturing's share of gross regional product, by the late 1960s, was well above that of agriculture. In the 1970s, Brazil began to earn more from the export of manufactures than from that of primary products. By the 1990s, more than half of Latin America's exports were at least processed. At the same time, however, the importation of capital goods and, in the case of most countries, of energy to fuel the industrialization process led to soaring debts and other problems.

While Latin America has been industrializing, or at least expanding export-processing, the United States has been moving in the other direction. Spurred by incentives, offered by both U.S. and foreign governments, and lured by cheap labor, U.S.-based corporations have shifted capital—and jobs—to the Third World, including Latin America. Thus, the United States, for several decades the virtually unchallenged provider of manufactured goods to Latin America, has itself become increasingly dependent upon foreign investment, the importation of manufactured goods, and the export of primary products, particularly wheat.

In most Latin American countries, as in the United States, the idea of stimulating the economy from the bottom up—of expansion of the domestic market and production to meet effective mass demand—has been abandoned in favor of production for export and/or for the relatively affluent. Modernization, in Latin America as in the United States, has meant increasingly capital-intensive—as opposed to labor-intensive—industry, resulting in chronic unemployment. In the absence of stunningly innovative policy, the unemployment problem in both Americas promises to get worse.

Since the Iberian conquest of the New World, the concentration of landownership has been among Latin America's most obstinate problems. Conquistadores and others favored by the Iberian monarchs carved out for themselves enormous estates complete with resident native American populations or imported African slaves to do the work. But the land grabs of the colonial period pale by comparison to those inspired since the mid-nineteenth century by the growth of export markets for primary products. Effective and enduring land reform has been rare in the twentieth century, and in some countries the ongoing process of seizure of peasant lands leaves an ever-increasing proportion of the rural population dependent upon seasonal work for large landholders. As semi-feudal estates are transformed into agribusinesses and machines replace workers, displaced peasants are left with neither land nor wages.

FREE MARKETS AND COSTLY POLITICS

In the 1970s, many Latin American governments, recognizing that their agricultural sectors had been neglected or milked while import-substitution industrialization was being promoted, turned their attention to the modernization of agricultural production and offered new incentives for the export of agricultural products. One consequence was that lands that had been used to produce staples for domestic consumption were converted into production for export. Export earnings, not usually redistributed in any form to the general population, have risen. Meanwhile, increasingly, basic foodstuffs must be imported, resulting in higher prices for the consumer and rising foreign debt, which in 2002 amounted to almost twice the total value of exports.

As is often pointed out in comparisons of Anglo-America and Latin America, Anglo-America was early blessed with a land tenure pattern of small holdings, or family farms. However, while the U.S. government, in the 1960s, spoke of the need for land reform in Latin America, the process of concentration of landholdings, favoring agribusiness conglomerates, assumed a dizzying pace in the United States. By the 1990s, the family farm was clearly an endangered species.

Denationalization, the process whereby the ownership or control of resources passes from national to foreign hands, has long been a major problem for Latin America. For the first century or so of independence, it was primarily the land and mineral resources that attracted foreign investors, with the diplomatic—and sometimes military—backing of their governments. Transportation, public utilities, and other infrastructural projects also were often undertaken and controlled by foreigners. By the mid-twentieth century, foreign firms and multinational corporations had begun to capture, or recapture, domestic markets for durable consumer goods and to buy out or squeeze out local industries. More recently, foreign firms have competed successfully for control of distribution and services as well. Even seemingly unalienable resources, like water, were falling under the control of foreign firms in the early 2000s.

For most of the century in Meso-America and for several decades in South America, the denationalizers have been predominantly U.S.-based corporations. Since the 1970s, however, firms based in Western Europe and Japan have been gaining rapidly in the competition for Latin American markets and for the fruits of Latin American land and labor. The same European and Japanese companies, along with those of East Asia and of Middle Eastern oil potentates, have also been increasing their shares of U.S. consumer markets, at the expense of U.S.-based companies, and increasing their shares of ownership of U.S. farmland and urban real estate, banks, and industries.

A kindred and more insidious problem in the United States, which has received less attention even though it is far more serious, is that of "delocalization." The same multinational banks, conglomerates, and chains that have displaced Latin American businesses and rendered Latin American economies dependent have also bought out or squeezed out local businesses in Tennessee and Michigan and New Mexico. Such companies, which pay campaign debts in Washington and taxes in the Bahamas, have no national or local allegiances. When they see greater profits to be made in São Paulo or Shanghai, they leave Nashville or Albuquerque jobless with no regrets; they were never a part of the community. Many of the companies that moved to Mexico in the early years of NAFTA are moving on now to China for even cheaper labor.

Several Latin American countries made headway in the 1960s and 1970s toward gaining control over their resources and their economies. Expropriation of mineral resources was particularly common, and was so popular that even the most *entreguista* right-wing military dictators rarely dared to try to reverse it. The doctrine that subsoil resources are national domain was inherited by most of the Latin American countries from the Spanish crown. Mexico, in 1917, declared its petroleum and other subsoil resources social property, to be owned and exploited by and for the people as a whole; it made the claim an economic reality with the nationalization of those resources in 1938. Most other Latin American countries subsequently established public corporations to manage the production, importation, or distribution of petroleum and other energy products. Meanwhile, in the United States, an ever-smaller number of companies make ever-larger profits, while consumers undergo a price-gouging energy crisis every fifteen to twenty years.

Attempts by Latin American nationalists to regain control of their economies have often been undertaken at great cost. Such attempts generally have the effect of adding the great weight of the multinational corporate community and the U.S. government to the ever-present schemes against popular governments. And foreign creditors and multilateral financial institutions weighed in heavily in the 1980s and 1990s with pressure for privatization and debt-for-equity swaps. Nevertheless, the extension of national control over the economy is central to the agenda of popular movements in Latin America. Political leaders have been forced at the turn of the twenty-first century, by the globalized control of credit conditionality, to backtrack on the issue. But the issue will surely be revisited, perhaps as regional (for example, MERCOSUR) rather than national challenges to global economic interests. In the United States, the ideas of public control over national or local resources and, in general, of placing public interest over private profit are still in the category of heresy.

For Latin America, the 1980s was a decade of turmoil. Civilian rule was restored in Argentina only after the military regime instigated and suffered humiliating defeat in a war with Great Britain over the Falklands/Malvinas

Islands. Military regimes held on in Chile and Paraguay until the end of the decade. In Central America, following upon the success of the Nicaraguan Revolution in 1979, insurgency and counterinsurgency raged throughout the 1980s in El Salvador and Guatemala; and efforts of the Reagan administration to reestablish U.S. hegemony in the region swept Honduras, Costa Rica, and even Panama into the turmoil. Such conflict exacerbated debt exposure and other economic disasters, resulting in what came to be known throughout Latin America as the "Lost Decade." After having grown since mid-century at rates averaging 4 to 6 percent annually, Latin American economies in the 1980s experienced a negative per capita growth rate of –8 percent, along with inflation levels ranging to more than 10,000 percent and high levels of unemployment and underemployment.[1] It was estimated in 1990 that three-quarters of the population was suffering from some degree or manifestation of malnutrition.

Economic growth was resumed in the 1990s in several countries, especially Mexico, Chile, Argentina, and finally Brazil, spurred largely by massive privatization of public assets and services. But spurts of growth have been followed by more prolonged recession—in the case of Argentina in 2001–2002 all-out economic meltdown. Moreover, new wealth did not trickle down. Overall income levels in the early 2000s are below those of 1980. The gap between rich and poor countries in Latin America, already the world region of greatest inequality, continues to grow. Likewise in the United States since the 1970s, the gap has been growing—generally the outcome not of policy failures but of policy decisions. In the United States, between 1983 and 1998, while the household net worth of the richest 1 percent of the population increased by 42 percent, that of the poorest 40 percent dropped by 76 percent; and the trend has since continued.

Meanwhile, the debt trap that is bankrupting so many Latin Americans is thereby destroying markets for U.S. manufacturers and wiping out jobs for U.S. workers. In fact, it is sadly ironic that even as the United States struggles against the encroachment of China, the European Union, and the newly industrializing countries on traditional markets, it continues, through unqualified support for the global creditor cartel, to destroy economies in the one area where it had the greatest trade advantages and to leave those countries with few profitable exports save the two least welcome, officially, in the United States: drugs and people. In fact, the largest source of foreign exchange for Latin America in 2004 was remittances from emigrant workers.

Moreover, like Third World debts in general (some US$800 billion in aggregate in 2001), Latin American debts are increasingly owed to private banks. To many of the same banks, and increasingly to banks in China, the United States now owes much of its national debt of some $7 trillion. The U.S. debt tripled in the 1980s, and, though the annual deficit dropped in the 1990s, both the debt itself and its proportional claim on the budget have mushroomed since 2000. To an even greater extent than is true of most Latin

American countries, the rising U.S. debt may be attributed to unproductive military spending.

Indices of health, education, services, and infrastructure suggest that the quality-of-life gap between the United States and Latin America has been narrowing steadily in the period since World War II. Even discounting the limitations of statistics and of index-making, this indicates very promising long-term progress for Latin America. In the shorter term, however—since the 1970s, for example—it also suggests slowed progress or even retrogression on the part of the United States. According to the U.S. Department of Education, more than 40 million, some 23 percent of American adults surveyed in 1993, were found to be functionally illiterate, almost twice the number so designated a decade earlier. The American Association of State Colleges and Universities reported a $500-per-student decline between 1980 and 1995 in state appropriations for public universities and colleges, largely a result of the increased state costs for prisons and health care. At the beginning of the twenty-first century, Americans were spending more per capita on health care than any other people in the world; yet some 44 million lacked any kind of medical insurance, and very few of the insured had full coverage. Immunization programs for children had been among the casualties of budget cuts in the 1980s, and cases of measles had multiplied tenfold in ten years. After a decade in which the number of pregnant women receiving no prenatal care climbed by 50 percent, the United States ranked twenty-second in the world in infant mortality prevention, placing it squarely in a Third World category. Life expectancy for non-Hispanic whites continued to rise, but for minorities it had begun to drop.

More than 14 million Americans who needed housing assistance in 2004 were not getting it, up from 3.5 million in the mid-1970s, and almost 40 percent of the homeless were children. The proportion of American children found to be in low-income families rose in the 1980s, dropped in the 1990s, and has risen again since 2000. According to a survey conducted by Columbia University's National Center for Children in Poverty, more than one-third of America's children were in low-income households in 2004.

Among the policy decisions reflected in these trends were changes in tax laws since the late 1970s that, according to the Congressional Budget Office, had left 90 percent of Americans paying more while the richest 10 percent paid up to a third less. Meanwhile, the richest 5 percent of the population enjoyed a real increase in their income of 64 percent between 1979 and 1998. In 2000, the wealthiest 10 percent of households owned more than 70 percent of all investment assets. The single richest individual had more wealth than 120 million people—40 percent of the population—combined.

While the gap between Latin America and the United States has been narrowing, the gap between the United States and the more prosperous and egalitarian states of Western Europe has been widening. As Latin America, in aggregate, becomes more nearly a part of the "developed" world, the United States becomes more nearly a part of America. Whether or not Latin America is perceived to have been developing in the late twentieth century depends upon which countries, which years, and which indices one chooses to emphasize. What is more readily apparent, however, is that the United States has been underdeveloping.

Even if Latin America and Anglo-America increasingly share the blessings and the curses of modernization—along with such problems as competition from stronger economies, excessive dependence on the export of primary products, concentration of landownership, the undermining of local businesses by multinational corporations, staggering debts, chronic unemployment, and a growing gap between rich and poor—is it not obvious that the two Americas are centuries apart in matters of government and politics? Perhaps. But there, too, similarities and convergences can be found.

From Anti-Communism to Anti-Terrorism

In the 1960s and 1970s, much of Latin America experienced the rise of a new and very modern kind of military dictatorship—institutional, technocratic, self-confident, and ruthless. In demobilizing civilian political organizations and imposing their new order, these military establishments were assisted by paramilitary, intelligence, and police networks with expertise in surveillance, torture, and assassination. This development is not unrelated to the economic problems mentioned above. Those who are left on the margins by modernization, who are needed neither as workers nor as consumers, and who are written off by the economic planners cannot simply be ignored. They are the ill-fed, ill-clothed, ill-housed masses who are presumed to constitute a threat to the established order. The greater their numbers and the greater their sophistication and potential for political organization, the more elaborate will be the apparatus of repression required to contain them. But there are limits to the efficacy of rule by brute force, and the wielders of economic power—domestic and foreign—have rediscovered the fact that a civilian government that is uninterested in acting upon or unable to act upon a popular mandate, and unwilling or unable to control military and paramilitary forces, is often a better hedge against social change than a repressive military government.

The 1980s witnessed the withdrawal of the generals from Latin America's presidential palaces and a process of "re-democratization." But the withdrawal has been only partial—not to a safe enough distance to allow democracy a free rein—and the new democracies, to a large extent, represent the victory of form over substance. Re-democratization has been accompanied by increasing indebtedness and surrender of economic sovereignty, the discrediting of reformist leaders and programs, and a return to economic elitism buffered by parties and parliaments and the ritual of elections. Civilian leaders have sometimes appeared to be virtual prisoners in their own presidential palaces, and violence, particularly against the poor, continues unabated.

Politics in Latin America has often been associated, in the minds of Anglo-Americans, with violence and petty corruption. But political assassination has been no stranger to the United States, and in the aftermath of Watergate, the Iran-Contra affair, and so many other scandals in the heart of the U.S. government—most recently, revelations of U.S. torture of prisoners in Iraq, Afghanistan, and elsewhere—Anglo-Americans should at least be learning humility. Meanwhile, Latin American politicians—democrats and demagogues alike—are drawing upon U.S. expertise in a more sophisticated, institutionalized form of corruption. Consultants, pollsters, and fund-raisers, credited with political miracles in the United States, are being hired by Latin American candidates to pass on the art of taking money from the rich and votes from the poor on the pretext of protecting each from the other. Media campaigns and media advisers for the most part replace political organizations and machines, and campaign contributions, legal and more substantial, replace under-the-table bribes. Even where elections in Latin America retain representational meaning, we are likely to see the increasing capitalization and frivolization of the process. In few Latin American countries, however, has voter turnout dropped as low as in the United States.

It should not go unnoticed in the United States that it was the most highly developed politically of the Latin American states that suffered the cruelest fate during the era of militocracy. Many of the same anti-egalitarian economic policies that were imposed on Brazil in the 1960s and the Southern Cone countries in the 1970s by counter-revolutionary military regimes have since been adopted in the United States without an open rupture in democratic processes. Perhaps the majority in the United States has been saved—by the myth of a classless society, the alienation of almost half of the eligible electorate, and the lack of effective political organization—from a fate worse than economic deprivation.

But not all U.S. citizens are spared the kind of official violence that is commonly employed in Latin America and elsewhere to contain a growing sector of marginalized, would-be workers. Such containment in the politically decentralized United States is carried out by increasingly autonomous local police forces. Police brutality, particularly against minority groups, is common from coast to coast. Amnesty International has called attention to such brutality on the part of the New York City police, and Human Rights Watch has cited the abuse of female prisoners in several state institutions. The U.S. federal prison population doubled in the 1980s and again in the 1990s. At more than two million in 2004, it was the largest prison population in the world, accounting for one-fourth of all the world's prisoners. Almost one in three African-American men in their twenties was in jail or on parole or probation.

Except for such brief skirmishes as those in response to the inner-city riots following the assassination of Dr. Martin Luther King and to Vietnam War protests, the United States has been spared the spectacle of troops on the streets. But it has not been spared the general trend toward militarism. The enhanced power of the U.S. military establishment during the Cold War was expressed primarily in the increasing militarization of the U.S. foreign policymaking apparatus and in the military's ever-increasing peacetime share of the national budget.

The role expansion of military establishments in the two Americas proceeded in tandem. The incorporation of Central America and the Caribbean into the U.S. sphere of influence in the early twentieth century, through military intervention and, in some cases, direct military occupation, left a more modern form of militarism firmly entrenched. In the 1950s and 1960s, the U.S. military, on the premise of the need for a global strategy in the face of a permanent global war, undertook the organizational and technological modernization of the South American military establishments as well. An aspect of the Cold War worldview, inculcated or reinforced through U.S. training, was the idea that the political arena is the battleground of the Cold War, and, as such, too important to be left to the politicians. It is not surprising, then, that the U.S. intelligence technicians and techniques employed to ferret out "subversives" in Latin America came to be unleashed on U.S. citizens as well. The people of the United States have reaped at home what they allowed the U.S. government to sow abroad. As the late U.S. senator Hubert H. Humphrey commented in 1973:

> With Watergate we have seen officials of our government commit criminal acts that strongly resemble the practices and methods directed against foreign governments and other peoples. Counterespionage, coverups, infiltration, wiretapping, political surveillance, all done in the name of national security in faraway places, have come home to haunt us. The spirit and the purpose of domestic policy is said to condition our foreign policy. The reverse is also true.[2]

Like Watergate, the more effectively suppressed Iran-Contra scandal of the 1980s proved once again that a democracy cannot maintain an empire without detriment to the essentials of its democratic character.

The end of the 1980s also marked the end of the Cold War. Soviet leader Mikhail Gorbachev had simply opted out. But as the Christmas season 1989 U.S. invasion of Panama demonstrated with great clarity, the end of the Cold War did not mean the end of U.S. intervention. The Cold War was never the reason for such intervention; it was only the rationale, and new rationales, including the war on drugs and the war on terrorism were already on the drawing board. After the September 11, 2001, attacks by Muslim terrorists on New York City and Washington, D.C., most Latin American leaders considered troublesome by the Bush administration were relabeled terrorists, and anti-terrorism became the all-purpose rationale for intervention.

WHAT KIND OF AMERICAN CENTURY?

Some seventy years ago, in times not so different from the early 2000s, when in the United States the lines outside soup kitchens were lengthening and the ranks of the homeless swelling, and when the United States was in disrepute beyond its own borders for such practices as gunboat diplomacy, a newly elected Democratic president, Franklin Delano Roosevelt, pledged nonintervention and ushered in a period of Good Neighborliness toward Latin America. Under cover of the Cold War, and more recently of the wars on drugs and on terrorism, subsequent U.S. presidents have failed to honor that pledge. But the gunboat diplomacy of the late twentieth and early twenty-first centuries has proved as subversive to the spirit of American democracy as did that of the last century's youth, and a renewed pledge of nonintervention is overdue.

Such a pledge must be understood to cover not only interventions undertaken for straightforwardly strategic or political motives previously covered by the now defunct Cold War. It must subsume also any and all substitute rationales for the ongoing pursuit of indefensible objectives. Given the recent history of military abuse of civil liberties and human rights in Latin America and given our professed intent to support fledgling democracies, there can be no excuse for continuing to extend aid in any form to Latin American military or paramilitary forces or for promoting arms sales—and thus arms races.

Little wonder that Latin America's democratic leaders, threatened at the least with trade disruption and credit freezes and all too often with military conspiracy or even U.S. military intervention if they moved to reward their own constituencies with a measure of economic democracy, have been skeptical of official U.S. protestations of common economic interests. The fact is, however, that the ordinary people of the United States and of Latin America, as opposed to the high-rollers who place their bets in a global game, occupy the same hemisphere. Now more than ever, as economic communities are roped off in Europe and Asia, Americans of North and South are destined to share either prosperity or destitution.

The economic time of troubles felt throughout the hemisphere in the 1980s has generally abated, at least in terms of the figures and purposes that matter most to economists, investors, and creditors. But policy continues to favor capital over labor, global enterprise over national and local business, financial sleight of hand over production and consumption for internal mass markets, and exploitation and depletion over conservation and regeneration. The same policies that have stripped Latin America of internally generated capital, obliterated social services, suppressed local markets, and kept labor cheap have served to draw U.S. capital—and jobs—abroad.

Having contributed, through unqualified support for a set of policies now known as "structural adjustment," to the impoverishment of the only area where the United States had a traditional trade advantage, the U.S. government proceeded to place already shortchanged U.S. workers in the position of competing for jobs with even more desperate Latin American workers. It cannot be said that this system has failed—every system works for somebody—but it has failed the people of the Americas, all of the Americas, and for the sake of us all it must be reversed.

The bureaucracies and mindsets generated by the Cold War and by an exploitative boom-and-bust approach to development are inappropriate for the challenges of the twenty-first century. If any government were to seek seriously to promote economic democracy in the United States, it would find that goal to be furthered by promoting economic democracy in Latin America as well. For better or worse, given NAFTA and other integrative initiatives, the economies of Anglo- and Ibero-America will be increasingly intertwined and the well-being of their peoples interdependent.

Though wiser policy might have delayed it, the passing of Pax Americana is not a matter of choice. And the "American Century" presaged by the inner circle of the incoming administration of George W. Bush, and clearly intended to be the American century all over the world, is a dangerous illusion. In the commercially driven New World order, the world's mightiest military machine is a devalued currency—just so much Confederate money. For half a century, the Cold War provided cover for the pursuit of private and bureaucratic interests in Latin America and for the use of Latin America in posturing and saber-rattling for domestic political advantage. The stripping away of that cover—and of subsequent substitute covers—should make it possible and even necessary, at last, to base policy on the legitimate interests of Americans and on a profound understanding of the common interests of the peoples of the Western Hemisphere.

NOTES

1. *The IDB* (Washington, D.C.), Vol. 16, No. 9–10, September–October 1989, pp. 6–9.
2. Hubert H. Humphrey, "The Threat to the Presidency," *Washington Post,* May 6, 1973.

Acknowledgments

In preparation of this fourth edition, I have benefited from the financial assistance of the Mark Fund and from the research and editorial assistance of my graduate assistants Michael Danielson, Janell Jenkins, and Catherine Grant. I am grateful for their assistance and, as always, for the all-purpose assistance of my husband, Martin C. Needler.

About the Book and Editor

This textbook, extensively revised and updated in this new fourth edition, introduces the student to what is most basic and most interesting about Latin America. The authors—each widely recognized in his or her own discipline, as well as among Latin Americanists—analyze both the enduring features of the area and the pace and direction of change. The book conveys the unifying aspects of Latin American culture and society, together with the distinct characteristics of major sub-regions and countries.

Highlights of the fourth edition include the traumatic impact of drugs and debt and the interventions they elicit throughout the hemisphere. Contributors also examine turn of the century trends, including emphasis on the export sector, pressure to privatize, general retrenchment with regard to social welfare programs, spurts of economic growth, steady growth in income gaps, and new threats to distinctive ecological zones. The burgeoning of new populist political parties and social movements in response to economic crises and extreme deprivation is also addressed here.

Jan Knippers Black is a professor in the Graduate School of International Policy Studies at the Monterey Institute of International Studies in California and a senior associate member at Saint Antony's College, Oxford. Previously, she has served as research professor of public administration at the University of New Mexico and as senior research scientist and chair of the Latin American Research Team in the Foreign Area Studies Division of American University.

About the Contributors

Diego Abente Brun is senior advisor to Paraguay's Ministry of Finance and president of his political party, Encuentro Nacional. Previously, he has served as Minister of Justice and Labor, as Ambassador to the Organization of American States and as Vice-President of the Senate of the Republic of Paraguay. He was elected to the Senate after about a decade as assistant and associate professor of political science at Miami University, Ohio. He is the author of several articles on the politics of Paraguay, Uruguay, and Venezuela that have appeared in scholarly journals, including *Comparative Politics, Latin American Research Review, Journal of Latin American Studies, Journal of Interamerican Studies*, and *The Americas*. He is currently working on a book on the politics of Paraguay.

Pablo Andrade A. is a professor at the Universidad Andina Simon Bolivar in Quito, where he is also the academic coordinator of the Masters Program in Latin American Studies. He is completing his Ph.D. dissertation on democratization processes in Ecuador in the Graduate Program in Social and Political Thought at York University in Canada. His research and publications have dealt with Latin American political thought, constitutional reform in Ecuador, Ecuador's foreign policy, and Ecuador's relations with the United States and with other countries of the Andean Region.

Peter Bakewell holds the Edmund and Louise Kahn Chair in History at Southern Methodist University in Dallas. He has previously taught at Cambridge University and at the University of New Mexico (where he also served as associate editor of the Hispanic American Historical Review), and Emory University in Atlanta. Among his many publications are definitive studies of colonial-era silver mining in Mexico and Bolivia. His recent books include *A History of Latin America: Empires and Sequels, 1450–1930* (1997, second edition 2003).

Jan Knippers Black is professor of international policy studies at the Monterey Institute of International Studies. She has also had teaching, research, or administrative appointments at several other institutions, including the University of New Mexico, American University in Washington, D.C., St. Antony's College, Oxford, and the University of Pittsburgh's Semester-at-Sea. A former Peace Corps volunteer in Chile, she holds a Ph.D. in international studies from American University in Washington, D.C. Dr. Black has served on more than two dozen editorial, advisory, or governing boards, mostly of NGOs, and she has visited more than 170 countries, lecturing or conducting research in most of them. She has authored or edited and co-authored a dozen books, co-authored another dozen, and published more than 150 chapters and articles in reference books, and anthologies, journals, magazines, and newspapers. Recent publications include *Development in Theory and Practice: Paradigms and Paradoxes* (2nd ed., 1999); and *Inequity in the Global Village: Recycled Rhetoric and Disposable People* (1999). She is now working on a book on human rights.

Peter Calvert is professor emeritus of comparative and international politics at the University of Southampton, England. He was educated at Campbell College, Belfast; Queens' College, Cambridge; and the University of Michigan, Ann Arbor. He took his doctorate at Cambridge. In 1964 he was appointed lecturer in politics at Southampton and in 1984 was appointed to a personal chair there. He retired in 2002 but continues to work on the politics and international relations of the Western Hemisphere, and to co-edit the journal *Democratization.* Among his recent publications are Politics and Society in the Third World , with Susan Calvert (2nd ed., 2001), *Comparative Politics: An Introduction* (2002), and *A Political and Economic Dictionary of Latin America* (2004).

Michael L. Conniff is director of the Global Studies Program at San Jose State University in California. Previously, he directed the Center for Latin American and Caribbean Studies and taught history at the University of South Florida in Tampa. He has published books on Brazil—*Urban Politics in Brazil* (1982), and Panama—*Black Labor on a White Canal* (1985) and *Panama and the United States* (1992). He has also worked extensively on populism, and, in 1999, published *Populism in Latin America.* He has edited several books, including *Latin American Populism in Comparative Perspective* (1982), *Modern Brazil* (1991, with Frank McCann), and *Africans in the Americas* (1994, with T. J. Davis), and *A History of Modern Latin America* (1998, with Larry Clayton) and *Populism in Latin America.* He has also served as executive secretary of the Conference on Latin American History.

Steve Ellner earned his Ph.D. at the University of New Mexico in Latin American history and has taught at the Universidad del Oriente in Puerto La Cruz, Venezuela since 1977. He is the author of *Organized Labor in Venezuela, 1958–1991: Behavior and Concerns in a Democratic Setting* (1993) and *Venezuela's Movimiento al Socialismo: From Guerrilla Defeat to Innovative Politics* (1988). He is co-editor of *Venezuelan Politics in the Chavez Era: Class Polarization and Conflict* (2003) and *The Latin American Left: From the Fall of Allende to Perestroika* (1993). He is a frequent contributor to several U.S. magazines, including *Commonweal* and *In These Times.*

David Fleischer received his Ph.D. in Political Science from the University of Florida and has taught at the University of Brasilia since 1972. He was visiting professor at George Washington University, the Federal University of Minas Gerais (UFMG), the State University of New York at Albany, and the University of Florida. He was a Peace Corps Volunteer in Brazil (1962–1964). He is the author of ten books, including: *Corruption in Brazil* (2002) and *Las Consecuencias Políticas del Sistema Electoral Brasileño* (1995), and co-author of *Brazil in Transition* (1983) and *Da Distensão à Abertura* (1988). He has contributed chapters to 48 books, including: *Reforming Brazil* (2004), *Corruption and Political Reform in Brazil* (1999), and *Brazil:*

A Country Study (1998). He has conducted research on legislatures, election and party systems, and corruption in South and Central America and Africa.

José Z. García is professor of political science and former director of the Latin American Institute at New Mexico State University in Las Cruces. He has lived in Ecuador and Peru and has done extensive research on military factionalism in Peru. More recently, he has done extensive research on the military in Central America, including preparation of a book on the Salvadoran military. Professor Garcia is experienced in practical politics as well; he served for several years as chair of the Democratic Party of New Mexico's Dona Ana County. He is currently serving on the governor's New Mexico-Mexico Border Commission.

William P. Glade is professor of economics at the University of Texas at Austin and director of the Mexican Center at the university's Institute of Latin American Studies. He has also served as senior scholar and acting secretary of the Latin American Program in the Woodrow Wilson International Center for Scholars, Smithsonian Institution, Washington, D.C. From 1989 to 1992, he was associate director in charge of educational and cultural affairs at the United States Information Agency. Recent publications include articles on systemic transformation in Latin America and the former centrally planned economies and two edited volumes—*The Privatization of Public Enterprises in Latin America* (1991) and *Bigger Economies, Smaller Governments: Privatization in Latin America* (1996)—and, with Charles Reilly, *Inquiry at the Grassroots: An Inter-American Foundation Fellowship Reader* (1993).

Alfonso Gonzalez is professor emeritus of geography at the University of Calgary in Alberta. Since receiving his Ph.D. from the University of Texas, Austin, he has been on the faculty at San Diego State College, Northeast Louisiana State College, Southern Illinois University, and the University of South Florida, where he served as chair of the Department of Geography. Professor Gonzalez specializes in Third World and Latin American geography, with particular attention to population, settlement, and socioeconomic development. He has performed field and archival research in several areas of Hispanic America and Spain and has presented and published numerous papers and book chapters. He has co-edited (with Jim Norwine) two editions of a book: *The Third World* (1988) and *The New Third World* (1998).

Fred R. Harris, a former member of the U.S. Senate (D-Oklahoma, 1964–1972), is a professor of political science at the University of New Mexico and a member of the Board of Directors of the North American Institute. He has been a Fulbright Scholar in Mexico, a visiting professor at the Universidad Nacional Autonoma de Mexico, a Distinguished Fulbright Lecturer in Uruguay, and he has taught and lectured extensively in Mexico and Latin America. He has produced sixteen non-fiction books (nine as author, seven as co-author or editor), including, with Lynn A. Curtis, *Locked in the Poorhouse: Cities, Race and Poverty in the United States (1998)* and, with David Cooper, Estudios sobre Estados Unidos y su Relacion Bilateral con Mexico (1986, with David Cooper). He is also an award winning author of three novels.

Jane S. Jaquette is Bertha Harton Orr Professor of political science at Occidental University in Los Angeles, California. She received her B.A. from Swarthmore College and her Ph.D. from Cornell University. A specialist in women's political roles in Latin America, she is a past president of both the Latin American Studies Association and the Association of Women in Development. Among the many works she has authored, edited, or co-edited are: ed., *The Women's Movement in Latin America: Feminism and the Transition to Democracy* (1989); ed., with Sharon Wolchik, *Women and Democratization in Latin America and Eastern and Central Europe: an Introduction* (1998); and ed., *Women's Movements in Latin America: Participation and Democracy* (1994). She is now researching the roles of women in democratization worldwide.

Shane Lewis is completing a master's degree in applied geography at Texas State University. He received an astronomy degree from the University of Texas in 1991 and stayed on to develop a human subject research management system for the UT Vice-President for Research. Since 1999, he has served as software developer for an international network of nongovernmental organizations seeking to document the ecological and human impacts of mining in the developing world. Current research projects focus on the complex ecological and economic trade-offs implicit in all attempts at sustainable development. These efforts have been supported by a fellowship from the prestigious Mexico-Norte research network.

Anthony P. Maingot is professor emeritus of sociology at Florida International University in Miami. He has previously taught at Yale University and at the University of the West Indies in Trinidad and served as acting dean of International Affairs at Florida International. Born in Trinidad, Professor Maingot studied at the University of Puerto Rico and the University of California, Los Angeles, before receiving his Ph.D. from the University of Florida. He was a member of the Constitutional Reform Commission of Trinidad and Tobago from 1971 to 1974 and president of the Caribbean Studies Association from 1982 to 1983.

Cynthia McClintok is professor of Political Science and international affairs and former director of the Latin American studies program at George Washington University in Washington, D.C. She is also a former president of the Latin American Studies Association. Her B.A. is from Harvard and her Ph.D. from the Massachusetts Institute of Technology. Professor McClintok is the author of many books, chapters and articles, particularly on Peruvian domestic and international politics including: *Peasant Cooperatives and Political Change in Peru* (1981); *Revolutionary Movements in Latin America: El Salvador's FMLN and Peru's Shining Path* (1998); and, with Fabian Vallas, *The United States and Peru: Cooperation–at a Cost* (2003). She also co-edited, with Abraham Lowenthal, *The Peruvian Experiment Reconsidered,* (1983). She has also served on the Council of the American Political Science Association and currently chairs its Comparative Democratization section.

Martin C. Needler is a former dean of the School of International Studies at the University of the Pacific and trustee of Saint Antony's College, Oxford. He has previously held teaching positions at Dartmouth College, the University of Michigan, and the University of New Mexico and postdoctoral fellowships or research positions at UCLA, Harvard, and the University of Southampton. He has published thirteen books, principally on Latin American politics and U.S. foreign policy, including *Political Development in Latin America* (1968), *Politics and Society in Mexico* (1971), *The Problem of Democracy in Latin America* (1987), and *Mexican Politics: The Containment of Conflict* (3rd ed., 1995). His *Identity, Interest, and Ideology: An Introduction to Politics* came out in 1996. Professor Needler holds a Ph.D. in political science from Harvard.

Jorge Nef is director of The Center for Latin American, Caribbean, and Latino Studies at the University of Southern Florida in Tampa. Previously he was professor of political studies and international development at the University of Guelph. He graduated from the University of Chile and has studied at Vanderbilt University, the Facultad Latinoamericana de Ciencias Sociales, and the University of California. A past president of the Canadian Association of Latin American and Caribbean Studies (CALACS) and editor of the Canadian Journal of Latin American and Caribbean Studies, he is a fellow of the Centre for Research on Latin America and the Caribbean (CERLAC) and the Centre for Refugee Studies (CRS), both at York University. *Human Security and Mutual Vulnerability* (1995) is among the numerous books, monographs and articles he has authored. He has been a consultant for national and international agencies in international development and a participant in the Expert Groups of the South Commission in Geneva (1989). In 1995 he traveled to Chile with 'Team Canada' during the prime minister's visit and was an expert witness for the Senate's Committee on Foreign Affairs.

Liisa L. North is professor of political science at York University and a fellow of York's Center for Research on Latin America and the Caribbean (CERLAC), where she has headed several international cooperation programs organized with the Latin American Faculty of Social Sciences (FLASCO) and various Andean NGOs. She has published monographs, book chapters, and articles on party politics, civil-military relations, and development processes in Chile, Peru, and Ecuador; on the civil wars, United Nations peacekeeping missions, and human rights and refugee crises in El Salvador and Guatemala; on Canadian-Latin American relations, with particular reference to Central America and the Organization of American States (OAS); and on rural development issues. She is co-editor, with John D. Cameron, of *Rural Progress, Rural Decay* (2003). Her articles have appeared in *Studies in Political Economy, Latin American Perspectives, Third World Quarterly, Ecuador Debate,* and *World Development*. She has also collaborated in various capacities with NGOs, including the former Jesuit Center for Social Faith and Justice in Toronto, OXFAM-Canada, and the Fondo Ecuatoriano Populorum Progressio (FEPP) in Quito.)

James Petras is professor emeritus of sociology at the State University of New York at Binghamton. He is the author of 40 books, published by leading U.S. and British presses and translated into 28 languages. He also has over 400 scholarly articles in refereed journals. His publications span a broad range of topics on Latin American and global developments, among them, *U.S. Hegemony Under Seige: Class Politics, and Development in Latin America* (1990); *Democracy and Poverty in Chile* (1994); and *La Continuacion de la Historia* (1996) and, with Henry Veltmeyer, *Globalization Unmasked: Imperialism in the 21st Century,* (2001). He is currently working as a freelance writer and an adviser to the landless workers' movement in Brazil.

James Lee Ray is professor of political science at Vanderbilt. He previously served on the faculties of State University College at Fredonia (New York), the University of New Mexico, and Florida State University. Professor Ray is author of *Global Politics* (8th ed., 2005), and has published articles in a number of journals, including the *British Journal of Political Science, International Interactions, International Organization, International Studies Quarterly,* and the *Journal of Theoretical Politics*. He has recently contributed chapters to *Progress in International Relations theory* (2003) and *The Scourge of War* (2004). He is currently working on a book with a working title of *American Foreign Policy and Political Ambition.*

Steve C. Ropp is professor of political science at the University of Wyoming. He is the author of *Panamanian Politics: From Guarded Nation to National Guard* (1982); co-editor (with James A. Morris) of *Central America: Crisis and Adaptation* (1984); and co-editor (with Thomas Risse and Kathryn Sikkink) of *The Power of Human rights: International Norms and Domestic change* (1999). Professor Ropp has taught courses on Latin American politics, U.S. foreign policy and international relations in Latin America, Asia, and Europe. At present, he is conducting research on various forces shaping and reshaping Panama, as well as on the political phenomenon of populism in the Americas and Europe.

Karl H. Schwerin is professor of anthropology at the University of New Mexico. Throughout his career he conducted fieldwork in several Latin American countries, with particular emphasis on economic and subsistence patterns, adaptive strategies, and processes of culture change. Professor Schwerin has served as president of the American Society for Ethnohistory and the University of New Mexico chapter of the scientific research society Sigma Xi. From 1987 to 1993, he chaired the Department of Anthropology at the University of New Mexico. He has published four books and numerous papers on a broad range of topics relating to Latin America and tropical societies worldwide. To mark the occasion of the 75th anniversary of the Department of Anthropology at the University of New Mexico, he has been writing a history of the department. A substantive and theoretical study of Carib warfare in Venezuela will appear shortly. Professor Schwerin also continues his long-term study on the ethnographic researches of the French explorer Alcide d'Orbigny.

Wendy Muse Sinek is a doctoral student at the University of California-Berkeley, specializing in Latin American politics. She holds an M.A. in International Policy Studies from the Monterey Institute of International Studies and has lived and worked extensively in Ecuador, Nicaragua, and the Dominican Republic. More recently, she has conducted fieldwork in Cuba and Brazil, with particular attention to the dynamics of social movements that emerge in response to economic crises.

Wayne S. Smith, an adjunct professor of Latin American Studies at the Johns Hopkins University in Baltimore and a senior fellow at the Center for International Policy in Washington, D.C., was a U.S. Foreign Service officer for over twenty-five years. When he left the service in 1982 because of profound disagreements with the Reagan Administration's policies, he was chief of mission at the U.S. Interests Section in Havana and was recognized as the Department of State's leading expert on Cuba. Smith holds three master's degrees, and his Ph.D. is from George Washington University in Washington, D.C. His published works include *The Closest of Enemies: A Personal and Diplomatic Account of U.S.-Cuban Relations Since 1957* (1987); *Portrait of Cuba (1991);* and *Toward Resolution: The Falklands/Malvinas Dispute* (1991), which he edited.

David Stea is professor of Geography and director of the Center for Texas-Mexico Applied Research at Texas State University-San Marcos. He is also president of the Association for Borderland Studies. Having a doctorate in psychology from Stanford

University, Dr. Stea has also been educated in aeronautical engineering and architecture. He lived for ten years in Mexico, spent extended periods in Puerto Rico and Brazil, and visited nine Central American and South American countries. Dr. Stea was nominated for the Right Livelihood Prize (the "alternative Nobel") in 1987 and received an honorary doctorate from the University of A Corunna, Galicia, Spain in 2003. He was invited to give the opening keynote at the 2004 meeting of the International Geographical Union in Glasgow, Scotland.

Nelson P. Valdes is professor of sociology at the University of New Mexico and Visiting Professor and Director of the Fundacion Amistad at Duke University. Born in Cuba, he came to the United States in 1961. Since 1977 he has traveled to Cuba on more than a dozen occasions. Professor Valdes holds a Ph.D. in history from the University of New Mexico and has published five books and numerous articles on Cuba. He founded and served as director from 1986 to 1996 of the Latin America Data Base, a computerized database that produced two electronic newsletters: the Central America Update and the Latin American Debt Chronicle. Professor Valdes has been a board member of the Center for Cuban Studies (New York) and the Instituto de Estudios Cubanos (Miami), and he has served as the Latin American analyst for the Pacific News Service. He is now a member of the Editorial board of the leading social science journal in Cuba, *Temas*. He is also project director of Cuba-L Project, a news and analysis distribution service of materials on Cuba, a spin-off of Latin America Database. In 1998 he established the Cuba Research and Analysis Group, a non-profit organization.

Arturo Valenzuela is Professor of Government and Director of the Center for Latin American Studies at Georgetown University. He served as Deputy Assistant Secretary of State for Inter-American Affairs in the first Clinton Administration. He is a member of the Council on Foreign Relations, Board Member of the National Democratic Institute for International Affairs, and former Board Member of America's Watch. He serves on the editorial boards of *The Journal of Democracy, The Third World Quarterly,* and *Current History.* The author or co-author of six books on Chilean politics, he is the co-editor and co-author with Juan Linz of *The Failure of Presidential Democracy* (1995). Professor Valenzuela previously taught at Duke University and has been a Visiting Scholar at Oxford University, the University of Sussex, the University of Florence, the University of Chile, and the Catholic University of Chile.

J. Samuel Valenzuela is professor and former chair of the Department of Sociology at the University of Notre Dame. He was formerly on the faculties at Yale and Harvard Universities and has been senior associate member at Saint Antony's College, Oxford University. He is the author of *Democratizacion via Reforma: La Expansion del Sufragio en Chile*, co-author of *Chile, A Country Study,* and co-editor of *Military Rule in Chile: Dictatorship and Oppositions* and of *Chile: Politics and Society*. He has also written numerous articles on the intersection between labor and politics and on democratization and electoral politics.

Henry Veltmeyer, is professor of sociology and international development studies at Saint Mary's University, Halifax, Nova Scotia, He also has a faculty appointment in the doctoral program in development studies at the Autonomous University of Zacatecas in Mexico. He has written and contributed to the publication of a wide range of articles and books on the dynamics of global development and Canadian political economy as well as the sociology of Latin American development. His publications include *Rethinking Development: Caribbean Perspectives, Canadian Corporate Power,* and, with James Petras, *Neoliberalism and Class Conflict in Latin America.* His most recent books are: with James Petras, *System in Crisis* (2003) and *Globalizacion en America Latina* (2004); and edited, *Globalization/Antiglobalization* (2004) and *Nongovernmental Organizations and Development* (forthcoming).

Christine J. Wade is an assistant professor of political science and international studies at Washington College in Chestertown, Maryland. She holds a Ph.D. in political science from Boston University. She is the author of *After the Peace: Postwar Politics in El Salvador* (forthcoming) and co-author, with Tommie Sue Montgomery, of *From Revolution to Reform: the Left in El Salvador* (forthcoming). Her current research focuses on revolutionary movements, the modern Left in Latin America, and U.S-Latin American relations.

Thomas W. Walker is professor emeritus of political science and director emeritus of Latin American studies at Ohio University. He holds a Ph.D. in political science from the University of New Mexico. He has been doing research in Central America for more than three decades and has served on international electoral observation teams in Nicaragua in 1984, 1990, and 1996. Walker is the author, editor/co-author, or co-editor of 10 books on the politics of Central America, including *Understanding Central America* (2nd ed., 1993), *Nicaragua: Living in the Shadow of the Eagle* (4th ed., 1991), and *Nicaragua Without Illusions: Regime Transition and Structural Adjustment in the 1990s* (1997).

Index

Abipón, 45
Abolengo, 393
Abreu, Leitão, 482
Acción Democrática, 183
Acción Democrática Nacionalista (ADN), 464
Acción Popular, 447, 449, 453
Accord of the Strengthening of Civilian Power and the Function of the Army (Guatemala), 323
Accord on Constitutional and Electoral Reforms (Guatemala), 323
Acuerdo Nacional, 572
AD. *See* Democratic Action
Adams, Grantly, 381
Adams, John Quincy, 252
Adams, Tom, 382
ADN. *See* Accion Democratica Nacionalista
Affirmative action, 355
  in Ecuador, 431
Afro-America, 44
  contemporary, 45–47
  indigenous population of, 46
Age structure, 24
Agrarian reforms, 141–143
Agricultural Modernization Act, 325
Agriculture, 303, 583
  in Caribbean, 384
  in Gulf-Caribbean Coastal Lowlands, 29–30
  in Honduras, 64
  in Indo-America, 51
  plantation-based, 44
Aguirre Cerda, Pedro, 511
AIDS, 189, 218
Air pollution, 66
Alarcón, Fabián, 430
Alkmin, José Maria, 474
Aleixo, Pedro, 477
Alemán, Arnoldo, 316
Alencar, José, 491
Alessandri, Arturo, 90, 510, 511
Alessandri, Jorge, 512, 518, 531
Alexander VI, 78
Alfonsín, Raúl, 93, 551
  presidency of, 547

Allende, Ignacio, 284
Allende, Salvador, 242, 259, 492, 501, 512, 514, 518.
  See also Chile
  administration of, 520
  Christian Democrats and, 524
  communists and, 521
  compromises of, 522–523
  inauguration of, 519
  United States and, 518–519
Alliance for Progress, 110, 258–259
Almond, Gabriel, 7
Alvarez, Gregorio, 561, 562
Alvarez, Gustavo, 324–325
Alvarez, Sonia, 16, 194, 198, 199
Alvear, Marcelo T. de, 543
Alywin, Patricio, 502
Amazon Basin
  deforestation of, 35–36, 63
Amazon River, 22–23, 35
Amazonia, 35–36
American Popular Revolutionary Alliance (APRA), 183, 445–447, 450
American Treaty of Reciprocal Assistance, 240
ANAPO. *See* National Popular Alliance
ANC. *See* National Constituent Assembly
ANCOM. *See* Andean Common Market
Andean Common Market (ANCOM), 241–242
Andean Community of Nations, 436
Andean Pact, 99, 109, 436
Anderson, Charles, 161
Andes, 22, 144
  population structure in, 51
Angeloz, Eduardo César, 549
Anti-Ballistic Missile Treaty, 274
Antilles
  population in, 30–31
APRA. *See* American Popular Revolutionary Alliance
April Package, 481
Araguaia National Park, 71
Aramburu, Pedro, 544
Arango, Doroteo. *See* Villa, Francisco "Pancho"
Araucanians, 45
Araya, Rolando, 329

Arbenz, Jacobo, 257
ARENA. *See* National Renovating Alliance
Argaña, Luis María, 575
Argentina, 16
  Catholic Church in, 544
  Constitution of 1994 of, 46
  constitutional reform in, 551–552
  counterrevolution in, 181
  crisis of 2001, 552–553
  currency of, 550
  debt of, 216
  dirty war and, 545–546
  economic crisis in, 135, 548–549
  Falklands and, 546–547
  foreign relations of, 553–554
  gender quotas in, 200–201
  geography of, 541
  Germany and, 239
  Great Britain and, 554
  history of, 541–543
  northwest, 38
  Peronists in, 544–545
  political parties of, 543–544
  post-Cold War, 244
  redemocratization of, 547–548
  Spain and, 541–542
  unemployment in, 144–145, 551
  United States and, 553–554
  women's rights in, 194
  World Bank support of, 548–549
Arias, Arnulfo, 336, 337, 341, 344
Arias, Oscar, 261, 327, 328
Aristide, Jean-Bertrand, 183, 184, 268
Aristocracy, 179
  political participation and, 180
Aristocratic Republic, 444–445
Army of National Liberation (ELN), 397, 403–404
Arnulfista Party (PA), 342
Arosemena Monroy, Carlos Julio, 438n4
Arts, 581
Arzú, Alvaro, 323
Asbún, Juan Pereda, 462
Association of Caribbean States, 387
Asunción, 556
Atlacatl Battalion, 319
AUC. *See* United Self-Defense Forces of Colombia
Audiencias, 80
Augustinians, 85
Austerity, 183, 184
Austral Plan, 548
Authentic Radical Liberal Party, 575
Authoritarian capitalism, 211–216
Authoritarianism
  bureaucratic, 11
  capitalism and, 211–216
Autogolpe, 450
  government following, 451–453
Aylwin, Patricio, 533
  government of, 534–535
Aztecs
  civilization of, 281

Bacha, Edmar, 471
Baja California, 31

Balboa, Vasco Nuñez de, 334
Baldez, Lisa, 205n45
Balladares, Pérez, 342
Balmaceda, José Manuel, 508
Banzer, Hugo, 462, 464, 465, 466
Barnes, Harry, 532
Barrientos, Rene, 462
Barrig, Maruja, 195
Barrios, Justo Rufino, 90
Barrow, Errol, 381
Bastide, Roger, 471
Batista, Fulgencio, 91, 313, 351
Bàtlle y Ordóñez, Jose, 90, 558
Battle of Avacucho, 232
Battle of Lircay, 502
Bay of Pigs, 252
  Castro, Fidel, and, 258
  CIA and, 352
Bechtel Corporation, 144, 466
Beef production
  deforestation and, 63–64
Behaviorist theory, 8–9
Belaúnde Terry, Fernando, 93, 447, 449
Benavides, Oscar, 446
Berger, Oscar, 324
Berlin Wall, 486
Betancourt, Rómulo, 92, 413
Betancur, Belisario, 401
Bethlem, Fernando, 480
Bignone, Reynaldo, 546
Bishop, Maurice, 261
Böhm, Bawerk, 103
Black, Jan Knippers, 441
Black Jacobins (James), 382–383
Black Power, 377. *See also* Slavery
  in Trinidad, 378
Blaine, James G., 253
Blanco, Jorge, 381
Blanco Party, 562
Bolaños, Enrique, 317
Bolívar, Simón, 89, 192, 232, 233, 443, 458
Bolivia, 16, 54, 181
  in Chaco War, 238, 460
  Chile and, 502–503
  coca production in, 464–466
  economy of, 459
  historical background of, 458–459
  language in, 467–468
  MNR in, 170
  neoliberalism in, 466–468
  Peru and, 458
  political stability of, 179
  post-Cold War, 244
  protests in, 136–137
  revolution in, 169, 170
  since 1982, 463–464
  United States and, 465–466
  at war, 234–235
  water privatization in, 466–468
Bolivian labor confederation (COB), 466
Bolivian Revolution, 169, 460–463
  class demolition following, 171
  institutionalization after, 172–173

power transfer in, 170
Bonder, Gloria, 195
Booth, John, 312
Bordaberry, Juan M., 561
Bordón, José Octavio, 551
Bosch, Juan, 211
Bourbons, 105
Boutros-Ghali, Boutros, 274
Box, Pelham H., 246
Boyer, Jean Pierre, 387
Brana-Shute, Gary, 385
Brana-Shute, Rosemary, 385
Branco, Castelo, 473, 474, 475, 478, 481
Brazil, 16, 46, 62–63, 81
    Cardoso, F.H., as president of, 488–491
    Collor disaster in, 486–487
    colonies in, 81–82
    counterrevolution in, 211
    debt of, 216
    deforestation of, 35–36, 63
    direct elections in, 485
    economic miracle in, 475–477
    exports of, 112
    feminism in, 198–200
    Franco interim in, 487–488
    highlands of, 36
    human rights in, 49
    indigenous population of, 44
    industrial expansion of, 8, 10
    Lula as president of, 491–494
    military coup in, 471–475
    petroleum in, 478
    political opening in, 477–483
    political stability of, 178–179
    political transition in, 483–485
    post–Cold War, 244
    protests in, 476
    in second restructuring, 105–106
    social duality in, 470–471
    in third restructuring, 106–107
    United States and, 480
    urban reform in, 143–144
    in World War II, 239
Brazilian Bar Association (OAB), 481
Brazilian Democratic Movement (MDB), 475, 478, 479
Brazilian Highlands
    climate of, 36
Brazilian Labor Party (PTB), 472, 473
Brazilian Social Democratic Party (PSDB), 486, 489
Brazilian Socialist Party (PSB), 491
British Labour Party, 382
Brizola, Leonel, 473, 480, 481, 486, 490
Brothers to the Rescue, 371
Brown, Lester, 64
Bucaram, Abdalá, 423, 428, 430
Budgetgate crisis, 488
Buenos Aires, 233
    provinces v., 541–543
Bulnes, Manuel
    presidency of, 503–504
Bureaucratic authoritarianism, 11
Burnham, Forbes, 382, 383
Busch, Colonel, 227n3
Bush, George H.W., 259, 262, 266, 333

on Cuba, 371
Bush, George W., 18, 186, 251, 263, 266, 268, 271, 272, 420, 592
    administrative attitudes of, 264
    on Cuba, 372
Bustamante, Alexander, 381, 446
Butler, Uriah, 382

Caballero Vargas, Guillermo, 575
Cabildos, 410
Cabrera, Manuel Estrada, 91
Cáceres, Andrés, 444
CACM. *See* Central American Common Market
Caldera, Rafael, 413, 415, 416
Calderón Fournier, Rafael, 327, 328
Calderón Sol, Armando, 320
Callejas, Leonardo, 325
Calles, Plutarco Elías, 94, 295, 296
Calvo, Carlos, 236
Calvo Doctrine, 236–237
Camata, Rita, 491
Cámpora, Héctor, 545
Canada
    Jamaica and, 377–378
Canal Zone, 333, 336, 337–338, 343
Capitalism, 107
    authoritarian, 211–216
    class and, 124–125
Capitalist class, 124–125
Caracazo, 409, 415
Carazo, Rodrigo, 327
Carbon dioxide, 66
Cárdenas, Lázaro, 94, 172, 296, 304
    land reform measures of, 296–297
Cárdenas, Víctor Hugo, 54, 464
Cardoso, Fernando Henrique, 9, 470, 476, 487, 492
    election of, 488–491
Carías Andino, General Turbicio, 227n3
Caribbean Basin
    agriculture in, 384
    basic statistics of, 376t
    in Cold War, 388
    communication in, 386
    crime in, 388–389
    diversity in, 387
    education in, 385
    future of, 389
    GDP of, 375
    geographically defining, 375
    globalization and, 388
    indigenous population of, 42
    literacy in, 385, 386
    modern-conservative societies in, 377–38
    modernity in, 386
    political economy of, 383–389
    political-ideological leadership in, 380–383
    religion in, 384
Caribbean Common Market (CARICOM), 99, 109, 381, 387
Caribbean Development Bank, 387
Caribbean Free Trade Area, 109, 113
CARICOM. *See* Caribbean Common Market
Carmona, Pedro, 417, 420
Carnegie Endowment for International Peace, 270

Carranza, Venustiano, 293, 294, 295
Carrera Damas, Germán, 411
Carter, Jimmy, 259–260
  Brazil and, 480
  Cuba and, 370
  on human rights, 321–322
Carter, Rosalyn, 480
Casa Alianza, 326
Casalta II, 62
Castañeda, Jorge, 16
Castello Branco, Humberto, 93
Castillo, Armas, 257
Castro, Cipriano, 411
Castro, Fidel, 92, 210, 244, 259, 273, 275, 357, 382
  Bay of Pigs and, 258
  in Cuban Revolution, 351
  economic reforms of, 366–367
  political positions of, 360
  on racial discrimination, 355–356
  reforms of, 355
  on socialism, 361
Castro, Raúl, 357
  political positions of, 360
Catholic Church, 5, 53, 161, 296
  in Argentina, 544
  in Chile, 507
  Chilean government and, 538
  Evangelism of, 84–86
  in Nicaraguan Revolution, 172
  in Paraguay, 572
Cauca Valley, 396
Caudillos, 90, 284–285, 296, 410, 542, 558
Cavallo, Domingo, 550, 551–552, 552
CC. *See* Central Committee
CEDAW. *See* Convention on the Elimination of
  Discrimination Against Women
Center-periphery model, 11
Central America
  redemocratization of, 181–182
Central American Common Market (CACM), 98–99,
  109, 113, 240
  problems for, 241–242
Central American Free Trade Area (CAFTA), 339
Central Committee of Communist Party (CC), 354, 355
Central de Obreros de Bolivia, 135
Central Intelligence Agency. See CIA
Central Labor Federation (CUT), 513
Cerezo, Vinicio, 322
Cerro de Pasco Corporation, 445
Césaire, Aimé, 382, 383
Ceuppens, Henry D., 569
CFCs. *See* Chlorofluorocarbons
Chaco War, 169, 238
  Bolivia during, 460
Chambers, George, 381
Chamorro, Violeta Barrios de, 316
Chant, Sylvia, 196
Chapare, 465
Chapman, Guillermo, 342
Chapultepec Park, 287
Charles, Mary Eugenia, 381
Charrúa, 45
Chaves, Aureliano, 481, 484, 486
Chávez, César, 148

Chávez, Federico, 568
Chávez, Hugo, 185, 415, 417, 420
  election of, 409–410
  oil policy of, 418–419
Cheek, James, 330n18
Cheyre, Emilio, 535, 536
Chiapas, 16, 54, 67, 136, 303
Chicago Boys, 528
Chile, 132, 181, 233–234. *See also* Allende, Salvador
  building democracy in, 533–538
  Catholic Church in, 507
  civil war in, 508
  Communist Party in, 510, 521, 537
  Conservative Party, 505, 506, 507, 509
  Constitution of 1833, 503
  Constitution of 1980, 531
  constitutional changes in, 536, 537
  copper in, 518
  demonstrations in, 523
  economic growth of, 220, 528
  feminism in, 198–200
  free trade agreements of, 534
  Frei, Eduardo, ruling, 517–519
  GNP of, 534
  human rights in, 534–535
  judicial system of, 536
  labor movements in, 509, 517
  land ownership in, 504
  mid-century political system of, 513–517
  middle, 37
  military government in, 525–528
  military in, 523
  mineral wealth of, 37
  mining in, 504
  oligarchy in, 502–505
  opposition to military government in, 529–530
  party system of, 508–510
  Peru and Bolivia and, 502–503
  political polarization in, 510–513
  post-Allende, 242
  religion in, 529
  social mobilization in, 518
  south, 37–38
  Spain and, 502
  state expansion in, 505–508
  trade liberalization in, 112
  transition to democracy in, 530–533
  United States involvement with, 259, 518–519
  urbanization of, 508–510
  wage readjustment in, 516
  at war, 234–235
Chilean counterrevolution, 167
Chlorofluorocarbons (CFCs), 267
Christian Democratic Party (DC), 512, 515
  Allende, Salvador, and, 524
  internal differences in, 521
  Popular Unity v., 522
  reforms of, 517
Christian Democrats (Ecuador), 432
Christian Democrats (El Salvador), 320
Christian Democrats (Paraguay), 572
CIA, 210
  Allende, Salvador, and, 518–519
  in Bay of Pigs invasion, 352

El Cielo Biosphere Reserve, 71
Científicos, 290
Cinco de Mayo, 288
Cipriani, Andrew, 382
Citizen's Action Party (PAC) of Costa Rica, 328, 329
City-States, 395–397
Civil-military relations, 220–222
Civil society organizations (CSO), 132
Civilista Party in Peru, 444
Clandestine Revolutionary Indigenous Committee, 136
Clark, J. Reuben, 255
Class
    capitalist, 124–125
    environmental problems and, 68–69
    middle, 125–126, 165, 168–169, 179–180
    ruling, 160, 168–169
    rural proletariat, 128–129
    structure of, 123t
    working, 126–129, 165–166, 209
Class struggle, 159
    dynamics of, 131–137
Clay, Henry, 249
Clayton-Bulwer Treaty, 236, 335
Clean Air Act, 268
Cleveland, Grover, 235–236
Climate, 23
    altitudinal zonation of, 34f
    of Brazilian Highlands, 36
Climate Change Convention, 267
Clinton, William, 263, 267, 419, 553
    on Cuba, 371
    on Peru, 452–453
CLOC. *See* Latin American Coordinating Body of
    Peasant Organizations
CM. *See* Council of Ministers
CNDM. *See* National Council on Women's Rights
COB. *See* Bolivian labor confederation
Coca production, 64, 65
    Bolivian, 464–466
Cocaine, 401, 465
Cochabamba, 466
CODELCO, 527
CODENPE. *See* National Council of the Indigenous and
    Black Peoples of Ecuador
Cold War, 210, 227, 258, 327, 512, 580
    Caribbean during, 388
    end of, 260–261, 262–263
    impact of, 256–257
    inter-American relations after, 243–246
    pardigmatic shift after, 14–16
    political climate after, 243–246
Colegiado in Uruguay, 559
Collapsible pyramid model, 163
Collor, Pedro, 487
Collor de Mello, Fernando, 93, 488
    impeachment of, 486–487
Collor Plan, 486
Colom, Alvaro, 324
Colombia, 16
    counterrevolutionaries in, 404–405
    as democracy, 392
    elections in, 223
    homicide in, 400
    human rights in, 400, 401–403

national front, 397–399
origins of oligarchy in, 393–394
Panama and, 340
partisan politics in, 394–395
reform in, 399–401
revolutionaries in, 403–404
social structure of, 395–397
United States and, 405–406
urbanization in, 397
violence in, 397
Colonia Miguel Hidalgo, 62
Colonial Spanish America
    beginning of, 79
    government of, 79–82
Colonialism, 160
Colorado Party, 558, 561, 562, 568, 570, 573
Colosio, Luis Donaldo, 299, 301
Columbus, Christopher, 78–79
Comedores populares, 132
Committees for the Defense of the Revolution, 353
Communication
    in Caribbean, 386
Communism, 257
    Cuban, 353–358
    global state of, 360
    Soviet collapse, 342
    terrorism and, 588–590
    United States against, 257–258, 318
Communist Party, 173, 259
Communist Party (Chilean), 510, 537
    Allende, Salvador, and, 521
Communist Party (Cuban), 353–358
Communist Party (France), 382
Communist Party (Venezuelan), 412–413
Community Action, 336
Community-based cooperation, 132–133
Comparative advantage, 15
Comparative indicators, 226t
Comptroller general of Chile, 514
CONAIE. *See* Confederation of Indigenous Nationalities
    of Ecuador
Confederation of Indigenous Nationalities of Ecuador
    (CONAIE), 135, 146–147, 149, 424, 428, 429,
    430
Confederation of Mexican Workers (CTM), 297
Confederation of Venezuelan Workers (CTV), 413–414,
    420
Congressional Budget Office, 587
Congressional Investigating Committee (CPI), 487, 488
Conquest, 42, 43
    of Latin America, 78–79
Conservation International, 65, 70
Conservative Party (Bolivia), 459
Conservative Party (Chile), 505, 506
    influence of, 509
    reforms of, 507
Conservative Party (Colombia), 394, 397–398
Conservative Unity (Uidad) in Costa Rica, 327
Constituent Assembly, 315
    in Brazil, 485
Contadora process, 261
Contras, 260, 315
Contreras, Eleazar López, 412
Contreras, Manuel, 535

Convention on the Elimination of Discrimination
Against Women (CEDAW), 190
Convertibility Law, 244
Convertibility Plan, 550
Coordinating Committee to Defend Gas, 467
Coordinator of Social Movements (CMS), 430
COPACAR, 567
COPAL, 567
COPEI, 409, 413, 416
Copper, 445
Chilean, 518
Cordilleran Ranges, 32–33
CORFO. *See* State Development Corporation
Coro, 411
Corporatism, 5–6
Corrales, José Miguel, 328
Cortas de ruta, 134
Cortes, Hernàn, 191, 281–282, 283
Costa e Silva, Arthur, 474–475
Costa Rica, 62–63
deforestation of, 63
economy of, 166
political evolution of, 165
political instability of, 327–329
revolution in, 186n4
social history of, 312–313
United States and, 327–328
Costa Rican Association for the Defense of Democracy
and Liberty, 328
Council of Ministers (CM) in Cuba, 359–361
Council of State (CS) in Cuba, 358, 359
Council on Foreign Relations, 277n30
Council on Violence Against Women, 199
Counterrevolution, 180
in Argentina, 181
in Brazil, 211
in Colombia, 404–405
decompression and, 178–179
economic transformation following, 176–177
facilitating factors of, 174–175
institutionalization following, 177
phases of, 176–177
political demobilization in, 176
Court system
of Chile, 514
Couto e Silva, Golbery do, 478
CPI. *See* Congressional Investigating Committee
Crafts
in Indo-America, 51–52
Craske, Nikki, 203
Crime
in Caribbean, 388–389
Criollos, 283, 284, 557
Cristiani, Alfredo, 318
CROM. *See* Regional Confederation of Mexican Labor
Cruz, Sor Juana de la, 191
Cruzado Plan, 487
CS. *See* Council of State
CSN Steel, 489
CSO. *See* Civil society organizations
CTM. *See* Confederation of Mexican Workers
Cuauhtémoc, 282
Cuba, 99, 251, 275, 313
American protectorate, 351

Carter, Jimmy, and
Communist party in, 353–358
Council of Ministers of, 359–361
economic efficiency in, 365
economic experimentation in, 361–370
European communism and, 361
Family Code of, 204n17
foreign trade with, 366
GMP in, 365–366
GNP of, 368t
gross internal investments of, 368
historical context of, 349
illiteracy in, 369–370
imports of, 367
independence of, 350
industrialization in, 363, 364
land reform in, 362
National Assembly of, 358–359
political system of, 353
population growth in, 369t
post-September 11, 264–265
socialism in, 352–353
Soviet Union and, 366
Spanish Colonialism and, 349–350
strategical vitality of, 249–250
sugar production in, 349–350, 364–365
unemployment in, 362
United States and, 253, 370–373
Cuban Confederation of Labor, 353
Cuban Democracy Act, 273
Cuban People's Party (PPC), 451
Cuban Revolution, 4, 5, 167
Castro, Fidel, in, 351
class demolition following, 171
as example, 348–349
historical context of, 349
impact of, 373
institutionalization after, 173
power transfer following, 170
reconcentration following, 173–174
redistribution following, 172, 363
U.S. government in, 210
Cuban Revolutionary Party (PRC), 350, 351
Cubás, Raúl, 576
Cuenca, 425
Cuitlahuac, 282
Cultural causation, 5
Culture Matters: How Values Shape Human Progress
(Harrison and Huntington), 6
Curaçao, 385
Currency
Argentinian, 550
in Ecuador, 433, 434
CUT. *See* Central Labor Federation
CVF. *See* Venezuelan Development Corporation
CVG. *See* Venezuelan Corporation of Guayana
CVP. *See* Venezuelan Petrolem Corporation
CVRD Mining, 489
Czechoslovakia
socialism in, 363–364

D'Aubuisson, Roberto, 319
D'Avila Mello, Ednardo, 479
DC. *See* Christian Democratic Party

De la Rúa Bruno, Fernando
    presidency of, 552–553
Death squads, 311
Debt, 2, 586
    dictatorships and, 213–214
    growth of, 216
    of selected countries, 215t
    Venezuelan, 183, 216
Debt-for-nature-swaps, 70
Debt management, 214
Decolonization, 380
Decompression, 178–179
    in Brazil, 477–483
Defense budgets, 229n25
Deforestation, 219, 267
    in Amazon Basin, 35–36
    in Latin America, 62–65
Delegacia da mulher, 199
Delocalization, 585
Democracy, 1–2, 182. *See also* Democratization;
        Redemocratization
    breakdown of, 225–226
    breakdown of, in Chile, 517–525
    breakdown of, in Uruguay, 560–563
    in Chile, 530–533
    development of, 217–218
    electoral, 455n10
    in Latin America, 4
    limited, 217–218, 222–224
    Peruvian, 448–451, 453–454
    in Uruguay, 557–560
    Venezuelan, 413–414
Democradura, 183
Democratic Action (AD), 409, 412, 413, 417
Democratic Labor Party (PDT), 482, 486
Democratic Party (Peruvian), 444–445
Democratic Revolutionary Party (PRD), 302, 341
Democratization, 93, 217–218
    of Ecuador, 426–428
    of Guatemala, 322–323
    of Paraguay, 574–577
Denationalization, 584
Dependency theory, 9–12
    core assumptions of, 10
    Marxism and, 12
    post-Cold War, 15–16
Depopulation, 42
Deutsch, Karl, 162
Development theory, 6–9, 12
    post-Cold War, 15
Díaz, Felix, 292
Díaz, Porfirio, 90, 170, 172, 295
    administration of, 289–291
Díaz del Castillo, Bernal, 281
Dictablanda, 183
Dictatorships, 91, 174. *See also* Military governments
    debt and, 213–214
    Uruguay, 564–565
Dirceu, José, 470, 493
Direct elections
    in Brazil, 485
Diriomo, 192
Disease, 84
    in Indo-America, 53

Dix, Robert H., 393
DNA. *See* National Anti-Narcotics Division
Dominican Republic, 378
    revolution in, 168
    United States involvement with, 259
Dominicans, 85
Dore, Elizabeth, 192
Dornelles, Francisco, 484, 485
Dosh, Paul, 148
Draft labor, 83
Drago, Luis, 236
Drago Doctrine, 236–237
Drug trade, 225, 262, 333
    in Colombia, 401
    in Ecuador, 437
    Peruvian, 453
    United States and, 265–267
Duarte, José Napoleón, 318
Duarte Frutos, Nicanor
    presidency of, 576–577
Due Obedience Law, 548
Duhalde, Eduardo, 550
    as president, 553
Dulles, Allen, 257
Dulles, John Foster, 256, 257
Durán-Ballén, Sixto, 424
Dutra, Olívio, 490
Duvalier, François, 383
Duvalier, Jean-Claude, 383
Duverger, Maurice, 475

EAP. *See* Economically active population
Earle, Rebecca, 191
Earth Summit, 267
Earthquakes, 23, 68
Echeverría Alvarez, Luís, 298
ECLA. *See* Economic Commission for Latin America
Economic activity
    structure of, 122t
Economic change
    grassroots reactions to, 139–141
Economic Commission for Latin America (ECLA), 9,
        98, 109, 212, 239–240, 370
    economic integration and, 240–241
Economic crisis
    in Argentina, 548–549
    in Mexico, 270
Economic cycles, 94–99
Economic development
    environment and, 60
    United States and, 268–272
Economic efficiency
    in Cuba, 365
Economic growth, 185, 586
    of Chile, 220, 528
    of Peru, 442, 453
Economic miracles, 220
    Brazilian, 475–477
Economic restructuring, 103–108
    Cuban, 361–370
    fifth, 110–114
    first, 103–105
    fourth, 108–110
    protesting, 133–134

second, 105–106
social impacts of, 129–131
third, 106–108
workplace protest and, 134–136
Economically active population (EAP)
  capitalist class, 124–125
  middle class, 125–126
  working class, 126–129
Economics, 8
Ecotourism, 70
Ecuador, 16, 55, 146–147, 239
  affirmative action in, 431
  austerity in, 184
  citizenship in, 431–432
  constitution of, 430–433
  in context, 438t
  currency in, 433–434
  democratization of, 426–428
  dependency of, 433–435
  drug trade in, 437
  export economy of, 425
  foreign policy in, 435–437
  GNP of, 423
  heads of state of, 428
  history of, 424–425
  literacy in, 429
  military reformers in, 426
  neoliberal policy in, 433–434
  new social movements in, 428–430
  Peru and, 453
  political parties in, 426–428, 438n3
  privatization in, 152
  protests in, 136–137
  redistribution in, 426
  residence in, 52
  SAPs for, 427
  urbanization of, 427
Ecuadorian Federation of Indigenous Evangelicals
    (FEINE), 429
Ecuadorian-Peruvian war, 222
Ecuentro Progresista, 565
Education
  in Caribbean, 385
  in Cuba, 369–370
  in Mexico, 305
EEC. *See* European Economic Community
Egeland, Jan, 403
Eisenhower, Dwight D., 256, 257
El Salvador, 181
  elections in, 223
  Honduras and, 241
  imperfect peace in, 319–321
  insurgency in, 317–319
  matanza of 1930, 169
  neoliberalism in, 320–321
  peace accords of, 331n22
  United States and, 318–319
Elbrick, Charles, 470, 477
Elections
  in Brazil, 485
  of Cardoso, Fernando Henrique, 488–491
  of Chávez, Hugo, 409–410
  in Colombia, 223
  in El Salvador, 223

  in Guatemala, 223
  in Paraguay, 183–184
  of Pérez, Carlos Andrés, 414
  of Stroessner, Alfredo, 571
  of Yrigoyen, Hipólito, 543
Electoral participation, 183–184, 223t, 229n28
  bids for, 159–161
Electoral systems
  in United States, 158
ELN. *See* Army of National Liberation
Embratel, 478
Emergency Social Fund (FSE), 488
Encomienda, 82–83
Encuentros, 196, 197
Endara, Guillermo, 341, 342
Endowment for Democracy, 186
Energy resources, 65–67
Environment
  basic issues regarding, 59–61
  class and, 68–69
  economic development and, 60
  gender and, 68–69
  human demension of, 67–68
  public policy and, 218–219
  solutions to problems in, 70–72
  United States on, 267–268
  urbanization and, 61–62
Errázuriz, Federico, 507
Erval Seco, 150
Escandón, Carmen Ramos, 203n3
Esquipulas Peace Accord, 322, 328
Estenssoro, Víctor Paz, 172–173, 187n5, 459, 460–461,
    463–464, 466
Estigarribia, José F., 567
Ethnic rights, 145–147
Euro-America, 42
  contemporary, 45–47
Europe
  Cuba and, 361
European Economic Community (EEC), 240
European Parliament, 360
Evans, Peter, 13
Evita. *See* Perón, Eva Duarte
Evolution
  of political process, 164–165
Exchange Reform Law, 560
Exclusionary socioeconomic agendas, 217–218
Exploitation
  of labor, 82–84
Exports, 94–96
  Brazillian, 112
  Ecuadorian, 425
External control
  social distance and, 168
Extractive industries, 65–67
EZLN. *See* Zapatistas

Fadul, Pedro, 576
Falklands, 585–586
  Argentina and, 546–547
Family
  in Indo-America, 52
Fanon, Frantz, 383
Farabundo Martí National Liberation Front (FMLN),

318–319
ARENA Party v., 320–321
FARC. *See* Revolutionary Armed Forces of Colombia
Fascell, Dante, 10
Feberistas, 567, 571
Febres, Cordero, 436
FEDECAMARAS, 417
Federation of Cuban Women, 353
Federation of Trade Unions, 134
Feijóo, María del Carmen, 195
FEINE. *See* Ecuadorian Federation of Indigenous
Evangelicals
Feminism, 193
attacks on, 202
in Brazil, 198–200
in Chile, 198–200
types of, 196
Ferdinand VII, 284, 542
Fernández Guadalupe Victoria, Manuel Félix, 285
Ferreira Aldunate, Wilson, 565
Fifth Republic Movement (MRV), 416, 417
Figueiredo, João Batista, 481
government of, 482
Figueres, José María, 327, 328
Filho, Fiel, 479
Filizzola, Carlos, 576
Fiscal Responsibility Law, 489
FLOMERES, 567
Flores, Francisco, 320
Flores, Lourdes, 453
Flores Facussé, Carlos, 326
FMLN. *See* Farabundo Martí National Liberation Front
FOB. *See* Forward Observation Base
Foreign debt, 212
regime crisis and, 213–214
of selected countries, 215t
Formal sector, 126–127
Fort-de-France, 382
Forward Observation Base (FOB), 437
Fossil fuels, 66
Fourth Declaration of the Lacandon Jungle, 153
Fox, Vicente, 94, 99, 184, 251, 270
France
Mexico and, 288–289
Franciscans, 85
Franco, Itamar, 487–488, 489
Franco, Julio C., 576
Franco, Rafael, 567
Franco, Francisco, 5
Frank, Andre Gunder, 10, 16
Free markets, 584–588
Free Trade Agreement of the Americas (FTAA), 18, 245,
270, 271, 339, 420, 554
Free Trade Area of the Americas, 149
Frei Montalvo, Eduardo, 512, 519
Chile under, 517–519
Frei Ruiz, Tagle, Eduardo, 533
Frente Amplio in Uruguay, 186, 561
Frondizi, Arturo, 544
Frota, Sylvio, 480
FSE. *See* Emergency Social Fund
FSLN. *See* Sandinista National Liberation Front
FTAA. *See* Free Trade Agreement of the Americas
Fujimori, Alberto, 93–94, 183, 201, 442, 450

government of, 451–453
Full Stop Law, 547
Funaro, Dilson, 485
Fundación Natura, 70

Gabeira, Fernando, 470, 494
Gadsden Purchase, 287
Gairy, Eric, 378
Gaitán, Jorge Eliécer, 394, 396
Galán, Luis Carlos, 401
Galtieri, Leopoldo F., 546
Galtung, Johan, 11
Gálvez, Mariano, 97
Galvo, Carlos, 236
GANA. *See* Great Alliance
García, Alán, 449, 450, 454
García, Lucas, 322
García, Paz, 324
García Meza, Luis, 462
Garotinho, Anthony, 491, 492
Garrastazú-Medici, Emilio, 207
GATT. *See* General Agreement on Tariffs and Trade
Gavíria Trujillo, César, 402
GDP. *See* Gross domestic product
Geisel, Ernesto, 474, 479, 480, 481
foreign policy of, 480
presidency of, 477–478
Gender, 17, 120–121, 131–132, 189
environmental problems and, 68–69
globalization and, 202–203
historical frame of, 191–193
labor force and, 120–121, 195–196
representation and, 197–198
social movements and, 190
Gender quotas
in Argentina, 200–201
General Agreement on Tariffs and Trade (GATT), 342
Gerardi, Juan, 323
Germany, 239
Gestido, Oscar, 561
Global Environmental Facility, 267
Global trade, 96
Globalization
Caribbean and, 388
gender and, 202–203
neoliberal, 17–18
GMP. *See* Gross material product
GNP. *See* Gross national product
Godkin, E.L., 253
Gold, 81, 283
Goldwater, Barry, 512
Gomes, Ciro, 490, 491, 492, 494
Gómez, Juan Vicente, 409, 411
Gómez, Laureano, 394, 395
Gómez, Máximo, 253
Gonçalves, Leonidas Pires, 484
González, Felipe, 494
González, Natalicio, 568
González Macchi, Luis, 576
Good Neighbor Policy, 210, 237
beginning of, 255
Gorbachev, Mikhail, 262, 330n5, 590
Goulart, João, 472, 473
Gran Colombia, 233

Great Britain, 262
  Argentina and, 554
  United States and, 235–236
Great Depression, 97–98, 109, 112, 209
Grenada, 259, 261, 378
Grenadian Revolution, 379
Gross domestic product (GDP)
  of Caribbean, 375
  of Paraguay, 569
Gross material product (GMP)
  Cuban, 365–366
Gross national product (GNP)
  of Chile, 534
  of Cuba, 368t
  of Ecuador, 423
  of Paraguay, 569, 570
Guanabara, 474
Guardado, Facundo, 320
Guatemala, 67, 181
  democratization of, 322–323
  elections in, 223
  government overthrow in, 210
  human rights in, 54
  indigenous population of, 43
  political instability of, 321–324
  poverty in, 219
  United States policy towards, 321–322
Guatemalan National Revolutionary Unity (URNG),
    184, 322, 323
Guatemalan Republican Front, 323
Guatemalan Revolution, 257
Guayaquil, 425, 434
Gueiler, Lydia, 462
Guerrero, 303
Guevara, Ernesto "Ché," 92, 364, 472
Guevara Arce, Walter, 461, 462
Guiana Highlands, 33–34
Guimares, Ulysses, 478–479, 484, 486
Guitierréz, Lucio, 424, 428
Gulf-Caribbean Coastal Lowlands, 29–30
  agriculture in, 29–30
Gulf of California, 31
Gunera de Mélgar, Nora, 326
Gutiérrez, Lucio, 185, 434, 494
Guzmán, Abimael, 451
Guzmán, Juan, 536
Guzmán Blanco, Antonio, 90, 411, 412

Hacendados, 160
Haiti, 183
  austerity measures in, 184
  development of, 268–269
  education in, 385
  independence of, 167
  modernity in, 386
  slave revolt in, 350
Harding, Warren G., 295
Harrison, Lawrence, 6
Haya de la Torre, Víctor Raúl, 446, 449
Hay-Pauncefote Treaty, 236
HDI. *See* Human Development Index
Heavily Indebted Poor Countries (HIPC) initiative, 326
Heavy Crude Pipeline, 434
Hegemony, 160

United States, 250
Helms, Jesse, 274
Helms-Burton Act, 273–274, 357, 371
Hernández, José Manuel, 411
Hernández-Martínez, General, 227n3
Herrera, Enrique Olaya, 394
Herrera Campins, Luis, 414
Herskovits, Melville, 375
Herzog, Vladimir, 479
Hidalgo y Costilla, Miguel, 284
Hierarchical systems, 164
Hinduism, 383, 387
HIPC initiative. *See* Heavily Indebted Poor Countries
    initiative
Hirschman, Albert O., 7
Hispanics, 582
HIV, 189, 218
Homeless Workers' Movement (MTST), 143
Homicide
  in Colombia, 400
Honduras, 69, 169
  El Salvador and, 241
  melon-raising in, 64
  neoliberal policy in, 326
  political instability in, 324–327
  poverty in, 219–220
  social history of, 312–313
  United States policy towards, 324–325
Hoover, Herbert, 237
Hoyos, José Azcona, 325
Htun, Mala, 17, 200
Huerta, Victoriano, 292
Human Development Index (HDI), 471
Human rights, 315, 326
  in Brazil, 49
  Carter, Jimmy, on, 321–322
  in Chile, 534–535
  in Colombia, 400, 401–403
  gender and, 194
  in Guatemala, 54
Human Rights Watch, 589
Humboldt, Alexander von, 105
Humphrey, Hubert H., 590
Hunting, 47–48
Huntington, Samuel, 6, 7
Hurricane Mitch, 317, 326
Hussein, Saddam, 244, 264
Hydroelectric power, 66
  in Paraguay, 569

Ibáez, Carlos, 227n3, 510, 512
Ibarra, José María Velasco, 92
ICJ. *See* International Court of Justice
Illia, Arturo, 544
IMF. *See* International Monetry Fund
Imperialism, 9
Import-substitution industrialization (ISI), 98
  goals of, 140
  initiation of, 110
Imports, Cuban, 367
Inacio da Silva, Luiz ("Lula"), 186, 244, 470, 486
  presidency of, 491–494
Income
  distribution of, 122t, 130–131, 140–141

Independence, 89–90
Indigenous populations, 40–41
  of Afro-America, 46
  of Brazil, 44
  of Mexico, 43
  movements, 198
  preconquest, 42–45
  rights of, 145–147
  social reforms and, 145–147
  Venezuelan, 49
Indo-America, 42, 43
  agriculture in, 51
  in colonial period, 50
  community structure in, 51
  crafts in, 51–52
  culture in, 53
  disease in, 53
  family in, 52
  population of, 50
  religion in, 53
Industrial Revolution, 95
Industrialization, 107, 112, 290
  Cuban, 363, 364
Inequality
  in electoral systems, 159–161
  structural poverty and, 219–220
Infamous Decade of Argentina, 543
Infant mortality, 24–25, 368–369
Informal sector, 127–128
  growth of, 131–132
Insecurity, 207–208
Institutional Revolutionary Party (PRI), 172–173, 297,
  341
  defeat of, 196
  dominance of, 300–301
  opposition to, 303
Institutionalization
  counterrevolution and, 177
  revolution and, 172–173
Inter-American Conference for the Maintenance of
  Peace, 237
Inter-American Development Bank, 103, 110, 128–129,
  240, 429
Inter-American Human Rights Commission, 264
Inter-American Juridical Committee, 273
Interdependence, 13
International Court of Justice (ICJ), 260
International Day of Farmers' Struggle, 143
International Feminist Congress, 192
International Labor Organization, 128, 144–145
International Monetary Fund (IMF), 119, 125, 133,
  415, 427, 433, 448, 560
International Petroleum Company (IPC), 447
International political economy (IPE), 13
Intra-elite alliances, 214–216
IPC. *See* International Petroleum Company
IPE. *See* International political economy
Iquique massacre of 1907, 509
Iraq, 264
ISI. *See* Import-substitution industrialization
Iturbide, Agustín, 89, 232, 284
IVSS. *See* Venezuelan Social Security Institute

Jackson, Andrew, 158

Jagan, Cheddi, 222, 381, 383
Jamaat al Muslimeen, 379
Jamaica
  Canada and, 377–378
James, C.L.R., 382
Jaquette, Jane, 17
Jaramillo, Bernardo, 401
Jereissati, Tasso, 486
Jesuits, 86
João VI (King of Portugal), 471
John Paul II, 199–200
Johnson, Lyndon, 211, 259, 512
Jonas, Susanne Bodenheimer, 9
Jones, Mark, 200
Juárez, Benito, 90, 97, 252, 280, 287, 288

Karinya, 47
Karl, Terry Lynn, 414
Kemmerer Mission, 435
Kennedy, John F., 210, 258
Kennedy-Khrushchev Understanding, 258
King Jr., Martin Luther, 158, 195, 589
Kirchner, Néstor, 244, 271, 553, 554
Kissinger, Henry, 259
Kissinger Commission, 314, 329n3
Korean War, 256
Krieger Vasena, Adalberto, 544
Kubitschek, Juscelino, 472

La Paz, 459
La Plata-Paraná Basin, 38–39
Labor. *See also* Working classes
  exploitation of, 82–84
  gender and, 120–121, 195–196
  growth of, 120–121
  reforms, 294
Labor movements, 161, 180
  in Chile, 509, 517
Lacalle Herrera, Luis A., 562–563
Lacayo, Antonio, 316
LAFTA. *See* Latin American Free Trade Association
Lagos, Ricardo, 494, 534, 535
Laíno, Domingo, 574, 575
Lambert, Jacques, 471
Land, 142
  ownership of, in Chile, 504
Land reform, 292, 294
  agrarian, 141–143
  of Cárdenas, 296–297
  Cuban, 362
Landless Rural Workers' Movement (MST), 142
  goals of, 149
Landscape, of Latin America, 22–23
Lanusse, Alejandro, 545
Latin America
  altitudinal zonation of climates in, 34f
  Amerindian population of, 46
  colonial governments of, 79–82
  colonial labor exploitation in, 82–84
  conquest of, 78–79
  corporatist model of, 5–6
  cultural causation in, 5–6
  deforestation in, 62–65
  democracy in, 4

dependency theory of, 9–12
development and modernization theory of, 6–9
economic cycles in, 94–99
economic dimensions of, 103t
fifth restructuring of, 110–114
fourth restructuring of, 108–110
liberation of, 232–233
natural regions of, 28f, 29t
nineteenth-century conflicts in, 233–235
physical characteristics of, 22–23
political generations of, 89–94
population characteristics of, 24–27
post-Cold War, 14–16
Roman Catholic Evangelism in, 84–86
settlement of, 79
social structure of, 120–123
urbanization in, 61–62
Latin American Coordinating Body of Peasant
    Organizations (CLOC), 143
Latin American Free Trade Association (LAFTA), 99,
    109, 113, 240
    problems for, 241–242
Law of Hydrocarbons, 412
Law of Political Parties and Elections, 432
Laws of Sale of Public Land, 566
League of Nations, 237
Lechín, Juan, 462
Legal systems, 179
Leguía, Augusto, 442, 445
LeMoyne, James, 403
León Carpio, Ramiro de, 323
Leoni, Raúl, 413
Lerdo de Tejada, Sebastián, 289
Lerner, Jaime, 62
Ley de Comunas, 426
Ley de lemas, 559–560
Liberal Front Party (PFL), 484
Liberal Party (Bolivia), 459
Liberal Party (Brazil), 491
Liberal Party (Chile), 506
Liberal Party (Colombia), 394, 396, 397–398, 399
Liberal Party (Honduras), 325
Liberal Party (Paraguay), 576
Liberal Party (Venezuela), 410–411
Liberal Radical Authentic Party
    (Paraguay), 572
Liberal Radical Party (Paraguay), 571
Liberalism, 96–97
    post-Cold War, 14–15
Lima, 132, 443, 444
    viceroys at, 80
Limantour, José Ives, 289–290,
    292
Limited democracy, 217–218
    in receiver states, 222–224
Linowitz Report, 214
Lista Abierta, 571
Literacy
    in Caribbean, 385, 386
    in Cuba, 369–370
    in Ecuador, 429
Lleras Camargo, Alberto, 394
Lleras Restrepo, Carlos, 400
Lodge, Henry Cabot, 257

Logging, 64–65
Lonardi, Eduardo, 544
López, Carlos Antonio, 234, 557
López, Francisco Solano, 234, 557
López, José Hilario, 97
López, Narciso, 252
López Michelsen, Alfonso, 399
Louisiana Purchase, 249–250
L'Ouverture, Toussaint, 89
Lula. *See* Inacio da Silva, Luiz
Lynch, Elisa, 234, 246n1

Madero, Francisco Ignacio, 291–292, 295
Madres of the Plaza de Mayo, 190, 194
Madrid, Miguel de la, 94, 298, 299, 302, 306
Maduro, Ricardo, 326–327
Mahuad, Jamil, 55, 428, 432, 434
Maisto, John, 419
Malan, Pedro, 489
La Malinche, 191
Maluf, Paulo, 483, 493
Malvinas War, 546–547
Manifest Destiny, 251–253, 286
Manley, Michael, 381, 382
Manley, Norman, 381, 383
Mannheim, Karl, 379
Mapuches, 48
Maquiladoras, 68, 69
Marcos (Mexico), 303
Mariátegui, José Carlos, 446
Marshall Plan, 110
Martí, José, 350, 387
Martinique, 382
Martz Jr., John D., 393
Marulanda, Manuel. *See Tirofijo*
Marx, Karl, 159
Marxism, 9, 162, 193, 352–353, 382, 383, 387
    dependency theory and, 12
    in Peru, 446
MAS. *See* Movement Towards Socialism
Massaccesi, Horacio, 551
Massera, Eduardo, 547
Matanza, 169
Maximilian, Ferdinand, 288
Maximilian of Hapsburg, 252
Mayans, 54
    rights organizations of, 146
Mbayá, 45
McCarthyism, 256
MDB. *See* Brazilian Democratic Movement
Measles, 84
Médici, Emilio Garrastazú, 8, 207
    government of, 477
Medina Angarita, Isaías, 412
Mejía Victores, Humberto, 322
Meirelles, Henrique, 492
Melgarejo, Mariano, 458
Méndez, Aparicio, 562
Menem, Carlos, 135, 205n48, 548, 551, 553, 554
    diplomatic relations of, 550
    presidency of, 549
Mercantilism, 283
Mercosur, 108, 113, 224, 243, 534, 554, 585
Mestizo-America

population of, 47
rural-to-urban migration in, 49–50
shamanism in, 48
villages in, 48
warfare in, 48
Mestizo-American populations, 42
Mestizos, 44
Mexican Constitution of 1824, 285
Mexican Constitution of 1857, 287–288
Mexican Constitution of 1917, 294, 296
Mexican Revolution of 1910–1920, 91, 192, 291–295
    class demolition following, 171
    end of, 295
    institutionalization after, 172
    power transfer in, 170
Mexican Revolutionary Party (PRM), 297
Mexico, 16
    bourgeoisie in, 124–125
    change in, 305–306
    economic crisis in, 270
    economic structure of, 303–305
    education in, 305
    extra-system opposition in, 303
    France and, 288–289
    historical foundations of, 280–281
    independence of, 284–285
    indigenous population of, 43
    labor reforms in, 294
    legacy of revolution in, 299–300
    missionaries in, 85
    new beginnings in, 300
    oil drilling in, 66–67
    political change in, 308
    political system of, 300–301
    Porfiriato, 289–291
    pre-Cortés, 281
    reform of, 287–288
    republic of, 285–286
    residence in, 52
    revolution in, 169
    since 1940, 298–299
    social structure of, 307
    United States and, 251, 293
    United States war with, 286–287
    War of Reform in, 97
Mexico City, 61, 193
    earthquake in, 68
    problems of, 307–308
    protests in, 134, 135
    viceroys at, 80
Middle class, 125–126
    political participation of, 165, 179–180
    ruling class and, 168–169
Military balance, 221t, 222
Military coup
    Brazilian, 471–475
    Panamanian, 340
Military governments, 177–178, 586. *See also*
    Dictatorships
    Chilean, 525–530
    opposition to, 529–530
    Peruvian, 447–448
    policy initiatives of, 527–528
Military interventions, by U.S., 236–237, 262

Military reform, 426
Militocracy
    establishment of, 180–181
Miller, Francesca, 191
Minas Gerais, 472, 483
Mining, 81, 83. *See also* Copper; Gold; Silver
    in Chile, 504
Ministry of Energy and Mines, 418
MIR. *See* Movement of the Revolutionary Left
Miranda, Francisco, 89
Miskitos, 49
Missionaries, 85
Mitre, Bartolomé, 90
Mitrione, Dan, 561, 564
Mitterrand, François, 492, 494
MNR. *See* National Revolutionary Movement
Moctezuma II, 281–282
Modern-conservative societies
    concept of, 377–380
Modernization theory, 6–9, 12
Molyneux, Maxine, 196
Monge, Luis Alberto, 327
Monroe, James, 260–261
Monroe Doctrine
    initiation of, 235
    invalidation of, 250–251
    Roosevelt Corollary to, 236, 254
    study of, 237
Montes Azules Biosphere Reserve, 67
Montesinos, Vladimirio, 450, 451, 452, 454
Montevideo, 556–557
Montoro, Franco, 478
Montt, Manuel, 505, 506
Moore Jr., Barrington, 571
Morales, Evo, 54, 465, 467
Morales Bermúdez, Francisco, 442, 448
Moran, Theodore, 13
Moreira Alves, Márcio, 476
Morelos y Pavón, José Maria, 284
Morínigo, Higínio, 567
Mortality rates, 368–369
Moscosco, Mireya, 342
Motherhood, 195–196
Mountain ranges, 32–33
Movement of the Revolutionary Left (MIR), 413, 464
Movement Towards Socialism (MAS), 416, 417, 465,
    467
Movimiento Todos Por la Patria (MTP), 548
MRTKL. *See* Tupac Katari Revolutionary Movement of
    Liberation
MRV. *See* Fifth Republic Movement
MST. *See* Landless Rural Workers' Movement
MTP. *See* Movimiento Todos Por la Patria
MTST. *See* Homeless Workers' Movement
MUPP. *See* Pachakutik United Pluricultural Movement

NA. *See* National Assembly
Nader, Ralph, 224
NAFTA. *See* North American Free Trade Agreement
Napoleon, Louis, 252
Napoleon Bonaparte, 542
Napoleon III, 234, 288, 557
Nariño, Antonio, 89
National Action Party (PAN), 184

National Agricultural Society (SNA), 513
National Anti-Narcotics Division (DNA), 437
National Assembly (NA), 430
  criticism of, 358
  functions of, 359
National Association of Indigenous Peoples, 134
National Association of Industrialists, 396
National Center for Children in Poverty, 587
National Constituent Assembly (ANC), 485–486
National Council of the Indigenous and Black Peoples of Ecuador (CODENPE), 432
National Council on Women's Rights (CNDM), 199
National Election Court (TSE), 475
National Endowment for Democracy (NED), 420
National Federation of Coffee Growers, 393, 396
National Front, 397–399
  dissolution of, 398
National Opposition Union (UNO), 173
National Party (Chile), 515
National Popular Alliance (ANAPO), 394, 399–400
National Renovating Alliance (ARENA), 475, 476, 479
  FMLN v., 320–321
National Revolutionary Movement (MNR), 170, 172–173, 457
  rise of, 460–463
  status of, 457
National Revolutionary Party (PNR), 296
National Security Council (Chile), 536, 537
National Security Council (Uruguay), 562
National Security Doctrine, 211
National System for Support of Social Mobilization (SINAMOS), 448
National Unity of Hope (UNE), 324
Nationalism, 185–186
Natural disasters, 23, 68
  relief efforts after, 69
Natural regions, 28f, 29t
Natusch Busch, Alberto, 462
Navarro, Raúl Béjar, 280
NED. *See* National Endowment for Democracy
Needler, Martin C., 7, 162
Neo-populists, 93–94
Neoliberalism, 135
  in Bolivia, 466–468
  criticism of, 15–16
  in Ecuador, 433–434
  in El Salvador, 320–321
  globalization and, 17–18
  in Honduras, 326
  impact of, 329
  post-Cold War, 14–15
  protest in, 133–134
Netherlands Antilles, 385
Netto, Delfim, 99, 476
Neves, Tancredo, 470, 473, 483, 484
New Jewel Movement, 261
New Orleans, 249–250
NGOs. *See* Nongovernmental organizations
Nicaragua, 181, 324
  constitutional period in, 315–316
  post-Sandinista, 316–317
  poverty in, 219
  Reagan administration and, 259–260
  revolution in, 91

Sandinista period of, 313–314
  transition period in, 314–315
  United States involvement in, 314–316
Nicaraguan Revolution, 167, 379
  class demolition following, 171–172
  institutionalization following, 173
Nixon, Richard, 259
  Chilean policy of, 518–519518
Nixon Doctrine, 211
Nobel Peace Prize, 261
Noboa, Gustavo, 424, 434
Nongovernmental organizations (NGOs), 198
  women's organizations and, 201
Noriega, Manuel, 262, 333, 341
Noriega, Roger, 275
Normalization, 208
North American Free Trade Agreement (NAFTA), 54, 60, 94, 113, 146, 184, 224, 243–244, 269, 307, 339, 389, 585, 592
North Korea, 250

OAB. *See* Brazilian Bar Association
Oakeshott, Michael, 377
OAS. *See* Organization of American States
Obrador, Manuel López, 302, 308
Obrajes, 283
Obregón, Álvaro, 94, 172, 293, 294, 295
O'Donnell, Guillermo, 11
Odría, Manuel, 442, 447
O'Higgins, Bernardo, 89
Oil Opening, 418
Olañeta, Pedro Antonio de, 458
Olds, Robert, 255
Oligarchies, 208, 209
  origins of, 393–394
  in Peru, 441–442, 445–447
Ollas comunes, 132
Olney, Richard, 250
Olson, Mancur, 150
OPEC. *See* Organization of Petroleum Exporting Countries
Opus Dei, 538
Ordáz, Gustavo Díaz, 298
Organic Law of Hydrocarbons, 416, 419
Organization of American States (OAS), 240, 243, 256, 264, 273, 436, 451
Organization of Petroleum Exporting Countries (OPEC), 140, 419
Organized labor, 165
Orinoco llanos, 33
Orozco Jr., Pazcual, 292
Ortega, Daniel, 92, 315, 317, 330n5
Ortega, Humberto, 316
Ortega-Alemán Pact, 317
Ospina Pérez, Mariano, 394
Oviedo, Lino, 575, 576

PA. *See* Arnulfista Party
PAC. *See* Citizen's Action Party
Pachakutik United Pluricultural Movement (MUPP), 427, 428
Pacheco, Abel, 327, 329
Pacheco Areco, Jorge, 561
Pacific Littoral, 31–32

Padilla, David, 462
Paéz, José Antonio, 90
Palocci Filho, Antônio, 492–493
PAN. *See* National Action Party
Pan-American Conference, 253, 254, 255
Pan-American League for the Advancement of Women, 193
Pan-American Women's International Committee, 192
Pan-Mayan movement, 146
Panama
   foreign policy of, 343
   geography of, 334
   global role of, 343–344
   history of, 334–337
   independence of, 335
   military coup in, 340
   political dynamics of, 339–343
   socioeconomic structures of, 337–339
   transit area growth in, 337–339
   United States invasion of, 262
Panama Canal Company, 335–336
Panama Canal Treaty, 343
Panama City, 335
Panamanian 1946 Constitution, 340
Panamanian Defense Forces (PDF), 333
Paniagua, Valentín, 453
Paraguay, 181
   Catholic Church in, 572
   in Chaco War, 238
   conflict in, 566–567
   democratization of, 574–577
   development of, 556
   elections in, 183–184
   GDP of, 569
   GNP of, 569, 570
   history of, 234
   militarism in, 567–568
   political process in, 570–574
   revolution in, 169
   socioeconomic structure of, 569–570
   Stroessner era in, 568
Paramilitaries, 404–405, 406
Pardo, Manuel, 444
Partido Justicialista, 546–547
Partido Liberal (PLH), 326
Partido Nacional (PN), 326
Partido Revolucionario Institucional (PRI), 94
Partisan politics, in Colombia, 394–395
Party of National Action (PAN), 301–302
Party of National Liberation (PLN), 327
Party of National Renovation (PRN), 486
Party of the Brazilian Democratic Movement (PMDB), 198, 483–484, 486
El Paso del Norte, 288
Pastrana, Andrés, 402
Patagonia, 38
Patiño, Simon, 459
Patria, Querida, 576
Patterson, Anne, 405
Paula Santander, Francisco de, 89
Paulistas, 44
Pauperization, 220
PB. *See* Political Bureau
PDF. *See* Panamanian Defense Forces

PDS. *See* Social Democratic Party
PDT. *See* Democratic Labor Party
PDVSA
   nationalization of, 417–419
Peace Corps, 580
Pearl Harbor, 239
Peasantry, 128–129
   land reforms and, 142
   transformation of, 209
   voting amongst, 160–161
Pedro I (Emperor of Brazil), 89, 471–472
Pedro II (Emperor of Brazil), 90
Pehuenche, 45
PEMEX. *See* Petróleos Mexicanos
Peñaranda, Enrique, 461
Penetration theory, 11
Peninsulares, 283
Pentagon, 263
People's National Movement (PNM), 378
Pérez, Carlos Andrés, 183, 417–418
   election of, 414
   impeachment of, 415
Pérez Jiménez, Marcos, 412–413
Pérez, José Joaquín
   administration of, 506
Perón, Eva Duarte, 92
   death of, 544
Perón, Juan, 92, 181, 410, 568
   reforms of, 543–544
Perón, María Estela Martínez de, 545
Peronists, 546, 547
   in Argentina, 544–545
   policies of, 549–551
Pershing, John, 254–255
Peru
   Bolivia and, 458
   Chile and, 502–503
   coca production in, 65
   colonial era in, 443
   democracy's return to, 453–454
   disputes involving, 238–239
   drug trade in, 453
   economic growth in, 442, 453–454
   Ecuador and, 453
   electoral democracy in, 448–451
   independence of, 443–445
   living standards in, 442
   Marxism in, 446
   military government in, 447–448
   mistrust in, 454n2
   oligarchy in, 441–442, 445–447
   post-*autogolpe*, 451–453
   privatization in, 152
   revolution in, 242–243
   riots in, 133
   Spain and, 443
   urban reform in, 144
   at war, 234–235
   women's organizations in, 195
Perú Posible, 454
Peruvian-Atacama Desert, 36–37, 54
Peso, 111, 134
Petrodollars, 166
Petróleos Mexicanos (PEMEX), 297, 304

Petroleum, 30, 66, 140, 295, 297, 303–304
  in Brazil, 477, 478
  production of, in Trinidad and Tobago, 377
  Venezuelan, 413, 417–419
PFL. *See* Liberal Front Party
Pineda, Rafael, 327
Pinochet, Augusto, 93, 190, 501, 529, 531, 535–536
  plebiscite and, 532
  prosecution of, 536
  regime of, 526–527
Piquetero, 145
  strategies of, 151
Pitanguy, Jacqueline, 199
Pius IX, 287–288
Pizarro, Francisco, 443
Plan Colombia, 225, 266, 402, 406, 420
Plan of Ayala, 292, 294
Plan of Ayutla, 287
Plan of Guadalupe, 293
Plan of San Luís Potosí, 291
Plantation agriculture, 44, 566
Platt Amendment, 253, 255, 351
Plebiscite, 532
PLH. *See* Partido Liberal
PLN. *See* Party of National Liberation
Plutocracies, 224
  in receiver states, 222–224
PMDB. *See* Party of the Brazilian Democratic Movement
PN. *See* Partido Nacional
PNM. *See* People's National Movement
PNR. *See* National Revolutionary Party
La Pola. *See* Salavarrieta, Policarpa
Policy Planning Bureau, 256
Political Bureau (PB), 354, 356
Political conflict
  power and, 161–162
Political generations, 89–94
Political participation
  aristocracy and, 180
  of middle class, 165, 179–180
  by social strata, 163
  of working classes, 165–166
Political parties, 160
Political process
  evolution of, 164–166
  revolution in, 166–179
  social change and, 163–164
Political representation
  of women, 190
Political systems
  arenas for, 161–162
  participation in, 159–160
Polk, James K., 252, 286–287
Popular Assembly, 462
Popular Colorado Movement, 572
Popular economy, 132–133
Popular Front, 259
Popular Front (Chile), 511
Popular Unity (UP), 518, 519, 520
  Christian Democrats v., 522
Population density, 24–25
  in Antilles, 30–31
Population distributions, 121t
Population growth, 24

Cuban, 369t
Euro-American, 46
Populism, 90–92, 185, 510
  neo, 93–94
  post-World War II, 98–99
  Uruguayan, 558
Porfiriato, 289–291
Portales, Diego, 90, 502, 503
Portillo, Alfonso, 323
Portillo, José López, 67, 298–299, 306
Portugal
  Brazil and, 105–106
  colonial governments of, 81
  colonial profits of, 81–82
  colonies of, 79
  influence of, 5
  labor exploitation by, 82–84
  religious ties of, 86
Portuguese America, 79
Potemkin democracy, 183–185
Poverty, 130
  growth of, 220t
  in Haiti, 184
  in Honduras, 219–220
  in Nicaragua, 219
  structural, 219–220
Powell, Colin, 420
Power, 159
  political, and religion, 160
  political conflict and, 161–162
  transfer, 170
Power capability, 161
Prado, Manuel, 446, 447
PRC. *See* Cuban Revolutionary Party
PRD. *See* Democratic Revolutionary Party
Prebisch, Raúl, 9
Precipitation, 23
Prestes, Luís Carlos, 91, 472
PRI. *See* Institutional Revolutionary Party
Prieto, Joaquín, 502
Private property, 384–385
Privatization, 111, 141
  movement strategies and, 152
  of water, 466–468
PRM. *See* Mexican Revolutionary Party
PRN. *See* Party of National Renovation
Professionalism, 125–126
Protest
  in Bolivia, 136–137
  in Brazil, 476
  in Chile, 523
  countryside, 136–137
  in Ecuador, 136–137
  in Mexico, 134–135
  against neoliberal restructuring, 133–134
  workplace, 134–136
PSB. *See* Brazilian Socialist Party
PSDB. *See* Brazilian Social Democratic Party
PTB. *See* Brazilian Labor Party
Public policies
  environmental effects of, 218–219
Puelche, 45
PUSC. *See* Social Christian
    Unity Party

Al Qaeda, 263, 264
Quadros, Jânio, 472, 478, 486
Quércia, Orestes, 478–479
Quichua, 429
Quirk, Robert E., 282
Quispe, Felipe, 467

Racial mixing, 43, 84
Racism, 355
Radical Party (Argentina), 543
Radical Party (Chile), 507, 509, 515
Reagan, Ronald, 259–260, 261, 314, 370, 436, 573
Reagan administration, 181
    aid to Guatemala under, 322–323
    Cuba and, 370
    Nicaragua and, 259–260
Real Plan, 488
Recabarrén, Luis Emilio, 509
Receiver states
    civil-military relations in, 220–222
    environmental public policy in, 219–220
    exclusionary socioeconomic agendas and, 217–218
    limited democracy in, 222–224
    plutocracies in, 222–224
    structural poverty in, 219–220
Reconcentration, 173
Recovery of Historical Memory (REMHI), 323
Redemocratization, 181–182, 184
    of Argentina, 547–548
    of Chile, 533–538
    of Uruguay, 565–566
Redistribution, 172
    Cuban, 361–370
    in Ecuador, 426
Reference Value Unit (URV), 488
La Reforma, 287–288
Reforms, 90. *See also* Social reforms; Urban reforms
    agrarian, 141–143
    labor, 294
    land, 142, 292, 294, 296–297, 362
    social impacts of, 129–131
Rega, José López, 545
Regime crisis
    foreign debt and, 213–214
Regional Confederation of Mexican Labor (CROM), 294
Reich, Otto, 420
Reina, Carlos Roberto, 325
Religion, 177, 311. *See also* Catholic Church
    in Caribbean, 384
    in Chile, 529
    colonial, 84–86
    in Indo-America, 53
    in Mestizo-America, 48
    political power and, 160
REMHI. *See* Recovery of Historical Memory
Remón, José Antonio, 337
Rengifo, Manuel, 502
Renovacíon Nacional (RN), 538
Repressive state, 211–216
Republican Party (Bolivia), 459
Revolution, 313. *See also* Counterrevolution
    agendas of, 348
    Bolivian, 169, 170–173, 460–463

class demolition following, 170–172
    in Colombia, 173, 397, 400, 403–404
    Costa Rican, 186n4
    Cuban, 4, 5, 167, 170–174, 210, 348–349, 363
    facilitating, 167–169
    Grenadian, 379
    institutionalization following, 172–173
    Mexican, 91, 169, 170–171, 192, 291–295, 297
    Nicaraguan, 91, 167, 171–173, 379
    Peruvian, 242–243
    power transfer in, 170
    reconcentration and, 173–174
    Spanish Liberal, 458
    strategy and, 92–93
Revolutionary Armed Forces of Colombia (FARC), 197, 397, 400, 403–404
Revolutionary Army of the People, 545
Revolutionary Democratic Party (PRD), 184, 186
Reyes, Walter López, 325
Ricardo, David, 15, 96
Rio Pact, 256, 273
Rio Protocol, 239
Rio Treaty, 210, 211
Ríos Montt, Efrain, 322
Riots, 133
RN. *See* Renovacíon Nacional
Robinson, William, 228n24
Roca, Julio, 90
Rockefeller Report of 1969, 211–212
Rodney, Walter, 377
Rodó, José Enrique, 3
Rodríguez, Andrés, 573
    presidency of, 574–575
Rodríguez, Miguel Angel, 327
Rodríguez, Victoria, 196
Rodríguez Lara, Guillermo, 426, 436
Rodríguez de Francia, José Gaspar, 557
Rojas Pinilla, Gustavo, 395, 399
Roldosista Party, 428
Romero, Oscar, 311
Roosevelt, Franklin, 91, 210, 236, 237, 255, 591
Roosevelt, Theodore, 210, 236, 254, 333, 336
Roosevelt Corollary, 237, 254, 255
Rosas, Juan Manuel de, 90, 542
Rostow, Walt W., 7
Ruling class, 160
    middle class and, 168–169
Rural proletariat, 128–129

Salamanca, Daniel, 460
Salas Romer, Henrique, 416
Salavarrieta, Policarpa ("La Pola"), 191
Salazar, Antonio de Oliveira, 5
Salinas de Gortari, Carlos, 127, 298, 301, 302, 306
Samper, Ernesto, 402
San Juan Bosco, 148
San Martín, Jose de, 89, 232, 443
Sánchez-Cerro, General, 227n3
Sánchez Cerro, Luis, 445, 446
Sanchez de Lozada, Gonzalo ("Goni"), 266, 457, 464, 465, 467
Sandinista National Liberation Front (FSLN), 49, 173, 189, 193, 259–260, 311, 315, 318
    constitutional period of, 315–316

period of, in Nicaragua, 313–314
transition period of, 314–315
Sandino, Augusto, 91
Sanguinetti, Julio María, 562
Santa Anna, José Antonio de, 90, 232, 280, 284–285, 285–286, 287
Santa Cruz, Andrés, 233, 458, 502–503
Santos, Eduardo, 394
Santos, Teotonio dos, 9
Sao Paulo, 199
São Paulo, 476
SAP. *See* Structural Adjustment Program
Sarmiento, Domingo Faustino, 3
Sarney, José, 93, 199, 470, 483, 484, 485
Sarney, Roseana, 491
Schild, Veronica, 202
Schneider, René, 519
Scott, Robert E., 393
Seaga, Edward, 381
Secretariat, 356
Selective incentives, 150
Seneildín, Mohammed Ali, 549
September 11, 2001, 263
Cuba after, 264–265
Seregni, Liber, 561, 565
SERNAM. *See* Servicio Nacional de La Mujer
Serpa, Horacio, 405
Serra, José, 491
Serrano, Jorge, 322
Service Elman, 42
Servicio Nacional de La Mujer (SERNAM), 199, 202
Seventh Inter-American Conference, 237
Shamanism, in Mestizo-America, 48
Shining Path, 449, 451
SIDOR, 414
Sierra Leone
income distribution in, 130
Siles Suazo, Hernán, 171, 179, 461, 462, 463
Silva, Hector, 321
Silver, 95, 458
SINAMOS. *See* National System for Support of Social Mobilization
Sitges Agreement, 398
Skeptical conservatism, 377
Slavery, 168, 350. *See also* Black Power
black, 83–84
Smallpox, 84, 282
Smith, Adam, 96
Smith, Gaddis, 250, 260–261
SNA. *See* National Agricultural Society
Soccer War, 169
Social analysis, 120
Social change
pressures for, 163
Social Christian Unity Party (PUSC), 327, 328
Social Darwinism, 3
Social Democratic Party (PDS), 470, 473, 482
Social mobilization, 162
in Chile, 518
in modern conservative societies, 379
revolution and, 167–168
Social movements
gender and, 190

goals of, 149–150, 157
member selection in, 147–148
strategies of, 151–153
Social reforms
agrarian, 141–143
indigenous people's rights, 145–147
unemployment, 144–145
urban, 143–144
Social security, 493
Social structure
of Colombia, 395–397
overview of, 123–124
Socialism
Castro, Fidel, on, 361
Chilean, 521
Cuban, 352–353, 363
models of, 363–364
Socialist party (Chilean), 510
Society for Industrial Advancement (SOFOFA), 513
SOFOFA. *See* Society for Industrial Advancement
Solís Fallas, Ottón, 328
Somocistas, 171–172
Somoza, Anastasio, 91, 170, 173, 227n3, 313
Sonoran Desert, 31
Sousa Mendes, Ivan de, 484
Southern Cone
hierarchical systems of, 164–165
Southern Cone Common Market, 566
Soviet Union, 250, 257, 258, 272
collapse of communism in, 342
Cuba and, 366
United States and, 262–263
Spain
Argentina and, 541–542
Chile and, 502
colonial government problems, 80
colonial profits of, 81
colonialism of, 283
Cuba and, 349–350
influence of, 5
labor exploitation by, 82–84
Liberal Revolution in, 458
liberation from, 232–233
Peru and, 443
religious ties of, 84–86
trade with, 104
Venezuela and, 410–413
Spanish-American War, 236
St. Lucia, 378
Standard Oil Company
nationalization of, 460
State Development Corporation (CORFO), 511
Stiglitz, Joseph, 271
Stroessner, Alfredo, 568, 570, 573
elections of, 571
Structural Adjustment Program (SAP), 214, 424, 433
for Ecuador, 427
provisions of, 119–120
Structural poverty
in receiver states, 219–220
Suazo Córdova, Roberto, 324, 325
Sugar
Cuban production of, 349–350, 363, 364–365
Summit of the Americas, 269

Sunkel, Osvaldo, 9, 16
Supreme Electoral Tribunal, 575
Suriname Revolution, 379
Swedish Electoral Commission, 315

Táchira, 411
Taft, William Howard, 210
Taliban, 263
Tapías, Fernando, 265
Tarahumara, 47
Tegucigalpa, 325, 326
Tehuelche, 45
Telebrás, 489
Teller Amendment, 253
Tenochtitlán, 282
Tequila crisis of 1994–95, 243
Terra, President, 227n3
Terrorism, 250
    communism and, 588–590
    United States and, 264–265
Texaco, 436
Texas, 286
Thatcher, Margaret, 262
Third World, 1
Thousand Day War, 394
Tiradentes, 89
Tirofijo, 404
Tobago
    oil production in, 377
Toledo, Alejandro, 452, 453, 494
Torres, Juan Jose, 462
Torricelli, Robert, 273
Torricelli Act, 357, 371
Torrijos, Martín, 343n10
Torrijos, Omar, 337, 338
Torrijos-Carter treaties, 333–334
Transnational impacts
    environmental problems and, 68–69
Treaty of Guadalupe Hidalgo, 287
Treaty of Neutrality, 343
Treaty of Tlatelolco, 554
Trilateral Commission, 218
Trinidad
    Black Power in, 378
    oil production in, 377
    social activism in, 382
Trujillo, Rafael, 91, 227n3
Truman, Harry S., 256
Truman Doctrine, 210
Truth and Reconciliation Committee, 535
TSE. *See* National Election Court
Tugwell, Franklin, 13
Tuna War, 438n4
Túpac, Amaru II, 443
Tupac Katari Revolutionary Movement of Liberation
    (MRTKL), 464
Tupamaro National Liberation Movement, 561, 564
Turbay Ayala, Julio César, 399
Turner, Stansfield, 330n11

Ubico, General Jorge, 227n3
UCR. *See* Unión Cívica Radical
UDI. *See* Unión Demócrata Independiente
ULF. *See* United Labour Force

UN Development Program, 261
Underdevelopment, 208–211
UNE. *See* National Unity of Hope
Unemployment
    in Argentina, 144–145, 551
    in Cuba, 362
Unidad Nacional (Peruvian), 453
Unilateralism
    United States' return to, 272–275
Unión Cívica Radical (UCR), 543, 546
Unión Demócrata Independiente (UDI), 538
Union of Young Pioneers, 353
United Fruit Company, 336
United Labour Force (ULF), 378
United Self-Defense Forces of Colombia (AUC),
    404–405
United States, 2, 582
    Argentina and, 553–554
    Bolivia and, 465–466
    Brazil and, 480
    Chile and, 259, 518–519
    Colombia and, 405–406
    against communism, 257–258
    Costa Rica and, 327–328
    Cuba and, 253, 370–373
    in Cuban Revolution, 210
    drug trade and, 265–267
    economic development and, 268–272
    El Salvador and, 318
    environmental protection and, 267–268
    Great Britain and, 235–236
    Guatemala and, 321–322
    hegemony asserted by, 250
    Honduras and, 324–325
    influence of, 9–12
    invasion of Panama by, 262
    involvement of, 225
    Manifest Destiny, 251–253
    Mexican war with, 286–287
    Mexico and, 251, 293
    military interventions of, 236–237, 262
    Nicaragua and, 314–316
    Panamanian policy of, 262, 343
    policy failure of, 272
    post-Cold War policy of, 263
    presidential campaigns in, 158
    protection of Cuba by, 351
    Soviet Union and, 262–263
    terrorism and, 264–265
    unilateralism of, 272–275
    Uruguay and, 563–564
    Venezuelan policy of, 419–420
United Workers Central (CUT), 400
UNO. *See* National Opposition Union
UP. *See* Popular Unity
Urban population, 228n21
Urban reform
    in Bolivia, 144
    in Brazil, 143–144
    in Peru, 144
Urbanization, 27, 582–583
    of Chile, 508–510
    in Colombia, 397
    of Ecuador, 427

environmental problems and, 61–62
Uribe Vélez, Alvaro, 403, 405
Uriburu, General, 227n3
URNG. *See* Guatemalan National Revolutionary Unity
Uruguay, 178, 180, 234
  breakdown of democracy in, 560–563
  democracy in, 557–560
  development of, 556–557
  dictatorship in, 564–565
  industrial sector of, 560
  political transition in, 564–565
  populism in, 558
  redemocratization of, 565–566
  stability of, 559
  United States and, 563–564
URV. *See* Reference Value Unit
U.S. dollar, 433, 550
U.S. War on Terrorism, 344
Utopia Unarmed (Castañeda), 16

Valenzuela, María Elena, 200, 205n44
Vance, Cyrus, 563
Vargas, Getúlio, 92, 165, 227n3, 472
Vargas, Ivette, 482
Vargas, Virginia, 201
Vargas Llosa, Mario, 441, 450
Vaso de Leche, 195
Vázquez, Tabaré, 565, 566
Velasco Alvarado, Juan, 442, 447–448
Venezuela, 185, 235–236
  colonial, 410–413
  debt crisis of, 183, 216
  economy of, 166
  indigenous population in, 49
  modern democracy in, 413–414
  petroleum in, 413, 417–419
  political crisis in, 415–417
  political evolution of, 165
  post-Cold War, 244
  Spain and, 410–413
  United States policy towards, 419–420
Venezuelan Corporation of Guayana (CVG), 413
Venezuelan Development Corporation (CVF), 412
Venezuelan Petrolem Corporation (CVP), 413
Venezuelan Social Security Institute (IVSS), 412
Venezuelan Solidarity Network, 420
Via Campesina, 143
Viceroys, 80
Videla, Jorge, 93, 545–546, 550
Vietnam, 582
Vietnam War, 518
Villa, Francisco "Pancho," 91, 292, 293, 295
Villarroel, Gualberto, 461
Viola, Roberto, 546
La Violencia, 395, 397, 401
Viva Rio, 144
Volcanoes, 32–33

Wage labor, 83
Wage readjustment laws, 516
Walesa, Lech, 494

Walker, Thomas W., 312, 330n11
Wallerstein, Immanuel, 11–12
War of the Pacific, 234–235, 238, 507
War of the Reform, 288
War of the Triple Alliance, 566
Wasmosy, Juan Carlos, 575
Watergate, 590
Water privatization, 466–468
Weber, Max, 386
Western Europe, 348
White, Robert E., 260
WHO. *See* World Health Organization
Who Will Feed China? (Brown), 64
Wiarda, Howard, 6
Wickham-Crowley, Timothy, 313
Williams, Eric, 378, 382, 383
  career of, 380
  death of, 381
Wilson, Henry Lane, 293
Wilson, Woodrow, 254, 293, 294
Women's Health Organization, 199
Women's movements. *See also* Feminism
  NGO-ization and, 201
  in Peru, 195
  of 1980's, 193–194
Workers' Party (PT), 470, 482, 490, 492, 494–495
Working classes
  formal sector, 126–127
  informal sector, 127–128
  peasantry, 128–129, 209
  political participation of, 165–166
Working conditions, 140–141
World Bank, 65, 119, 245, 427, 433
  Argentina supported by, 548–549
  HIPC initiative of, 326
World Health Organization (WHO), 143, 554
World Soccer Cup, 478
World Summit on Sustainable Development, 60
World systems theory, 11–12
  IPE and, 13
World Trade Center, 263
World Trade Organization (WTO), 274, 306
  demonstrations against, 17–18
World War I, 237
World War II, 239–240, 435
  industrial growth after, 338–339
World Wildlife Fund, 70
WTO. *See* World Trade Organization

Yanomamö Indians, 49
Yrigoyen, Hipólito, 90
  election of, 543
Yucatán peninsula, 30

Zamora, Jaime Paz, 464, 466, 467
Zamora, Rubén, 319
Zapata, Emiliano, 91, 292, 294–295, 303
Zapatistas (EZLN), 16, 54, 67, 136, 193, 299, 303, 404
  strategies of, 152–153
Zedillo, Ernesto, 299, 301, 306